Henri Lefebvre and the Theory of the Production of Space

Christian Schmid is a geographer, sociologist, and urban researcher. He is professor of sociology at the Department of Architecture, ETH Zürich. In the 1980s and 1990s, he was an urban activist and worked in the cultural centre Rote Fabrik in Zurich. He is a founding member of the International Network for Urban Research and Action (INURA). His scientific work is on planetary urbanisation, comparative urban analysis, and theories of space and the urban. He is a co-editor of *Space, Difference, Everyday Life: Reading Henri Lefebvre* (with Kanishka Goonewardena, Stefan Kipfer, and Richard Milgrom; Routledge, 2008) and *Urban Revolution Now: Henri Lefebvre in Social Research and Architecture* (with Łukasz Stanek and Ákos Moravánszky; Ashgate, 2015). Together with architects Roger Diener, Jacques Herzog, Marcel Meili, and Pierre de Meuron, he co-authored *Switzerland: An Urban Portrait* (Birkhäuser, 2006), a pioneering analysis of extended urbanisation. At the ETH Future Cities Laboratory Singapore, he led a long-term research project on the comparison of eight large metropolitan areas across the world, which will be published in *Patterns and Pathways of Urbanization: A Comparative Approach* (with Monika Streule; Birkhäuser). With Neil Brenner he is working on the theorisation and investigation of planetary urbanisation, and with Milica Topalović he is leading a research project on extended urbanisation, which will be published in *Extended Urbanisation: Territories, Processes, Struggles* (Birkhäuser).

Henri Lefebvre and the Theory of the Production of Space

Christian Schmid

Translation by Zachary Murphy King

VERSO

London • New York

This English-language edition first published by Verso 2022
Translation © Zachary Murphy King 2022
First published as *Stadt, Raum und Gesellschaft: Henri Lefebvre und die Theorie der Produktion des Raumes*
© Franz Steiner Verlag, 2005

This translation was made possible by funding from the Börsenverein des Deutschen
Buchhandels and the Department of Architecture at ETH Zürich.

1 3 5 7 9 10 8 6 4 2

Verso
UK: 6 Meard Street, London W1F 0EG
US: 388 Atlantic Avenue, Brooklyn, NY 11217

versobooks.com

Verso is the imprint of New Left Books

ISBN-13: 978-1-78663-700-0
ISBN-13: 978-1-78663-701-7 (UK EBK)
ISBN-13: 978-1-78663-702-4 (US EBK)

British Library Cataloguing in Publication Data
A catalogue record for this book is available from the British Library

Library of Congress Cataloging-in-Publication Data
Names: Schmid, Christian (Sociologist), author. | Murphy King, Zachary,
    translator. | Schmid, Christian (Sociologist). Stadt, Raum und
    Gesellschaft.
Title: Henri Lefebvre and the theory of the production of space / Christian
    Schmid ; translation by Zachary Murphy King.
Other titles: Stadt, Raum und Gesellschaft. English
Description: London ; New York : Verso, 2022. | Includes bibliographical
    references and index.
Identifiers: LCCN 2022034716 (print) | LCCN 2022034717 (ebook) | ISBN
    9781786637000 (trade paperback) | ISBN 9781786637024 (ebook)
Subjects: LCSH: Lefebvre, Henri, 1901-1991. | Cities and towns—Research. |
    Sociology, Urban.
Classification: LCC NA2765 .S2913 2022 (print) | LCC NA2765 (ebook) | DDC
    307.76—dc23/eng/20220826
LC record available at https://lccn.loc.gov/2022034716
LC ebook record available at https://lccn.loc.gov/2022034717

Typeset by Hewer Text UK Ltd, Edinburgh
Printed and bound by CPI Group (UK) Ltd, Croydon CR0 4YY

Contents

Foreword

The story of this book begins in May 1980, on the streets of Zurich. The shattered remains of bank and luxury-store windows lay on the ground, trash containers are on fire, demonstrators storm through the streets, and policemen in combat gear are shooting with rubber bullets, their water cannon taking aim at anything that moves. The object of the struggle is the city: 'We want the whole city!' was the slogan that captured the explosion of rage, fantasy, and lust for life that put Zurich in a state of emergency for almost two years. Today, this may seem like simply one of the many, many urban revolts and uprisings that shaped the stories of urbanisation around the globe over the past several decades. For us, however, fighting with all that we had, everything was at stake.

That Zurich, of all places, had become the scene of such fierce, bitter, and prolonged conflict was astonishing in every respect. Zurich had been one of the quietest and most prosperous cities in the world, relatively small and well controlled. It had no strong social conflicts and a long history of social integration; a quarter of all housing was social housing, the political system was based on direct democracy, and, for many years, a large governing coalition had represented all of the major political parties. Of anywhere in the world, why did such a violent uprising occur in this city?

I was a young student at the time and participating in a research project on community media in cultural anthropology, which used action research and video to investigate social movements and youth culture in Zurich. As it later turned out, we had, without realising it, documented the series of events leading to the Zurich revolt. We recognised how the first protests formed against the demolition of affordable housing, against inner-city highway projects, against the

glaring lack of social spaces and cultural venues, against the socio-cultural stagnation, against a repressive and 'frozen' social climate that held this city in its icy
grip. We documented how long-suppressed demands resurfaced – for an alternative culture, for a more open society – and how politicisation processes began,
resulting in happenings, demonstrations, squats, imaginative and fun actions,
and absurd slogans: 'Down with the Alps! We want to see the Mediterranean!'
This slogan was obviously inspired by Dadaism, another movement that – in the
midst of the First World War – also originated in Zurich.

One of the actions was a small demonstration in front of the Opera House
on 30 June 1980, directed against the narrow-minded cultural politics of the
city. Suddenly, out of nowhere and without any warning, the situation escalated
into the 'Opera House Riot', which made headlines in the international media
and marked the beginning of 'the Zurich movement'.[1] Once again, we were
there with our video camera. When we showed our recordings at the first
public general assembly of 'the movement' a few days later, we immediately
found ourselves in the middle of the controversy. The government of the canton
of Zurich intervened and forced the university to deprive us of the video equipment, ordered the immediate termination of our research, and dismissed
Heinz Nigg, the director of our project. We organised resistance right away,
brought the movement to the university, and were, from then on, involved as
activists in the movement.[2]

Our experience was what Lefebvre called philosophy's 'becoming practical',
'becoming worldly' – and this can be quite dangerous, as we quickly learned in
the context of what was sometimes a violent conflict. The personal experience
of such a revolt propels one almost immediately and irreversibly on a different
path in life. But we also learned a second lesson: understanding the course of

---

1   The 'Zurich movement' was one of the fiercest urban revolts in Western Europe at
that time. It lasted for almost two years, demonstrations and actions happened at a near
weekly pace, hundreds of people were seriously injured due to police violence, and thousands faced legal prosecution (see for example Nigg, *Wir wollen alles, und zwar subito!*;
Schmid, 'The Dialectics of Urbanisation in Zurich').
The Zurich movement has to be understood in the context of a wider range of movements, starting with punk (and later European ska) in England and 'il movimento del '77',
an autonomous movement in Italy, which was based in (mostly squatted) social centres
(*centri sociali*). In 1980 and 1981, a series of revolts and movements erupted throughout
Western Europe, such as the squatter movement in Berlin (*Hausbesetzerbewegung*) and
Amsterdam (*kraakers*), the fights against Runway 18 West in Frankfurt, and the riots that
erupted in several inner-city neighbourhoods in Britain in 1981. Movements and mobilisations also emerged in smaller cities, such as Freiburg in Germany and Lausanne in
Switzerland ('Lôzane bouge'). The history of these movements is only partially written
(see for example Andresen and Van der Steen, *A European Youth Revolt*).
2   Schmid, 'Researching the City with Video'.

events requires interpretation. Why did we take to the streets? What were we rebelling against? What were we fighting for? We knew the domesticated and controlled everyday life, the narrow-minded and repressive social and cultural climate that prevailed in this city, and we ourselves felt the rage that drove us to the streets; we knew what we were fighting for: a different life, a different society, a different culture, the possibility of being able to realise alternative ways of living. But why here, in Zurich? We had empirically investigated the history of the events ourselves, and we were also involved in many of the activities and actions. But we were, in fact, quite ignorant. We lacked knowledge, we lacked theory.

Soon, another group of students formed at the Department of Geography at the University of Zurich, rebelling against the conservative and reactionary professors, demanding a different, open-minded, socially relevant geography. We knew each other from the demonstrations and actions, and began to ask questions and initiate discussions together. While outside in the streets the revolt was still raging, inside in the seminars we were challenging our professors armed with epistemology and critique of science, and so we also learned about the practical value of theory.[3] We soon formed a 'subgroup' that began to work on the urban question. We knew that urban development had been crucial to this revolt, which we would later call an 'urban revolt', and we wanted to better understand this relationship. Since there was almost no urban research in Zurich at the time, we had to come up with this urban theory ourselves. So, we started from scratch and taught ourselves what we needed to know. Collectively exploring new fields of knowledge and action and self-organised forms of learning was quite common during this revolt. In those turbulent but also extremely productive years, many new worlds had opened up – in punk music, in graphic art, in photography, in video and film, in theatre and dance – and many people had explored new cultural territories, developed and realised new ideas together, invented new cultural forms and styles. Zurich, once so provincial and boring, turned into a cosmopolitan metropolis that radiated far and wide.

We now tried the same with urban theory. We had no teachers, no instructions; we had some suggestions from critical students from Germany, with whom we soon entered into a lively exchange.[4] We read Castells, Harvey, Lefebvre, Engels, Marx, the Chicago School, and also some economic theory.

---

3   Bernhard et al., *Geografe nüme schlafe!*

4   We had joined forces with other students from Germany and Austria, who were also resisting conservative German geography, to form the Arbeitskreis Wissenschaftstheorie und Wissenschaftskritik (Working Group on the Theory and Critique of Science), and, together, we developed a critical geography over a period of years, with joint work on feminism, fascism in geography, and urban development (see ibid.).

Lefebvre proved to be, by far, the most compelling of all our readings. We were particularly inspired by his thesis about the complete urbanisation of society, his concept of the urban revolution, and his understanding of the urban as a process, which provided us with some important guidelines for our research. We organised retreats together, in which we learned to understand the constructions and nuances of these theories and to recognise their differences. Because we read the original texts, we understood how unfairly and polemically Castells had attacked his former colleague Lefebvre, how Castells misquoted him, and how misleading his presentation of Lefebvre's theory was. Since we also educated ourselves politically in the meantime, we understood very well that Castells represented the political point of view of the French Communist Party and considered Lefebvre to be an anarchist – which, in a certain sense, he was. And, finally, we also noticed the shaky construction of Castells's theory. While reading together, we actually laughed out loud at certain passages. It was a liberating laugh that ended our fear of theory forever.[5]

'Theory', for us, was not only a means of analysing and understanding our own situation, it was also a very practical, powerful, and joyful instrument that we applied in our activism. We founded the Ssenter for Applied Urbanism (SAU), and confronted our theoretical insights with the practical world.[6] We produced a multimedia show about the history of Zurich, wrote articles, organised public events, discussions, happenings, 'urban safaris' (public city tours), and ambitious thematic weeks, which we organised in the cultural centre Rote Fabrik.[7] Inspired by Lefebvre, we developed our own transductive approach to urban research in which our conceptualisations informed and inspired our more practical endeavours; concomitantly, the experience we acquired through our activism constantly challenged our theoretical reflections, thus stimulating us to revise our concepts.

We also sought alternatives to the prevailing academic industry. In conservative German geography, none of us – including most of our colleagues from Germany and Austria – had any chance of having an academic career. In 1991,

---

5   We turned these analyses into a book, which our professors did not accept as our diploma thesis, but which many students then used to study for their exams (see Hartmann et al., *Theorien zur Stadtentwicklung*).

6   The group that we named 'Ssenter for Applied Urbanism (SAU)' consisted of Roger Hartmann, Hansruedi Hitz, Richard Wolff, and the author. The word 'Ssenter' does not exist in any language – it is a joke; it results in the acronym SAU. The word *Sau* means 'pig' in German.

7   The alternative cultural centre Rote Fabrik was one of the concrete results that the Zurich movement had achieved and in which we worked for many years; see Wolff, 'A Star Is Born'; IG Rote Fabrik, *Bewegung tut gut*; Klaus, 'Die Bedrohung durch die Stadt'.

with a group of friends, we founded the International Network for Urban Research and Action (INURA) in Zurich and Salecina, an organisation that brought together activists, practitioners, and researchers from various countries and disciplines. INURA continues its work today, after more than three decades. The annual meetings of this network have become an important place of exchange beyond the academic industry, inspiring us again and again and encouraging us to continue with our own critical urban research. Together, we explored different 'possible urban worlds' and learned a lot about other cities and other urban practices and struggles.[8]

In Zurich, we investigated more and more aspects of urban development and thus directly experienced the paradigm shift in urban research emerging in the 1980s. We analysed the housing question and housing struggles, gentrification and urban regeneration, and the emergent globalisation of Zurich – which, during those years, became one of the centres of the global financial system – and we also discovered the enormous changes on the urban periphery, where various new centralities emerged. These theoretical and empirical efforts enabled our Zurich group to develop an analytical framework that integrated a range of new approaches developed at the time, such as the new urban-regional economy, global city theory, theories of gentrification, and analyses of the new developments on the urban periphery, as well as regulation theory, which allowed us, after some revisions, to establish a useful periodisation of Zurich's urban development.[9] Together with the group 'urbi et orbi' from Frankfurt, we engaged in a comparative project on politics and urban development in the two financial metropolises of Frankfurt and Zurich,[10] and working with a group of architects from Geneva, we discussed and developed the regulation approach and combined it with Lefebvrian concepts to make it applicable to a comparison of urban development in Geneva and Zurich.[11]

Eventually, I decided to accept an offer from Benno Werlen to return to the academic industry and begin a dissertation. I wanted to explore the paradigm

8   INURA, *Possible Urban Worlds*; INURA and Paloscia, *The Contested Metropolis*; Lehrer and Keil, 'From Possible Urban Worlds to the Contested Metropolis'.

9   Hitz, Schmid, and Wolff, 'Zurich Goes Global'; Hitz, Schmid, and Wolff, 'Urbanization in Zurich'.

10   This project introduced, among other concepts, global city theory and the analysis of the new centralities in the urban periphery, as well as some Lefebvrian applications into German-speaking urban studies. It brought together Roger Keil and Klaus Ronneberger from Frankfurt, and Hansruedi Hitz, Ute Lehrer, and Richard Wolff from Zurich, as well as the author (see Hitz et al., *Capitales Fatales*).

11   See DuPasquier and Marco, *Régulations fordiste et post-fordiste en Suisse depuis 1937*; Groupe Genève 500 mètres de villes en plus, *Genève, projet pour une métropole transfrontalière*; Schmid, 'Urbane Region und Territorialverhältnis'; Schmid, 'Raum und Regulation'; Schmid, 'Specificity and Urbanization'.

shift in urban research and systematise our empirical and theoretical findings. However, at a certain moment, these new urban concepts had revealed their limits. They were basically middle-range concepts addressing specific aspects of urban development, which made it difficult to integrate them into a more encompassing analytical framework. And they could not provide answers to the big question that had preoccupied me for so long: what is the urban? So, after much hesitation, I returned to Lefebvre and thus to an adventure with an uncertain outcome.

Lefebvre was largely absent from scholarly debates at this point. Though there had been a great wave of interest in French philosophy in Anglo-American academia, Lefebvre's work had been largely ignored. While his work is part of 'Western Marxism', it is also very unusual, heterodox, and open-ended. It is different from the solidly constructed and systematically designed theory of Marx and its German adaptations. It is also different from an Anglo-American political economy oriented towards critical realism. And it is in direct opposition to the structural 'Structural Marxism' of Althusser and his group with its clear rules and structures, which dominated French Marxism in the 1970s. Lefebvre had always strongly criticised structuralism, and he had bitterly opposed Althusser's anti-humanist Marxism from the beginning. Then there was Castells's devastating critique, as well as Harvey's reception which, while sympathetic, was nevertheless very cursory and distant. All of this meant that Lefebvre's texts did not find their way into international critical urban and regional studies, and they were only translated into English after significant delay.

Most of Lefebvre's older texts on everyday life, Marxism, metaphilosophy, and the urban were available in German, but not *The Production of Space* – this book had long languished without attention. I went to Paris on a scholarship, which helped me improve my French enough to read Lefebvre in the original, and which also allowed me to criss-cross the city that was so important to Lefebvre. To understand Lefebvre's work, one must understand Paris. When Lefebvre speaks of *la ville*, he (always also) means Paris. And I soon also came to understand that Paris was very different from Chicago, which, at the time, still served as the standard model of Anglo-American urban studies. Even before the LA School proposed its exciting theses, it was clear to me that the Chicago model, which we ourselves had analysed in our theory book, was basically a special case and that urban development needed to be understood much more broadly: urban development is always specific, and has to be analysed as the result of manifold determinations.

Lefebvre developed an original theoretical approach that cannot be fitted into any category. It is inspired by the activism he himself had experienced, by

Dadaism, Surrealism, Situationism, and May 1968 in Paris. In Lefebvre's work, dialectics is the core that drives the theory. But dialectics is poorly understood, especially in Anglo-American philosophy. It took Harvey many years to finally write a chapter on dialectics, and when he did, he introduced it with 'rules'.[12] Anyone who has been socialised in the German traditions of critical theory and philosophy would never explain dialectics through rules, since dialectics means interaction, contradiction, movement – the opposite of rules. Lefebvre, however, goes far beyond Hegel and Marx; he incorporates Nietzsche's poetry, and thus develops a three-dimensional dialectic in which he constitutively includes lived experience in the formation of theory. For this, he also draws on elements of phenomenology, from Heidegger, from Merleau-Ponty, and from Bachelard, which opens a materialist access to the unspoken, to the subterranean and unconscious. These, it should be noted, are theoretical ingredients that are viewed by many – and not only by Marxists – with a great deal of suspicion.

While I was writing my dissertation, Lefebvre was 'rediscovered' by postmodern geography, a current that included Soja, Gregory, Dear, and many others, who saw him as a precursor of postmodernism. But postmodernism, and, by extension, the poststructuralism that forms its theoretical basis, was hardly compatible with Lefebvre's epistemology, which is neither 'postmodern' nor 'poststructuralist'. He engaged intensely and critically with modernity, not in order to establish a 'postmodernism' but rather to radicalise the project of modernity and develop it into a critical humanism. And he, who was always a vehement critic of structuralism, could not become a poststructuralist either. We discussed Harvey's (and also Jameson's) sharp critique of postmodernism intensively. I agreed with them on much but not everything, especially the thesis that 'culture' was ultimately just a superstructural phenomenon of late capitalism. As someone who had lived through a cultural awakening and had worked for years in a cultural centre, I knew from my own experiences that culture is always a central element of political struggle – and that in a capitalist society, of course, there is always a tendency to commodify this awakening. Lefebvre's theory gives culture a much more active role, not as 'culture' – a term he himself always put in quotation marks – but as an activity and as a representation that both is connected to power but also draws on lived experience and is able to transcend everyday life with its poetry.

And, so, I also wrote my own analysis of Lefebvre's theory against the backdrop of its then-dominant postmodern interpretation, which has a place in this book, even if postmodernism has since disappeared from the political and

---

12   Harvey, *Justice, Nature and the Geography of Difference.*

academic agenda. Fortunately, I was not alone in my critique. Others were also rediscovering Lefebvre and were unhappy with the postmodern interpretation. We began to organise ourselves, gathering at INURA meetings, organising joint sessions at conferences, and, finally, publishing a book together.[13] Thus the appropriation of Lefebvre's theory also became a collective project and, at the turn of the century, a 'third wave' of Lefebvre appropriation emerged, offering a systematic yet open interpretation of Lefebvre's work. It contributed to a new understanding of the three-dimensional theory of the production of space and, consequently, of the three-dimensional dialectic. It utilised the thesis of complete urbanisation and its implications as a central starting point for analysis. It uncovered Lefebvre's concepts of the urban – centrality, mediation, and difference – and opened up his understanding of levels and scales. It made Lefebvre's theory of the state and his concept of 'state space' accessible. It explored Lefebvre's own empirical studies and his involvement in architectural projects. Finally, it also stimulated postcolonial appropriations of Lefebvre's thought and applied his work in a wide variety of fields (see section 1.4). My own book, published in German, on which this revised and extended English version is based, was a part of this 'third wave'. It specifically contributed a detailed reconstruction of Lefebvre's understanding of the urban, of his theory of the production of space, and of his three-dimensional dialectics.[14]

When my book on Lefebvre finally found its way onto my kitchen table, there was already a second one that had come off the press at almost the same time: *Switzerland: An Urban Portrait* by ETH Studio Basel, which is, in many ways, a practical application of Lefebvre's theory.[15] ETH Studio Basel was a small research unit, an offshoot of the Department of Architecture at ETH Zurich located in Basel, founded by four well-known architects – Jacques Herzog, Pierre de Meuron, Marcel Meili, and Roger Diener – and me, the geographer. I had the role of 'scout' in exploring the terrain of urbanisation that was unfamiliar to architects. We had one research question: what is urban Switzerland? But we had no answers, and neither a theory nor a method. Together with our students, we systematically explored Switzerland for years, using Lefebvre's thesis of complete urbanisation as a guideline. Over the course of the project, we developed an adapted,

---

13   Specifically, this was the ISA RC21 session in Berlin in 1997, a panel at the World Congress of Sociology in Montreal in 1998, sessions at the annual conferences of the American Association of Geographers in New York City (2001), Los Angeles (2002), Philadelphia (2004), and Denver (2005), and at the conference Studies in Political Economy of Scale in Toronto in 2005. We published the results of these discussions in Goonewardena et al., *Space, Difference, Everyday Life*.

14   Schmid, *Stadt, Raum und Gesellschaft*.

15   Diener et al., *Switzerland*.

practice-oriented version of Lefebvre's three-dimensional conception of the production of space, which allowed us to capture and map urbanisation processes across the terrain of Switzerland. We also developed a distinctive multidimensional methodology and discovered cartography as a crucial analytical tool. Thus, we learned from our own experience that Lefebvre's theory can ultimately be grasped only in application: one must immerse it in social reality, and develop it further in confrontation with this reality. Thus, a novel territorial approach emerged, which we used to study a wide variety of urban areas.[16] In the framework of the Future Cities Laboratory Singapore, a research branch of ETH Zurich, we continued this work in several comparative transdisciplinary research projects analysing urbanisation processes in large urban regions and in territories of extended urbanisation across the globe, broadening Lefebvre's theory with postcolonial urban approaches. All these projects are thus much more than just applications of Lefebvre's theory. Following the principle of transduction, they are effective developments of his theory.[17]

Inspired by these and other new insights, Neil Brenner and I sought to extend Lefebvre's theory in a way that would allow us to capture and conceptualise the various new forms of urbanisation we were then investigating. We drew on Lefebvre's concept of planetary urbanisation and expanded it with the concepts of concentrated, extended, and differential urbanisation.[18] The publication of these new concepts sparked heated debates, some of which were ignited by the style of our intervention, but also raised fundamental questions: What is the relationship between theoretical abstraction and concrete empirical research? What do urbanisation and the urban actually mean? What forms of urbanisation can be identified? How does the relationship between city and countryside present itself today? What role do peripheralisation and centrality play? These are all questions that will be discussed further in this book.

Re-reading my book fifteen years after its first publication in preparation for its translation, I realised how much critical urban and regional research has changed since then. 'Postmodernism' is a term of the past, and poststructuralism has dissolved into different, often empirically oriented strands. At the same time, a new, postcolonial urban studies has emerged, challenging the dominance of Western models of urbanisation and opening the field to new and inspiring investigations across the globe. The reception of Lefebvre's work has

---

16   Diener et al., *The Inevitable Specificity of Cities*; Diener et al., *Territory*.

17   Schmid et al., 'Towards a New Vocabulary of Urbanisation Processes'; Schmid and Streule, *Patterns and Pathways of Urbanization*; Schmid and Topalović, *Extended Urbanisation*; Topalović, *Hinterland*.

18   Brenner and Schmid, 'Planetary Urbanization'; Brenner and Schmid, 'The "Urban Age" in Question'; Brenner and Schmid, 'Towards a New Epistemology of the Urban?'.

also changed. It has become a part of many analyses and is applied to a wide variety of questions and contexts. This created a strange situation for me in revising my German book for English publication: to some extent, what I had originally written as a basis for further analysis has been realised and also informed a number of theoretical projects. Much of what I had envisaged and explored in my analysis has since been effectively applied and developed, not least through a whole series of projects in which I myself was involved. This book, therefore, needed significant revision; after all, it was not intended to remain a historical document but to provide orientation for current thinking. So, although I have included large parts of the original manuscript unchanged, I have re-contextualised them and also substantially expanded them in places. This is especially true of chapter 7, which elaborates and extends Lefebvre's dialectical-materialist theory of society. It was part of the original manuscript of my dissertation, but I was advised to omit it from the submitted PhD and the published book because its explicit Marxist orientation posed a problem for German geography, even at the turn of the twenty-first century. In addition, there were other aspects that I could not pursue further at the time, or that only later re-emerged as relevant, such as the concept of the right to the city, the question of concrete utopias, the conceptualisation of levels and scales, or Lefebvre's understanding of planetary urbanisation. The current book therefore additionally explores these themes. Finally, I also had to adapt the book to the prevailing reading conventions of Anglo-American academia.

In this updated form, this book is now available to an English-speaking audience as an introduction to Lefebvre's thought, a systematic overview of the theory of the production of space, and as an inspiration and stimulus to explore contemporary urban worlds.

Introduction

The starting point of Lefebvre's theory of the production of space is a problematic that has changed fundamentally in recent decades: the problematic of urban space. Since the second half of the twentieth century, the process of urbanisation has been constantly expanding over the earth, new geographies have emerged at all scales, everyday world orientations have been reshaped, and living conditions have been fundamentally transformed for large parts of the planet. These transformations have led to considerable confusion about the specificity of the urban, its form, its definition, and its limits; they have also challenged the basic social categories of 'space' and 'time'. How can the urban be conceived theoretically? What categories can be used to analyse the changing spatio-temporal configurations that define our world today? What terms and concepts can capture the manifold urbanisation processes that are both shaping and destroying our planet? In the past decades, disciplines concerned with the urban question have seen many initiatives to develop new understandings of the fundamental concepts of space and time and to elaborate new conceptions of related social theories.

In this theoretical and empirical reorientation, the work of Henri Lefebvre has been of exceptional importance. In the 1970s, when the process of a comprehensive urbanisation of the planet was only beginning to emerge, he outlined a theory of the production of space that remained unrecognised for a long time, and was only slowly received more broadly, developing its full impact several decades later. The importance of this theory lies in the fact that it systematically embeds the categories of 'urban' and 'space' in a general social theory and makes it possible to map, capture, and analyse the production of space at all scales. Its multidimensional conception allows it to consider the material production of space, the production of knowledge and concepts, and the production of everyday world meanings in their relational interplay. Accordingly, this theory has attracted interest from a wide variety of disciplines: in geography, sociology, and cultural anthropology, the political sciences, literature, cultural studies and the arts, philosophy, and in architecture, urban design, and planning.

The theory of the production of space that Lefebvre developed in a mere decade, between the mid-1960s and the mid-1970s, is a very unusual theory. It offers a great openness for different appropriations, allows for many interpretations, and can be applied to a wide range of empirical and practical questions. In particular, it connects to various fields of practice, and appeals not only to theorists and researchers, but also to activists and practitioners. At its core, it is an independent dialectical theory of social practice, building on ideas from Marx, Hegel, and Nietzsche, which also integrates considerations from phenomenology and semiotics. It combines cultural, linguistic, political, social, and economic aspects of spatial production in a multi-layered conception. It is a dynamic theory that does not stop at the analysis of urban phenomena, but opens onto a horizon of possibility, a concrete utopia of another, urban society.

The reader of Lefebvre, however, faces significant difficulties in understanding this theory: Lefebvre developed it continuously, incorporating ongoing social changes into his theorising. Furthermore, it is embedded in French philosophical discussions of the time, which were extremely rich and fruitful in those years, but also complex and contradictory. The reception of Lefebvre's theory has long struggled with these peculiarities, and has been characterised by various misunderstandings and simplifications, especially because its distinctive social and epistemological context has not been sufficiently taken into account. Much has been written about Lefebvre's wide-ranging work, but, to date, very few studies analyse in depth the fundamental concepts and categories of his theory.

This book presents a comprehensive reconstruction of Lefebvre's theory of the production of space. It frames its epistemological and theoretical context and offers an analysis and critique of its central categories and concepts on the basis of a systematic immanent reading. The aim of this book is to reveal the basic principles of this theory and to make it accessible for further analysis and application. It thus provides a comprehensive analytical framework to help readers engage productively with Lefebvre's analysis, situating and explaining a wide variety of spatial phenomena and to apply his ideas for empirical research. Finally, in the spirit of Lefebvre's commitment to praxis, the book also offers insights for everyday practice in a rapidly changing, opaque, and illegible urban world.

Lefebvre's Project

Henri Lefebvre addressed a wide variety of issues over the course of his long life as, in his own words, a philosopher, sociologist, activist, and 'metaphilosopher'. In more than 60 books and some 300 articles, he devoted himself to, among other things, the critique of philosophy, metaphilosophy, and dialectics, linguistics and semiotics, the development of a theory of social practice, rural sociology, the critique of everyday life and modernity, and rhythmanalysis, as well as the development of a new theory of the state. Within this broad corpus, the texts on questions of the urban and space, written in a brief period from the late 1960s to the mid-1970s, occupy a special place. They treat a specific historical problematic, which was addressed in the contemporary debates as a 'crisis of the city'. This term refers to a historical moment in the long history of urbanisation in which the morphology of the city began to dissolve, the everyday qualities of urban spaces were fundamentally transformed, and the opposition of city and countryside was fundamentally questioned.

Lefebvre's approach to this problematic was strongly influenced by his studies of everyday life and the modernisation of society, which he had begun in France after the Second World War and which he continued for decades. In the course of these studies, he encountered the phenomenon of urbanisation that would subsequently preoccupy him more and more. After writing various essays, some of which are assembled in the anthology *Du rural à l'urbain*, in 1968 he published *The Right to the City*, his first attempt to theorise the urban crisis, in which the search for a new theory of the city took centre stage. As a result of his analysis, he formulated the demand for a 'right to the city': by this term he understood the right not to be expelled from the city, the right to access the possibilities and opportunities of the urban, the right to a renewed urbanity. Only two years later, Lefebvre expanded these initial thoughts into a general theory of urban society in *The Urban Revolution*. This book started with the most radical of all possible theses on the urban: the complete urbanisation of society. It involved a radical critique of existing theories on the city, and indicated a fundamental change of perspective, a reorientation of analysis from the object of the 'city' to the process of urbanisation. This dynamic analysis was directed towards a virtual, possible vanishing point: the urban revolution and the resulting emergence of an 'urban society' replacing the extant 'industrial society'.

The analysis of urban society raised the question of the connection between the urban problematic and the development of society as a whole. In order to shed light on this connection, Lefebvre again shifted the focus of analysis and placed the urbanisation process in the context of the more general theoretical category of social space. This led to one of his most complex and difficult works, *The Production of Space*, from 1974, considered by many to be his magnum opus, in which, as the title indicates, he outlines a comprehensive theory of the social production of space. This text, whose key insights only become accessible through a meticulous reconstruction, is then the central work analysed in this book. Lefebvre complemented these analyses of the urban and of space with an encompassing analysis of the state. In the four-volume work *De l'État*, published between 1976 and 1978, Lefebvre presented a new grounding for state theory, in which he develops the concept of a 'state space' that reveals the active role of the state in the production of space.

In their entirety, Lefebvre's texts on everyday life, the city, the state, and space contain a general theory of society in which society is consistently conceived in its spatio-temporal dimensions. This heterodox theory, which is positioned outside of all current approaches and schools, received little attention in the academic world for a long time. Although Lefebvre was considered one of the most important French philosophers, and other parts of his work were widely received, his texts on the urban and on space presented considerable difficulties. They drew readers into a new field of knowledge that had hardly been theoretically explored at the time of their publication. Whoever makes the effort to engage with this theory, however, will experience a fascinating theoretical world that holds many insights, and also many surprises.

Troubles with Lefebvre[1]

Lefebvre is among the large number of French authors in philosophy and social theory who have been translated into English and has been accordingly resituated in a different epistemological context in recent decades. In this respect, Eleonore Kofman and Elizabeth Lebas strongly emphasise the problem of transferring concepts from their original context to other contexts in which they might no longer be applicable.[2] They grasp this problem with the apt phrase 'lost in transposition': the transfer from one (historical) place, or from one linguistic, political, and social context, to another. In this process, a work is detached from the conditions in which it was produced and from its relation to other intellectual currents with which it was associated, and inserted into a new environment, a new place and time, with its different language, problematics, and conditions. While new interpretations and contextualisations of a

---

1   This section is based on Schmid, 'The Trouble with Henri'.
2   Kofman and Lebas, 'Lost in Transposition'.

work can always generate new knowledge, it must also be kept in mind that important aspects of this work can at the same time be obscured. This is particularly evident in those receptions of Lefebvre's work which, while acknowledging its inspirational qualities, deny it any theoretical coherence. For example, Don Mitchell, who has long studied Lefebvre's texts, writes:

> But as with so much of his work, his arguments are only coincidentally coherent. Lefebvre's value is not as a theorist so much as a generative thinker adept at being suggestive. This is, surely, one reason he is so attractive to the rest of us all these years after his intellectual heyday: he opened up all manner of avenues for continued investigation.[3]

However, to suggest an absence of theoretical coherence in Lefebvre's oeuvre displays a lack of knowledge of the historical, theoretical, and epistemological context of Lefebvre's work. The same can be said for many confusions and misunderstandings which have become evident in the interpretation of his work.[4] A better and more adequate understanding of Lefebvre's theory requires attention to aspects of his work that are relatively unfamiliar, especially to the Anglo-American academic industry: 1) the open epistemological position that Lefebvre characterises as *metaphilosophy*; 2) his heterodox and open-ended *dialectical materialism*; 3) his *three-dimensional dialectic*; 4) the dialectical relationship between theory and praxis that Lefebvre captures in the concept of *transduction*; 5) the *strategy of cognition* that sets Lefebvre's theory in constant motion; 6) and, last but not least, Lefebvre's *language*, which oscillates between analysis and poetry.

The fact that Lefebvre always developed and refined his theoretical concepts in interaction with the current social developments of his time is fundamental to understanding his thought. Lefebvre lived in a specific urban situation in Paris, with its exceptional intellectual climate, and he was biographically intertwined with the history of movements that ranged from the artistic and avant-garde currents of the turbulent 1920s, especially Dadaism and Surrealism, to the critical urbanist experiments and actions of the Situationists in the late 1950s and early 1960s, to the 'explosion' of May '68. His epistemological position was decisively shaped by these everyday, artistic, and activist experiences, which recur in various forms in all his texts. These experiences inspired his ambitious project of a revolutionary humanism. Lefebvre's goal, then, was not to solve puzzles, as is so often the case in the academic industry, but to advance social change, and he used analysis itself as an instrument to achieve this

---

3   Mitchell, 'Revolution and the Critique of Human Geography', 10.
4   See also Kipfer et al., 'On the Production of Henri Lefebvre'.

change. Such an analysis is always both a critique and a project: a radical critique of what exists that opens up a possibility for practical (and radical) change.[5] It was in this way that Lefebvre transcended the field of philosophy and developed a *metaphilosophy* that aims to make philosophy 'of the world'. The realisation of philosophy, then, means that it becomes worldly – not as philosophy, but as a 'project that is realised in the world and, by its very realisation, negates itself in the process of sublation'.[6]

Lefebvre's theoretical point of departure was his critical engagement with the philosophical debates of the 1920s. In familiarising himself with Western philosophy, he appropriated a wide variety of theories and incorporated them into his reflections in a critical manner. Not only did he strongly contribute to introducing Hegel and the early work of Marx into French discussions,[7] but, in the process, he developed his own heterodox *dialectical materialism*. In this, he relied essentially on two sources: First, he drew on a nineteenth-century school of thought that I will call, from the French perspective, 'German dialectics'. Specifically, the three most complex, controversial, and enigmatic figures in this strand of thought were precisely the ones most appreciated and cited by Lefebvre: Hegel, Marx, and Nietzsche. The adoption of this body of thought by Lefebvre involved, on his part, a transposition under the intellectual conditions of the interwar period in France, shaped by this specific situation with its own 'zeitgeist' and its own problematics. Second, essential elements of Lefebvre's work are based on phenomenology. This includes parts of Heidegger's work as well as the work of Maurice Merleau-Ponty and Gaston Bachelard. Lefebvre brought together these two traditions of thought – German dialectics and Franco-German phenomenology – in a highly creative way, and from them he developed an original theoretical world that transcends disciplinary boundaries and cannot be assigned to existing 'schools'.

The epistemological core of Lefebvre's work is his original formulation of a *three-dimensional dialectic*, which is still poorly understood, especially in the Anglo-American academy, where dialectical thinking is less widespread. It is an unusual version of dialectical thinking, which Lefebvre himself explained fully only in his late writings. Unlike the dialectic of Hegel and Marx, Lefebvre's version is three-dimensional, that is, it places three concepts in interdependence. This is a basic principle that he hints at in his early writings, which he gradually develops throughout his texts until he finally unfolds it in its full breadth in *The Production of Space*, where he makes it the centrepiece of his three-dimensional theory of the production of space. This dialectic has

---

5   Stanek, *Henri Lefebvre on Space*.
6   Lefebvre, *Métaphilosophie*, 51. Translation by the author.
7   See particularly Marx, *Morceaux choisis de Karl Marx*; Hegel, *G. W. F. Hegel, Morceaux choisis*.

enormous potential, but it is difficult to access, understand, and apply. This is because for Lefebvre the dialectical movement of concepts must be grasped in its entirety. Often, however, attempts are made to circumvent this dialectic and use only individual aspects of his concepts. But if Lefebvre's concepts are applied undialectically, they lose their dynamism and complexity, and thus an essential part of their analytical sharpness and effectiveness.

Based on his dialectic, Lefebvre developed his own understanding of the relationship between theory and praxis. He was not only a philosopher and theorist, he was also an activist, constantly engaged in the political realities and social developments of his time, and he participated as well in the elaboration of a number of concrete architectural and urbanistic projects. Thus, his concepts are largely based on his own experiences and research, and also on the work of his colleagues, collaborators, and students, as Łukasz Stanek has shown in great detail.[8] This research directly informed his theories, since, true to his dialectical approach, he developed his theoretical concepts in close inter-action with empirical research, in the sense not of classical deduction, but of dialectical *transduction*, in the movement from praxis to theoretical abstrac-tion and back to concrete application:

> Transduction elaborates and constructs a theoretical object, a possible object from information related to reality and a problematic posed by this reality. Transduction assumes an incessant feedback between the conceptual framework used and empirical observations . . . It introduces rigor in invention and knowledge in utopia.[9]

Thus, Lefebvre understands transduction as a dialectical movement: a first moment consists in empirically analysing a specific, concrete social practice, while also getting rid of the allegories, metaphors, pseudo-concepts, and repre-sentations that try to define and dominate this practice. A second moment focuses on approaching the fullness of the lived experience analytically without destroying it. Finally, in a third moment, the concept is developed in a way that allows it to analyse the extant society, to articulate a critique of the present, and to illuminate the horizon of future developments.[10] To engage in this dialectical procedure is to think along with this movement.

The procedure of transduction directly affected the character of Lefebvre's concepts, which he developed through a specific *strategy of cognition*.[11]

8   Stanek, *Henri Lefebvre on Space.*
9   Lefebvre, *Right to the City*, 151.
10   Lefebvre, *La présence et l'absence*, 37; see also *Right to the City*, 165–6.
11   Lefebvre, *Everyday Life in the Modern World*, 28.

Lefebvre's metaphilosophical epistemology prohibited him from attempting to systematise concepts on the basis of a predetermined speculative principle (whether an old one, such as offered by a Kantian schema, or newer ones), and to develop an ontology from it. Alfred Schmidt remarked on this point, 'Opposed to every ontology ... [Lefebvre] developed himself into a critical Marxist whose standards grew out of a materialist analysis of the course of history.'[12] Lefebvre did not seek to fix or set his concepts ontologically. Instead, he explored the changing meaning, content, limits, and ultimately the conditions of the social validity of these concepts. This meant employing a double-edged procedure: the critique of concepts by praxis, and the critique of praxis by concepts. Theoretical abstraction thus relates to a concrete reality, to a real confrontation. This means, then, to take concepts as a guide to recognising society, or even to confront the philosophical concepts with the unphilosophical world.[13] Thus, one cannot simply 'apply' Lefebvre's theoretical concepts, that is, take them as a theoretical framework by which one could analyse and explain a wide variety of empirical examples. Rather, the task is to confront these concepts with reality, or even immerse them into reality, and allow them to become generative. Accordingly, Lefebvre often introduces his concepts as approximations, as 'strategic hypotheses' whose scope and areas of validity he explores in the course of his investigation. With a strategic hypothesis, he centres his reflections around a particular focal point, the core of a concept, then expands it in repeated approximations. He examines its validity and tests possible areas of application, only to develop it further and often to merge it into a new concept. This strategy may or may not be successful; it may last for a shorter or longer time, after which it splits, decentres, or dissolves altogether. It does not aim at any eternal truth, but remains related to the moment and thus necessarily subject to revision.[14]

Accordingly, a 'final' definition of these concepts can hardly ever be assumed; they change in the course of Lefebvre's theoretical forays, but not arbitrarily, rather within the confines of an inherent movement (which can and must be reconstructed). This procedure also characterises his books, which usually begin with a provisional definition of a concept that he then develops as the book progresses. As he himself explained, the 'truth' of a concept is revealed only at the end of the book, as the result of a search that reveals the dynamic character of the concept.[15] Thus, the definition of his concepts cannot be clarified simply on the basis of individual passages in the text – a very common mistake in the

---

12   Alfred Schmidt, 'Henri Lefebvre and Contemporary Interpretations of Marx', 325.
13   Lefebvre, *Everyday Life in the Modern World*, 28; Lefebvre, *Metaphilosophy*, 50, 114.
14   Lefebvre, *Production of Space*, 60.
15   Lefebvre, *La présence et l'absence*, 16.

interpretation of Lefebvre's texts. Accordingly, Lefebvre's theory is in a perpetual dialectical movement. It has, so to speak, a deep structure which is fluid. It goes without saying that this process will not stop at the end of the book, because the concept will continue to unfold in theoretical discussions and in praxis. As a consequence, therefore, the theory as a whole must also be continuously developed. It must not stand still, or it will lose its generative power.

Therefore, finally, the *language* used by Lefebvre is of great importance, something that has been almost completely ignored in previous interpretations. Any engagement with Henri Lefebvre's 'metaphilosophical meditations' conveys first and foremost a 'reading experience' that is exceptional in academia: his texts can offer the sensual experience of an inspiring and pleasurable read with rich undertones and overtones that often convey something more than logical analysis would suggest. Michel Trebitsch describes Lefebvre's writing style as 'between flexibility and vagueness, where thinking is like strolling, where thinking is rhapsodic'.[16] As Wolfgang Altenhoff notes, Lefebvre deliberately dispensed with the accepted tools and conventions of scholarly writing, with 'verbalised' scientificity and the norms implicit in it.[17] This is a consequence of his critique of language derived from Nietzsche, who understands language as a system and as a deadly power that can only be overcome by poetry, by a new alliance of concept and imagination. This practice results in a specific terminology that often does not correspond to our current understanding of the terms used. This problem is particularly evident in translations, some of which have caused considerable confusion and left certain concepts completely obscure.

Lefebvre thus developed an often playful, while also redundant and fragmentary, writing style that provokes emotional responses by poetic means. His texts are strewn with polemics, abrupt musings, digressions seemingly unmotivated by the immediate context, questions that arise suddenly which he often leaves open or answers with his famous 'yes and no'. As Kofman and Lebas noted:

> Being Lefebvrian, it has been said, is more a sensibility, rather than a closed system; and indeed, many have found his theoretical insights difficult to apply due to the fluidity, dynamic and openness of his thought. It is probably encapsulated to perfection by one of his most common responses, 'yes and no'.[18]

---

16   Trebitsch, preface to *Critique of Everyday Life*, vol. 1, xi.
17   Altenhoff, foreword to *Sprache und Gesellschaft*, 9–10.
18   Kofman and Lebas, 'Lost in Transposition', 8.

In order to understand this writing style, it is also important to take the production process of these texts into account, since, as Rob Shields points out, Lefebvre's preferred method of writing was dictation:

> His writing practice is anchored in the duality of his voice and the activity of his typists. Dictating all of his most important books and articles 'live' while his female companions typed, a conversation is implicit in the rambling quality of his works. If they are hard to read or analyze, this is because they are cut up by theoretical questions and because they consist of dictated material, and discussions that were the unacknowledged contributions of those typists, which filled in a lengthy outline of key points that Lefebvre wrote up ahead of time.[19]

Finally, the richness of his presentation of the many facets and multiplicity of diverse phenomena, linguistically 'captured' and melted into the flow of argumentation, testifies to his search for a comprehensive theoretical project and consistent effort to grasp the totality of social processes.[20] This includes a conscious use of symbolic figures, of metaphor and metonymy. It is precisely such aspects that make Lefebvre's texts extremely attractive and at the same time pose serious problems for any analytical reading, as Neil Brenner and Stuart Elden noted: 'Lefebvre's writing style – with its dense theoretical argumentation, its many implicit references, its elusive organisational structure and its frequent digressions – can prove extremely challenging, and at times downright frustrating, even to French-language readers of his texts.'[21]

The Thesis of Coherence

As shown above, Henri Lefebvre developed an extraordinarily sophisticated and far-reaching general theory of society, which provides important and extremely fruitful starting points for the analysis of spatio-temporal social processes. The aim of this work is to analyse the contemporary historical and epistemological context of this theory, to reconstruct its inner structure and logic, and thus to make it more accessible for empirical research and for practical applications.

This project is motivated by a certain conception of theory. It understands theory as a tool that can guide and drive the process of 'cognition'. Interestingly,

---

19 Shields, *Lefebvre, Love and Struggle*, 6–7.
20 Altenhoff, foreword to *Sprache und Gesellschaft*, 11.
21 Brenner and Elden, 'Henri Lefebvre in Contexts', 767.

English has no clear equivalent to the German *Erkenntnis* or French *connaissance*, which are often used to describe the exciting moment in which research or a discussion creates a new insight and thus helps to better recognise the world. While 'knowledge' (*Wissen* in German, *savoir* in French) can be understood as a completed and canonised form of knowledge, and thus also an instrument of power, 'cognition', in the sense of *Erkenntnis* or *connaissance*, is open to discovery. For Lefebvre, knowledge involves a clandestine connection to power, a crude or subtle intermingling with political practice and ideology. While knowledge is in the service of power, critical and subversive cognition does not accept that power. It contains both a critique of its own insights, which it relativises, and a critique of the status quo, which it opens towards the real and towards the possible: it provides an orientation, which opens pathways and reveals a horizon.[22] A theory should therefore not simply systematise the existing body of knowledge and consolidate it into a canon but, on the contrary, critically question supposed certainties again and again, test the existing concepts, and dynamically develop them further. Cognition is a process, a constant questioning of what exists and an exploration of possibilities, an expansion of the horizon of canonised knowledge.

Lefebvre's theory is therefore not to be confused with a framework into which one could simply plug empirical data without further reflection. Rather, this theory should be seen as an active tool that can have a generative power. It can guide one to investigate certain questions that would otherwise have gone unnoticed, and its internal logic can drive thinking and lead to certain conclusions, whether one likes them or not – this is the practical value of a theory. It illuminates reality, and at the same time it animates the future. One should therefore not adopt or apply Lefebvre's theory without examination, but should develop it further, in constant confrontation with social reality. What is needed is an open and creative approach to this theory.

For this to be possible, however, it is necessary to understand the principles of the construction of this theory, the logic of its connections, its mode of explanation, the definitions of its terms and concepts, the dynamics of its method, and the relation of the theory to praxis. Therefore, the initial methodological thesis of this work is the thesis of coherence: the following analysis assumes that Lefebvre's work is characterised by a continuity of concepts and terms that are linked in a consistent way. To assume the coherence of a work means to carry out a systematic reading and to undertake an *immanent* reconstruction and critique of its central concepts and categories. Thus, the following analysis examines Lefebvre's theory not according to some external

---

22   Lefebvre, *Production of Space*, 367–8, 10; Lefebvre, *Urban Revolution*, 66.

standards and theoretical positions but according to its inner logic. It thus differs substantially from most previous presentations of Lefebvre's theory. The aim here is to work out the fundamental principles of his epistemology and to expose the basic lines of his general spatio-temporal social theory.

In doing so, it is important to take into account both the developmental lines of Lefebvre's thought and the context of his respective works. As Kipfer notes, this requires

> a methodologically pluralist approach to Lefebvre's work that incorporates contextual, textual and intertextual readings of Lefebvre and analyzes both content and form, problematic and method of Lefebvre's texts. Such an approach should be aware of the structure of Lefebvre's work, which is neither an arbitrary collection of fragments nor an integrated system. In Lefebvre's own terms, his combined work can be seen as a fluid constellation of concepts with a loose meta-theoretical orientation and multiple, moving conceptual centers of gravity. It is an open totality that resembles the time-space dynamics that Lefebvre observed during May 1968 in Paris.[23]

Kofman and Lebas have shown that such an interpretation requires a simultaneously synchronic and diachronic movement through his work. This means, on the one hand, to work synchronically through the concepts and theories that are developed in a text, and to reflect on references and connections to other texts; and on the other hand, to run diachronically along the lines of the historical development of the overarching concepts and to analyse continuities and ruptures in Lefebvre's thought. This necessitates a compilation and confrontation of numerous texts and concepts, some of which span a considerable period of time. In order to counteract the danger of an overly schematic systematisation, and to let the rich undertones and overtones that Lefebvre employs in his texts resonate, extensive passages of text will be quoted directly or paraphrased at length throughout this book.

On this basis, Lefebvre's theory of the production of space is subjected to a systematic and critical immanent reconstruction. Accordingly, I have not attempted to develop alternative readings of Lefebvre's theory, or to seek points of contact for possible combinations with other theories, as some other interpretations have done. This book takes a fundamentally different approach: it tries to think through the inner laws and logics of his theory consistently to the end, to elucidate its dialectical linkages and argumentations, the

---

23   Kipfer, 'The Relevance of Henri Lefebvre in the 1990s', 7.

movement of thought and action, the interplay of theory and reality as it arises in practical confrontation and interaction, but also in empirical investigation. Accordingly, it places great emphasis on epistemology, the conditions under which knowledge can be gained. Thus, this book is about theory as an indispensable tool of cognition, and at the same time as an adventure in thought.

A Guide through the Book

The structure of this book follows the developmental logic of Lefebvre's thought: beginning with his critique of philosophy and his engagement with the dialectic, it presents his critique of everyday life, his thesis of the complete urbanisation of society, and his theorisation of the urban; analyses his three-dimensional theory of the production of space and its implications; looks at his theorisation of the state; and finally presents the outline of a general theory of society in which society is consistently conceived in its spatio-temporal dimensions.

The introductory chapter, 'On the Reception of Lefebvre's Theory', situates the reception and interpretation of the theory of the production of space in its historical context. It first sheds light on the problematics that motivated this theory and outlines the broader theoretical context of the concepts of the 'urban' and of 'space'. It situates this theory among contemporary debates, and analyses the main lines of the reception of Lefebvre's work, which in turn have influenced these debates in a complex interaction – especially given the delays in English translation. The fluctuating history of the reception of Lefebvre's theory also serves as a transdisciplinary introduction to the history of urban and regional studies in the past fifty years. The exposition of the chapter follows the historical development of the problematics of space and the urban and highlights in detail the three waves of Lefebvre interpretation that have been associated with them. It discusses, first, the 'urban crisis' that initiated the emergence of neo-Marxist-oriented critical urban studies in the 1970s. Second, it analyses the poststructuralist and postmodernist interpretation of the 1990s, which was marked by the emergence of a new spatial problematic and the 'spatial turn' in the social sciences and humanities. This reception was followed by a third wave of interpretation which insisted on a historical-materialist and dialectical understanding of Lefebvre and pursued a systematic interpretation and critical appropriation of his theory. The chapter concludes with an overview of the wide reception that Lefebvre's theory has achieved in recent times.

The second chapter, 'The Three-Dimensional Dialectic', analyses the epistemological and metaphilosophical foundations that are crucial for an understanding of the theory of the production of space. The fact that Lefebvre did not follow particular schools of thought and defied existing disciplinary boundaries necessitates a detailed analysis of these foundations. In the process, three major lines of his thought can be reconstructed. First, he developed a specific understanding of social praxis, which was decisively influenced by his activist experiences and his interactions with the Dadaists, the Surrealists, and later also the Situationists. Second, this understanding of praxis led him to his radical critique of philosophy and science, which strives to make philosophy worldly and which he called 'metaphilosophy'. Third, he oriented himself epistemologically in relation to a philosophical current that I call, as noted above, 'German dialectics'. From his appropriation of the thought of Hegel, Marx, and Nietzsche, he gradually developed a three-dimensional version of dialectics that is highly unconventional and stands without precedent in the history of theory. This chapter thus reconstructs the basic outlines of a theory of social praxis and introduces Lefebvre's three-dimensional dialectical thought.

The epistemological and theoretical consequence of Lefebvre's metaphilosophy was to turn to a question that classical philosophical traditions had systematically excluded: everyday life, and thus the 'unphilosophical', the banal and ordinary, and the concrete world as experienced and suffered by human beings. In the course of his investigations of everyday life in France, Lefebvre came across the new social phenomenon of urbanisation. The third chapter, 'Urbanisation and Urban Society', traces Lefebvre's efforts to understand urbanisation in its historical breadth and depth and to anchor it in social theory. Starting from the provocative thesis of the complete urbanisation of society, he developed the idea of an urban revolution, which opens the prospect of the (possible) rise of an urban society. Two theoretical steps or operations can be identified in this analysis: in the first step, Lefebvre reconstructs the historical development of the city of the West, from the political city of antiquity to the possible end point of the complete urbanisation of society, the dissolution of the city, and the dialectical sublation of the contradiction of city and country. In a second step, Lefebvre analyses the same history of the city from the perspective of the entire society and identifies a sequence of three spatio-temporal fields or 'continents': the rural, the industrial, and the urban. These three fields, which he understands as overlapping modes of thought, action, and life, can each be characterised by a particular characteristic: while the rural field is determined by need and the industrial one by work, the urban field opens up the historic possibility for enjoyment and pleasure as defining characteristics. Lefebvre ultimately concludes that the transition from the industrial to the urban field is part of an urban revolution, comparable in its dimensions and effects to the industrial revolution. He identifies the possibility that in the course of this revolution an urban society could emerge. With this concrete utopia of an urban society, Lefebvre went far beyond contemporary analyses of urbanisation. He did not stop at a critique of urbanisation, but rather explored its inherent possibilities. In doing so, he shed light on a number of phenomena and processes that are only now fully developing, and which this chapter discusses and defines: the dialectic of urbanisation manifested in the double process of implosion–explosion, the urbanisation of everyday life, the rediscovery of the urban, and the planetary reach of urbanisation unfolding in the last decades.

Starting from the thesis of complete urbanisation and the dissolution of the 'city' as a morphological, economic, social, and political entity, the fourth chapter, 'The Urban Level', pursues the question of what meaning the term 'city' still has in an urbanised society. Lefebvre tried to discover this by means of a third theoretical operation in which he identified three levels or orders of social reality: first, a private level, the near order, that of everyday life; second, a general level, the far order, dominated by the state and the world market; and third, in between, he situated a middle level – the level of the urban, which he conceived as a level of mediation between the near and the far order, between the private and the general. This analysis allowed him to identify the specificity of the urban: centrality. He understood centrality as a form that brings together the most diverse elements of society and in this way becomes productive. Centrality can therefore be understood as a social resource. In capitalism, centrality is determined by the fundamental contradiction of access or exclusion, which expands on a planetary scale to the dialectic of centralisation and peripheralisation. Lefebvre derived from this analysis the demand for a right to the city, which he understood as a right to centrality, the right to access the possibilities and opportunities of the centre, the right for self-determination in the creation of urban space.

The analysis of the urban as a specific level of social reality leaves an open question: how is the urban produced in social praxis? Answering this question again requires a change of perspective: the city must be analysed in a general sense as a spatio-temporal configuration. The analysis thus approaches the central concept of this study in chapter 5 – 'The Production of Space'. According to Lefebvre, the social process of the production of space can be examined along three dimensions that are dialectically related to each other: the perceived (*le perçu*), the conceived (*le conçu*), and the experienced (*le vécu*). In spatial terms, this involves spatial practice, the representation of space, and the spaces of representation. This double triad of dialectical terms at the heart of Lefebvre's theory remains the subject of extensive debate and speculation to this day. Its basic characteristics are only revealed through a meticulous reconstruction of his work. In a critical examination of selected, especially postmodern interpretations, the foundational elements and lines of argumentation of Lefebvre's theory are elaborated and some widespread misunderstandings are explained. Finally, Lefebvre's independent, three-dimensional variant of the dialectic is exposed and further developed.

With a more precise definition of the three dimensions of the production of space to hand, the sixth chapter, 'On the History of Spaces', follows the account of the history of the West as presented by Lefebvre himself. This chapter serves to further determine and specify the three dimensions of the production of space, drawing on Lefebvre's own examples and illustrations. It also presents Lefebvre's unconventional history of space, which unfolds in three stages: from absolute space to abstract space to differential space. This history outlines a movement from nature to the dominance of a socially produced 'second nature'. It finally finds, at a higher level, the urban, which can be conclusively defined here: the urban is a product that emerges in the complex interplay of spatial practice, the representation of space, and spaces of representation, or perceived, conceived, and lived space. It is a differential space-time in which social differences recognise, respect, and interact with each other. The urban is a possible-impossible, a concrete utopia, a utopia that is not located in the far future or in an abstract space-time, but can become realised in everyday life, in the here and now.

The seventh chapter, 'The Commodification of Space', brings together the concepts discussed so far with the basic categories of Marxist social theory. This chapter was part of the original manuscript of this book but was never published. It shows how consistently Lefebvre introduces space or space-time into Marxist social theory. He recognises in the production of space a second circuit of capital that overlaps and complements the first circuit of the production of goods – an analysis that David Harvey made a key element of his own political economy of space. Lefebvre, however, goes a decisive step further by consistently following the process of exchange that is constitutive of capitalism and thus the dialectic of exchange value and use value. He reveals how social space becomes commodified, not only the land and real estate, but the entire space of the planet, which also includes formerly 'natural elements', such as air, water, and earth. In the process, urban space itself, with its specific qualities, and everything it contains, along with the people who constitute it, also becomes a commodity. Lefebvre then shows how social relations are incorporated into space: every social relation entails a material 'support' that forms the very basis of the spatial-material order of a society. Addressing the question of how this material support is produced, he develops a new, spatial understanding of the state that goes beyond the classical Marxist base–superstructure theorem. With the commodification of space, the state becomes the central actor directing and supervising the production of space. Lefebvre identifies the fundamental role of the state in capitalism as the equalisation of the unequal, and thus the regulation and control of the conditions of exchange. Lefebvre recognises that this creates a multiscalar 'state space'. Moreover, he argues that the ever-widening expansion of urbanisation is only possible with an enormous expansion of state control and surveillance. The earth as a planet finally becomes the new horizon of the production of space. The result of Lefebvre's enormous theoretical efforts is therefore nothing less than a reformulation and expansion of Marxist theory. The broad scope of Lefebvre's theory has not yet received the recognition it deserves: he developed not only a political economy of space, but a general spatio-temporal social theory.

Finally, summarising the reconstruction carried out through the book, the concluding chapter, 'A Spatio-Temporal Theory of Society', presents the general outline of Lefebvre's spatio-historical and dialectical-materialist theory of society. It can be presented as an analytical matrix of the production of social space and social time, composed of three basic categories: dimensions, levels, and configurations of social reality. The first, which determines the other categories of the theory, can be understood as *the spatio-temporal dimensions of social reality*. The production of space can be understood analytically as the totality of three dialectically interrelated processes of production that dialectically imply each other: the production of material conditions, the production of knowledge, and the production of meanings. The second category is formed by *the spatio-temporal levels of social reality*. These refer to the broader social context of the production of space and follow a threefold subdivision into the global level or distant order dominated by the state and the market, the private level or near order that determines everyday life, and an intermediate and mediating level in between, the urban level. The urban appears here in three different ways: as the form of centrality, as the level of mediation, and as a differential space-time. Finally, the third category, *the spatio-temporal configurations of social reality*, refers to the historicity and temporality of the production of space. Lefebvre identified in his historical excursions several attempts to develop a periodisation of the modes of production of space. However, he introduced this category only in an approximate way and left it in an incomplete state. This opens new possibilities for a substantial expansion of Lefebvre's theory that have emerged in recent years, especially with the rise of postcolonial urban studies and an emphasis on the historically and geographically varied nature of space and the urban.

With this conceptual overview – it is hoped – an analytical tool is now available that can be productively used for exploring a wide range of questions, and that might create possibilities for a renewal of social theory, empirical research, and political practice.

1

On the Reception of Lefebvre's Theory

The aim of this introductory chapter is to reveal the social problematics that motivated Lefebvre's theory of the production of space and to outline the theoretical debates in which his understandings of the 'urban' and of 'space' are to be situated. This chapter will also explore the reception of Lefebvre's contribution, which, in turn, influenced these debates in a complex interaction. It will thus lay out a number of reasons to explain why his spatio-temporal social theory still strongly inspires ongoing debates in social sciences and humanities, including philosophy, sociology, human geography, cultural anthropology, regional and urban economy, cultural studies, literature, arts, planning, urban design, and architecture.

A theory of urban space involves two basic problems: first, the question of how social space is constituted, constructed, or produced, and how it is theoretically anchored in a social theory. Second, we must explore the fundamental properties of urban space and ask how the specificity of the urban can be defined. I will approach these problematics from the perspective of the urban question. Epistemologically, the critique of urbanisation and urbanism formed the starting point of Lefebvre's theory of the production of space, and it can accordingly only be understood through his analysis of urbanisation and of urban society. In the history of social theory, 'the city' has been one of the privileged 'objects' of theory building and research since the beginning of the social sciences, while 'space' remained an under-theorised category in social theory until the 1980s (section 1.1).

The reception of Lefebvre's theory of the production of space has undergone various shifts. It can be divided into three clearly distinguishable phases in which different interpretations of Lefebvre's work were produced, some of which even appear to be incompatible. The first phase was marked by the broad stream of social protests of the late 1960s and is situated in the problematic of the 'crisis of the city' (*crise de la ville*) and the 'rediscovery of the urban'. Lefebvre's works on the urban and urbanisation, especially his books *Right to the City* and *The Urban Revolution*, became the starting point of a paradigm shift in which a neo-Marxist critical urban theory emerged. These books were mainly read by activists, however, and had hardly any influence on academic discussion. In contrast, two other theoretical approaches gained great importance at this time, both of which strongly built on Lefebvre's analyses. David Harvey, one of the founders and leading exponents of *radical geography*, developed a theory of the political economy of urbanisation and the production of the built environment influenced by Lefebvre's work. Despite its far-reaching ambition, however, Harvey's theory has a narrower focus than Lefebvre's wide-ranging project of a theory of the production of space. In parallel, Manuel Castells developed his theory of collective consumption, which took Althusser's structuralist Marxism as its basic orientation. This theory, which formed the core of the *new urban sociology*, was likewise based on Lefebvre's analysis, although Castells himself understood it as an alternative to Lefebvre's. This first, neo-Marxist phase of the appropriation of Lefebvre's work on the urban and space was thus ambivalent: on the one hand, Lefebvre's work formed the logical starting point and the theoretical basis of the newly emerging critical urban studies; on the other hand, however, his own writings were not widely received and were relegated to the margins of intellectual discussions (section 1.2).

In the course of the fundamental social changes of the 'long 1980s', which were characterised by the crisis of the Fordist–Keynesian development model in the Western industrialised nations, by the disintegration of the socialist bloc, and by the establishment of a neoliberal world order, another paradigm shift developed in critical urban and regional research. On the empirical level, the intertwined processes of globalisation and urbanisation raised new questions and revealed problems that could no longer be satisfactorily explained by the old approaches. On the epistemological level, there was a simultaneous change of perspective from modernism to postmodernism and from structuralism to poststructuralism. Subsequently, new theoretical approaches emerged that increasingly placed space at the centre of their analysis. As a consequence, a *spatial turn* in the social sciences and humanities emerged, in which *postmodern geography* played a decisive role. In this context, Henri Lefebvre's work was rediscovered. This second phase of the appropriation of Lefebvre's theory thus took place under completely different conditions to the first. It was less interested in his concepts of urbanisation and the urban than in a particular theoretical perspective: to show the importance of space for understanding current social processes. Accordingly, *The*

Production of Space became the book that everyone read but no one really understood. This reception was also characterised by a selective reading, one that placed Lefebvre in almost arbitrary theoretical constellations and often seamlessly included him in the gallery of postmodern ancestors. Thus, this second wave of reception did not exploit the full potential of his theory on either a theoretical or an empirical level (section 1.3).

A third phase of reception emerged around the turn of the twenty-first century, some of which explicitly opposed postmodernist and poststructuralist interpretations and insisted on a historical-materialist and dialectical understanding of Lefebvre's theory. A new generation of scholars sought ways out of the theoretical vacuum left by the postmodern and poststructuralist turn and attempted to develop a new understanding of Lefebvre's central theoretical categories and concepts. It is in this current of a simultaneously systematic interpretation and critical appropriation of Lefebvre's theory that the present work situates itself. Today, the reception of Lefebvre's work encompasses a broad field of research. His theory is related in various ways to a wide range of questions and has also been applied successfully in many empirical studies (section 1.4).

1.1 The Specificity of the Urban and the Question of Social Space

> How to think about the City . . . without conceiving clearly the space it
> occupies, appropriates (or 'disappropriates')?[1]

The questions of city and space have been treated in very different ways in social theory, yet both are crucial to understanding and contextualising Lefebvre's theory. Therefore, this introductory section provides a short, critical overview of some of the main concepts and definitions of the 'city' and relates them to understandings of 'space' in social theory.

Since the beginning of the social sciences, the 'city' has been a privileged field of theoretical reflection and empirical research. This can be attributed, among other things, to the fact that urban development repeatedly posed new problematics, which inspired new theorisations, and gave rise to new concepts of the urban from which different schools and approaches emerged. In contrast, 'space' played a subordinate role in the social sciences for a long time. It is true that space (like time) was one of the fundamental categories of classical

---

1   Lefebvre, 'Preface to the New Edition', in Elden, Lebas, and Kofman, *Henri Lefebvre*, 208.

philosophy, from Aristotle to Descartes, Newton and Leibniz to Kant and Spinoza (see section 5.1). However, most social theories are part of seemingly 'non-spatial' approaches that give epistemological priority to time and historical development. The history of social theories shows a remarkable similarity between otherwise very different theoretical traditions. In most classical approaches, time and history were the dominant categories of analysis; the core questions were related to the entire society and oriented towards an understanding of social change. With the constitution of nation states, society presented itself as a national unit, and theory production was primarily concerned with the (historical) development of this national society. In this context, social space and spatial differentiation appeared at best as secondary questions, but mostly as derived aspects which were not in themselves significant for the development of society.[2]

The Specificity of the Urban

Whoever sets out to explore the specificity of the urban in the history of social theory is confronted with a bewildering variety of definitions.[3]

In his famous analysis of the medieval city in the West, Max Weber defined the ideal type of the 'urban community' (*Stadtgemeinde*) as follows:

> [An] urban 'community' in the full meaning of the word [occurred where] the settlement had ... a relative predominance of trade-commercial relations with the settlement as a whole displaying the following features: 1. a fortification, 2. a market, 3. a court of its own and at least partially autonomous law, 4. a related form of association, and 5. at least partial autonomy and autocephaly, thus, also, an administration by authorities in the election of whom the burghers participated.[4]

With this definition, Weber attempted to capture the fundamental social, economic, and political changes that took place in the medieval cities of the West, where a bourgeoisie based on trade and craftsmanship established itself and acquired a certain political independence. Compared to the surrounding

---

2   See for example Konau, *Raum und soziales Handeln*; Saunders, *Social Theory and the Urban Question*; Gottdiener, *The Social Production of Urban Space*; Soja, *Postmodern Geographies*; Werlen, *Society, Action and Space*.

3   See Saunders, *Social Theory and the Urban Question*; Hartmann et al., *Theorien zur Stadtentwicklung*.

4   Max Weber, *The City*, 54–6.

countryside, this city presented itself as a 'haven of freedom'. If a serf managed to escape from the countryside to the city and stay there for a while, he could obtain citizenship in the city and thus 'freedom'. This is where the famous German saying 'Stadtluft macht frei!' (urban air makes you free) comes from, which to this day remains an ideological remnant in urban areas that have long since lost their political, social, and economic independence.

However, the serf who came to the city was free in two senses: he was no longer chained to the land and the landlord, but he was also free of any means of production and thus forced to sell his labour power. It was Karl Marx who illuminated this other side of the coin, and accordingly he found a different answer to the question of the specificity of the urban:

> The foundation of every division of labour which has attained a certain degree of development, and has been brought about by the exchange of commodities, is the separation of town and country. One might well say that the whole economic history of society is summed up in the movement of this antithesis.[5]

The dialectical contradiction of city and countryside thus formed for Marx the decisive basis for the development of capitalism. Accordingly, he did not define 'city' as a specific category, but as a category of society as a whole, which can only be understood in the dialectical relationship between city and country.

But even this definition refers to a specific historical situation, which in turn gradually lost its specificity in the course of the rise of capitalism and the advent of industrialisation in Europe. The city became the place where the means of production and the labour force were concentrated, and thus also a place where the contradictions of industrial society collided in all their sharpness. One of the earliest and at the same time best-known depictions of this problem can be found in Friedrich Engels's impressive description of Manchester in *The Condition of the Working Class in England*. Here, he recognised the tendency towards the centralisation of population and capital inherent in industrial capitalism, which would later be conceptualised as 'agglomeration economies'. At the same time, it was in the city that the contradictions between capital and labour were brought to a head: 'The great cities are the birthplaces of labour movements; in them the workers first began to reflect upon their own condition, and to struggle against it; in them the opposition between proletariat and bourgeoisie first made itself manifest.'[6]

---

5   Marx, *Capital*, trans. Fowkes, 472.
6   Engels, *The Condition of the Working Class in England*, 418.

These contradictions opened a long tradition of reflections that examined the social significance of the city and that understood the urban as the focal point of social development. In his famous essay 'Metropolis and Mental Life' of 1903, the German sociologist Georg Simmel linked the forms of social relations in big cities to three criteria: the division of labour, the money economy, and size.[7] He understood the city as a cultural form and postulated a connection between (urban) morphology and the social organisation of coexistence. At the same time, he also recognised the differentiating power of the urban: The concentration of people in large metropolises not only leads to an increased level of social interaction, but also gives much greater significance to the money economy and hence to exchange values and the market. This, in turn, forces individuals to specialise their professional skills in order to make a living. Thus, urban differences emerge based not only on immigration or inhabitants' different origins but also on the social division of labour and the related generation of cultural, economic, and social inventions in large metropolises.

This body of thought found its way across the Atlantic via Robert Park, who had studied under Simmel, and formed one of the important foundations of the Chicago School of Sociology, which was ground-breaking in many respects. Park and his colleagues, especially Ernest Burgess and Roderick McKenzie, viewed the social antagonisms of Chicago of the 1920s and 1930s, strongly marked by diverse waves of immigration, as a social laboratory or biotope in which the most diverse processes of urban society could be studied.[8] Following bioecology, they understood the city as a socio-ecological unit in which specific processes such as invasion, succession, and segregation take place. They saw these processes as closely related to the spatial form of a city: Burgess sketched a city model with concentrically arranged rings, each representing a different socio-ecological habitat. Although it was originally intended merely as a working sketch, it became the most famous model of urban development, even though its theoretical foundations and the terminology of the Chicago School with its strong reference to bioecology and social Darwinism were controversial. By contrast, the extremely rich empirical studies conducted within the framework of the Chicago School received far less attention.

This conception of the city as a socio-ecological unit proved to be difficult to maintain over time. It was challenged by the process of urbanisation itself, which seemed to overcome all morphological and socio-spatial boundaries. Accordingly, it became increasingly difficult to define the limits of the city empirically, and the idea of the city as an organism became untenable. Even

---

7   Simmel, 'Metropolis and Mental Life'.
8   Park, Burgess, and McKenzie, *The City*.

before the Second World War, Louis Wirth, a member of the Chicago School, tried to find a way out of this dilemma. In his 1938 article 'Urbanism as a Way of Life', one of the most famous essays on urban sociology to date, he defined the city, partly by reference to Simmel, as a 'way of life' based on three material characteristics determining urban social life: size, density, and heterogeneity.[9] This conception had the great advantage of allowing for different shades of urban and rural, depending on the quantitative values these characteristics assumed. In this logic, the larger, the denser, and the more heterogeneous a city is, the more 'urban' it is. However, also in this conception the city theoretically forms a unit, a definable and delimitable settlement space.

The concept of agglomeration offered another solution to the problems of defining and delimiting urban areas. It first emerged in demography and was used particularly to analyse census data. It took account of the continuous expansion of cities by applying a dynamic definition of urban space through the identification of catchment areas, essentially based on commuter linkages. It thus tried to escape the strong dependence on the morphology of settlement areas. However, this approach still treats the city as a bounded spatial unit, and the delimitation of an urban area remains of central definitional importance. Furthermore, these definitions became more complicated as urban areas began to overlap and intertwine, and new terms were coined with more open definitions, from 'conurbation' to today's 'urban mega-region'.[10]

A completely different approach was taken with concepts that sought to grasp the urban in architecture and urban planning, such as the famous Athens Charter, which was drawn up and discussed at the 4th CIAM Congress, 'The Functional City', in 1933, and which Le Corbusier later published in a revised form. It defines the city as a unit of four key functions: living, working, recreation, and transportation. A central goal of the charter was to counter the observed 'image of chaos' of contemporary cities with an efficient functional urban design. In Le Corbusier's formulation: 'The city will take on the character of an enterprise that has been carefully studied in advance and subjected to the rigor of an overall plan . . . Subordinated to the needs of the region, assigned to provide a framework for the four key functions, the city will no longer be the disorderly result of random ventures.'[11] This functional definition of the city was used for concrete analyses and urban design proposals and dominated the architectonic discourse for decades.[12]

---

9 Wirth, 'Urbanism as a Way of Life'.
10 For a discussion of the agglomeration question, see Brenner and Schmid, 'The "Urban Age" in Question'.
11 Le Corbusier, *The Athens Charter*, 99–100.
12 Van Es et al., *Atlas of the Functional City*.

At the same time, the German geographer Walter Christaller made the first serious attempt to understand the economic foundations of urban development with his dissertation *Central Places in Southern Germany* from 1933.[13] His aim was to comprehend the economic laws that determine the number, distribution, and size of cities in a given area. To this end, he approached the city from the perspective of centrality, which he regarded as its specific economic function in social life. However, he considered only one aspect of centrality, namely the optimal provision of goods and services to the population of an area. Based on these assumptions, he arrived at an ideal distribution of cities in space, which corresponds to a hierarchical hexagonal system. He thus considered cities from the perspective of the national territory, and designed a universal system that could be applied to the systematic planning of the entire (national) territory (see also section 4.5).

All these concepts were finally called into question in the course of the 1960s, when a new problematic began to dominate the urban discussion: the 'crisis of the city'. The radically reorganised cities which emerged in the wake of the widespread application of functional planning had lost so much of their everyday qualities that public criticism and social protest arose in various places, demanding urban qualities and leading to a 'rediscovery of the urban'. It was precisely this crisis that became one of the starting points of Henri Lefebvre's theory.

The wide diversity of definitions of the urban apparent from this brief review suggests three basic conclusions. First, the city and the urban are *theoretical categories*: they are not directly observable 'objects', but complex phenomena that must necessarily be conceived and defined theoretically. Their definition depends crucially on the perspective from which they are viewed, and they are therefore also determined by divergent research interests and questions. All of the definitions presented above, a list that could be extended as desired, look at the urban from very different perspectives. Not only do they illuminate different facets, but they are also often incompatible or even contradictory.

Second, these definitions are always bound to a given period. They refer to very specific historical problems that raise questions at a certain point in time and urgently demand answers. As the urban problematic is always posed anew, the city and the urban are therefore not universal but necessarily *historical categories* that must be redefined according to the current social situation. They are thus always grasped in new – explicit or implicit – definitions.

---

13   Christaller, *Central Places in Southern Germany.*

Third, the city and the urban are always *specific categories*. It is interesting to see that many definitions can be traced back directly to concrete, spatially and historically situated urban constellations that guide and inspire a theoretical perspective. Some definitions thus constitute generalisations of concrete examples, such as Manchester, Berlin, Paris, Chicago, or Los Angeles. In this way, the concrete experiences of the researchers become part of these definitions, even if unstated and implicit, and the definitions are often not questioned but taken as a 'given'. We essentially learn as children what a 'city' is, through the experience of a (certain) place at a (certain) time. Anticipating one of Lefebvre's central conclusions, we can postulate that we cannot see a space without having first conceptualised it, and that we cannot conceptualise it without having first experienced it.

These considerations raise the question of how the urban can be theoretically defined at all. First, the urban presents itself as a complex and multidimensional phenomenon that various concepts and theories illuminate from different perspectives, usually covering only certain facets. Second, it is always embedded in a historical development and thus determined by changing problematics. And third, it is always embedded in very concrete and thus specific situations. The generalisation of such necessarily limited perspectives and specific examples entails major problems. Postcolonial urban research has clearly demonstrated the limitations of the construction of 'paradigmatic examples' and pointed to the great diversity of urban developments that exist and coexist in the world, which Jennifer Robinson has expressed in the well-known formulation 'ordinary cities'.[14] Based on these reflections, ETH Studio Basel has posed the question of how to theoretically and empirically grasp the inevitable specificity of urban spaces.[15] The question of the specificity of the urban – how to define the nature of the urban – thus rests on the specificity of (historically and geographically) concrete places, which requires a fundamentally different approach.

This conclusion raises the question of more general categories that could be used to capture the constitution of the urban as a social process. Accordingly, placing the 'city' as a specific category in a larger, more general context seems like an obvious step. On the one hand, this is time and thus history, and on the other, space. This shifts the problem to an epistemological level: what actually is space (and time)?

---

14 Robinson, *Ordinary Cities*.
15 Diener et al., *The Inevitable Specificity of Cities*; Schmid, 'Specificity and Urbanization'.

The Question of Space

Even more than in the case of the urban, the problem of defining 'space' is a fundamental one: it brings us to epistemological questions that are generally treated in the history of science under the rubric of the 'ontological status of space' (and time).

These questions inevitably lead into dangerous waters. Those who engage in them are forced to navigate between Scylla and Charybdis: on one side stand the cliffs of the 'reification of space' and thus the naturalisation of social facts; on the other side lurk the rocky shoals of the 'derivation thesis', which understands 'space' as a mere expression of overall social processes.

The reification of space is at the core of a debate with which geography, in particular, has struggled since its beginnings as a scientific discipline. It refers to an objectified, naturalist conception of space that conceives of space 'in itself' as a physical entity or 'substance' and regards it as an 'object' that becomes socially active. Such reifying conceptions ascribe an effect on human bodies and human activities to material space.[16]

While the reification of space appears as the result of a naïve materialism, of the unquestioned belief in the 'reality' of the visibly apparent, the derivation thesis is conversely based on a central premise of social theory: on the primacy of the theoretically conceived. It leads to the well-known formulation that certain social laws, processes, or structures are 'expressed' in space. However, such a position already presupposes the existence of a pre-given, physical-material space, and it fails to recognise that what we commonly call 'space' does not present itself as a pristine surface to the footprint of history.

Both conceptions of 'space' thus prove to be problematic: on the one hand, no effective forces can be attributed to physical 'space in itself'; on the other hand, space is not a mere expression of superordinate processes and developments that directly imprint themselves on the physical materiality of the earth's surface.

There are no easy ways out of this dilemma. Attempts to shift the problematic of space to the level of discourse and to see space as discursively constituted, for example, or to reduce it pragmatically to procedural questions, such as in planning and urban design, miss the problem at the heart of the discussion on space: it is not 'abstract space', the space of discourse or space as a purely analytical category that seems to pose almost insurmountable difficulties, but its physical-material aspect. The analytical challenge of any 'spatial' theory remains the question of the materiality of space.

---

16   See Werlen, *Sozialgeographie alltäglicher Regionalisierungen*, 143ff.

On this slippery terrain, more recent debates have at least reached a certain agreement. Space is neither a substance nor an object in the conventional sense of the word: 'space in itself does not exist'. If one can agree on this sentence, there still remain a number of questions. Is space an a priori category, a theoretical concept, a dimension of social reality? Does it exist without time, or is it a historical phenomenon?

Even a brief look at one of the classical debates on space in physics shows this problem in all its acuity: the dispute on Newton's concept of absolute space and Leibniz's concept of relative space (see also section 5.1). Is (physical) space in itself an absolute given, an immovable and unchanging container in which the material particles it contains can be absolutely localised – or is it a relative one whose qualities only arise from the relational position of material objects and events? It was not until hundreds of years later that the theory of relativity seemed to have settled this debate, since it was based on a relative rather than an absolute conception of space. However, this conclusion would be ill-informed. Albert Einstein himself rejected Leibniz and agreed with Newton, considering the conception of absolute space to be the only possible, and the only productive, foundation for Newton's mechanics, given the state of science at that time.[17]

This leads to the significant conclusion that 'space' is not an unchangeable 'fact' or 'object' and that the question of the 'right' conception of space can only be answered in relation to the given problem and the underlying theory. Even if approaches in the social sciences rightly insist on their epistemological difference from the natural sciences, this question reveals a remarkable analogy: 'space' does not exist prior to theory. This shifts the problem to the relation between spatial theory and social theory.

Spatial theory and social theory are not independent of one another, but mutually dependent: every theory of space is based on a certain conception of society, and every social theory implies a certain conception of space. Accordingly, they cannot be discussed as separate subjects.

If one follows this line of argument, there are basically two possible approaches to the theorisation of 'space'. One possibility is to look for the 'appropriate' spatial concept for an existing socio-theoretical conception. In recent years, this classical social-scientific approach has led to a number of theories of social space, exemplified by the historical-materialist concept of David Harvey and the action-theoretical concept of Benno Werlen.[18]

Another possibility is to adopt a historical approach and to connect the respective spatial theories or concepts back to the development of society.

---

17 Einstein, foreword to Jammer, *Concepts of Space*.
18 Harvey, *Limits to Capital*; Werlen, *Society, Action and Space*.

What is sought in this case is no longer a theory of space (and time), but a theory of the *production* of space. If space is a social product, then this product, this produced space, can be analysed. This was the approach taken by Henri Lefebvre.

City and Space as Products

Lefebvre's fundamental thesis, which also serves as a guideline for this work, is that society produces its space, that space is a social product.

The idea of 'producing space' may sound strange, as Lefebvre himself conceded.[19] But by this formulation he wanted to indicate that 'space' can only be understood from within a given society. Space is a social product, a human-made 'second nature'.

Lefebvre did not want to create a spatial theory or a spatial concept – he wanted to analyse the process of the production of space itself. From this perspective, spatial theories or spatial concepts become a constitutive component of the production of space. Lefebvre does not stop at such an analysis, however, but dialectically relates these theories or concepts of space back to a material production process and to a process of the production of meaning. In this way, a three-dimensional dialectic of the production of space emerges that cannot simply be deduced. To understand it, it is necessary to engage with Lefebvre's dialectical theoretical world.

The orientation of such an analysis is fundamentally historical, and thus time comes to the fore. 'Space' cannot be understood without the time that produces it and that emerges from it. The key to understanding the production of space is thus historical analysis.

From this point of view, it can no longer be a matter of examining the 'city', but rather the process of its production. Lefebvre accordingly made a fundamental shift in the perspective of urban studies from the analysis of an 'object' – the city – to the analysis of a process – urbanisation. From these reflections emerge the outlines of a comprehensive spatio-temporal theory of social practice.

---

19   Lefebvre, *Production of Space*, 23.

1.2 Critical Urban Theory

> The urban phenomenon is universal, which would be sufficient justification
> for the creation of a university devoted to analytic research on the subject.[20]

The historical starting point of Lefebvre's theory of the production of space is the 'crisis of the city' (*crise de la ville*), as described in the 1960s in Western Europe and North America. This crisis can be traced back to multiple aspects of the modernisation of society that were connected to urbanisation and functional approaches to urbanism in the post-war period: the standardisation of society through the production of uniform, monofunctional, and monotonous housing estates and zones of detached houses in the banlieues and suburbs, the expansion of central business districts and the concomitant expulsion of parts of the population from their neighbourhoods, the destruction of a lively everyday world with its social networks, the gradual disintegration of the inner cities and the increasing social unrest caused by urban poverty and racism. This urban crisis formed one of the starting points of diverse countermovements that led to the broad current of social protest in the late 1960s. In retrospect, it can be postulated that the urban crisis was a central aspect, if an under-studied one, of the 'crisis of Fordism'.

The urban crisis also provoked a fundamental upheaval in academic debates, as the various disciplines involved in urban studies at the time had hardly any significant answers to offer to the radically changing social situation. The 'quantitative revolution' that had taken hold in the social sciences in the course of the post-war period had frozen urban studies in empiricism and model fetishism. Thus, the disintegrating 'Fordist city' with its explosive social problems appeared as terra incognita through which new paths of theory had to be forged. The urban crisis immediately became a crisis of urban research in all the disciplines involved.

In this context, Henri Lefebvre's work on the question of the urban was a real breakthrough. It became the starting point of a paradigm shift that led to the emergence of a new, *critical* urban studies, involving diverse disciplines. Although they subsequently branched out widely, in retrospect two theoretical pivot points can be identified, each with a different focus, but both strongly influenced by Lefebvre. One pivot was the theory of collective consumption, which came from French structuralist Marxism and was fundamentally influenced by the work of Manuel Castells. It developed into the dominant critical

---

20 Lefebvre, *Urban Revolution*, 54.

urban theory in France and also radiated into Anglo-American *new urban sociology* and neighbouring disciplines such as urban political economy and urban political sciences.[21] The second pivot was David Harvey's theory of the production of the built environment. It emerged within the framework of *radical geography* and formed the basis of an urban political economy that also influenced critical political economy as well as urban political sciences and urban planning.[22]

Until the mid-1980s, the theories of Castells and Harvey remained the two most influential and debated contributions to critical urban studies, and they are discussed in all relevant overviews.[23] Both theories offer a comprehensive analysis of the urban, and both follow Lefebvre's perspective of understanding the city as a socially produced spatio-temporal configuration and of analysing social space from the perspective of urbanisation.

Post-war Urban Research

In post-war urban studies, *urban sociology* had become the central discipline. Applying concepts of urban social ecology derived from the Chicago School of Sociology, it developed a quantitatively oriented mainstream, which processed ever-larger data packages using ever more sophisticated statistical methods. *Urban economics* also depended predominantly on quantitatively oriented approaches, above all developing specialised location and land use theories, which were mostly designed in the form of neoclassical equilibrium models.[24] *Urban geography* was also characterised by a quantitative mainstream, at that time subsumed under the rubric of 'spatial science': on the one hand, it applied a solid canon of location theories, ranging from von Thünen's land use theory, Alfred Weber's industrial location theory, and Christaller's theory of central places, to Lösch's theory of market networks.[25] On the other hand, it relied on the quantitative variant of urban social ecology to explain the internal differentiation of cities.[26]

---

21   See for example Pickvance, *Urban Sociology*; Harloe, *Captive Cities*; Mayer, Brandes, and Roth, *Stadtkrise und soziale Bewegungen*; Walton, 'Urban Sociology'.

22   See Tabb and Sawers, *Marxism and the Metropolis*; Cox, *Urbanization and Conflict in Market Societies*; Dear and Scott, *Urbanization and Urban Planning in Capitalist Society*.

23   Saunders, *Social Theory*; Gottdiener, *The Social Production of Urban Space*; Hartmann et al., *Theorien zur Stadtentwicklung*; Katznelson, *Marxism and the City*; Soja, *Postmetropolis*; Merrifield, *Metromarxism*.

24   See for example Alonso, *Location and Land Use*.

25   See for example Carter, *The Study of Urban Geography*.

26   See for example Berry and Kasarda, *Contemporary Urban Ecology*.

Initially, 'space' posed few problems to these approaches – at least, there was hardly any corresponding awareness of a problem. This is evidenced, for example, by David Harvey's *Explanation in Geography*, the most important overview of the spatial discussion in geography at the height of the quantitative paradigm.[27] At the end of a chapter on the 'language of spatial form', Harvey gives the following advice:

> The lesson that should be learned is that there is no need to take a rigid view of the spatial concept itself either for philosophical purposes nor for purposes of empirical investigation. The concept itself may thus be regarded as flexible – to be defined in particular contexts, to be symbolised in particular ways, and to be formalised in a variety of spatial languages.[28]

Insofar as the category of space was explicitly addressed at all within the framework of such quantitative functionalist approaches, it was based – in accordance with the abstract explanatory models used – on the purely geometric, homogeneous, isotropic, two-dimensional concept of Euclidean space.[29] Thus a 'spatial science' emerged, which in one form or another always presupposed a predefined 'space' as an empirical object of research.[30]

The limitations of all these approaches were already problematised in contemporary discussions: the 'quantitative paradigm' offered only partial theories and, with its pronounced empiricism, had led to a dramatic loss of theoretical depth compared to older approaches. What weighed even more heavily than such theoretical deficits, however, was their increasing empirical barrenness. They remained wedded to a technicist logic and had no answers to the emerging urban crisis and the newly emerging problematics associated with it.

Significantly, the first impetus for the renewal of urban research came from 'outsider' critics who began to interrogate post-war urban design and planning and its unforeseeable social consequences, such as the young journalist Jane Jacobs, who influenced generations of urban researchers and planners with her book *The Death and Life of Great American Cities*, or the philosopher and psychoanalyst Alexander Mitscherlich, whose book title *Die Unwirtlichkeit unserer Städte* (*The Inhospitality of Our Cities*) would resonate far into the future.[31] The polemics and experimental methods of the

---

27 Harvey, *Explanation in Geography*.
28 Ibid., 228.
29 Ibid., 191–2.
30 Werlen, *Society, Action and Space*.
31 Jacobs, *The Death and Life of Great American Cities*; Mitscherlich, *Die Unwirtlichkeit unserer Städte*.

Situationists also expressed a fundamental critique of functional urbanism (see also section 3.2).

However, these criticisms, which are only singled out here as examples, remained essentially limited to aspects of urban design and planning. The first to address the 'crisis of the city' systematically and on a solid theoretical basis was Henri Lefebvre. Although he was inspired by these critiques, he launched a much broader theoretical project: he not only saw the urban crisis as a consequence of functionalist urbanism, but placed it within the framework of a comprehensive process of *urbanisation* that was engulfing and transforming both the countryside and the city. And he postulated that contemporary society was undergoing a fundamental social change: an 'urban revolution'.

The Theory of Collective Consumption and the New Urban Sociology

The first response to Lefebvre's provocative thesis came from Althusserian structural Marxism. In 1972, only two years after the publication of Lefebvre's *The Urban Revolution*, the sociologist Manuel Castells, a collaborator and colleague of Lefebvre who had fled Spain's dictatorship, presented a neo-Marxist replica under the programmatic title *The Urban Question*. Despite being strongly influenced by Lefebvre's analysis, this book presented itself as a 'truly' Marxist alternative. In France, Lefebvre's humanist Marxism had already been challenged in the late 1960s by Louis Althusser, who developed a structuralist interpretation of Marx that was diametrically opposed to Lefebvre's dialectical and open materialism on many points, and which became the dominant Marxist current in France in the course of the 1970s.

Just the title *The Urban Question* already points to the author's ambition and intentions: it is an explicit reference to Friedrich Engels's *Housing Question*. In the extremely influential collection of essays published under this title, Engels had analysed the pressing housing crisis in the industrial cities of his time as a derived process that could only be grasped within the framework of a comprehensive critique of capitalism. Accordingly, the housing crisis could not be solved by urban reforms, but only by a social revolution: 'It is not that the solution of the housing question simultaneously solves the social question, but that only by the solution of the social question, that is, by the abolition of the capitalist mode of production, is the solution of the housing question made possible.'[32] As long as capitalism exists, the housing crisis will perdure – this,

---

32   Frederick Engels, *The Housing Question*, 347–8.

then, is his provocative thesis, and to this day the empirical evidence for it cannot be denied.

Analogous to Engels's classical analysis, Castells's writings tried to show that the 'urban question', which was on the agenda a good hundred years later, did not constitute an independent field, but had to be traced back to general social processes. And, like Engels, Castells sharply criticised both 'right-wing' and 'left-wing' ideologies that conceded this question a certain degree of independence. He criticised the concept of 'urban culture', as represented by Simmel, the Chicago School of Sociology, and Wirth, for suggesting that cultural phenomena were produced by the city as a specific ecological form, rather than by capitalist industrialisation.[33] In contrast, he understood 'urban culture' as a myth that narrated human history in an ideological way. His sharp criticism of Lefebvre, which was ignited by Lefebvre's concept of an 'urban revolution', aimed in the same direction. Castells accused him of substituting an urbanist theorisation of Marxist problematics for a Marxist analysis of the urban phenomenon.[34] In the context of the Marxist discussion at the time, this was a devastating critique. In addition to a barely veiled politically motivated critique of Lefebvre's views on self-organisation and autogestion, and especially his rejection of the 'dictatorship of the proletariat', Castells took particular issue with Lefebvre's understanding of the urban. He argued that, similar to Wirth's conception of urban culture, Lefebvre suggested a production of the social content, the urban, through a trans-historical form, the city.[35] Despite this heavy critique, however, he conceded that Lefebvre had linked the urban question to the extended reproduction of the labour force and had thus opened a decisive path in urban research.[36] Castells then placed this point at the centre of his own analysis of the urban question (see also section 3.5).

The starting point of this analysis was a specific reading of Lefebvre's thesis that the city represents a projection of society onto the terrain or into space. Lefebvre had developed this thesis in a critical way, however, as part of his three-dimensional theory of the production of space (see section 4.2).[37] Castells, in contrast, while adopting this thesis, cautioned against the 'false evidence' of space: whatever theoretical perspective one adopted, it had to be accepted that every space was constructed. Here, again, he seems to follow Lefebvre's theory of the production of space. However, Lefebvre's *production* means something different to Castells's *construction*. While Lefebvre focuses

---

33   Castells, *The Urban Question*, 73ff.
34   Ibid., 86ff.
35   Ibid., 89.
36   Ibid., 94.
37   Ibid., 92, 115.

on a general process of the development of society and thus regards space as produced by social practice, Castells, in the tracks of Althusser, considers the 'theoretical praxis' of the construction of theory. Thus, for him, every space is constructed in theory, and if the space under consideration is not defined on a theoretical level, this means that one is referring to a culturally determined – and thus ideological – definition. This statement is the consequence of the elementary epistemological postulate of Althusser's Marxist structuralism: that every object of analysis is necessarily constructed.[38] Accordingly, for Castells there could be no theory of space that was not, at least implicitly, specified as an integral part of a general theory of society.[39]

From Castells's structuralist perspective, 'space' is thus the concrete expression of social development, and the analysis has to reveal the structural and conjunctural laws that determine its existence and transformation.[40] It follows that the 'spatial' particularity of a social structure can only be the 'evident' expression of the particularity of that social structure.[41] This is an almost paradigmatic example of a derivation thesis.

According to Althusser's famous schema, a social structure can be related to three instances: the ideological, the political-legal, and the economic. In this context, delimiting or defining a space means determining the relations between the elements of the social structure within a unit of these three instances. Castells ultimately postulates that each of these instances and their sub-elements generate their own space, whereby all of these spaces change continuously through class struggle.[42]

Then, using this structuralist concept of space, Castells attempted to determine the specificity of the urban, conforming to the structuralist scheme, through a systematic reductionist analysis: is the urban an ideological entity? No, says Castells, because this position refers to the thesis on urban culture, according to which the city represents a specific form of civilisation – a thesis that he had already rejected before as 'urban ideology'. Is the urban a political entity? Under certain historical conditions, he saw the urban as a unity of political-legal apparatuses, such as in the Greek polis or the medieval city. In advanced capitalism, however, there is an almost complete mismatch between political boundaries and the specificity of their social content. Is the urban an economic entity? As a last resort, Castells had to necessarily agree with this question. He justified this with one of Althusser's foundational theses that in

38   Ibid., 234–5.
39   Ibid., 115.
40   Ibid.
41   Ibid., 234–5.
42   Ibid., 234–7.

capitalism the economic is the dominant instance that overdetermines the political-legal and ideological instances. But the organisation of the labour process and the circulation of commodities were no longer bound to a fixed location in monopoly capitalism: in Castells's understanding, space was increasingly irrelevant to production. And he added the famous passage: 'It is a question of the tendential elimination of space as a source of specificity. Whereas time, on the other hand, becomes increasingly central to the process, fragmenting into specific operations according to the differential speed of realisation. This, of course, has still to be shown.'[43]

This leaves labour power, and the process of its reproduction, as the last economic element to be considered in relation to the urban. And it is precisely here, as foreshadowed by Lefebvre (see section 7.3), that Castells finds what he is looking for – a direct relationship between the city and a specific aspect of the economic instance:

The spatial organisation of the reproduction of labour power seems . . . to lead to very familiar geographico-social realities, namely, the urban areas [agglomerations], in the banal statistical sense of the term. What is an 'urban area'? . . . An urban unit is not a unit in terms of production. On the other hand, it possesses a certain specificity in terms of residence, in terms of 'everydayness'. It is, in short, the everyday space of a delimited fraction of the labour force. This is not very different from the definition, current among geographers and economists, of an urban area on the basis of the map of commutings.[44]

Castells does not stop at this definition, and continues by breaking down the reproduction of labour power further into individual and collective consumption, whereby he understands collective consumption as consumption whose economic and social organisation does not take place via the market, but through the state apparatus. Castells has thus finally found the central definition of the urban: the city is a unit of collective consumption.

In summary, this appears to be a consistent structuralist conception of space and the city: 'space' is derived from superordinate social-theoretical premises and the 'city' in turn is nothing other than a well-defined 'section' of this 'structural' space. Its definition takes place through the identification of the element central to its constitution: collective consumption.

This also makes it possible to define the social starting point and the

---

43 Ibid., 443.
44 Ibid., 444–5. Translation amended.

political goal of Castells's urban analysis: the 'urban social movements'. Castells uses this term to refer to the most diverse groups that resist capitalist urban development, whether in the inner cities threatened by urban restructuring or in the chronically undersupported settlements of state-orchestrated mass housing in the banlieues. The urban social movements thus appeared to a certain extent as 'logical' actors of collective consumption and as central addressees of the political analysis resulting from this theory.

This highly formalised theory was relatively easy to implement empirically. Castells and his colleagues subsequently undertook extensive research on urban development and urban struggles in France and later in other parts of the world.[45] Castells's theory formed the core of an intense but brief flowering of French neo-Marxist urban sociology, with such famous figures as Francis Godard, Jean Lojkine, Edmond Préteceille, Christian Topalov, and many others.[46]

However, the schematic conception of this theory gave rise to extensive debates. Castells himself acknowledged these weaknesses early on and concretised and modified his theory over the years. This was already evident in the epilogue to the second edition of *The Urban Question* in 1975, in which he unambiguously – though not openly – took up elements of Lefebvre's book *The Production of Space*, which had appeared in the meantime. He made a range of further revisions in the following years; despite all efforts, however, he could not transcend the structuralist rigour and limits of the basic concept.[47] The problem is already apparent at the level of the theoretical assumptions: the city remains, in the final analysis, merely a manifestation of social structures. If these superordinate structures change, space and thus the city will also change. The concepts of 'space' and 'city' thus ultimately remain purely abstract categories derived from wider contexts, and, in this way, aptly illustrate the functioning of a classical thesis of derivation.

Nevertheless, this theory allowed for a critical analysis of a central aspect of the urban crisis of the 1960s and 1970s in Western countries: the crisis of the Keynesian welfare state. At the same time, it provided the chance to link urban social movements conceptually with other political movements, trade unions, and left-wing parties, thus bringing the urban question into the general

---

45　Castells, *Luttes urbaines et pouvoir politique*; Castells, *The City and the Grassroots*; Castells and Godard, *Monopolville*; Castells et al., *Crise du logement et mouvements sociaux urbains*.

46　See for example Topalov, 'A History of Urban Research'.

47　Castells, *City, Class and Power*; Castells, *The City and the Grassroots*. See also Gottdiener, *Social Production of Urban Space*; Saunders, *Social Theory*; Merrifield, *Metromarxism*.

political debates and political struggles of those years, not only in Western Europe and North America, but also in many countries in Latin America, Asia, and Africa, where rapidly accelerating urbanisation also turned collective consumption into an explosive question.

By the 1980s, Castells's approach began to lose its appeal, and was soon condemned in Paris as 'concrete Marxism' (marxisme de béton). On the one hand, Althusser's Marxism had passed its zenith and was increasingly criticised as rigid and dogmatic, and on the other hand, with the neoliberal turn, it was precisely social reproduction that came under massive political pressure. With spreading policies of privatisation, cuts in social expenditures, and the withdrawal of the state from many areas of society, the topic of collective consumption fell off the political agenda and, from the mid-eighties onwards, visibly disappeared from the academic debate. Castells himself turned to the 'informational city' and the 'network society', and eventually abandoned Marxism altogether.[48] However – and this is often forgotten in epitaphs for the theory of collective consumption – the social problem that existed at that time was by no means off the table. It has appeared again and again in different forms in various places, for example in the form of the social and economic polarisation of urban areas and of manifold processes of peripheralisation (see section 4.5).[49]

Another important consequence of this theory was that it had a strongly negative influence on the reception of Lefebvre's analyses in both the French- and the English-speaking worlds. Castells's critique was a central reason why Lefebvre's works on the urban and on space received little attention for a long time and were not translated into English. Castells made a remarkable departure from his earlier criticism of Lefebvre in his highly influential *The City and the Grassroots*.[50] However, he continued to regard Lefebvre as a 'philosopher of the city' who did no research and who 'had not the slightest idea of the real world'.[51] Accordingly, his 'rehabilitation' of Lefebvre was hardly noticed.

Radical Geography and the Project of a Historical Geography

The second important starting point for critical urban theory in the 1970s was Anglo-American geography. Here, under the influence of the social upheaval

---

48   Castells, *The Informational City*.

49   See for example Marcuse, ' "Dual City" '; Sassen, *The Global City*; Brenner, Marcuse, and Mayer, *Cities for People, Not for Profit*.

50   Castells, *The City and the Grassroots*.

51   Catterall, 'Citizen Movements, Information and Analysis', 146. See also Castells, *The City and the Grassroots*, 300; Merrifield, *Metromarxism*; Pinder, 'Reconstituting the Possible'.

of the late sixties, a *radical geography* had formed, a heterogeneous movement that saw itself as a countermovement to the mainstream in geography and its irrelevance to pressing current issues. It neither dealt with a specific problematic nor developed a coherent theory; *radical geography* united a whole bundle of diverse concepts, thematic fields, and theoretical orientations.[52]

The most spectacular and also most influential book of radical geography was *Social Justice and the City* by David Harvey.[53] Like Castells's *The Urban Question*, this title also announces a programme – and it defines two of the central themes of radical geography in the years to come. Even more decisive, however, was the paradigm shift that took place in this book: Harvey, who only five years earlier had presented the standard work of the quantitative paradigm within anglophone geography with *Explanation in Geography*, made the paradigm shift to radical geography in the book itself. If the first part treats 'liberal approaches' and their limitations, the second part turns to critical political economy and historical materialist approaches.

In contrast to Castells, Harvey was highly impressed by Lefebvre's analysis. In his concluding chapter he wrote:

> Unfortunately, the essays in this volume were completed before I had the opportunity to read Lefebvre's *Marxist Thought and the City* and *The Urban Revolution* . . . There are parallels between his concerns and mine and there are similarities in content (which is reassuring) and some differences in interpretation and emphasis (which is challenging).[54]

Subsequently, Harvey developed his own Marxist approach to urbanisation, in which he returned to Lefebvre's work again and again.

However, while Lefebvre developed a comprehensive theory of the production of space, Harvey pursued a narrower project: to design a political economy of space that built directly on Marx's *Capital*. Thus, it was a short passage from *The Urban Revolution* that aroused Harvey's interest: here Lefebvre sketched a secondary circuit of capital that runs parallel to the circulation of capital in industrial production and is fed by productive investments in space (see section 7.1).[55] Harvey constructed his theory of the production of the built environment on Lefebvre's analysis, which he fully developed in his *Limits to Capital* of 1982. The aim of this book is the consistent introduction of space into Marx's theory of value, whereby, as the title programmatically announces, it systematically

---

52 For an early overview, see Peet, *Radical Geography*.
53 Harvey, *Social Justice and the City*.
54 Ibid., 302–3.
55 Lefebvre, *Urban Revolution*, 159–60.

explores the limits of capital accumulation. According to a historical-materialist understanding, these limits are rooted in capitalism's inherent tendency to crisis. However, this crisis can be interpreted differently. From Harvey's point of view, Marx had opened different 'windows' on the process of capital accumulation with his theory: depending on the perspective adopted, the question of the limits to capital finds a different answer in each case. As a result of his investigation, Harvey presented a 'three-cut crisis theory'.

The first, and classical, view of capitalist crisis is based on the law of the tendency of the rate of profit to fall and the crises inherent in the nature of the reproduction of capital. Accordingly, Harvey begins with the classical reproduction scheme of capital as developed by Marx. Crisis theory, the core of all Marxist analysis, is based on the observation that the circulation of capital is disturbed and the reproduction of capital falters. The question of what exactly leads to these crises has been the subject of protracted debates ever since this theory appeared.

From Harvey's spatial-theoretical perspective, however, this 'classical' form of crisis is only the first aspect, or the 'first cut' theory of crisis. He expands it by introducing Lefebvre's observations into this schema: in times of over-accumulation and falling rates of profit, the initial conditions of the first crisis, capital can be diverted from the first circuit of capital into a second one, which Harvey defines as investment in the 'built environment'. This second circuit, which can partially absorb the shocks of the first, differs from the latter mainly in its different temporality: the time horizon here is oriented towards long-term investment, and thus towards the future rather than the present.[56]

The production of the built environment means a productive investment of capital that drives the urbanisation process and fundamentally changes the space-time configurations of the world. As a consequence, spatio-temporal barriers become less important and the globe shrinks: a process that Harvey calls 'space-time compression'.[57] But this also gives rise to the fundamental problem of this second cycle: capital is invested and thus immobilised in a material infrastructure that conflicts in the long run with the dynamics of technological change and capital accumulation. The value of investments in the built environment thus becomes uncertain, and the continuous circulation of capital is threatened by serious collapse. The second circuit thus offers only a temporary way out of the crisis tendency inherent in capital. Transformed via the financial system, it can arrive at a crisis once again – the 'second cut' crisis.[58]

But Harvey does not stop there. He opens a third 'window' that reveals a

---

56   Harvey, *Limits to Capital*, xvi.
57   Harvey, *Condition of Postmodernity*.
58   Harvey, *Limits to Capital*, xvi.

view of ground rent and the processes associated with it, the geographical mobility of capital and labour. From the generalisation of these processes, he extracts a concept he calls *spatial fix*, which denotes the production of relatively coherent and stable socio-spatial configurations, as nations or regions.[59] He sees urban space as a central anchor of this spatial fix. Urban spaces function in his analysis to a certain extent as the basic units of the processes of social production and reproduction.[60] The crisis-prone nature of capitalist accumulation requires the creation of ever-new spatial fixes, however, and thus also implies the geographical expansion of the capitalist process of value production: through exports, through productive investment, and through the expansion of the mass of 'free labour'. But even with these means, the tendency of capitalist accumulation to produce crises cannot be resolved in the long run. This results, for example, in imperialist wars and the reproduction of social contradictions on an enlarged scale, which ultimately lead to the 'third cut' crisis.[61] The result of this comprehensive reconstruction and spatial-theoretical extension of Marx's *Capital* is a 'historical geography' of capitalism. Harvey later applied the theoretical framework of *Limits to Capital* in concrete historical studies, such as the analysis of postmodernity and the regime of 'flexible accumulation' and his study of the historical conditions of the Paris Commune.[62]

What role does the city play in this spatial version of the reproduction of capital? It appears in the general schema laid out here under a dual aspect: on the one hand, it is an essential element of the built environment that must be analysed in the context of the urbanisation process. On the other hand, the city is also a spatial fix, a geographically bounded, regulative unit that can be defined by the working day. Harvey calls this unit 'structured coherence'. It no longer corresponds to a city in the classical sense, but rather to an urban region that extends far into the surrounding hinterland. A structured coherence is composed of specific economic and technological structures, organisational forms, and a dominant set of social relations that together define (regional) consumption and production models.[63] Harvey is, however, cautious enough to speak of a *tendency* to structured coherence, for it exists in the midst of a maelstrom of forces that tend to undermine it. The urban region is a precarious, fragmented, and splintered entity, fractured by multiple political and ideological-cultural boundaries. This conception reveals some surprising relationships. On the one hand, it takes

---

59   On this, see also Brenner, 'Between Fixity and Motion'; Brenner, *New Urban Spaces*.

60   Harvey, *Urbanization of Capital*, 145.

61   Harvey, *Limits to Capital*, 431ff.

62   Harvey, *Condition of Postmodernity*; Harvey, *Consciousness and the Urban Experience*.

63   Harvey, *Urbanization of Capital*, 140.

up essential elements of the regulation approach, particularly the regulation of social relations and the emergence of new accumulation regimes (see section 1.3). On the other hand, it also shows certain parallels to Castells's concept of collective consumption. The spatial dimension of the reproduction of labour power is at the centre of Harvey's definition of the urban region, which is defined, as in Castells's theory, in the classical geographical sense of the agglomeration, and thus by the labour market or the commuter catchment area.

Harvey's approach, like Castells's, is guided by a decidedly theoretical perspective in which the concepts of 'space' and 'city' are derived from a general social theory. In contrast to Castells, the focus is not on social structures but on the classical Marxist concepts of political economy. His ambition is to embed 'city' and 'space' in the heart of Marxian theory and to place them in direct relation to the law of value and the reproduction process of capital. However, this does not result in new definitions of 'space' or the 'city', as in Castells, but in new theoretical categories: on the one hand, the 'built environment', an analytical concept that refers directly to the schema of capital circuits; and on the other hand, the spatial fix and thus generally conceived socio-spatial units such as 'urban region' or 'nation'. Significantly, the term 'space' is mentioned only a few times in *Limits to Capital*. Harvey ultimately sticks to his relativistic conception of space, which he had already presented in *Explanation in Geography*.

Nevertheless, Harvey essentially followed Lefebvre's change of analytical perspective from the object of the 'city' to the process of urbanisation, which Harvey understood as constitutive of as well as constituted by various social processes.[64] In the following years, he extended his analyses to ever-wider fields, treating questions of culture, the environment, the body, difference, and urban utopias. In many of these reflections, Lefebvre was a central point of reference and an important source of ideas, themes, and concepts. However, Harvey's references to Lefebvre remained selective, and he was also sceptical of Lefebvre's dialectics (see section 5.7). Ultimately, Harvey has hardly ever stepped outside the field of a classical critique of political economy, and the basic elements of a political economy of space developed in *Limits to Capital* still form the foundation of his theoretical reflections today.

The First Wave of Lefebvre Interpretation

As has become evident in the course of this chapter, Lefebvre's theoretical reflections played an ambivalent role in the first phase of critical urban theory.

---

64   Harvey, *Justice, Nature and the Geography of Difference*.

Although they undoubtedly were the point of departure for the entire debate, they were not often taken up or developed on their own terms. Either they served mainly as negative examples, as they did for Castells, or they formed an almost invisible guideline in the background, as in Harvey's case.

In Anglo-American urban studies, Lefebvre's work was nevertheless treated in two important overviews, Saunders's influential *Social Theory and the Urban Question* and Mark Gottdiener's encompassing study *The Social Production of Urban Space*, in which Lefebvre's texts on the urban, on space, and on the state are presented in detail.[65] Otherwise, however, Lefebvre's texts received little attention. This is particularly evident in the comprehensive overview of Marxist urban theory by Ira Katznelson, who describes Lefebvre's work exclusively from the point of view of Harvey and Castells, and obviously had not read Lefebvre's texts, most of which had not yet been translated into English.[66] For example, in referring to Harvey's positive appraisal of Lefebvre in *Social Justice and the City*, Katznelson comments: 'Lefebvre may have shown Marxism the way back to the city, but having reached its gates, he entered by bidding Marxism's project of social theory farewell.'[67] His conclusion is typical of the attitude of many Marxist scholars of the time:

> In my discussion of Lefebvre, I treat this corpus as a unity at the price of moving too rapidly over differences in these texts and losing much of the nuance in the argument. I think this is a justifiable approach because, as will be apparent quite soon, I think Lefebvre should be quickly left to his place of honour, more as a pioneer who raised and pursued long dormant questions than as an analyst who succeeded in putting answers to them.[68]

The same disregard for Lefebvre's work was also evident in Anglo-American histories of philosophy, as Lynn Stewart notes: 'References to Lefebvre's work have been confined almost exclusively to accounts of the history of Marxism, many of which do not seem to know what to make of the man or his work.'[69] As Kipfer, Goonewardena, Schmid, and Milgrom observe, studies of Western Marxism have either ignored Lefebvre altogether or mentioned him only in passing.[70] Martin Jay devotes a brief and cursory passage to him in *Marxism and Totality*, and Perry Anderson refers to him only very rarely in *Considerations of*

---

65   Saunders, *Social Theory*; Gottdiener, *Social Production of Urban Space*.
66   Katznelson, *Marxism and the City*.
67   Ibid., 101.
68   Ibid., 94.
69   Stewart, 'Bodies, Visions, and Spatial Politics', 609.
70   Kipfer et al., 'On the Production of Henri Lefebvre'.

Western Marxism.[71] In contrast, Mark Poster discussed Lefebvre's relationship to French existentialism in detail, and Michael Kelly excavated debates on materialism and idealism in Lefebvre's early writings, and later examined his conceptualisation of everyday life and his relationship to Roland Barthes.[72]

In the Francophone world, Lefebvre almost completely disappeared from the scene in urban studies in the course of the 1970s. The only notable exception is the work of Geneva geographer Claude Raffestin, who presented a ground-breaking dissertation on the production of territory, in which he combined elements of Lefebvre and Foucault in a highly productive manner. This work became the starting point of the 'territorial approach', further developed mainly in Italy and Switzerland (see section 1.4).

In contrast, Lefebvre's work found a much warmer reception in the German-speaking world. Alfred Schmidt, an undogmatic member of the second generation of the Frankfurt School, introduced Lefebvre's anti-ontological and dialectical materialism into the German debate.[73] Kurt Meyer, who had studied with Lefebvre in Nanterre, published an introduction to Lefebvre's revolutionary romanticism in 1973, and followed up with a book on urban society after a long hiatus in 2007.[74] Thomas Kleinspehn wrote a very lucid introduction to Lefebvre's Marxist critique of everyday life, Jens Peter Schwab discussed Lefebvre's understanding of Marx's concept of alienation, and Heinz Sünker examined Lefebvre's metaphilosophy and his conception of colonisation.[75] While Lefebvre played an important role in German discussions on everyday life and alienation, he did not appear at all in German geography, which remained very conservative until the end of the twentieth century. In urban research he was only introduced in the course of the 1980s by the two action and research groups 'urbi et orbi' in Frankfurt and 'Ssenter for Applied Urbanism' in Zurich (see section 1.4). Klaus Ronneberger provides a good overview of the German-language discussion of Lefebvre's work.[76]

The situation was somewhat different in Latin America, where Lefebvre's texts on the urban were translated relatively early and were very influential, with two opposing camps forming around Castells and Lefebvre. This

---

71 Jay, *Marxism and Totality*; Anderson, *Considerations of Western Marxism*.

72 Poster, *Existential Marxism in Postwar France*; Kelly, *Modern French Marxism*; Kelly, 'The Historical Emergence of Everyday Life'; Kelly, 'Demystification'.

73 Alfred Schmidt, *Beiträge zur Marxistischen Erkenntnistheorie*; Alfred Schmidt, 'Henri Lefebvre and Contemporary Interpretations of Marx'.

74 Meyer, *Henri Lefebvre*; Meyer, *Von der Stadt zur urbanen Gesellschaft*.

75 Kleinspehn, *Der verdrängte Alltag*; Schwab, '*L'homme total*'; Sünker, *Bildung, Alltag und Subjektivität*.

76 Ronneberger, 'Henri Lefebvre and Urban Everyday Life'.

discussion was not translated into English, and thus has remained isolated from international scholarship, a situation that is changing only slowly today.

1.3 Postmodern Geographies

The fact is that space 'in itself' is ungraspable, unthinkable, unknowable.[77]

In retrospect, the first phase of critical urban and regional research analysed in the preceding chapter had an important, but overall rather limited, significance. As early as the mid-1980s, a paradigm shift was emerging that was essentially determined by two closely interrelated developments. On the one hand, it was the consequence of an epistemological reorientation within the social sciences and humanities from modern to postmodern and from structuralist to poststructuralist approaches, which postulated a departure from 'grand theories' and their search for comprehensive analyses. Even though Harvey's classical, Capital-oriented Marxism differed from Castells's structural Marxism in many respects, critics accused them both of latent or overt economism and determinism and of ignoring many important aspects and processes. While Castells's theory of collective consumption soon disappeared from the scene, Harvey's political economy of space – not least thanks to his consistent and persistent work – has retained an important position within critical urban research to this day.

On the other hand, this paradigm shift also reflected the dramatic transformation of the capitalist world system in the long 1980s, which was linked to fundamental transformations in spatial development, driven by the interconnected processes of urbanisation and globalisation. In the course of this change, a wide variety of new urban phenomena emerged that demanded new explanations. Thus, from the mid-1980s onwards, new approaches were developed that dealt with the discovery of new, empirically observable phenomena, emphasised the contingency of urban and regional developments, and increasingly placed space at the centre of analysis. As a result, a 'spatial turn' emerged in the social sciences and humanities. This turn was also associated with a rediscovery of Henri Lefebvre.

---

77   Lefebvre, *Production of Space*, 218.

New Urbanisation Processes

The long 1980s marked a decisive turning point in urban development world-wide. The deep economic and political crisis of national-developmentalist regimes of accumulation, the collapse of state socialism, and the subsequent intensification of various processes of global exchange led gradually to the establishment of a contradictory and heterogeneous new world order. New geographies of uneven spatial development emerged throughout the world with the stepwise unravelling of the global financial system; the microelec-tronic revolution with all its effects on global communication, on production and consumption networks, and on everyday life; the flexibilisation of produc-tion processes and labour relations; and the deregulation of national norms and rules. Explosive processes of globalisation and urbanisation and various forms of stagnation, shrinkage, and marginalisation often developed in close proximity to one another and crystallised in a mosaic of socio-spatial uneven-ness across the globe. These different and contradictory transformations demanded new explanations and, accordingly, new concepts and new theorisations.

Various strands of the regulation approach analysed these dramatic trans-formations as a change in the regime of capitalist accumulation. Following Gramsci, they interpreted the economic crisis of the 1970s and the subsequent political change in the Western industrial nations as a crisis of Fordism. The question of possible ways out of this crisis and of the typical characteristics of the emerging social development model after Fordism was answered with concepts such as 'post-Fordism', 'flexible accumulation', and the 'liberal-productivist development model'.[78] Finally, at the beginning of the twenty-first century, 'neoliberalism' and 'neoliberalisation' became the dominant terms to characterise the new model of social development.[79] However, these terms did not imply the idea of a homogeneous spatial development on a worldwide scale. The Paris Regulation school had already emphasised that Fordism did not exist 'as such', but only different national variants of Fordism.[80] In the same vein, Brenner, Peck, and Theodore developed the term 'variegated neoliberali-sation' to indicate that it subsumes very different social models.[81] For years, these concepts inspired an extensive debate on the typical features and

---

78   See, respectively, Hirsch and Roth, *Das neue Gesicht des Kapitalismus*; Schoenberger, 'From Fordism to Flexible Accumulation'; Harvey, *Condition of Postmodernity*; Alain Lipietz, *La société en sablier*.

79   Peck and Tickell, 'Neoliberalizing Space'; Harvey, *Brief History of Neoliberalism*.

80   Aglietta, *A Theory of Capitalist Regulation*.

81   Brenner, Peck, and Theodore, 'Variegated Neoliberalization'.

characteristics of post-Fordist or neoliberal spatial development.[82] However, the applications of these concepts to the analysis of spatial development brought a whole range of problems with them.[83]

The radical social change also challenged the dominance of the nation state, whose status had gone almost completely unquestioned in social sciences for decades. A critical confrontation with the idea of the national territory as a homogeneous structuring framework of spatial development began, further driven by the unequal development dynamics that were also becoming apparent within individual nation states. As Michael Storper argued, the region was thus rediscovered 'as a fundamental unit of social life in contemporary capitalism'.[84] This shift is exemplified by Doreen Massey's *Spatial Divisions of Labour*, which, in the tradition of 'radical geography', initiated a departure from structuralist interpretations of the 'regional question'. As Massey stated: 'It is indeed time that regional and local particularities were reinstated as a central focus of geographical thinking.'[85] At the same time, the insight began to take hold that these 'new' regional economies are integrated in a highly variable way into transnational production networks, and a dialectical figure emerged in which globalisation and regionalisation were understood as mutually interrelated, interdependent processes.[86] As a result, many researchers demanded to abandon the fixation on ontologically given and a priori defined geographical configurations and instead to address these restructuring processes as a 'scale question'.[87] As Erik Swyngedouw observed: 'Scale becomes the arena and moment, both discursively and materially, where sociospatial power relations are contested and compromises are negotiated and regulated. Scale, therefore, is both the result and outcome of social struggle for power and control.'[88]

This also led to a redefinition of the urban question. Strictly speaking, what emerged as a 'new regional economy' no longer described *regional* economies in the classical sense – but rather new forms of *urban* economies, indicating a fundamental reconfiguration of the urban.[89] The range of

---

82   Hirsch and Roth, *Das neue Gesicht des Kapitalismus*; Brenner and Theodore, *Spaces of Neoliberalism*.

83   See Leborgne and Alain Lipietz, 'New Technologies, New Modes of Regulation'; Schmid, 'Urbane Region und Territorialverhältnis'.

84   Storper, *The Regional World*, 3.

85   Massey, *Spatial Divisions of Labour*, 120.

86   Amin and Thrift, 'Neo-Marshallian Nodes in Global Networks'; Schmid, 'Urbane Region und Territorialverhältnis'.

87   Swyngedouw, 'The Mammon Quest'; Brenner, 'The Limits to Scale?'.

88   Swyngedouw, 'Neither Global nor Local', 140.

89   See also Scott, *Regions and the World Economy*.

'new' urban production systems extended from peripheral, crisis-ridden regions to thriving small-town 'industrial districts' and new high-tech clusters and specialised service complexes in booming metropolises. Already by the beginning of the 1980s, Robert Cohen had established a connection between the restructuring of the world economy, the reorganisation of global corporations, their increased need for business-oriented services, and the development of certain urban centres into sites of strategic coordination and control for the world economy, which he called 'global cities'.[90] Saskia Sassen used these observations to analyse global cities as specific production systems that produce 'global control capability'.[91] Meanwhile, John Friedmann and Goetz Wolff coined the term 'world city' for those cities that are preferred destinations for both international flows of capital and a large number of migrants.[92] Both approaches observed a structurally conditioned polarisation of labour markets and life worlds, which Sassen understood as the common presence of centre and periphery and Friedmann and Wolff paraphrased with the metaphor of 'citadel and ghetto'. The border between privileged and precarious areas, between North and South, now ran right through the centres of the world economy, which became 'contested terrains' where the contradictions of the new global order clashed in concentrated form.[93]

These developments also drew attention to the new social divisions that were emerging in urban areas throughout the world, the precarisation and outsourcing of industrial activities and the rise of new urban middle classes, the new economic significance of urbanity, and the associated emergence of various forms of urban restructuring. Processes of urban regeneration and gentrification became important new fields of research and also a theoretical and ideological battlefield around the question of the urban.[94] However, it was not only the centres of the metropolises that were being transformed, but also, increasingly, their urban peripheries. While skylines rose in inner cities as symbols of global capitalism, new urban configurations emerged in various places on the urban periphery, which Robert Fishman called 'technoburbs' and Joël Garreau 'edge cities'.[95] Edward W. Soja, analysing the new urban configuration of Orange County in the Los Angeles region, coined the

---

90   Cohen, 'The New International Division of Labor', 300.
91   Sassen, *Global City*; Sassen, *Cities in a World Economy*.
92   Friedmann and Wolff, 'World City Formation'; Friedmann, 'The World City Hypothesis'.
93   Sassen, *Cities in a World Economy*, 165ff.
94   Smith, *The New Urban Frontier*; Libby Porter and Shaw, *Whose Urban Renaissance?*.
95   Garreau, *Edge City*; Fishman, *Bourgeois Utopias*.

term 'exopolis' to describe these developments in an encompassing way.[96] Even though these new forms of urbanisation were first studied and described in North America, they soon became apparent in Europe, where new archipelagos and clusters of the global economy also emerged.[97] As a consequence, extended and polycentric metropolitan regions developed, characterised by strong political, social, and cultural fragmentations and the overlap of catchment areas around diverse centralities. Not only had the historical form of the 'city' finally blown up, but 'functional spaces' such as agglomerations or urban regions could no longer be identified and delimited without problems. Taken together, all these tendencies indicated a fundamental reconfiguration of the urban, radically questioning the classical form and understanding of the 'city'.

In all these discussions, Lefebvre's theory of the urban and of the production of space, with very few exceptions, played practically no role, although it would have been eminently suitable for a comprehensive analysis of these processes (see sections 3.5 and 4.5).

Postmodernism and Poststructuralism

In parallel to these political-economic analyses, a second debate developed in architecture, art, and philosophy that addressed this 'new era' in terms of aesthetics, culture, and epistemology, and which was summarised under the label 'postmodernism'. It comprised a whole series of highly heterogeneous currents and tendencies, some of whose roots reach far back into the critiques and protests of the 1960s, which in one form or another had already articulated a farewell to modernism.

In architecture, the influential 1972 manifesto *Learning from Las Vegas* by Robert Venturi, Denise Scott Brown, and Steven Izenour is generally regarded as the initial spark of postmodernism.[98] In *Complexity and Contradiction in Architecture*, Venturi had already subjected the architecture of the modern age to a sharp critique.[99] Criticism of modern architecture and urban planning was, however, nothing new at the time (see section 3.2). What was new were their proposals for a practical way out of the impasse of functionalist architecture: *Learning from Las Vegas* postulated nothing less than the

---

96   Soja, *Thirdspace*.
97   See for example Ronneberger and Schmid, 'Globalisierung und Metropolenpolitik'; Prigge, *Peripherie ist überall*; Veltz, *Mondialisation, villes et territoires*.
98   Venturi, Scott Brown, and Izenour, *Learning from Las Vegas*.
99   Venturi, *Complexity and Contradiction in Architecture*.

dissolution of the boundary between high culture and 'commercial mass culture', and it took elements of everyday or 'popular' architecture from Las Vegas as the role model for a renewal of architecture. At the same time, a version of postmodernism in architecture also emerged in Europe. As early as 1966, the Italian Marxist Aldo Rossi had formulated a sharp critique of modern architecture in *L'architettura della città*, based on an analysis of the 'European city', and demanded that urban planning should continue to develop traditional urban structures in a historically critical manner.[100] Although there were very different ideas about this 'new' architecture, the term 'postmodern architecture' coined by Charles Jencks was subsequently used extensively to characterise a movement and a style.[101] In practice, however, postmodern architecture became a fashion trend that faded away relatively quickly.

A second strand of postmodernism can be identified as a broad movement in culture and art, ranging from pop art to punk to video art. This movement was adopted, received, and disseminated primarily by art and literary critics and quickly diffused into other disciplines, where it stimulated a *cultural turn* in social sciences and humanities characterised by the increasing inclusion of cultural aspects into a wide range of analyses.

Finally, a third current emerged that was originally deeply rooted in French philosophy and can be subsumed under the term 'poststructuralism'. This heterogeneous current, which includes such diverse thinkers as Michel Foucault, Jean Baudrillard, Jacques Derrida, Gilles Deleuze, Félix Guattari, and many others, promoted a rejection of rigid structuralism in its classical and neo-Marxist versions. In his study *The Postmodern Condition*, Jean-François Lyotard brought all these currents together in the term 'postmodernism', which was already widely used in North America.

Postmodernism could thus not be clearly defined; it was a very broad and heterogeneous current with various political, cultural, and epistemological offshoots. What they had in common was that they turned against totalising narratives, demanded a departure from a theoretical 'central perspective', and relied on the 'play of differences'. Feminist and postcolonial approaches found their place in it, as did critical cultural studies or 'post-Marxist' approaches. The epistemological and political assessment of postmodernism was, of course, controversial: while for some it meant nothing more than the 'cultural logic of late capitalism', as it had for Fredric Jameson, or flexible accumulation, for David Harvey, others, such as Rosalyn Deutsche and Doreen Massey, pointed

---

100   Rossi, *The Architecture of the City*.
101   Jencks, *The Language of Post-modern Architecture*.

to its critical roots in feminism, art, and the new social movements and emphasised its emancipatory potential.[102]

This debate on postmodernism and poststructuralism had a direct and last-
ing influence on critical urban studies, and, conversely, urban studies intervened decisively in this postmodern debate. As Deutsche noted, the contribution of urban studies was based on a 'winning combination' in bringing together
critical discourses on both space and culture.[103] Anglo-American 'postmodern
geography' became the central discipline of this new approach to urban
research, thereby partly integrating elements of the 'old' radical geography.[104]

The 'Spatial Turn'

Taken as a whole, all of these new approaches in regional and urban research at
the end of the twentieth century had one thing in common, which was also
explicitly addressed in one form or another in many texts: they postulated a
new importance of the 'spatial'. As early as 1984, Jameson announced:

> We have often been told, however, that we now inhabit the synchronic
> rather than the diachronic, and I think it is at least empirically arguable
> that our daily life, our psychic experience, our cultural languages, are
> today dominated by categories of space rather than by categories of time,
> as in the preceding period of high modernism.[105]

In geography, Doreen Massey and John Allen declared programmatically:
'Geography Matters!'[106] And Edward W. Soja and Derek Gregory, two well-
known representatives of 'postmodern geography', postulated a far-reaching
change of perspective from the historical to the spatial.[107] The 'rediscovery' of
space as a central category of the social sciences, or 'the reassertion of space in
social theory', as Soja programmatically declared in the subtitle of his book,
became the most important obsession of postmodern geography for the next
few years. However controversial the context of this spatial turn may have
been, there is no disputing the renewed interest in 'spatial' issues, not only in

---

102   Jameson, *Postmodernism*; Harvey, *Condition of Postmodernity*; Deutsche, *Eviction*;
Massey, *Space, Place and Gender*.

103   Deutsche, *Eviction*.

104   See for example Soja, *Postmetropolis*; Dear, *The Postmodern Urban Condition*.

105   Jameson, 'Postmodernism', 16.

106   Massey and Allen, *Geography Matters!*.

107   Soja, *Postmodern Geographies*; Gregory, *Geographical Imaginations*.

geography but also in sociology, in literary and cultural studies, and also in economics, where economic geography was to a certain extent rediscovered.[108]

It was in this way that 'space', a long-neglected category of theoretical reflection, reappeared on the stage of current problematics in the social sciences and humanities. This initiated a debate on space that was in many cases closely intertwined with the question of the urban. As discussed in section 1.2, critical urban theory had already addressed the question of space, starting, like Lefebvre, from the 'urban question'. In the changed social and theoretical context of the neoliberal or postmodern era, however, there was a shift in meaning: while, in the debate of the 1970s, 'space' was a cipher for an overarching general structure and for the worldwide homogenisation of social processes, in the 1980s it became a symbol for complexity, contingency, and difference. This change can be seen very clearly by comparing the central postulates on the meaning of space across these decades. While Castells had proclaimed the end of space as a source of specificity and Harvey had referred to Marx's dictum of the 'annihilation of space by time', empirical studies by the end of the century provided countless arguments for the opposite: 'space' did not become more homogeneous and uniform, but, on the contrary, it appeared more and more differentiated and complex. Accordingly, Anthony King proclaimed the emergence of a global 'regime of difference'.[109]

This 'new meaning of the spatial' is, however, a result not only of social development, but also, as discussed above, of a changed conception of space that is closely connected to the 'postmodern turn'. The affinity of postmodernism to spatial metaphors is not surprising, if we consider its starting points in the critique of modern architecture and in poststructuralism, which made 'difference' a central concept of its analyses. The 'spatial' connotation of the term 'difference' is ambiguous, however, denoting on the one hand the simultaneity of heterogeneous social conditions, and on the other a 'decentring of knowledge', the rejection of a 'totalising central perspective' in favour of diverse and divergent points of view. The transition from modernism to postmodernism can thus also be understood as a transition from privileging a linear overall social development to emphasising social differentiation and the simultaneity of the unequal.

However, the new interest in 'spatial questions' initially fell into a theoretical

---

108   In sociology, see Giddens, *The Constitution of Society*; Bourdieu, 'Social Space and Symbolic Power'. In literary and cultural studies, see Jameson, *Postmodernism*. For economics, see Michael E. Porter, *Competitive Advantage*; Fujita, Krugman, and Venables, *The Spatial Economy*.

109   King, *Culture, Globalization and the World System*.

vacuum. No 'spatial theories' or at least 'spatial concepts' were available to directly address the new postmodern questions in social science. In all relevant disciplines, 'space' had remained a theoretically underdeveloped category, and a systematic theoretical reorientation got under way only very slowly. In retrospect, several important and influential anthologies of the time that took up this problem read like an intriguing search for the enigma of space.[110] A new problematic, the problematic of space, was open to a new epistemological exploration.

Henri Lefebvre and Postmodern Geography

In this changed context, the works of Henri Lefebvre experienced a renaissance, especially in Anglo-American scholarship and in geography. Michael Dear summarised the central aspect of this rediscovery as follows: 'Most social theorists are by now aware that Lefebvre's project is aimed at a reorientation of human inquiry away from its traditional obsession with time and toward a reconstituted focus on space.'[111] In this situation, a book by Lefebvre that had previously received little attention took on a new significance: *The Production of Space*. John Allen remarked: '*The production of space* is one of those books which, when it was finally published in 1991, seemed to hold out the promise of revealing all that we desperately wanted to know about space, but never quite knew how to ask.'[112] Jameson also referred to Lefebvre in his theorisation of postmodernism, even if he did not discuss the French theorist's work in detail. Years later, he returned to Lefebvre again in his book on dialectics.[113]

The new interest in the question of space, however, was not the only reason for this renaissance of Lefebvre's theory. It was also important that his reflections proceeded from an epistemological position to which the critique of 'grand theory' did not seem to apply. Lefebvre himself was one of the most vehement critics of structuralist, economistic, and reductionist approaches, and he spanned a theoretical horizon that sought to include the most diverse elements, but especially cultural, psychoanalytical, and semiotic analyses. Deutsche, for example, praised him: '[Lefebvre's] analysis of the spatial exercise of power as a construction and conquest of difference, although it is thoroughly grounded in Marxist

---

110   See for example Gregory and Urry, *Social Relations and Spatial Structures*; Wentz, *Stadt-Räume*; Benko and Strohmayer, *Space and Social Theory*.

111   Dear, *The Postmodern Urban Condition*, 47.

112   Allen, *Lost Geographies of Power*, 160.

113   Jameson, *Postmodernism*; Jameson, *Valencies of the Dialectic*.

thought, rejects economism and opens up possibilities for advancing analysis of spatial politics into realms of feminist and anti-colonial discourse.'[114]

The second wave of Lefebvre reception thus took place under very different conditions to the first. What in the 1970s had given rise to harsh criticism or was at least passed over with disapproving silence now appeared promising in a postmodern and poststructuralist light. His poetic metaphilosophical reflections opened up a wide scope for creative interpretations and offered themselves as a projection screen or a 'quarry' for ideas and concepts, in which selected passages or concepts were isolated, reformulated, and incorporated into postmodern narratives. In the process, postmodern writers often ignored the fact that terms such as 'space', 'urban society', 'modernity', 'everyday life', 'language', and 'difference' are each based on specific definitions within Lefebvre's work, definitions which in many cases do not coincide with their corresponding postmodern or poststructuralist meanings.

This difficulty appears, for example, in Soja's interpretation of Lefebvre. His 'ontology of space', developed in *Postmodern Geographies*, uses a reifying, undynamic, and undialectical understanding of Lefebvre's concept of space at crucial points.[115] In his next book, *Thirdspace*, he takes up Lefebvre's three-dimensional dialectic of space, but is unable to resolve it.[116] The key concept of the book – 'thirdspace' – arose from a creative misunderstanding of Lefebvre's theory, as did his concept of a 'trialectics', which he used to characterise Lefebvre's three-dimensional dialectic. Although Soja sought to counterpose his 'trialectics' to the classic figure of 'thesis–antithesis', the term 'dialectics' has nothing to do with 'two', but is based on the Greek prefix 'dia', which means 'through' (for a detailed critique, see section 5.7).

A similar problem arises in another important book of geographical postmodernism, in which Lefebvre is again assigned the central position of advocate: *Geographical Imaginations* by Derek Gregory.[117] Here, too, Lefebvre appears in a 'postmodern' light, and the 'rediscovery' of his work serves in part as material for a reckoning with radical geography and especially the political economy of David Harvey. The fact that the two thinkers ultimately pursued very different projects is mentioned, but hardly taken into account either in the analysis or in the evaluation. It is precisely this juxtaposition that clearly shows the thrust of Lefebvre's postmodern reception: what is appealing about Lefebvre is his broad thematisation of 'cultural' aspects, not least his language, which oscillates between polemic and poetry. Lefebvre's theory offers the possibility of

---

114   Deutsche, 'Uneven Development', 29.
115   Soja, *Postmodern Geographies*.
116   Soja, *Thirdspace*.
117   Gregory, *Geographical Imaginations*.

constitutively including processes that had so far been ignored in orthodox Marxist analyses or devalued as cultural 'superstructure phenomena', and to overcome the deterministic and economistic concept of material-economic base and ideological-cultural superstructure (see section 7.3).

However, most postmodern and poststructuralist interpretations ignore the fact that Lefebvre's materialist and dialectical social theory connects these cultural phenomena and processes back to a material process, a concrete everyday practice. Lefebvre, who had always been decidedly and fundamentally opposed to structuralism, was therefore logically just as much at odds with poststructuralist approaches. He was also far from developing a culturalist theory, as he was very critical of the concept of 'culture'. In essence, such appropriations of Lefebvre's theory miss not only the author's intention, but also the quality and potential of his approach. As far as the 'spatial imagination' is concerned, for Lefebvre this does not simply consist of images that are produced or reproduced in our heads in an ultimately inexplicable way but is based on concrete everyday spatial practices which produce these imaginaries and which are in turn transformed by them. It is precisely this reciprocal relationship that forms the explosive core of the theory of the production of space.

The Second Wave of Lefebvre Interpretation

This second wave of interpretation of Lefebvre's work thus had quite ambivalent effects. On the one hand, a Lefebvre industry emerged that incorporated his work into almost every conceivable kind of theoretical context. On the other hand, it was through this often inaccurate interpretation that Lefebvre's work was widely introduced and discussed in the social sciences and humanities. Nonetheless, it had a major impact on various conceptualisations and raised awareness of the fact that social space is not given in itself but is the result of a process of production, however this process is understood and theorised.

Doreen Massey, for example, drew heavily on Lefebvre, as is already evident in her use of the term *space/time*.[118] However, her concept of 'relational space' is very general, and also more inspired by Harvey than it might seem at first glance. Jameson also relied on Lefebvre in his theorisation of postmodernism, even if he did not discuss the French theorist's work in detail.[119] John Allen referred to Lefebvre at length in formulating his topology of space, and together with Michael Pryke he examined the production of the abstract space of finance

---

118   Massey, *Space, Place and Gender*.
119   Jameson, *Postmodernism*.

in London, contrasting the everyday lives and spaces of those who work in the financial markets and those who work in the low-income support sector of the financial industry.[120] Michael Keith and Steve Pile also tried to ground their conceptualisation of place and identity in Lefebvre's theory, and Kevin Hetherington consulted Lefebvre in his non-reductionist analysis of identity politics of social movements.[121]

Besides these theoretical (and ideological) debates and controversies, the concrete applications of Lefebvre's theory remained rather modest. Even the 'postmodern' Los Angeles School mainly used extant political-economic approaches, and in Allen Scott and Edward Soja's important collection *The City*, Lefebvre is not mentioned once.[122] However, despite his theoretical difficulties with Lefebvre's theory, Soja demonstrated a remarkable sensitivity for everyday experiences in his empirical texts and exemplified the potential of combining a political-economic perspective with an analysis of 'lived space', however interpreted.[123]

Overall, these encounters with Lefebvre's theory remained rather short episodes. They were largely isolated, struggling with the enormous scope and vast complexity of Lefebvre's work and the fact that only a few of his texts had been translated into English. His theoretical references, unusual for the Anglo-American academy, his heterodox Marxism, his specific dialectics, his references to Hegel and Nietzsche often posed great difficulties for a postmodern reception.

Subsequently, poststructuralist urban studies turned to other topics. Scholars focused on questions of social difference (see section 6.4), worked with Foucault's concepts of power/knowledge relations, governmentality, and biopolitics, dealt with the deconstruction of all kinds of texts, and later mobilised actor–network theory and assemblage theory. Most of these approaches, theories, and concepts are largely incompatible with Lefebvre's dialectical materialism. Thus, the second phase of Lefebvre's interpretation gradually faded out at the beginning of the twenty-first century, as did the term 'postmodernism' itself.

120   Allen, *Lost Geographies of Power*; Allen and Pryke, 'The Production of Service Space'.
121   Keith and Pile, *Place and the Politics of Identity*; Hetherington, *Expressions of Identity*.
122   Scott and Soja, *The City*.
123   Soja, *Thirdspace*; Soja, *Postmetropolis*.

1.4 Critical Research with Lefebvre

> Between the fundamental project and the radical critique, there is a
> reciprocity of perspective. Criticism opens an outlet; the project shows
> itself in this opening.[124]

While Lefebvre was the great absent presence in critical urban studies of the
1970s, his postmodern 'rediscovery' in the 1990s pushed his work into the centre
of the debate, but at the same time also confined it in an ontological corset,
misinterpreted it in many ways, and, moreover, was confronted with many theoretical riddles. It was only slowly that another more systematic and dialectical
interpretation of Lefebvre's theory emerged, which first had to oppose these postmodern interpretations. As Kofman and Lebas noted: 'There seems currently to
be an attempt amongst those labelling themselves postmodern geographers to
appropriate any thinker who "prioritises" space, as if this accolade automatically
makes a geographer.'[125] They criticised the then-dominant Anglo-American
postmodern interpretation of Lefebvre for its ostentatious privileging of space
over time and the accompanying reduction of Lefebvre's theory to spatial aspects.
They also accused it of approaching his work in a homogenising manner and
adopting, without any differentiation, definitions and concepts that had arisen in
a different social and epistemological context. This, they claimed, had led to
many oversimplifications and misunderstandings.

Rob Shields specifically criticised the postmodern simplifications and incor-
porations of Lefebvre by Soja and Gregory, who had created a kind of 'Lefebvre
Chorus': 'For a Lefebvrian geography,' he wrote, 'we get an amalgam of postmodern writers on identity, community, and the city.'[126] Stefan Kipfer and Richard
Milgrom were similarly critical: 'The "Lefebvrian industry" that has developed in
the Anglo-American world since the English language publication of *The
Production of Space* in 1991, has not necessarily clarified the current relevance of
his work.'[127] Stuart Elden took the same line: 'It would ... be harsh, but not
perhaps unfair, to suggest that Lefebvre's work has suffered as a result of being
read in English and appropriated for a certain type of academic work by certain
types of scholars.'[128] Finally, in a programmatic text, Neil Brenner and Stuart
Elden called for a critical review of previous (postmodern) interpretations.

---

124 Lefebvre, *Metaphilosophy*, 104–5.
125 Kofman and Lebas, 'Lost in Transposition'.
126 Shields, *Lefebvre, Love and Struggle*.
127 Kipfer and Milgrom, 'Henri Lefebvre – Urbanization, Space and Nature', 38–9.
128 Elden, 'Politics, Philosophy, Geography'.

First, to what degree have readings and appropriations of Lefebvre reflected a breadth of theoretical understanding, an attention to exegetical detail and a sensitivity to his own political-historical context? Second, and relatedly, to what extent have these engagements with Lefebvre succeeded in excavating intellectual and political impulses within his writings that resonate productively with contemporary questions, concerns and projects?[129]

Engaging with probing questions such as these, a new wave of appropriation of Lefebvre's thoughts emerged around the beginning of the twenty-first century.

The Third Wave of Lefebvre Interpretation

This third wave of Lefebvre interpretation was based on a critical appropriation of his theory and included a much broader part of his work than earlier receptions – this, of course, also presupposed a knowledge of French. For many scholars, Lefebvre's theory promised a way out of the dilemma created by the confrontation between historical-materialist and poststructuralist approaches and allowed them to take political-economic aspects as well as representations and everyday life experiences into account. As Christian Schmid, Łukasz Stanek, and Ákos Moravánszky wrote, this third wave of Lefebvre interpretation 'not only bridged the gap between "political-economic" and "cultural" readings but understood Lefebvre's consistent integration of questions of political economy, state theory, language theory, architecture, everyday life and lived experience in an encompassing materialist and dialectical framework as the decisive advantage of his theory'.[130]

The starting points of this third wave were small, networked circles of researchers in Frankfurt, Zurich, London, Toronto, and New York, who jointly organised Lefebvre panels at various conferences (see Foreword). This work resulted in a special issue on Lefebvre in *Capitalism Nature Socialism* (June 2002) and in the edited volumes *Space, Difference, Everyday Life: Reading Henri Lefebvre* and *Urban Revolution Now: Henri Lefebvre in Social Research and Architecture*, which together provide a comprehensive overview of the themes, the discussions, and also the empirical approaches of this third constellation of Lefebvre readings.[131]

---

129 Brenner and Elden, 'Henri Lefebvre in Contexts', 764.
130 Schmid, Stanek, and Moravánszky, 'Theory, Not Method'.
131 Goonewardena et al., *Space, Difference, Everyday Life*; Stanek, Schmid, and Moravánszky, *Urban Revolution Now*.

This new attempt at interpretation was multifaceted and polyphonic, but showed certain commonalities: first, it constituted the beginning of a profound engagement with Lefebvre's theory. In the English-speaking world, Rob Shields presented a detailed reappraisal of Lefebvre's philosophical roots, having already drawn heavily on Lefebvre's theory in his widely acclaimed analysis of places on the margin. Bud Burkhard illuminated Lefebvre's early philosophical work of the interwar period and his central role in introducing and popularising Marxism in France. Stuart Elden published the first thorough and detailed theoretical overview of Lefebvre's oeuvre, and Andy Merrifield followed up with a compact and accessible introduction to Lefebvre's life and work.[132] In addition, a growing number of translations of Lefebvre's texts paved the way for a wider appropriation of Lefebvre's theory in the English-speaking world.[133] In German, Ulrich Müller-Schöll presented a meticulous study of Lefebvre's metaphilosophy.[134] This was followed by my own book *Stadt, Raum und Gesellschaft: Henri Lefebvre und die Produktion des Raumes* of which the present book is a greatly expanded and revised version; some parts of this book were also later published in English.[135]

Second, it was in this context that Lefebvre's texts on the city, which had received only limited attention in the critical urban studies of the 1970s and 1980s, but also in the postmodern discussion of the 1990s, finally found greater appreciation. A real breakthrough here came with the translation of large parts of *The Right to the City*, carefully edited and extensively annotated and contextualised by Eleonore Kofman and Elizabeth Lebas.[136] With *Metromarxism*, Andy Merrifield presented an interpretation that gave Lefebvre his due central place in critical urban studies.[137] Finally, *The Urban Revolution* was translated into English in 2003, with a foreword by Neil Smith, which meant recognition in Anglo-American critical urban theory.

Third, these interpretations acted as a bridge by rejecting the dualism between 'political economy' and 'cultural studies' that had so strongly characterised theoretical debates until then, and by showing how an open-minded

---

132   Shields, *Lefebvre, Love and Struggle*; Shields, *Places on the Margin*; Burkhard, *French Marxism between the Wars*; Elden, *Understanding Henri Lefebvre*; Merrifield, *Henri Lefebvre*.

133   These include, in particular, the carefully selected, edited, and commented text collection in Lefebvre, *Key Writings*. Another important collection which presents a selection of previously almost inaccessible texts on the state is Lefebvre, *State, Space, World*.

134   Müller-Schöll, *Das System und der Rest*.

135   Schmid, *Stadt, Raum und Gesellschaft*; Schmid, 'Henri Lefebvre's Theory of the Production of Space'; Schmid, 'Henri Lefebvre, the Right to the City'; Schmid, 'The Trouble with Henri'.

136   Lefebvre, *Writings on Cities*.

137   Merrifield, *Metromarxism*.

appropriation of Lefebvre's dialectical, metaphilosophical epistemology could combine political-economic analyses with the study of lived practices and symbolic meanings. Kipfer emphasises in this context: 'Lefebvre's Marxism defies dichotomies (between political economy and cultural studies, universality and particularity, class and other social relations) that shaped the reception of Lefebvre in the 1980s and 1990s.'[138] This statement also refers to attempts to pit Marxist approaches against postcolonial ones.

Fourth, there was an increased effort to develop Lefebvre's theory further, to apply it to various contexts and thus make it fruitful for novel reflections and analyses. These include Brenner's examination of Lefebvre's theory of the state, which he links to the debates on the scale question, Kipfer's approach of developing Lefebvre's work in dialogue with Gramsci and Fanon, and my own efforts to complement Lefebvre's theory with the regulation approach and thus gain a theoretical basis for the comparative analysis of urban development. Finally, the postcolonial extension of Lefebvre's theory, advanced consistently by Kipfer and Goonewardena, was a crucial opening to Lefebvre scholarship (see below).

In France there was also a gradual rediscovery of Lefebvre. On the basis of extensive interviews with Lefebvre, Rémi Hess wrote a detailed biography shortly before Lefebvre's death that provides a very helpful historical grounding for his concepts with many theoretical cross-references.[139] It aroused a new interest in Lefebvre in the francophone world and also received attention beyond it. In addition, there was a small group of friends who had worked together with Lefebvre, such as Armand Ajzenberg, who had collaborated with Lefebvre on one of his last books and continued to publish consistently thereafter; Pierre Lantz, whose supervisor was Lefebvre; and Michel Trebitsch, who started to analyse Lefebvre's texts from the point of view of the history of science.[140] This renewed interest in Lefebvre in France was particularly marked by the 1994 collection of articles in the journal *Espaces et Société* – which had been founded by Lefebvre. This project was initiated by Monique Coornaert and Jean-Pierre Garnier, and was partly animated by the Anglo-American (postmodern) revival of Lefebvre.[141] Another important stage was the conference on the 100th anniversary of Lefebvre's birth in 2001 at the Université Paris 8 in St Denis, which also attracted a new generation of activists and researchers. Thanks especially to the efforts of Rémi Hess, a long series of new editions of Lefebvre's books appeared in the following years, some of which had long

---

138 Kipfer, 'Pushing the Limits of Urban Research', 478.
139 Hess, *Henri Lefebvre et l'aventure du siècle*.
140 Lefebvre and Groupe de Navarrenx, *Du contrat de citoyenneté*; Lantz, 'La fin de l'histoire'; Trebitsch, 'Henri Lefebvre et l'autogestion'.
141 Coornaert and Garnier, 'Actualités de Henri Lefebvre'.

been out of print. An important role in this new wave was then played by Hugues Lethierry, who not only wrote a new intellectual and political biography of Lefebvre, but also launched a broader discussion of Lefebvre's work.[142] Finally, a new generation of researchers also entered the discussion, organising a Lefebvre conference at the Paris Nanterre University in 2011.[143]

To summarise, the third wave of Lefebvre interpretation started from an undogmatic reading, took Lefebvre's work as a starting point for further thinking, and was at the same time more precise and more open than the previous receptions. In addition to these renewed and expanded theoretical discussions, another major step was that Lefebvre's theory finally found its way into empirical research. The legend spread by Castells, among others, that it is extremely difficult, if not impossible, to apply Lefebvre's theory stubbornly persisted for a long time. This changed when Stanek presented his meticulous historical review of Lefebvre's own empirical research and that of his collaborators, and also shed light on his cooperation in architectural projects (see section 6.5).[144]

The enriched understanding of Lefebvre's work made empirical applications possible that not only cited Lefebvre's work, as had already been done almost routinely in certain fields of scholarship, but also included his theories and concepts constitutively in their investigation and, following his principle of transduction, developed them further. Today, contributions informed by Lefebvre's theory may be found in fields as diverse as geography, sociology, cultural anthropology, urban studies, architecture and urban design, planning, cultural studies, literary studies, art history, pedagogy, history, and even legal studies. They are operating with different understandings, often stretch across several disciplines, and thus constitute transdisciplinary fields of research. Additionally, the postcolonial turn in urban studies has sparked a renewed interest in Lefebvre's work and further advanced the dissemination and application of his concepts around the world.

At this point, an account of the current receptions of Lefebvre would be appropriate. However, I have had to abandon a comprehensive approach to this endeavour. It is no longer possible to attain even a rough overview of the various topics and fields of research that engage with Lefebvre's work in one way or another. Such an overview would probably not be useful either, because it would simply show that Lefebvre's theory is widely available today. To conclude this

---

142 Lethierry, *Penser avec Henri Lefebvre*; Lethierry, *Agir avec Henri Lefebvre*; Ajzenberg, Lethierry, and Bazinek, *Maintenant Henri Lefebvre*.

143 This conference was documented in the journal *L'Homme et la Société* (no. 185–6, 2012), which provides a very good overview of current research topics.

144 Stanek, *Henri Lefebvre on Space*.

chapter, I will therefore limit myself to giving some indications of current tendencies in working with Lefebvre's theory, without any claim to completeness.[145]

Everyday Life, Public Space, and Concrete Utopia

Lefebvre's comprehensive work on everyday life, which spans almost half a century, in many ways constitutes an independent field of scholarly discussion. While there have been substantial engagements with his work in the German-speaking world since the 1970s,[146] in-depth accounts in Anglo-American academia only emerged when the three volumes of *Critique of Everyday Life* were gradually translated into English. The prefaces written by Michel Trebitsch for each volume present an important and rich first-hand source.[147] Subsequently, a whole series of remarkable overviews and interpretations appeared. Peter Osborne discussed Lefebvre's concept of everydayness at the end of his ground-breaking book on modernity and the avant-garde. Michael Gardiner contextualised Lefebvre's 'everyday utopianism' in the philosophical debates of the twentieth century, and Kanishka Goonewardena highlighted the revolutionary relationship between Marxism and everyday life at the beginning of the twentieth century. John Roberts analysed Lefebvre's dialectic of the everyday as a philosophy of praxis and as a critique of commodity production. Lefebvre's account on the dialectics of the modernisation of everyday life in the post-war period was presented by Ben Highmore in his comprehensive overview of theories on everyday life, which he accompanied with a reader offering a wide-ranging selection of original texts; he then applied this theory in his own empirical studies. Additionally, Michael Sheringham examined Lefebvre's contributions in the context of the prolific phase of French studies on everyday life from the 1950s to the 1970s. Finally, Anne Raulin wrote a concise overview of Lefebvre's body of work on everyday life from the perspective of French urban anthropology.[148]

---

145 The following account is strongly based on the reviews in Kipfer et al., 'On the Production of Henri Lefebvre'; Kipfer, Saberi, and Wieditz, 'Henri Lefebvre: Debates'; Schmid, Stanek, and Moravánszky, 'Theory, Not Method'.

146 This includes Meyer, *Henri Lefebvre*; Kleinspehn, *Der verdrängte Alltag*; Sünker, *Bildung, Alltag und Subjektivität*.

147 Trebitsch, prefaces to Lefebvre, *Critique of Everyday Life*, 3 vols.

148 Osborne, *Politics of Time*; Gardiner, *Critiques of Everyday Life*; Gardiner, 'Everyday Utopianism'; Goonewardena, 'Marxism and Everyday Life'; Roberts, *Philosophizing the Everyday*; Highmore, *Everyday Life and Cultural Theory*; Highmore, *The Everyday Life Reader*; Highmore, *Ordinary Lives*; Sheringham, *Everyday Life*; Raulin, 'La vie quotidienne, entre colonisation et émancipation'.

Many researchers made this wide theoretical body of work fruitful for the analysis of concrete situations. Literary scholar Kristin Ross encountered Lefebvre's theory starting from the concept of social space and then applied it in a very thorough way to the analysis of the modernisation of everyday life in post-war France; this revolutionary understanding of everyday life also permeates her books on May 1968 in Paris and the Paris Commune.[149] The historian Harry Harootunian has used Lefebvre's conceptualisation of modernity and everyday life to better understand the modern history of Japan. Fraya Frehse applied Lefebvre's regressive–progressive method in her anthropological studies of the everyday uses of São Paulo's public spaces. In the German-speaking world, Anne Vogelpohl has investigated the spaces and times of everyday life at the level of different urban neighbourhoods, and Sabine Knierbein has been pursuing the ambitious project of using the concept of lived space in everyday life as an analytical bridge between the study of urban culture and of public space on a theoretical, empirical, and didactic level for years. As Knierbein's engagement in the didactics of planning and architecture shows, Lefebvre's work was also applied in pedagogy. Sünker had developed his analysis on education, everyday life, and subjectivity in the context of social pedagogy, and more recently, Sue Middleton published a very inspiring book on her experiences with Lefebvre's theory in various pedagogical projects.[150]

A rousing appropriation of Lefebvre's theoretical and activist engagements was presented by the legendary journalist and rock music critic Greil Marcus, who wrote a provocative kaleidoscopic history of twentieth-century counter-cultures, assembling accounts on the punk movement, Dadaism, the Lettrist International and the Situationist International, various theorists, writers, poets, artists, graffiti and filmmakers, and protesters and activists to create a profound critique of everyday life.[151]

Lefebvre's posthumously published book *Rhythmanalysis*, which was translated into English only in 2004, is a very important complement to his analyses of everyday life, as he considers in this work everyday life not from the point of view of space but from the point of view of time and the rhythms of life. This

149   Ross, *The Emergence of Social Space*; Ross, *Fast Cars, Clean Bodies*; Ross, *May '68 and Its Afterlives*; Ross, *Communal Luxury*.

150   Harootunian, *History's Disquiet*; Frehse, *O tempo das ruas na São Paulo de fins do Império*; Frehse, 'For Difference "in and through" São Paulo'; Vogelpohl, *Urbanes Alltagsleben*; Knierbein, *Die Produktion zentraler öffentlicher Räume*; Knierbein, 'Public Space as Relational Counter Space'; Sünker, *Bildung, Alltag und Subjektivität*; Middleton, *Henri Lefebvre and Education*.

151   Marcus, *Lipstick Traces*.

book has opened up a new research strand of its own and has become an important source of inspiration in urban studies.[152]

Urbanisation and Urban Development

Lefebvre's analysis of urbanisation forms a second central field of scholarly debate and interpretation. As the above discussion has shown, both Castells and Harvey built on Lefebvre's work in key points, but Castells's devastating critique and Harvey's positive yet cursory reception did not contribute to a wider dissemination of his texts in academia. His texts were, however, eagerly read by many activists, in French, in German, and in some other language areas where translations were available. In Latin America, Lefebvre's thought had a much wider circulation not only among activists but also among academics, as French philosophy and sociology were widely discussed there and several of his texts were available in Spanish and Portuguese early on.[153]

The situation in Anglo-American academia changed dramatically with the postmodern wave of Lefebvre's reception, which indeed largely neglected his texts on the urban, but instead mobilised *The Production of Space* for the analysis of urban developments, as Soja's work shows in an exemplary manner.[154] At the same time, another current of Lefebvre interpretation emerged in the German-speaking world, with the groups 'urbi et orbi' in Frankfurt and 'Ssenter for Applied Urbanism' in Zurich, which relied strongly on his urban texts, critically analysed the urban development of these two metropolitan regions, and also intervened in local public debates. Both groups, which soon began collaborating, developed similar theoretical approaches, integrating Lefebvre's writings with theorisations of urban struggle, the global city concept, accounts of the urban periphery, the regulation approach, and conceptualisations of urbanity and difference.[155] Some of these works also became accessible in English and

---

152 The edited volumes by Edensor, *Geographies of Rhythm*, and Mels, *Reanimating Places*, contain a wide selection of application examples. Interesting contributions also come from Meyer, 'Rhythms, Streets, Cities', and Seigworth and Gardiner, 'Rethinking Everyday Life'.

153 An overview of recent research in various Latin American countries is provided by Mattos and Link, *Lefebvre revisitado*.

154 Soja, *Thirdspace*; Soja, *Postmetropolis*.

155 See for example Hartmann et al., *Theorien zur Stadtentwicklung*; Hitz et al., *Capitales Fatales*; Hitz, Schmid, and Wolff, 'Boom, Konflikt und Krise'; Prigge, *Zeit, Raum und Architektur*; Prigge, 'Urbi et orbi'; Prigge, *Urbanität und Intellektualität im 20. Jahrhundert*; Ronneberger, *Peripherie und Ungleichzeitigkeit*.

eventually fed into the third wave of Lefebvre reception.[156] In the Anglo-American discussion, it was Andy Merrifield, in particular, who not only introduced Lefebvre's theory on the urban into critical urban theory, but also repeatedly pushed it forward with new ideas and concepts.[157] Having developed a comprehensive analysis of Lefebvre's theory, Kanishka Goonewardena and Stefan Kipfer created a critical postcolonial approach to urban studies based on Lefebvre's concepts of centrality, difference, and levels of social reality, and applied it to analyses of Toronto and Paris.[158]

In the following years, Lefebvre's theory has been used by many to develop a more comprehensive, multidimensional, and dialectical understanding of processes of urban restructuring, urban regeneration and gentrification, and the related urban struggles.[159] While Mark Davidson searched for a comprehensive Lefebvrian understanding of gentrification, others developed specific applications. Martin Phillips, for example, investigated gentrification processes in two villages in south-east England, and Thomas Dörfler analysed urban redevelopment processes in Berlin and Hamburg focusing particularly on the symbolic surplus value of the urban. Jean-Pierre Garnier examined the process of *embourgeoisement* through the designing and implementation of the encompassing state-led infrastructure and redevelopment project for 'Greater Paris'. Rahel Nüssli and I analysed the process of urban intensification in the former urban periphery of Zurich. Ng et al. and Agnes Shuk-mei Ku presented two thorough Lefebvrian analyses of the political mobilisations provoked by the demolitions of the Star Ferry pier and the Queen's pier in Hong Kong.

There have also been various activist contributions. Kike España, for

---

156   For example, Hitz, Schmid, and Wolff, 'Urbanization in Zurich'; Hitz, Schmid, and Wolff, 'Zurich Goes Global'; Keil and Ronneberger, 'Going up the Country'; Schmid, 'The Dialectics of Urbanisation in Zurich'; Prigge, 'Reading the Urban Revolution'; Ronneberger, 'Henri Lefebvre and Urban Everyday Life'; Schmid, 'Journeys through Planetary Urbanization'.

157   Merrifield, *Metromarxism*; Merrifield, *The Politics of the Encounter*; Merrifield, *The New Urban Question*.

158   Goonewardena, 'The Urban Sensorium'; Goonewardena, 'Henri Lefebvre'; Goonewardena and Kipfer, 'Spaces of Difference'; Kipfer, 'How Lefebvre Urbanized Gramsci'; Kipfer, 'Neocolonial Urbanism?'; Kipfer, *Le temps et l'espace de la (dé)colonisation*; Kipfer and Goonewardena, 'Henri Lefebvre and "Colonization"'.

159   Davidson, 'Gentrification as Global Habitat'; Davidson, 'Displacement, Space and Dwelling'; Phillips, 'The Production, Symbolization and Socialization of Gentrification'; Dörfler, *Gentrification in Prenzlauer Berg?*; Dörfler, 'Antinomien des (neuen) Urbanismus'; Garnier, *Une violence éminemment contemporaine*; Garnier, ' "Greater Paris" '; Nüssli and Schmid, 'Beyond the Urban–Suburban Divide'; Ng et al., 'Spatial Practice, Conceived Space and Lived Space'; Ku, 'Remaking Places and Fashioning an Opposition Discourse'.

example, activist of the anti-austerity 15M movement, analysed municipalist practices in the 'gentle city' Málaga in south Spain. With these practices, activists tried to produce 'gentle holes' apart from tourism and gentrification and thus to propose a radical reformulation of urban life. Christoph Schäfer drew a whole series of large-format cartoons on the history of the city in the footsteps of Lefebvre, which he used at activist events and which he also published as a book. And the Kollektiv Quotidien Berlin combined theory, urban politics, the arts, and activism in an easily accessible presentation of Lefebvre's concepts.[160]

The Right to the City

If Lefebvre has really found a global reach today, then the concept and the battle cry of 'the right to the city' has played a key role in this. Since the turn of the century, it almost completely replaced the concept of 'urban social movements', which was mainly based on Castells's theory of collective consumption and dominated academic debates in urban studies for decades. As Mayer has shown, research on urban social movements focused mainly on the study of relatively well-organised movements that challenged insufficient public transport, infrastructures, and services and demanded more participation in decision-making processes in urban design and planning, even though there have of course always been more radical and spontaneous urban movements and uprisings.[161]

This situation changed significantly towards the end of the century. As new rounds of urban restructuring led to massive displacements and various forms of dispossession worldwide – igniting new waves of urban protest and struggle – social movements, political organisations, and academics alike increasingly took up Lefebvre's concept of 'the right to the city'. Unlike Castells, Lefebvre did not conceptualise urban social movements as such, but understood them in the broader context of the dialectical contradiction between urbanisation and social struggle.[162] His political stance and his demand for autogestion had led him to take the self-organisation and self-determination of social movements seriously, instead of defining and structuring them in advance according to

---

160   España, *Die sanfte Stadt*; Schäfer, *Die Stadt ist unsere Fabrik*; Kollektiv Quotidien, *Lefebvre for Activists*.

161   Mayer, 'The "Right to the City" in Urban Social Movements'; Mayer, 'Neoliberal Urbanism and Uprisings across Europe'.

162   See for example Schmid, 'Dialectics of Urbanisation in Zurich'; Uitermark, 'Looking Forward by Looking Back'.

theoretical concepts. Thus, in the context of the May 1968 movement in Paris, he remarked: 'A theory of the movement has to emerge from the movement itself, for it is the movement that has revealed, unleashed, and liberated theoretical capacities.'[163]

In the changed context of urban development and urban struggle of the early twentieth century, Lefebvre's concept of 'the right to the city' experienced an incredible rise in adoption and adaptation.[164] Initially used only rarely, the term soon became a kind of master key for very different situations and contexts and all kinds of urban movements, alliances, actions, mobilisations, and struggles across the world (this discussion is addressed in detail in section 4.4).

Planetary Urbanisation

Lefebvre's theory became an important starting point for the analysis of urban development and urban struggle after the turn of the century, but more recently, another aspect of his theory has gained prominence: the planetary extension of urban areas. His thesis of complete urbanisation invites us to broaden our view and examine the urbanisation of seemingly 'rural' or 'non-urban' areas. Inspired by Lefebvre, the book *Zürich ohne Grenzen* (*Zurich without Borders*), had already addressed precisely this cross-border and borderless kind of urbanisation in the 1980s. ETH Studio Basel took up this analysis with the project *Switzerland: An Urban Portrait*. By systematically examining urbanisation processes across the entire territory of Switzerland, it also identified different urban configurations in sparsely settled territories, and it developed a method that allows researchers to capture the urbanisation of all types of territories, even outside dense settlement areas and agglomerations.[165]

Based on these and other experiences and observations, Andy Merrifield as well as Neil Brenner and I launched the concept of planetary urbanisation, which was directly inspired by Lefebvre's thesis of complete urbanisation and his understanding of the planetary (see section 4.3).[166] Brenner's edited volume *Implosions/*

---

163   Lefebvre, *The Explosion*, 103.

164   A very good overview of the French discussion of this concept from its beginnings in the late 1960s to the 2000s with precise theoretical explanations can be found in Costes, *Henri Lefebvre*.

165   Ginsburg et al., *Zürich ohne Grenzen*; Diener et al., *Switzerland*; Diener et al., *Territory*.

166   Brenner and Schmid, 'Planetary Urbanization'; Brenner and Schmid, 'The "Urban Age" in Question'; Brenner and Schmid, 'Towards a New Epistemology of the Urban?'; Merrifield, 'The Right to the City and Beyond'; Merrifield, *The Politics of the Encounter*.

Explosions, whose title refers to Lefebvre's definition of urbanisation, documents much of the early discourse.[167] This planetary perspective inevitably calls into question familiar positions in urban studies, and has triggered correspondingly fierce reactions. The first texts on planetary urbanisation provoked so many responses and critiques that it is impossible to give a brief overview.[168] A first broad critique related to the style of the articles and their lack of recognition of feminist and queer theoretical approaches. Some responses criticised from a feminist position the Lefebvre interpretation underlying the approach of planetary urbanisation.[169] Further controversies erupted about the conception of the complete urbanisation of society, the critique of city-centric approaches, the agglomeration question, the existence or non-existence of an 'outside of the urban', the transformation of the historical opposition between city and countryside, and the resulting question of the redefinition of the urban. These are questions that are discussed in detail in this book from the perspective of Lefebvre's theory. Another important aspect of the controversy concerned the question of how abstract and general processes can be linked to the analysis of concrete developments.[170] This question is also addressed in detail in this book, based on Lefebvre's dialectic, his combination of general conceptions with concrete analyses through the procedure of transduction, his understanding of concrete abstraction, and his concept of levels of social reality.

Beyond these debates and controversies, the perspective of planetary urbanisation has opened up a wide field for the analysis of new forms of urbanisation. In particular, the concept of *extended urbanisation*, which is derived from Lefebvre's thesis of complete urbanisation, allows us to understand and conceptualise urbanisation processes and urban protests beyond dense settlement areas and agglomerations. This concept was first conceived and empirically applied by Roberto Luís Monte-Mór to analyse the urbanisation of Amazonia, and it was independently developed again a few years later by Brenner and me in the context of our theorisation of planetary urbanisation with a slightly different emphasis.[171]

167   Brenner, *Implosions/Explosions*.

168   For a broad selection of voices in this controversy including Neil Brenner's and mine, see the special issue in *Society and Space, Environment and Planning D*, 36, no. 3, (2018).

169   See particularly Ruddick et al., 'Planetary Urbanization'; Buckley and Strauss, 'With, against and beyond Lefebvre'; Hart, 'Relational Comparison Revisited'.

170   Some answers to this can be found in Goonewardena, 'Planetary Urbanization and Totality', and Schmid, 'Journeys through Planetary Urbanization'.

171   Monte-Mór, 'Modernities in the Jungle'; Monte-Mór, 'Extended Urbanization and Settlement Patterns'; Monte-Mór, 'What Is the Urban in the Contemporary World?'; Monte-Mór and Castriota, 'Extended Urbanization: Implications'; Brenner and Schmid, 'Towards a New Epistemology of the Urban?'

The Latin American academic research contributed many important studies on extended urbanisation, particularly on the operationalisation of resource extraction.[172] The edited volume from Nancy Couling and Carola Hein discusses the multi-layered process of urbanisation of the North Sea, and Nikos Katsikis comprehensively analyses the urbanisation of the global hinterlands. The edited volume *Emerging Urban Spaces* from Horn, Alfaro d'Alençon, and Cardoso shows the great breadth of current research on extended urbanisation with a mainly postcolonial orientation, much of which explicitly refers to Lefebvre.[173] In-depth theoretical and empirical examinations of various processes of extended urbanisation can be found in the long-term collective project led by Milica Topalović and me on territories of extended urbanisation across the planet.[174] More detailed accounts on extended urbanisation can be found in sections 3.5 and 4.5.

The Production of Space: Theory, Research, and Practice

After being completely neglected for almost fifteen years, *The Production of Space* became a pivotal point of Lefebvre interpretation following its English transla-tion in 1991 and its postmodern 'rediscovery'. It was applied in a wide variety of contexts and served as an inspiration for many scholars, even if they often mentioned Lefebvre only in passing or not even explicitly. To this day, the three-dimensional dialectic developed in this book remains a key question of any inter-pretation of Lefebvre. However, an undialectical and schematic application of this dialectic is still widespread today, as the postmodern misunderstandings of it continue to circulate. Soja's misleading formulation of a 'trialectic' still pervades many recent texts, and there are ongoing attempts to construct an 'ontology of space', despite the fact that Lefebvre's dialectic defies any kind of ontology. One of the central starting points for the third wave of Lefebvre appropriation was to develop a consistent interpretation and application of the three-dimensional dialectic. This also forms a central component of the present book.

---

172   Arboleda, 'In the Nature of the Non-City'; Arboleda, 'Spaces of Extraction, Metropolitan Explosions'; Arboleda, *Planetary Mine*; Wilson and Bayón, 'Concrete Jungle'; Wilson and Bayón, 'Black Hole Capitalism'; Wilson, *Reality of Dreams*; Castriota and Tonucci, 'Extended Urbanization in and from Brazil'; Castriota, 'Extractivism and Urban Struggle'; Kanai, 'On the Peripheries of Planetary Urbanization'.

173   Couling and Hein, *Urbanisation of the Sea*; Couling, 'Ocean Space and Urbanisation'; Katsikis, 'From Hinterland to Hinterglobe'; Brenner and Katsikis, 'Operational Landscapes'; Horn, Alfaro, and Cardoso, *Emerging Urban Spaces*.

174   Schmid and Topalović, *Extended Urbanisation*; see also Topalović, *Hinterland: Singapore*.

The three-dimensional concept of the production of space has huge potential and has allowed for very diverse applications, especially in architecture, ethnography, and geography. It is not possible here to go into the whole breadth and length of these contributions, but only to mention a few highlights. Exemplary applications of the three-dimensional concept include Stanek's analysis of the socialist industrial town of Nowa Huta near Krakow, and my own analysis of the complete urbanisation of Switzerland based on an analysis of an experimental documentary film. A dramatic application was presented by Eugene McCann, who analysed the segregated and discriminatory everyday life in a predominantly African American government housing development north of downtown Lexington, Kentucky. Yonn Dierwechter mobilised Lefebvre's theorisation of modernities in his analysis of urban planning and economic survival in Cape Town's post-apartheid townships, Elisa Bertuzzo analysed everyday life in a densely populated settlement in Dhaka, and Felicity Chan discussed the production and negotiation of differences in three Los Angeles neighbourhoods. Ulrich Best explored lived spaces and the 'spatial politics of affect' in the controversies about the future use of the defunct Tempelhof airport in Berlin. A whole range of important contributions on various aspects of the production of space and on planetary urbanisation came from Japhy Wilson, who analysed the consequences of abstract space and explored the concrete utopia of differential space in Lefebvre's theory and in urban developments in Mexico and Ecuador.[175]

ETH Studio Basel took a great step further here and developed its own version of Lefebvre's three-dimensional analysis, which uses the three dialectically linked concepts of 'networks, borders, differences' and makes it possible to identify and analyse the most diverse forms of urbanisation.[176] This approach was further developed towards a three-dimensional conception of urbanisation processes distinguishing material production processes, processes of territorial regulation, and socialisation and meaning processes in their dialectical interplay. This conception has been shown to be particularly productive in a long-term comparative project on the patterns and pathways of urbanisation processes in large urban territories across the world, led by Christian Schmid (see also section 8.1).[177]

---

175   Stanek, 'Architectural Project and the Agency of Representation'; Schmid, 'Travelling Warrior and Complete Urbanization in Switzerland'; McCann, 'Race, Protest, and Public Space'; Dierwechter, 'Lefebvre's Modernities'; Chan, *Tensions in Diversity: Spaces for Collective Life in Los Angeles*; Bertuzzo, *Fragmented Dhaka*; Best, 'The Debate about Berlin Tempelhof Airport'; Wilson, ' "The Devastating Conquest of the Lived by the Conceived" '; Wilson, 'Plan Puebla Panama'; Wilson, 'Notes on the Rural City'; Wilson, *Reality of Dreams*.

176   Diener et al., *Switzerland*; Diener et al., *The Inevitable Specificity of Cities*.

177   Schmid et al., 'Towards a New Vocabulary of Urbanisation Processes'; Streule et al., 'Popular Urbanization'; Schmid and Streule, *Patterns and Pathways of Urbanization*.

The theory of the production of space has also entered the field of architecture, with the development, at the end of the 1990s, of a counter-current to the increasingly formal and fashionable designs of postmodernism. This new current criticised the alienation of architecture from lived experience, and applied the intellectual and political critique of consumer society and commodification of the late 1960s, drawing particular inspiration from Lefebvre. As Mary McLeod pointed out in her detailed introduction to Lefebvre's theoretical work and his collaboration with practising architects, Lefebvre's dialectical approach allowed him to vigorously critique the oppressions of daily existence and at the same time supported his conviction that everyday life harbours the desires that generate transformation.[178] Thus, Harris and Berke called for an unspectacular 'architecture of the everyday' and Chase, Crawford, and Kaliski took reflections by Lefebvre, Debord, and De Certeau as entry points for examinations of urban life and as incentives for design activities in Los Angeles and New York. A similar approach was taken by Borden, Kerr, Rendell, and Pivaro, who analysed architecture as part of the production of social space. Furthermore, Iain Borden showed how the urban practice of skateboarding contains a critique of the modes of operations of contemporary cities and tests the possibility of a differential space.[179]

In the 2010s, a new generation of scholars again mobilised Lefebvre's theory of the production of space in architecture and urban planning. Lehtovuori used Lefebvre's theory in a comprehensive way to analyse the production of public urban space. Tornaghi and Knierbein explored research and education in planning and architecture, arts, and activism, and Knierbein and Viderman presented a selection of case studies across the world on emancipatory practices emerging from lived space.[180] In this context, Lefebvre's numerous references to the Situationists, and in general to the debates on architectural and urbanist (concrete) utopias, also played an important role. They are discussed in detail in section 6.5.[181]

---

178   McLeod, 'Henri Lefebvre's Critique of Everyday Life'.

179   Berke and Harris, *Architecture of the Everyday*; Chase, Crawford, and Kaliski, *Everyday Urbanism*; Borden et al., *The Unknown City*; Borden, *Skateboarding, Space and the City*.

180   Lehtovuori, *Experience and Conflict*; Tornaghi and Knierbein, *Public Space and Relational Perspectives*; Knierbein and Viderman, *Public Space Unbound*.

181   An excellent overview is provided in Pinder, *Visions of the City*; see also Pinder, 'Reconstituting the Possible'. Important contributions can also be found in Sadler, *The Situationist City*; Gardiner, *Critiques of Everyday Life*; Gardiner, 'Everyday Utopianism'; Hughes and Sadler, *Non-plan*; Cunningham, 'Triangulating Utopia'. Milgrom takes the Situationist architecture of Lucien Kroll as a starting point to demonstrate how Lefebvre's method can be applied for concrete differential urban design practice: Milgrom, 'Lucien Kroll'.

Finally, it is worth mentioning Lefebvre's own engagements with architectural projects, which have been extensively reviewed by Stanek and also discussed by McLeod.[182] Stanek also published Lefebvre's lost manuscript *Toward an Architecture of Enjoyment*, which addresses architecture directly. In addition, another architectural project for Novi Beograd in which Lefebvre was directly involved was unearthed by Ljiljana Blagojević; it is documented and analysed in detail in *Autogestion, Or Henri Lefebvre in New Belgrade*.[183]

State and Regulation

Like his book *The Production of Space*, Lefebvre's important and extensive analyses on the state were almost completely neglected for a long time. In his imposing four-volume work *De l'État* he sketched out a new Marxist theory of the state that contains great potential, and here he also considerably expanded the theoretical basis of his theory of the production of space. However, these efforts found practically no reception for many years, as theoretical discussions in France were heavily dominated by structuralist and poststructuralist variants of Marxist state theory, and by various strands of regulation theory. Since this book has never been republished in French and has still not been translated into any other language, its reception remains limited to this day. In the German-speaking world, Hajo Schmidt presented a comprehensive analysis of Lefebvre's theory of the state, focusing particularly on the state's intrinsic violence through the process of commodification, while Corell Wex illuminated the connection of Lefebvre's theorisation of the state with the production of space, thereby developing the concept of the 'logistics of power'.[184]

By far the most influential contribution in this field comes from Neil Brenner, who comprehensively analysed and further developed Lefebvre's theorisation of the state as the dominant actor in the production of space. Brenner particularly took up Lefebvre's concept of scale, expanded it into a flexible and multidimensional version of the 'scale question', and developed Lefebvre's concept of 'state space' into a powerful analytical tool in urban and regional research. Brenner's major achievement is his incorporation of Lefebvre's open theory of the state into his own multiscalar theorisation of state

---

182   Stanek, *Henri Lefebvre on Space*; McLeod, 'Henri Lefebvre's Critique of Everyday Life'.

183   Bitter and Helmut Weber, *Autogestion*.

184   Hajo Schmidt, *Sozialphilosophie des Krieges*; Wex, 'Logistik der Macht'.

restructuring and the transformation of statehood. He thus conceived a new, dynamic understanding of the historical geographies of state power, which is particularly suitable for analyses of urban developments.[185]

From a postcolonial perspective, Manu Goswami adopted Lefebvre's understanding of the modern state as a spatial framework of power to analyse the emergence of a contradictory Indian nationalism in the second half of the nineteenth century and the production of India as a 'colonial state space'. Bringing Lefebvre together with subaltern and postcolonial studies, she analysed the complex ensemble of practices, ideologies, and state projects that underpinned the restructuring of the institutional and spatio-temporal matrices of colonial power and everyday life. More recently, Kit Ping Wong used Lefebvre's and Brenner's concepts of state space for her analysis of the contradictory role of the Chinese state in the urbanisation of the Pearl River Delta.[186]

There is another project which still remains to be completed: combining Lefebvre's theory of the production of space with the regulation approach to enable a historical analysis of urban developments. Based on the concept of the *rapport territorial* (territorial social relation) of DuPasquier and Marco, I have developed a conceptualisation that brings together elements of the French Regulation school with Lefebvre's theory.[187] Starting from this theoretical basis, we collectively developed an independent 'territorial approach' at ETH Studio Basel, which can also capture dual-land regimes with traditional and market forms of territorial regulation, and which has already been applied in various research projects (see also section 8.3).[188]

Greig Charnock has critically remarked that Lefebvre's 'open Marxism' cannot be combined with 'closed', structuralist-regulationist Marxist approaches, against which Lefebvre himself had always stood in vehement opposition.[189] While Lefebvre indeed heavily criticised structuralist (and post-structuralist) approaches, it is nevertheless possible, however, to draw his work into engagement with 'open' versions of the regulationist approach, especially on the basis of dialectical German interpretations and the work of Alain Lipietz,

---

185　Brenner, 'Global, Fragmented, Hierarchical'; Brenner, 'Between Fixity and Motion'; Brenner, 'The Urban Question as a Scale Question'; Brenner, 'The Limits to Scale?'; Brenner, *New State Spaces*; Brenner, *New Urban Spaces*.

186　Goswami, *Producing India*; Wong, 'Territorially-Nested Urbanization in China'.

187　DuPasquier and Marco, *Régulation fordiste et post-fordiste*; Schmid, 'Urbane Region und Territorialverhältnis'; Schmid, 'Raum und Regulation'.

188　Diener et al., *The Inevitable Specificity of Cities*; Schmid, 'Specificity and Urbanization'; Schmid et al., 'Towards a New Vocabulary of Urbanisation Processes'; Karaman et al., 'Plot by Plot'.

189　Charnock, 'Challenging New State Spatialities'.

who sought to combine structure and agency in his own understanding of regulation (see also section 8.3).[190]

Feminist Appropriations

Many exponents of feminist and queer theory approaches recognised the potential of Lefebvre's work early on. His combination of economic and cultural aspects of social development, and also his references to psycho-analysis opened up a promising potential for feminist appropriations.[191] Gibson-Graham saw in Lefebvre an unusual openness for a Western Marxist who also directly addressed and embraced feminist concerns. Jenny Bauer presented a feminist interpretation of Lefebvre's theory of the production of space by exploring references to Judith Butler.[192] Doreen Massey noted that Lefebvre insisted on the importance of lived practices and symbolic mean-ings of particular spaces and recognised in his depiction of Picasso's repre-sentation of the space of modernity that 'he is concerned centrally with its very particular gendering and sexualization'.[193] Lynn Stewart also praised Lefebvre's sensitivity to feminist concerns, which is especially evident in her discussion of the objectification of women, and the pernicious role phallo-centrism plays in the marginalisation of women. However, Virginia Blum and Heidi Nast criticised Lefebvre's heteronormativity in this context, although they still found his analysis of space and politics ground-breaking (see section 6.3).[194]

As Frehse, Knierbein, and Vogelpohl point out in their works, Lefebvre's thematisation of everyday life and thus also of the sphere of reproduction spoke directly to the core of feminist studies. Most importantly for feminists, he treated everyday life not as a specialised discipline but as part and parcel of his analysis of capitalism, and took it consistently as the starting point of his general theory of society, thus establishing direct links to urbanisation and the production of space. Mary McLeod, who has examined Lefebvre's relevance for

---

190   Alain Lipietz, 'Accumulation, Crises, and Ways Out'; Alain Lipietz, 'From Althusserianism to "Regulation Theory" '; see also Kipfer, Saberi, and Wieditz, 'Henri Lefebvre: Debates'.

191   This was pointed out, for example, in Deutsche, 'Uneven Development'; Deutsche, *Eviction*; Blum and Nast, 'Where's the Difference?'; Robinson, 'Feminism and the Spaces of Transformation'.

192   Gibson-Graham, *The End of Capitalism*, 74ff.; Bauer, *Differentielles Denken*; Bauer, *Geschlechterdiskurse um 1900*.

193   Massey, *Space, Place and Gender*, 182, 251.

194   Stewart, 'Bodies, Visions and Spatial Politics'; Blum and Nast, 'Where's the Difference?'

feminist conceptions of ordinary architecture, emphasised that Lefebvre's writing

> combines a deep respect for everyday existence with a commitment to creativity and change. He not only delineates the mundane and routinised dimensions of our daily lives, but also underscores those special, uplifting, pleasurable moments that give us glimpses of richer possibilities . . . His writings, although they contain some blatantly sexist phrases, convey a deep understanding of the joys and oppressions of women's daily existence.[195]

Frigga Haug has also discussed his theorisation of everyday life and emphasised his references to materialist feminist and anti-racist Marxist approaches, and, as mentioned above, Ross also relied on Lefebvre in her analysis of the gendered relationships between domestic and late-colonial culture in urban France.[196] In contrast, Tovi Fenster, among others, challenged Lefebvre's concept of the right to the city because it fails to devote sufficient attention to patriarchal power relations. Vacchelli and Kofman, as well as Vogelpohl, however, show ways for conceptualising the right to the city in a gendered perspective in urban contexts beyond Anglo-American knowledge production.[197]

Some feminists engage with Lefebvre's phenomenological conception of the production of space and thus open up very interesting new perspectives for a deepened understanding of lived space (see section 5.6). Lynn Stewart showed that Lefebvre regarded the body as a producer of difference, through rhythms, gestures, and imagination. Kirsten Simonsen argued that Lefebvre's thinking could usefully contribute to feminist (and other) approaches on 'body politics' and 'performativity'. And in a thorough and fascinating essay, Eden Kinkaid addressed Lefebvre's and Merleau-Ponty's accounts of bodily practices as an important source for a critical phenomenology of social space that supports critical race, postcolonial, feminist, and queer perspectives on differential embodiment.[198]

---

195   McLeod, 'Mary McLeod interviewed by Gevork Hartoonian', 112ff.; McLeod, 'Everyday and "Other" Spaces'.

196   Haug, 'Questions Concerning Methods in Feminist Research'; Haug, 'Alltagsforschung'; Ross, *Fast Cars, Clean Bodies*.

197   Fenster, 'The Right to the Gendered City'; Vacchelli and Kofman, 'Towards an Inclusive and Gendered Right to the City'; see also Vogelpohl, 'Henri Lefebvres "Recht auf Stadt" feministisch denken'.

198   Stewart, 'Bodies, Visions, and Spatial Politics'; Simonsen, 'Bodies, Sensations, Space and Time'; Kinkaid, 'Re-encountering Lefebvre'.

Finally, Michelle Buckley and Kendra Strauss provide an excellent overview of feminist appropriations of Lefebvre, and highlight in particular the potential for further engagement of feminist, critical race, and queer urban research with his work, noting his 'invitations to revolutionize the day-to-day practice of intellectual knowledge production' and calling for a corresponding epistemological plurality and interdisciplinary cooperation in critical urban studies.[199]

The Postcolonial Turn

The final discussion of this chapter is devoted to postcolonial approaches, which have not only gained great importance in urban studies in recent years, but also started to shape Lefebvre interpretations in decisive ways. Postcolonial urban studies have expanded the early postcolonial critiques of a Eurocentric, modernist, and often linear historiography with a critique of the dominance of Western models of urbanisation in scientific discourse and have thus revealed a multitude of different urban worlds across the globe.[200] In doing so, as Kanishka Goonewardena stated, they have also provided a critique of 'the role of urbanisation in the uneven development of capitalism' and advanced the search for emancipatory political possibilities in this process.[201] Postcolonial urban studies include a dual procedure: engaging in the analysis of the various forms and processes of urban development outside Europe and North America and, at the same time, problematising the colonial past and present in the imperial centres themselves.

Lefebvre's work was not spared from postcolonial critique: the bias of his Western Marxism is obvious, as the following chapters will show. The empirical basis of his analyses was France, particularly Paris and the Pyrenees. Even though he increasingly included international developments in his later work, as he became acquainted with them in his travels, his historical excursions in *The Urban Revolution* and *The Production of Space* were essentially limited to the history of the West, from ancient Greece and Rome through the European Middle Ages to the French Revolution, the Commune of 1871, and then Paris May 1968 (see sections 4.4 and 6.2). Lefebvre himself was well aware of these shortcomings, as the following quote reveals, reflecting on the traps that captured intellectual thinking in France, from which he sought to escape: 'We

---

199   Buckley and Strauss, 'With, against and beyond Lefebvre'.
200   Robinson, 'Thinking Cities through Elsewhere'; Roy and Ong, *Worlding Cities*.
201   Goonewardena, 'The Country and the City', 219.

might well note an embarrassing Euro-centrism, which never misses the occasion to confine itself to a somewhat provincial Paris-centrism.'[202]

Following this path of reflection, the editors of *Space, Difference, Everyday Life* called for Lefebvre to be globalised, and they also outlined a possible postcolonial development of his work.[203] In subsequent years, Kipfer and Goonewardena's major project was to connect 'metropolitan Marxism' with anti-colonial traditions, and to produce a new orientation in Lefebvre scholarship by putting counter-colonial aspects in Lefebvre's oeuvre to good analytical use.[204] They noted that writing on Lefebvre has generally proceeded as if 'the colonial' mattered little if at all in his work, as his anti-colonial insights either remained unacknowledged or were only weakly developed. They also showed, theoretically as well as empirically, that Lefebvre's concept of 'colonisation', which theorises the organisation of territorial relations, opens possible paths towards postcolonial theorisations (see also sections 4.5 and 8.3).[205]

Other postcolonial scholars also moved in this direction by integrating basic elements of Lefebvre's theory into their own approaches. Crystal Bartolovich, for example, relied on Lefebvre for her Marxist conception of everyday life in postcolonial studies: 'Lefebvre insisted on taking seeming trivialities seriously, believing that anyone devoted to resisting capitalist domination could not afford to ignore its permeation into the nooks and crannies of all aspects of our lives.'[206] Bahriye Kemal, for her part, applied Lefebvre's understanding of space production as well as his rhythmanalysis for her postcolonial analysis of anglophone, hellenophone, and turkophone literatures of Cyprus. Fernando Coronil drew on Lefebvre's three-dimensional conception of the production of space and his theorisation of ground rent and land commodification. For Coronil, the land question, in which the state plays a decisive role, has a fundamental importance for the development of (post)colonies, and its study helps to decentre Eurocentric conceptions that often reduce the analysis of capitalist development to a dialectic of capital and labour.[207] The land question is also a key starting point of Wing-Shing Tang's analyses of the urbanisation of Hong Kong, in which he makes repeated references to Lefebvre's theoretical framework. In

---

202   Lefebvre, 'Au-delà du savoir'.

203   Kipfer et al., 'Globalizing Lefebvre?'.

204   Kipfer and Goonewardena, 'Urban Marxism and the Post-colonial Question', 77.

205   Goonewardena, 'The Country and the City'; Kipfer, 'Fanon and Space'; Kipfer, 'The Fractures of Worldwide Urbanization'; Kipfer, 'Pushing the Limits of Urban Research'; Kipfer, *Le temps et l'espace de la (dé)colonisation*; Kipfer and Goonewardena, 'Lefebvre and "Colonization"'.

206   Bartolovich, 'Introduction', 6.

207   Kemal, *Writing Cyprus*; Coronil, 'Beyond Occidentalism'; Coronil, 'Towards a Critique of Globalcentrism'.

doing so, he also recognises the limitations of Lefebvre's theorisation, which is based on a historical urban–rural relationship specific to Europe that must be modified for postcolonial analyses and, in the case of China, to allow that country's unique dual rural–urban system to be included in the analysis.[208] The important role of conflicting dual-land regimes in shaping urbanisation processes has also been noted by Karaman, Sawyer, Schmid, and Tang in their analysis of plotting urbanism in Shenzhen, Lagos, and Istanbul.[209]

Further postcolonial engagements with Lefebvre include Jennifer Robinson, who delved deep into the theoretical foundations of Lefebvre's dialectical Marxism as part of her comparative postcolonial approach. She found that his view of totality provided him with a distinctive starting point for a vital, heterodox, open, and dynamic Marxist theorisation of space and also brings into consideration some alternative approaches to abstraction and conceptualisation in the Marxist tradition. In a similar way, Gillian Hart notes that her own relational approach to comparison is strongly influenced by Lefebvre, particularly by his conception of the production of space-time, by his focus on praxis, and his critique of everyday life, and by his regressive–progressive method. Ananya Roy has also referred to Lefebvre and based her own understanding of urbanism on his theorisation of planning as a representation of space and his emphasis on everyday life and on social struggles over urban space.[210] In the meantime, Lefebvre's conceptualisations have become more widespread within postcolonial urban research, particularly in Latin America (see above).

Beyond Lefebvre?

The various postcolonial appropriations of Lefebvre, as well as the recent studies on planetary and extended urbanisation, and many further theoretical developments and combinations with other approaches, have led to a much more open and diverse treatment of Lefebvre's theory in recent years. As Kipfer, Saberi, and Wieditz remind us, Lefebvre's quest for a genuinely global and multipolar form of critical knowledge production needs to be translated, actualised, and de- and recontextualised.[211] This means fully appropriating his work, and enriching and deploying it in constant interaction with practice, to

---

208   Tang, 'Where Lefebvre Meets the East'.
209   Karaman et al., 'Plot by Plot'.
210   Robinson, 'Thinking Cities through Elsewhere'; Hart, 'Relational Comparison Revisited'; Roy, 'Urbanisms, Worlding Practices and the Theory of Planning'.
211   Kipfer, Saberi, and Wieditz, 'Henri Lefebvre: Debates', 121.

bring it into dialogue with other approaches and eventually to develop new concepts and research perspectives.

In this sense, there have been various calls to go beyond Lefebvre and to develop 'post-Lefebvrian' approaches. This discussion must be left open here because the various strands of research and theorisation that rely on Lefebvre's work are developing in very different directions. In a sense, the question of post-Lefebvrian approaches is also posed incorrectly: Lefebvre's theory has to be developed further if it is to remain alive. This theory is developed in dialectical relationship to practice, in the movement of transduction, and the appropriate way to engage with it is to continue this movement.

2

The Three-Dimensional Dialectic

This chapter lays out the epistemological foundations of Lefebvre's theory of the production of space. A general lack of familiarity with these foundations has led to a number of misunderstandings, misinterpretations, and reductions. As a consequence, the theory's potential has not been fully recognised or utilised to this day (see section 1.2).

As the following reconstruction demonstrates, Lefebvre's thinking was shaped primarily by two intellectual traditions spanning his entire oeuvre from its beginnings in the 1920s to his last writings in the 1980s: the first is that of a radical, open, and poetic thinking strongly influenced by the specific urban situation of Paris in the early 1920s, with its exceptional intellectual and artistic climate inspired by Surrealism and Dadaism. Lefebvre's engagement with philosophy flowed into a fundamental critique of philosophical thought, a rejection of intellectualism and a turn towards praxis and action. Second, Lefebvre produced a highly independent dialectical thought based on the nineteenth-century 'German dialectic', proceeding from its most trenchant and important representatives – Hegel, Marx, and Nietzsche. In their basic outline, Lefebvre's epistemological foundations can be characterised as a specific variant of German dialectics with a distinctly 'actionist', twentieth-century French flavour (see section 2.1).

Consequently, Lefebvre's engagement with these three great German thinkers is at the heart of this chapter. The debates they initiated deal, ultimately, with nothing less than the great questions of humanity: being and consciousness, object and subject, form and content, the self-creation of human beings and the end of history, the absolute state and the great revolution, the death of God and the creation of the *Übermensch*. These debates not only are deeply enmeshed in Western thought, but also exhibit a specifically German hue – in terms of German history, but also the German language. The idiosyncrasies and capabilities of this language shape their principles of construction, their specific vocabulary, and their rhetorical figures. This is one of the reasons why the dialectical argumentation which Lefebvre takes from these thinkers is often flattened out to the point of unrecognisability in translation.

This chapter thus dives into a philosophical world which may strike many readers as antiquated and detached from contemporary problems and questions. Lefebvre wrote of these debates: 'It is still a combat among giants, dragons, and cyclopes; the struggle of gods and goddesses, ideas and concepts.'[1] In the contemporary Anglo-American academic industry, where the dominant view understands epistemological positions fundamentally as perspective-based, relative, and context-dependent, the goal of drafting a general theory of society and thinking about humanity in an all-encompassing manner may appear presumptuous, perhaps even incurring outright rejection. Nevertheless, a degree of familiarity with this philosophical world is essential if we are to develop a deeper understanding of Lefebvre's theory. Three particularly important themes from the broad field of Lefebvre's philosophical investigations emerge: the concept of praxis, the question of dialectics, and the outlines of 'metaphilosophy'. For reasons of length, other important aspects must unfortunately be excluded from this volume, most notably Lefebvre's understanding of alienation (and appropriation), his humanistic concept of the 'total man', and his understanding of an open totality.[2]

The first step in the reconstruction of Lefebvre's approach which I offer in this chapter clarifies the materialist concept of praxis that Lefebvre developed by retracing the Marxian critique of idealism (section 2.2). Praxis is the point of departure and object of all of Lefebvre's theoretical endeavours, and many of his theoretical reflections remain incomprehensible if this central point of reference is not taken into account. Praxis does not, however, mean the kind of cooperation between academic inquiry and the political and economic establishment so often advocated today, but rather involves (political) action and (revolutionary) social conflict: Lefebvre views praxis from the perspective of concrete activity, of action, and thus from the perspective of possible social transformation. His open and revolutionary understanding of praxis, which goes beyond Marx, provides him with a broad conception of production transcending the narrow definition of political economy, and allows him to apply

---

1   Lefebvre, *Marxist Thought and the City*, 21.
2   See for example Meyer, *Henri Lefebvre*; Elden, *Understanding Henri Lefebvre*; Schwab, *'L'homme total'*; Kipfer, 'The Relevance of Henri Lefebvre in the 1990s'; Goonewardena, 'Henri Lefebvre'; Goonewardena, 'Planetary Urbanization and Totality'.

his theoretical concepts to numerous empirical and practical fields such as everyday life, urban space, the state, and ultimately the production of space itself.

The next step outlines the essentials of classical dialectics as adopted by Lefebvre in critical reference to Hegel in *Dialectical Materialism* (1939) and *Logique formelle, logique dialectique* (1947). While Hegel's dialectic takes place exclusively within the world of thought and is hermetically enclosed within itself, Lefebvre uses Marx to search for a simultaneously materialist and open understanding of the dialectic, anchored in praxis. Thus, he seeks to access the fundamental social dynamic which constitutes the internal movement of the contradiction – from the affirmation, to the negation, to the negation of the negation (see section 2.3).

The third step follows Lefebvre's radical critique of thought, of language, and of philosophy, building upon Nietzsche and opening itself towards the becoming-worldly of philosophy and poetic transcendence, as Lefebvre expounds in *Metaphilosophy* (1965) (see section 2.4).

Ultimately, a fundamentally different, three-dimensional dialectic emerges in interaction with the three moments of the dialectic Lefebvre identifies in Hegel, Marx, and Nietzsche. It evolves in his writings only gradually, first in his reflections on everyday life, subsequently forming the epistemological foundation of his theory of language, and finds its fullest elaboration in his three-dimensional theory of the production of space (see sections 5.6 and 5.7). The formal explanation of this dialectic is found only near the end of his life, primarily in *La présence et l'absence* (1980) and *Le retour de la dialectique* (1986). With these insights, we can offer a precise interpretation of Lefebvre's three-dimensional dialectic. The few existing depictions of his dialectical thought primarily limit themselves to interpretations of *Dialectical Materialism*, sometimes complemented by original reflections on Nietzsche.[3] A deeper engagement with *Metaphilosophy* can be found in the work of Ulrich Möller-Schöll and Heinz Sünker.[4]

It goes without saying that an introductory chapter will not be able to depict such enormous intellectual endeavours in all of their breadth, depth, and complexity. While Lefebvre's engagement with the 'early' Marx can be fairly precisely traced due to his own relatively narrow selection of reference literature (although I limit myself to the *Theses on Feuerbach* and the *Economic and Philosophical Manuscripts* here), a more substantial discussion of

---

3   Schwab, *'L'homme total'*; Shields, *Lefebvre, Love and Struggle*; Elden, *Understanding Lefebvre*; Stanek, *Henri Lefebvre on Space*.

4   Müller-Schöll, *Das System und der Rest*; Sünker, *Bildung, Alltag und Subjektivität*.

Nietzsche was not possible (due, at least in part, to my own limited knowledge). A more thorough engagement with Hegel would far exceed the scope of this volume. It is made even more difficult by the circumstance that Hegel's dialectic appears here in a double appropriation: first, in Marx's critique, and second in Lefebvre's adaptation of this critique. For reasons of pragmatism, this chapter comprises not a (critical) appraisal of these great German theoreticians, but rather the depiction of their positions which Lefebvre offers to both his audience and himself. Thus, Hegel and Marx constitute both the points of departure and the prime opponents of his own theoretical efforts. The heart of this chapter is thus the reconstruction of this depiction by Lefebvre, rather than its confrontation with other interpretations of the foundational texts.

Dialectical thought means thinking in and with contradictions, and is thus also a kind of thinking which finds itself in constant motion, developing in the historical flow of praxis and thought. This chapter is, consequently, also in constant motion, written in interaction with the various philosophical positions, tracing their dialectical cascades towards a richer, more comprehensive understanding of social reality through the three-dimensional dialectic.

The translation of these thoughts has posed considerable problems. In fact, it is basically a double translation – from German into French for Lefebvre, and from French to English for this book. To this day, there is still no agreement as to how to translate certain fundamental German philosophical terms into French and into English. While Lefebvre's own translations from German are of course consistent, the English translations of Hegel, Marx, and Lefebvre as well show a remarkable variation. This applies especially to two key terms in this chapter, *das Aufheben des Widerspruchs* and *der Geist*, which are translated – even for the same (often famous) quotes – in different words, depending on the work and the edition. *Der Geist*, which denotes the non-corporeal essence of a being in Hegel (and more generally in German philosophy), was translated as *l'Esprit* by Lefebvre and in English translations as 'Spirit' or 'Mind'. For *aufheben*, a key concept in dialectics, Lefebvre uses *dépasser*; it appears in English translations, depending on philosophical orientation and context, as 'to transcend', 'to overcome', 'to supersede', or 'to sublate'. I will use 'spirit' and 'to sublate' in this text, a choice that I cannot discuss here at greater length.

2.1 Henri Lefebvre: *L'aventure du siècle*

> To understand what is happening in order to transform it, to seize the
> 'lived' in order to beat a path towards life.[5]

Born at the turn of the century in 1901, Henri Lefebvre's life passed through
most of the political and intellectual phases constituting Eric Hobsbawm's
'short twentieth century'.[6] In this sense, his oeuvre holds up a mirror to this
century's theoretical and social developments, reflected from the perspective of
a French intellectual living in Paris. Accordingly, Rémi Hess chose a fitting
subtitle for his biography of Lefebvre: '*L'aventure du siècle*'.[7]

One could compile a long list of publications summarising Lefebvre's life
and work: beginning with David Harvey's renowned afterword to the English
translation of *The Production of Space*;[8] to the extensive biographical overviews written by Rémi Hess, Rob Shields, and Andy Merrifield; Stuart Elden's
comprehensive presentation of Lefebvre's theoretical concepts; and Łukasz
Stanek's detailed reconstruction of Lefebvre's development of the theory of the
production of space in connection with his empirical sociological research and
concrete engagements in architecture and urban design.[9] These are complemented by Lefebvre's own biographical writings, *La somme et le reste* (1959)
and *Le temps des méprises* (1975). Here, rather than repeating these depictions
of Lefebvre's work and life, I draw out several constants which run through his
wide-ranging oeuvre and which ground the interpretation I offer here: first, his
emphatic relationship to praxis and poetry; second, his radical critique of
philosophy and the academic industry; third, his undogmatic and heterodox
approach to Marxism; and fourth, his highly unconventional understanding of
dialectics.

The Romantic Revolutionary

Lefebvre left his parents' home in Mourenx in the Pyrenees as a teenager to attend
the Lycée Louis-le-Grand in Paris. He began studying philosophy at the Sorbonne
in 1919 – a course of study which left him deeply dissatisfied in light of the

---

5   Lefebvre, *Survival of Capitalism*, 61.
6   Hobsbawm, *The Age of Extremes*.
7   Hess, *Henri Lefebvre et l'aventure du siècle*.
8   Harvey, afterword to Lefebvre, *Production of Space*.
9   Shields, *Lefebvre, Love and Struggle*; Merrifield, *Henri Lefebvre*; Elden, *Understanding Lefebvre*; Stanek, *Lefebvre on Space*.

turbulent changes going on in the world at the time. He had read neither Marx nor Hegel at this point, and attempted to formulate his own philosophical foundation with Spinoza, Schelling, and Nietzsche (whom he began reading at fifteen years of age).[10] At the same time, he witnessed the collapse of inherited values and encountered a highly creative avant-garde suffused with revolutionary ideas and optimism. Lefebvre was particularly attracted to Dadaism, which not only denounced eurocentrism, logic, and 'logocentrism', but also demanded: '*Changer la vie!*' (Change life!).[11] This exciting world contrasted with the hermetic philosophy of his teachers (among them Léon Brunschvicg and Henri Bergson), who celebrated an almost pure intellectuality but failed to provide answers to the burning questions of the time. Lefebvre founded the *Philosophies* group together with his Sorbonne classmates Georges Friedmann, Norbert Guterman, Pierre Morhange, and Georges Politzer. They published the magazine *Philosophies* from 1924 to 1926, followed by two issues of a publication titled *L'Esprit*.[12] The *Philosophies* group rejected both dominant ideologies of positivism and intellectualism, turning towards an engagement with the unphilosophical and thus with everyday life. The group's postulate of finding a 'different pathway' to change the world would lead it into proximity of the Surrealists.[13] Yet, while the latter sought a poetic strategy to overcome everyday life, the *Philosophies* sought a revolutionary path (see section 3.1).

Lefebvre's attitude towards these experiences later in life was characterised by a degree of ambivalence: while distancing himself from an unconscious, undialectical, and unmaterialistic – even 'idealistic' – attitude, he repeatedly invoked the 'living' kernel of these experiences, which allowed both the submerged past and possible futures to flash through one's mind. He later wrote:

> Those who did not go through this period (and through its critique) seem to lack an experience . . . Dadaism, Surrealism, and a grim (untenable) romanticism – which also meant contempt for the world's platitudes and the prose, a disgust with mundane delights and miseries. But it also meant taste and the sense of the miraculous, the surprising, and thus the exceptional *moment* . . . the impossibility of rejecting the subjective force, enthusiasm, the taste for freedom . . . In this sense, I cannot do otherwise but remain a revolutionary romantic.[14]

---

10   Lefebvre, *Qu'est-ce que penser?*, 144ff.
11   Lefebvre, *Le temps des méprises*, 39, 45.
12   On this, see Burkhard, *French Marxism between the Wars*.
13   Lefebvre, *Le temps des méprises*, 37.
14   Lefebvre, 'Henri Lefebvre par lui-même', 292. Translation by author. See also Lefebvre, 'Vers un romantisme révolutionnaire'.

Lefebvre would encounter a group with similarities to the Surrealists two decades later as a professor in Strasbourg: the Situationist International, an actionist group operating at the intersections of art, philosophy, and architecture. A tension-filled relationship would develop between Lefebvre and the Situationists – several of whom, including Guy Debord, were his students in Strasbourg – influencing Lefebvre at least as heavily as he would the group itself.[15] The Situationists' original project of provoking new situations by means of diverse interventions into social reality aligned with Lefebvre's attempt to develop a theory of the 'moment' within the context of his analysis of everyday life. This concept proposed a counterpart to the 'situation' of the Situationists – arguably, the former observed social reality from the perspective of time, while the latter did so from that of space.[16] The results of this shared work can be seen, for example, in his interpretation of the Paris Commune of 1871, to which Lefebvre dedicated a lengthy volume featuring a key argument developed together with the Situationists:

> The Paris Commune? This was first of all an immense, great festival (*fête*), a festival that the people of Paris gave to themselves and the world. It was magnificent and joyful, a spring festival in the city, a festival of the revolution, a total festival, the greatest of modern times.[17]

This passage led to a bitter disagreement with the Situationists, who accused him of plagiarism.[18]

A further decisive activist moment for Lefebvre came in the form of May 1968 in Paris, which he dissected theoretically in *The Explosion: Marxism and the French Upheaval* (1968) and *La manifeste différentialiste* (1971).[19] At the time, he was a professor at the Paris Nanterre University, whose campus was still under construction in a run-down banlieue in western Paris. This university became the starting point of the movement of 1968 in Paris, when activists occupied the professors' halls on 22 March 1968 in protest against the Vietnam War, unacceptable campus conditions, and the state authorities more generally. Lefebvre, whose packed, energetic lectures on modernity and everyday life were legendary,

---

15   On this, see Lefebvre, *Le temps des méprises*, 214ff.; Sadler, *The Situationist City*, 44ff.; Merrifield, *Henri Lefebvre*, 21ff.; Gardiner, *Critiques of Everyday Life*.

16   See Lefebvre, *Critique of Everyday Life*, vol. 2, 340ff.; Hess, *Henri Lefebvre et la pensée du possible*.

17   Lefebvre, *La proclamation de la commune*, 20–1. Translation by author.

18   See Trebitsch, preface to Lefebvre, *Critique of Everyday Life*, vol. 2.

19   See, among others, Stanek, *Lefebvre on Space*, 179ff.; Merrifield, *Henri Lefebvre*, 39ff.; Kipfer et al., 'Globalizing Lefebvre?'.

interpreted these events as follows: 'In March 1871 as in May 1968, people who had come from the outlying areas into which they had been driven and where they had found nothing but a social void assembled and proceeded together toward the reconquest of the urban centers.'[20] He would subsequently interpret the 1871 Paris Commune as an 'urban revolution.'[21]

This moving history flowed into Lefebvre's theoretical reflections and grounded his specific understanding of the relation between theory and praxis. For Lefebvre, theory was never to be an end in itself, but rather was always linked to social practice and social movements. The central points of reference for his theoretical project were the brief moments of liberation, which always included existential experiences bound to physicality and concrete material conditions. In this sense, Lefebvre's materialism is rooted in existential experiences: a social movement is not a discourse, nor is discourse its goal. Whatever motivations may drive it forward, it is first and foremost an immediate experience occurring in a concrete space in a concrete time.

The Critique of Philosophy

A second constant of Lefebvre's thought emerges immediately from this relation between action and praxis: his radical critique of philosophy, first cultivated by the *Philosophies* group as discussed above. Building on his actionist roots, Lefebvre accused philosophy of a fundamental lack of practical relevance and criticised speculative thinking, systematisation, ontology, and metaphysics. For him, philosophy as such always remained subsumed under ideology.[22]

For Lefebvre, however, philosophy was (despite its speculative abstractions) never fully external to praxis, as its controversies with religion or its conflicts with the state clearly indicate. Moreover, the goals of cognition and action as established by the philosophers seemed to be acceptable to him: freedom, justice, truth, the formation of authentic relationships between humans through the complete mutual acknowledgment of free consciousness. That said, however, philosophy could never achieve these goals through the powers of theory or the spirit alone. Only activity and action in the course of a (practically and theoretically) effective critique of existing society could make possible their entrance into life and their practical realisation.[23]

20　Lefebvre, *The Explosion*, 117–18.
21　Lefebvre, *Urban Revolution*, 110–11.
22　Lefebvre, *Metaphilosophy*, 19; Lefebvre, *Right to the City*, 98.
23　Lefebvre, *Metaphilosophy*, 19–20.

From this position, Lefebvre not only criticised classical philosophy from Plato to Hegel, but also launched repeated assaults on contemporary philosophy and theory, most notably (French) structuralism, as well as phenomenology and existentialism. In *L'existentialisme* (1946) he criticised primarily Heidegger and Sartre, sketching out his own path from existentialism to Marxism, while *Au-delà du structuralisme* (1971) argues against the classical structuralism of Claude Lévi-Strauss as well as the neo-Marxist structuralism of Louis Althusser, whom he accused of turning away from the dialectic and returning to philosophical thinking. In *Position: Contre les technocrates* (1967), he focuses his criticisms primarily on scientism and the unreflected use of 'models' and 'systems'. He repeatedly criticises the parcellation and specialisation of knowledge in academic life, fundamentally questioning the claims to power of various disciplines.

Engaging with Marxism

In light of his sharp critique of philosophy and idealism, it comes as little surprise that Lefebvre began moving towards historical materialism quite early. Like his colleagues from *Philosophies* and several Surrealists, he joined the French Communist Party in 1928, which would ultimately expel him for his critique of Stalinism in 1958.[24]

Lefebvre's relationship to Marxism was always characterised by a deep ambivalence, yet Marx's work would nevertheless remain Lefebvre's central point of reference throughout his life. This can be seen not only in the underlying structures of his argumentation and his fundamental theoretical concepts (see chapter 7) but also in the impressive number of books and other publications devoted to Marx and Marxism, such as *Pour connaître la pensée de Karl Marx* (1947), *Le marxisme* (1948), *Problèmes actuels du marxisme* (1958), *Marx* (1964), or *The Sociology of Marx* (1966). In his book *Le fin de l'histoire* (1970), he asks, in reference to Marx: 'How can one determine the goal, the end, the conclusion, the finality of history, without invoking a transcendence, a secularized divinity, the idea, rationality, or humanity?'[25] Accordingly, Lefebvre always opposed a narrow and scholastic reading of Marx's work and criticised the ossification of critical thinking caused by blind dogmatism. He identified two fundamental errors or illusions: on one side, Marxism was treated as a closed system to be applied to already existing reality; while, on the other, it was

---

24 Hess, *Henri Lefebvre*, 75–6, 154ff.
25 Lefebvre, *La fin del l'histoire*, 39.

abandoned or destroyed under the pretext of radical critique.[26] For Lefebvre, then, one could neither accept Marxism *en bloc* nor reject it in its entirety.[27] He saw Marx's works not as a closed theoretical structure to be merely interpreted nor treated as an end point of thought but rather as a point of departure, as a historical moment of thought, which is necessarily challenged by ongoing social development.[28]

Lefebvre's central point of reference was thus not *Capital*, which he accused of having a rigorous but stunted form, a reductive approach, and a homogenising rationality. He instead pointed to the *Grundrisse* for the critique of political economy, in which he saw the outlines of another, richer project: its less strict construction, the limited extent of its formal cohesion, and its less developed formalisation and axiomatisation allowed for historical context and the practical conditions of the 'world of the commodity' to be addressed.[29]

Lefebvre's primary references were, however, the fragmentary sketches Marx developed in Paris in 1844, and which appeared in English for the first time in 1959.[30] Lefebvre uncovers the roots of Marxist thought in these early texts: German philosophy, French actionism, and English economy. For Lefebvre, these manuscripts – which he translated into French and published together with Norbert Guterman in 1933 (initially in the periodical *Avant-Poste*, appearing as *Morceaux choisis de Karl Marx* in 1934) – were not only the point of departure for his appropriation of Marx, but Marx's most seminal text altogether. Although he rarely made explicit reference to sources, Lefebvre quoted from this text repeatedly in both early and later works, often in the form of lengthy passages. In these often spurned 'juvenilia', he found the philosophical root of what were for him central and hitherto misunderstood concepts – praxis, alienation, the total man – and a rediscovery of Hegel.[31]

From this reading, Lefebvre developed a specific interpretation of Marxist thought which rejected both philosophism and economism, refusing to reduce Marx's legacy to either a philosophical system (dialectical materialism) or a theory of political economy.[32] Consequently, Lefebvre developed a unique theoretical approach, which – although fundamentally built on the classical writings of Marx and Engels – went far beyond them in decisive points. Hajo

---

26   Lefebvre, *Production of Space*, 321–2.
27   Lefebvre, *Survival of Capitalism*, 10.
28   Lefebvre, *Production of Space*, 321–2.
29   Ibid., 102.
30   Marx, *Economic and Philosophical Manuscripts*.
31   Lefebvre, *Dialectical Materialism*, 49.
32   Lefebvre, *Everyday Life in the Modern World*, 30.

Schmidt ascribes to Lefebvre a remarkably impartial relationship to Marx and the Marxist tradition.[33] Looking back on his own work, Lefebvre wrote:

> If somebody counters: 'You are finding thoughts in Marx's works that are not there!' I will respond: 'Maybe, but what interest could we have today in repeating what Marx has written or said in inferior words . . .? Why not clearly express what can only be found in Marx as potential? Does it not mean to detect the thinking of Marx in applying his own procedure?[34]

The German Dialectic: Hegel, Marx, and Nietzsche

Historical materialism also brings us to a further constant in Lefebvre's oeuvre: the dialectic. What does the dialectic mean? To begin with, it means a deep conviction that human reality is internally characterised by contradictions and can only be truly grasped through an understanding of these contradictions. In Lefebvre's depiction, this fundamental conception is presented as follows: 'The law of logic says: "No thought or reality without coherence." The dialectic proclaims: "There is neither thought nor reality without contradictions." '[35]

At the core of the dialectic is a concept whose deeper meaning is only revealed in German: '*das Aufheben des Widerspruchs*' (the sublation of the contradiction). Hegel used the term '*Aufheben*' precisely because of its shimmering ambiguity, which is completely lost in the French (*dépasser*) and English (to sublate). Lefebvre remarks that the concept of *Aufheben*

> does not have the simplicity, clarity and distinctness that the habit of Cartesian thought leads us to seek in concepts. At the origin of this essential notion, what is it that we find? A play on words, an untranslatable pun – nothing formal and perhaps nothing that can be formalized in a perfectly coherent discourse.[36]

If formal logic states 'no proposition can be both true and false', Lefebvre's dialectic contends: 'If we consider the content, if there is a content, an isolated proposition is neither true nor false; every isolated proposition must be transcended; every proposition with a real content is both true and false, true if it

---

33 Hajo Schmidt, *Sozialphilosophie des Krieges*, 162.
34 Lefebvre, *Une pensée devenue monde*, 213. Translation by author.
35 Lefebvre, *Rhythmanalysis*, 22.
36 Lefebvre, *Metaphilosophy*, 22.

is transcended, false if it is asserted as absolute.'[37] This passage is the key to Lefebvre's renowned rhetorical figure, by which he prefers to answer self-imposed questions with 'yes and no'.

It is decisive, then, that Lefebvre's conception of dialectics does not simply follow Marx, but rather seeks to return to Marx's foundations and thus to Hegel. In doing so, he discovered the conflictual relationship between Marx and Hegel, a relationship which he would continue to trace and analyse from his earliest works until his last.

Marx and Hegel are complemented by a third, no less profound source in Lefebvre's dialectic: Nietzsche. Lefebvre was well aware of the ambivalences running through Nietzsche's oeuvre, yet nevertheless viewed him throughout the decades as his most important ally alongside Marx against philosophical thought.[38] He stated that while Hegel had revealed an unbearable reality – the state, which establishes and asserts itself and thereby blocks social development – Marx revealed the *objective* social and political possibility of a revolutionary breakthrough. Nietzsche, however, demonstrated a *subjective* possibility for a breakthrough through the application of the pure act: the 'yes' to life, the belonging to the present. Lefebvre identifies herein a poetic praxis which holds the potential to create subjective differences.[39]

'This is not a matter of forcibly bringing Nietzschean thought into the concepts of Marxist thought, or attempting an eclecticism condemned in advance.'[40] Lefebvre identifies in Nietzsche's writings a specific form of the dialectic, yet is fully aware that Nietzsche's *Überwinden* (overcoming) is radically different from Marx's and Hegel's *Aufheben*: it retains nothing, nor does it raise the hitherto existing conditions onto a higher plane – it is more subversive than revolutionary.[41]

Based on these three dialectical thinkers, Lefebvre would unfold an undeniably original and unique version of the dialectic over his long career – the three-dimensional or triadic dialectic, which is absolutely central to an understanding of his theory of the production of space. In the following, we will elaborate the nature of this dialectic and its implications and consequences for social theory.

---

37   Lefebvre, *Dialectical Materialism*, 30.
38   On this, see Hajo Schmidt, *Sozialphilosophie des Krieges*; Kofman and Lebas, 'Lost in Transposition'; Merrifield, 'Lefebvre, Anti-Logos, and Nietzsche'; Müller-Schöll, *Das System und der Rest*; Elden, *Understanding Lefebvre*.
39   Lefebvre, *Hegel, Marx, Nietzsche*, 203.
40   Lefebvre, *Metaphilosophy*, 122.
41   Lefebvre, *Hegel, Marx, Nietzsche*, 26.

2.2 The Concept of Praxis

Au commencement fut l'action.[42]

As outlined in the introductory section, the concept of praxis is the pivotal point of Lefebvre's theoretical work. Beginning with his early writings in *Philosophies*, Lefebvre places a central emphasis on praxis, which he views as fundamental and inexhaustible. Praxis is both the point of departure as well as the objective of all his theoretical endeavours, which, in turn, must flow back into praxis – this, in short, captures Lefebvre's main philosophical principle.

While his understanding of praxis emphasised spontaneity and activism during his eventful years with the *Philosophies* group, Lefebvre would look for a more solid theoretical foundation rooted in Marxism over the coming years. Initial sketches of this foundation can be seen in *La conscience mystifiée* (1936), published together with Norbert Guterman. With *Dialectical Materialism* (1939), Lefebvre presented shortly thereafter an elaborated and coherent version of this foundation. The book's title is on the one hand programmatic, insofar as Lefebvre seeks to develop a materialist dialectics (see section 2.3), while simultaneously misleading, because his understanding of Marxism is anything but a recapitulation of Stalin's dogmatic 'Diamat' (dialectical materialism), meant to provide party leaders with a 'scientific' and thus 'true' Marxism. In fact, the opposite is the case, as Lefebvre noted in his preface to the fourth French edition of the book, published in 1957: 'This book was written in resistance . . . it sought to *restore Marxist philosophy and Marxism as philosophy.*'[43] Although Lefebvre would later – particularly in *Metaphilosophy* – radically discard any and all notion of philosophy whatsoever (see section 2.4), the praxis-based dialectical and materialist philosophy he developed in *Dialectical Materialism* continued to resonate in *Metaphilosophy* and beyond, with only minor refinements. Stefan Kipfer's introduction to this book offers a very concise and helpful guideline through its main arguments.[44]

---

42 Lefebvre and Guterman, *La conscience mystifiée*, 22.
43 Lefebvre, *Dialectical Materialism*, x.
44 Kipfer, 'Preface to the New Edition', in Lefebvre, *Dialectical Materialism*.

The Self-Production of the Human Being

The cornerstone of Henri Lefebvre's theoretical framework is the notion of the 'self-production of man', which Marx took from German idealism and adapted to materialism:

> By way of Hegel, Marx's thought holds all philosophers within it: the project of man proposed by each, the moment of project proposed by philosophy as a whole. History, for its part, is the natural history of man, and the prehistory of his finally human reality. It is the story of his laborious and painful birthing, with its detours and errors, its alienations.[45]

This same basic principle serves as the leitmotif of Marx's *Economic and Philosophical Manuscripts*: 'A being sees himself as independent only when he stands on his own feet, and he only stands on his own feet when he owes his existence to himself.' Furthermore: 'History itself is a real part of natural history and of nature's becoming man.'[46] For Marx, human beings are fundamentally part of nature; they are natural beings. They produce and produce themselves, creating their world and with it themselves. Lefebvre thus builds on a core concept of Marxist thought when he posits:

> 'Inasmuch as he is a natural being, man is given' says the *Manuscript* of 1844. At the starting-point of his 'production' therefore we find biological and material Nature, with all its mystery and tragedy. Transformed yet present, this Nature will constantly be appearing in the content of human life.[47]

Shortly after this phrase, however, he moves beyond this position, arguing: 'To start with, Man was a biological possibility, although this possibility was able to be actualized only after a long struggle, in which Man has increasingly assumed responsibility for his own Being. His activity becomes power and will.'[48] And, further: 'The modern consciousness is only just beginning to sense the depth of the natural "will-to-live", with its contrasts and ambivalences: its intimate blend of aggressiveness and sympathy, its tumultuous energies and its periods of calm, its destructive furies and its joy.'[49]

Here, we see the explosive mixture inherent in the axiomatic foundations of

---

45   Lefebvre, *Metaphilosophy*, 39–40.
46   Marx, *Economic and Philosophical Manuscripts*, 355–6.
47   Lefebvre, *Dialectical Materialism*, 102.
48   Ibid., 102–3.
49   Ibid., 102. Translation amended.

Lefebvre's thought: alongside the figure of Marx grappling with Hegel, it is fairly easy to recognise Nietzsche in these passages, whom Lefebvre almost seamlessly amalgamates with Marx's notion of the 'self-production of man'. The full consequences of this theoretical mixture will be explored in section 3.4. First, though, it is helpful to give a more detailed account on Lefebvre's engagement with the early Marx.

Labour and Action

From Marx, Lefebvre took the idea of the self-production of human beings – the production of human beings by themselves – as the point of departure for his historical, dialectical, and materialist theory. This, in turn, raises a decisive question: how do human beings create themselves?

Marx's answer is clear: human labour creates human beings and is the defining trait of human existence, as the following passage states:

> But since for socialist man the whole of what is called world history is nothing more than the creation of man through human labour, and the development of nature for man, he therefore has palpable and incontrovertible proof of his self-mediated birth, of his process of emergence.[50]

This thought even applies to the production of the five senses: 'The *cultivation* of the five senses is the work of all previous history.'[51]

Lefebvre, by contrast, takes this argument in a different direction:

> By acting man modifies Nature, both around and within him. He creates his own nature by acting on Nature. He transcends himself in Nature and transcends Nature in himself. By shaping it to his own requirements he modifies himself in his own activity and creates fresh requirements for himself. He forms himself and grasps himself as a power by creating objects or 'products'. He progresses by resolving in action the problems posed by his action.[52]

For Marx, human beings are created through 'labour', whereas for Lefebvre they are created through 'activity', through *action*: activity and not labour is thus, for Lefebvre, the fundamental category of being, of becoming human, of

---

50   Marx, *Economic and Philosophical Manuscripts*, 357.
51   Ibid., 353.
52   Lefebvre, *Dialectical Materialism*, 106.

the self-production of human beings. With programmatic flair, he and Guterman posited: '*Au commencement fut l'action*' – in the beginning was the act.[53] With this phrase they not only confirmed their resolutely materialist standpoint, but also established their central concept: action. In the following decades, this distinctive element marked Lefebvre's Marxist approach: where Marx writes of 'labour', Lefebvre almost consistently uses the terms *activité*, *action*, and *acte* – activity, action, act. He stands by this view until his late writings. In *De l'État*, he quotes both Goethe: '*Am Anfang war die Tat*' (at the beginning was the act), and Nietzsche: '*Das erste ist die Handlung*' (the first thing is activity), and does so in German. However, he distinguishes his own position from those two quotes. He is keen to avoid his postulate being understood genealogically – the act as historical origin – but rather genetically: the act as foundation, as the basis of society (see also sections 3.1 and 7.4).[54]

Because Lefebvre deploys the terms *activité* or *action* self-evidently and subsumes 'labour' under them, it is rather difficult to conclusively identify their philosophical roots. This circumstance has been the subject of several controversies. According to Schwab and Shields, these terms were taken from Lefebvre's early philosophy teacher, Maurice Blondel, whom he deeply respected.[55] Blondel, a philosopher heavily influenced by Christian metaphysics, developed in his dissertation a science of praxis based on experience of the Christian faith.[56] Although it is certainly plausible that Blondel's philosophy influenced Lefebvre to some degree, Schwab and Shields were only able to present clues rather than concrete evidence of this argument. In the texts consulted for this book, Lefebvre makes no reference to Blondel whatsoever.

In order to develop a deeper understanding of Lefebvre's concept of praxis, we must first take the semantic context of these two terms into account: while 'activity' and 'action' are relatively neutral words in the English language, the French *activité* and *action* in particular possess a deeper horizon of meaning: thus, in Lefebvre's work, the term *action* implies far more than a mere action, but rather contains within it also resistance and thus a liberating moment, encompassing the living manifestation of human existence in its totality (see section 3.4).

The history of Lefebvre's intellectual development, both his philosophical disputes and 'actionist' roots in tumultuous 1920s Paris, among the *Philosophies* and in the milieu of the Surrealists with their empathetic emphasis on action, their disdain for philosophical speculation, and their scepticism towards the

---

53   Lefebvre and Guterman, *La conscience mystifiée*, 22; see also ibid., 39.

54   Lefebvre, *De l'État*, vol. 3, 54.

55   Schwab, '*L'homme total*'; Shields, *Lefebvre, Love and Struggle*, 33.

56   Blondel, *L'action*. On this, see Schwab, '*L'homme total*', 57ff. and Hess, *Henri Lefebvre et l'aventure du siècle*, 25.

concept, suggests a Dadaist, surrealist, or spontaneistic origin of his concept of praxis – a certain colouring, which it always carries within it as an undertone.

Regardless of what Lefebvre's early sources of inspiration may have been, it remains uncontroversial that *Tätigkeit* (activity) and *Praxis* were core concepts of eighteenth- and nineteenth-century German philosophy, from German idealism and the philosophical interventions of Marx and Engels to Nietzsche's philosophical writings. Lefebvre refers to this history of philosophical development consistently and explicitly in his work, beginning with *La conscience mystifiée* in 1936 until his last writings.

Praxis between the Spirit and the World

So for Lefebvre, the declared point of departure of 'praxis'[57] is Hegel: 'What does the "positive" element bequeathed by Hegel consist of? According to us, the notion of praxis.'[58] According to Lefebvre, Hegel had developed a concept of praxis in his *Philosophy of Right* which incorporated its complexity and its contradictions. However, this text is highly ambivalent: 'The theory of praxis is here. And yet, it is not here: the whole of praxis is attached to speculation, and finally absorbed in the state.'[59] Marx excavated a rational and real kernel from Hegelianism, and developed it step by step into a materialist concept of praxis in his *Economic and Philosophical Manuscripts*, *Theses on Feuerbach*, *The Holy Family*, and *The German Ideology*:[60] 'From the first, Marx *thought* as a man of action.'[61]

In fact, Marx also proceeds from praxis and activity in his early texts, writing in the *Economic and Philosophical Manuscripts* that 'the product is simply the résumé of the activity'.[62] His depiction of the 'self-creation of man', subsequently adopted by Lefebvre, had already been a key element of German idealism, as evidenced by the reflective philosophy of Johann Gottlieb Fichte, who had a strong influence on Marx:

> The self's own positing of itself is thus its own pure activity. The self posits itself, and by virtue of this mere self-assertion it exists, and conversely, the self exists and posits its own existence by virtue of merely existing. It

---

57 Lefebvre, *Sociology of Marx*, 29.
58 Lefebvre, *Metaphilosophy*, 36.
59 Ibid., 33. See also Lefebvre, *Sociology of Marx*, 29.
60 Lefebvre, *Metaphilosophy*, 35; Lefebvre, *Sociology of Marx*, 29.
61 Lefebvre, *Sociology of Marx*, 27.
62 Marx, *Economic and Philosophical Manuscripts*, 326.

is at once the agent and the product of action; the active, and what the activity brings about; action and deed are one and the same, and hence the 'I am' expresses an Act, and the only one possible, as will inevitably appear from the *science of knowledge* as a whole.[63]

Of decisive importance, however, is the fact that activity – the positing of the self – is conceptualised in German idealism not at the practical level, but rather belongs to the realm of the spirit (see section 3.3). Marx adopts this figure, subjects it to a materialist interpretation, and thereby realises historical materialism's central epistemological insight: because human beings are objective beings, activity is also to be understood as objective activity, not merely the abstract activity of the spirit.

> When real, corporeal *man*, his feet firmly planted on the solid earth and breathing all the powers of nature, establishes his real, objective *essential powers* as alien objects by externalization [*Entäusserung*], it is not the *establishing* [*Setzen*] which is subject; it is the subjectivity of *objective* essential powers whose action must therefore be an *objective* one. An objective being acts objectively, and it would not act objectively if objectivity were not an inherent part of its essential *nature*. It creates and establishes only objects because it is established by objects, because it is fundamentally nature. In the act of establishing it therefore does not descend from its 'pure activity' to the *creation* of *objects*; on the contrary, its *objective* product simply confirms its *objective* activity, its activity as the activity of an objective, natural being.[64]

In his engagements with early materialism and with Feuerbach's materialist philosophy in particular – which proceeded from physical matter and objects as central categories of reality – Marx develops a materialist concept of praxis not only in opposition to this 'naïve' objective materialism, but with explicit reference to idealism. His renowned *Theses on Feuerbach* serves as a paradigmatic example of this thinking:

> The chief defect of all previous materialism (that of Feuerbach included) is that things [*Gegenstand*], reality, sensuousness are conceived only in the form of the *object, or of contemplation*, but not as *sensuous human activity*, *practice*, not subjectively. Hence, in contradistinction to

---

63   See Schwab, 'L'homme total', 23; Fichte, *The Science of Knowledge*, 97.
64   Marx, *Economic and Philosophical Manuscripts*, 389.

materialism, the *active* side was set forth abstractly by idealism – which, of course, does not know real, sensuous activity as such. Feuerbach wants sensuous objects, really distinct from conceptual objects, but he does not conceive human activity itself as *objective* activity.[65]

Marx makes unmistakably clear that his concept of praxis ('the active side') was developed from idealism and counterposed to early materialism, and particularly to Feuerbach, which 'regards the theoretical attitude as the only genuinely human attitude', and thus 'does not grasp the significance of "revolutionary", of "practical-critical", activity'. He concludes that 'the question whether objective truth can be attributed to human thinking is not a question of theory but is a *practical* question. Man must prove the truth, i.e. the reality and power, the this-worldliness of his thinking in practice.'[66] These reflections are crowned by his well-known eleventh thesis: 'The philosophers have only *interpreted* the world in various ways; the point is to *change* it.'[67]

The *Theses on Feuerbach* constitute something like the theoretical concentrate of Marxian philosophy, while simultaneously marking its point of inflection, the programmatic postulate of philosophy becoming worldly through a revolutionary praxis (see section 3.4). They contain a dual critique: of the hitherto existing forms of materialism on the one hand, which proceeded from an undialectical concept of the 'thing' or the 'substance', and of idealism, which conceived human beings only in terms of their consciousness, on the other.

Lefebvre proceeds from precisely this concept of activity and praxis as developed in the *Economic and Philosophical Manuscripts* and the *Theses on Feuerbach*, referring back to and discussing them extensively at prominent points in his analyses of Marx.[68] According to Lefebvre's interpretation, the foundation of Marxian thought can be described as follows:

Feuerbach, who rejected Hegelian philosophy in the name of a materialist anthropology, did not succeed in getting beyond the philosophical attitude. Although he emphasizes the world of sense, he overlooks the subjective aspect of sensory perception: the activity that fashions the object, that recognizes it, and itself in it. Feuerbach does not see that the object of perception is the product (or the work) of a creative activity, at once sensory and social. Because he neglects the practical-sensory

---

65   Marx, 'Theses on Feuerbach', 3.
66   Ibid.
67   Ibid., 5.
68   See for example Lefebvre, *Dialectical Materialism*, 53ff.; Lefebvre, *Problèmes actuels du marxisme*, 47ff.; Lefebvre, *Sociology of Marx*, 32ff.

activity, he all the more neglects the practical-critical, i.e., revolutionary activity. In opposition to a philosophical materialism which did not take praxis into account, idealism developed the subjective aspect of human thought, but only abstractly, ignoring sensuous activity.[69]

In this way, Lefebvre acquires a concept of praxis from his engagement with Marx's early writings that is opposed to philosophy and speculation,[70] simultaneously exhibiting a critique of idealism and of (early) materialism: the 'substance' of the materialists is the metaphysically obscured nature, arbitrarily separated from human beings. Conversely, the consciousness of the idealists is the metaphysically obscured spirit, arbitrarily separated from nature. Materialism and idealism are interpretations of the world which fail to sustain revolutionary praxis. For Lefebvre, the unique particularity of Marxism is thus not its materialist approach but rather its practical character, that it overcomes speculation – that is, philosophy – and thus both idealism and materialism.[71] Lefebvre explicitly refers to the young Marx's materialist humanism, which he approaches as both scientific and political guide: 'Here we see how consistent naturalism or humanism differs both from idealism and materialism and is at the same time their unifying truth. We also see that only naturalism is capable of comprehending the process of world history.'[72] Lefebvre's 'Marxism' is thus fundamentally historical, acknowledging the historicity of cognition as well as the historicity of human beings, thereby enabling the (epistemological) possibility of change.[73] 'It is not therefore a question of defining man and the human, but rather of dismissing those representations that claim to define him, leaving him free to define himself in praxis.'[74]

The kernel of Lefebvre's concept of action and praxis – which has caused so much confusion for readers of his work and which does in fact emerge practically out of nowhere at various points – is thus revealed: for Lefebvre, praxis is Hegel's fundamental concept, which Marx accepted, developed, and unfolded but did not entirely clarify, and which later interpretations of Marxism tended to obfuscate.[75] According to Lefebvre, praxis is conceived as beginning and end in the *Economic and Philosophical Manuscripts*, as the origin of all thought and source of all solutions, as the fundamental relation between living human

69   Lefebvre, *Sociology of Marx*, 33.
70   Ibid.
71   Ibid., 31–2.
72   Marx, *Economic and Philosophical Manuscripts*, 389.
73   Lefebvre, *Sociology of Marx*, 32.
74   Lefebvre, *Metaphilosophy*, 294.
75   Ibid., 35, 102.

beings and nature, and their own nature. The critical study of political economy thus flows seamlessly into the analysis of social praxis.[76]

Production in the Narrow and Broad Sense

Directly connected to the (materialist) concept of praxis is the concept of 'production': human beings create themselves from nature through activity. As demonstrated above, this concept initially had an encompassing meaning in Marx's work, which Lefebvre takes up: 'The term *production* acquires a more forceful and a wider significance, when interpreted according to Marx's early works (though still bearing *Das Kapital* in mind).'[77]

The concept of 'production', like 'praxis', also stems from Hegel's thought:

> In Hegelianism, 'production' has a cardinal role: first, the (absolute) Idea produces the world; next, nature produces the human being; and the human being in turn, by dint of struggle and labour, produces at once history, knowledge and self-consciousness – and hence that Spirit which reproduces the initial and ultimate Idea.[78]

In referring to political economy and clarifying the Hegelian concept of production, Lefebvre argues, Marx was seeking a rationality immanent to that concept and to its content (that is, activity).

> A rationality so conceived would release him from any need to evoke a pre-existing reason of divine or ideal (hence theological and metaphysical) origin. It would also eliminate any suggestion of a goal governing productive activity and conceived of as preceding and outlasting that activity. Production in the Marxist sense transcends the philosophical opposition between 'subject' and 'object', along with all the relationships constructed by the philosophers on the basis of that opposition.[79]

An ambiguous concept of production emerges in this process,[80] regarded by Lefebvre as highly fruitful for precisely this reason. Broadly speaking, Lefebvre subsumes everything that human beings as social beings create under the

---

76 Lefebvre, *Dialectical Materialism*, 89.
77 Lefebvre, *Everyday Life in the Modern World*, 30.
78 Lefebvre, *Production of Space*, 68. Translation amended.
79 Ibid., 71.
80 Lefebvre, *Survival of Capitalism*, 7–8.

concept of production: their own lives, history, consciousness, social relations, the world (including social time and social space):

> There is nothing, in history or in society, which does not have to be achieved and produced. 'Nature' itself, as apprehended in social life by the sense organs, has been modified and therefore in a sense produced.[81]

Even the logical form – an abstract form, which could easily be perceived as timeless and non-produced, that is, metaphysical – was, in Lefebvre's view, produced. Production, in the broad sense, thus cannot be reduced to the fabrication of products nor is it limited to things or exchangeable material goods, but rather includes knowledge, artworks, and even joy, pleasure, and crime. And he quotes – in several texts – the ironic fragment in which Marx celebrates the criminal:

> A philosopher produces ideas, a poet poems ... A criminal produces crimes. If we take a closer look at the connection between this latter branch of production and society as a whole, we shall rid ourselves of many prejudices.[82]

Marx and Engels, however, did not leave the concept of production in this state of indeterminacy. Their deepened analysis of bourgeois society and their encounter with the political economy of Adam Smith and David Ricardo increasingly led them to narrow their definition of the concept until it had been reduced to its purely economic meaning – the production of things – and only referred to a single category: labour.[83]

The concept of production would find its completion in *Capital*, where 'labour' would become the central aspect of activity and the foundation of Marxist theory, with its fundamental laws of motion of capital, labour, value, and the commodity. In Lefebvre's view, this entailed a limitation of perspective, a reduction of the analysis of the economic realm which ignores substantial aspects of human life and activity. He concedes, however, that economic questions and production in the strict sense deserve a prominent place in the analysis of capitalist society. Consequently, the economy and the critique of political economy were the main topics of *Capital*, marginalising other aspects of praxis, and pushing the broad (poetic, or rather poietic) concept of the production of

---

81   Ibid., 68.

82   Marx, *The Production Process of Capital*, 306; Lefebvre, *Marxist Thought and the City*, 126; Lefebvre, *Production of Space*, 68.

83   Lefebvre, *Production of Space*, 69; Lefebvre, *Survival of Capitalism*, 21–2.

human beings through themselves, through their manifold works over the course of history, into the background.[84] The more Marx and Engels restricted and clarified the concept of production, however, the more it lost its creative and imaginative connotations.[85]

The Critique of Political Economy

That Lefebvre relied on a broader and more open understanding of production, activity, and praxis from the outset is striking. As far as the term 'labour' was concerned, however, he remained largely indifferent. Although he repeatedly refers to Marx's fundamental concepts such as productive forces, social relations of production, and mode of production (see chapter 7), he sought to embed them in a comprehensive, almost poetic context (see section 2.4). The theoretical kernel of *Capital* – the theory of value – remained more part of a diffuse Marxist 'substructure' than a concept guiding his investigation. In this sense, we can construe a contradiction between Lefebvre's understanding and Marxist theory, and – depending on one's standpoint – interpret it either as a regression back to idealism or as a transcendence of Marxian thought.[86]

Lefebvre himself would have brushed off both criticisms. In line with his rejection of canonisation and dogmatism, as well as his striving to grasp Marxist thought in its totality and thus also in its historical movement, he disapproved of the often applied division between Marx's allegedly philosophical and speculative 'early works' and his scientific, economic 'late works' – a division he considered artificial and superficial. Production and praxis could not, in Lefebvre's view, be reduced to the economic; he read Marx's 'late works' consequently and persistently in the broad sense of production, relating the mode of production not only to the economy and to labour, but to all human activities, including the self-production of human beings. In this all-encompassing conception of production, 'labour' is ultimately not the central category of the definition of human beings, but rather a historical category, the dominant principle of capitalism – and the central concept of its fundamental critique.[87]

Consequently, Lefebvre's texts attempt to restore the original meaning of the 'critique of political economy' as a *critique of the dominance of the economic*:

---

84   Lefebvre, *Metaphilosophy*, 101–2.
85   Lefebvre, *Production of Space*, 69.
86   On corresponding critiques of Lefebvre, see for example Schwab, 'L'homme total', 103–4. Further examples are cited in Kleinspehn, *Der verdrängte Alltag*, 21.
87   Hajo Schmidt, *Sozialphilosophie des Krieges*.

The first of Marx's great investigations into economics was 'a critique of political economy'. If we want to understand the fundamentals of his thought this word 'critique' must be taken in its widest sense. Political economy . . . has got to be criticized and transcended.[88]

Against this backdrop, the concept of activity remains more general to that of labour: as creation, as creative activity (*activité créatrice*):

Labour must not be reduced to its most elementary form but, on the contrary, thought of in accordance with its higher forms: total labour then takes on its creative or 'poetic' meaning. The creation that is pursued in the Praxis, through the sum of individual acts and existences, and throughout the whole development of history, is the creation of man by himself.

As if to emphasise the distance, Lefebvre quotes Marx in the next sentence: 'The so-called history of the world is nothing other than the production of man through human labour'.[89]

That this recourse to creation exposes idealistic roots is confirmed by Lefebvre himself: 'The long tradition of idealist philosophy must not be dismissed. On the contrary. It contains the abstract – but to a certain degree valid – expression of the creative activity of man'.[90]

However, Lefebvre is in agreement with Marx on this point, who (as described above) also returned to idealism at this juncture. Nevertheless, two very distinct optics can be observed in Lefebvre and Marx: whereas Marx sees human beings as creating themselves through labour from the realm of necessity, in order to (in the distant future) develop themselves in self-determined labour as humans, for Lefebvre, creation and creative activity are part of the self-creation of human beings from the outset – an always already existing possibility of liberation.

---

88   Lefebvre, *Dialectical Materialism*, 85.
89   Ibid., 117.
90   Lefebvre, *Problèmes actuels du marxisme*, 43.

2.3 The Dialectical Movement

> The dialectic is back on the agenda. But it is no longer Marx's dialectic,
> just as Marx's was no longer Hegel's.[91]

After having reconstructed Lefebvre's materialist concept of praxis, and thus
the fundament of his epistemology, we turn now to his dialectic, and thus to
the key for his way of reasoning. Dialectical thought is very difficult to convey
and apply. In contrast to binary or formal logic, no clear relations or rules of the
logical connection of sentences, of the truth and falsehood of propositions, can
be construed. There thus exists considerable danger of dialectics merely being
used as an analytical black box to dissolve unresolved questions into diffuse
contradictions, and synthesise alleged oppositions into questionable compromises. This difficulty is compounded by the existence of markedly varied
understandings of the dialectic, which often interpret the classics of dialectics
in deeply contradictory ways.

Lefebvre began studying the dialectic as a young philosophy student (see
section 2.1). He traced Marx's engagement with Hegel and attempted to clarify
the relationship between these two great German dialecticians and render it
fruitful for his own theory – a labour which would accompany him for the rest
of his life and repeatedly pose new questions for his work. In this engagement,
he developed his own unique and original interpretation of the dialectic, which
remains difficult to decipher and has yet to be systematically reconstructed to
this day.

Presenting a compact and 'valid' depiction of Lefebvre's dialectic is impossible here for this reason, even more so given how often he modified and
expanded it. Multiple intertwined lines of development can thus be identified.
This problem proves even more challenging as Lefebvre presented his arguments dialectically in many of his analyses, making them impossible to grasp
without an understanding of his dialectical thought. This section thus merely
seeks to sketch out the beginnings of Lefebvre's dialectic, as developed through
his engagements with Marx and Hegel. Even this endeavour can be performed
only fragmentarily here, as his multi-layered presentation and interpretation of
the Hegelian dialectic alone would exceed the dimensions of this volume.

As in the concept of praxis, the essential elements of Lefebvre's dialectic can
already be found in *La conscience mystifiée*. A broader discussion of Hegel's
dialectic and Marx's critique thereof is presented in *Dialectical Materialism*,
while the most extensive and sophisticated elaboration of Lefebvre's early

---

91 Lefebvre, *Survival of Capitalism*, 14.

dialectic can be found in *Logique formelle, logique dialectique* (first published in 1947), intended as the first volume and introduction of a highly ambitious, eight-volume series on dialectical materialism. For simplicity's sake, the following deliberations are primarily restricted to a presentation from the perspective of *Dialectical Materialism*.

Dialectical Thought

According to Lefebvre, the central element of Hegelian philosophy Marx salvaged in his theory was the dialectic, and with it, Hegel's fundamental conviction that all thought moves in contradictions.[92] Lefebvre begins his depiction of the Hegelian dialectic with a critique of formal logic, schematically illustrated with the following example: 'A is A. If A is B and B is C, then A is C.'[93] For Lefebvre, this example represents, in a sense, a pure logical form which can be arbitrarily applied to various content. It implies the notion that content can be captured with form. This notion, however, simultaneously produces a division between form and content, which can be understood as externally oppositional: on the one side, an abstract logical form; on the other, a concrete content, captured by this logic.[94] It would thus appear that form has achieved total independence from content,[95] or, as Hegel wrote: 'as though the movement of thought were something independent, unaffected by the object of thought'.[96]

But, Lefebvre asks, is it possible to conceptualise two entirely separate logics – an abstract logic of form and a concrete logic of content?[97] The consequence thereof would be to place rationality outside of the real, in the ideal: 'Logic becomes the concern of a fictive being, pure thought, for whom the real will seem impure. Conversely, the real finds itself being rejected and handed over to the irrational.'[98] Lefebvre concludes from this that formal logic studies change in a purely analytical fashion, drawing conclusions in which thought only has to do with itself. Formal thought obeys only its own pure identity with itself.[99]

As Hegel had shown, however, the pure, abstract form is a thing of

---

92 Lefebvre, *Metaphilosophy*, 25.
93 Lefebvre, *Dialectical Materialism*, 9.
94 Ibid., 10.
95 Ibid., 9.
96 Hegel, *Lectures on the History of Philosophy*, 220.
97 Lefebvre, *Dialectical Materialism*, 9.
98 Ibid., 13.
99 Ibid., 9.

impossibility. According to Hegel, the simple, void identity cannot even be formulated. Lefebvre illustrates this as follows:

> When the logician who has just posited 'A' posits 'not-A', and asserts that 'A is not not-A', he is adopting the form of negation without having justified it; he is thus positing the 'other' of A, the difference or non-identity, and is even positing a third term, 'A', which is neither 'plus A' nor 'minus A'. The term 'not-A' is posited only to vanish, but in this way identity becomes a negation of the negation, a distinction within a relation.[100]

Tracing the contours of Hegel's dialectic, Lefebvre's line of argument thus begins at the terminological level. The identity of the term is only understood in relation to other terms, and thus to its negation. To posit a term thus always means to posit its opposite, that is, the term only accrues its identity out of the dialectical relation to its opposite. This, however, produces a third term, which negates and contains both the term and its negation simultaneously. The identity of the initial term only emerges, then, as the result of the movement of affirmation–negation–negation of the negation. In Lefebvre's understanding, the pure form thus always possesses content: the difference, or rather the contradiction, which is produced in this dialectical movement.[101] The logical form 'A is A' thus exhibits a hidden, unexpressed, and inapparent content, emerging out of the internal contradiction and its dialectical movement.

Positing a term thus initiates that term's self-movement, as captured in the renowned figure of thesis–antithesis–synthesis: the initial term, the affirmation, contains within it its negation, which both negates and completes it simultaneously. By virtue of their internal relation the two terms act on each other, react and generate the 'Third Term'. Within the Third Term the first term is found again, only richer and more determinate, together with the second term, whose determination has been added to the first determination. The Third Term turns back to the first term by negating the second one, by negating therefore the negation and limitation of the first term, destined to be negated. From this, Lefebvre draws the somewhat ironic conclusion:

> The contradiction which thrust each term beyond itself, uprooting it from its finitude and inserting it into the total movement, is resolved. The Third Term unites and transcends the contradictories and preserves what

---

100   Ibid., 10.
101   Ibid., 11; see also 28.

was determinate in them. Unity triumphs after a period of fruitful discord.[102]

The German word *aufheben*, meaning both overcoming and preserving at once, takes on crucial dialectical significance in this context:

> The German '*aufheben*' ('to sublate' in English) has a twofold meaning in the language: it equally means 'to *keep*', 'to "preserve"', and 'to cause to cease', '*to put an end to*'. Even 'to preserve' already includes a negative note, namely that something, in order to be retained, is removed from its immediacy and hence from an existence which is open to external influences. – That which is sublated is thus something at the same time preserved, something that has lost its immediacy but has not come to nothing for that. – These two definitions of 'to sublate' can be cited as two dictionary *meanings* of the word. But it must strike one as remarkable that a language has come to use one and the same word for two opposite meanings. For speculative thought, it is gratifying to find words that have in themselves a speculative meaning . . . Something is sublated only in so far as it has entered into unity with its opposite; in this closer determination as something reflected, it may fittingly be called a moment.[103]

In a dialectical sense, a 'moment' can thus be understood as the result of a sublation, of the self-movement of the term.

As Lefebvre asserts, formal logic is incapable of recognising this self-movement of the term. It attempts to deduce content from form, proceeding logically from the thinking to the existing being and construing the relation between form and content as participation. Formal identity is thus made into a schema of identification. Lefebvre describes this as 'magical' thinking, often tied to a metaphysics of being, in which identity becomes an inner and substantial objective trait of being: 'Being . . . is identical to itself and thus defines itself.'[104]

In dialectical thought, however, being cannot exist without its 'other', its negation: nothingness. Nothingness is thus contained in being itself, as both 'its' other and its negation: 'Being is not, non-Being is; they are by virtue of each other. In thought as in reality they pass into one another all the time, and are thus set in motion and enter into the Becoming.'[105] 'Becoming' is thus the mediating

---

102   Ibid., 22.
103   Hegel, *The Science of Logic*, 81–2.
104   Lefebvre, *Dialectical Materialism*, 11.
105   Ibid., 20.

third term, which emerges from the contradiction between the first term – being, stripped of all content and thereby free of presuppositions – and nothingness. Lefebvre, however, views this synthetically acquired dialectical unity as mere deduction, positing that which was already contained in the term. Conversely, however, becoming is the first determined being, the first concrete thing, the abstract moments of which are pure being and pure nothingness: 'Once they are joined dialectically abstractions regain the concrete, and return into that fluid unity which had been broken by the abstractive understanding. There is nothing in heaven or earth which does not contain within it Being and Nothingness.'[106] He closes by quoting Hegel's renowned dictum: 'The being as such of finite things is to have the germ of this transgression in their in-itselfness: the hour of their birth is also the hour of their death.'[107]

The Promise of Becoming

The Hegelian dialectic appears to open itself in becoming, yet in Hegel this becoming strives towards absolute knowledge as is expressed in his dialectical sequence of abstract–concrete–absolute. Hegels dialectic is, in this sense, self-contained.

> Hegel seeks to perfect Logos: philosophical discourse as such. He wants to grasp the totality, which includes life. This is his aim. For him, the word makes itself not flesh but systematic discourse, a system completed and presented as such: a circle that imitates the great circle of the universe, the idea returning to itself.[108]

Hegel wrote:

> For this reason, Spirit necessarily appears in Time, and it appears in Time just so long as it has not grasped its pure Notion, i.e. has not annulled Time . . . Time, therefore, appears as the destiny and necessity of Spirit that is not yet complete within itself.[109]

Lefebvre adds: 'The universal system, in completing time, filling it, thus also terminates history.'[110] This assertion constitutes one of Lefebvre's central

---

106   Ibid., 21.
107   Hegel, *The Science of Logic*, 101.
108   Lefebvre, *Metaphilosophy*, 24.
109   Hegel, *Phenomenology of Spirit*, 487.
110   Lefebvre, *Metaphilosophy*, 50.

criticisms, running through his early and later writings: 'The trouble with the Hegelian system was that it made history culminate in the present, represented a sort of "end of history", and thereby paralyzed the hope of action.'[111]

Lefebvre opposes to this enclosed Hegelian system an understanding of dialectics which insists upon a more open conceptual pairing of contradiction and sublation. Contradiction does not find its final truth and determination in its sublation but rather in its transformation – overcome, yet simultaneously preserved and further developed in this double determination.[112]

In this radical sense, *Aufhebung* does not mean, as in Hegel, uncovering a higher, quasi-eternal truth, nor does it mean resolution, reconciliation, compromise, and so on. The contradiction tends towards its own sublation, but because sublation does not simply eliminate the old contradiction but rather simultaneously preserves and raises it to the next level, it carries the germ of the new contradiction within it. This understanding of the dialectic is therefore characterised by a deeply historical and dynamic conception of development and history. Lefebvre observes that movement is thus a sublation,[113] an assertion which can be legitimately inverted: sublation means (historical) movement. In Lefebvre's understanding, Hegel prioritised the aspect of becoming, and gave human consciousness an historical dimension. However, his systematisation of philosophy also entailed a termination of thought, which ultimately halted time; he declared the achievement of the process of becoming in the state and within his own system, thereby nullifying his most valuable contribution. Marx adopted and unfolded this approach by grasping nature and society historically, thereby opening up a perspective on the future:[114] 'With Marx, time reappears, inexhaustible, and with it, unlimited creative capacity in praxis.'[115]

Although Lefebvre oriented himself clearly towards Marx, his conception of the dialectic is further radicalised: in his materialist approach, the term *Aufhebung* designates an act, a creative force, thus not so much the 'real' as a realisation, a becoming. For Lefebvre, between the two determinations of sublation – the 'abolishing' and the 'raising'– there is indeterminacy, openness: the possibility of realising through an action, a project.[116] This becoming cannot be formalised or exhausted in discourse: 'We would rather say that the "concept" of "*dépassement*" [sublation] indicates what in living (productive,

111   Lefebvre, *Sociology of Marx*, 27.
112   Lefebvre, *Metaphilosophy*, 22.
113   Lefebvre, *Dialectical Materialism*, 24.
114   Lefebvre, *Sociology of Marx*, 28.
115   Lefebvre, *Metaphilosophy*, 35.
116   Ibid., 22.

creative) activity does not pertain to the concept as such. Why? Because this creative power cannot be completely defined, and thus exhausted.'[117] Logical and analytical reason – coherent, formal discourse – cannot capture becoming, the movement of *Aufhebung* in the creative act, for it also carries within it the risk of potential failure, as well as the possibility of accomplishment – a promise.[118]

The Alienation of Thought

The initial critique of Hegel discussed above also contains a second point: as much as Hegel's dialectical thought may appear as a fascinating intellectual breakthrough (as it did to both Marx and Lefebvre), it remains abstract. It does not come into the world. 'For Hegel, the tree of knowledge . . . becomes man himself. Man is no longer the demon gardener or the divine farmer who maintains this fine tree among others. He identifies himself with this privileged work. Knowledge and existence coincide.' Nonetheless: 'The tree of knowledge is not the tree of life.'[119]

For Hegel, dialectical movement unfolds in the concept, and thus in thought itself. It is here that the materialist critique begins, initiated by Feuerbach. Marx adopted this critique in his *Economic and Philosophical Manuscripts* and enriched it. Lefebvre, for his part, draws on this specific Marxian critique in his own work, extensively reviewing and elaborating it in order to then, in his own way, 'sublate' it.

In the *Manuscripts*, Marx discovered in Feuerbach the only figure to have cultivated a serious, critical relation to the Hegelian dialectic, and the 'true conqueror of the old philosophy' more generally.[120] According to Marx, Feuerbach's great contribution consisted of being the first to prove that philosophy is nothing more than religion, channelled into thoughts and performed through thinking, and thereby also a form of alienation of human existence. Second, he founded true materialism by making relations between humans the basic principle of his theory. Third, he opposed to the negation of the negation the positive, based on and positively grounded in itself.[121]

For Marx, the Hegelian system begins with pure, speculative thought, the absolute and fixed abstraction, the infinite. In a second step, this infinite

---

117   Ibid., 23.
118   Ibid.
119   Ibid.
120   Marx, *Economic and Philosophical Manuscripts*, 381.
121   Ibid.

sublates itself by positing the actual, the sensuous, the finite, the particular. In a third step, then, this negation is sublated, the spirit returns to itself and becomes absolute knowledge, self-aware, self-confirming, absolute abstract spirit.[122] For his materialist critics, however, Hegel's spirit had not in this way grasped the world, but merely itself in its own alienation from the world: the philosophical spirit is nothing 'but the estranged mind of the world thinking within its self-estrangement, i.e. conceiving itself abstractly'.[123] Logic, 'the *currency* of the mind', as Marx quips, is only the speculative thought-value of humans and nature, their unreal, estranged character, thought abstracted from nature and real humans, that is, abstract thought. Nature is external to such thought, its loss of self. The spirit is ultimately nothing more than thought returning to its own place of birth, discovering and affirming itself as absolute knowledge and receiving its conscious and appropriate existence. The true existence of the spirit is therefore the abstraction.[124] Or, as Lefebvre comments: 'Hegel's Spirit feeds off the world and devours it, causing it to disappear.'[125]

Marx observes a double fallacy of thinking in Hegel's figure of thought, as laid down in *The Science of Logic*: first, Hegel conceptualises the objects of human beings as being alienated from human existence. The human being objectifies itself unlike and in opposition to abstract thought – this constitutes the posited essence of alienation to be sublated. In this philosophical sense, then, alienation is understood as the opposition of '*in itself*' and '*for itself*' of consciousness and self-consciousness, of object and subject, of abstract thought and sensuous reality within thought itself.[126] Second, it follows that the objectified essence can only appear as a spiritual essence, as for Hegel 'Spirit alone is the *true* essence of man'.[127] As Marx follows Hegel through the entire cascade of sublations, he ultimately arrives at the absolute idea.

But what is this absolute idea? How does it sublate itself? It starts again from the beginning and contents itself to being either a totality of abstractions or a self-affirming abstraction. 'But the abstraction which comprehends itself as abstraction knows itself to be nothing.'[128] In the dialectic, however, nothing calls for its opposite, for its sublation. Marx infers from this that the abstraction must relinquish itself again and thus arrive at a being, that is its direct opposite – nature: 'Hence the whole of the *Logic* is proof of the fact that abstract thought

---

122   Ibid., 382–3.
123   Ibid., 383.
124   Ibid., 383–4.
125   Lefebvre, *Dialectical Materialism*, 39. Translation amended.
126   Marx, *Economic and Philosophical Manuscripts*, 384.
127   Ibid., 385. Translation amended.
128   Ibid., 397.

is nothing for itself, that the absolute idea is nothing for itself and that only *nature* is something.' Abstraction (that is, the abstract thinker) must thus resolve to relinquish itself and establish its otherness, its particular, its determined in place of its nothingness, its universal, and its indeterminateness, thereby releasing nature – which it contained only as abstraction – and to look at nature freed from abstraction: 'The abstract idea, which directly becomes *intuition*, is quite simply nothing more than abstract thought which relinquishes itself and decides to engage in *intuiting*.'[129] For the abstract thinker, this constitutes a transition from abstracting to intuiting, which is difficult to realise: 'The *mystical* feeling which drives the philosopher from abstract thinking to intuition is *boredom*, the longing for a content.'[130]

However, the abstract thinker never comes to this content, to nature, because '*nature as nature*, i.e. in so far as it is sensuously distinct from the secret sense hidden within it, nature separated and distinct from these abstractions is *nothing*, a *nothing proving itself to be nothing*, it is *devoid of sense*, or only has the sense of an externality to be superseded [*aufgehoben*]'.[131]

Marx drew the following conclusion from these considerations: Hegel, as a dialectical philosopher, understands his own alienation from the world as alienation in general; he views the real, sensuous world – its objects and elemental powers – as alienated and thereby unreal, while viewing his own, spiritual world which he acquired through his dialectical method and which gives him his self-consciousness as philosopher as the real world. Yet, if one adopts, like Marx, the standpoint of the real, sensuous world, then the abstract, philosophical world stands on its head. The world which appears to Hegel as real is in fact the unreal, and thus the philosopher himself is an unreal or alienated essence: 'The man alienated from himself is also the thinker alienated from his *essence*, i.e. from his natural and human essence. His thoughts are therefore fixed phantoms existing outside nature and man.'[132]

Lefebvre agrees with this assessment. By viewing people of praxis and the non-philosophical world as 'alienated', philosophy had, by definition, placed itself on the wrong side. Marx, however, by demonstrating the existence of philosophical alienation, unified philosophical and non-philosophical human beings under one and the same concept.[133] In order for praxis and cognition to appear according to their truth, it is necessary first of all to cast aside the illusion of philosophical existence, taken to its culmination by Hegel and so

129   Ibid., 398.
130   Ibid.
131   Ibid., 399.
132   Ibid., 398. Translation amended.
133   Lefebvre, *Metaphilosophy*, 296.

perfectly expressed that it becomes intolerable.[134] Only an actually existing, practical energy can solve actually existing problems:

> Only an active, poietic (creative) thought, a form of energy that is practical and based on a praxis, can cross the point at which differences, contraries, oppositions, contradictions, confront one another and rigidify in an endless confrontation.[135]

Or, in Marx's words:

> It can be seen how the resolution of the *theoretical* antitheses themselves is possible only in a *practical* way, only through the practical energy of man, and how their resolution is for that reason by no means only a problem of knowledge, but a *real* problem of life, a problem which *philosophy* was unable to solve precisely because it treated it as a *purely* theoretical problem.[136]

This progression through the dialectic brings us back to Lefebvre's point of departure: praxis. But how is praxis to be expressed as a concept?

Form and Content

With the concept of praxis comes, again, the question of its content, which in Hegel's system is constituted in thought alone. Lefebvre asks: 'Yet did Hegel really grasp the entire content of human experience? Did he grasp it in its authentic movement? Did he really set out from the content and extract the form from it without falsifying it?'[137] In light of the discussion above, Lefebvre is compelled to answer this question in the negative. First, a single individual cannot purport to comprehend the infinite richness of reality. Every epoch or individual discovers a new content, a surprising aspect in every great work of art. Development never stands still – new lines of conflict emerge and with them new content, new topics, and new problems, which demand to be raised to the level of intellectual life.[138] Second, Hegel proceeded from thought rather

---

134   Ibid., 16.
135   Ibid., 49.
136   Marx, *Economic and Philosophical Manuscripts*, 354.
137   Lefebvre, *Dialectical Materialism*, 36.
138   Ibid., 36–7.

than action. Lefebvre retorts angrily: 'Il y a l'action! (there is action).[139] Hegel may have conceived of the absolute Idea as a unity of praxis and knowledge, of creative activity and thought, but the Spirit sublates the immediate, reshaping it and assimilating it.[140] For Hegel, spiritual freedom is not determined by an appropriation of content through 'becoming aware', but rather as a setting-free of Spirit in relation to the content as such – experience, life, or action – by means of the concept and the idea.'[141] In contrast, for Lefebvre, action is the actual content of concepts, resolving the contradictions of thought – it alone is creative. Abstraction refers to a concrete history, a real confrontation. One only reaches the concept through a comparison of the elements of an ensemble and the individual parts of a multiplicity. Praxis cannot be deduced from concept, but rather the other way around: the concept emerges with and from praxis; praxis is the origin and the site of concepts.[142]

Herein lies the core of Lefebvre's materialist dialectic: praxis is the content of concepts, and concepts are only its abstract form. For Lefebvre, form and content can only be united when it is shown how content produces its form.[143] According to this line of thinking, one cannot deduce content from form, but rather quite the opposite: the concept itself can only be determined by praxis. This position earned Lefebvre accusations of postulating a 'logic of content'.[144] That an oversimplified opposition between form and content can be observed in Lefebvre's texts is undeniable – but where exactly is the problem? As worked out above, Lefebvre understands Hegel's dialectic as the dialectic of the concept, emerging in the self-movement of the concept. In this dialectical logic, content is not external to the concept but in fact emerges from it, in and with thought. However, Lefebvre insists, truth is not conceived as a unity of form and content in Hegel 'but is defined by the agreement of the form with itself, by its internal coherence, by the formal identity of thought'.[145]

This line of argument contains a contradiction. Even if the passage from Marx cited above suggests that the philosopher in his abstractness cannot reach the content – nature – this means neither that the form of this nature is a concept, nor that the abstract form lacks content. The quintessence of the Marxian critique of Hegel is something else: the content of an abstract form can only be an abstraction, a content derived from the abstraction from all

---

139   Ibid., 38.
140   Ibid.
141   Ibid., 40.
142   Ibid., 40; Lefebvre, *Metaphilosophy*, 7, 43.
143   Lefebvre, *Dialectical Materialism*, 11–12.
144   See Schwab, 'L'homme total', 62ff., 87ff.
145   Lefebvre, *Dialectical Materialism*, 39.

content.[146] This abstract content is a nothing, albeit a dialectical nothing, which in turn points to the positive, the practical content – nature (see above). From this we can conclude that for Marx, the real content is in fact the concrete content, which can hence be interpreted as 'action'. Nevertheless, this insight tells us nothing about the form of this concrete content.

At the same time, Marx also acknowledges the positive elements of Hegel's accomplishments, particularly in establishing

> *determinate concepts*, the universal *fixed thought-forms* in their inde-
> pendence of nature and Spirit, as a necessary result of the universal alien-
> ation of human existence, and thus also of human thought, and to
> comprehend them as moments in the process of abstraction.[147]

The 'determinate concepts' have thus objectified themselves vis-à-vis nature and the spirit, and this objectification is the necessary result of the alienation of human existence and thus of human thought: concepts are moments of a process of abstraction from a human's being and thought.

For Marx, the relation between thought and reality is thus not the contra-diction between form and content, nor that between the abstract and the concrete. Forms are a component of social reality, and abstraction is a social process which occurs not only in thought but also in concrete praxis (see section 7.2). The contradictions between form and content, between the abstract and the concrete, unfold both in thought and in reality, which Marx conceives in their dialectical unity: 'It is true that thought and being are distinct, but at the same time they are in unity with one another.'[148]

Lefebvre follows this argument when declaring: 'The word and the concept finally fix the object, and immobilize it by separating it from Nature.'[149] Yet he goes further by concluding that every object is turned both towards nature and towards human beings. Every object is concrete and abstract: concrete because of its materiality which flows into activity 'by resisting or obeying it'; abstract due to its specific, measurable contours, and because it has the potential to enter into social existence and become a bearer of social relations, which add to its materiality – both in language and in social meaning.[150]

This argumentation leads to a degree of confusion: Lefebvre appears to follow Marx almost seamlessly, while seemingly contradicting him at the same

---

146 Marx, *Economic and Philosophical Manuscripts*, 396–7.
147 Ibid., 397. Translation amended.
148 Ibid., 351.
149 Lefebvre, *Dialectical Materialism*, 107.
150 Ibid.

time. The entire course of his argument loses coherence, and it becomes increasingly unclear what exactly Lefebvre understands as the dialectic. Obviously, there is another dimension in his dialectic that has not been illuminated in this reconstruction so far.

Thought and Action

What is the kernel of the dialectical problem of form and content in Lefebvre's work? It can be found in his understanding of activity, of *action*.

> Action has specific laws, whether it be a relapse from contemplation and the inner life or, which is more likely, a fertilization of the mind through contact with the outside world or, alternatively, a distinct essence, parallel with thought and juxtaposed with other essences, their unity being transcendent.[151]

In this passage, Lefebvre presents us with a broad range of variations, all of which address the relation between thought and action, leading to an intersection opening up multiple possible interpretations. We can conclude that Lefebvre assumes that action follows specific laws, and is thus not free as such. But what constitutes these laws?

Lefebvre sees a first possibility in the 'relapse' of action from contemplation. Little can be said about this. Thought and action must somehow be mediated through spontaneity and the unconscious, yet it remains unclear how thought, activity, and the spontaneous converge.

The second possibility, which Lefebvre considers more likely, is 'a fertilization of the mind through contact with the outside world' – an argument which continually re-emerges in his writings. He grounds this variant in *Dialectical Materialism* as follows: every productive activity seeks to isolate a certain object from the material universe, to abstract it from this universe. This abstractness, however, is simultaneously a concrete-practical force. A concrete unity of subject and object forms out of every human effort which acts upon an object. Subject and object are opposed to each other in this relation, forming a dialectical whole.[152] Yet the starting point for this dialectical whole is, for Lefebvre, practical activity and not thought:

---

151   Ibid., 38.
152   Ibid., 108.

The starting-point for this abstraction is not in thought, but in the practical activity; the essential characteristics of sensuous perception cannot be correctly deduced from an analysis of thought, but from an analysis of the productive activity and of the product. Abstraction is a practical power.[153]

Active human beings go from product to themselves and then from themselves to the product. Consciousness is formed practically:

In this way a painter tests himself out and discovers himself in his earliest attempts, after which he perfects his technique and modifies his style. It would be absurd to suppose that a painter might develop his gift and become conscious of it without actually putting brush to canvas; for him, painting is not merely an excuse, an occasional manifestation of a hidden talent which existed beforehand.[154]

Put simply, Lefebvre sees a dialectical contradiction between thought and activity, between abstraction and praxis, but the starting point for this contradiction lies in praxis and only resolves itself in praxis. Inverted, concepts form not through thought, but through praxis and knowledge of praxis.

This line of argument exhibits a certain appeal as a deeply materialist formulation: being determines consciousness. Yet is it not humans' nature to be both active and thinking beings? Would then the fundamental contradiction of humans not be that they posit themselves in thought and action at the same time? And would not the problem of philosophy then be that it posits *either* thought *or* action? Asserting the absolutely established primacy of action appears in this light as inconsequential; the question of the starting point of the dialectic poses a false problem: if the starting point is thought, then it will return to thought, as Marx demonstrated using the example of Hegel's dialectic. If the starting point is practical reality, even if conceived as 'substance' or 'activity', the dialectic will return to this practical reality, leaving behind thought as a mere reflection or illusion. Rather, the starting point must be movement, and thus the contradiction between thought and practical activity.

This consideration appears to follow Lefebvre's third suggestion quoted above: activity is a 'distinct essence, parallel with thought and juxtaposed with other essences, their unity being transcendent'.[155] As will be demonstrated in

---

153   Ibid., 109.
154   Ibid., 112.
155   Ibid., 38.

the following discussion, this third suggestion grounds Lefebvre's specific three-dimensional dialectic. Nevertheless, the other two versions remain present in his argumentation as under- and overtones, from time to time generating strange interferences and incoherencies in his analysis.

2.4 Towards a Three-Dimensional Dialectic

Love must be reinvented. –Rimbaud
Revolution must be reinvented. –Lefebvre[156]

The following conclusion can be deduced from the analysis of Lefebvre's dialectic thus far: Lefebvre draws his dialectic from Hegel, which he understands as a dialectic of the concept. He criticises this dialectic using Marx: it cannot be applied to reality, as it only unfolds in the mental, in thought. The contradictions of life, however, are not merely thought but are in fact real. Hegel's thought is thus alienated from life and can only convey this life in alienated form. Accordingly, the task at hand is to conceive real life in its very contradictoriness.

For Lefebvre, the problem with Hegel is rooted not only in the fact that this thought cannot exhaust praxis because it is alienated; nor is it only because it blocks the pathway to praxis and thus to freedom. For Lefebvre, the problem is of a much more fundamental nature: such thought prevents humans' liberation by seeking to dominate praxis, and it allies with power in doing so, even becoming power itself. Closely linked to this problem is the question of ideology, which I refrain from discussing here, as Lefebvre himself grasps the problem more fundamentally: in the practical power and violence of abstraction – of thought, writing, and language.

The critique of alienated thought and the violence of abstraction is a leitmotif running through Lefebvre's entire oeuvre, from his beginnings with the *Philosophies* to *De l'État* and beyond. It also constitutes the foundation of his pointed and often furious attacks on contemporary philosophy and science, as well as on urban planning and architecture, and it is also linked to his understanding of the violence of abstract space and the state (see sections 6.3 and 7.2). Although this critique unfolds in various forms throughout Lefebvre's writings, it finds its most consistent form in *Metaphilosophy*, his key work on this problematic.

---

156   Lefebvre, *Critique of Everyday Life*, vol. 2, 70.

The Violence of Abstraction

The point of departure for Lefebvre's critique of thought is a specific under-standing of formal logic which he views as inherent in Hegel's dialectical logic. Lefebvre postulates that Hegel's dialectic does not abolish formal logic, but rather sublates it. Thus, by giving it concrete meaning, it preserves and rescues it. Formal logic is the logic of the instant, of the affirmation; it isolates objects and protects them in their isolation: 'It is the logic of a simplified world.'[157] This logic serves to communicate isolated meanings: this table is a table and not a book. But in isolating it, this logic views the table outside of all its relations to creative activity, it abstracts it from the ravages of time. For Lefebvre, formal logic is thus the logic of common sense – and also the logic of abstraction as such.[158] Its content is the pure, abstract thing, and thus stability in general: 'Its reign extends with that of commodity production, with the domination of the privileged form that is exchange value.'[159]

Lefebvre thus views formal logic – logical thought – as a means, as an instru-ment to dominate reality. Reason is concerned with stabilities, constructing and consolidating equilibriums and structures: 'From the day that a man held in his fist a pebble removed from the becoming of nature and hammered into a tool, analytical understanding existed as a potential, with its characteristics of an active abstraction, defined determinations, and concepts fixed in language.'[160] Reason, by establishing determinations and separations, is in this sense a concrete force. For Hegel, it was even the 'absolute power': 'The activity of dissolution [separation] is the power and work of the *Understanding*, the most astonishing and mightiest of powers, or rather the absolute power.'[161]

Formal logic strives to create abstract stabilities and thus entails for Lefebvre a double imposition: the imposition of coherence and the imposition of reduc-tion. It implies a homogenising strategy and the capability, linked to violence, of separating that has hitherto been joined together, to fracture all existing unities.[162] This strategy necessarily reduces the inexhaustible complexity and richness of life to abstract categories and concepts. For Lefebvre, this reduction is institutionalised in two specific systems: science and the state.

Under the banner of scientificity, reductionism constructs oversimplified models in order to then transform them into absolute knowledge. While

---

157   Lefebvre, *Dialectical Materialism*, 25.
158   Ibid., 25–6.
159   Lefebvre, *Metaphilosophy*, 14.
160   Ibid., 27–8.
161   Hegel, *Phenomenology of Spirit*, 18.
162   Lefebvre, *Production of Space*, 411–12.

methodological reduction dialectically calls for the restoration of a content, reductionism venerates the simplified form, the internal logic and coherence of the process.[163] No theory or philosophy could, however, fully conceive reality: 'Is there anyone who is free of all illusion?'[164] The illusion of philosophy consists, for Lefebvre, in its belief in being capable of enclosing the entire world in its system. Every philosopher believes his or her system to be a step forward compared to its predecessors, leaving nothing unaccounted for and enclosing everything even more hermetically: 'Yet there is always more in the world than in any philosophical system.'[165]

For Lefebvre, systematic reduction ultimately corresponds to a praxis; it serves the state and political power as a means to reduce social contradictions, not simply in the form of ideologies, but explicitly as knowledge.[166] This critique ultimately leads Lefebvre to a noteworthy distinction between knowledge (*le savoir/das Wissen*) and 'cognition' (*la connaissance/die Erkenntnis*): for Lefebvre, *le savoir* contains a covert pact with power, a subtle or rough intermingling with political practice and ideology. In contrast, critical and subversive *la connaissance* explicitly refuses to acknowledge this power. It contains both its own critique, as well as a critique of existing conditions, opening it up to the real and the possible.[167] Critical thought does not seek to construct models but to give an orientation, which reveals a horizon and opens up pathways to a possible future (see also the discussion in the introduction).[168]

The Transcendence of Poetry

For Lefebvre, Logos is the foundation of all power and authority.[169] Dialectical reason, which introduces the negative, discovers the specific negativity of reason, which only seemingly appears positive and determinate. By positing these determinations while maintaining their separation, 'the power of the understanding is none other than that of death'.[170] Hegel himself had already proclaimed:

---

163 Ibid., 105–6.
164 Lefebvre, *Urban Revolution*, 152.
165 Ibid.
166 Lefebvre, *Production of Space*, 106.
167 Ibid., 367–8, 10.
168 Lefebvre, *Urban Revolution*, 66.
169 Ibid., 135.
170 Lefebvre, *Metaphilosophy*, 26.

Death, if that is what we want to call this non-actuality, is of all things the most dreadful, and to hold fast what is dead requires the greatest strength. Lacking strength, Beauty hates the Understanding for asking of her what it cannot do. But the life of Spirit is not the life that shrinks from death and keeps itself untouched by devastation, but rather the life that endures it and maintains itself in it.[171]

Following Hegel at a critical distance, Lefebvre suggests that 'the system' emerges from a magical operation, through a kind of witchcraft

that transforms into absolute positivity, accomplished, finished and perfected, the uncertainty of becoming and the terrible power of death that haunts becoming. It is not that becoming understands itself according to being, but rather that becoming metamorphoses into 'being', grasped, determinable and determinate: metaphysical. By this magic, becoming vanishes and the historical evaporates. By the stroke of a speculative sorcerer's wand, the determinate is lost and fixed, each determination in its place, its degree.[172]

When thought becomes a certainty, an accomplished thing, it becomes unreal at the same time: 'The System is the truth, and it is the end and death.'[173] The roots of this position go back to the legendary *Philosophies*: '*Se représenter l'être, c'est cesser d'être*' (to represent being is to end being), as Lefebvre wrote as early as 1926.[174] Forty years later, he would go on to insist that the 'prose of the world has killed poetry. The Rose, for its part, is either plucked or perished. Time (the world) is terminated, thus dead. The dead grabs hold of the Living.'[175]

It is here that Lefebvre returns to Nietzsche and his vicious critique of religious figures and metaphysical thinkers who express fury and contempt for life.[176]

It is a miserable story: man seeks a principle through which he can despise men – he invents a world so as to be able to slander and bespatter this world: in reality, he reaches every time for nothingness and construes

---

171   Hegel, *Phenomenology of Spirit*, 19.
172   Lefebvre, *Metaphilosophy*, 30.
173   Ibid., 32.
174   Lefebvre, 'La pensée et l'esprit', 20.
175   Lefebvre, *Metaphilosophy*, 35.
176   Ibid., 122.

this nothingness as 'God', as 'truth', and in any case as judge and condemner of *this* state of being.[177]

In the same sense, language and signs also embody Hegel's 'terrible power of negativity'. They signify a terrible abstraction, function as weapons, threaten the visible, embody death. With the written word comes power: signs are doublings of things, doublings which disarticulate, shatter, and destroy the 'beings' and enable their restoration in another form, the construction of another world.

> As compared with what is signified, whether a thing or a 'being', whether actual or possible, a sign has a repetitive aspect in that it adds a corresponding representation. Between the signified and the sign there is a mesmerizing difference, a deceptive gap: the shift from one to the other seems simple enough, and it is easy for someone who has the words to feel that they possess the things those words refer to. And, indeed, they do possess them up to a certain point – a terrible point.

Here Lefebvre quotes Goethe's *Faust* – in German: '*Ich kann das Wort so hoch unmöglich schätzen*' ('I cannot grant the word such sovereign merit').[178]

How is it possible to define and evaluate knowledge without grasping language? In Lefebvre's view, contemporary thought has subjugated language to knowledge by declaring linguistics to be absolute knowledge. The real problem, however, was the other way around: 'pure' knowledge has to be investigated as a problem of language. For Lefebvre, Nietzsche was the only one to correctly pose the problem of language by proceeding from the truly spoken rather than from a 'model', and he also connected meaning to values and knowledge to power and the will to power.[179]

With recourse to Nietzsche, Lefebvre opposes to the deadly power of the sign the metamorphosis of the sign – poetry. Over the course of a struggle which overcomes the opposition between work and play, the poet wrests the written word from death – a struggle as terrible as the shifting terrain upon which it is conducted. Yet the poet finds help and support – from musicians, dancers, actors, who share the same frightening path, for which they are compensated with 'incomparable pleasures'.[180]

'God is dead' – Nietzsche's 'saying with immense resonance, genuinely

---

177   Nietzsche, *The Will to Power*, 253.
178   Lefebvre, *Production of Space*, 134–5.
179   Lefebvre, *Survival of Capitalism*, 62.
180   Lefebvre, *Production of Space*, 135.

poietic'[181] – serves as Lefebvre's guide in this endeavour. Not in the sense of previous readings, however, which struck him as powerless, nor as a radical critique of traditional thought, the abstract conception of the transcendental or as rehabilitation of the practicosensuous which Marx had already ensured, nor as a critique in the sense of a materialist and atheistic philosophy which postulates the vanishing of superstition and the emergence of a profane, laicistic, and humanist morality, tolerating religious belief as an individual choice.[182] No, Lefebvre boldly asserts the strongest and most dangerous hypothesis, albeit with a degree of 'philosophical irony': '*God did exist. He has died.*'[183]

Humanity experienced divinity. Religion was not an institution founded on human weakness alone, not merely a human-made projection of their own powers onto the canvas of the clouds. Rather, it was the consciousness of a finite existence, seeking to emerge from the endless universe. This eternal consciousness of finite existence was soon obliged to obey the law of the world: finitude. All that forms in the universe and is born into the world is always finite. The presence of the holy and the divine showed a god who sought to be – an attempt together with its counterpart, the diabolical and the accursed.[184] In order to exist, humans had to kill God, an unthinkable act: 'What could the divine be? Absolute spontaneity, the pure birth of what arises, the paradisiac encounter, or the chance of such an encounter, between man and nature.'[185]

'Who is responsible for the murder of God? Philosophy and the philosopher. They did not succeed.'[186] While religion sought its salvation in transcendence, philosophy did so in immanence:

> For religion, man contained in himself neither the reason of his being nor the reason of his reason, nor the meaning of his life. Philosophies proclaimed that man contained in himself his raison d'être. Yet they never managed to escape the dilemma raised by religion: 'Man does not have his being in himself. And this is why there is the being of man, human being.'[187]

The fundamental dilemma of philosophical alienation is located in this dialectical spiral; with this alienation's sublation thus disappears what defines human

---

181   Lefebvre, *Metaphilosophy*, 85.
182   Ibid.
183   Ibid., 86.
184   Ibid.
185   Ibid., 87.
186   Ibid.
187   Ibid., 88.

beings: 'God is dead – all is permitted. Nothing any longer limits cruelty, violence, arbitrariness. All is permitted – all is possible. And so man becomes possible.'[188]

With this example of a radical and simultaneously poetic reading of Nietzsche, Lefebvre seeks to unleash fantasy and the poetic exploration of the impossible, making possible that which lies beyond the possible.[189] We find in this 'poetry' the third basic element of Lefebvre's dialectical trilogy, alongside the primacy of praxis (Marx) and dialectical thought (Hegel) – transcendence. Lefebvre locates this neither in the beyond (as in religion) nor in thought (as in philosophy), and neither in pure praxis and the historical determination of a social class (as Marx). He seeks a dialectical third, which negates thought and praxis alike and preserves them by raising them to a higher, poetic, or poietic, level.

'For Nietzsche, truth is poetic in kind.' Truth is brought forth and grasped in an act of thought, which produces it by articulating it: 'Truth grasps the person who grasps it. This double grasping transforms him: he is one thing and becomes another. He becomes what he is. This action is accompanied by poetic speech; only speech, which runs through discourse, can speak.'[190]

The secret of poetry, which transforms sensation and sensuous perception, is for Nietzsche an active principle, the will of the poet, the absolute will. 'The instant becomes moment, eternity. Word becomes action. The act of this thought simultaneously reveals depths and detects possibilities. Poetic speech . . . seizes from the accomplished its secret, that of the possible.'[191]

The Inexhaustibility of Being

The 'real' is thus traversed by a broad, conflictual becoming, which philosophy termed 'cosmos', 'world', 'God', 'divine providence', 'life', 'will', and so on. 'At each level of stability, this becoming seems exhausted. It seems reduced to a "residue". Then contradictions resurge: becoming recommences. It breaks or dissolves the stabilities.'[192]

What characterises this becoming, this inexhaustible 'third'? What is its driving 'force'? Lefebvre deliberately leaves this 'it' indefinite. He makes clear that it is located in this world and on the earth, and that it is experienceable, but

---

188   Ibid., 90.
189   Ibid., 86.
190   Ibid., 124.
191   Ibid., 124–5.
192   Ibid., 2.

inexhaustible and impossible to fully grasp theoretically. He gives it many names throughout his work: *désir*, *élan vital*, creative power, poiesis, imagination, spontaneity, will to power, basic instinct, human energies.

Here, Rob Shields sees influences from Schopenhauer,[193] whom Lefebvre had read in his youth, in his emphasis on 'will' as opposed to 'intellect' and in the conception of the adventure as a spontaneous expression of individual creativity.[194] Jens Peter Schwab, in contrast, views the term *élan vital* with scepticism and concludes (correctly) that it does *not* come from Bergson.[195] Rémi Hess attempts to show how Spinoza's notion of objective thought functioning in living organisms and all of nature also influenced Lefebvre via Schelling.[196] Lefebvre wrote a long introduction to a translation of Schelling's *Philosophical Inquiries into the Essence of Human Freedom* in which he also discussed Schelling's notion of 'intuition': this careless, lively, and adventurous intuition rooted in nature was a desire, a liberating and revolutionary want. 'Lefebvre thus sees in Schelling the integration of desire and love, production and risk, adventure and play, understanding and drama into philosophy.'[197] Lefebvre, however, also saw the limits of this philosophy: it remained philosophy and failed to depict the current and the contemporary.[198] Lefebvre later wrote that creative power in human history did not give philosophy the right to construct an ontology under its banner: 'We must not "ontologize" history.'[199]

Nietzsche's will to power also belongs to the 'essential powers' evoked by Lefebvre. While this concept appears in his early work only sporadically, it would become a central explanatory category of state violence and power in *De l'État*.[200]

Finally, we come to the most important of these concepts, the non-philosophical and simultaneously most poetic of them which Lefebvre uses most often and which for him represents the most central and general category: *le désir*, desire. For Lefebvre, *le désir* means adventure, the unknown, that which was overlooked by philosophy and must first be restored through the sublation of philosophy.[201] Lefebvre sees here, in the Nietzschean sense, the grand struggle between Logos and Anti-Logos: while Logos classifies, orders, cultivates knowledge and places it in the service of power, the great desire (*le Grand Désir*), in contrast, seeks to

---

193   Shields, *Lefebvre, Love and Struggle*, 9.
194   Hess, *Henri Lefebvre et l'aventure du siècle*, 22.
195   Schwab, *'L'homme total'*, 58.
196   Hess, *Henri Lefebvre et l'aventure du siècle*, 65.
197   Ibid., 64. Translation by author.
198   Ibid., 65–6.
199   Lefebvre, *Metaphilosophy*, 2.
200   On this, see Hajo Schmidt, *Sozialphilosophie des Krieges*, 202ff.
201   Lefebvre, *Metaphilosophy*, 322.

overcome the divisions between needs and desires. The psychoanalytical formulation of the struggle between the pleasure principle and the reality principle provides, in Lefebvre's view, only an abstract and vague impression of the grand struggle – this great dialectical movement from Logos to Eros, from domination to appropriation, from technology to poetry.[202]

Lefebvre localises desire in the proximity of needs; it is, in a sense, the dialectical sublation of need and its inherent contradiction: satisfaction and dissatisfaction. While culture positions itself on the level of satisfied or unsatisfied needs, desire forms the level of poetry: the 'desire for creative work, for refined pleasure, in violence or cruelty, in wisdom or grandeur'.[203] It transcends the conflict between natural and artificial needs, between the determined, limited satisfactions and the dissatisfaction, which seeks to break through these limitations. It proceeds from need, sublates it, and returns, as in love and through love, back to its origin, to nature. Nature is older than the precise localised need. Desire is endless, infinitely vulnerable, and yet carries its certainty within itself: 'Creation and re-creation rising back to the source, the heart of the new totality – is this not Hegel's Rose of the World? Hegel was mistaken in finding this flower in knowledge. Marx, in the wake of Goethe, rediscovered it in total life.'[204]

Here, the difference between Lefebvre and Marx becomes evident. While Lefebvre celebrates the elegant, illuminated, light, buoyant, pervasive, and truly transcendent *désir*, Marx proclaims the earthy, suffering, tortured, acquiescent, and dark – passion: 'Man as an objective sensuous being is therefore a *suffering* being, and because he feels his suffering [*Leiden*], he is a *passionate* [*leidenschaftliches*] being. Passion is man's essential power vigorously striving to attain its object.'[205]

Passion, which realises itself as humanity's essential power in and through labour – or desire, through which humans return to nature? The distinction signifies more than a mere dialectical game. According to Lefebvre, Marx was evidently of the opinion that nature would reveal itself in the course of social praxis. But, if the transforming of nature *into* humans occurs at the same time as the becoming of nature *through* humans, Lefebvre asks, how and why is this possible?[206] Do nature and being, which create human beings, exist in the absolute outside of human existence, before it and without it? Lefebvre responds with his typical dialectical 'yes and no'. Yes, because nature births the human

---

202 Lefebvre, *Production of Space*, 391–2.
203 Lefebvre, *Metaphilosophy*, 76, 322.
204 Ibid., 322.
205 Marx, *Economic and Philosophical Manuscripts*, 390.
206 Lefebvre, *Metaphilosophy*, 131–2.

being, preceding it in material history and biological life. No, if it is true
that being and nature are determined to bring forth and accomplish the human
being and that which sets it apart from natural existence: thought. It is here that
Lefebvre locates humanity's potential.[207]

This position, this hope, also forces Lefebvre to accept a deeper truth in philosophical, psychological, and poetic words: the 'inexhaustibility of "being" '.[208]
If this phrase is taken seriously, then the origin of Lefebvre's terms matters little,
as it is precisely the inexhaustible, the residual of every analysis, which defies
every conceptual, philosophical, and analytical grasp. It can only be experienced
in praxis, in the dialectical movement of 'becoming'.

The Strategy of Residues

'Shall we insist on Nietzsche's defeat? Yes . . . the most poetic speech is not
enough to change praxis.'[209] For Lefebvre, the objective cannot be to think of
being – even if in poetic words – but rather to create it. This necessitates,
however, a clear decision for an action, for a strategy.[210] Lefebvre sketched out
several strategies over the course of his multifaceted and wide-ranging engagements with praxis: the revolution of everyday life, the urban revolution, and
the production of a differential space (see sections 4.1, 4.4, and 6.4). He developed his most fundamental strategy, however, in *Metaphilosophy* – the strategy
of residues.[211]

Residue is the non-reducible element which every systematic operation
necessarily brings forth. If it is impossible to grasp all of life theoretically, a
living remainder always remains, which eludes both abstraction and control:
'becoming shows itself inexhaustible, despite being actual and present. In the
face of operations of understanding and discourse, a residue always persists.'[212]
This residue contains valuable and essential qualities, for which Lefebvre gives
several notable examples:

> *Religion*, despite its efforts, has left and still does leave an irreducible:
> fleshly life, spontaneous vitality. *Philosophy* casts light on . . . the every-
> day, the non-philosophical that it makes manifest by expelling it.

---

207   Ibid., 132–3.
208   Ibid., 131.
209   Ibid., 125.
210   Ibid., 11.
211   On this point, see also Müller-Schöll, *Das System und der Rest*.
212   Lefebvre, *Metaphilosophy*, 23, see also 11; Lefebvre, *Production of Space*, 135.

Mathematics casts light on drama . . . *Technology* and machinery point a finger, as it were, towards what resists them: sex, desire, the deviant and unusual . . . The state bitterly opposes freedom and thus also indicates it . . . *Art*, having become culture, leaves behind the residue of 'creativity'. *Bureaucracy* in vain hunts out the individual, the singular, the deviant. *Organization* cannot exterminate spontaneous life and desire. As for everydayness, despite itself, it opens onto the totality, reprised and renewed by poiesis.[213]

Lefebvre's strategy thus consists of assembling these irreducibilities and creating a more real and truer universe in praxis. This is a poietic strategy, resting on difference, the non-convergence of different worlds, their discrepancies, disharmonies, and dysfunctions – and thus, their conflicts.[214] 'Promoting a residue, showing its essence (and its essential character) against the power that crushes it and demonstrates it by trying to crush it, is a rebellion. Gathering the residues is a revolutionary thought.'[215]

The aim of this poietic revolt? The appropriation of human nature – a new, reclaimed spontaneity irreducible to models, behaviours, and attitudes which encompasses lucidity and action: 'This spontaneity higher and deeper than the elementary is reason and resultant of poiesis, residue among residues, fundamental rebellion. Not "wild thought" but "wild desire".'[216] Lefebvre refers here to the famous book *La pensée sauvage*, in which Claude Lévi-Strauss analyses 'wild thought' in its untamed state as distinct from thought cultivated or domesticated for the purpose of yielding a return. With *désir sauvage*, in contrast, Lefebvre proposes the poietic exploration of the unknown aspects of love, sex, and pleasure.[217]

Metaphilosophy

A substantial component of Lefebvre's strategy of residues is the radical rejection of philosophy and knowledge in the service of power. In order to enter the world and at the same time transcend reality, philosophy must be sublated.[218]

---

213 Lefebvre, *Metaphilosophy*, 301–2.
214 Ibid., 11, 302.
215 Ibid., 302.
216 Ibid., 304. Translation amended.
217 Ibid., 305. See also Lévi-Strauss, *The Savage Mind*.
218 Lefebvre, *Metaphilosophy*, 17–18.

Philosophy must become world, not as philosophy, but as a project that is realized in the world, negated by its very realization. Then the philosophical world and the non-philosophical world will lose their one-sidedness and will both be overcome. The realization of philosophy will make simultaneously for its grandeur and its loss. Time will continue, fertilized by philosophy and in no way destroyed by it.[219]

Philosophy is realised by being sublated, and sublates itself by realising itself: the revolutionary project consists, in Lefebvre's view, of the world becoming philosophy and philosophy becoming world.[220] This argument refers to Marx's renowned passage: 'The result is that as the world becomes philosophical, philosophy also becomes worldly, that its realisation is also its loss.'[221]

For Lefebvre, the becoming worldly of philosophy is accomplished only in the concrete praxis of concrete subjects. This requires that philosophy turns to that which the philosophical tradition systematically obscures: the everyday, the banal and diffuse, in human praxis.[222] Such an approach is, however, no longer philosophy in the classical sense of the word, and therefore Lefebvre calls it 'metaphilosophy'. Metaphilosophy confronts traditional philosophy with social and political praxis, with everyday life, with the possibilities and impossibilities appearing in the modern world, and not least with the project of a radical transformation of everydayness.[223]

Lefebvre sealed his fate as a philosopher with this project: 'Are we then going to continue to philosophize, despite claiming to supersede [sublate] philosophy? Not quite. We are going to grasp our praxis renewed by a poietic decision and say what it reveals.'[224]

Outlines of a Three-Dimensional Dialectic

This metaphilosophical outlook on everydayness (see section 3.1) reveals the basic outlines of Lefebvre's epistemology. Although he repeatedly references other thinkers such as Freud, Heidegger, or Sartre, he explicitly identifies three nineteenth-century German thinkers as key figures in understanding

219 Ibid., 51.
220 Ibid., 17–18.
221 Marx, *Difference between the Democritean and Epicurean Philosophy of Nature*, 85.
222 See Hajo Schmidt, *Sozialphilosophie des Krieges*, 170.
223 Lefebvre, *De l'État*, vol. 2, 169; Lefebvre, *Metaphilosophy*, 113.
224 Lefebvre, *Metaphilosophy*, 315.

modernity: Hegel, Marx, and Nietzsche.[225] From his early engagements with philosophy to his later works on the everyday, the urban, space, and the state, this philosophical triumvirate forms the theoretical foundation of his intellectual oeuvre.

His appropriation of the 'German dialectic' provides him with a renewed, three-dimensional dialectic unparalleled in philosophy and the history of science. It is a dialectic which begins classically with Hegel, and accomplishes the materialist inversion through Marx, to ultimately find its unexpected sublation in Nietzsche. Hegel, Marx, and Nietzsche each stand for a specific moment of the dialectic: Marx forms the affirmation, the positing of being through praxis. In contrast, Hegel stands for the concept, the word and thus the negation – death. Nietzsche, lastly, embodies the negation of the negation: poetry, which wrests the word away from death, transcends the concept and the world alike, raises it to a higher level, and thus – and only thus – achieves a higher dialectical truth.

Lefebvre describes this dialectic somewhat profanely as a radical critique of Hegel rooted in Marx's social praxis and Nietzsche's views on art.[226] Generally speaking, Lefebvre's fundamental dialectical figure can be understood as a contradiction between (social) thought and (social) activity, which is joined by the creative, poetic, and poietic act as the third moment: for Lefebvre, the work of art is the unity of the finite and the infinite, endlessly determined and alive.[227] He is less interested in 'high art' as in quotidian art, the poetry of the everyday, the art of life: 'Marxist rationality thus links up with Nietzschean thought in the justification of becoming.'[228]

Lefebvre thus formulates a three-dimensional figure of social reality: the first moment is formed by material praxis as the starting point of life and analysis. It stands in contradiction to the second moment – thought, word, and writing – which Lefebvre understands as abstraction and concrete power, as imposition. The third moment is constituted by poetry, desire, the will to power as forms of transcendence, which help becoming to break through death. Yet Lefebvre does not halt with this sublation in transcendence and poetry, nor does he drift into metaphysics, but rather returns with the movement of the dialectic to praxis, to action.

This three-dimensional figure changes the character of the dialectic in a decisive way: the sequence of affirmation–negation–negation of the negation, which then becomes the new affirmation and in this dialectical movement unfolds the course of history, is in a sense sublated in itself: the three dialectical moments are relating to each other equally. In this way, Lefebvre goes far beyond Hegel *and*

---

225   Ibid., 49ff.
226   Lefebvre, *Production of Space*, 406.
227   Lefebvre, *Dialectical Materialism*, 36–7.
228   Lefebvre, *Metaphilosophy*, 130.

Marx, because his dialectic sublates the initial contradiction between a dialectic of spirit and a dialectic of praxis by positing a third term that he does not clearly define and name, but relates to the experienced, the lived.

Lefebvre would only clearly define this 'three-dimensional dialectic' late in his career, particularly in *Le retour de la dialectique*. In his own words, the concept had taken a subterranean pathway, only to emerge later on.[229] He views the basic three-dimensional figure as a further development of the dialectic, which he opposes to the dialectic of his renowned predecessors, Hegel and Marx. The Hegelian dialectic claimed to *construct* becoming, yet this proved to be an illusion, as it had only constructed a representation. In contrast, the Marxist dialectic claimed to *produce* becoming yet failed to realise this grand objective. It would appear, concludes Lefebvre, that history consisted less of depths, surprises, and unbridgeable gaps than of junctions, volte-faces, and detours which the dialectic had failed to grasp. As an orientation, he offers his own version of the dialectic, the 'triadic' or 'ternary' analysis. It posits equivalent concepts which stand in shifting relations and complex movements to one another, where one soon confirms one or the other concept, the negation of one or the other.[230] In this way, Lefebvre's dialectic opens a horizon of becoming – of possibilities, uncertainties, and chances. Moreover, it allows for the formulation of a strategy, albeit without any certainty of reaching its goal.

Triadic Analysis

How can these insights be implemented? What does this triadic analysis, the 'analysis of becoming', mean? Lefebvre approached this form of dialectics only gradually. He took initial steps towards this triadic analysis in the second volume of *Critique of Everyday Life* by differentiating three dimensions of analytical understanding.[231] He begins with the dimension of analytical understanding and formal logic, which refers to only one aspect or variable and for this reason tends towards one-sidedness. This is followed by dialectical logic, the domain of dichotomies and mutual exclusions, and thereby the operational technologies to define and grasp polarised relations, reciprocities, and interactions. He subsequently introduces three-dimensionality, and with it the level upon which dialectical movement can first be grasped – a movement based on

---

229   See Lefebvre, *Le retour de la dialectique*, 41–2.
230   Ibid., 42.
231   Lefebvre, *Critique of Everyday Life*, vol. 2, 153–5.

inherent conflicts advancing through successive sublations, which thus cannot be entirely exhausted by analytical understanding.

In the same book we can find the first examples of such triads, such as 'body–mind–soul', the constants of Western philosophy, as well as the triad 'form–structure–function' which repeatedly arises in Lefebvre's writings and served as the foundation for his sharp critique of formalism, structuralism, and functionalism.[232] This triad also offers an answer to the protracted problem of form and content, which had created so much difficulty for Lefebvre in *Dialectical Materialism*. Of particular importance is further the triad 'need–labour–pleasure', which Lefebvre would later identify as a central characteristic of the rural, the industrial, and the urban in *The Urban Revolution* (see section 3.4).[233]

This three-dimensionality would also play a constitutive role in Lefebvre's theory of language developed in the 1960s, distinguishing a paradigmatic, a syntagmatic, and a symbolic dimension of language according to this very triadic principle (see section 5.7). In *Rhythmanalysis*, the triad appears as 'melody–harmony–rhythm'.[234] In *La présence et l'absence*, he asks: 'Is there ever a relation between two terms, if not in representation? There are always Three. There is always the Other'.[235] In the same book, he presents an entire list of triads relating to the most diverse aspects of reality.

The culmination of this three-dimensional dialectic is constituted in *The Production of Space*, where it provides the key to understanding the famous double triads: 'perceived, conceived, and lived space', and 'spatial practice, representation of space, and spaces of representation'. This fundamental three-dimensional conception of the production of space is discussed extensively in chapter 5.

The End of History

After this journey through the depth and heights of dialectical thinking, we have to ask where these dialectics end. In his book *La fin de l'histoire*, published in the same year as *The Urban Revolution*, Lefebvre has extensively engaged with this question. This book is itself part of a metaphilosophical triad. The first volume, *Introduction to Modernity*, with the subtitle *Préludes* in the French original, explores the state and condition of the modern world in a comprehensive way. The second volume of this trilogy is *Metaphilosophy*, bearing in the original version the subtitle *Prolégomènes* (prolegomena), which in the strict

---

232   Ibid.; see also Lefebvre, *Au-delà du structuralisme*, 347–69.
233   Lefebvre, *Critique of Everyday Life*, vol. 2, 154.
234   Lefebvre, *Rhythmanalysis*, 12.
235   Lefebvre, *La présence et l'absence*, 143. Translation by author.

sense means an ensemble of preliminary notions of a science. As we have seen, this work examines the becoming worldly of philosophy and declares the end of philosophy. The third volume, *La fin de l'histoire*, bears the subtitle *Épilégomènes*, which means a concluding summary of some of the foundational ideas of a work; it asks the question where history will lead us.[236] The word *fin* in French can mean both 'end' as well as 'goal' – a wonderful dialectical ambiguity, which Lefebvre consciously plays with here.

Thus, in this book Lefebvre sets again the stage for the three protagonists of his metaphilosophical drama, Hegel, Marx, and Nietzsche. He struggles once more with Hegel's legacy, the philosophy of history, and its consequence, the finality of history, which he tries to direct towards a truly materialist and open-ended conception of history as the becoming of the human being. In this struggle, he tries to escape the cliffs of Western philosophy – historicism emphasising continuity and antihistoricism which he accuses of being unable to recognise the general movement of social development, a tendency that he locates particularly in structuralism.[237] In many ways, *La fin de l'histoire* marks the end point of Lefebvre's philosophical project and, on his reaching the age of seventy, the beginning of a thorough engagement with the urban, the production of space, and the state. He would only return to the great philosophical debate some years later with the work *Hegel, Marx, Nietzsche, or, The Realm of Shadows*:

> In myth, from the poetry of Homer to the *Divine Comedy*, the realm of shadows possessed an entrance and exit, a guided trajectory and mediating powers. It had gates, those of an underground city, overshadowed by the earthly city and the city of God. Today, where are the gates of the realm of shadows? Where is the way out?[238]

At the end, philosophy resides in the underworld, and the outcome of history is indeterminate: Lefebvre can outline some paths toward a different society, but he is confronted with a simultaneously bitter and hopeful truth: the openness of history, and, most importantly for Lefebvre, the openness of the historical project of a radical humanism.

---

236   Lefebvre, *La fin de l'histoire*.
237   Lefebvre, *De l'État*, vol. 3, 15.
238   Lefebvre, *Hegel, Marx, Nietzsche*, 48.

3

Urbanisation and Urban Society

The preceding chapter reconstructed the epistemological foundations of Lefebvre's thinking, highlighted the key role of praxis in his approach, and explored his understanding of dialectics. On this basis, this and the following chapters will uncover, step by step, the historical development of Lefebvre's theory of the production of space, outline its basic elements and internal construction, and analyse its social, theoretical, and epistemological contexts.

The first step in this reconstruction is the analysis of Lefebvre's understanding of the phenomenon of urbanisation, which preceded his writing on space. In the long trajectory of his intellectual life, the question of urbanisation emerged relatively late – at the beginning of the 1960s. For Lefebvre, the process of urbanisation was a real discovery, and even caused a kind of shock, when he encountered the construction of a new town in the midst of the rural landscape near Navarrenx, his home town in the Pyrenees. This 'discovery' has to be placed in the context of two crucial aspects of his theoretical work: first of all, it is based on his own empirical research, which Łukasz Stanek has reconstructed in detail.[1] Second, it results from his specific approach to this research, focusing on the exploration of everyday life.

Lefebvre's specific understanding of everyday life is directly linked to his philosophical position, examined in the previous chapter. It is the consequence of his dialectical conceptualisation of the becoming worldly of philosophy and his epistemological starting point, social praxis (see section 2.2). How can social praxis be understood? By investigating everyday life. Consequently, Lefebvre developed a research strategy which he characterised by the term

---

1   Stanek, *Henri Lefebvre on Space*.

'metaphilosophy'. This meant to analyse what the philosophical tradition had systematically ignored: the banality and triviality of human practices. Metaphilosophy designates the end of philosophy and the starting point of a new project that would occupy him until the end of his life: the study of everyday life, which he explored both theoretically and empirically in its manifold facets (section 3.1).

Lefebvre came to the question of urbanisation from his study of everyday life, and thus from a phenomenological perspective, so to speak. The 'phenomenon of urbanisation' initially presented itself to empirical analysis as the process of urban sprawl, a process that equally transformed both urban and rural areas. Lefebvre thus understood urbanisation as a comprehensive process of social transformation, an approach that was fundamentally new at that time. In his search for a theoretical basis for his analysis of urbanisation, he found some clues in Marx and Engels, along with some inspirations in contemporary critiques of urbanism, particularly the idea of the 'explosion of the city' and the related diagnosis of a 'crisis of the city'. On this basis, Lefebvre started a new theoretical endeavour: he projected the urbanisation process into the future, and thus developed his central, provocative, and enormously productive thesis: the thesis of the complete urbanisation of society (section 3.2).

He took this thesis as the starting point for a historical reconstruction of the process of urbanisation, which he carried out in two steps. As a first step, he analysed the history of the Western city along a 'space-time axis' of urbanisation. This analysis reveals that the city has repeatedly taken on a different status and meaning in different social formations. Lefebvre begins his analysis in the ancient times, examines the central role of the city in the development of capitalism, follows the industrialisation that led to an urban explosion, and finally ends with the present as a critical zone in which urbanisation is increasingly covering the entire planet. Thus, the 'city' proved to be a historical category that has a tendency to dissolve in the process of urbanisation. In this process, Lefebvre observed that the historical contradiction of city and country was dialectically sublated and thus fundamentally transformed. This requires a new analysis: the city can no longer be regarded as an isolated, delimited entity, but must instead be analysed in the context of the development of the entire society (section 3.3).

This finding led to Lefebvre's second step, to analyse the same history of urbanisation from the perspective of the entire society, thereby also opening up a view over the entire territory. This analysis resulted in the discovery of a succession of three historical sequences, 'continents', or 'fields': rural society, industrial society, and, finally, urban society. Thus, a process became apparent that had remained invisible by focusing only on cities: urbanisation is, so to speak, the other side of industrialisation: these are directly interrelated but also conflicting processes. The industrialisation of society produces urbanisation, which, in turn, contains a potential, a chance, a possibility: the emergence of an 'urban society'. Lefebvre thus uncovers a process that has otherwise remained hidden: an ongoing urban revolution. This revolution opens itself to a possible future, an urban society on a planetary scale (section 3.4).

This twofold historical analysis reveals the specific dialectic of the urbanisation process. Urbanisation must be distinguished from urban society. Urbanisation is a process that implies the potential of an urban society, but does not automatically lead to it. An urban society can only be realised through social struggle and social movements – in and through an urban revolution. It is impossible to overestimate the importance of this analysis. It went far beyond existing attempts to explain urbanisation and provoked a fundamental reorientation in the theoretical understanding of the urban. In recent years, these findings have been taken up again and further developed in various ways: in the relation between industrialisation and urbanisation, the question of the urbanisation of everyday life, the rediscovery of the urban as a social process, the varied nature of the contradictions of city and country in different contexts, and, in particular, the thesis of complete urbanisation, which found a new theorisation in the concept of planetary urbanisation (section 3.5).

As pointed out in chapter 1, it took a long time before Lefebvre's texts on urbanisation developed their full potential in scholarly practice. While his works on everyday life were widely discussed early on, his texts on the urban have long been neglected and misunderstood. Nonetheless, they were highly appreciated by activists, especially in Germany and France, and they quickly became a fixture in urban studies in Latin America. In the Anglo-American academic world, however, it took more than thirty years for the two most important books to be translated (*The Right to the City* was published in 1996, and *The Urban Revolution* finally appeared in 2002). Today, these two books are well known and are cited extensively. But there are still substantial debates on how to interpret these texts, owing largely to the fact that they are rarely read systematically, and are not considered in relation to Lefebvre's wider theoretical project.

The two central concepts explored in this chapter are 'urbanisation' (*urbanisation*) and 'urban society' (*société urbaine*). In contrast to English (or German), the term *urbanisation* in French has both an active and a passive meaning: on the one hand, certain actors (for example, state organs or private companies) might 'urbanise' an area, but on the other hand it can be said that an area has been urbanised. Although Lefebvre himself does not define the term *urbanisation* in a precise way, he does not use it to simply describe the 'growth of cities', or of urban populations, as most classical texts do.[2] For him, it instead denotes a complex, multidimensional social process that will be gradually unpacked over the following chapters. In a similar sense, 'the urban' – synonymous for urban society in Lefebvre's texts – does not simply mean urban territories, urbanism, or urbanity for Lefebvre, but refers to a fundamental social transformation: it is the result of an urban revolution.

3.1 The Critique of Everyday Life

Man will be everyday or he won't be at all.[3]

As we saw in the introduction, Lefebvre developed his understanding of urbanisation and the urban revolution from his critique of everyday life. He had already formulated this critique before he began to work on Marx and dialectical materialism – it emerged in the context of the *Philosophies* group (see section 2.1). Their fundamental critique of philosophy had led to the call to investigate practical life, which also meant engaging with the question of everyday life. This was a concern that the *Philosophies* shared with another, related group, the Surrealists. Rémi Hess reported on a dispute over the idea of everyday life between the Surrealists and the *Philosophies* around 1925;[4] both groups essentially agreed on the eminent importance of a critique of everyday life. They were divided, however, on the question of how everyday life could be sublated. The Surrealists had a project: their bet was on poetry. Surrealism was, initially, a way of life, one that wanted to escape from everyday life through poetry and poetic action.[5] In contrast, the *Philosophies* postulated a different approach: for them, changing everyday life meant revolution (see section 2.1).

Following on from these debates, the concept of everyday life served Lefebvre as a guideline for the cognition of society. He first deepened his critique of everyday life in the book *La conscience mystifiée* (*The Mystified Consciousness*) from 1936, which he wrote together with Norbert Guterman, another member of the *Philosophies*. An examination of the question of consciousness, written in the context of fascism's ascendance in Europe, this book also included a critique of the mystification of the realities of

---

2   See for example Brenner and Schmid, 'The "Urban Age" in Question'.

3   Lefebvre, *La somme et le reste*, 266.

4   Hess, *Henri Lefebvre et l'aventure du siècle*, 51–3.

5   From a conversation with Lefebvre, quoted in ibid., 52; see also Lefebvre, *La somme et le reste*, 394–6.

contemporary society.[6] This study opened the way for a deeper examination of the question of everyday life and everydayness. Lefebvre began his doctoral thesis on the history of the everyday life of the peasant communities in the Vallée de Campan in the Pyrenees while the Second World War was still under way.[7] And, immediately after the war, he began an ambitious theoretical and empirical project on the critique of everyday life that was to occupy him for forty years, right up to the end of his life.

The three-volume *Critique of Everyday Life*, which Lefebvre would only complete in 1981, stood at the centre of this project, which was confined primarily to the analysis of French society.[8] The first volume, published in 1947, bore the title *Introduction*. Looking back, Lefebvre characterised its 'theoretical postulate' as follows: 'The rational core, the real centre of praxis is located in everyday life.'[9] The analysis developed in this book was influenced by the reconstruction process in the aftermath of the Second World War. As Lefebvre noted later, many then believed that they were creating a different society, while at the same time they were working to restore the old social conditions in only slightly altered form.[10] The second volume of the *Critique*, entitled *Foundations for a Sociology of the Everyday* and published in 1962, develops the theoretical foundations of an analysis of everyday life. It conveys a wealth of concepts, categories, and theories, but contains few empirical or historical analyses. These, however, can be found in another book published in the same year, *Introduction to Modernity*, which illuminates the connection between everyday life and modernity, an idea central to Lefebvre's thought.

The book *Metaphilosophy*, published in 1965, finally laid the epistemological foundations for Lefebvre's investigations into everyday life. In this book, he also explicitly turned his attention away from philosophy and towards praxis (see also section 2.4). In 1968, he published *Everyday Life in the Modern World*, a kind of interim report or inventory from his wide-ranging project. It is on this book that I will especially focus in the following section. Only in 1981 did Lefebvre finish the third volume of his trilogy on everyday life, which he had already announced in 1968: *From Modernity to Modernism: Towards a Metaphilosophy of Everyday Life*. The book *Elements of Rhythmanalysis* (1992), which appeared only after his death and focuses on temporality, must also be seen in the context of a comprehensive analysis of everyday life and

---

6   See Burkhard, *French Marxism between the Wars*, 205–7.
7   Lefebvre, 'Henri Lefebvre par lui-même'; see also Stanek, *Henri Lefebvre on Space*, 5–7.
8   See Lefebvre, *Everyday Life in the Modern World*, 30.
9   Ibid., 31. Translation amended.
10   Ibid., 42.

everydayness.[11] It forms a very important complement to his predominantly 'spatial' analyses in the preceding works on everyday life, urbanisation, and space.[12] Overall, this comprehensive and wide-ranging body of work on everyday life was relatively well received, and provided Lefebvre with a permanent place in theories and research on everyday life.[13]

The Concept of Everydayness

The concept of everydayness (*la quotidienneté*) does not originate from the experience of everyday life: it comes from philosophy and cannot be understood without it. It designates the non-philosophical for and through philosophy. In contrast to the ideal of philosophy, daily life presents itself as the real world. In contrast to the practical banality and triviality of everyday life, philosophy strives towards higher spheres and portrays itself as something abstract, absent, distanced, disinterested – as both a radical and a futile critique of the everyday. In this sense, philosophy and everyday life are directly opposed to one another, as are their alienations: philosophical alienation is truth without reality; everyday alienation is reality without truth.[14]

As Lefebvre understood it, this confrontation between philosophy and everyday life can only be ended through philosophy's continuation on the path to its own realisation and thus its dialectical sublation, when it ceases to postulate the separation of the philosophical and the non-philosophical, the higher and the lower, spiritual and material, the theoretical and the practical, the 'cultivated' and the 'uncultivated':[15] 'We have, then, asserted that everyday life is the object of philosophy precisely because it is non-philosophical.'[16]

The everyday is the prose of the world. It is that which lacks a date, the ensemble of banal activities, the triviality of repetitions, of gestures at work and out of work, the modest and the solid, the (obviously) insignificant and the self-evident whose fragments are chained together in a routine, without having to check the

---

11   See also Kofman and Lebas, 'Lost in Transposition', 7.

12   See Mels, *Reanimating Places*; Meyer, *Von der Stadt zur urbanen Gesellschaft*; Vogelpohl, *Urbanes Alltagsleben*; Edensor, *Geographies of Rhythm*.

13   See for example Sünker, *Bildung, Alltag und Subjektivität*; Osborne, *The Politics of Time*; Gardiner, *Critiques of Everyday Life*; Highmore, *Everyday Life and Cultural Theory*; Sheringham, *Everyday Life*; Roberts, *Philosophizing the Everyday*.

14   Lefebvre, *Everyday Life in the Modern World*, 14; Lefebvre, *Metaphilosophy*, 104; Lefebvre, *Critique of Everyday Life*, vol. 3, 15–16.

15   Lefebvre, *Everyday Life in the Modern World*, 16.

16   Ibid., 17.

articulations of these fragments.[17] The everyday produces an 'ethics of the time-table and an aesthetics decorating the use of time'.[18] Everyday life denotes the site of conflict between the rational and the irrational. It is the place where the concrete problems of production are, broadly speaking, given expression, and it thus also represents the way in which human social existence as a whole is produced.[19] 'It is in everyday life that [people] enjoy and suffer: here and now'.[20]

This conception contains clear parallels to existentialism. But Lefebvre criticises existentialism, and Sartre in particular, for their entrenchment of a *philosophical* project: 'One of the aspects of existentialism was the description of the everyday in its triviality, using terms that were still philosophical'.[21] In contrast, Lefebvre, inspired by his time with the *Philosophies* group, was convinced of the need to both recognise and sublate everydayness.[22]

The Regressive–Progressive Procedure

How can we recognise everyday life? And how can we explore it empirically? In order to answer these questions, a brief introduction to Lefebvre's 'regressive-progressive method' is indispensable. It has already been presented and analysed in various publications.[23]

Lefebvre insists that his method is nothing other than the method that Marx outlined in his famous *Introduction* to the *Grundrisse*: to understand the past from the most developed forms of the present. In doing so, Marx had reversed the 'usual' historical procedure.[24] Marx writes in *Capital*:

> Reflection on the forms of human life, hence also scientific analysis of those forms, takes a course directly opposite to their real development. Reflection begins *post festum,* and therefore with the results of the process of development ready to hand.[25]

---

17   Ibid., 14, 29.
18   Ibid., 24. Translation amended.
19   Ibid., 27.
20   Ibid., 21.
21   Lefebvre, *Metaphilosophy*, 71.
22   Ibid.
23   This includes, among others, Hess, *Henri Lefebvre et l'aventure du siècle*, 178–92; Hajo Schmidt, *Sozialphilosophie des Krieges*; Stanek, *Henri Lefebvre on Space*, 159–61; Frehse, 'For Difference "in and through" São Paulo'.
24   Lefebvre, *Une pensée devenue monde*, 99.
25   Marx, *Capital*, vol. 1, 168.

Marx's method essentially consists in descending from the concrete to the abstract, only to ascend again to the concrete. It seems to be the right thing to do, writes Marx in *Grundrisse*, to start with the real and the concrete in political-economic analysis, such as with the population. But the population consists of the most diverse elements, and is therefore a chaotic idea of the whole. That is why one must analytically descend from the concrete to increasingly abstract concepts, until one reaches the simplest definition. From there, the journey must then be taken backwards, in order to arrive at the population again, this time not at a chaotic conception of the whole, but at 'a rich totality of many determinations and relations'.[26] This reflection ends with the famous passage: 'The concrete is concrete because it is the summary of many provisions, that is, unity of the manifold.' In thinking, therefore, the concrete appears as a process of summarising, as a result, not as a starting point, although it is the real starting point and therefore the starting point of contemplation and imagination.[27] The method of ascending from the abstract to the concrete is then also, for Marx, the way of thinking, of appropriating the concrete, of reproducing it as a concrete-in-thought, but it is not the process of creating the concrete itself.[28]

From these elements found in Marx, Lefebvre develops his own dialectical procedure for analysing social reality: the regressive–progressive procedure.[29] Lefebvre prefers the term 'procedure' (*démarche*) to that of 'method', since it is not a question here of precise instructions for action, but rather of a movement that is adapted to the specific object and the specific problem.[30] He presented this procedure for the first time in a 1953 essay on the perspectives of rural sociology,[31] which is based on his own empirical work in the French Pyrenees.[32] He later also applied it in *The Urban Revolution* and in *The Production of Space*, but only briefly mentioned it there.[33] In *De l'État* he used this procedure to analyse the different forms of the state, explicitly referring back to his earlier article on rural sociology.[34] It is interesting to note that Jean-Paul Sartre himself took precisely this article as the starting point for his own method and quoted from it extensively.[35]

---

26 Marx, *Grundrisse*, 100.
27 Ibid.
28 See ibid., 39.
29 Lefebvre, *De l'État*, vol. 3, 37.
30 Ibid., 63–5; Lefebvre, *Hegel, Marx, Nietzsche*, 47.
31 See Lefebvre, 'Perspectives on Rural Sociology'.
32 See, particularly, Lefebvre, *La Vallée de Campan*.
33 Lefebvre, *Urban Revolution*, 23–4; Lefebvre, *Production of Space*, 79–81.
34 Lefebvre, *De l'État*, vol. 2, 65.
35 Sartre, *La critique de la raison dialectique*, 41–2; see Hess, *Henri Lefebvre et l'aventure du siècle*, 182–4.

In his studies on the Pyrenees, Lefebvre had recognised that rural life presents a double complexity: on the one hand, there is a horizontal complexity, because in the social formations and structures of the same historical time decisive differences manifest themselves, which can go so far as to be antagonistic. On the other hand, a vertical complexity can be observed as the coexistence of different social formations originating from different times.[36] In order to be able to grasp these two forms of complexity, Lefebvre proposed a 'very simple' method that includes three moments:[37]

a) The description: This first moment is based on observation, but with a view informed by experience and a general theory. The focus here is on participant observation in the field. In addition, there is the cautious use of other research techniques, such as interviews, questionnaires, statistics, and so on.

b) The *analytical-regressive* or *genealogical* analysis:[38] This is the analysis of the described reality and the attempt to date its origins accurately. It goes back in time, starting from the present, in order to search in the broadest sense for the conditions that have made this present possible. This analysis must therefore go back through the various historical social formations to find the origin, or rather the beginning, of a historical process.

c) The *progressive-synthetic* or *historical-genetic* analysis:[39] This analysis attempts to classify social formations and structures within the framework of an overall process. The aim is to return to the present, which is thus illuminated, understood, and explained.[40] It is thus a matter of capturing the historical movement of the production of the present, starting from the identified, more or less distant conditions, through the concatenation of determinisms, events, contingencies, and conscious decisions.[41]

Like Marx, Lefebvre is thus concerned with the production and reproduction of the object under consideration in thought. The concept, the theoretical conception, captures a 'reality'; yet it does not simply reflect a general process

---

36 Lefebvre, 'Perspectives on Rural Sociology', 112–13.
37 See on the following ibid., 117.
38 Lefebvre, *Une pensée devenue monde*, 101.
39 Ibid.
40 Lefebvre, 'Perspectives on Rural Sociology', 117
41 Lefebvre, *De l'État*, vol. 2, 28; Lefebvre, *Une pensée devenue monde*, 101.

onto a theoretical surface, but seeks to reproduce its historical dynamics in thought.[42]

In *De l'État*, Lefebvre elaborates further on the distinction between the genealogical (regressive) and genetic (progressive) analysis: The genealogical analysis searches for the origin (*origine*) of a historical process; it insists on the site of origin, the contexts, and the connections. The genetic analysis, in contrast, looks for the fundamental dynamics (*fondement*) of the present moment and attempts to restore the genesis of a general process.[43] Hajo Schmidt comments, 'If the genetic approach captures the recognisable trajectory, the continuity and the inner cohesion of a historical movement, the genealogical approach emphasises the discontinuity and contradiction of this movement, the shifting balance of power and political intervention.'[44]

Lefebvre uses this regressive–progressive procedure to reconstruct how a given social order came into being, and thus seeks to recognise the production of the present as well as its unfinished virtualities or possibilities.[45] In *The Urban Revolution*, Lefebvre took this procedure a decisive step further by also pursuing the possibility of using this procedure to uncover a hidden potential, the possible future of a historical process. Progressive analysis, then, having advanced from the obsolete and finished to the present, highlights also, in this movement, the possible end point of a process. Thus, at the same time as tracing a historical process, the progressive analysis illuminates what is possible, what is to come, or what is new.[46]

The Society of Controlled Consumption

To recognise everyday life according to Lefebvre's procedure means, first of all, to reveal its genesis and its characteristic traits through historical analysis. Though everyday life has existed as long as society, the concept of everydayness (*le quotidien*) did not appear until much later.[47]

> Certainly, there was a 'life' in the past: the repetition of habitual gestures, eating, drinking, sleeping, working. For the majority of people it was a hard job to gain this life that was hardly more than survival. But this life

---

42   Lefebvre, *De l'État*, vol. 3, 10, 37.
43   Ibid., 37; Lefebvre, *De l'État*, vol. 2, 65.
44   Hajo Schmidt, *Sozialphilosophie des Krieges*, 183. Translation by author.
45   Lefebvre, *Une pensée devenue monde*, 101.
46   Lefebvre, *Urban Revolution*, 23; Lefebvre, *De l'État*, vol. 2, 64.
47   See Hess, *Henri Lefebvre et l'aventure du siècle*, 51.

of each day was enveloped by great cycles and systems: the months, the seasons, the years, life and death. Religion, the sense of the sacred, later morality, penetrated it and metamorphosed it.[48]

Thus, Lefebvre asks whether one could even speak of everyday life in the context of earlier societies. He considers the term 'style' more appropriate for these societies: style of life, of works, of civilisations.[49] 'Our own everyday life is typical for its yearning and quest for a style that obstinately eludes it.'[50] Lefebvre sees the consolidation of everyday life as a specific characteristic of modern societies, closely linked to the spread of the money economy and consumer culture in the nineteenth century.[51] 'From then on the prose of the world spread, until now it invades everything – literature, art and objects – and all the poetry of existence has been evicted.'[52]

On this basis, Lefebvre identifies the social significance of everyday life more precisely: everyday life, and not 'the economic in general' is the level at which current capitalist society is established. However, as Lefebvre points out, everyday life is nevertheless shaped by the requirements of enterprises and adjusted to corporate rationality.[53] In this sense, everydayness (*le quotidien*) refers to the totality of actions that are strung together day by day to form a whole. Eating, dressing, and sleeping are not isolated acts; they are acts that are embedded in a social context and thus also in a social space and a social time, and they are therefore determined by existing social relations.[54]

Applying this analysis, Lefebvre tries to determine the specific quality of post-war society. What should this society be called? 'Industrial society or technological society? Society of abundance or of leisure? Society of labour or of non-labour? State capitalism? Socialism? Civilisation of the image? Era of the gadget, the jukebox, of nylon, plastic, the atom bomb, idols and "celebrities"?'[55] He dismisses all these suggestions one by one: The 'industrial society' identifies a part of the essential facts but only a part (see section 3.4) and tends to mythologise industrialisation.[56] The 'technical society' (*société technicienne*) suggests a technical environment that is opposed to the 'natural

---

48 Lefebvre, *Metaphilosophy*, 107.
49 Lefebvre, *Everyday Life in the Modern World*, 42; Lefebvre, *Metaphilosophy*, 108.
50 Lefebvre, *Everyday Life in the Modern World*, 29.
51 Lefebvre, *Metaphilosophy*, 108; Lefebvre, *Everyday Life in the Modern World*, 29.
52 Lefebvre, *Everyday Life in the Modern World*, 29.
53 Lefebvre, *Urban Revolution*, 30; Lefebvre, *Survival of Capitalism*, 72.
54 Lefebvre, *Critique of Everyday Life*, vol. 3, 15–16.
55 Lefebvre, *Metaphilosophy*, 107.
56 Lefebvre, *Everyday Life in the Modern World*, 46.

environment' and characteristic of that society.[57] The term 'affluent society' conceals the material misery that still exists in these societies, as well as all those cultural and social needs that remain deeply unsatisfied.[58] The term 'leisure society' conceals the routines and the constraints that dominate everyday life.[59]

Finally, Lefebvre decides to characterise French post-war society using a precise – albeit also complicated and inelegant – term: 'the bureaucratic society of controlled consumption'. He intends this term to both emphasise the rational character of this society and to point to the limits of this rationality, as well as to name the object that this bureaucratic society organises: consumption.[60] If businesses had previously produced haphazardly for an uncertain market, consumption – and therefore everyday life – was becoming increasingly organised and structured: 'Everyday life was cut up and laid out on the site to be put together again like pieces of a puzzle, each piece depending on a number of organisations and institutions, each one – working life, private life, leisure – rationally exploited (including the latest commercial and semi-programmed organisation of leisure).'[61]

As a result of the organisation of work, which is divided and assembled, measured, and quantified according to criteria of productivity, the reign of quantitative measurement has spread to the whole of society. Everyday life's specificity lies in the fact that, through a relentless analytic practice, reality is split into separate, functional, organised, structured sectors of living: work, private life, leisure – a separation that is also recognisable in the organisation of urban areas. Lefebvre understands the modern 'tearing apart' of human beings to be a result of society's systematic functionalisation and institutionalisation. What constitutes the unity of these separate sectors? In Lefebvre's view: repetitiveness, passivity, conditioning, and non-participation.[62] 'That era resulted in the constitution of an everydayness, a social environment of sophisticated exploitation and carefully controlled passivity.'[63] Everyday life represents, accordingly, the spread of industrial rationality by means of the state and institutions. Qualitative criteria all but disappear, and rationality, abstraction, and absolute quantification triumph – albeit with certain limits that cannot be exceeded. As Lefebvre points out, another possibility always

---

57   Ibid., 48.
58   Ibid., 51.
59   Ibid., 52.
60   Ibid., 60.
61   Ibid., 58–9.
62   Lefebvre, *Critique of Everyday Life*, vol. 3, 26; Lefebvre, *Metaphilosophy*, 108–9.
63   Lefebvre, *Urban Revolution*, 140.

remains beyond this rational conditioning. Life can never be completely controlled.[64]

The Revolution of Everyday Life

'Everydayness cannot be tolerated. It is insufferable, unacceptable. People conceal it, deny it, misconstrue it. No one accepts it.'[65] Radical critique of everyday life leads Lefebvre to identify a radical negativity. In his understanding, everyday life cannot be recognised without an accompanying rejection and desire to change it. His critique of everyday life also questions the totality of the modern world: culture, the state, technology, institutions, structures, constituted groups, and analytical and operational thinking.[66]

What is the target of this critique? How should everyday life be changed? Lefebvre took his first answer from the Surrealists, who proposed a possible antidote to the alienation from everyday life: poetry. Citing Hölderlin – 'man lives as a poet' – Lefebvre affirms: even if people surround themselves with the worst kitsch, caricatures of poetry, it shows their desire to live poetically. If human beings do not have the ability to live poetically or to invent poetry, they will produce it in their own ways:

> Even the most derisive everyday existence retains a trace of grandeur and spontaneous poetry, except perhaps when it is nothing more than a form of advertising or the embodiment of a world of commodities, exchange having abolished use or overdetermined it.[67]

At the same time, however, Lefebvre's earlier experience with surrealism had already shown him the limits of a poetic strategy. The poetic word and its verdict on everyday life quickly lost their authenticity. The creation of a style may succeed to some extent in literature, but it fails in life, and thus in practice.[68]

How can a poetic project be set free from more than a century of poetic tradition? How do you merge it with a thinking that comes from philosophy but liberate it from the one-sidedness of philosophy? Lefebvre sees the answer

---

64   Lefebvre, *Critique of Everyday Life*, vol. 3, 26–7.
65   Lefebvre, *Metaphilosophy*, 298.
66   Ibid., 297–8.
67   Lefebvre, *Urban Revolution*, 82–3.
68   Lefebvre, *Metaphilosophy*, 121.

in the project of changing everyday life by restoring the richness it has lost.[69] This is his metaphilosophical 'strategy of residuals' (see section 2.4). In his eyes, to liberate the creative activity inherent in the everyday would be a revolutionary project:[70] 'A revolution takes place when and only when, in such a society, people can no longer lead their everyday lives; so long as they can live their ordinary lives the old relations are constantly re-established.'[71]

This view corresponds to the Situationists' position, who also exposed the misery and alienation of everyday life and whose interventions sought to change it radically.[72] Lefebvre's meeting with them in the early 1960s had an enormous influence on both sides.[73] The Situationists adopted and radicalised Lefebvre's concept of everyday life, as evidenced in the text 'Perspectives for Conscious Alterations in Everyday Life' by Guy Debord, which appeared in the journal *Internationale Situationniste* no. 6 in 1961. And Debord's famous book *The Society of the Spectacle* from 1967 provides a thorough analysis of the commodification of everyday life that turns even art into a mere commodity: the experience of real life is transformed into mere images, into pure spectacle. Despite all their differences, both the Situationists and Lefebvre saw everyday life as the starting point of all social change.

Analysing everyday life, Lefebvre had in the early 1960s already recognised the growing malaise that was to culminate in the 1968 revolt.

> We can thus detect a generalized latent malaise, and also points of crystallisation for discontent and rejection (art or what is already replacing it; questions of housing and urbanism; those of education and training, etc.). We can discover direct contestations (in the action of social and political forces) and also indirect ones (in the clumsy attempt to rediscover playful activity, for example) . . . The totality of contestations and the contestation of totality, that is, negativity, are only reconstituted on the basis of the everyday.[74]

---

69   Ibid., 122.
70   Lefebvre, *Everyday Life in the Modern World*, 65–6.
71   Ibid., 32.
72   See Lefebvre, *Hegel, Marx, Nietzsche*, 156ff.
73   See Roberts, *Philosophizing the Everyday*, 77–9; Merrifield, 'Lefebvre and Debord'.
74   Lefebvre, *Metaphilosophy*, 298.

Everyday Life under Fordism

The originality of Lefebvre's analyses of everyday life lies in the attempt to comprehend society through its triviality and thus gain a radically different perspective on social processes. He developed these analyses continuously over more than forty years. At the beginning of this work, immediately after the Second World War, everyday life was, in many respects, unusual as a field of scientific research. Prevailing academic norms of the time did not sanction going into the 'lowlands' of everyday life, while an exploration of everyday life conflicted with the dominant position in Marxist approaches, that work and production were to be treated as central categories of social analysis. Looking back, Lefebvre noted that his first volume of *Critique of Everyday Life* had given rise to conflicting criticisms: one that insisted on the purity of scientific research, and another that proceeded in the name of taking action.[75] It was not until the early 1980s that Lefebvre saw a change, both in philosophy and in the social sciences, which increasingly tried to grasp the concreteness and the reality of everyday life. He remained sceptical of such studies, however, because his aim was to produce a *critique* of everyday life that would be capable of realising its transformation.[76]

Lefebvre's investigations, as previously mentioned, can also be distinguished from related approaches through his specific understanding of praxis as the starting point and goal of all theoretical reflections. From this point of view, the poetic project of Surrealism, as well as Nietzsche's poetic 'strategy', seemed idealist, while existentialism, from Heidegger to Sartre, was still attached to philosophy.

From Lefebvre's materialist position, everyday life could be revealed only through historical analysis; the essential characteristics of post-war society were distilled in his concept of the 'bureaucratic society of controlled consumption'. Without dwelling on the various aspects that Lefebvre presents in his work on this concept, it can be understood as an early version of the concept of 'Fordism' developed by the French Regulation school in the 1970s.[77] According to this concept, a specific development model prevailed in the Western industrialised nations in the post-war period that was based on a combination of mass production and mass consumption mediated by the nation state through Keynesianism and the expansion of the welfare state. The Fordist–Keynesian development model not only included the standardisation of the production

---

75   Lefebvre, *Survival of Capitalism*, 72.

76   Lefebvre, *Critique of Everyday Life*, vol. 3, 4.

77   Aglietta, *A Theory of Capitalist Regulation*.

process, but also a specific model of consumption based largely on the standardised construction of housing, mass transport, and the mechanisation of domestic labour through new consumer goods, from vacuum cleaners to washing machines. The state programming of everyday life described by Lefebvre accordingly sheds light on a central aspect of Fordism as it emerged at the level of private life (discussed in more detail in section 4.3).

Following Lefebvre's analysis, Kristin Ross took a detailed look at the massive changes to everyday life in France during the post-war economic boom, the *trentes glorieuses* (thirty glorious years), by analysing the production of the new Fordist middle class, its lifestyle, its way of habitation, and its career patterns. She examines the important role of women in this process, the change of domestic work and the political economy of domestic work by the modernisation process orchestrated by the state, which concerns the household, personal hygiene, and the private car, among other things.[78] And she also highlights what is lacking in most analyses of modernisation in France, including that of Lefebvre – a consideration of the consequences of colonisation and the traumatic effects of the Algerian war, which inscribed themselves into everyday life in multiple ways. The concept of the colonisation of everyday life, which Lefebvre and Debord developed to analyse the state's and capital's dominance over everyday life, is applied by Ross in its full meaning (see also sections 4.4 and 7.4).[79]

Beyond its relevance for contemporary history, Lefebvre's project of studying everyday life is of central importance in epistemological terms. It connects the analysis of social reality to concrete everyday practices, thus using these practices as starting point for understanding the 'world'. The theoretical framework gained from this analysis formed the basis of Lefebvre's analyses of urbanisation, the production of space, and the state, which will be analysed in this and the following chapters.

3.2 The Complete Urbanisation of Society

> I'll begin with the following hypothesis: Society has been completely urbanized.[80]

With his studies of everyday life, Lefebvre had laid the foundation for a systematic investigation of social practice, which he pursued continuously, under

---

78   Ross, *Fast Cars, Clean Bodies*.
79   See also Kipfer and Goonewardena, 'Lefebvre and "Colonization"'.
80   Lefebvre, *Urban Revolution*, 1.

shifting hypotheses, from the end of the Second World War. During the course of these studies, he stumbled upon a phenomenon which would subsequently occupy him ever more intensely: that of urbanisation.

Lefebvre experienced his decisive encounter with the phenomenon of urbanisation near his birthplace of Navarrenx in the western Pyrenees. In Mourenx, a planned new town built around the industrial complex of Lacq in the middle of a traditional rural area, he examined the shock which this radical invasion of modernity had caused in rural society. In a comprehensive essay, he presented his most important finding, that the monotony of the work process and the order of a functionalised and bureaucratised city produced the new plague of the modern world: boredom. 'The battle against boredom begins. We don't know if this public enemy will be defeated. On this battle and this challenge depends – up to a certain point – the meaning and the destiny of "modernity".'[81]

In the sporadic texts he dedicated to urbanisation in the early 1960s, Lefebvre considered it as a process that primarily affected rural areas and was directly linked to industrialisation. In the following years, however, his perspective changed radically, documented in the collection *Du rural à l'urbain*. No longer exclusively focused on rural areas, he began to look also at the transformations caused by the process of urbanisation in the cities. These empirical studies are comprehensively documented and analysed by Stanek.[82]

By the end of the decade, Lefebvre's analyses of everyday life had shifted to focus on the question of urban life, and he began to develop his own theory of the urban. In 1968, the year of the May events in Paris, he published his first approach on this theory in *The Right to the City*, in which he developed a wide range of concepts. They remain deeply relevant, as attested in Eleonore Kofman and Elizabeth Lebas's meticulously prepared, English-language edition of parts of this work.[83]

Only two years later, Lefebvre published his most important book on the urban question, *The Urban Revolution*, which historically marks the beginning of critical urban theory. For a very long time, however, this book did not enjoy the reception and appreciation it deserved, particularly in francophone and anglophone urban studies. Only in 2003 was it finally translated into English. In 1972, with *Marxist Thought and the City*, he additionally presented an overview on Marx's and Engels's sparse texts on the urban question.[84] The

---

81 Lefebvre, 'Les nouveaux ensembles urbains', 128. Translation by author. See also Lefebvre, *Introduction to Modernity*, 117–26.

82 Stanek, *Henri Lefebvre on Space*.

83 Lefebvre, *Right to the City*.

84 Lefebvre, *Marxist Thought and the City*.

phenomenon of urbanisation and the urban society also play a central role in *The Production of Space* (see sections 6.4 and 6.5).

City and Country in Marx and Engels

The first problem for Lefebvre was to grasp his empirical observations on urbanisation in theoretical terms. The 'phenomenon of urbanisation' had hardly been a subject of theoretical discussion at all, and therefore there was no analytical framework available for its investigation. The classical disciplines of urban studies were stuck in a quantitative mainstream that offered no starting point for a critical problematisation of urbanisation (see section 1.2). Even in historical materialism, the city and urban society had hardly drawn attention. Looking back on his own investigations, Lefebvre held that so-called Marxist thinking had long ignored questions of the city and of space. Consciousness of these problematics, in his view, had only recently developed.[85]

Addressing this lack of theorisation, Lefebvre first returned to Marx and Engels's classic texts, to obtain a preliminary foundation for a deeper understanding of urbanisation. From the very beginning it was clear to him that he would not find a coherent theory on the city there:

> Throughout the work of Marx and Engels there are references to the city and urban problems, but these references were never systematized by the founders of scientific socialism. They do not form a body of doctrine that would rest on a given methodology or a specialized 'discipline' such as philosophy, political economy, ecology, or sociology. Generally speaking, these fragments are presented in terms of other, broader topics: the division of labor, productive forces and the relations of production, historical materialism.[86]

Lefebvre's investigation began with *The Condition of the Working Class in England* by Friedrich Engels, a work which has been well regarded and received in urban studies.[87] In this text, where the young Engels describes and analyses the industrial revolution in England in great detail, the city occupies a prominent place. Engels pays particular attention to Manchester as a 'model case'.[88]

---

85   Lefebvre, *De l'État*, vol. 4, 264–5.
86   Lefebvre, *Marxist Thought and the City*, 15.
87   See for example Saunders, *Social Theory and the Urban Question*; Hartmann et al., *Theorien zur Stadtentwicklung*; Katznelson, *Marxism and the City*.
88   Lefebvre, *Marxist Thought and the City*, 10.

This early text already contained significant insights that would fall by the wayside but be rediscovered later. Engels already recognised, for example, the immanent tendency of industrial capitalism towards centralising labour power and capital in cities:

> The greater the town, the greater its advantages. It offers roads, railroads, canals; the choice of skilled labour increases constantly, new establish-ments can be built more cheaply, because of the competition among builders and machinists who are at hand, than in remote country districts, whither timber, machinery, builders, and operatives must be brought; it offers a market to which buyers crowd, and direct communication with the markets supplying raw material or demanding finished goods. Hence the marvellously rapid growth of the great manufacturing towns.[89]

The city appears here as the most developed social arena of industrial society and thus also as the site where its contradictions collide most violently.[90]

Marx, on the other hand, makes no reference to the city in this early period. Lefebvre combed through his treasured *Paris Manuscripts* again (see section 2.2), in which Marx confronted the leading theoretical views of his day. Lived experience (*vécu*) appeared in commentaries and digressions, noted Lefebvre, who went on to claim that Marx's theoretical considerations only derived their meaning and scope from a specific social context: urban reality.[91]

It was in Marx and Engels's collaboratively written *The German Ideology* that Lefebvre found Marx's first explicit statements on the city – primarily in their observations on antiquity and the Middle Ages, where they identified the historical foundations of the dialectical contradiction between city and coun-try.[92] Marx took up these considerations again in the *Grundrisse*, where he made the noteworthy distinction between two different historical configura-tions of the city: for Marx, the classical city-state of antiquity still bore the mark of rural rule over the city.[93] The field, he claimed, appeared as a territory of the city, but the village was not a mere accessory of the land. War was the great common enterprise, and the concentration of residences in the city was the foundation of this martial organisation.[94] The city became the centre of country

---

89   Engels, *The Condition of the Working Class in England*, 326.
90   Ibid.
91   Lefebvre, *Marxist Thought and the City*, 21.
92   Marx and Engels, *The German Ideology*, 32; Lefebvre, *Marxist Thought and the City*, 25–6.
93   Marx, *Grundrisse*, 474, 484–5.
94   Ibid., 474.

life, as the rural worker's place of residence, and as the centre in waging war: 'The history of classical antiquity is the history of cities, but of cities founded on landed property and on agriculture.'[95] In contrast to this, the medieval (Germanic) community was not concentrated in the city: 'The Middle Ages . . . begin with the land as the seat of history, whose further development then moves forward in the contradiction between town and countryside; the modern [age] is the urbanisation of the countryside, not ruralisation of the city as in antiquity.'[96]

On the basis of these observations, Marx and Engels analysed the contradiction between city and country in the context, on the one hand, of the division of labour between manual and intellectual labour, and, on the other, in the context of the separation of capital and landed property. They noted that the city formed the crucial condition for the formation of capital and its independent existence from landed property. A new form of property emerged whose basis existed only in labour and exchange.[97] According to Marx and Engels, the contradiction of city and country developed into the historical differentiation of two opposing modes of production and therefore played a crucial historical role in the development of capitalism.

Lefebvre saw it as one of historical materialism's essential contributions to the question of the city that it had placed this conflictual relation between city and country at the heart of the analysis. Marx, he finds, attributed the transition from feudalism to capitalism to the city, which shattered the medieval feudal system.[98] Lefebvre reconstructs three parallel conflicts in this first great struggle among Europe's main social formations: first, that of the bourgeoisie against feudal rule; then that between mobile private property and communal and landed property; and, finally, that between city and country. Something new eventually formed out of this conflict-ridden, and therefore extremely productive, moment: capitalism and the world market.[99]

For Lefebvre, however, this analysis bore the mark of its time, and therefore had its limitation within its own historical moment as well. Marx and Engels had hardly experienced the process of urbanisation:

Marx was unable to observe more than the first indications of an immense transformation. He noted the anti-natural, factitious, practically abstract character of the great modern cities, in which he saw at the same time how

---

95   Ibid., 479.
96   Ibid.
97   Marx and Engels, *The German Ideology*, 64.
98   Lefebvre, *Marxist Thought and the City*, 6, 30.
99   Ibid., 23–4, 32.

in the factories, the natural context of proletarian action, the working-class population was concentrating and becoming aware of itself.[100]

There were no answers to be found here for Lefebvre's urgent questions on urbanisation and the crisis of the city. Lefebvre noted laconically in *The Right to the City*: 'The works of Marx (notably *Capital*) contained precious indications on the city and particularly on the historical relations between town and country. They do not pose the urban problem.'[101]

The Crisis of the City

As this account shows, Lefebvre initially had no viable theory with which to analyse urbanisation. Marx and Engels had only experienced the beginning of the process, and they were unable to recognise its far-reaching historical and social significance. In contrast, urbanisation *had* been problematised in some contemporary critiques of urban development, which all confirmed a 'crisis of the city'.[102] The most influential of these critiques were the work of a team of young journalists from the American business magazine *Fortune*. They appeared between September 1957 and April 1958 as a series of articles and were published shortly thereafter in book form under the title *The Exploding Metropolis*.[103] The introduction begins with the sentence: 'This is a book by people who like cities.'[104] What follows is an urban, cosmopolitan manifesto, an engaged, well-researched critique of urbanisation and post-war urban planning in North America. The aspects considered include 'urban sprawl' and the problems of the 'car-friendly city', as well as the consequences of functional segregation and inner-city restructuring. Not long after this, Jane Jacobs, one of the authors of the *Fortune* series, took up and expanded this critique in her book, *The Death and Life of Great American Cities*, focusing in particular on urban planning. It is still one of the most well-known and influential books on the subject.

At the same time in Europe, an equally radical critique came from the Situationists, which worked at the limits of art, politics, and architecture (see section 2.1). In their texts and pamphlets, the group produced biting criticisms of the European variants of urbanisation. In *Internationale Situationniste* no. 6

---

100   Lefebvre, *Metaphilosophy*, 110.
101   Lefebvre, *Right to the City*, 130.
102   See Stanek, *Henri Lefebvre on Space*.
103   Whyte, *The Exploding Metropolis*.
104   Ibid., 7.

they identified the primary evil in contemporary functional urban design (*urbanisme*).

> Until it merges with a general revolutionary praxis, urbanism is necessarily the first enemy of all possibilities for human life in our time. It is one of those fragments of social power that claim to represent a coherent whole, and which tend to impose themselves as a total explanation and organization, while doing nothing except to mask the real social totality that has produced them and which they preserve.[105]

Against the totalitarian power of ruling urbanism, the Situationists proposed the concept of 'unitary urbanism' (*urbanisme unitaire*), a concept which complemented the other interventionist, actionist, and Situationist methods which had made the group famous, such as 'psychogeography', '*dérive*', and the 'Situationist intervention'.[106]

Lefebvre knew these texts, and they clearly made a deep impression on him. He mentions *The Exploding Metropolis* as early as his *Metaphilosophy*, and refers to Jane Jacobs in *The Production of Space*.[107] He also knew the Situationists' critique very well, as some of them had been students of his in Strasbourg (see section 2.1). Urbanisation was one of the key points of their discussions at that time, and their positions on urbanism were reflected in Lefebvre's biting critique of post-war functionalist urban design (see section 6.3).[108] Lefebvre's first reflections on the process of urbanisation are largely embedded in these early critiques of modern urban planning. However, he also placed his own analysis in the wider context of the contradiction between city and country, as defined by Marx and Engels. He identified a twofold process engulfing both city and country which led to the transformation of both and changed the nature of the contradiction: a worldwide crisis of the traditional city accompanied, incorporated, and exacerbated a worldwide crisis in traditional agriculture.[109] Thus, he analyses urbanisation from a double perspective: on the one hand, he looks at how rural areas are transformed by urbanisation, and, on the other, he observes how the city loses both its autonomy and its distinct form.

---

105 Situationist International, 'Editorial Notes: Critique of Urbanism', 103.
106 See for example Sadler, *The Situationist City*; Pinder, *Visions of the City*.
107 Lefebvre, *Metaphilosophy*, 111n4; Lefebvre, *Production of Space*, 364.
108 On this, see also Hess, *Henri Lefebvre et l'aventure du siècle*, 214–16.
109 Lefebvre, *Right to the City*, 126.

The Urban Fabric and the Explosion of the City

During his years studying farming communities in the western Pyrenees, Lefebvre had already observed that the industrialisation of agriculture dominated all other problems, and that the associated loss of autonomy in agricultural production would result in a fundamental transformation of rural space.[110] This process led to depopulation and at the same time to the 'depeasantisation' (*dépaysannisation*) of the areas that were still rural. They were robbed of those very elements that once constituted country life: traditional trades, crafts, and small local centres. The traditional community of peasant life, the village, was losing its rural specificity and was being absorbed into larger social units.[111]

From these observations, Lefebvre developed a view of the future in the mid-1960s whose relevance remains undiminished even at the beginning of the twenty-first century:

> In a short time from now, in the most developed regions and countries, the rural population will undoubtedly have disappeared, making way for town-dwellers engaged in agricultural production with improved methods and industrial technologies. Agriculture is being aligned with industry, and steadily ceasing to constitute a distinct sector of the economy, almost autonomous on account of its technical backwardness. Cities and agro-cities will replace villages, reduced to an antediluvian, folkloric or touristic existence.[112]

Lefebvre uses harsh words to describe this process: the expanding cities invade, corrode, and dissolve the countryside.[113] In order to grasp this process, he borrows a term from semiotics which he uses in an intentionally metaphorical way: the 'urban fabric' (*tissu urbain*). 'The urban fabric grows, extends its borders, corrodes the residue of agrarian life.'[114] Lefebvre does not define this term clearly and does not limit its meaning only to morphology: the urban fabric, he writes, forms the economic basis of urban society, the (material) support through which urban life pervades rural areas.[115]

---

110   Lefebvre, *Du rural à l'urbain*, 9.
111   Lefebvre, *Right to the City*, 76; Lefebvre, *Urban Revolution*, 3.
112   Lefebvre, *Metaphilosophy*, 110–11.
113   Lefebvre, *Right to the City*, 122–3.
114   Lefebvre, *Urban Revolution*, 3.
115   Lefebvre, *Right to the City*, 71.

This expression, 'urban fabric', does not narrowly define the built world of cities but all manifestations of the dominance of the city over the country. In this sense, a vacation home, a highway, a supermarket in the countryside, are all part of the urban fabric.[116]

A whole urban system of material objects and infrastructure is realised as part of this fabric: water supply, electricity, gas, automobiles, television, plastic utensils, 'modern' furniture. An urban system of values also develops parallel to this: urban amenities, urban clothing, the rapid adoption of new fashions as well as a mode of rationality spread through urbanisation. Lefebvre calls these 'sociological trivialities', although he notes that they have far-reaching implications.[117]

This does not necessarily lead, as Lefebvre points out, to a homogenisation of space: the *tissu urbain* is more or less densely spun, and smaller and larger islands of 'rurality' (*ruralité*) survive between its meshes; hamlets, villages, even entire regions stagnate or decay and remain reserved for 'nature'.[118]

Urbanisation not only transforms traditional agrarian societies, however, it also leads to fundamental changes in cities. From this inverse perspective, the phenomenon of urbanisation manifests itself in the expansion of urban agglomerations, in the extension of urban networks of banks, trade, and industry, and in the emergence of remote urban peripheries (such as residential areas packed with second homes).[119] Lefebvre sees cities everywhere splintering, whether in the developing world, in highly industrialised countries, or in state socialism.

As this global process of industrialization and urbanization was taking place, the large cities exploded, giving rise to growths of dubious value: suburbs, residential conglomerations and industrial complexes, satellite cities that differed little from urbanized towns. Small and midsize cities became dependencies, partial colonies of the metropolis.[120]

These observations led Lefebvre to the 'most extreme of all' hypotheses, which he borrowed from *The Exploding Metropolis*:[121]

---

116   Lefebvre, *Urban Revolution*, 3–4.
117   Lefebvre, *Right to the City*, 72.
118   Ibid., 71–2; Lefebvre, *Urban Revolution*, 4.
119   Lefebvre, *Right to the City*, 71.
120   Lefebvre, *Urban Revolution*, 4.
121   Whyte, *The Exploding Metropolis*.

By the process of growth, the city has itself shattered; it is perhaps in the process of disappearing. This is a hypothesis not exempt from risk, not verified up until now, but seductive and fruitful, precisely as an extreme strategic hypothesis.[122]

The Strategic Hypothesis

With the two theses of the explosion of the city and the expansion of the urban fabric over the countryside, Lefebvre had found his first principles for analysing urbanisation. Evolving from his initial Marxist analysis of the contradiction between city and country, both theses indicate that the 'urban question' – on a planetary scale – contains a dual crisis: a crisis of the city and a crisis of agrarian civilisation. Both crises appear at once and transform each other. While the practical and ideological foundations as well as the manifest forms of these dual crises differ according to political regime and the social relations in individual countries, they nevertheless call society as a whole into question.[123]

A point of convergence appears when the double crises of city and country are considered together. Lefebvre argues that world society is approaching a critical point in which the contradictions between city and country will be dialectically sublated: 'In the highly industrialized countries, the ancient conflictual relationship between town and country . . . is tending today to be resolved in an unexpected fashion. The town absorbs the countryside – though not without the resistance of those affected, or without convulsions.'[124]

Lefebvre creates a new 'strategic hypothesis' from these observations. At the very beginning of *The Urban Revolution* he postulates *the complete urbanisation of society*. This extreme thesis, the conclusion of insights and observations gathered over a long period, now serves as a starting point for a new investigation and for the drafting of a new theory of urbanisation. It signals a paradigmatic shift on the theoretical level: the analytical perspective shifts from the city as 'object' to the process of urbanisation.

'The hypothesis is anticipatory. It prolongs the fundamental tendency of the present.'[125] Lefebvre's 'strategic hypothesis' even surpasses the Marxian principle of comprehending the past with the most developed categories of the present: it projects the current tendency into the future in order to illuminate

---

122 Lefebvre, *Metaphilosophy*, 111.
123 Lefebvre, *Right to the City*, 145.
124 Lefebvre, *Metaphilosophy*, 110.
125 Lefebvre, *Urban Revolution*, 4.

the present.[126] If both the 'city' and the 'country' are in the process of dissolving, this tends towards a (virtual, because only anticipated) point of convergence that indicates the complete urbanisation of society and eventually announces the transition to the 'urban society'.

What does this hypothesis imply? It postulates, first of all, society's complete urbanisation in both spatial and sectoral terms: it includes, on the one hand, all aspects of society, and, on the other, the entire globe. 'The urban problematic is worldwide . . . Urban society can only be defined as planetary.'[127]

At the same time, the hypothesis entails a definition, that of the 'urban society': 'An "urban society" is a society that results from a process of complete urbanisation. This urbanisation is virtual today, but will become real in the future.'[128] Lefebvre uses the term 'urban society' only for societies that result from industrialisation, a process that dominates and absorbs agricultural production. With this definition, Lefebvre is able to eliminate the ambiguity and vagueness of the term 'urban', under which all kinds of cities had long been subsumed – the Greek polis, the oriental and medieval city, the commercial and industrial city, the town and the megalopolis.[129] This is a decisive distinction from other definitions that attempt to give the terms 'urbanisation' and 'urban society' a universal, transhistorical meaning (see section 1.1).

It is tremendously important to understand how Lefebvre defines the concept of the 'urban society' or, succinctly, 'the urban'. Lefebvre uses the term 'the urban' (*l'urbain*) explicitly as an abbreviation of 'urban society': 'the urban' does not express a final state, a fait accompli, but rather a tendency, a direction, a virtual reality.[130] Lefebvre constructs the urban society as a 'virtual object' which stands for urban life and urban reality, but which is, in its essence, incomplete. It is a possibility, a potential, a 'reflection of the future', which illuminates the horizon and invites realisation: the reality of the phenomenon of urbanisation constitutes itself as a virtual object, an urban society that covers the entire earth.[131]

The urban society is therefore both a hypothesis and a definition, referring to an 'object' who might not yet be existent:

Even though this 'object' is located outside any (empirical) fact, it is not fictional. We can assume the existence of a virtual object, urban society;

---

126   Ibid., 23.
127   Ibid., 166–7. Translation amended.
128   Ibid., 1.
129   Ibid.
130   Ibid., 16.
131   Ibid., 3, 16, 60, 161; Lefebvre, *Right to the City*, 165.

that is, a possible object, whose growth and development can be analysed in relation to a process and a praxis (practical activity).[132]

Towards an Epistemology of the Urban

The urban is on the rise and is slowly taking hold of the realm of epistemology to become an episteme of the time. 'History and the historic grow further apart. Psychoanalysis and linguistics, like economy and politics, reach their apogee and begin to decline. The urban begins its ascendance.'[133]

What does the urban comprise? At first, it is withdrawn from view. It constitutes a 'blind field' (champ aveugle). This paradoxical combination of a subjective word – blind – and an objective designation – field – is conceived neither as a literary image nor as a metaphor. It marks what is blinding and what is blinded, what knowledge misconceives and misrecognises. This blind field thus also involves the power of ideology and the power of language. It presents itself to be studied: as a virtual reality for knowledge and as a possibility for action.[134]

From this angle, Lefebvre identifies a new meaning of the 'crisis of the city': This crisis marks a critical zone, and with it a transition. In this zone, the terrain evaporates under our feet: 'Within this zone, the terrain flies before us, the ground is booby-trapped. Although the old concepts no longer work, new concepts are beginning to take shape. Reality isn't the only thing to go; thought itself begins to give way.'[135] The crisis of the city thus contains a moment of possibility: it allows new aspects of urban reality to emerge, shining light upon what had been poorly understood, and revealing what was badly conceived.[136]

The critical zone, the blind field, reveals a gap: the lack of an epistemology of the urban. The source of this gap is not only the 'blindness' of industrial logic, but also, as Lefebvre notes, the organisation of knowledge production, the parcelling out and specialisation of knowledge. The 'science of the city', he finds, takes its methods, experiments, and concepts from partial sciences, thereby making its synthesis doubly fleeting: on the one hand, it can only achieve a systemisation and strategic programming by means of its partial analyses. On the other hand, by relying on these partial analyses, its object, the city, disintegrates. Cognition, he continues, sees before it an already-changed

---

132 Lefebvre, *Urban Revolution*, 3, see also 5, 16.
133 Ibid., 191.
134 Ibid., 30–1, 166–7.
135 Ibid., 166.
136 Lefebvre, *Right to the City*, 100.

historical city, but then parcel it in order to assemble it again from the resulting analytical fragments.[137]

> What does this analytical practice retain of the city and the urban whose results one can detect on the ground? Aspects, elements and fragments. It places before our eyes the spectre, the spectral analysis of the city. When we speak of spectral analysis, its meaning is almost literal and not metaphorical.[138]

And even more explicitly:

> Before our eyes, under our gaze, we have the 'spectre' of the city, that of urban society and perhaps simply of society. If the spectre of Communism no longer haunts Europe, the shadow of the city, the regret of what has died because it was killed, perhaps guilt, have replaced the old dread. The image of urban hell in the making is not less fascinating, and people rush towards the ruins of ancient cities to consume them touristically, in the belief that they will heal their nostalgia.[139]

The dominant scientific industry can therefore only produce a spectral analysis of the city, or a 'spectre' of the city – Lefebvre plays here with the dual meaning of the French word *le spectre,* which can mean both spectrum and spectre. The urban, he claims, cannot be expressed through the separation of content into fragments, nor through their murky unification. 'The urban phenomenon is universal, which would be sufficient justification for the creation of a university devoted to analytic research on the subject.'[140]

To understand the urban would require a complete reading which would bring different, partial readings together. For what is at issue here is a totality – the totality of urban society.[141] This totality cannot be grasped directly, only step by step: a difficult advance, where obstacles must be avoided and risks must be accepted at every step.[142] The concept of totality plays an important role in Lefebvre's work and is not limited to the urban question. It is discussed in more detail by Jens Peter Schwab and Kanishka Goonewardena.[143]

---

137   Ibid., 106, 126; Lefebvre, *Urban Revolution*, 6–7.
138   Lefebvre, *Right to the City*, 142.
139   Ibid., 142–3.
140   Lefebvre, *Urban Revolution*, 54.
141   Ibid., 18, 49, 56, 173–4.
142   Ibid., 49.
143   See Schwab, '*L'homme total*'; Goonewardena, 'Planetary Urbanization and Totality'.

Urbanisation, Urban Society, Urban Practice

With the thesis of the complete urbanisation of society, Lefebvre defines a process (urbanisation), a virtual object (urban society) which points towards the end point of this process, and a concrete (urban practice), which leads to this end point. He thus identifies the virtual, the future and utopian starting point, from which he will analyse the process of urbanisation.

From today's point of view, this thesis may seem banal. It should be kept in mind, however, that it was formulated in 1970, at a time when the phenomenon of urbanisation was hardly discussed in public discourse and in scientific research. In addition, this thesis has to be understood comprehensively. For Lefebvre, urbanisation does not simply mean the geographical extension of cities; it involves complex, multi-layered, and contradictory processes that include cultural, social, economic, and linguistic aspects. In retrospect, this thesis can be characterised as truly visionary.

Having started from the vanishing point of this thesis, Lefebvre embarks on a journey through time to analyse the historical dimensions of the 'phenomenon of urbanisation'. The term 'phenomenon' is chosen deliberately: Lefebvre initially approaches the urbanisation process phenomenologically, in a certain sense. He discovers a phenomenon that presents itself to him as a comprehensive reality that contains the totality of social practices. This reality cannot be understood directly; it is not immediately apparent.[144] Lefebvre therefore approaches this unknown 'phenomenon of urbanisation' from different perspectives and tries to narrow it down and define it through two analytical operations: the construction of a space-time 'axis' of urbanisation and the definition of three spatio-temporal 'fields', comprehensive modes of thinking, acting, and living: the rural, the industrial, and the urban. The following two sections deal with these two ways to grasp the urban in turn.

3.3 The Space-Time Axis of Urbanisation

We can draw an axis as follows:
0------------100%[145]

Lefebvre starts his analysis of the urbanisation process with a historical reconstruction. The object of analysis is the (Western) 'city', which was the starting

---

144   Lefebvre, *Urban Revolution*, 50, 61–2.
145   Ibid., 7.

point for the strategic hypothesis of the complete urbanisation of society presented above. This analytical operation follows the regressive–progressive method Lefebvre had developed in his analysis of everyday rural life (see section 3.1). With this method, he first descends from the present to the past, in order to explore the genealogy of a process or phenomenon, and then, in a second step, reconstructs its genesis in an ascending movement. In his analysis of urbanisation, however, he starts in the future, which he has already illuminated with his thesis of complete urbanisation, and then proceeds in the descending, regressive movement from the prospective and virtual to the present and from there to the past. He subsequently performs an ascending, progressive analysis going from the obsolete and terminated to the new and open.[146]

In his reconstruction, Lefebvre begins by drawing an axis: from the degree zero of urbanisation, 'pure nature', to the complete urbanisation of society. This axis begins with the non-existence of the city, the complete dominance of the countryside, of peasant life and agricultural production, and ends with 100 per cent urbanisation, the absorption of the countryside by the city, the complete domination of industrial production, even in agriculture:

> This axis is both spatial and temporal: spatial because the process extends through space, which it modifies; temporal because it develops over time. Temporality, initially of secondary importance, eventually becomes the predominant aspect of practice and history.[147]

The Political City

Where is the degree zero of urbanisation? Lefebvre locates it as the domain of hunter-gatherers who marked and named space, invented field names, and set landmarks. The transition to settled life and the foundation of the village went hand in hand with the generation of local agriculture, craft production, the beginnings of child rearing.[148] Lefebvre notes, however, that almost everywhere in the world, the city accompanies or closely follows the establishment of organised social life, agriculture, and the village:

> The representation according to which cultivated land, the village, and farm civilisation slowly secreted urban reality reflects an ideology . . .

---

146   Ibid., 23–4.
147   Ibid., 7; see also Lefebvre, *Right to the City*, 122.
148   Lefebvre, *Metaphilosophy*, 8–9; Lefebvre, *Urban Revolution*, 7.

Agriculture was little more than gathering, and was only formalized through pressure (authoritarian) from the urban centres, generally occupied by skilful conquerors who had become protectors, exploiters, and oppressors, that is, administrators, the founders of a state, or the rudiments of a state.[149]

This claim, which, among other things, refers to the high cultures of Mesopotamia and Egypt, was based primarily on analyses of the 'Asiatic mode of production', especially by the critical geographer Karl August Wittfogel, a member of the Frankfurt School. Although Lefebvre also mentions works by French Marxist anthropologists Jean Chesneaux and Maurice Godelier, he neglects many examples of alternative paths of development, such as in Africa or South East Asia.

Lefebvre calls this first form of the city the 'political city' and places it at the beginning of the space-time axis. What are this city's traits? 'It is completely given over to orders and decrees, to power.'[150] It was inhabited by the nobility, priesthood, and warrior class and dominated what was often a vast agricultural area. It lived off this land, taking the fruits of the fields and farm work as its tribute. It therefore had a double character in relation to the countryside: it was the seat of a social group which, on the one hand, collected the surplus product of rural society, and on the other hand it was equipped with administrative and military power and thus also provided a protective function. Sometimes one aspect would become more important, sometimes the other.[151]

In this way, the city lived in an often difficult symbiosis with the rural space it controlled. The city-state established a firm centre, a centre in time and in space, constituting itself as a place of privilege surrounded by a periphery that bore its stamp:

The town seems to gather in everything which surrounds it, including the natural and the divine, and the earth's evil and good forces. As image of the universe (*imago mundi*), urban space is reflected in the rural space that it possesses and indeed in a sense *contains*. Over and above its economic, religious and political content, therefore, this relationship already embodies an element of symbolism, of image and reflection: the town perceives itself in its double, in its repercussions or echo; in self-affirmation, from the height of its towers, its gates and its campaniles, it

---

149   Lefebvre, *Urban Revolution*, 8.
150   Ibid.
151   Lefebvre, *Production of Space*, 234–5; Lefebvre, *Urban Revolution*, 8; Lefebvre, *Right to the City*, 118–19.

contemplates itself in the countryside that it has shaped – that is to say, in its work. The town and its surroundings thus constitute a *texture*.[152]

The political state thus formed an economic, religious, and political centre, and, in most cases, stood in a conflictual relationship to the country around it. The separation of city and country corresponded to the division of labour between material and intellectual work. The functions of organisation and leadership, political and military activities, philosophy and science were concentrated in the city. Correspondingly, the city became the seat of Logos: in contrast to rurality, the country life exposed to nature, the sacred earth and its dark power, urbanity presented itself as reasonable and decent. Reason had its birthplace and its homestead in the city.[153]

The Merchant City

The cities, thanks to the growing surplus of agricultural products, began to accumulate objects, treasures, and capital, but also knowledge, techniques, and artistic objects (artworks, monuments). Bartering and trade rose in importance. Nevertheless, trade remained a 'low' occupation for hundreds of years, one which was banished to particular districts or even to the space beyond the city gates. The process of integrating the market and goods into the city took centuries, and it only ended when the city itself was integrated into a social structure based on exchange, long-distance communication, and money:

> The political city resists this with all the power at its disposal, all its cohesiveness; it feels, knows, that it is threatened by markets, merchandise, and traders, by their form of ownership (money, a form of personal property, being movable by definition) . . . In truth, it is only in the European West, at the end of the Middle Ages, that merchandise, the market, and merchants were able to successfully penetrate the city.[154]

Over the course of the long struggle between merchants and the landed aristocracy, which turned out to be very productive, particularly in the West, trade developed into an urban function. The market replaced the public gathering space (agora, forum) and established itself as the centre between the church

---

152   Lefebvre, *Production of Space*, 235, see also 234.
153   Lefebvre, *Right to the City*, 81, 143.
154   Lefebvre, *Urban Revolution*, 9; Lefebvre, *Right to the City*, 89, 122.

and the town hall. 'Architecture follows and translates the new conception of the city. Urban space becomes the meeting place for goods and people, for exchange. It bears the signs of this conquered liberty, which is perceived as Liberty – a grandiose but hopeless struggle.'[155] And, so, the merchant city appears in Europe in the fourteenth century, grafted onto the political city. It marked an approximate midpoint in the space-time axis of urbanisation.[156]

With the upswing of merchant capital, an event occurred at some point which remained unnoticed, despite the consequences it would have: a society founded on the land and land ownership had metamorphosed into a society dominated by the money economy. At the very moment when the significance of agricultural production fell below the significance of craft production, the market and exchange value appeared, the first critical phase and a tipping point in the history of urbanisation. This point can be situated in Europe in the sixteenth century: the city got the upper hand over the country, not only in economic and political terms but also in social terms. It was an event which could not be given a date; it was not an institutional shift and it was not a process that could be clearly identified by economic measurements – there was never an absolute break. But, in a few decades, depending on the perspective, everything had changed – or everything continued as before.[157] The city grew in significance in the social order to such an extent that this order fell apart:

> From this moment on, the city would no longer appear as an urban island in a rural ocean, it would no longer seem a paradox, a monster, a hell or heaven that contrasted sharply with village or country life in a natural environment. It entered people's awareness and understanding as one of the terms in the opposition between town and country. Country? It is now no more than – nothing more than – the town's 'environment', its horizon, its limit. Villagers? As far as they were concerned, they no longer worked for the territorial lords; they produced for the city, for the urban market. And even though they realized that the wheat and wood merchants exploited them, they understood that the path to freedom crossed the marketplace.[158]

This fundamental transformation went together with a change in thinking. Thinking human beings no longer saw themselves as part of nature, of a dark

---

155   Lefebvre, *Urban Revolution*, 10.
156   Ibid., 11, 13.
157   Lefebvre, *De l'État*, vol. 3, 13; Lefebvre, *Production of Space*, 268–9; Lefebvre, *Urban Revolution*, 12; Lefebvre, *Right to the City*, 120.
158   Lefebvre, *Urban Revolution*, 11.

world, at the mercy of mysterious powers. The reality of the city became an important mediator between nature and humans' thinking and being. For Lefebvre, this was related to the rise of reason: 'The logos was reborn, but its rebirth was not attributed to the renaissance of the urban world but to transcendent reason. The rationalism that culminated in Descartes accompanied the reversal that replaced the primacy of the peasantry with the priority of urban life.'[159] An expression of this reversal was the emergence of the image of the city and the development of its own form of writing: the map. The first city maps appeared in the sixteenth and seventeenth centuries.

> These are not yet abstract maps, projections of urban space onto geometric coordinates. A cross between vision and concept, works of art and science, they displayed the city from top to bottom, in perspective, painted, depicted, and geometrically described. This perspective, simultaneously idealist and realist – the perspective of thought and power – was situated in the vertical dimension, the dimension of knowledge and reason, and dominated and constituted a totality: the city.[160]

The Industrial City

The transition from a mercantile and banking capitalism to one of competition, and from craft production to industrial production, was accompanied by a massive crisis which also affected the city. Industry posed a new analytical problem: what was the nature of its connection to the city? Initially, industrial plants were mainly established outside the city. As Lefebvre writes, industry was no longer dependent on a concrete place to the same extent as agriculture was, but it was nevertheless still subject to concrete conditions. Industrial plants were located according to the availability of energy sources (rivers, wood, coal), raw materials, means of transport (rivers and canals, and, later, railways), and labour power.[161] In the city, industry found itself in the proximity of capital, the market, and abundant and cheap labour. The city, like the workshop, allowed for the concentration of the means of production, of tools and machinery, raw materials and workers. In the end, it made no difference where industry was established – it could be located anywhere, 'but sooner or later made its way into existing cities or created new cities'.[162]

---

159   Ibid., 12.
160   Ibid., 12–13.
161   Ibid., 13, 117; Lefebvre, *Right to the City*, 68–9.
162   Lefebvre, *Urban Revolution*, 13.

With the rise of industry and the expansion of the market, the historical city was attacked from all sides. What had kept it distinct and separated it from the rural surroundings – the ramparts, guilds, local oligarchies, small markets – dissolved. Over the course of a process reaching enormous proportions, capitalism took hold of the historical city, smashed it into pieces, and created a new social space whose material basis was formed from private enterprise and the division of labour.[163]

In this dramatic transformation, urban reality lost the characteristics ascribed to it in the preceding epoch: an organic whole, an inspiring image, a space which is dominated and ordered by splendid edifices. Urban reality morphed into command: a repressive order, dominated by signals, signs, and rules (such as traffic rules). Buying and selling, commodities and markets, money and capital seemed to sweep all obstacles out of their way. The industrial city thus often became a formless agglomeration with little urban character, a conglomerate of cities and settlements.[164] Does the city even still exist? 'It is a phantom, a shadow of urban reality, a spectral analysis of dispersed and external elements that have been reunited through constraint.'[165]

Urbanisation revealed itself in a double movement: it was on the one side a monstrous expansion of urban fragments; on the other a 'conquest' and a partial destruction of the historical city as it had existed before capitalism.[166] In order to describe this double historical process, which no one expression can completely capture, Lefebvre borrows a metaphor from atomic physics: implosion–explosion. It is 'the tremendous concentration (of people, activities, wealth, goods, objects, instruments, means, and thought) of urban reality and the immense explosion, the projection of numerous, disjointed fragments (peripheries, suburbs, vacation homes, satellite towns) into space'.[167]

The industrial city thus marks a rupture in the reality of the city.

Yet something strange and wonderful was also taking place, which helped renew dialectical thought: the non-city and the anti-city would conquer the city, penetrate it, break it apart, and in so doing extend it immeasurably, bringing about the urbanisation of society and the growth of the urban fabric that covered what was left of the city prior to the arrival of industry.[168]

---

163 Lefebvre, *Production of Space*, 364; Lefebvre, *Survival of Capitalism*, 26.
164 Lefebvre, *Urban Revolution*, 14.
165 Ibid., 35.
166 Lefebvre, *De l'État*, vol. 4, 265.
167 Lefebvre, *Urban Revolution*, 14.
168 Ibid., 13–14.

As the urbanisation process finally approaches the 100 per cent point on the space-time axis, a second critical phase or zone announces itself, a second tipping point. The implosion–explosion can also be seen as a prelude on the way to the urban society. It is a part of the problematic of this society as well as the critical phase that announces this problematic.[169]

The City as a Historic Configuration

The space-time axis of urbanisation is discussed at length here because it contains the key to Lefebvre's understanding of the urban society. From today's perspective, it might appear to be a rhetorically impressive, but not very original and indeed quite Eurocentric, outline of the development of the city, a sketch that postulates a seemingly one-dimensional line of development from the Greek city-state through the medieval city to the industrial city of Western Europe. As Lefebvre himself admits, the 'historic city' described here borrows significantly from the history of Paris.[170] This Eurocentric view does not only result in an inadmissible generalisation and simplification of the historical process of urban development. It also creates substantial problems for understanding the enormous multiplicity of urban forms and processes. Lefebvre's view is thus justifiably and sharply criticised in various recent texts, particularly by Kipfer, Goonewardena, and Tang.[171]

Additionally, Lefebvre's account depends heavily on Marx's and Engels's preliminary observations on the Western city (see section 3.2): Lefebvre's 'political city' corresponds to the 'classical city of antiquity' in Marx, the city as the centre of rural life based on land holdings and agriculture. The (medieval) 'merchant city' is the birthplace of capitalism, and thus also the site of the initial confrontations between the aristocracy and the bourgeoisie. Finally, the industrial city is based, as Engels had written, on the concentration of labour power and the means of production, thus forming a privileged stage for the class struggle between the bourgeoisie and the proletariat. This reconstruction is obviously derived, as Lefebvre acknowledged, from the classic periodisation of (Western) history sketched by Marx and Engels and later cemented in Marxist orthodoxy: ancient modes of production, feudalism, merchant capitalism, industrial capitalism, monopoly capitalism. From this we can also deduce a direct relationship between modes of production

---

169   Ibid., 169–70.
170   Lefebvre, *De l'État*, vol. 4, 265.
171   See for example Kipfer, 'The Fractures of Worldwide Urbanization'; Goonewardena, 'The Country and the City'; Tang, 'Where Lefebvre Meets the East'.

and urban development (on this see sections 6.6 and 7.4). And Lefebvre indeed makes the claim that

> each mode of production has 'produced' (not in the sense of any ordinary thing but as a privileged work) a type of city, which 'expresses' it in a way that is immediately visible and legible on the environment, by making the most abstract relationships – legal, political, ideological – tangible.[172]

Lefebvre's analysis nevertheless contains much more than a trite reconstruction of a one-dimensional 'model of development': it is an attempt to understand the 'city' as a historic configuration. Considered in its historical movement, the city has undergone critical phases: 'destructurations and restructurations' follow one another in time and space.[173] He thus also makes clear that the 'city' and the 'city-country opposition' change radically over time, and with this the dominating and defining social contradictions are also transformed. Neither 'city' nor 'country' nor their mutual relationship can be defined in a universal way. This insight has massive consequences for the understanding of the urban (see sections 1.1 and 3.5).

Lefebvre's account of the historical development of the 'city' is therefore not to be taken at face value: it should be conceived, rather, as the development of a concept, as a 'figure of thought', as a guiding principle, which more powerfully emphasises the phenomenon of urbanisation. As he notes,

> In this book I have not, for the most part, followed the historical method as it is generally understood. Superficially it may appear that I have been describing and analysing the genesis of the city as object and its modifications and transformations. But my initial concern has been with a virtual object, which I have used to describe a space-time axis. The future illuminates the past, the virtual allows us to examine and situate the realized.[174]

Sublating the Contradiction between City and Country

The end point of Lefebvre's analysis, the second critical phase, is therefore decisive in the space-time axis of urbanisation. Here the contradiction between city and country nears the point of its dialectical sublation. This is where the

---

172 Lefebvre, *Urban Revolution*, 24.
173 Lefebvre, *Right to the City*, 106.
174 Lefebvre, *Urban Revolution*, 23.

fundamentally novel character of Lefebvre's analysis comes to the fore in relation to the debates on urban development of his time: his space-time axis
reveals a historical movement from 'nature' to the city–country contradiction
and, finally, to the sublation of this contradiction.

In dialectical thinking, the two configurations of 'country' and 'city' can
only emerge as a mutually contradictory pair that constantly transform one
another (see section 2.3). First, Lefebvre shows us the city as an island,
surrounded by the ocean of the countryside. Then a precarious balance develops in which the two worlds face one another as equals. In the first critical
phase, with the rise of trade and craft production and the beginning of capitalism, the balance tips in favour of the city. The city finally explodes during
industrialisation, spreading over the country and announcing the arrival of the
second critical phase.

What happens to the contradiction between city and country in this second
critical phase? How is this contradiction sublated? For Marx and Engels, the
sublation of this contradiction was one of the first conditions for the creation
of the (communist) collective, and Engels had even explicitly insisted that the
elimination of the metropolises was a precondition for this development.[175] In
the *Communist Manifesto*, Marx and Engels demanded in their ninth measure
the combination of agricultural and industrial production and the gradual
abolition (not sublation) of the difference between town and country. According
to the classical Marxist view, this abolition was supposed to lead to a tendency
towards urban villages or country towns, with industrial settlements spread
equally over the land – a vision which in part became (an often unfortunate)
reality in 'actually existing socialism'.[176]

Lefebvre sees the sublation of this contradiction in a completely different,
radical light: industrialisation generates a process of urbanisation that leads to
the negation of the country and the dissolution of the city, that is, not to a
compromised synthesis, but to a completely new constitution of the urban.
Urbanisation as the end of both city and countryside? Would this be the unexpected conclusion of the sublation of the city–country dialectic postulated by
Marx and Engels? In his typically dialectic style Lefebvre answers both yes and
no:

Will the urban fabric, with its greater or lesser meshes, catch in its nets
all the territory of industrialized countries? Is this how the old

---

175   On the conditions for the formation of the collective, see Marx and Engels, *The
German Ideology*, 64; on the elimination of the metropolises, see Engels, *Anti-Dühring*, 283.
176   On the classical Marxist urban vision, see Schnaidt, 'Les marxistes ont-ils un projet
urbain?'.

opposition between town and country is overcome? One can assume it, but not without some critical reservations. If a generalized confusion is thus perceived, the countryside losing itself into the heart of the city, and the city absorbing the countryside and losing itself in it, this confusion can be theoretically challenged. Theory can refute all strategies resting on this conception of the urban fabric. Geographers have coined to name this confusion an ugly but meaningful neologism: the rurban. Within this hypothesis, the expansion of the city and urbanization would cause the urban (the urban life) to disappear. This seems inadmissible. In other words, the overcoming of opposition cannot be conceived as a reciprocal neutralization ... The 'urbanity–rurality' opposition is accentuated rather than dissipated, while the town and country opposition is lessened. There is a shifting of opposition and conflict.[177]

The contradiction is thus deferred: while the opposition of city and country diminishes, the opposition between 'the urban' and 'the rural' intensifies. This means that neither the urban nor the rural can be understood any longer in their conventional categories. On the one hand, city and country should not be reduced to a static spatial morphology, as they are integral parts of society. On the other hand, however, they cannot be understood as aligned with two different modes of production, as they had been in Marx's and Engels's analysis, as they are both now dominated by industrialisation. The contradictions are no longer to be found between city and country. The essential contradiction must be sought within the phenomenon of urbanisation itself.[178]

Lefebvre's historical reconstruction of urbanisation breaks off, however, at the point of the industrial city, the 'anti-city'. Thus, the central question remains open: what happens in the second critical phase, when urbanisation approaches the 100 per cent mark? This question points to two interrelated problems: first, in relation to the urban society, whose character and internal contradictions must be more closely specified. This aspect will be explored in the next section. Second, the problem of the spatial form of the urban arises: what is the role of the city – or: what is the city – in the urban society? This question is the subject of chapter 4.

---

177 Lefebvre, *Right to the City*, 120.
178 Lefebvre, *Urban Revolution*, 170.

3.4 The Urban Society

> Life has not yet begun.[179]
> Urban life has yet to begin.[180]
> The period of urban revolutions has begun.[181]

Lefebvre's first attempt at defining the phenomenon of urbanisation considered the city as a historical configuration. Its main insight was that of the dialectical sublation of the city–country contradiction: urbanisation proves to be a 'total' phenomenon that encompasses the entire society, and thus both 'the city' and 'the country'.[182]

This insight, however, leads to the loss of the object of analysis: the city spreads over the entire territory and in this sense can only be understood as a total social phenomenon. This necessitates a second attempt at defining urbanisation, one which does not depend on the historical category of the city and instead draws on the nature of society as a whole. If the city or the city–country contradiction stood at the centre of the first (historical) analysis, a broader scope of analysis, covering the entire society, is necessary for the second step. Lefebvre changes his lens, as it were: from the city *in* a particular society to the urban *as* society.

Lefebvre identifies three spatio-temporal 'fields' or 'continents' in this second analytical operation: the rural, the industrial, and the urban. He sees these three fields or continents, which he sometimes calls layers, epochs, or moments, as fields of forces and conflicts characterised by specific social contradictions and confrontations.[183] They form, so to speak, projection screens on which not only social phenomena become visible, but also sensations and perceptions, time and space, image and representation, language and rationality, social theories and social practices.[184]

Three Spatio-Temporal Continents

As Lefebvre points out, the spatio-temporal fields or continents emerge in the dynamics of social development and can be discovered historically – like

---

179 Lefebvre, *Metaphilosophy*, 105.
180 Lefebvre, *Right to the City*, 150.
181 Lefebvre, *Urban Revolution*, 43.
182 Ibid., 48.
183 Ibid., 28, 30.
184 Ibid., 28–9, 32.

mathematics, physics, or history.[185] With this passage Lefebvre refers directly to Louis Althusser without, however, even mentioning him. Althusser had postulated that Marx opened up a 'continent of human knowledge', the continent of history, analogous to the contributions of Thales to mathematics or Galileo to physics.[186]

In contrast to Althusser, however, Lefebvre understands these continents in a much more encompassing sense as modes of thinking, acting, and living. They should not be understood as successive or overlapping layers of facts and phenomena, and there are no 'ruptures': these continents can coexist, in time *and* space.[187] This is another allusion to Althusser, who postulated in *For Marx* an 'epistemological rupture' between the works of the young ('Hegelian') Marx and his later ('scientific') writings, which opened up the 'continent of history'.

For Lefebvre, however, these continents are not conceived or discovered, but emerge in a historical process, a process he had described in another context (the reproduction of relations of production; see section 7.3):

> It is not the kind of continent which a navigator or solitary explorer sees looming out of the mist. It rises from the waves. The navigator cannot conjure it up with some magic spell; he has to pilot his ship into the midst of the reefs in order to reach the continent as it rises. No one can claim the distinction of having discovered it themselves.[188]

And elsewhere in the same book, in similarly poetic words: 'Neither the adventurer in knowledge nor the mere recorder of facts can sight this "continent" before actually exploring it.'[189] Lefebvre here implies that there is a dialectical relationship between the production of knowledge and social development. These 'continents' equally designate both concept and reality. The concept emerges along with its 'object', and cannot be constructed, but only arises from a multidimensional practice.[190]

Lefebvre differentiates three such spatio-temporal fields or continents: the rural, the industrial, and the urban. These fields, as with the space-time axis of urbanisation, indicate not only a historical progression, but also a spatial juxtaposition: these fields are superposed, telescoped, and sometimes absorbed into one another. As an example, Lefebvre mentions the countries of the 'third world', which experience the rural, the industrial, and the urban field all at

---

185   Ibid., 32.
186   Althusser, 'Lenin and Philosophy', 22.
187   Lefebvre, *Urban Revolution*, 32.
188   Lefebvre, *Survival of Capitalism*, 59.
189   Ibid., 7.
190   Ibid., 59.

once.[191] These three fields can then also be accordingly understood as rural, industrial, and urban social formations, or, in a more comprehensive sense, as time-space/space-time (*temps-espace/espace-temps*) or as social space-time configurations (see section 8.3). As in the space-time axis of urbanisation, critical phases or critical zones appear in the relations between these fields, marking painful transitions or turning points.[192]

The Rural Continent

The rural continent is determined by agriculture and peasant life. It is characterised by the dominance of 'necessity'. Scarcity reigns. Production is limited and essentially based on agriculture, which installs itself in 'nature'. Time and space do not disrupt the cycles of farming production but blend in with them and are generally dependent on their particularities. The space-time of this society is therefore cyclical and emphasises local characteristics.[193]

The city of the rural field is the political city (see section 3.3), and although it is as deeply rooted at the farming communities which surround it and leave their imprint upon it, a fundamental social division of labour already begins to take shape: the division between material and intellectual labour, between production and trade, between agriculture and craft – and by extension the separation of city and country. But this political city is still distant from the urban society, and hardly even affords a presentiment of what that might be.[194]

The Industrial Continent

The first critical phase or zone marks the transition from the rural to the industrial field. Lefebvre assigns the concept of 'labour' to the industrial field, and it is correspondingly the field that is dominated by the economic. Industry takes hold of nature and consumes its energies in order to produce goods for exchange. Productivity is raised to the status of fetish, and 'nature', including human nature, becomes devastated.[195]

A project of universal rationality forms in the industrial field, a project of comprehensive order that corresponds to the logic of the commodity. The

---

191   Lefebvre, *Urban Revolution*, 32, 125.
192   Ibid., 28.
193   Ibid., 33, 38, 117.
194   Ibid., 35, 43.
195   Ibid., 33, 117.

industrial continent aspires towards homogeneity, towards a rational unity enforced by planning. The division of labour is applied to ever-wider social spheres. According to Lefebvre, the great plan of the industrial era consists in organising the entirety of the social division of labour in a way to match the efficiency of industrial production – a project that, though it may be begun again and again without end, can never be completed.[196]

This expansion of the industrial form of the division of labour to the entire society also leaves its mark on social space. It replaces presumably natural particularities – in accordance with its quantitative rationality – with a calculated, methodically and systematically imposed homogeneity. Places become randomly available; they are homologous and differ from one another only in the degree of their distance from one another. Space is represented as objective and measurable, related to the criteria of production. Its use is calculated according to optimisation: the costs of overcoming distances, of transporting objects, and of information become primary. The space-time organisation of the industrial field evokes the semblance of absolute rationality, because it consists of order and compulsion. Industrial practice strives to create a homogeneous structure but splits everything up into particles, whose relations to one another are only illusionary (see also section 6.3).[197]

From the perspective of the urban society, the industrial field therefore appears different than it appeared to itself:

> From its own perspective, it was productive and creative, in control of nature, substituting the freedom of production for the determinism of matter. In fact – in truth – it was radically contradictory and conflictual. Rather than dominating nature, industry ravaged it, destroyed it completely. Claiming to substitute a consistent rationality for the chaos of spontaneity, it separated and dissociated everything it touched, it destroyed connections by instituting a reign of homogeneous order. For industry, the means became an end and the end a means: production became strategy, productivism a philosophy, the state a divinity.[198]

For Lefebvre, this definition of the industrial field contains a critique not only of capitalism, but also of actually existing socialism:

---

196 Ibid., 34–5, 37–8.
197 Ibid., 34–5, 123.
198 Ibid., 176.

It is a period of warfare and revolution, which abort as soon as they appear to realize themselves in the cult of the state and the fetishism of production, which is itself the realization of the fetishism of money and commodities.[199]

The Urban Continent

In the second critical phase, another upheaval takes place: industrialisation produces urbanisation, and the latter becomes a dominant process that eventually encompasses the entire earth. Lefebvre regards industrialisation as a precondition to urbanisation. Industrialisation forms the starting point of urbanisation; it provides the conditions, creating the possibility of a fundamental transformation of society. Over the course of a deep crisis – the crisis of the city – the problematic of industrialisation shifts and becomes that of urban development. Industrialisation morphs from a *dominant* and coercive force into being itself a *dominated* actuality, the reality dominated by urbanisation.[200]

There are several problems inherent in these cryptic formulations that Lefebvre makes again and again on the subject of urbanisation. For example, what determines the qualities of urbanisation? What are its prospects?

Lefebvre, first of all, recognises a crucial difference between (economic) growth and (social) development: industrialisation designates the quantitative side, while urbanisation designates the qualitative one. The development of society can only be realised in urban life, through the creation of the urban society.[201]

Industrialisation and urbanisation should not, therefore, be considered independently from one another. They must be understood as a highly complex and conflictual double process, as a process with two dominant aspects: growth and development, economic production and social life. The two aspects of this process form a conflicting, dialectical unity: industrialisation provides the conditions and the means of urbanisation, and the urban society forms the orientation, the meaning, the goal of industrialisation, and industrial production. Lefebvre understands industrialisation and urbanisation as dialectically linked concepts that contain urban life within them: the urban society will eventually emerge from their contradictions.[202]

---

199 Ibid., 36.
200 Lefebvre, *Right to the City*, 74, 128–9; Lefebvre, *Urban Revolution*, 16–17, 87, 138.
201 Lefebvre, *Right to the City*, 130, 164.
202 Lefebvre, *Urban Revolution*, 151–2; Lefebvre, *Right to the City*, 85, 132, 144, 177–8.

Urban society, meanwhile, remains a virtual reality, the possible result of social development. What is the 'meaning' of this development? What does the urban society 'stand for'? Lefebvre gives a surprising answer: *jouissance*. This term has several meanings, and also erotic and sexual connotations. It is usually translated into English as 'pleasure' or 'enjoyment', which does not fully cover the full spectrum of the word *jouissance* (see also section 6.5).

The Urban as the Site of Desire

Lefebvre postulates that the three spatio-temporal fields or continents correspond to the three moments that can be identified in every social process: *need–labour–enjoyment*.[203]

Using these three concepts, he again takes up the reflections sketched in his *Metaphilosophy*, and here too finds the decisive reference in Marx.[204] In the *Paris Manuscripts*, Marx had discussed at length the social relationship between need and enjoyment and their historical relation to labour and accumulation. Once again, Lefebvre's interpretation of this text is both daring and original at the same time: Marx, he writes, shows the metamorphosis of needs through the mediation of productive labour towards the capacity for enjoyment, towards a consciousness that is simultaneously individualised and socialised.[205] It is important here to once again address problems of translation. Marx uses here the word *Genuss*, which has several meanings, including 'enjoyment' and 'pleasure', but also 'consumption' in a more generic sense. While most translations of Marx use 'consumption', Lefebvre, for his part, translates this word with *jouissance*, hence enjoyment or pleasure. These are not minor differences, of course, and they illustrate in an exemplary way the ambivalences language can express: human beings, by necessity, consume goods, but one hopes that this is not only a necessity, but also a pleasure.

Provocatively, Lefebvre places *labour* in the historical context of his three dialectical fields: labour corresponds to the capitalist phase, the dominance and the terror of economic forces. But it is a transitory phase, says Lefebvre, that leads from the origin, from need, to the true humanisation of humanity and, through that, to pleasure.

For Lefebvre, the origins of today's society lie in an initial state of non-labour, in a nature that creates without effort, in which bounty is hardly

---

203   Lefebvre, *Urban Revolution*, 32.
204   Lefebvre, *Metaphilosophy*, 115.
205   Ibid., 73; see also Marx, *Economic and Philosophical Manuscripts*, 349–51, 358–60.

distinguishable from savagery. In our present era, modernity arduously paves the way to non-labour, to the actual goal of the accumulation of technologies, knowledge, and machines. That would be the conclusion of this seemingly endless period of work, of accumulation and reduction through knowledge and power.[206] 'While it is true that during the industrial period the "reality principal" overwhelmed the "pleasure principle", hasn't the moment for its revenge arrived within urban society?'[207]

Lefebvre sees his theory of the urban as an expansion and extension of Marx's analysis, as the latter did not quite capture the double process of industrialisation and urbanisation. The incompleteness of Marx's theory and of Marxist thinking, claims Lefebvre, is misunderstood:

> For Marx himself, industrialization contained its finality and meaning, later giving rise to the dissociation of Marxist thought into economism and philosophism. Marx did not show (and in his time he could not) that urbanization and the *urban* contain the *meaning* of industrialization. He did not see that industrial production implied the urbanization of society, and that the mastery of industrial potentials required specific knowledge concerning urbanization.[208]

According to Lefebvre, Marx recognised only one side of the double process, (quantitative) industrialisation, while Lefebvre considered the other side, (qualitative) urbanisation. At the same time, this is also a sharp critique of an economic rationality, of a science and politics oriented towards quantitative growth, a critique explicitly directed at Marx himself:

> Marx distinguished growth and development only because he wanted to avoid any confusion between quantity and quality. But for Marx the growth (quantitative) and development (qualitative) of society could and must occur simultaneously. Unfortunately, history shows that this is not the case.[209]

It took two centuries for industry to produce the rise of the commodity. While the commodity of course predated industrialisation, its significance had been nevertheless limited by the material, social, and political structures of agrarian production and the mercantile cities. Industrialisation permitted the virtually

---

206   Lefebvre, *Production of Space*, 264, 409.
207   Lefebvre, *Urban Revolution*, 85.
208   Lefebvre, *Right to the City*, 130.
209   Lefebvre, *Urban Revolution*, 168.

unlimited expansion of exchange value. For Lefebvre, the commodity did not only incorporate humans into overarching social relations, but also created a logic, a language, a world. The commodity cleared all hurdles, and, he suggests, this process is far from over. The car, the current 'pilot-object' in the world of commodities, is on the way to removing the last barrier to the expansion of exchange value: the city (see section 7.1).[210]

The industrial epoch was dominated by political economy in both its variants: liberal economy and planned economy. For Lefebvre, the sublation of economism is emerging on the horizon today, a sublation through and in praxis. Use value, which for centuries has been subordinated to exchange value, can again prevail – in and through the urban society which emerges from the reality that still resists, and which preserves the image of use value: the city.[211]

City and urban society thus emerge, for Lefebvre, from use value. He sees the most important use of the city, of the streets and squares, of buildings and monuments, as for public celebration and festivity, which are consumed unproductively, with no purpose but fun and pleasure.[212] He asserts that the satisfaction of elementary needs is not enough to extinguish the non-satisfaction of fundamental desires. Through the cracks in industrial society sprouts the desire for imbalance and surprise, for the release from normalcy and constraints, for moments of play and spontaneity. The site of this desire, the place where Eros and Logos are perhaps to be found together again, is the city, urban space.[213] 'For the individual, the surrounding city is the place of desire (that which stimulates, multiplies, and intensifies the desires), and also the totality of constraints weighing on the desires, inhibiting desire.'[214]

It is, accordingly, from this position that Lefebvre also pleads for a new architecture – an architecture of enjoyment. In a long-missing manuscript, which Łukasz Stanek found in Saragossa and later published in English, Lefebvre examines in detail the conditions required for a potential 'architecture of enjoyment', as an alternative to the violence of industrial society, as a negation of the everyday, and as the realisation of a concrete utopia of another, urban society (see section 6.5).[215]

210　Lefebvre, *Right to the City*, 166.
211　Lefebvre, *Urban Revolution*, 168.
212　Lefebvre, *Right to the City*, 102.
213　Lefebvre, *Urban Revolution*, 85, 176; Lefebvre, *Right to the City*, 88, 92.
214　Lefebvre, *De l'État*, vol. 4, 270. Translation by author.
215　Lefebvre, *Toward an Architecture of Enjoyment*, 147–8; Stanek, 'Introduction: A Manuscript Found in Saragossa'.

The Urban Revolution

For Lefebvre, the current situation may be compared to a certain degree to that which Marx experienced in relation to industrialisation: in both cases, radical critique is supposed to pave the way for thought and action.[216] Through this lens, the programmatic concept of 'urban revolution' marks a fundamental shift similar to that of the 'industrial revolution'. Lefebvre understands the industrial revolution in a dual manner: on the one hand as a (revolutionary) transformation of productive forces, and on the other as the possibility of a social revolution. The 'urban revolution' is correspondingly also to be read through these dual meanings: on the one hand it refers to

> the transformation that affects contemporary society, ranging from the period when questions of growth and industrialization predominate (models, plans, programs) to the period when the urban problematic becomes predominant, when the search for solutions and modalities unique to urban society are foremost.[217]

On the other hand, these transformations can nevertheless only be achieved through a social revolution. 'The words "urban revolution" do not in themselves refer to actions that are violent. Nor do they exclude them.'[218]

Lefebvre's hopes for the urban revolution amount, in the end, to nothing less than the creation of a new humanism, after the old humanism's practical rejection by so-called industrial society, capitalist or not.[219] 'The path that has been opened leads toward the reconstruction of some form of humanism in, by, and for urban society.'[220] A new conception of human being thus emerges from the urban society: urban beings that are polyvalent, polysensorial, capable of complex and transparent relationships with the 'world', for whom and through whom the city and life in the city will become an oeuvre, an appropriation, use value.[221] On the way to the urban society, it will be important to heed and detect new social needs, knowing that these needs can only be discovered in the course of their emerging and only reveal themselves in the process of exploration. The urban revolution must produce this new subject, the confident human being capable of experiencing pleasure, whose capacities are fully developed:

---

216 Lefebvre, *Urban Revolution*, 135.
217 Ibid., 5.
218 Ibid.
219 Ibid., 65.
220 Ibid., 68–9.
221 Ibid., 64; Lefebvre, *Right to the City*, 124, 167.

the total human being, who will now become the urban human being. Lefebvre even claimed in *Metaphilosophy*: 'Life has not yet begun',[222] an idea he repeats in *The Right to the City* as 'Urban life has yet to begin.'[223]

It is from this perspective that the urban society comes to be the last stage on the long road of humans' self-becoming. What the industrial revolution left undone is now left to the urban revolution to complete: the end of the reign of the economic, the liberation of *désir*, the discovery of the continent of enjoyment, the restoration of use value – a revolution that exceeds what Marx envisioned, a total revolution.

But Lefebvre's ambiguous, dual understanding of historical development, as presented programmatically in *Metaphilosophy*, must nevertheless still be taken into account even when reading these hopeful pronouncements (see section 2.4): 'For Marx, the revolution was to constitute a historic moment, a leap into freedom, the end of alienations. We know that this will take a long time.'[224]

Lefebvre is well aware that the realisation of an urban society in the here and now is impossible, and that even in the future its development will remain highly uncertain. It is precisely for this reason that he defines the urban society not as an achieved reality, but as a prospect, as a shimmering virtuality, as a projection on the horizon, or – in his favourite formulation – as the 'possible-impossible', that which imparts a meaning and a goal to the possible, to the act.[225]

> Can theoretical knowledge treat this virtual object, the goal of action, as an abstraction? No. From this point on, it is abstract only in the sense that it is a *scientific*, and therefore legitimate, abstraction. Theoretical knowledge can and must reveal the terrain, the foundation on which it resides: an on-going social practice, an urban practice in the process of formation.[226]

The (virtual) urban society marks a tendency: 'We shouldn't confuse trends with realization. Today's society is undergoing a transition and can best be understood in this sense.'[227] The urban revolution that will, in its turn, lead to a real urban society does not result from ongoing urbanisation as a historically necessary consequence. It is a possibility in the present, an option to be realised.[228]

---

222 Lefebvre, *Metaphilosophy*, 105.
223 Lefebvre, *Right to the City*, 150.
224 Lefebvre, *Metaphilosophy*, 20.
225 Lefebvre, *Right to the City*, 181; Lefebvre, *Urban Revolution*, 17, 40, 179.
226 Lefebvre, *Urban Revolution*, 17.
227 Ibid., 138.
228 Ibid., 64.

The Urban as Totality and Virtuality

This conception of the urban revolution reveals the whole scope of the divergence between Marx and Lefebvre, as elaborated in chapter 2. It need not be reiterated here that Marx's idea of the goal of the great revolution differed significantly from Lefebvre's. For Marx, labour and enjoyment were dialectically entangled, and eliminating alienation meant that all members of society should enjoy the fruits of their labour. The 'end of labour' or 'non-labour' was completely alien to his thinking (and the reality of his time).

Lefebvre's idea of 'non-labour' and enjoyment can be interpreted in several ways: first of all, it is a provocation and a radical critique of industrialisation, of productivist rationality, of the economism that dominates society, rules everyday life, and is devastating the planet. The fact that this critique does not emerge from the zeitgeist, but developed continuously and consistently from his analyses of everyday life beginning in the 1950s (see section 3.1), is noteworthy for a non-conservative thinker. This critique, which appeared again and again in various forms in his work, was also radical for France in the early 1970s. It was not aimed at adapting industrial production to the requirements of the 'environment' and has nothing in common with fashionable mainstream ideas, which passed under the label of 'qualitative growth' in the 1980s and flowed into debate on 'sustainability' in the 1990s. In political slogans such as 'a better life' or 'a different life' or 'quality of life', which are associated with the 'environment' and 'protecting nature', Lefebvre saw only the pale reflection of a radical utopia that had fallen back into idealism. Rather, the utopia he envisaged was of an urban society that, beyond productivism and the work ethic, would devote itself to the important things in life – play, pleasure, desire.[229]

Lefebvre maintained an unbroken and seemingly naïve belief in the idea that technical progress will one day liberate humanity from labour. This belief, which repeatedly shines through in Lefebvre's work, should, however, be placed in the larger context of his critical analysis of the urbanisation process, which he does not fundamentally reject, nor want to undo or even limit: rather, he sees urbanisation as an opportunity and a possibility. As vague as the concept of the virtual urban society seems to be, it forms a vanishing point that has lost none of its relevance even at the beginning of the twenty-first century.

---

229   Lefebvre, *The Production of Space*, 30–1.

3.5 The Dialectic of Urbanisation

> The urban . . . rises above the horizon, slowly occupies an
> epistemological field, and becomes the episteme of an epoch.[230]

> The urban revolution is a planetary phenomenon.[231]

Based on the analysis of Lefebvre's texts on the city and on urbanisation developed in this book so far, it is possible to formulate a provisional summary.
First, Lefebvre developed a new theory of the urban out of the rudimentary
approaches he had found in the contemporary critique of urbanism and in the
classic texts of Marx and Engels. Second, he consistently placed the urban
question in a general social and historical context and identified an underlying
process that dialectically sublates the dominant urban–rural contradiction:
urbanisation. And, third, he not only theorised urbanisation and the crisis of
the city, but also tried to point out a possible future: the urban revolution that
leads to the emergence of an urban society.

With his theory of the urban, Lefebvre laid a central foundation for critical
urban studies. He also anticipated crucial aspects that have been to a certain
extent 'rediscovered' in the course of the years and decades which followed.
The first of these is the Janus-faced process of industrialisation and urbanisation, which Lefebvre encapsulated with the metaphor of 'implosion–explosion'.
The industrialisation of society leads to a concentration of capital, means of
production, and labour power, but it also generates an ever-increasing expansion of urban areas and the emergence of a worldwide urban fabric. From this
observation he developed the thesis of the complete urbanisation of society,
which has proved to be visionary and extraordinarily fruitful, but which has
also given rise to considerable debate and misunderstanding. Connected with
this thesis is the question of the sublation of the urban–rural contradiction,
which is still the subject of controversy today. Finally, it has also given rise to
the recent heated debate about 'planetary urbanisation' – a concept that was
also sketched by Lefebvre.

A second important insight is Lefebvre's analysis of the urbanisation of
everyday life, anticipating Manuel Castells's concept of collective consumption,
but conceiving it in a much more dynamic and fundamental way, most of all by
opening it up to a possible urban future. This future is determined by the
contradictory relationship between urbanisation and urban society: while

---

230   Lefebvre, *Urban Revolution*, 191.
231   Ibid., 113.

urbanisation describes a historical process, urban society stands for the possible, for a potential that is inherent in urbanisation. This, ultimately, gives rise to the conception of the urban revolution, which has been foreshadowed in a wide variety of urban movements and revolts and a long history of the rediscovery of the urban.

Industrialisation and Urbanisation

To better understand Lefebvre's concept of urbanisation, it is key to examine his understanding of industrialisation, the starting point of his analysis. He came to the remarkable conclusion that the industrialisation of society always entails processes of urbanisation. It was industrialisation that set the historical process of urbanisation in motion, which subsequently led to the emergence of the contemporary encompassing form of urbanisation. Accordingly, Lefebvre clearly opposes the idea, still widespread today, that urbanisation should be understood as a universal process that extends from antiquity to the present. For Lefebvre, urbanisation is a historical process directly linked to industrialisation, and for this reason cannot be a universal category.

The metaphor of 'implosion–explosion' allowed him to grasp this connection between industrialisation and urbanisation. On the one hand, as Engels had already recognised (see section 3.2), the internal dynamics of industrialisation led to a concentration of labour and the means of production, and thus to the formation of urban agglomerations. The German economist, geographer, and sociologist Alfred Weber (the brother of Max Weber) had developed this insight further, showing that the concentration of enterprises and the expansion of transport systems could lead to economic advantages, which he called 'the power of agglomeration' (*die Agglomerationskraft*).[232] This concept subsequently became a central part of urban economics under the label of 'agglomeration economies'. Allen Scott and Michael Storper recently elevated agglomeration economies to a transhistorical, universal principle capturing the very 'nature of the city'.[233] This concept, however, has many ambiguities and weaknesses. The reasons and causes for 'the growth of cities' always present themselves differently in their historic and regional specificity and must be examined in detail in each individual case.[234] It is nevertheless undisputed that agglomeration economies only became effective on a large scale through

---

232   Alfred Weber, *Theory of the Location of Industries*.
233   Scott and Storper, 'The Nature of Cities'.
234   See also Schmid, 'Specificity and Urbanization'; Schmid, 'Extended Urbanization'.

industrialisation. With the industrial revolution, urbanisation became a comprehensive process, first in Europe and then in more and more places worldwide. This was due, first, to the unprecedented increase in economic productivity unleashed by industrialisation, and, second, to the mechanisation of agriculture and improved transport conditions that loosened the rigid socio-metabolic relationship between cities and their agrarian hinterlands.[235] To be sure, large cities were possible even earlier, but only under very specific political, economic, and agricultural conditions.[236]

At the same time as the 'implosion' of the city, however, Lefebvre also saw an urban 'explosion', as urban areas began to expand without end and disjointed urban fragments spread over the countryside. Industrialisation is not limited to the operation of factories, because it also requires a material basis, in particular, transportation and communication facilities, but also energy, raw materials, and all sorts of other resources. Lefebvre coined the term 'urban fabric' to refer to this phenomenon. The urban fabric, which is always expanding and becoming more densely woven across the globe, includes not only buildings but also infrastructure for energy production, transport, and communication, from telephones to satellite connections; and also entails the general spread of everyday consumer goods, first and foremost the automobile, then the refrigerator, the television, and so on. It includes as well a wide variety of social processes and practices, such as the rapid adoption of fashions, urban entertainment, and the enforcement of an 'urban rationality'.[237] This concept of the urban fabric inspired a broader understanding of urbanisation and was further developed, particularly by Neil Brenner and Andy Merrifield.[238] It subsequently became a central element in arguments for the concepts of planetary and extended urbanisation (see below).

Harvey addressed this process of the extension of the urban fabric with the concept of the *production of the built environment* (see section 1.2). He demonstrated that investment in the built environment forms a 'second circuit of capital' – an idea he took directly from Lefebvre. This circuit fundamentally changes the spatio-temporal configurations of the world: The spatial barriers to the production process become less important, and the globe shrinks – a process he called 'space-time compression'. Thus, ever-larger amounts of capital are locked into the built environment for the long term, which in turn drives the process of urbanisation even further. Harvey expressed this connection in

---

235   Scott and Storper, 'The Nature of Cities'; Harvey, *Justice, Nature and the Geography of Difference*, 44.

236   See for example Bairoch, *Cities and Economic Development*.

237   Lefebvre, *Right to the City*, 72.

238   See for example Brenner, *New Urban Spaces*; Merrifield, *The New Urban Question*.

the notion of the *urbanisation of capital*, which can be understood as a political economy variant of Lefebvre's general thesis of complete urbanisation (see section 7.1).[239] It is important to note, however, that Lefebvre's thesis goes beyond political economy and includes a more comprehensive conception of urbanisation, expressed in his notions of the urban fabric and the production of space. As the preceding section argues, if he speaks of industrialisation and urbanisation, he means not only the industrial production of goods and the production of buildings and infrastructure, but the industrialisation and the urbanisation of society.

The Dialectical Sublation of the Contradiction between City and Country

In the context of industrialisation and urbanisation, the transformation of the contradiction between city and country is crucial. I cannot go into detail here about the sprawling debates on this question, which encompass many aspects. I would like to emphasise, in particular, the highly provocative character of Lefebvre's thesis of the complete urbanisation of society in his time. It broke with the widespread idea that social developments could still be explained by the contradiction between city and country. Lefebvre did not claim that this contradiction had been eliminated, though, but postulated that it was transformed by the urbanisation process and had become a new contradiction between centre and periphery (see sections 3.3, 4.5, and 7.1).

Lefebvre's basic claim can be summarised as follows: the contradiction between city and country still exists, but it is in the process of transformation. In a dialectical understanding, the 'sublation' of this contradiction means that it is eliminated in one sense, but simultaneously preserved and elevated to a higher level (see section 2.3). Lefebvre was, to a certain extent, a contemporary witness of this process, and he had done empirical research on this transformation in his sociological studies of rural life. His research results became an important basis for his analysis of urbanisation, as he described and analysed a whole series of fundamental social changes in the 'countryside'.

To begin with, Lefebvre addressed the industrialisation of agriculture, which had itself become part of the global economy. As a result, it had long ceased to be the largest sector of the economy in Western countries but was increasingly characterised by industrialisation and rationalisation.[240]

---

239 Harvey, *Limits to Capital*; Harvey, *Condition of Postmodernity*.
240 Lefebvre, *Urban Revolution*, 3.

Second, Lefebvre observed the dissolution of the village community:

The traditional unit typical of peasant life, namely the village, has been transformed. Absorbed or obliterated by larger units, it has become an integral part of industrial production and consumption ... The urban fabric ... corrodes the residue of agrarian life.[241]

In this context, Lefebvre also noted the emergence of agricultural towns, not only in the Soviet Union, but in many other parts of the world.[242] Although Lefebvre does not mention it, the much-discussed book *The Vanishing Peasant* from 1967 by agricultural sociologist Henri Mendras seemingly made a great impression on him. This book looks at the industrialisation of agriculture in France and shows in detail the changes that France's peasant society underwent in the process. Mendras defined peasantry by the relative autonomy of rural communities from the society that encompassed them. 'In a word, the peasant is defined in relation to the city. If there is no city there is no peasant, and if the society is *entirely urbanized* there is no peasant either.'[243] This passage indicates that the urban–rural question was being widely discussed in France in the late 1960s. It has to be emphasised that Mendras's book was published *before* Lefebvre's books on the subject appeared. Although neither Mendras nor Lefebvre ever made explicit references to one another, the parallels between their analyses are striking, as the following quotation from Lefebvre in *Metaphilosophy* (from 1965) shows: 'In a short time from now, in the most developed regions and countries, the rural population will undoubtedly have disappeared, making way for town-dwellers engaged in agricultural production with improved methods and industrial technologies.'[244]

Third, as shown above, Lefebvre observed that the urban fabric is encroaching further and further into rural areas, covering them with motorways, supermarkets, industrial complexes, and satellite towns.[245] This is also accompanied by a massive change in the peasant way of life, a process Lefebvre called the urbanisation of everyday life (see below). Further, Lefebvre also observed the tremendous growth of tourism, which integrates and exploits the rural, ultimately contributing to the commodification of space (see section 7.1).

Despite all these tendencies, Lefebvre insisted that the 'rural' was not being eliminated. It still existed in various forms and gradations: local and regional

---

241 Ibid.
242 Ibid., 4.
243 Mendras, *The Vanishing Peasant*, 7. Emphasis added.
244 Lefebvre, *Metaphilosophy*, 110.
245 Lefebvre, *Urban Revolution*, 4.

forms of rurality survived, and between the meshes of the urban fabric smaller and larger islands of 'rurality' remained left out, with entire regions stagnating or decaying.[246] In this way, the contrast between rurality and urbanity may even intensify as the contradiction between city and country weakens even further.[247] This means that certain elements of the rural survive and serve a new function within urban society. This is not only about material spatial practices but also about representations and experiences, agrarian myths, and their ideological extensions.[248] On that point, Stefan Kipfer observes, 'In this sense, city and country can outlive their eras and relate to core-periphery relations variably. Not necessarily anachronistic, they continue to produce space, also through nationalism, reactionary or otherwise.'[249]

It is crucial to note, as emphasised in section 1.1, that depending on the situation and theory, very different definitions of the 'city' and the 'urban' exist and coexist. The same applies accordingly to the 'countryside' and the 'rural'. Without going into further detail here, there are correspondingly quite different definitions of the rural: the dominance of agricultural production, the absence of larger cities, a certain way of life, a certain cultural form, the prevalence of certain traditions and forms of socialisation, and so on. In addition, there are also various political and planning definitions of 'rural areas', which are often associated with specific land use regulations or forms of governance.

In much scholarly writing, it is therefore highly unclear what is in fact meant by 'urban' and 'rural'. Very often, the urban–rural relationship is treated as universal, and spoken of as *the* urban–rural contradiction. This formula is misleading, however, because this relationship inevitably depends on concrete situations and circumstances, conditions, and constellations. Lefebvre himself has vividly described the multiple transformations of the urban–rural relationship in Europe from antiquity through the Middle Ages to the present-day 'sublation' of this relationship (see section 3.3). It is quite clear that in other parts of the world there are quite different conditions and power relations, which result accordingly in different urban–rural relationships. For example, Wing-Shing Tang has pointed out that the situation in contemporary China is fundamentally different from Lefebvre's account of the contradictory relationship between city and country in the West, and this is very much related to the different power relations and institutional forms of control over land.[250]

---

246   Lefebvre, *Right to the City*, 71–2.
247   Ibid., 120.
248   Lefebvre, *Urban Revolution*, 103.
249   Kipfer, 'Pushing the Limits of Urban Research', 479.
250   Tang, 'Where Lefebvre Meets the East'.

It is also important to abandon notions of separate urban and rural life worlds, since these are effectively interconnected in many ways. The 'classic' migration from rural to urban areas alone, which still accounts for much of urban growth, establishes long-lasting relationships between the migrants' places of origin and their destinations. In large areas of Africa and Asia, moreover, processes of circular migration have long established close ties and exchange relationships between rural and urban areas, which are now multiplied and further differentiated by massively expanded spatial mobility. For contemporary West Bengal, for example, Elisa Bertuzzo describes different forms of mobilities and sporadic migrations, which she calls 'translocalisations'. Similarly, in the West African corridor, Alice Hertzog has explored the very complex relationships that emerge through mobilities and movements, producing entirely new urban configurations. And Stefan Kipfer shows that indigenous identities and affiliations in Canada take on meanings that are in no way confined to Western notions of 'city' and 'country'.[251] For many people around the world today, urban and rural are no longer (and have long not been) opposites but are rather different modalities or phases of their everyday lives.

Kanishka Goonewardena further points to the close economic relationships and interdependencies between 'city' and 'country', in contemporary and earlier times.[252] He sees clear parallels between Lefebvre's *The Urban Revolution* and Raymond Williams's book *The Country and the City*, which addresses, among other things, the production of the 'country' as a site of commodity production, dispossession, and underdevelopment through emerging capitalism, colonialism, and imperialism. In doing so, he also makes a direct connection between 'enclosure' in England at the time of the industrial revolution and the parallel developments in the colonies through deportations, the destruction of rural and traditional livelihoods, and the precarisation of living conditions.

Stefan Kipfer shows for the twentieth century how divides between colonial towns and 'rural' plantations were materially instituted through deportations, forced sedentarisation, and ghettoisation in colonial and postcolonial plantation economies in the Caribbean. Similarly, colonial and neocolonial policies in Canada resulted in the exclusion of indigenous peoples from cities and their forced resettlement in reserves. Japhy Wilson confronts Lefebvre's analysis of the new town of Mourenx with a series of new towns recently constructed in Chiapas, Mexico, in which the region's indigenous and peasant population has

---

251   Bertuzzo, *Archipelagos*; Hertzog, 'Movement and Urban Fabric along the West African Corridor'; Kipfer, 'Pushing the Limits of Urban Research'.
252   Goonewardena, 'The Country and the City'.

been relocated and their cultural practices erased. This shows that the 'country', especially under colonial and neocolonial conditions, often involves relations of violence, as a result of many different processes and power relations. It points to the need for broadening Lefebvre's analysis of the city–country contradiction beyond the Western experience.

The Urbanisation of Everyday Life

This returns us to the analysis of everyday life, with which we began this chapter. Lefebvre did not limit his analysis of urbanisation to economic processes alone, for the starting point of his encounter with the phenomenon of urbanisation was, after all, his study of everyday life, in which he noted a close connection between the formation of everydayness and the urbanisation process. Thus, urbanisation goes hand in hand with an initially slow but increasingly comprehensive transformation and modernisation of everyday life, from the spread of the automobile and the accompanying mass motorisation, which first made the expansion of urbanised areas possible on a large scale, to the industrialisation of housing, be it mass housing or the standardised production of single-family homes, to the spread of consumer society, and thus the commodification of more and more spheres of daily life.

In consistent continuity with Lefebvre's argumentation, it can be postulated that the social enforcement of (programmed) everyday life was only possible through and with the urbanisation process. As Lefebvre noted, the critique of everyday life has a somewhat surprising role: while it does not capture the entirety of social practice in the industrial field, it does capture its essential results.[253] Lefebvre condensed these results in the concept of the 'bureaucratic society of controlled consumption', a term that precisely characterises the (Fordist) post-war society of France (see section 3.1). In his later texts, Lefebvre positioned this society in the broader context of urbanisation and invited us to go further, to examine the form of this new urban society, and to strengthen the germ of the urban that sustains itself in the cracks of the planned and programmed order.[254] Thus, through the analysis of urbanisation, the 'bureaucratic society of controlled consumption', still subject to industrial rationality, is relativised and dialectically sublated in the 'urban society'. The switch between these two terms thus marks precisely the epistemological transition between the two continents, the industrial and the urban.

---

253   Lefebvre, *Urban Revolution*, 139–40.
254   Lefebvre, *Right to the City*, 129.

Conversely, it can also be postulated that the 'crisis of the city' was initially a crisis of everyday life and consumption, and thus moved the question of social reproduction and gender roles to the centre of the urban question, as Kristin Ross depicted in such a lucid way.[255] It was precisely following this thesis that Manuel Castells developed his own theory of the city in *The Urban Question*, in which he defined the urban as a unit of collective consumption (see section 1.2). However, Lefebvre had countered such a limited optic even before the publication of Castells's book by arguing that urban reality not only was tied to consumption but also influenced production and relations of production.[256] He then criticised the theory of collective consumption after its appearance, without mentioning Castells by name, for reducing urban phenomena to the question of the reproduction of labour power. He argued that this analysis, which he considered structuralist and non-dialectical, was not wrong. It was, however, trivial and without historical specificity, and could apply equally to both an English town in the late eighteenth century and a modern megalopolis.[257] What Lefebvre saw as lacking in this theory, then, is not only the economic aspect of the urban, but, in particular, the historical perspective that suggests a dynamic opening to a possible future.[258]

If the analysis of the 'bureaucratic society of controlled consumption' can be read as an apt analysis of Fordist society, the vision of an urban society contains essential elements of a post-Fordist society. In this sense, the transition from Fordism to post-Fordism or to a neoliberal development model can also be understood as a transition from a bureaucratic society of controlled consumption towards an urbanising society. This transition can be, to a certain extent, vividly experienced through Lefebvre's texts. If in his first texts he described the boredom of a programmed everyday life as the core problem of the urbanised world, in his subsequent texts he identified the potential of a desire that he characterised as urban: the desire for urbanity, for encounter, for the possibility of creating a 'different' society, centred no longer on labour, but on pleasure and enjoyment.

---

255   Ross, *Fast Cars, Clean Bodies*.
256   Lefebvre, *Urban Revolution*, 47.
257   Lefebvre, *Survival of Capitalism*, 66; see also Lefebvre, *De l'État*, vol. 4, 267–8.
258   Lefebvre, *Production of Space*, 391.

Urbanisation and Urban Society

This fundamental social change therefore directly raises the question of the connection between urbanisation and urban society. The intrinsic quality of Lefebvre's analysis lies precisely in the fact that he did not stop at a critique of the urbanisation process, but rather continued to think about this process in its prospective, possible further development. In contrast to many contemporary and subsequent analyses, he did not depict an urban horror scenario, nor did he operate with dystopian visions of the future, such as the film *Blade Runner*, evoked by Mike Davis and Edward Soja, or Isaac Asimov's Planet Trantor, which Andy Merrifield used as a metaphor of a completely urbanised world.[259] Rather, Lefebvre sought to explore the possibilities inherent in the process of urbanisation. In doing so, he made a notable distinction between urbanisation and urban society. Urbanisation is a process linked to industrialisation that brings about a fundamental change in living conditions. This does not mean, however, that it necessarily results in an urban society. Rather, the urban is a possibility, a potential that is inherent in urbanisation, but its realisation requires a fundamental social change – an urban revolution.

It was precisely on this point that Lefebvre's analysis went substantially beyond that of contemporary critics of the 1960s (see section 3.2). Like the Situationists or the North American critics of modern urbanism, Lefebvre loved the city.[260] But his critique was not limited to lamenting a lost world and calling for an urban renaissance. Rather, with the concept of the urban revolution, he tried to advance theoretical understanding of the process of urbanisation, unveiling a potential that he programmatically labelled 'urban society'. In this sense, urbanisation is a comprehensive social process, while the urban appears as a specific quality. As urbanisation proceeds and transforms both urban and rural areas, it also produces the potential for the creation of new urban situations and thus for the emergence of urbanity.

Largely based on Lefebvre's analysis, the distinction between *urbanisation* and *urbanity* subsequently became an important argument in urban studies. For example, Jean-Pierre Garnier has described the ongoing transformation of Paris into a 'Greater Paris' as urbanisation without urbanity.[261] In a similar way, ETH Studio Basel placed this distinction at the core of its urban analysis of Switzerland and considered the uncovering of 'urban potentials' in a wide

---

259   Davis, *Ecology of Fear*; Soja, *Postmetropolis*; Merrifield, *The Politics of the Encounter*.
260   Whyte, *Exploding Metropolis*; Jacobs, *The Death and Life of Great American Cities*.
261   Garnier, ' "Greater Paris" '.

range of urban configurations as the central goal.[262] And Roberto Luís Monte-Mór interpreted this distinction as a call to struggle for urbanity.[263]

The Rediscovery of the Urban and the Urban Revolution

Based on this distinction between urbanisation and urbanity, the transition from industrial to urban society postulated by Lefebvre becomes more tangible. Since the mid-1960s, the crisis of the city provoked a long and multifaceted history of the rediscovery of the urban, which was manifested, among other things, in a wide variety of urban movements and revolts, a history whose beginnings Lefebvre himself had witnessed and which he himself also helped to advance with his analyses and interventions.[264] A first climax of this confrontation came with the widespread urban mobilisations at the end of the 1960s including May '68 in Paris, which made such an impression on Lefebvre (see section 4.4). But many other struggles also put the urban question on the agenda in many parts of the world.[265]

One example of such struggles is the 1980s movement in Western Europe, which, as Lüscher and Makropoulos recognised, demanded an 'urban promise'. The following passage is not only motivated by the urban revolt in Zurich, but obviously also inspired by Lefebvre:

These urban revolts are not revolts against urbanisation, but against the lack of urban forms of life in the city. They claim a promise that cities continually make and continually break . . . The all-encompassing possibility of freely developing forms of life is initially fiction. That this fiction can become as real as anything can become real is the pivotal point of the urban promise. But the spark of the urban revolt is that the fiction, in most cases, remains stuck before the point where it might be experienced in its full intensity.[266]

These urban movements, struggles, and revolts appeared in many shapes and

---

262   Diener et al., *Switzerland*.

263   Monte-Mór, 'What Is the Urban in the Contemporary World?'.

264   Schmid, 'Henri Lefebvre, the Right to the City'.

265   See for example Mayer, Brandes, and Roth, *Stadtkrise und soziale Bewegungen*; Castells, *The City and the Grassroots*; INURA, *Possible Urban Worlds*; Harvey, *Rebel Cities*; Kipfer et al., 'Globalizing Lefebvre?'; Brenner, Marcuse, and Mayer, *Cities for People, Not for Profit*; Mayer, Thörn, and Thörn, *Urban Uprisings*.

266   Lüscher and Makropoulos, 'Vermutungen zu den Jugendrevolten 1980/81', 123, 126. Translation by author.

forms, as squatter movements, as struggle for social centres, as struggle against large urban projects, or as urban revolts.[267]

In the following years, urban revolts and uprisings erupted in many places across the world, manifesting a fundamental dissatisfaction with a functionalised, commodified, and controlled everyday urban life, and increasingly also against racism, social exclusion, unemployment, austerity politics, and precarity. Thus, a wide variety of groups fought with diverse actions and everyday appropriations against the transformation and modernisation of entire neighbourhoods, against the expansion of central business districts and the creation of new business zones, and against gentrification, housing shortages, and displacement. They demanded social openness, old and new forms of urbanity, (autonomous) meeting places, (alternative) culture, street life and public spaces, the preservation of popular districts, the possibility to live other lifestyles, urban democracy, and self-determination. As different as all these struggles are, many can be understood as urban struggles, struggles for a renewed urban life, for access to the material and immaterial resources of the city, for centrality, for difference. We will consider these struggles from different angles in other parts of this text: Lefebvre's concepts of the 'right to the city' and the 'struggle for centrality' will be discussed in more detail in sections 4.4 and 4.5, the struggle for difference in section 6.4.

In and through these struggles, the understanding of the urban fundamentally changed, as did urban spaces themselves. Countless initiatives created meeting places and venues – various forms of open urban spaces, solidarity networks, and alternative everyday practices, open to cultural, ethnic, racial, and sexual differences. Thus began a long and varied history of the 'rediscovery of the urban'. Subsequently, more and more social groups discovered the advantages of 'urban life', the diverse social and cultural venues and activities, the meeting places and public spaces, and the opportunities and chances that urban centres had to offer, while also recognising the economic potentials of 'urban values'.

Gradually, at different speeds, out of the crisis of the city in the 1960s emerged an 'urban renaissance'. The urban became mainstream, a consumable commercial offer. Many urban neighbourhoods were degraded into places of consumption and spectacle, as Debord had already recognised, and urban life itself became a commodity to be bought and sold. The privatisation of public spaces, state-led upgrading and beautification processes, and globalised gentrification processes led to the domestication and normalisation of the urban, to the point where many residents had to fight to stay in the city at all (see sections 4.4, 4.5, 6.4, and 7.1).

---

267   See also Schmid, 'The Dialectics of Urbanisation'.

Thus, the urban revolution that Lefebvre proclaimed with overwhelming pathos presents itself in a different light to today's perspective: even if we are far from inhabiting a different, non-capitalist 'urban' mode of production today, or realising an urban society, we still live in a different – urban – world. The urban problematic has evolved. In the public consciousness, however, the extent of this change is often overlooked. It could be measured, and here, too, Lefebvre provides the guiding principle, precisely through an analysis of everyday life.

The Urbanisation of the Planet

These considerations finally bring us back to the visionary thesis of the complete urbanisation of society. As Lefebvre's 'implosion–explosion' metaphor implies, this thesis indicates on the one hand the massive transformation of urban centres and, on the other, the endless expansion of the urban fabric, which makes the idea of bounded and delimitable urban spaces obsolete. In the meantime, urban research has explored the most diverse facets of these new urban realities and identified a wide variety of new urban configurations that no longer have anything in common with the classical forms of the 'city' but rather resemble Lefebvre's 'anti-city' or 'non-city' (see section 3.3). The 'city', in the classical sense of the word, which can be clearly distinguished morphologically and socially from and in relation to its rural hinterland, is now only a relic of a bygone era. The former cities have merged into larger units, into agglomerations and urban regions, into overarching polycentric catchment areas such as metropolitan regions or global city regions, or even into 'urban galaxies' and 'mega-regions', which can be seen as agglomerations of agglomerations.[268]

At the same time, however, once 'non-urban' areas are themselves being transformed by a wide variety of urbanisation processes. Lefebvre's thesis of complete urbanisation invites us to examine the most diverse places of this planet in search of new forms of urbanisation. While many critics of Lefebvre's thesis lament its indifference to divisions between 'rural' and 'urban', and speak of 'the urbanisation of everything', one can also take the thesis as a starting point for serious urban research and ask, 'Is the Matterhorn city?', 'Is the Mediterranean urban?', 'Is the jungle urbanized?'[269] What is important here, of course, is less the answers but more the resulting concrete analyses.

---

268 See for example Soja and Kanai, 'The Urbanization of the World'; Harrison and Hoyler, *Megaregions*.

269 Meili, 'Is the Matterhorn City?'; Brenner and Katsikis, 'Is the Mediterranean Urban?'; Monte-Mór, 'Modernities in the Jungle'. See also the critical examination by Roy, 'What Is Urban about Critical Urban Theory?'

To grasp these multifaceted transformations we need new approaches, new methods, and concepts. In the project *Switzerland: An Urban Portrait*, ETH Studio Basel applied Lefebvre's thesis of complete urbanisation by systematically scanning and analysing the entire area of Switzerland. In doing so, it developed new terms to characterise areas that are still declared 'rural' in official statistics but which have been urbanised in a variety of ways. It identified basically two different situations: on the one hand, areas experiencing a strong pressure of urbanisation ('quiet zones'), and on the other, areas marked by a continuous loss of social and economic activities ('Alpine fallow lands'). ETH Studio Basel subsequently developed this procedure and the corresponding methods into a 'territorial approach' and applied it to a wide variety of areas across the world, seeking to understand and characterise the different territories of urbanisation.[270]

These theoretical considerations, methodological innovations, and concrete empirical investigations were one of the starting points for the concept of 'planetary urbanisation'. This intervention, initiated by Andy Merrifield and by Neil Brenner and me, takes Lefebvre's metaphorical figure of the 'implosion–explosion' of the urban as a starting point and postulates that urbanisation has assumed a planetary scope. This requires decentring the analytical perspective on urbanisation, and adopting an ex-centric position, starting no longer from the centre, but from the (urbanised) peripheries.[271]

This planetary aspect of urbanisation was already clearly seen by Lefebvre in *The Urban Revolution*: 'The urban problematic is worldwide. The same problems are found in socialism and in capitalism – along with the failure to respond. Urban society can only be defined as planetary. Virtually, it covers the planet.'[272] He further argues that the urban revolution is a planetary phenomenon and that urban society, as a virtual object, is nothing other than planetary society.[273] The precise meaning of the term 'planetary' in Lefebvre is discussed in detail in section 4.3.

Lefebvre's last text, published in May 1989 in the French monthly journal *Le monde diplomatique*, evokes the possible 'planetarisation of the urban' and, two decades after the publication of *The Urban Revolution*, asks some burning questions:

---

270   Diener at al., *Switzerland*; Diener et al., *The Inevitable Specificity of Cities*; Diener et al., *Territory*.

271   Merrifield, *Politics of the Encounter*; Merrifield, *The New Urban Question*; Brenner and Schmid, 'Planetary Urbanization'; Brenner and Schmid, 'The "Urban Age" in Question'; Brenner and Schmid, 'Towards a New Epistemology of the Urban?'; Schmid, 'Journeys through Planetary Urbanization'.

272   Lefebvre, *Urban Revolution*, 166–7. Translation amended.

273   Ibid., 17, 113, 169.

Are new forms arising in the entire world and imposing themselves upon the city? Or, on the contrary, is an urban model gradually expanding to the world wide scale? A third hypothesis suggests that we are currently in a transitory period of mutations in which the urban and the global cross-cut and reciprocally disrupt each other.[274]

Planetary and Extended Urbanisation

In order to apply the concept of planetary urbanisation empirically, and to capture the double movement of implosion and explosion in more precise terms, Neil Brenner and I have developed the interrelated concepts of concentrated, extended, and differential urbanisation.[275] In this way, urbanisation can be understood analytically as the simultaneity of processes of concentration and extension: any form of urbanisation not only generates a concentration of people, the means of production, goods, and information that lead to concentrated urbanisation, but also inevitably and simultaneously causes a proliferation and expansion of the urban fabric, thus resulting in extended urbanisation. Food, water, energy, and raw materials must be brought to urban centres, requiring an entire logistical system that ranges from transport to information networks. Conversely, areas that are characterised by extended urbanisation can also evolve into new centralities and urban concentrations. Thus, concentrated and extended forms of urbanisation exist in a dialectical relationship to each other and can, at times, seamlessly merge.

Similarly basing his work on Lefebvre, Roberto Luís Monte-Mór had developed a related concept of extended urbanisation in his seminal work on the urbanisation of Amazonia in Brazil. He had noted that, for decades, this region has not been the rural region or even the 'pristine jungle' it is often portrayed as. Directly inspired by Lefebvre, he presents the extension of socio-spatial relations as a dialectical unity of urban centres and the urban fabric. Thus, he identifies the extension of urban forms, processes, and practices far beyond cities and agglomerations, integrating rural with urban-industrial spaces. This leads to a multiplication of 'urban frontiers', as extended urbanisation penetrates along various transportation corridors and communication networks into hitherto non-urbanised spaces, as well as into old industrial regions and the islands of rural life in the hinterlands of the big metropolises.[276]

---

274   Lefebvre, 'Dissolving City, Planetary Metamorphosis', 567.
275   Brenner and Schmid, 'Towards a New Epistemology of the Urban?'; Schmid, 'Analysing Extended Urbanisation'; Schmid, 'Extended Urbanization'.
276   Monte-Mór, 'Modernities in the Jungle'; Monte-Mór, 'What Is the Urban in the

The concepts of planetary urbanisation and extended urbanisation have initiated a broad discussion and have opened up the field of urban studies to analyses of the entire planet. This opening is quite in line with Lefebvre's intention:

It is the analyst's responsibility to identify and describe the various forms of urbanization and explain what happens to the forms, functions and urban structures that are transformed by the breakup of the ancient city and the process of generalized urbanization.[277]

It is precisely along these lines that researchers have used Lefebvre's theory in recent years to investigate a wide variety of urbanisation processes and their economic, social, and political consequences. Detailed studies include (see also section 1.4), the analysis of the urbanisation of Amazonia by Monte-Mór, Castriota, Tonucci, Kanai, and Wilson; the operationalisation of resource extraction in Chile and Colombia by Arboleda; the construction of a pipeline across Canada connecting a tar sand extraction site in the province of Alberta with global markets by Kipfer; various aspects of the urbanisation of the oceans, particularly by Couling and Hein; the operationalisation of agriculture in the corn belt of the North American Midwest by Katsikis, and in the palm oil plantations in South East Asia by Topalović; the effects of the planning of large infrastructure projects, such as the Plan Puebla Panamá or the Manta-Manaus multimodal transport corridor by Wilson and Bayón; the forced corridor urbanisation across India by Nitin Bathla; and the rural industrialisation of Dongguan in the Pearl River Delta by Wong.[278] An overview of such highly diverse forms of extended urbanisation is provided in the book *Extended Urbanization*, edited by Milica Topalović and me.[279] As these examples show, the perspective of planetary urbanisation in no way assumes that living

---

Contemporary World?'; Monte-Mór, 'Extended Urbanization and Settlement Patterns'; Monte-Mór and Castriota, 'Extended Urbanization: Implications'.

277   Lefebvre, *Urban Revolution*, 17.

278   Monte-Mór, 'Modernities in the Jungle'; Castriota, 'Extractivism and Urban Struggle'; Castriota and Tonucci, 'Extended Urbanization in and from Brazil'; Kanai, 'On the Peripheries of Planetary Urbanization'; Wilson, *Reality of Dreams*; Arboleda, 'In the Nature of the Non-city'; Arboleda, 'Spaces of Extraction, Metropolitan Explosions'; Arboleda, *Planetary Mine*; Kipfer, 'Pushing the Limits of Urban Research'; Couling and Hein, *Urbanisation of the Sea*; Couling, 'Ocean Space and Urbanisation'; Katsikis, 'Operational Landscapes of Primary Production'; Brenner and Katsikis, 'Operational Landscapes'; Topalović, 'Palm Oil'; Wilson, 'Notes on the Rural City'; Wilson and Bayón, 'Concrete Jungle'; Wilson and Bayón, 'Black Hole Capitalism'; Bathla, 'Delhi without Borders'; Wong, 'Territorially-Nested Urbanization in China'.

279   Schmid and Topalović, *Extended Urbanisation*.

conditions are being levelled out across the planet, but on the contrary high-lights the profoundly uneven and contradictory character of contemporary urbanisation processes.

Analysing the Urbanisation Process

The presentation of the urbanisation process in this chapter, following Lefebvre's method, traced the entire process of discovery: starting from the postulate of philosophy becoming worldly, Lefebvre began the study of everyday life, which he understood as a historical product that had only emerged with the industri-alisation and commodification of society. As this analysis progressed, it became apparent that everyday life was increasingly dominated by the process of urbanisation. This process can be defined in two ways: as the progressive spread of urban areas and as the fundamental transformation of cities. By observing the phenomenon of urbanisation and analysing the double crisis of city and countryside, Lefebvre developed his strategic hypothesis of the complete urbanisation of society.

This hypothesis marks a first, decisive stage on the way to a new theory of the urban. It makes it possible to grasp urbanisation in terms of the entire soci-ety and to understand it as a historical phenomenon. Lefebvre approaches this phenomenon analytically in two steps or operations. In the first step, on the basis of an historical analysis, he constructs a space-time axis of urbanisation. This perspective entails the loss of the 'object' of the city – urbanisation ulti-mately results in the complete urbanisation of society; the city dissolves and thus proves to be a historical configuration.

In a second step, Lefebvre constructed a sequence of three spatio-temporal fields or continents: the rural, the industrial, and the urban. This analysis looks at the same process of urbanisation from a comprehensive perspective and shows that the rural field is captured by industrialisation, which in turn gener-ates urbanisation. This double analytical movement, along the time-space axis of urbanisation and across the spatio-temporal fields, reveals a virtual object – urban society. Lefebvre does not define it as an already achieved reality, but as a prospect, as an enlightening virtuality: urban society is the possible.

It is in this context that the 'crisis of the city', as crises of everyday life and the functional industrial organisation of the city, which formed the starting point of this investigation, can be situated more precisely. For Lefebvre, it marks a transition, the transition from industrial to urban society. Accordingly, the phenomena and processes that today determine everyday life and the produc-tion process must be analysed in terms of this urban society. Thus, the urban represents the episteme of contemporary society. Walter Prigge notes with reference to Lefebvre's considerations: 'The urban is the condition of the possibility of the cognition of society today; here its present truth appears.'[280] He concludes that the challenge and the task of urban research is finding a new approach to social theory building from the analysis of the urban.

This crisis of the city is therefore not only a material and social crisis, but also an epistemological one: the 'critical zone' on the space-time axis of urbanisation constitutes a 'blind field' that reveals an important gap: the absence of an epistemology of the urban. When the urban becomes pervasive, how can it be recognised at all? How can it be grasped and analysed? A new problem springs directly from Lefebvre's analysis – the loss of the city as object of urban research. His theory of the urban is still incomplete. What does 'city' mean in an urbanised world? This question will be explored in the following chapter.

---

280   Prigge, 'Urbi et orbi', 180. Translation by author.

4

The Urban Level

The analysis presented in chapter 3 reconstructed the first part of Lefebvre's theoretical engagement with the phenomenon of urbanisation. Starting from the thesis of the complete urbanisation of society, he developed the outlines of a (possible) urban society as a result of an ongoing urban revolution.

At the time Lefebvre published these thoughts, they represented a radical break with the conventional (Western) understanding of the city: he regarded 'the city' as a historical category dissolving in the process of urbanisation. As a consequence, the city could no longer be analysed as an object, as a bounded and delimited unit. Instead, he shifted his analysis to focus on a transformation process – urbanisation – and on the inherent possibility of the emergence of an urban society. He already established the basis for this fundamental change – which indeed can be understood as a paradigm shift – in *The Right to the City*, but he completed his analysis in a comprehensive way in *The Urban Revolution*, where he consistently used the term 'city' in a critical sense (section 4.1).

With this change, however, Lefebvre lost not only the object of his analysis – the city – but also the theoretical instruments for grasping urban reality. Nevertheless, the process of urbanisation does not mean that the city disappears as a built form and as a social reality, nor does it mean that all urban areas become uniform and homogeneous. But it does signify a fundamental change, and it raises the question of how to understand the urban. What is the 'city' in an urban society? What concepts can be used to characterise it?

To define the specificity of the urban in an urbanised world requires a radical analytical reorientation, a change in perspective: the urban must be analysed in the overall context of the entire society. Lefebvre structures this context by identifying three levels or orders of social reality. First, he posits a private level

P, the near order, which is determined by everyday life, the dwelling, the private. Second, he defines a general level G, the far order, which is determined by the (national) state and the world market. In between, he places a middle level M – the urban level, which mediates between the general and the private levels. In this way, Lefebvre designs a general dialectical framework that allows him to integrate everyday life, the urban, and the state into the analysis (section 4.2).

This framework implies a decidedly historical approach to spatial configurations. The levels of social reality are not given a priori, but have developed historically, and each level is in constant transformation. The general level G shows the tendency to expand from the national scale to the planetary scale. Lefebvre used the concept of *mondialisation* to characterise this process, long before the English term 'globalisation' was coined. The private level P is also changing radically, as it is increasingly dominated by an industrial rationality and a market logic, resulting in the development and expansion of everydayness. Between these two levels lies the urban level, the middle and mediating level, which, however, is being eroded through the urbanisation process and is in danger of disappearing (section 4.3).

By applying the most extreme hypothesis, the dissolution and disappearance of the city, Lefebvre reveals the specific quality of the urban level: it is a social resource; its productivity lies in bringing together the most diverse elements of society. In this way, Lefebvre arrives at a new definition of the urban: it is a specific form – centrality. The question of the specificity of the urban in an urbanised world can now be clarified more precisely: upon and amid the ruins of the old city, new urban practices emerge, which rediscover and recreate the 'urban' (section 4.4).

Centrality can be understood as a social resource. With *mondialisation*, the decision-making power over the worldwide production process has been increasingly concentrated in certain privileged cities, which have been restored as centres of economic control and decision-making. As a result, large portions of the population have been excluded from centrality and banished to the periphery. The struggle for centrality thus emerges from this analysis as the fundamental contradiction of the urban in the late twentieth century. Lefebvre derived from this conclusion the demand for a right to the city, which he understood as a right to centrality, the right to access the possibilities and opportunities of the centre, and the right for self-determination in the creation of urban space. At the beginning of the twenty-first century, 'the right to the city' became increasingly popular as a slogan and battle cry, and also as a theoretical concept. It has been used by a wide variety of groups and institutions, in activist milieus and radical movements, but it has also been used by reformist initiatives and organisations. In addition, a rapidly increasing number of academic publications have applied the concept to a wide variety of urban movements and situations, while also modifying its meaning in many ways (section 4.5).

Placed into the context of the planetary reach of urbanisation, however, centrality can no longer be considered from the perspective of an individual urban area. The relationship between centre and periphery extends to planetary scale, and must be considered from this perspective. The question of centrality thus expands to the dialectic of centralisation and peripheralisation. New centralities are emerging in various locations across the planet, while many previously agrarian and industrial areas are facing sometimes dramatic processes of peripheralisation. This results in a complex urban topography, which is characterised by the simultaneity of different processes of peripheralisation and centralisation (section 4.6).

4.1 The City in an Urbanised World

> And now we go back to the city. The concept of the city, as such, belongs
> to history; it is a *historical category*.[1]

The starting point of Lefebvre's analysis of the urbanisation process was the 'crisis of the city'. As it turned out, this crisis was a crisis not only in practice, but also of theory. It revealed the problems with previous definitions of the urban, whose 'object' – the 'city' – is disappearing: the city explodes, dissolves into fragments, and urbanisation becomes general. This observation led Lefebvre to a change in perspective: from the definition and analysis of an object, the 'city', to the analysis of a process, urbanisation.

Lefebvre made this transition mainly in between writing his main works on the question of the urban. In *The Right to the City*, he was still defining the city as a (spatial) object.[2] He had, accordingly, considerable problems with clearly distinguishing the terms 'city' and 'urban society' from one another. The question which arose, then, was this: how are the dimensions and the manifold contradictions of the urban society developing on the ruins of the city to be conceptualised? For Lefebvre, this question marked the 'critical point' of a practical and theoretical rupture in the development of the city.[3]

In *The Urban Revolution*, Lefebvre considered this 'critical point' from a new

---

1   Lefebvre, *Marxist Thought and the City*, 116.
2   Lefebvre, *Urban Revolution*, 194.
3   Lefebvre, *Right to the City*, 126.

perspective. He states that the city as an entity has only a historical existence: 'The concept of the city no longer corresponds to a social object. Sociologically, it is a pseudo-concept.'[4] Instead, Lefebvre introduces the terms 'urbanisation' and 'urban society' into his analysis, because the term 'city' is to be understood as an object, whereas a theoretical approach requires a critique of this object and a more complex concept of a possible object: the urban society.[5] From this perspective, Lefebvre argues, there can be no science of the city (such as urban sociology or urban economics), but only an emerging cognition of the general process of urbanisation.[6] For this reason, Lefebvre consistently substituted in his texts the terms 'urban' or 'urban society' for 'the city'. However, this change is only partly due to the results of Lefebvre's historical analysis. It is also the consequence of Lefebvre's theoretical premises, which accorded epistemological priority to activity and the production process over the result and the product (see section 2.2).

With this change in perspective, however, Lefebvre has also lost the 'object' of his analysis: the city. The epistemological shift from 'city' to 'urbanisation' does not fundamentally solve the problem of identifying the object of analysis. In Lefebvre's understanding, urbanisation is a 'total' phenomenon, which for this reason alone evades any 'objectification'. It cannot therefore represent a scientific 'object'.[7] Even the construction of 'urban society' as a 'virtual', utopian 'object' does not bring a solution. This is not only due to the virtual character of this object, but also because it is located on a different level of analysis, that of society as a whole. Thus, although Lefebvre rejects the 'city' as a concept and replaces it with 'urban society', he is still confronted by the 'city' in his analysis.

Definitions of the City

To theoretically situate the problematic Lefebvre faced, it is helpful to return to earlier debates on the specificity of the urban (see section 1.1). In principle, there are two different approaches to this question: on the one hand, the city can be defined as a distinct (spatial) unit which can be delimited, and which is defined by certain characteristics; on the other hand, it can be analysed in the context of the contradiction between the city and its counterpart, the country.

The first approach corresponds to the ideal type of the city as defined by

---

4   Lefebvre, *Urban Revolution*, 57.
5   Ibid., 50.
6   Ibid., 16.
7   Ibid., 57.

Max Weber:[8] the city forms a distinct unit that is constituted by a political body, the city community. This political body has its own rules and laws, and separates itself from the outside world with its walls and ramparts. The Chicago School of Sociology had a similar idea, taking bioecology as its point of departure and conceiving of the city as a social organism subject to its own (socio-ecological) laws.[9]

Even as theorists responded to the 'crisis of the city', the idea that the city forms a social unit has persisted, and there have been repeated attempts to reconstruct this unity within the dissolving urban areas. This has included attempts to identify commuter zones and define agglomerations or urban regions accordingly. Even critical urban studies have not been able to give up these ideas completely (see section 1.2). The theory of collective consumption, for example, defines the city as a unit for the reproduction of labour power, which, as Castells himself noted, hardly differs from the definition of agglomeration as it is used in demographics, geography, and economics – an agglomeration in the statistical sense, starting from the spatial form of commuting.[10] In a similar way, Harvey defined the city or urban region as a physically distinct social unit, using the working day as a temporal measure to define this unit.[11] In the recent history of urban research, the perimeter of this urban unit has been continuously extended in various attempts to delimit the sprawling urban areas, up to 'metropolitan regions' and 'urban megaregions', with their overlapping, functionally linked, polycentric catchment areas.[12]

Marx and Engels applied a fundamentally different way of defining the city, one that does not pose the problem of the urban boundary. They placed the dialectical contradiction of city and country at the centre of their analysis and examined its development over time. In their conception, this contradiction ultimately leads to its dialectical sublation, which they imagined as taking the form of industrial towns closely linked to the surrounding agrarian hinterland (see section 3.2). One of Lefebvre's most important achievements was to have interpreted the sublation of this contradiction differently – as the complete urbanisation of society.

Louis Wirth brought a different approach into play by trying to capture the urban way of life using the criteria of size, density, and heterogeneity.[13] This approach made it possible to determine a gradual transition from the 'rural' to

---

8   Max Weber, *The City*.
9   Park, Burgess, and McKenzie, *The City*.
10 Castells, *The Urban Question*.
11 Harvey, *Urbanization of Capital*.
12 See for example Harrison and Hoyler, *Megaregions*.
13 Wirth, 'Urbanism as a Way of Life'.

the 'urban' way of life, explicitly referring to the ethnological concept that Robert Redfield called the 'folk-urban continuum'.[14] However, Wirth's definition, which was based on the theory of the Chicago School, still rested on the idea of a bounded (material) 'settlement space' and thus postulated a spatial unity of the urban, from which it derived cultural and social characteristics based on material conditions, an approach that has been strongly criticised for its spatial determinism.

Taking these difficulties into consideration, Peter Saunders called for a radical departure in urban sociology from attempts at defining the city in spatial terms. In his book *Social Theory and the Urban Question*, one of the most influential urban sociological treatises of the 1980s, he argued, drawing on classical concepts developed by Marx, Weber, and Durkheim, that the city had played a historically specific role in the development of Western capitalism, but that it could no longer be considered a significant category of analysis from a sociological point of view.[15] He tried to prove that although most of the questions relevant to urban sociology occur in cities, they are, ultimately, questions of the entire society. Urban sociology, he argued, had therefore lost the city as a specific object of analysis.[16] He conceded, particularly with reference to Lefebvre, Harvey, and Massey, that the city still has a significant function as a spatial configuration in the process of capital accumulation and that the city is thus a valid object for political-economic analyses. At the same time, however, he maintained that the problem of space must be separated from the analysis of specific social processes and accordingly called for a 'non-spatial' urban sociology.[17]

At first glance, this position seems to follow Lefebvre's argument and take up his concept of urban society: from a sociological point of view, the entire society has to be examined, and the city is relevant only as a historical category. However, Lefebvre never intended to analytically remove the city from consideration. On the contrary: his idea of the urban society consisted precisely in restoring the specificity of the urban as a concrete, material reality.

---

14   Redfield, 'The Folk Society'.

15   Saunders, *Social Theory and the Urban Question*, 204; see also Brenner and Schmid, 'The "Urban Age" in Question'.

16   Saunders, *Social Theory and the Urban Question*, 203–4.

17   Ibid., 178–93, 203.

In Search of the Specificity of the Urban

As was to be expected, Lefebvre articulated a fierce critique of existing theories of the city. However, with the exception of the works of Marx and Engels (see section 3.2), he did not engage with other theories. He merely argued that the extant theoretical concepts of the city or urban reality were composed of facts, representations, and images borrowed from the pre-industrial or even the pre-capitalist city. In practice, however, the core of the city, the essential part of the image and the concept of the city, had exploded. As a result, such analyses of the city and urbanisation had become obsolete, as they were no longer able to understand the current urban reality:[18]

> Until recently, theoretical thinking conceived the city as an entity, as an organism and a whole among others . . . One would thus see in it a simple result, a local effect reflecting purely and simply general history. These representations . . . did not contain theoretical knowledge of the city and did not lead to this knowledge; moreover, they blocked at a quite basic level the enquiry; they were ideologies rather than concepts and theories.[19]

Lefebvre's general critique of previous representations of the city thus contains two key points. First, the city had been conceived of as an entity, an idea that he rejected with his thesis of complete urbanisation. His second critique is that the city had been seen as a local 'reflex' of universal history – a version of the deduction thesis, discussed in section 1.1. However, as the previous chapter noted, Lefebvre does not regard the city as a mere expression of general history and society, but on the contrary as a place which is historically generative and plays an important role in the production of society.

These considerations, however, leave Lefebvre confronted with a central contradiction brought to light by his own analysis. On the one hand, the city dissolves in the urbanisation process and reveals a virtual point of convergence: urban society. On the other hand, it still persists as an image, an ideology, but also as a built form.

> However, the city has a historical existence that is impossible to ignore. Small and midsize cities will be around for some time. An image or representation of the city can perpetuate itself, survive its conditions,

---

18   Lefebvre, *Right to the City*, 74; see also Lefebvre, *Urban Revolution*, 125–6.
19   Lefebvre, *Right to the City*, 100.

inspire an ideology and urbanist projects. In other words, the 'real' sociological 'object' is an image and an ideology![20]

To escape this urban ideology, it might seem logical to separate the social
('urban society') from the material morphology ('the city'). The city would
thereby become an immediately present reality, a practical, sensual, architectural fact. In contrast to this material reality, urban society would be conceived
as a social reality composed of relationships that could only be constructed or
reconstructed in thought.[21] This solution to the problem corresponds in large
parts to that proposed by Saunders (see above). For Lefebvre, however, separating the social from the material was dangerous: the urban would be detached
from the soil and the material morphology and would be conceived of as a kind
of imaginary transcendence according to the speculative mode of existence of
being, spirit, and soul. According to this conception, urban society would be
understood merely as a possibility that sought its embodiment in urbanistic
thinking, in knowledge or reflection. But Lefebvre insists that the urban is not
a spirit, not a philosophical being: 'Urban life, urban society, in a word the
urban, cannot go without a practico-material base, a morphology.'[22]

Thus, a new definition of the city is needed, one which does not seek to
conceptualise it as a unity, as a whole, or as an object, but which also does not
deprive it of a material or morphological basis. A definition is needed which
includes the historical city, but is open to urban society. Lefebvre's search for
such a new definition of the urban will be reconstructed in the following
sections. However, even if Lefebvre rejected the term 'city', it nevertheless
demonstrates an astonishing persistence, and it will continue to appear in this
text. This is partly because Lefebvre developed his strong critique of 'the city'
only in *The Urban Revolution* and of course used the term 'city' in his older
texts. More importantly, however, he could not abandon this term completely
even in his subsequent texts. Everyday language permeates his work and is
tenacious because it contains ideas and images that cannot be easily replaced,
since we learned them as children and associate them with very specific
experiences.

---

20   Lefebvre, *Urban Revolution*, 57.
21   Lefebvre, *Right to the City*, 103.
22   Ibid., 103.

4.2 The Urban Level: Mediation

The urban space is concrete contradiction.[23]

The starting points for Lefebvre's redefinition of the urban are the two analytical operations he used to identify the characteristics of the urbanisation process. With his first operation, the construction of a space-time axis of urbanisation, he recognised the 'city' as a specific historical formation that changes in and with history and ultimately dissolves: the city explodes, disintegrates into fragments, and urbanisation becomes generalised (see section 3.3). The second operation approached the city anew from the perspective of the entire society and analysed it as part of the general economic and social development,[24] an analysis that eventually revealed the urban society (see section 3.4).

These two operations leave an analytical lacuna: how the development of the city is linked to the overall development of society. Lefebvre tries to address this question with a third analytical operation. He introduces the concept of 'levels' (*niveaux*): spatio-temporal levels of social reality. He distinguishes three such levels: the private level P, which comprises dwelling and everyday life; the general level G, which is dominated by the state and the (world) market; and a middle or mediating level M, the level of the 'urban'.

Lefebvre's writing style and research procedure pose serious problems for a coherent presentation of his conceptualisation of levels. He presented an introductory, and still very incomplete, sketch in *The Right to the City*, and further developed this analysis in *The Urban Revolution*. There, however, he was primarily interested in the urban level and paid little attention to the private level, which he had already analysed in detail in his studies on everyday life (see section 3.1). Indeed, he had already affirmed in his *Metaphilosophy* that everyday life had been established and consolidated as a 'level' of social reality.[25] In contrast, level G remains abstract and diffuse in Lefebvre's texts on the urban: it is the level of the world market and the nation state, and these units mostly interested him as background, as instances of domination and power which remain attached to the process of industrialisation and which he sought to transcend with his concept of the urban revolution. Only in his later works, in *The Survival of Capitalism*, in *The Production of Space*, and especially in *De l'État*, did he pay greater attention to level G. However, and this complicates the following theoretical

---

23   Lefebvre, *Urban Revolution*, 39.
24   Ibid., 80.
25   Lefebvre, *Metaphilosophy*, 108.

reconstruction, the concept of levels still plays only a secondary role in these texts. In *The Production of Space*, Lefebvre presents it explicitly, but in a very cursory way and without any commentary.[26] In *De l'État*, the work that treats level G most directly, the concept of levels appears, but rather implicitly and mixed with the concept of 'scale' (*échelle*) (see section 7.5).

The concept of the levels of social reality presented in the following sections is therefore the result of a reconstruction that cannot be found in this direct form in Lefebvre's texts. It is the result of an attempt to bring together scattered passages and make them fruitful for analysis.

Spatio-Temporal Levels of Social Reality

We shall begin with level P. It denotes the private (*le privé*), or the 'near order' (*l'ordre proche*). Lefebvre defines it as the level of practico-sensual reality (*réalité pratico-sensible*), as the level of direct, personal, and interpersonal relations between individuals and the social groups that constitute society. These groups can be smaller or bigger and more or less organised and structured. Lefebvre includes the family, the neighbourhood, organised bodies, professions, and corporations, and so on. The near order is the level of family life, of sexual life, of dwelling but also of the division of labour. It is linked to particular ways of living and modulating the everyday. In a comprehensive sense, level P is thus the level of everyday life.[27]

Lefebvre contrasts this near order with the far order (*l'ordre lointain*), the most general level of social reality. This is the level of society as a whole, and it is also the level of action of the powerful institutions that organise and regulate society, such as religious institutions or the state.[28] Lefebvre therefore calls this level the *niveau global* or level G. It should be noted that the French term 'global' means general, overall, and not worldwide, so it should not be translated into English as 'global' – which is, however, the case in almost all translations so far. The *niveau global* thus refers to the general, superordinate level and not necessarily to the level of the entire world. In an early formulation, Lefebvre also calls this level the *niveau supérieur* (the upper level),[29] and a passage in *De l'État* indicates that Lefebvre subsumes the region, the nation, and the world under this level.[30]

---

26   Lefebvre, *Production of Space*, 155–6.
27   Lefebvre, *Right to the City*, 112–14.
28   Ibid., 112.
29   Ibid., 115.
30   Lefebvre, *State, Space, World*, 228; Lefebvre, *De l'État*, vol. 4, 273.

This general level or far order is endowed with power. It encompasses moral and legal principles, religions, state power, political strategies, 'class logics'; it is represented by a legal code (which may or may not be formalised), and is regulated by 'culture' and by contexts of meaning (*ensembles signifiants*). The general level is an abstract, formal, supra-sensory (*suprasensible*), and transcendental phenomenon; it is the level where general, abstract relations come into play, such as the capital market, spatial planning, or the planning of industrial production, and where general processes predominate, such as industrialisation or the exchange of commodities.[31]

Between these two levels, the private and the general, Lefebvre situates an intermediate level, level M. This letter stands for *moyenne*, *mixte*, or *mediation*; it is a middle, mixed, mediating level. This is the urban level in the true sense. It has a specific code that is oriented around certain institutions, such as the municipal authorities with their services, information channels, distribution networks, and decision-making power.[32]

These three levels correspond to specific practices and processes: the general level G is the level of the overarching processes of industrialisation and urbanisation, the level of the nation state and state power; level M is the level of urban society; and the private level P is the level of the modalities of dwelling and the modulations of the everyday.[33] The three levels also correspond to three specialised disciplines or competencies: planning and economics on level G, 'urbanism' (urban design and urban planning) on level M, and architecture on level P.[34]

The Urban as Mediation

From a general perspective, the urban level thus forms an intermediate level between, on the one hand, the far order, the state, knowledge, institutions, and ideologies; and, on the other, the near order, everyday life, and dwelling:[35] '[The city] is situated at an interface, half-way between what is called the *near order* . . . and the *far order* . . .'[36] The city is only an intermediate level, but for Lefebvre it is of decisive importance, because it serves as a mediating instance between the general and private levels:[37]

---

31   Lefebvre, *Right to the City*, 123, 144, 167, 170; Lefebvre, *Urban Revolution*, 83, 90.
32   Lefebvre, *Right to the City*, 119, 124; Lefebvre, *Urban Revolution*, 79.
33   Lefebvre, *Right to the City*, 130.
34   Lefebvre, *Production of Space*, 12.
35   Lefebvre, *Urban Revolution*, 89.
36   Lefebvre, *Right to the City*, 101.
37   Ibid., 142.

The city is a *mediation* among mediations. Containing the *near* order, it maintains it; it fosters relations of production and property; it is the place of their reproduction. Contained in the *far order*, it supports it; it incarnates it.[38]

Thus, level G lies both above and within the city. The social structure appears and becomes perceptible in the city. Conversely, the city is part of society: it contains and embodies institutions and ideologies and makes them perceptible.[39] At the same time, the city forms, in a certain sense, an 'envelope' for dwelling. It is the surrounding of 'private' life, the beginning and end point of networks that allow the exchange of information and also transmit commands, thus imposing the far order on the near order.[40] Everyday life, which is directed and regulated by institutions from 'above', is thus constituted at the urban level, where it is consolidated by multiple constraints:[41] 'It is in the urban that the everyday is establishing itself, constituting itself, forming itself.'[42] In summary, the three spatio-temporal levels of social reality can be characterised as follows: as the near or immediate, the urban or mediating, and the distant or mediated.[43]

The Urban as Text

From these considerations, Lefebvre gains a 'first' definition of the city: it is a projection of society on the ground. 'We therefore here propose a first definition of the city as a *projection of society on the ground*, that is, not only on the actual site, but at a specific level, perceived and conceived by thought, which determines the city and the urban.'[44]

Once again, a problem of translation arises here: *projeter* means not only to project, but also to throw or to hurl. Society is thus thrown onto the ground, not only onto a sensually palpable terrain, but also onto a specific level that is conceived by thinking. The far order manifests itself through and in immediacy; it becomes visible by inscribing itself into reality.[45] This reality, this level,

---

38   Ibid., 101. Translation amended.
39   Ibid., 112.
40   Ibid., 114.
41   Ibid., 143.
42   Lefebvre, *De l'État*, vol. 4, 270. Translation by author.
43   Ibid., 273.
44   Lefebvre, *Right to the City*, 109.
45   Ibid., 109, 115.

this terrain, is the city. This thought can also be expressed the other way around: it is the city which projects the far order, the social order, onto the terrain and onto the surface of immediate life. It inscribes this order and translates it into commands and instructions that regulate action and the use of time. It stipulates a meticulous hierarchy of places, moments, occupations, people.[46] 'In the form of meaning, in the form of simultaneity and encounters, in the form, finally, of an "urban" language and writing, the city dispatches *orders*. The *far order* is projected into the *near order*.'[47]

The city could therefore also be read as a social text, which to a certain extent contains a compendium of society: 'Yes, the city can be read because it writes, because it was writing.'[48] The writing (or voice) of the city, then, is the buildings, the monuments, but also the streets and squares, the empty spaces, the spontaneous theatricality of the meetings, the celebrations, the ceremonies.[49] Lefebvre specifies though that what is inscribed into the urban space is not only a far order, a mode of production, a general code, but also times and rhythms: 'The city is heard as much as music as it is read as a discursive writing.'[50]

It could also be said, therefore, that the different levels are represented in the urban reality in and by different 'materialities' or 'artefacts'.[51] Level G would thus be represented by monuments, large-scale urban projects, ministries, and religious buildings, but also by motorways and by the general structure of the urban fabric. These buildings and infrastructures presuppose control by superior organisational powers, and they project their worldview onto the ground. They do not coincide with the dominant social relations, but they represent their social 'presence'.[52] In the same sense, level M would be represented by streets, squares, avenues, public buildings (town halls, schools, and so on), while level P includes private buildings, apartment blocks, single-family homes, villas, shanties, and so forth.[53] The three levels can therefore also be understood linguistically as semiotic levels inscribed in the terrain: the semiology of power – signifying the general level – the properly urban semiology, and the semiology of daily life – signifying ways of living and dwelling.[54]

---

46   Ibid., 109, 115, 153; Lefebvre, *Urban Revolution*, 41.
47   Lefebvre, *Right to the City*, 114.
48   Ibid., 108.
49   Ibid., 113–14.
50   Ibid., 109.
51   Ibid., 112.
52   Ibid., 112; Lefebvre, *Urban Revolution*, 27, 72.
53   Lefebvre, *Urban Revolution*, 80–1.
54   Lefebvre, *Right to the City*, 116.

However, the city's messages are not clear, and even the far order is rarely coherent. There are religious, political, and moral orders, and each of them relates to an ideology with practical implications.[55] Furthermore, general processes and relations are only inscribed in the urban text as transferred by ideologies and political strategies. Therefore, it is difficult to conceive the city as a single semantic, semiotic, or semiological system, as an 'urban language' consisting of a totality of signs. In the course of its projection onto a specific level, the general code of society is modified. The specific code of the urban is a modulation of it, a version, a translation. It is not enough to examine this text without referring to the context, to that which remains to be deciphered above and below the urban text: institutions and ideologies on the one hand; and on the other, everyday life, sexual and family life – the 'unconscious of the urban', which hardly expresses and writes itself, but instead conceals itself in the inhabited spaces. The city can therefore not be understood as a single system of meaning, sense, or value: the different levels of reality forbid any such systematisation.[56]

For Lefebvre, therefore, semiotics cannot exhaust the practical and ideological reality of the city. The theory of the city as a system of meaning tends to become an ideology itself. It separates the urban from its morphological basis, and from social practice, by reducing it to the relationship of signifier and signified and abstracting it from actually perceived meanings.[57] In most cases, the semiotics of the city remains rooted in the historical city and thus in a historical configuration that has long since been disintegrated by the urbanisation process.

As social text, this historic city no longer has a coherent set of prescriptions, of use of time linked to symbols and to a style. This text is moving away. It takes the form of a document, or an exhibition, or a museum. The city historically constructed is no longer lived and is no longer understood practically. It is only an object of cultural consumption for tourists, for a[n] aestheticism, avid for spectacles and the picturesque. Even for those who seek to understand it with warmth, it is gone.[58]

---

55   Ibid., 114.
56   Ibid., 108, 114.
57   Ibid., 114–15.
58   Ibid., 148.

The Dimensions of the Urban Level

To conclude: for Lefebvre, the urban forms a partial and open totality, which is itself a level of more comprehensive totalities (the nation, the national territory, the state).[59] In this sense, it is an intermediate level between abstract social processes and practical-sensual reality. Lefebvre characterises the urban as a mediation between the private and the general level, as a projection of the far order into the near order, and as a social text that translates different orders into instructions for action, without, however, achieving coherence and clarity.

The indeterminacy of these formulations, which Lefebvre varies again and again, indicates that he is circling around a theoretical object which he cannot yet identify and fully explain conceptually. As we will see in chapter 5, this object is space, whose 'levels' Lefebvre elaborates in *The Right to the City* and *The Urban Revolution*, but whose other characteristics still remain in the dark at this stage. In *The Production of Space*, he will approach and conceptualise these characteristics with the category of 'dimensions'. However, as we have just seen, this category already exists implicitly in *The Urban Revolution*. In a short passage, Lefebvre distinguishes between three 'dimensions' or 'essential charac-teristics' of the urban level. First, it is a projection of social relations onto the terrain. Second, it is the terrain on which different strategies or logics collide – in this capacity, he sees it as a means of mediation, a tool for action by institu-tions and social organisations. And third, it forms a specific social reality, the level of an urban practice.[60]

In *The Production of Space*, Lefebvre will assign precise terms to these 'dimensions': the city as projection (and as text) is a 'space of representation', the city as a terrain of strategies is a 'representation of space', and the urban practice is, in a comprehensive sense, a 'spatial practice'. The concept of 'dimen-sions' will be discussed and analysed in detail in chapter 5, as key to the analy-sis of the production of space. However, it is helpful for the following explana-tions to keep in mind this 'dimensionality', which cuts across the levels (discussed in detail in section 8.2).

---

59   Lefebvre, *De l'État*, vol. 4, 270.
60   Lefebvre, *Urban Revolution*, 87.

4.3 The General and the Private

> A new space *tends* to develop, at the world scale, integrating and
> disintegrating the national and the local.[61]

The previous section presented an exposition of the three spatio-temporal
levels of social reality and a first characterisation of the specificity of the urban
level as a level of mediation between the near and far orders. As became apparent, Lefebvre does not conceive of these three levels as closed units, but as
partial and open totalities that are linked to other totalities.[62] They can only be
separated from each other by abstraction. One should therefore neither separate these levels nor fuse them, but rather explore their various connections,
their articulations and disarticulations, the projections from one level to the
other. The meaning of the levels is relative: they overlap and interpenetrate
each other, which causes interferences; their logics collide and sometimes crash
into each other.[63]

This conception allows Lefebvre to present the development of the urban
level in relation to the other two levels. It is therefore necessary to clarify how
the general level G and the private level P are constituted and which processes
shape these levels. In particular, the question arises of how the urban level M is
articulated with the other two levels, how these articulations change in the
course of historical development, and how the urban level is influenced by
these changes.

On the one hand, there is the general level G. Lefebvre explores this level
mainly in the context of his analysis of the state in his four-volume work *De
l'État*. This level is characterised by the process of *mondialisation*, which leads
to the extension of state control and the world market to the entire globe. As
Lefebvre notes in the introduction of *De l'État*, the 'state' is, therefore, not actually the object of this book, but rather its *mondialisation*, a process on the path
to realisation.[64] The object of analysis is thus the 'world system of states'.[65]

As Brenner and Elden have noted, the French term *mondialisation* cannot
be translated as 'globalisation', because the two terms denote different
processes.[66] *Mondialisation* is derived from *le monde* (the world), and has been

---

61   Lefebvre, 'Preface to the New Edition', 212.

62   Lefebvre, *De l'État*, vol. 4, 270.

63   Lefebvre, *Right to the City*, 112; Lefebvre, *Urban Revolution*, 86, 88–9; Lefebvre,
Production of Space, 387.

64   Lefebvre, *De l'État*, vol. 1, 41.

65   Ibid.; Lefebvre, *De l'État*, vol. 3, 253.

66   Brenner and Elden, introduction to *State, Space, World*, 22.

used in the French-speaking world since the early twentieth century to describe the worldwide expansion of organisations and of capitalism in general. Lefebvre gives this term additional meanings, which will be analysed in more detail below. In contrast, the term 'globalisation' was not widely used until the 1980s. As an economic term it describes the emergence of global networks of interaction, exchange, and production, which have emerged on a large scale since the crisis of Fordism.[67] Initially, this term was strongly contested by the anti-globalisation or counter-globalisation movements of the late 1990s, and was thus also a political term. To mark the difference between the two terms and the concepts they designate I will, like Brenner and Elden, use the term *mondialisation* in the French original in the following, as well as the terms *mondial* and *mondialité* derived from it, which are often translated as 'worldwide' and 'worldliness', though these terms do not really capture the scope of meaning of the French terms.

The counterpart of the general level G is the private level P, the level of the everyday and the private. It is characterised by the contradiction between *habiter* (habitation, dwelling) and the 'habitat'. While *habiter* for Lefebvre describes an experienced activity, he takes the term 'habitat' from the field of architecture and urban planning and uses it to indicate the industrial rationality that dominates everyday life.

In this context, it is revealing that Lefebvre refers directly to two texts by Heidegger in his discussion of both *mondialisation* and *habiter*. Because of Heidegger's intellectual and political affinity to National Socialism, this reference has triggered some heated discussions in recent times, as shown, for example, in Geoffrey Waite's furious attack on 'Left-Heideggerian' approaches.[68]

Lefebvre had an ambivalent relationship to Heidegger. They had personally exchanged ideas before the Second World War, and Heidegger's phenomenological philosophy did influence Lefebvre, although, I believe, much less than Elden claims.[69] In his *L'existentialisme* of 1946, Lefebvre sharply criticised Heidegger's 'backward-looking' and 'profascist' philosophy, his fundamental pessimism, and his anti-humanistic mystifications.[70] At the same time, he saw in his thinking 'underground currents'[71] that interested him – and that influenced his concepts of the lived and of everyday life. Heidegger thus became, together with Bachelard and Merleau-Ponty, an important inspiration for the concept of *l'espace vécu*, lived space (see section 5.6).

---

67   Schmid, 'Urbane Region und Territorialverhältnis'.
68   Waite, 'Lefebvre without Heidegger'.
69   Elden, *Understanding Henri Lefebvre*, 78–80.
70   Lefebvre, *L'existentialisme*, 175–7.
71   Hess, *Henri Lefebvre et l'aventure du siècle*, 54.

Mondialité *and* Mondialisation

As explained in the previous section, the general level G is the space of institutions, and thus primarily the level of the state, the nation, and the national territory.[72] However, this national configuration is not absolute; it is a historical product and as such subject to constant change. The central aspect for Lefebvre is that this level shows a tendency to expand to a world-wide scale, a process directly linked to the expansion of the world of commodities: 'The world market flourishes, so to speak. The worldwide [*la mondialité*] realizes itself as a concrete abstraction. "Everything" (the total-ity) is bought and sold.'[73]

For Lefebvre, the extension of the general level G to the entire globe is the core of the process of *mondialisation*. A new concrete totality emerges, which is not limited to the world market, but incorporates wider processes. As Lefebvre discussed in detail in *Metaphilosophy*, *mondialisation* is rooted in industrialisation and essentially coincides with modernity: 'From particular cultures (humanism and classicism, with their abstract universality; culture of peasant origin; bourgeois culture; proletarian culture; national cultures) we pass to "Mondial" or world culture, which initially consists in the worldwide consumption and destruction of all past and dead cultures.'[74] *La mondialité* marks a transition from a life that is controlled and organised by institutions and ideas ('the sacred', 'culture') to a life left to itself, an abandoned life, from rootedness (in the soil, in the city, in the milieu) to 'uprooting', from a limited but concrete human being to a human being of perfect abstraction.[75]

Which sectors are transformed by *mondialisation*? According to Lefebvre, it is first of all exchange and trade, which produce the world market. Then comes the state, which forms a world system of states with its state-centred technoc-racy. But everyday life also becomes 'mondialised'.[76] *Le mondial* thus rises to the horizon in a paradoxical way, as a possibility that is already partially and fragmentarily realised, thus already introduced and produced, but which is also counteracted by the divisive forces of modernity and states. Nevertheless, *le mondial* tends to break down boundaries and overcome the obstacles that stand in its way. In this context, Lefebvre evokes the multi- or rather suprana-tional corporations that out-manoeuvre states and use them to consolidate

---

72   See Lefebvre, *Urban Revolution*, 79; Lefebvre, *De l'État*, vol. 4, 270.
73   Lefebvre, *Production of Space*, 341. Translation by author.
74   Lefebvre, *Metaphilosophy*, 305. Translation amended.
75   Ibid.
76   Lefebvre, *State, Space, World*, 283; Lefebvre, *De l'État*, vol. 4, 432.

their domination.[77] And he also discusses, more than a decade before the 'globalisation debate', the *mondialisation* of production and production cycles, the investment and accumulation of productive capital by firms operating on a worldwide scale, the *mondialisation* of capital markets, and thus the transfer of surplus value. The term 'internationalisation' would undervalue the scope of these phenomena, he notes, because the relationship between capital and labour has changed its (spatial) scale. At the same time, however, the relations of production remain tied to the national scale. In this way, he sees a contradictory, fractured planetary space emerging, in which the nation states retain their functions – control, hierarchisation, regulation –while, at the same time, some subnational regions become stronger and states internally more differentiated, and supranational companies emerge.[78] Thus, a new space is forming on a planetary scale that integrates and disintegrates the national and the local. This is a process full of contradictions, linked to the conflict between a worldwide division of labour and the effort to create a new world order associated with a different rationality.[79] Lefebvre calls this new emerging space a 'homogeneous-fractured space' (*espace homogène-brisé*), which will be discussed in detail in section 6.3.

It is remarkable how Lefebvre anticipated the debate on globalisation and regionalisation that would fully unfold only in the 1980s. He thereby specifically addressed the double movement of the emergence of global production networks on the one hand and the regionalisation of production systems on the other (see section 1.3).

The Mondial *and the Planetary*

It is important to note that the historical developments described above form only one aspect of Lefebvre's use of the term *mondialisation*. Its epistemological background lies deeper and includes a definition that goes back to Heidegger and his famous quotation 'The world worlds.' Lefebvre writes:

> When Heidegger utters 'Die Welt weltet' (the world worlds [*le monde se mondifie*]), this statement, which is almost a tautology, has great meaning. He means to say that the worldwide conceives itself in and by itself and not by another thing (history, spirit, labour, science, etc.). The world

---

77 Lefebvre, *State, Space, World*, 275; Lefebvre, *De l'État*, vol. 4, 415–16.
78 Lefebvre, *State, Space, World*, 246–7; Lefebvre, *De l'État*, vol. 4, 314–16; Lefebvre, *Production of Space*, 351.
79 Lefebvre, 'Preface to the New Edition', 212.

becomes world, becoming what virtually it was. It transforms itself by becoming worldwide. In it discovery and creation converge. It does not exist before it creates itself, and yet, it proclaimed itself, possible/impossible, through all the powers, technology, knowledge, art.[80]

Heidegger said, 'The world worlds.'[81] It should be noted that the verb '*welten*' does not exist in German – it is an invention by Heidegger, a play on words that he introduced in his text 'The Origin of the Work of Art' to show that art 'puts truth to work' and thereby 'founds a history'. For Heidegger, the work of art opens up a world, whereby this 'world' is not necessarily extending across the entire globe. Thus, Heidegger could also say, analogous to the colloquial use of the word, 'The farmer's wife has a world.' Heidegger's word '*welten*' has a shimmering indeterminacy. It evokes associations with 'becoming worldwide' but also with 'becoming worldly or mundane'. Lefebvre deliberately plays with this ambiguity when he writes: '*Le monde se fait monde*' (the world becomes worldly; but also, the world becomes world), because becoming worldly means '*devenir monde*' in French.[82]

Lefebvre, however, also made a further reference to the term 'becoming worldly', namely to one of the famous phrases from Marx – 'philosophy's becoming worldly' (*das Weltlich-Werden der Philosophie*; see section 2.4). Thus, shortly after the passage on Heidegger quoted above, he writes that Marx understood the world from the starting point of philosophy and its sublation.[83] Marx had written in his doctoral dissertation: 'The result is that as the world becomes philosophical, philosophy also becomes worldly, so that its realisation is simultaneously its loss.'[84] But, at the same time, explains Lefebvre, Marx also recognised the other side of *mondialisation*: the worldwide expansion, which first takes the form of the world market – a spatial configuration. For Marx, the world market is already multi-layered and differentiated; there are the market of goods, which existed before capitalism, the market of capital, the market of labour, and so on. The domination of a political power and a centre – in Marx's time, England – establishes and controls this spatial configuration that regulates and dominates the flows of production and capital.[85] In this sense, *mondialisation* in Lefebvre means 'becoming worldly' and 'expanding worldwide' at

---

80   Lefebvre, *State, Space, World*, 276; Lefebvre, *De l'État*, vol. 4, 416.

81   Heidegger, 'The Origin of the Work of Art', 170.

82   Lefebvre, *Metaphilosophy*, 44.

83   Lefebvre, *De l'État*, vol. 4, 420.

84   Marx, *Difference between the Democritean and Epicurean Philosophy of Nature*, 85. Translation amended.

85   Lefebvre, *State, Space, World*, 277; Lefebvre, *De l'État*, vol. 4, 419.

the same time, and *le mondial* would have to be translated accordingly as 'worldwide/worldly' in English.

At this point, another central concept comes into play: the earth (*la terre*), or the planet Earth, and the planetary (*le planétaire*). This distinction also originates from the same text by Heidegger quoted above. Here the 'earth' is in conflict with the 'world':

> World and earth are essentially different from one another and yet are never separated. The world grounds itself on the earth, and the earth juts through world. Yet the relation between the world and the earth does not wither away into the empty unity of opposites unconcerned with one another. The world, in resting upon the earth, strives to surmount it. As self-opening it cannot endure anything closed. The earth, however, as sheltering and concealing, tends always to draw the world into itself and keep it there.[86]

Stuart Elden has shown that Lefebvre's interpretation of Heidegger's text was strongly influenced by Kostas Axelos, a good friend and frequent discussion partner, whose book *Vers la pensée planétaire* from 1964 resonates in many of Lefebvre's texts.[87] In a review of Axelos's book Lefebvre explains:

> For human beings, 'earth' is the fundamental point of stability: soil without a horizon, a sphere. The spherical form is also the immutable figure of perfection. When practical action and understanding are removed, this earth appears as a unity of cycles, self-regulating, stable systems: waters, winds, air, light, soils, and sediments.[88]

With the modern world, human-made systems (physical, chemical, economic, and so on) are beginning to use and cover the earth. In this way, the 'human world' constructs itself: 'Around us and for us, planet earth is the world.'[89]

But this world is a broken totality: the planet only enters into our horizon through ruptures, fractures, and separations (between the East and West) and in the threat of nuclear destruction:[90] 'Metaphilosophical thought encompasses this fragmentary, broken totality, en route towards "something else":

---

86   Heidegger, 'The Origin of the Work of Art', 174.
87   See Elden, 'Mondialisation before Globalization'; Axelos, *Vers la pensée planétaire*.
88   Lefebvre, *State, Space, World*, 255.
89   Ibid., 256.
90   Ibid., 257; see also Lefebvre, *Metaphilosophy*, 106.

towards a planetary totality that is totally new.'[91] Already in *Metaphilosophy* Lefebvre sketches out the distinction between the worldwide/worldly (*le mondial*) and the planetary (*le planétaire*),[92] a distinction which then appears repeatedly in his later works. In *Metaphilosophy* he wrote: 'The earth is our world, and what extends to the whole earth worlds itself [*se mondialise*].'[93] In *De L'État*, like an echo, and with direct reference to Axelos, he says: 'For us the planetary is the only figure accessible to the worldwide. Thus goes the world without truce, without end.'[94] 'End', like the French original *fin*, should be understood clearly in its ambiguity: as both end and goal.

So, what is the world? As Lefebvre ironically stated, all great thinkers have thought – and at the same time missed – the totality of the world. The *mondial* cannot be defined by nature – nature opens itself to the *mondial*, but only as transformed into a second, produced nature (see section 6.1). What remains is the planetary, a totality of places, and with it the totality of produced space, which is at the same time a product and a work. Planet Earth stands at the origin and end of productive and creative activity: 'Planetary space gives itself to the human species as theatre and scenario, field of the possible and sudden appearance of the un-foreseen.'[95] Planetary space cannot be explained through the historical past, but is, rather, created by the development of productive forces, by the application of techniques and strategies, by productive investments in infrastructures and energy systems.[96] One could also say that the planet is the material support on which we build our world – or our worlds. In this sense, the planetary is a material support, and, at the same time, a horizon. It is precisely for this reason that urbanisation could also take on a planetary reach (see sections 3.5 and 7.5).

As can be seen here, Lefebvre ultimately created a very independent and dialectical concept of the *mondial* and the planetary, which contains various ingredients. While the *mondial* denotes the world society, and, in a certain sense, also the possibility of a 'world revolution', the planetary signifies the material reality and condition of human existence. In this way, Lefebvre integrated Heidegger's concept into a materialistic and dialectical theory, though one he did not fully develop. It must be said, however, that Heidegger's idea of the *Erde* (earth) could also suggest a completely different interpretation, especially in the historical-political context of its creation. His seemingly harmless

---

91 Lefebvre, *Metaphilosophy*, 307.
92 Ibid., 54.
93 Ibid.
94 Lefebvre, *State, Space, World*, 277; Lefebvre, *De l'État*, vol. 4, 419.
95 Lefebvre, *State, Space, World*, 278; Lefebvre, *De l'État*, vol. 4, 421.
96 Lefebvre, *De l'État*, vol. 4, 95.

philosophical reflection on the work of art is not so innocent when one considers the metaphorical and real meaning of 'earth' and 'soil' under National Socialism.

It should be mentioned here that Heidegger's word creation *welten* ('worlding') subsequently had a career of its own. For example, Gayatri Chakravorty Spivak – with explicit reference to Heidegger – made 'worlding' a central concept in her analysis of colonialism and political inequality.[97] The term has thus also spread into postcolonial urban research, as the book *Worlding Cities* by Ananya Roy and Aihwa Ong shows.[98] At the same time, the term 'planetary' has also experienced a resurgence in recent years, for example in *The Planetary Turn* by Elias and Moraru – again strongly inspired by Spivak, especially by her book *Death of a Discipline*.[99] Although there are some very interesting aspects and parallels, a discussion of these concepts is beyond the scope of this book.

Habiting and Habitat

The transformation of the world affects not only level G, but also the other levels of social reality. As a result, everyday life has also 'become worldly' and has become an integrating and integrated part of this world.[100] In order to define this level more precisely, Lefebvre introduced a fundamental distinction: that between *l'habitat* ('habitat') and *l'habiter* (which is translated either as 'habiting' or 'dwelling'). Habitat, 'a caricatural pseudo-concept', is for Lefebvre the technocratic reduction of living to a mere function.[101] He argues that at the turn of the century, a school of urban thought pushed 'habiting' aside and created the concept of 'habitat', a simplified function that reduced the human being 'to a handful of basic acts: eating, sleeping, and reproducing'. Lefebvre sees in this concept the essence of industrialised everyday life: the habitat, a homogeneous and quantitative space, had been installed from above in ideology and practice, and had forced lived experience to be enclosed in boxes, cages, and even 'dwelling machines' (on the concept of 'lived space', see section 5.5).[102]

In contrast, habiting 'was an age-old practice, poorly expressed, poorly articulated linguistically or conceptually, seen sometimes as vital and

---

97   Spivak, *A Critique of Postcolonial Reason*.
98   Roy and Ong, *Worlding Cities*.
99   Elias and Moraru, *The Planetary Turn*; Spivak, *Death of a Discipline*.
100 Lefebvre, *State, Space, World*, 283; Lefebvre, *De l'État*, vol. 4, 432.
101 Lefebvre, *Urban Revolution*, 81.
102 Ibid.

sometimes as degraded, but always concrete'.[103] In order to find and express habiting and its meaning, Lefebvre requires concepts and categories that descend into the here and now of the 'lived experience' of the inhabitants, into the unknown and unrecognised realm of everyday life.[104] He refers explicitly to Nietzsche and – once again – to Heidegger: 'It required the metaphilosophical meditations of Nietzsche and Heidegger' to restore the meaning of the term 'habiting'.[105]

In 'Building Dwelling Thinking', one of his most famous lectures, Heidegger said: 'Residential buildings do indeed provide lodgings; today's houses may even be well planned, easy to keep, attractively cheap, open to air, light, and sun, but – do the houses in themselves hold any guarantee that *dwelling* occurs in them?'[106] Heidegger saw dwelling as the basic character of being, as the way mortals are on earth. Dwelling, he said, also means staying, residing, and the basic character of dwelling is to spare, to preserve that which protects from harm and threat. Dwelling, then, is the basis of humanity, in the sense of mortals' sojourn on earth.[107] Here the 'earth' reappears again, as discussed in detail above. In 'The Origin of the Work of Art', Heidegger wrote: 'Upon the earth and in it, historical man grounds his dwelling in the world.'[108]

Lefebvre summarises Heidegger's thoughts as follows: 'This means that the relation of the "human being" to nature and its own nature, to "being" and its own being, is situated in habiting, is realized and read there.'[109] Lefebvre clearly sees the reactionary side of Heidegger, but he asserts that even if his 'poetic' critique of habitat can be seen as a right-wing critique, 'nostalgic and atavistic', it has nevertheless introduced the problematic of space: in habiting, the relationship to the possible and the imaginary is realised. It should no longer be treated as a residue, as a trace or result of so-called superior levels. A more radical thinking confirms the permanent primacy of habiting. It is the source or foundation of meaning.[110]

---

103   Ibid.
104   Ibid., 82; Lefebvre, *Right to the City*, 76.
105   Lefebvre, *Urban Revolution*, 81.
106   Heidegger, 'Building Dwelling Thinking', 348.
107   Ibid., 353, 362.
108   Heidegger, 'The Origin of the Work of Art', 172.
109   Lefebvre, *Urban Revolution*, 82.
110   Ibid., 82, 85.

The Banlieues of Paris

The dominance of habitat over habiting or dwelling is most evident to Lefebvre in the construction of the banlieues, the monofunctional settlements on the outskirts of the core cities, which he and his research teams analysed in detail over the years, as Stanek has shown.[111] In *The Right to the City* he summarises this development in Paris as follows: With the construction of the *banlieue* a process was set in motion that decentred the city. A de-urbanised periphery was established around the city, which nevertheless remained dependent on the city. But the inhabitants of the *banlieues* did not stop being urban, even if they lost their consciousness of this and believed themselves to be close to nature, the sun and the green. If urban reality is defined by dependence on the centre, the *banlieues* are urban. If the urban order is defined by a perceptible and legible relationship between centre and periphery, they are 'de-urbanized'.[112] Lefebvre sees a 'unique paradox' in this development: 'One could call it a de-urbanizing and de-urbanized urbanization to emphasize the paradox.'[113]

In a first phase, at the end of the nineteenth and beginning of the twentieth centuries, this process was characterised above all by the relatively disordered, often spontaneous spread of simple single-family houses, called '*pavillons*' (bungalows).[114] In this phase, Lefebvre notes, the notion of 'habitat', which planners used in the term '*habitat pavillonaire*', remained somewhat 'uncertain'.

> Individual owner-occupation will enable variations, particular or individual interpretations of *habitat*. There is a sort of plasticity which allows for modifications and appropriations. The space of the house – fence, garden, various and available corners – leaves a margin of initiative and freedom to *inhabit*, limited but real.[115]

It was only after the Second World War that in Paris (as well as in the rest of France) the construction of state housing on a large scale began. The surge in industry, demographic pressure, and immigration from peripheral areas led to a housing shortage that took on catastrophic proportions and exceeded the capabilities of private companies. Furthermore, they were not interested in the construction of housing because they did not consider it profitable enough.

---

111   Stanek, *Lefebvre on Space*.
112   Lefebvre, *Right to the City*, 78–9.
113   Ibid.
114   Ibid.
115   Ibid., 79.

The state could no longer limit itself to regulating housing developments and confining real estate speculation, but was forced to intervene in housing production itself. The demand for the 'right to housing' was awakened in society's consciousness, triggered by dissatisfaction with the housing crisis and by indignation over the dramatic fates of individuals. But the demands were limited to 'more housing', and state housing construction did not change its market-economy conception and orientation. The initiatives of public and semi-public organisations were not guided by an urban thinking, but merely consisted in providing as many apartments as possible in the shortest possible time and at the lowest possible costs.[116]

The result of this rational urban planning was the construction of the '*grands ensembles*', large-scale, uniformly conceived, and standardised housing estates, each with thousands of apartments. For Lefebvre, state rationality is pushed to the limit here. In the new housing estates, habitat is established in its purest form, as 'a burden of constraints'. To a certain degree, the *grands ensembles* realised the concept of habitat, by excluding habiting, the plasticity of space, and the appropriation by groups and individuals of the conditions of their existence. It results in 'complete everydayness': functions, prescriptions, and a strict use of time are inscribed and signify themselves in this habitat.[117]

One could say, Lefebvre adds, that the 'urbanist thinking' of the new estates had bitterly pursued the urban and the city in order to uproot them. Every perceptible urban reality disappeared: the streets, the squares, the monuments, the meeting places, even the bistro had apparently drawn the ire of the ascetic city builders. They had to push the limit of the destruction of urban reality to the point of provoking the demand for its restoration. And it was only slowly and timidly that some elements of urban reality reappeared there: the café, the shopping centre, the street, some so-called 'cultural' amenities.[118]

According to Lefebvre's analysis, the urban order is attacked from two directions: the *grands ensembles* and the *banlieues pavillonaires*. But the disorder of the banlieue harbours a new order, one that is a direct result of the contrast between apartment block and single-family home, and which tends to constitute an urban 'system of significations'. In and through the thinking of the inhabitants, each form of housing defines itself in relation to the other, against the other. While the inhabitants of the apartment blocks install themselves in the 'logic of the habitat', in the seemingly rational organisation of space, the inhabitants of the single-family houses entrench themselves in the imaginary

---

116   Ibid., 78–9.
117   Ibid., 79.
118   Ibid., 79–80.

of the habitat, in dreams, nature, health, apart from the bad and unhealthy city. The consciousness of the urban reality blurs and even seems to disappear.[119]

Under the rule of habitat and the supposed rationality of urbanism, Lefebvre argues, the relationship of the human being to the world, to nature, and to its own nature – its desire, its corporeality – has been plunged into a misery as never before.[120] Excluded from the city, the proletariat will lose its sense of the 'oeuvre'. Excluded from the sites of production, available for work at scattered enterprises, the proletariat loses its creative capacity and its conscience. Under the rule of habitat, society is ideologically and practically oriented to problems other than those of production, and is directed towards everyday life and consumption.[121]

The End of the City

Lefebvre interprets this development as a disappearance of the city: the 'city' – the historical city as well as the virtual urban society – is torn apart between the general and the private level.[122] The 'old spaces', from the neighbourhood and village to the national territory, tend to burst.[123] From this perspective, the dictum of complete urbanisation can be interpreted as the 'moment' of *mondialisation*, an interpretation that Lefebvre himself supports. In *The Right to the City*, for example, he writes that the crisis of the city is a dominant aspect of *mondialité* in progress.[124] And, in *The Production of Space*, he asks: how is this new space of capitalism, which ensures its survival, produced? Under the pressure of the world market, through and with urbanisation.[125]

The attack from above, from level G, comes from a general project that starts with the demands of industrialisation and includes a general coercion motivated by technology. The entire national territory must be planned; the particularities of place and location must disappear. The attack from below, from level P, is based on habitat, on individualism and the destruction of dwelling associated with it. According to Lefebvre, the state and private enterprise are jointly trying to absorb the city and abolish it as such. The state proceeds from above, private enterprises from below, by securing housing and the function of

---

119   Ibid., 80.
120   Lefebvre, *Urban Revolution*, 83.
121   Lefebvre, *Right to the City*, 77.
122   See Lefebvre, *Urban Revolution*, 94.
123   Lefebvre, *Right to the City*, 194; Lefebvre, *De l'État*, vol. 4, 265–6.
124   Lefebvre, *Right to the City*, 124.
125   Lefebvre, *Production of Space*, 326.

dwelling, but also recreational facilities, even culture and social promotion. According to Lefebvre, sociological thinking, political strategy, and urbanistic reflection also tend to jump from the level P, architecture, directly to the level G, general planning, thus passing over the middle level, the urban.[126]

Thus, two groups of questions masked the problems of the city and urban society: on the one hand, the question of housing and habitat; and on the other hand, the question of industrial organisation and overall planning. Thus, the first, from below, and the second, from above, have produced a rupture in the traditional morphology of cities, while the urbanisation of society took its course.[127] For Lefebvre, state power and economic interests follow almost exclusively a single strategy: to devalorise, degrade, and destroy urban society.[128] In the society of controlled consumption, the city is oriented towards industry. It becomes a material device for organising production and controlling consumption: 'It serves to regulate, to lay one over the other, the production of goods and the destruction of products with that devouring activity, "consumption".'[129] But can the authorities and powers do without the mediation of the city? Can they completely abolish the urban? Productivist rationality, which tends to eliminate the city on the level of general planning, rediscovers it on the sector of organised and controlled consumption.[130]

This situation calls for a double reversal of the relations: it is not the global that should define habiting, but the other way around: starting from habiting, the city and the world should be reconquered. Industrialisation, the economy, the global should be subordinated to the urban, and the global to habiting.[131] Thus, urban space must be reconquered from the point of view of habiting. The habiting, the low, the subordinate, must return to the foreground. 'The predominance of the general, the logical and the strategic, is still part of the "inverted world" that we need to overturn.'[132]

The Dissolution of the Urban Level

Lefebvre provides in these passages an apt analysis of urban planning in France in the 1950s and 1960s. From today's perspective, they can also be read as an

---

126 Lefebvre, *Right to the City*, 123; Lefebvre, *Urban Revolution*, 97–8.
127 Lefebvre, *Right to the City*, 176.
128 Ibid., 128.
129 Ibid., 126.
130 Ibid., 142.
131 See Lefebvre, *Urban Revolution*, 100.
132 Ibid., 85. Translation amended.

astonishing analysis of the Fordist city, starting from the thesis that the Keynesian regulation of society presupposes a control of the city. Lefebvre illuminates the reproduction side of Fordism as a functionalisation of the urbanisation process and as a direct control over everyday life: the city becomes a mere reproduction machine, a production-oriented system that dominates everyday life.

If we combine this analysis with that of everyday life in Lefebvre's earlier works, particularly in *Everyday Life in the Modern World* (see section 4.1), the 'society of controlled consumption' is placed in a broader – urban – context. Everyday life is a specific spatio-temporal level of social reality, which is overlaid and dominated by other levels. From this analysis, Lefebvre also gains a new interpretation of the 'crisis of the city' in Fordism: this crisis is basically a crisis of everyday life, which reveals itself on the mediating urban level. It is precisely the result of the elimination of the mediating function of the city through the control of the nation state and the private economy.

Only from this perspective does the construction of the three levels unfold their full analytical potential: Lefebvre observes the destruction and the dissolution of the city through the pincer movement of the general and the private levels. This dissolution leads to a generalisation of the urban, and thus potentially to the complete urbanisation of society.

4.4 The Urban Form: Centrality

> The fact that any point can become central is the meaning of urban space-time.[133]

The analysis of the levels of social reality presented above had the goal of determining the specificity of the urban. It enabled a new understanding of the 'crisis of the city': On the one hand, a state order is established on the general level G, which tends to homogenise all differences. On the other hand, the private level P is subjected to an industrial logic that leads to the functionalisation and control of everyday life. As a consequence, the two levels seem to coincide, and the city as a specific level of social reality threatens to disappear. What has been lost in this process? In the most extreme thesis of the disappearance of the city, the specific quality of the urban becomes visible: it forms the level of mediation that articulates the general and the private levels with one another. In this capacity, the urban level has a specific social function: it brings

---

133   Ibid., 116.

the different elements of society together and thus makes them effective, fruit-ful, innovative. These considerations led Lefebvre to a new definition of the city: it is a centre, and it is defined by its centrality.

According to Lefebvre, the city has always been the site of accumulation. It gathers, concentrates, accumulates: people, products, symbols, knowledge, techniques, money, and finally also capital:[134] 'There can be no city or urban reality without a center . . .. There can be no sites for leisure, festivals, knowl-edge, oral or scriptural transmission, invention, or creation without centrality.'[135]

Lefebvre does not refer to other theories in his definition of the city as centrality. To a certain extent, it is part of his entrenched knowledge, and appears repeatedly in his texts, often abruptly. Nevertheless, at least three possible sources of this definition can be identified. First, Lefebvre explicitly follows the Greco-Latin thesis that the city is the centre, the privileged place, the cradle of thought and invention.[136] Second, precisely this definition is already found in Marx and Engels. In *The German Ideology* they wrote: 'The town [*Stadt*] is in actual fact already the concentration of the population, of the instruments of production, of capital, of pleasures, of needs, while the country demonstrates just the opposite fact, isolation and separation.'[137] Third, this defi-nition also reflects links to the concepts and activities of the Situationists (see section 3.2).

Centrality and the Logic of the Simultaneous

For Lefebvre, 'city' means exchange, rapprochement, convergence, assembly, meeting – a centrality that brings together everything that exists in the world. The city creates a specific situation, the 'urban situation', in which different things come together and no longer exist separately. As a place of encounter, communication, and information, the city is also a place where constraints and normalities dissolve, a place of playful and unpredictable moments and events.[138]

The urban is defined as the place where people step on each other's toes, where they find themselves in front of and amid a heap of objects, where they intertwine until they have lost the thread of their own activity, where

---

134   Lefebvre, *Production of Space*, 101; Lefebvre, *Urban Revolution*, 24.
135   Lefebvre, *Urban Revolution*, 96–7.
136   Lefebvre, 'Preface to the New Edition', 208.
137   Marx and Engels, *The German Ideology*, 64.
138   Lefebvre, *Right to the City*, 172; Lefebvre, *Urban Revolution*, 37, 118–19.

they entangle their situations with each other in such a way that unfore-
seen situations arise.[139]

For Lefebvre, this definition of urban space contains a virtual 'zero vector':
urban space is a space in which any point can attract anything, in which the
space-time vector, the distance between content and what it contains, tends
towards zero. Every point can become a focal point, a privileged place where
everything converges: 'Everything that occurs within the urban reality does
so as if everything that constituted that reality could converge.'[140] Although
this is impossible and utopian in Lefebvre's sense (see section 6.5), it characterises the dialectical movement, the immanent contradiction of urban
space-time: the city is the virtual cancellation, the negation of distances in
space and time. Every urban space contains this possible-impossible, its own
negation:[141] 'the cancellation of distance haunts the occupants of urban space.
It is their dream, their symbolized imaginary, represented in a multiplicity of
ways.'[142]

For Lefebvre, the city, the urban, centrality, is thus not defined as a system or
by a system, not as timeless substance, nor as object or subject. It is defined
through the unification and encounter of what exists together in space. Thus,
centrality resembles a logical form. Its logic stands for the simultaneity that it
contains, the result of which is the simultaneity of everything which can be
brought together at or around a point:[143] 'The urban is, therefore, pure form: a
place of encounter, assembly, simultaneity. This form has no specific content,
but is a center of attraction and life. It is an abstraction, but unlike a metaphysical entity, the urban is a concrete abstraction, associated with practice.'[144]
Centrality is a form that is empty, but demands a content. This content can be
anything: fruits of the field, products of industry, works of humans, objects and
instruments, actions, signs and symbols, and so on.[145]

Centrality constitutes itself both as an act of thinking and as a social act. As
a mental form, centrality is the simultaneity of events, perceptions, of the
elements of a whole in the 'real'. As a social form, it is the meeting and gathering of goods and products, riches, activities. Centrality can therefore be defined
as neither attached to nor detached from a material morphology. It is a field of

---

139 Lefebvre, *Urban Revolution*, 39. Translation amended.
140 Ibid., 116–17. Translation amended.
141 Ibid., 39–40, 96, 123.
142 Ibid., 39.
143 Lefebvre, *Right to the City*, 143, 166; Lefebvre, *Production of Space*, 149, 331–2.
144 Lefebvre, *Urban Revolution*, 118–19.
145 Ibid., 39–40, 118–19; Lefebvre, *Production of Space*, 331–2.

relations that encompasses especially the relationship between space and time.[146]

There is a dialectical contradiction between this urban form and its relationship to content: something always happens in urban space. Emptiness, the absence of action, can only be apparent. The void (for instance, a square) attracts: a crowd can gather, a festival can unfold. The fascination of urban space lies precisely in this potential of centrality. At the same time, this space can exclude content, become a place of power: through hierarchical structures, through visible and invisible borders, through administrative regulations.[147]

The City as a Centre of Decision-Making

Centrality is thus a mere form – its content remains theoretically undetermined. This definition has the consequence that the urban can always mean something different, depending on the concrete social situation. Accordingly, the determination of the content of the urban requires a historical analysis.

As Lefebvre observes, even before capitalism the city was a place of meeting, receiving, and reuniting, which in this capacity was endowed with religious sites. With the formation of capitalism, the assembly of then still-artisan production units in the city formed the analogy of the combination of tools and machines in the workshops and manufactures. As a result, the city was no longer just the passive site of production or of the concentration of capital. Rather, it became an instrument for production. In its capacity as a centre, the city acquired an economic function that is essential to the capitalist mode of production: the city became a productive force (this thesis and its consequences are discussed in detail in section 7.1).[148]

What is the specificity of centrality in contemporary society? For Lefebvre, it takes on a new quality thanks to information and data-processing techniques: knowledge and information from all over the world can be brought together and processed at one point. This increases the capacity for meeting and association, and simultaneity is thereby intensified and condensed; communication accelerates to the point of quasi-immediacy (*quasi-instantanéité*).[149] In this context, a reference that Lefebvre made as early as 1974 to the tertiarisation of production is also revealing: because the conception of products gains in

---

146   Lefebvre, *Right to the City*, 164, 172; Lefebvre, *Production of Space*, 332.

147   Lefebvre, *Urban Revolution*, 130.

148   Lefebvre, *Right to the City*, 73–4; Lefebvre, *Urban Revolution*, 15; Lefebvre, *De l'État*, vol. 4, 269.

149   Lefebvre, *Right to the City*, 170; Lefebvre, *Production of Space*, 334.

importance, it requires an increase in the variety of information that leads to an increasingly complex organisation of productive labour. Producer services, subcontractors, and suppliers multiply. As a result, urban centralities fulfil the task of advancing the intellectualisation (*intellectualisation*) of the productive process.[150]

All these developments result in a new or renewed centrality based on information. However, this kind of centrality is more a strategy than a philosophy: it excludes peripheral elements and condenses wealth, means of action, knowledge, information, 'culture'. And, finally, it produces the highest power, the concentration of powers: decision-making.[151]

From these considerations, Lefebvre finds the new content of centrality in contemporary society: 'The creation which corresponds to our times, to their tendencies and (threatening) horizons, is it not the *centre of decision-making*?'[152] The new centres combine design and information, organisational and institutional decision-making, and they appear like a project on the way to the realisation of a new centrality – the centrality of power.[153] Today, urban centres function as centres of decision-making, centres of power, which unite the constitutive elements of society in a limited territory, and which can thus be used by and for power.[154]

The preliminary end point of the urbanisation process is thus not the dissolution of the city and the sprawl of urban areas, but, on the contrary, a social redefinition of the city and its reconstitution as a power centre at the highest level, as a decision-making centre. This conclusion also requires a reinterpretation of the dual process of industrialisation and urbanisation and the sublation of the contradiction between city and countryside (see section 3.4).

As Lefebvre noted, in an initial period the process of industrialisation invades and devastates the pre-existing urban reality, to the point of its destruction by practice and ideology and its eradication in reality and consciousness. Industrialisation thus proves to be a negative force against urban reality; the urban society is negated by the industrial economy. In the second period, urbanisation spreads and urban society generalises. Urban reality reveals itself – in and through its own destruction – as socio-economic reality. Society discovers that it is in danger of disintegrating if it lacks the city and centrality: an essential component for the planned organisation of production and consumption has disappeared. Finally, in the third period, an attempt is made

---

150   Lefebvre, *Production of Space*, 390.
151   Ibid., 332–3.
152   Lefebvre, *Right to the City*, 73.
153   Ibid.
154   Lefebvre, *Production of Space*, 333; Lefebvre, *Urban Revolution*, 43–4.

to restore centrality and reintroduce urban reality: the disintegrating old centres are replaced by the centre of decision-making.[155]

Industrialisation thus at first produces urbanisation in a negative sense. The historical city, its morphology, its practical-sensual reality, splinters. But then urban society emerges on the ruins of the historical city and its agricultural surroundings. And, in the course of this change, the relationship between industrialisation and urbanisation is transformed: the city is no longer merely the passive container of products and production. That which persists and is consolidated in the disintegrating urban reality, the decision-making centre, becomes a means of production and a system for the exploitation of social labour by those who control information, culture, and decision-making.[156]

Thus, although urban reality is dominated and destroyed by industrialisation, it nevertheless shows an astonishing tendency to reproduce itself.[157] Urban society survives on its shaken foundations, and in fact even intensifies: 'Social relations continue to become more complex, to multiply and intensify through the most painful contradictions. The form of the urban, its supreme reason, namely simultaneity and encounter, cannot disappear.'[158]

The New Athens

These considerations finally provide an answer to the questions posed at the beginning of this chapter regarding the specificity of the urban and the redefinition of the city in an urban society: the process of complete urbanisation means not only the explosion of the city and the expansion of urban areas, but also the formation of new centralities.[159]

Despite urbanisation, the urban cores, disintegrated by the rampant urban fabric, are not disappearing. They resist by transforming themselves. They remain centres of urban life, in which their aesthetic quality plays an important role. They contain not only monuments and seats of institutions, but also spaces suitable for festivities, parades, and entertainment, from nightclubs to the splendour of opera houses. They become a premium product of consumption and survive thanks to this double role: as places of consumption and as consumable places. Thus, the old centres enter into

---

155   Lefebvre, *Right to the City*, 74.
156   Ibid., 178.
157   Lefebvre, *Production of Space*, 386.
158   Lefebvre, *Right to the City*, 128.
159   Lefebvre, *Production of Space*, 391.

exchange and become exchange value, not without remaining at the same time use value.[160]

As a consequence, the centre of decision-making and the centre of consumption unite, and decision-making power and the ability to consume coalesce. Based on their strategic convergence, their alliance creates an exorbitant centrality on the terrain: the capitals and the metropolises are consolidated as centres of power, the population is 'made elite' (*élitisé*), production and the working class are driven to the peripheries.[161] The urban cores become citadels of power, places where wealth and power accumulate to enormous density.[162] These decision-making centres contain all channels of information, all means of cultural and scientific development. The image of the 'new city' is already represented by New York and Paris, among other cities: the new masters occupy and inhabit this privileged space, this place of rigorous spatial programming, without necessarily owning it completely. Around them, distributed in space according to formalised principles, human groups are placed which Lefebvre does not wish to call by the terms slaves or serfs, nor vassals, nor proletarians. What should they be called? They have various 'services' to perform for the masters of this state that is firmly established in this city. 'Could this not be the true New Athens, with its minority of free citizens, possessing and enjoying social spaces, dominating an enormous mass of subjugated people, in principle free, genuinely and perhaps voluntarily servants, treated and manipulated according to rational methods?'[163]

Thus, already by the end of the 1960s, Lefebvre had developed this haunting and polemical analysis that is strikingly consistent with the situation in many metropolises of the twenty-first century.

The World City

These observations led Lefebvre to define the contemporary role of the city in an urbanised world: Although the contradiction between city and countryside is sublated and the city no longer represents a specific mode of production or a distinct way of life, and thus no longer develops any social specificity, it does not lose its specific function of centrality. On the contrary, it had been restored as a centre of economic control and decision-making. Under these conditions, the historical-dialectical role of centrality means that decision-making power over a global production process is concentrated in certain privileged places in

---

160   Lefebvre, *Right to the City*, 73, 170.
161   Ibid., 162; Lefebvre, *De l'État*, vol. 4, 265–6.
162   Lefebvre, *Urban Revolution*, 79, 97.
163   Lefebvre, *Right to the City*, 161.

the world. With this conception, Lefebvre anticipated the core of the 'world city' and the 'global city' concepts in an astonishing way. The correspondence even goes as far as the term *ville mondiale*, which Lefebvre used in *The Urban Revolution* – more than a decade before John Friedmann and Goetz Wolff would introduce the concept of 'world city' into urban theory.[164] Lefebvre, however, did not use the term *ville mondiale*, which he attributed to Maoism, uncritically. He argues that this term could only be used with reservations, because it extrapolates the concept and the classical image of the city – as a political administrative centre, as the centre for the protection and exploitation of a vast area of land – to the world level. Urban society, however, will only emerge from the ruins of the classical city.[165]

Both the 'world city' and the 'global city' concepts situate the central social contradiction in the contrast between a highly qualified economic sector and a precarious low-income sector, which Friedmann and Wolff described with the metaphor 'citadel and ghetto'. Saskia Sassen emphasised the fact that both sectors are economically related to each other and must therefore necessarily be located in the same place.[166] From this 'simultaneity', this coexistence of both privileged and disadvantaged social groups and the resulting conflicts, she derived the central contradiction of a global city, and she found a formulation that could be borrowed directly from Lefebvre: the city as a 'contested terrain'.

Lefebvre, however, goes a decisive step further. For him, it is not only socio-economic polarisation that characterises the central contradiction of metropolises, but above all the fact that a large portion of the population is excluded from centrality and banished to the periphery. The struggle for centrality emerges from this analysis as the fundamental contradiction of the urban. In order to understand this contradiction, he delves far back in the history of Paris, true to his regressive–progressive method, to the legendary Commune of 1871, and then ascends back to the present.

From the Commune of 1871 to Paris May 1968

Nowhere was the struggle for centrality more dramatic for Lefebvre than in nineteenth-century Paris under the regime of Napoleon III and his prefect Baron Haussmann. In an unprecedented strategic intervention, Haussmann had imposed a new order on the city of Paris, which continues to occupy

---

164   See Lefebvre, *Urban Revolution*, 17, 169ff.; Friedmann and Wolff, 'World City Formation'.

165   Lefebvre, *Urban Revolution*, 169.

166   Sassen, *Cities in a World Economy*.

generations of architects and urban scholars to this day. With the construction of the famous boulevards, he cut through the narrow and dense, socially and functionally mixed urban fabric and fundamentally reorganised the city. For Walter Benjamin, Paris thus became the capital of the nineteenth century, with its magnificent boulevards and monuments, and was at the same time opened up to the commodity – and to the bourgeoisie.[167]

In Lefebvre's analysis, the fifteen-year restructuring of Paris led to the destruction of large parts of the central neighbourhoods, the deportation of the proletariat to the periphery, the simultaneous invention of the banlieues and of habitat, the 'bourgeoisification' (*embourgeoisement*) and depopulation of the centre.[168] At the same time, however, this intervention manifested an inherent class logic, driving the rational coherence of the absolute state to its end. It is thus the highest instance, the state itself, and not just any institution that intervened. But to contemporaries, the ideology that underpinned and supported this rationality did not appear as such. Many admired the new Paris; others lamented the loss of its soul. But the truth that the city had been destroyed by becoming bourgeois hardly occurred to anyone at that time. What did it take for the truth to manifest itself? Revolutionary urban practice, with its concrete utopia.[169] In 1871, only a few years after the end of Haussmann's urban transformation, the famous uprising occurred: the Paris Commune shook the city to its core, and became a wake-up call and a model for so many revolutionaries. Lefebvre said: 'The workers, chased from the center of the city to its outskirts, returned to the center occupied by the bourgeoisie. Through a combination of force, luck, and good timing, they took control of it.'[170]

In *La proclamation de la Commune*, Lefebvre meticulously reconstructed the chronology of events on the basis of detailed archive work. Inspired by his discussions with the Situationists, he interpreted the 1871 uprising as the great attempt to elevate the city to the arena and the ground of human reality (see section 2.1). By the middle of the nineteenth century, industrialisation and the state had established their domination of Paris, unsettled it, and exploded its core. Was the Parisian proletariat aware of this situation? Obviously not, as Lefebvre notes – its historical consciousness and class consciousness were different. The 1871 uprising had various, sometimes contradictory, objectives, but it culminated in a festival without end that restored the city to its glory, beauty, and raison d'être. The Communards made history, and history made its way through them – with their creative inventions, their attempts and detours, their blind heroism – until the

---

167 Benjamin, 'Paris, the Capital of the Nineteenth Century'.
168 Lefebvre, *Urban Revolution*, 109–10.
169 Ibid.
170 Ibid., 110. See also Lefebvre, *The Explosion*, 117–18.

tragic end.[171] 'The Commune, which became a foundation of the Marxist analysis of revolutions, was a revolution that went without a Marxist analysis.'[172] Finally, Lefebvre asked: 'Why is it that the Commune was not conceived as an urban revolution but as a revolution of an industrial proletariat moving towards industrialization, which does not correspond to historical truth?'[173]

Almost 100 years after the Commune's uprising, Lefebvre himself experienced an urban uprising in Paris: May 1968, where he saw his analysis of the Commune, which he had completed shortly before, confirmed. As is well known, the May 1968 uprising in Paris began at the Paris Nanterre University, where Lefebvre was teaching at the time. It had been built as an extension of the famous Sorbonne University, located in the central Latin Quarter, and, as Stanek describes, was located on an isolated campus in the poor municipality of Nanterre in a banlieue of Paris.[174] In his treatise *The Explosion*, which in the French original has the title *L'irruption – de Nanterre au sommet* (The outbreak – from Nanterre to the summit), Lefebvre describes in detail the situation in this peripheral space, cut off from urban life: 'In March 1871 as in May 1968, the people come from the periphery, from the outside where they had been driven, where they found only a social vacuum, assembled and headed towards the urban centres in order to reconquer them.'[175]

The Contradictions of Centrality

These two historical moments in Paris – the Commune of 1871 and May 1968 – clearly show the contradictions of centrality. As Lefebvre explains, despite the crushing dominance of power, the centre remains a place of unrest and movement, a melting pot, a focal point. This development is highly contradictory, Lefebvre says. On the one hand, political power and the hegemonic class would have no interest in extinguishing this source of fire if they want the city to maintain its worldwide reputation, which it owes precisely to its audacity, its exploration of the possible and the impossible, its so-called cultural development, its highly diverse actions and actors – the people, the intelligentsia, students, artists, and writers. On the other hand, the political powers and the economically ruling bourgeoisie fear this fermentation:[176]

---

171 Lefebvre, *La proclamation de la Commune*, 22, 32.
172 Ibid., 34. Translation by author.
173 Lefebvre, *Urban Revolution*, 111.
174 Stanek, *Henri Lefebvre on Space*, 179–81.
175 Lefebvre, *The Explosion*, 117–18.
176 Lefebvre, *Production of Space*, 386.

The centralized management of things and of 'culture' tries to avoid this intermediary tier, the city. And more: the State, centres of decision-making, the ideological, economic and political powers, can only consider with a growing suspicion this social form which tends towards autonomy, which can only live specifically, which comes between them and the 'inhabitant', worker or not, productive or unproductive worker, but human and citizen [*citoyen*] as well as city dweller [*citadin*]. Since the last century, what is the essence of the city for power? It ferments, full of suspect activities, of delinquency, a hot bed of agitation.[177]

Here, finally, the full contradiction of centrality becomes apparent: if on the one hand it is a means and instrument of power, it contains on the other hand the possibility of radical social change.[178]

It is thus theoretically impossible not to support urban concentration, together with the attendant risks of saturation and disorder, and the opportunities for encounters, information, and convergence. To attack or destroy it implies a form of empiricism that begins with the destruction of thought.[179]

Centrality has to be understood dialectically, and this distinguishes the conception of Lefebvre from other, apparently similar conceptions: centrality is a form, and what this form contains or should contain, its content, is the subject of struggle.

4.5 The Right to the City

The city is a machine of possibilities.[180]

As this reconstruction has shown so far, 'the city' for Lefebvre is bound to centrality and always involves some degree of confrontation and struggle over the content of centrality. At the end of the 1960s, Lefebvre saw centrality as being dominated by decision-making powers. However, there was also manifold resistance to this occupation of centrality by capital and the state. From this perspective, centrality becomes a political issue, as political forces

---

177 Lefebvre, *Right to the City*, 128.
178 Lefebvre, *Urban Revolution*, 97.
179 Ibid., 96–7.
180 Lefebvre, *Survival of Capitalism*, 16. Translation amended.

challenge or consolidate the centre of decision-making. For Lefebvre, resolving this question was a central criterion of democracy.[181]

In 1968, Lefebvre therefore demanded, programmatically, what the title of his book announced: *The Right to the City*. Two years later, in *The Urban Revolution*, in accordance with the critique of the concept of the 'city' developed therein, he reformulated this right as 'the right to centrality' or 'the right to the street'.[182] However, all these designations mean the same thing: the right to access the possibilities and opportunities of the centre, the right not to be forced out of society and culture into a space produced for the purpose of discrimination, the right not to be excluded from centrality and its movement.[183]

Lefebvre related this right to the other rights that define civilisation: the right to work, to education, to health, to housing, to leisure, to life. The 'right to the city' does not refer to the former city, however, but to urban life, to centrality, to places of meeting and exchange, to rhythms of life and a use of time that allows a full and complete use of these moments and places.[184] This right cannot therefore be understood as a simple right to visit or to return to traditional cities. It can only be formulated as the right to a transformed, renewed urban life. The urban, the place of encounter, must find a morphological basis, a practico-sensual realisation that gives priority to use value.[185]

How does Lefebvre imagine the realisation of this right to the city? He criticised a so-called urban thinking, which is limited to 'optimising' industrialisation and its consequences, or to mourning the alienation that has occurred in industrial society, or even to advocating a return to the ancient city community. He regarded such supposed models as nothing more than variants of the urbanistic ideology (see section 5.3). Thus, Lefebvre remained sceptical of the possibilities of urban reform: 'Can it protect existing urban institutions? Possibly. Can it promote them? Can it develop criteria and models? Can it extend to urban society (virtual and possible) the institutions and ideologies drawn from the city (of the past)? No. That would be impossible.'[186] And even more clearly:

> It is impossible to envisage the reconstitution of the old city, only the
> construction of a new one on new foundations, on another scale and in

181 Lefebvre, *Right to the City*, 121, 163; Lefebvre, *Urban Revolution*, 95.

182 Lefebvre, *Urban Revolution*, 150, 194.

183 Lefebvre, *Survival of Capitalism*, 35; Lefebvre, *Urban Revolution*, 150.

184 Lefebvre, *Right to the City*, 178.

185 Ibid., 158.

186 Lefebvre, *Urban Revolution*, 89.

other conditions, in another society. The prescription is: there cannot be a going back (towards the traditional city), nor a headlong flight, towards a colossal and shapeless agglomeration.[187]

The city must, therefore, be reinvented. It is crucial to understand the urban in its movement, as a process: 'It is impossible to bring urban reality to a complete stop. To do so would kill it.'[188]

The call for the right to the city is of course strongly related to the question of citizenship. It is clear that an 'urban citizenship' must be conceptualised in a radically different way to the citizenship of a national state. I cannot go further into this wide-ranging topic here, but mention the 'Groupe de Navarrenx', which formed around Lefebvre in the 1980s and was named after his birthplace, where the group regularly met. In 1991, this group published an extensive discussion on the question of citizenship, to which Lefebvre himself contributed the introduction.[189] Here, following in the footsteps of Rousseau, he outlines a new 'social contract' that contains a whole series of new citizens' rights, including, of course, the right to the city.

Commodification and Dispossession

The reconstruction of Lefebvre's conceptualisation of centrality presented so far leads to an important preliminary conclusion: although the city dissolves in the process of urbanisation and loses both its morphological form and its social and political unity, centrality remains its main defining characteristic. Accordingly, the essential contradiction of urban society is no longer to be found in the contradiction of city and country, but in the interior of the phenomenon of urbanisation: between the centrality of power and other forms of centrality, between the centre and the peripheries, between integration and exclusion.

This conclusion, which Lefebvre formed in 1970, has not lost its actuality – on the contrary. The fundamental transformations of the 'long 1980s' opened the world to global capitalism, spurring a worldwide push to urbanisation and the extension of global networks of production and information. Across the globe, new strategic nodes and command centres of the world economy were installed, which became not only places of power and control, but – precisely because of

---

187   Lefebvre, *Right to the City*, 148.
188   Lefebvre, *Production of Space*, 386.
189   Lefebvre and Groupe de Navarrenx, *Du contrat de citoyenneté*.

their global interconnectedness – also important centres of innovation and incu-
bators of new economic and social developments (see section 1.3).

After the concepts of the 'world city' and the 'global city', which still took a
critical look at these developments, mainstream economics soon recognised
the renewed importance of centrality and praised the creativity and innovative
power of the flourishing world metropolises, with texts such as *Cities and the
Creative Class*, *The Triumph of the City*, or *Welcome to the Urban Revolution*.[190]
These and similar interventions were strongly criticised for exhibiting an
'urban triumphalism' that presented metropolises across historical and regional
contexts as engines of innovation, civilisation, prosperity, and democracy, but
without addressing any negative consequences of such developments.[191] On a
practical level, a 'new metropolitan mainstream' emerged, promoting strategies
of gentrification, urban regeneration, and urban renewal, and materialising in
cultural and architectural flagship projects and new prestigious business,
consumer, and leisure zones.[192] At the same time, all kinds of urban megaprojects have been launched, particularly in the Global South, which plough up
not only the centres of urban regions, but increasingly also their urban peripheries, and are often accompanied by massive displacements.[193]

Lefebvre had already commented on such developments with great pessimism at the end of the 1980s: 'All that remains are, on the one hand, centres for
power and decision-making and, on the other, fake and artificial spaces.' He
further noted that 'the urban centre is not only transformed into a site of
consumption; it also becomes the object of consumption, and is valued as
such.'[194] As a consequence, urban space itself becomes a commodity that is sold
and bought.[195] Collectively generated urban qualities are commodified and
financialised, and their exchange value siphoned off via the ground rent (see
section 7.1). Entire inner cities were thus transformed into privileged spaces of
the global urban elites, while countless people, working class, urban poor,
migrants, are displaced, evicted, dispossessed, and expropriated from the social
networks and urban values they themselves helped to create.

190   See, among others, Fujita, Krugman, and Venables, *The Spatial Economy*; Florida,
Cities and the Creative Class; Glaeser, *Triumph of the City*; Brugmann, *Welcome to the Urban
Revolution*.
191   Brenner and Schmid, 'Towards a New Epistemology of the Urban?'; Peck,
'Struggling with the Creative Class'; Peck, 'Economic Rationality Meets Celebrity
Urbanology'; Krätke, 'The New Urban Growth Ideology of "Creative Cities" '.
192   See Schmid, 'Henri Lefebvre, the Right to the City'.
193   See Datta and Shaban, *Mega-Urbanization in the Global South*; Sawyer et al.,
'Bypass Urbanism'.
194   Lefebvre, 'Dissolving City, Planetary Metamorphosis', 567.
195   Lefebvre, *Production of Space*, 154.

Lefebvre had used the term *embourgeoisement*, which is common in France, to describe such processes. It was translated into English as 'gentrification' without further explanation.[196] It is important, however, to insist that the term *embourgeoisement*, which Harvey also uses in this context, is not the same as gentrification.[197] It denotes a process that can no longer be explained solely by the realisation and absorption of the rent gap, and it goes far beyond the gradual renovation of neighbourhoods.[198] The process under consideration is much broader and more fundamental than gentrification. It results from the domination and commodification of centrality itself, and can lead to the transformations of entire urban regions. Accordingly, this process requires a different terminology.

Merrifield has called this process, in the footsteps of Lefebvre, 'neo-Haussmanization', defined as a 'global-urban strategy that has peripheralized millions of people everywhere'.[199] While this term might fit urban development in Paris, it is less suitable for export to the entire world, in order to avoid once again universalising a very specific term from a city in the West, as was already the case with the term 'gentrification', which was based on the experience of London. It would be much more appropriate here to use more specific concepts and to differentiate the various processes more clearly.[200]

At the core of this process is the struggle for centrality and for access to centrality, resistance against the extraction of urban value created by the population, the privatisation and thus expropriation of collectively created resources, and the destruction of popular centralities. All these processes have massive effects on large parts of the population in an urban region.

Struggles for Centrality

With the beginning of the twenty-first century, struggles for centrality have fuelled ever new waves of mobilisations, in urban centres as well as in many urban peripheries. They can be roughly divided into four groups: a first group of struggles happened mainly in Europe and North America and was directed against various forms of gentrification and urban regeneration, large-scale redevelopment and urban megaprojects, and the privatisation and

---

196   Lefebvre, *Urban Revolution*, 109–10.

197   Harvey, *Justice, Nature and the Geography of Difference*, 405. See also Préteceille, 'Is Gentrification a Useful Paradigm'.

198   See Smith, *The New Urban Frontier*.

199   Merrifield, *The New Urban Question*, 29.

200   See Schmid et al., 'Towards a New Vocabulary of Urbanisation Processes'; Hanakata, Schmid, and Streule, 'Incorporation of Urban Differences'.

commodification of urban spaces.[201] A second group of struggles erupted in peripheralised, neglected, and racialised neighbourhoods, which developed into territorial traps affected by stigmatisation and exclusion, precarisation and hopelessness. A typical example of this is the repeated revolts and uprisings in various banlieues in Paris and other French cities, which were caught in a downward spiral and experienced an unprecedented social, economic, and everyday peripheralisation, a development that far exceeded Lefebvre's fears.[202] Third, with the global financial crisis of 2007–08, anti-austerity movements emerged, especially in Southern and Eastern Europe, which can also be understood as struggles over centrality that directly demanded a different urban politics of solidarity. Fourth, revolts and struggles arose in many popular neighbourhoods in Latin America, Africa, and Asia that were threatened by slum clearing, urban renewal, and large-scale urban and infrastructure projects that dispossessed and displaced millions of people.

Finally, the historic global moment of 2011 should also be mentioned here, when a great wave of protest swept around the world, challenging the whole range of urban problematics. There was the protest against the domination and commodification of centrality by the neocolonial state in Hong Kong and the fierce struggle for centrality in Istanbul.[203] There were the mobilisations against austerity politics and precarisation in Athens, Madrid, Barcelona, and many other cities in Southern and Eastern Europe that developed new urban strategies of solidarity.[204] The struggle for urban space and centrality also played a crucial role in the Arab Spring, highlighted by the enormous social and political importance of central squares.[205] The Occupy movement also manifested the importance of centrality for exchange, mobilisation, and politicisation with its plaza occupations across the world. Despite the fact that social media was decisive in all these mobilisations, experiences showed that the role of centrality and thus of material physical space was not weakened by the virtual social space of social media but, on the contrary, strengthened.

---

201   See for example Thörn, Mayer, and Thörn, 'Re-thinking Urban Social Movements'.

202   See on this, among others, Dikeç, *Badlands of the Republic*; and Kipfer, 'Neocolonial Urbanism?'.

203   Ng et al., 'Spatial Practice, Conceived Space and Lived Space'; Ku, 'Remaking Places and Fashioning an Opposition Discourse'; Kuymulu, 'Reclaiming the Right to the City'; Erensü and Karaman, 'The Work of a Few Trees'.

204   Petropoulou, 'From the December Youth Uprising to the Rebirth of Urban Social Movements'; Martínez López, 'Between Autonomy and Hybridity'; Vaiou and Kalandides, 'Practices of Solidarity in Athens'; Islar and Irgil, 'Grassroots Practices of Citizenship and Politicization in the Urban'.

205   Kanna, 'Urban Praxis and the Arab Spring'; Lopes de Souza and Barbara Lipietz, 'The "Arab Spring" and the City'.

The Many Meanings of the 'Right to the City'

The very different struggles described above have initiated an astonishing renaissance of the term 'the right to the city', both as a theoretical concept and as a political slogan. Lefebvre himself had chosen this term, as we have seen, as the title of his first, still-preliminary reflections on urbanisation, in order to name a social problematic – the 'crisis of the city' – and also to issue a call to action. The book was published shortly before the outbreak of May 1968 in Paris, and it was soon among the texts eagerly read by activists. A very good overview of the significance and history of 'the right to the city' in France is provided by Laurence Costes, who not only gives a valuable introduction to Lefebvre's theory, but also analyses in detail the prehistory and consequences of this book.[206]

Only two years later, in his conceptually and theoretically more elaborated work *The Urban Revolution*, Lefebvre then critically questioned the term 'city' and abandoned it in favour of his thesis of complete urbanisation. There, he even described the term 'city' as an ideological pseudo-concept (see section 4.1). Accordingly, he defined 'the right to the city' as 'the right not to be excluded from centrality and its movement', and he also explicitly demanded a 'right to centrality'.[207]

But the slogan 'the right to the city' had already entered the world, and Lefebvre could no longer take it back. The term had its own career, becoming increasingly independent of Lefebvre's work and often used without reference to it. A significant part of the term's appeal lies in the flexible interpretive possibilities it offers for both research and practice. A wide variety of groups and institutions have used it, including activist milieus and radical movements, but also reformist initiatives and organisations. In addition, a rapidly increasing number of academic publications have applied the concept to a wide variety of urban movements and situations, while also modifying its meaning in many ways. It is not possible here to even begin to address the numerous publications that have dealt with 'the right to the city' in one form or another, nor to cover the diverse actions and campaigns that have taken place using this slogan. Therefore, only a very cursory outline of some important developments is included here. On the level of *collective practice*, highly diverse movements and mobilisations have gathered under the rallying cry 'the right to the city' across the world and have repeatedly given it different meanings, including struggles against urban regeneration, urban renewal, gentrification, housing shortages,

---

206   Costes, *Henri Lefebvre: Le droit à la ville.*
207   Lefebvre, *Urban Revolution*, 150, 194.

and displacement, such as in Hamburg and Berlin, in Zagreb and Belgrade, and in several Polish cities.[208] It also became a slogan for forming alliances: in the United States, with community organisations from different urban regions joining together to form a broad 'Right to the City Alliance', with a strong multi-racial commitment to low-income and precarious workers.[209] In Latin America and South Africa, 'the right to the city' is understood as a comprehensive right to decent living conditions in urban spaces, affordable and adequate housing, urban infrastructure, education, and health.[210] Still other demands are made by various settler and squatter movements as well as by indigenous movements fighting for the legalisation and consolidation of popular settlements.[211]

'The right to the city' has also become the slogan of *reform-oriented* organisations and institutions. In France, an early split evolved between a radical, Lefebvre-oriented position and a reform-oriented, social democratic position trying to integrate Lefebvre's slogan into official politics.[212] As Gilbert and Dikeç describe, 'The right to the city' formed the opening article in the French 'Urban Development Act' (*Loi d'orientation pour la ville*) of 1991, but this did not fundamentally change the situation in the peripheralised banlieues.[213]

'The right to the city' subsequently became increasingly popular internationally. It was written into the constitution in Colombia in 1997 and in Brazil in 2001, discussed at the Social Forum of the Americas in Quito in 2004 and the Urban Forum in Barcelona in the same year, sponsored by UNESCO, and it has also been placed on the official agenda of UN-Habitat. These forms of appropriation were not without opposition and have sparked heated debates about reformist versus radical urban strategies.[214] In addition, the question of

---

208　Domaradzka, 'Urban Social Movements and the Right to the City'; Blokland et al., 'Urban Citizenship and Right to the City'; Dolenec, Doolan, and Tomašević, 'Contesting Neoliberal Urbanism on the European Semi-Periphery'; Pluciński, 'Henri Lefebvre's Second Life'.

209　Liss, 'The Right to the City'; Fisher et al., 'We Are Radical'.

210　La Llata, 'Operation 1DMX and the Mexico City Commune'; Rolnik, 'Ten Years of the City Statute in Brazil'; Diani, Ernstson, and Jasny, ' "Right to the City" and the Structure of Civic Organizational Fields'.

211　Horn, 'Indigenous Peoples, the City and Inclusive Urban Development Policies in Latin America'.

212　On the former, see Coornaert and Garnier, 'Actualités de Henri Lefebvre'; Garnier, *Une violence éminemment contemporaine*. On the latter, see Castro, *Civilisation urbaine ou barbarie*.

213　Gilbert and Dikeç, 'Right to the City'; Dikeç, *Badlands of the Republic*.

214　UNESCO, *Urban Policies and the Right to the City*; UN-Habitat, *The Right to the City*; Sugranyes and Mathivet, *Cities for All*; Fernandes, 'Constructing the Right to the City in Brazil'; Huchzermeyer, 'The Legal Meaning of Lefebvre's the Right to the City'.

'the right to the city' has come to include discussions about the status of legal rights and the related question of citizenship.[215]

In the *academic industry*, 'the right to the city' has played a different role. Initially it expressed a general conception of urban struggles and urban protest that goes beyond the narrow definition of the concept of 'urban social movements', which focuses on the question of 'collective consumption' inspired by Castells.[216] In particular, it was used to address urban protests and revolts that occur spontaneously and do not necessarily constitute themselves as movements or organisations.[217] However, it was not until the beginning of the twenty-first century that Lefebvre's version of 'the right to the city' was used on a larger scale as a conceptual or theoretical framework for the analysis of urban mobilisations. A good overview of the early debates can be found in a special issue of *GeoJournal* from 2002, edited by Lynn A. Staeheli, Lorraine Dowler, and Doris Wastl-Walter, and more detailed accounts can be found in the texts by Mark Purcell, who has consistently explored, applied, and developed Lefebvre's concepts as well as his own notion of revolutionary democracy over the years.[218]

Often, however, the specific character of Lefebvre's theoretical project is less important in academic texts, and the concept serves more as a heuristic that allows researchers to anchor (and theoretically position) their analyses. Mitchell, for example, in his much-cited book *The Right to the City*, in which he addresses struggles in and around public space, hardly mentions Lefebvre at all and refers instead to Harvey's concept of social justice.[219] Other authors understand the concept as the core of Lefebvre's theory, and thus often reduce it to the point of unrecognisability. In this context, Marcelo Lopes de Souza criticises the concept's 'trivialisation and corruption' and the danger of a vulgarisation and domestication of Lefebvre's phrase by institutions that have no commitment to upend the status quo: 'In many cases it seems to mean just the right to a more "human" life in the context of the capitalist city and on the basis of a ("reformed") representative "democracy".'[220]

---

215   See for example Attoh, 'What *Kind* of Right Is the Right to the City?'.
216   Mayer, 'The "Right to the City" in Urban Social Movements'; Mayer, 'Neoliberal Urbanism and Uprisings across Europe'.
217   Schmid, 'The Dialectics of Urbanisation in Zurich'.
218   Staeheli, Dowler, and Wastl-Walter, 'Social Transformation, Citizenship, and the Right to the City'; Purcell, 'Excavating Lefebvre'; Purcell, *Recapturing Democracy*. From the perspective of legal studies and the question of citizenship, Chris Butler has explored the concept in great depth and detail: Butler, *Henri Lefebvre*; Butler, 'Abstraction beyond a "Law of Thought" '. The book *Cities for People, Not for Profit*, edited by Brenner, Mayer, and Marcuse, also provides a broad and advanced theoretical discussion.
219   Mitchell, *The Right to the City*.
220   Lopez de Souza, 'Which Right to Which City?'.

As Uitermark, Nicholls, and Loopmans note, there is always the additional problem that the concept structures social reality and is applied to movements that do not use the term themselves.[221] In particular, they see the problematic aspect that the movements themselves are influenced by it, so that claims for local democracy and rights come into view while claims articulated on a larger scale move into the background. In this way, many applications of the term – intentionally or unintentionally – also generate a localism, and reconstitute 'the city' as a social or political unit, which in turn can exclude certain social groups and interests. This was precisely one of the reasons why Lefebvre himself had criticised the term 'city' so vehemently. In the German discussion, among academics as well as activists, this very aspect is emphasised more strongly by no longer using the correct German translation, 'Das Recht auf *die* Stadt', but 'Das Recht auf Stadt', which means, approximately, the 'right to the urban': without the definite article, the term 'city' no longer denotes a (concrete) object, but a general property.[222]

Some well-known theorists have also taken up 'the right to the city' anew and, relying on Lefebvre to differing extents, filled it with their own meanings. John Friedmann, for example, proclaimed in his text 'The Right to the City': 'A city can truly be called a city only when its streets belong to the people.'[223] David Harvey, in his widely received text on the subject, defines the right to the city as the right to control the process of urbanisation and to introduce new forms of urbanisation, a position he further elaborates in his book *Rebel Cities*.[224] In contrast, Peter Marcuse criticises the overarching, sweeping, and simplistic nature of the term. He paints a nuanced picture of the various economically and culturally disadvantaged and excluded social groups in diverse urban spaces, and points out that this can also lead to a split between the 'discontented' and the 'dispossessed'.[225]

Andy Merrifield has also critically examined the term and argues that it has completely lost its meaning in the face of planetary urbanisation.[226] In its place he has promoted the concept of the 'politics of encounter' – strongly inspired by the mobilisations of the Arab Spring and the Occupy movement. The city, in Merrifield's view, was the site but not the object of the protests, which he sees as related to more general social demands. This position is reminiscent of the

---

221   Uitermark, Nicholls, and Loopmans, 'Cities and Social Movements'.
222   Holm and Gebhardt, *Initiativen für ein Recht auf Stadt*.
223   Friedmann, 'The Right to the City', 139.
224   Harvey, 'The Right to the City'; Harvey, *Rebel Cities*.
225   Marcuse, 'Whose Right(s) to What City?'.
226   Merrifield, 'The Right to the City and Beyond'; Merrifield, *The Politics of the Encounter*.

discussions surrounding the May 1968 movement in Paris, which also called for general and, above all, worldwide changes; as shown above, however, it was Lefebvre who addressed the urban side of this movement and took it as an important starting point for his urban theory.

This turbulent history of a term that Lefebvre had actually rejected, but which was so catchy and became so popular that he could not discard it from his vocabulary, is revealing. It shows the possibilities and the limits, the opportunities and the dangers of theory. As Lefebvre himself pointed out, the researcher always takes a risk in coining terms and concepts. Once sent out into the world, they begin a life of their own, are detached from their original context, and are appropriated, transferred to other contexts, and filled with new content and meaning. While this is often a popular tactic in academic competition, and much intellectual labour is frustrated or even destroyed in the process, as Lefebvre's own story shows, productive moments can also arise from it. However, it remains surprising that such diverse struggles and movements have come together under this one term. This demonstrates the resilience of the term 'city', which in all its indeterminacy and vagueness presents itself as a projection surface for the most diverse demands, and thus allows groups with diverse interests to establish common ground and form alliances. The implicit meanings evoked by 'the right to the city', the various experiences, wishes, and desires, amid the processes of self-organisation and appropriation of urban space, can point in very different directions, which is both the term's strength and its weakness.

The spread of the slogan 'right to the city' thus made many things possible, but it also moved the discussion in a direction that led away from Lefebvre's grand theoretical project of better understanding the conditions and consequences of complete urbanisation. Thus, important processes were left out of these discussions, in both theory and practice. These overlooked processes have nevertheless become increasingly important, especially in recent years, and often take place outside the dissolving dense agglomerations. De Souza has therefore suggested replacing the term 'the right to the city' with 'the right to the planet' – a suggestion that makes perfect sense in this context.[227]

Lefebvre himself continued to use the term 'the right to the city' until the end of his life, but almost always framed it with other terms: 'right to centrality', 'right to difference', 'right to (urban) space'. And he always linked it to a revolutionary concrete utopia of generalised autogestion and urban citizenship (see section 6.5).

---

227   Lopes de Souza, 'From the "Right to the City" to the Right to the Planet'.

4.6 The Dialectic of the Urban

Centers and peripheries presuppose and oppose one another.[228]

The initial question of this chapter was: what is the specificity of the urban in a completely urbanised society? As has been shown, Lefebvre defined the urban on the one hand as a specific level of social reality, as a middle level between the general and the private, as a level of mediation. On the other hand, he defined the urban as a material form that corresponds to this level: centrality.

The connection between these two definitions becomes clear only on a second glance. Centrality is a logical, geometric construction that manifests itself only on the intermediate, middle level: it cannot be discerned on the general level of society, nor on the private level of individual actors. Lefebvre accordingly notes that the concept of centrality connects the punctal with the general.[229]

Lefebvre defines centrality as a pure form that says nothing about its content. Depending on the historical situation, the city assembles and centralises different elements of society, and therefore the determination of the content of centrality always requires a historical analysis. Additionally, Lefebvre conceives centrality dialectically and thus tries to reach its inner dynamics: the assembly and encounter of different elements has the concrete effect that something unexpected, surprising, innovative might result. Thus, centrality is to be understood as a productive force: the productivity of the urban lies in the fact that it brings the most diverse elements of a society together and allows them to react to each other (see also section 7.1).

This double definition of the urban as the mediating level of social reality and as the form of centrality allows Lefebvre to approach the urban both as a general and as a specific (and thus historical) category, without losing it theoretically. As a general form, centrality can be found in many different societies. Lefebvre notes that every epoch, every mode of production, and every specific society has produced its own centrality, depending on the form of religious, political, commercial, cultural, or industrial centres.[230] This also implies that the specificity of the urban does not disappear in the course of the urbanisation process: 'The disappearance of centrality is neither called for theoretically nor practically.'[231] On and in the ruins of the old city, a new urban practice emerges; the city is, so to speak, rediscovered and recreated. However, as Lefebvre noted,

---

228   Lefebvre, 'Dissolving City, Planetary Metamorphosis', 567.
229   Lefebvre, *Production of Space*, 332.
230   Ibid.
231   Lefebvre, *Right to the City*, 120.

the urban phenomenon is thereby fundamentally transformed, and a double paradox, or rather a double contradiction, emerges. On the one hand, more and more urban centres become centres of power and decision-making, expelling large parts of the population and excluding them from access to centrality. This process also limits and domesticates the urban. On the other hand, the 'dialectisation' of social relations through urbanisation leads to a second paradox: 'centers and peripheries presuppose and oppose one another. This phenomenon, which has deep roots and infamous historical precedents, is currently intensifying to such a degree, that it encompasses the entire planet.'[232] We must now connect these findings to the overall development of society and analyse them from the broader perspective of the urban level.

As noted earlier, Lefebvre's elaboration of his concept of levels only exists in fragments. A reconstruction was necessary in order to be able to apply it, which of course leaves open a relatively large space for interpretation. Other scholars, particularly Kanishka Goonewardena, Stefan Kipfer, and Neil Brenner, have also looked closely at this concept and discovered additional aspects and facets of it.[233]

A series of questions arises from this reconstruction. First of all, there is the fundamental problem of the constitution of these levels. Lefebvre had not only introduced the concept of levels, but also used the concept of scale in his later work, which caused considerable confusion needing to be addressed. Related to this, secondly, is the question of centrality and its mode of operation as a level. In this context, the contradictory dynamics of centrality must be elucidated, which consist in the fact that, on the one hand, *mondialisation* leads to an intensification of the hierarchy of centres, while, on the other, urbanisation results in the dispersion of centrality and the emergence of polycentric urban configurations. In order to understand this dynamic, it is necessary to broaden our view to the whole territory, and to analyse the complex pattern of centres and peripheries, and of centralisation and peripheralisation, that has developed in the past decades.

Finally, the question of the articulation of the levels arises: How can the urban level mediate between the general level G and the private level P? Which regulations and institutions are necessary for this? What role do political processes and political mobilisations play?

---

232   Lefebvre, 'Dissolving City, Planetary Metamorphosis', 567.
233   See for example Goonewardena, 'The Urban Sensorium'; Kipfer, 'Why the Urban Question Still Matters'; Kipfer et al., 'Globalizing Lefebvre?'; Brenner, *New Urban Spaces*.

Level or Scale?

When discussing the question of levels, we should first point out an often over-looked but important distinction that Lefebvre himself introduced, but which still causes some confusion today: the distinction between 'scale' and 'level'. As early as *The Production of Space*, but especially in *De l'État*, Lefebvre used the concepts of both level (*niveau*) and scale (*échelle*) to capture the 'vertical' structuring of spatial processes. This distinction has been partially lost in English translations: in *The Production of Space*, for example, both terms are consistently translated as 'level'.[234] Brenner has analysed this distinction and made an important contribution to the debate on the 'scale question' using Lefebvre's reflections on *échelle*.

The starting point of this debate, which in the 1990s proliferated in urban studies, social geography, regional economy, and critical political economy, and which formed a central element of the spatial turn in the social sciences, was the combined processes of globalisation and urbanisation (cf. section 1.3). On the one hand, the global scale was strengthened by the formation of global networks of production and interaction and the emergence of a new international division of labour. This was associated with the creation of new forms of global regulation, and the establishment of numerous new inter- and transnational organisations. On the other hand, the process of urbanisation had broken up the morphology and catchment areas of cities and agglomerations to such an extent that new regional forms of regulation and governance were created in many places. Both processes increasingly challenged the role of the nation state as the central framework of territorial organisation, as new institutions and new forms of regulation emerged that were situated below and above the scale of the nation state. Such re-scaling processes had partly been going on for a long time, but they were clearly intensified in the context of neoliberal strategies and policies.[235]

As has been shown, Lefebvre had already provided important starting points for a theorisation of these processes decades earlier, with his contributions on urbanisation and *mondialisation*, and his open conception of the production of space. He had also forged a way out of the rigid understanding of the state as a fixed institutional framework of social relations that dominated most approaches and theories of the time (see section 7.5). As Brenner noted, Lefebvre's notion of the superimposition and interpenetration of social spaces

---

234   Brenner, *New Urban Spaces*, 62, 65–6.
235   See for example Brenner, *New State Spaces*; Keil and Mahon, *Leviathan Undone?*; Swyngedouw, 'The Mammon Quest'; Swyngedouw, 'Neither Global nor Local'.

allowed him to theorise the relational, mutually interdependent character of geographical scales under capitalism.[236] Brenner referred in particular to Lefebvre's metaphor of social space as a millefeuille, the many-layered puff pastry dessert, to explain the polymorphic character of sociospatiality.[237]

Thus, different scales are always involved in the production of urban spaces, and a multiscale approach is required to capture their transformation. These considerations led Brenner to his central thesis that the urban question is ultimately a scale question: 'multiscalar methodologies are now absolutely essential for grasping the fundamental role of cities as preconditions, arenas and outcomes of the current round of global capitalist restructuring.'[238]

As inspiring and far-reaching as Lefebvre's reflections and Brenner's interpretations and further developments are, a theoretical puzzle remains: how are Lefebvre's concepts of scales and levels related? Lefebvre himself did not really solve this riddle. Thus, in both *The Production of Space* and *De l'État*, the terms 'level' and 'scale' often appear abruptly side by side. In the context of protest movements, for example, Lefebvre writes in *De l'État*: 'They emphasise the relations between people (individuals, groups, classes) and space with its different *levels*: the neighbourhood and the immediate, the urban and its mediations, the region and the nation, and, finally the worldwide . . . These movements are experimenting with modes of action at diverse *scales*.'[239] This passage allows us a wide range of interpretations. Another passage in *The Production of Space*, however, reveals that Lefebvre is thinking of levels and scales together: there he distinguishes between 'the "micro" level (architecture, dwelling and habitat, neighbourhood), the "medium" level (the city, urbanism, the town–country relationship) and the "macro" level (spatial and territorial planning, the national territory, the general and the worldwide).'[240]

Lefebvre's distinction between level and scale only becomes clear when the implications of applying these concepts are considered. Thus, Kipfer pointed out in a remarkable reply to Brenner that with the one-sided focus on the scale question an essential insight of Lefebvre has been lost: that the urban forms a level of social reality that allows the urban to be grasped as centrality and as mediation.[241] In this sense, as Kipfer has shown, each individual level constitutes a multiscalar reality. The general level G, for instance, is characterised by

---

236 Brenner, 'Between Fixity and Motion', 466.
237 Brenner, 'A Thousand Leaves'.
238 Brenner, 'The Urban Question as a Scale Question', 375. See also Brenner, *New Urban Spaces*.
239 Lefebvre, *State, Space, World*, 228; Lefebvre, *De l'État*, vol. 4, 273. Emphasis added.
240 Lefebvre, *Production of Space*, 388. Translation by author.
241 Kipfer, 'Why the Urban Question Still Matters'.

the nation state as well as by various supranational entities. Likewise, on the urban level M the multiscalar reality becomes almost constitutive. Finally, everyday life and thus level P are also multiscalar: everyday mobility leads to multilocal daily and weekly routines, and also to the most diverse short- and long-term forms of migration, which connect different, often very distant territories and places with each other. Scales are thus vertical, hierarchical frameworks that shoot through and penetrate the different levels. Lefebvre spoke in this context of territorially defined 'space envelopes' as relatively stable boundaries and hierarchies of social relations. It is important to see that these scales interact, and therefore need to be understood in relation to each other.[242]

Lefebvre postulates that in a situation of increased territorial complexity, only the urban, as a level of mediation and centrality, can bring together and connect the manifold elements of social reality. The concepts of levels and scales should therefore not be played off against each other but should be used as concepts that deal with different aspects and thus also make different processes visible.

Centre and Periphery

Having discussed the difference between levels and scales, a second question arises: How can centrality, which is, after all, point-shaped, be imagined in the context of levels? How can the production of centrality be thought of as a comprehensive process? If we look at centrality from the perspective of the levels, and thus place it in the larger social context, the fundamental dialectic of the urban becomes visible: the centre cannot be thought without its complement, its dialectical opposite – the periphery. Centrality is thus a relational concept; it does not exist without periphery, or peripheries.

So far in this chapter, we have considered centrality from the perspective of an individual city and analysed the struggle for centrality and against selective access to or exclusion from centrality. This is consistent insofar as, in Lefebvre's historical analysis, centrality first coincides with the city: the city arises as a centre, and it embodies centrality. The urbanisation process dissolved this unity of city and centre. As early as the nineteenth century, peripheries, suburbs, banlieues, and barrios developed, settlement spaces that 'belong' to the city but lack centrality. Accordingly, one can live in urban areas and still be cut off from centrality. This phenomenon was introduced into urban studies with the relatively vague and generic term 'urban periphery'. In parallel,

---

242   Lefebvre, *Production of Space*, 350–1.

however, as Lefebvre has shown (see section 3.3), the countryside was also being urbanised, in multiple ways. In the 1980s, the term *periurbanisation* was introduced in France to characterise a process in which the peripheries become urbanised, or vice versa: the 'countryside' becomes the 'periphery'. In this context the thesis of complete urbanisation means that the relationship between centre and periphery extends to the entire territory, and thus must be considered from this perspective. Finally, in this renewed and changed meaning of centrality, Lefebvre finds the dialectical sublation of the urban–rural contradiction. Through urbanisation it is transformed into the contradiction between centre and periphery (see section 7.1).

Interestingly, the problem of centrality was not introduced into urban theory until the 1930s, when the geographer Walter Christaller published his famous 'central place theory', which he understood as an economic theory of the city and also considered an important tool for spatial planning, which at the time was only at its very beginning (see section 2.1). Christaller's project was the creation of a rational spatial order, looking not at the industrial production process, but at the process of consumption. He was therefore not concerned with the question of agglomeration and the general logic of location (see section 3.5), but was instead interested in how to supply the population with goods and services in the most efficient way. He also took temporality into account, that is, the question of how often a product is in demand, and thus distinguished functions of low centrality (such as bakeries) from those of high centrality (such as hospitals). Christaller's level of analysis was the national territory, and thus level G. As was common at the time, he considered the state as a container in which a wide variety of 'places' were located. Seen from a planning rationality, a hierarchically graded hexagonal distribution pattern of 'central places' proved to be the most efficient way to supply the entire population. He thus drew the now-famous picture of hexagonal structures extending from the most central place (*Oberzentrum*) down to the market town (*Markt-Ort*) with about 800 inhabitants, and from there even further on to the village and to the individual farm. Central place theory can be understood as a universal concept of spatial development guided by the postulate of an 'equality in space'. It is an attempt to construct a comprehensive, equal, and at the same time hierarchical arrangement of centralities in space. The urban–rural opposition disappears completely in this system, as do the peripheries. The whole territory is thus uniformly planned, and all levels, the nation state (G), the 'central places' (M), and the individual households (P), are brought together in one single spatial system. Central place theory is thus a prime example of the dominance of the state and the state-planned and organised space over the urban level.

This system is so universal that it was applied (with certain adaptations) first in fascist Germany, and then, after the Second World War, in Israel (as the basis for the Sharon Plan), in Poland, in parts of the Soviet Union, and in many countries of the West.[243] It has had a career in academia and planning, particularly in the United States and France, and was even written into the constitution of the Federal Republic of Germany. Christaller himself, who was still close to the communist KPD in the early 1930s, joined the Fascist NSDAP in 1940 and contributed his concept to the 'Generalplan Ost' as a staff member in the Stabshauptamt Planung und Boden, which was responsible for spatial planning in the newly conquered territories in Poland and the Soviet Union.[244]

To my knowledge, Lefebvre did not refer to Christaller anywhere in his writing, but he must have known the theory of central places, as it was one of the dominant concepts in spatial planning in post-war France. In many passages of his work, he addressed and criticised the overarching state logic that produced a unitary system and even caused the distinction between city and country to disappear.[245] This is also a precise description of Christaller's conception.

Central place theory allows us to better understand Lefebvre's concept of centrality: first, in contrast to Christaller, his concept is not static but dynamic, because he embeds it in the context of the urbanisation process; second, he sees centrality not only as an instrument of state domination but also as a productive force that generates new possibilities and potentials; and third, his dialectical concept allows us to detect the unequal development of centralities and peripheries and thus the highly contradictory processes of centralisation and peripheralisation.

Polycentrality

Centralisation is clearly a double-edged process: on the one hand, it tends to sharpen urban hierarchies, leading to the development of decision-making centres on a global scale. On the other hand, the process of urbanisation, with the continuous expansion of the urban fabric, leads to the dispersion of centrality, and thus to polycentrality. As Lefebvre observed, the dominant centres tend to dissolve into partial centralities whose concrete relations are difficult to determine.[246] This opposition of dispersion and centralisation, of urban fabric

---

243   Kegler, 'Zentrale Orte'; Trezib, Die Theorie der zentralen Orte in Israel und Deutschland.

244   Rössler, 'Wissenschaft und Lebensraum', 174–6.

245   See for example Lefebvre, Urban Revolution, 79.

246   Ibid., 97, 119–20.

and centrality, requires, according to Lefebvre, the introduction or even the invention of new urban forms: polycentric cities, differentiated and renewed centralities, and moving or floating centralities.[247] 'Neither traditional city (separated from the country to better dominate it), nor the Megalopolis without form or fabric, without woof or warp, would be the guiding idea.'[248]

With these ideas Lefebvre anticipated concepts developed in the late 1980s, when numerous new centralities were suddenly 'discovered' in seemingly monotonous and monofunctional suburbs and banlieues, some of which had been developing for some time but had hardly been discussed before. New terms were coined for these 'new' urban configurations, such as 'edge city' or 'technoburb',[249] or, in Edward W. Soja's general formulation, 'exopolis': 'The new metropolis is exploding and coalescing . . . in improbable cities where centrality is virtually ubiquitous and the solid familiarity of what we once knew as urban melts into air.'[250] More recent research has also coined terms such as 'postsuburbanisation' or 'new urban intensity' to describe these processes.[251] Lefebvre's proposal for dealing with such new urban configurations is still very relevant today: ultimately, they cannot be prevented, but only productively developed further.

The same applies to areas located outside large agglomerations, where new forms of centrality have also developed. The new forms of this peripheral centralisation were analysed by Pierre Veltz in one of the most concise analyses of *mondialisation*, globalisation, and metropolisation to date.[252] This work has never been translated into English and is therefore hardly known outside France. Veltz does not explicitly refer to Lefebvre, but to a certain extent he logically extends Lefebvre's thinking. He shows that not only metropolitan areas but also small and medium-sized centres represent a clear break with Christaller's regular model of centrality.[253] These centres become economically specialised and, simultaneously, increasingly interconnected, thereby forming networks of cities. In addition, new centralities emerge at transport nodes, at places with certain economic, cultural, or scenic qualities, in emerging tourist regions, or even in favourably located peripheries (where, for example, special economic zones are created). Veltz calls these new territorial configurations 'territories *by* networks' (*territoires en réseaux*), which replace the former 'territories *of* networks' (*territoires de réseaux*).

247   Lefebvre, *Right to the City*, 120.
248   Ibid.
249   Garreau, *Edge City*; Fishman, *Bourgeois Utopias*.
250   Soja, *Thirdspace*, 239.
251   Nüssli and Schmid, 'Beyond the Urban–Suburban Divide'.
252   Veltz, *Mondialisation, villes et territoires*.
253   Ibid., 62.

This new form of territory is constituted by centralities that form nodes in a gigantic system of global networks in which manifold flows meet and are thereby articulated and mediated with each other. Such territories are thus no longer clearly defined units within a nested hierarchy (as in Christaller's model), but interconnected condensation nuclei in an immense and indecipherable network on a planetary scale. Together, these nuclei form a complex and extremely dynamic 'archipelago economy' (économie d'archipel).[254] The large metropolises do not lose their importance in this system, however. Instead, they become 'fantastic machines of commutation – actual and potential – of energies, competences, desires'.[255] Veltz thus describes a simultaneity of different developments: while exorbitant global centralities develop, new centralities emerge in former urban peripheries and in areas outside of large agglomerations. It is clear that these planetary developments, which Lefebvre had only sketched, but whose full extent he could not yet recognise, require a radical further re-evaluation of his theory (see also section 8.2).

Peripheralisation and Colonisation

In addition to the centralities, the 'peripheries' must now be brought into focus, because new peripheries are also emerging hand in hand with the new centralities, and many previously agrarian and industrial areas are facing sometimes dramatic processes of peripheralisation. This development had already become apparent in the 1960s, was intensified with the crisis of Fordism in the 1970s, and has continued ever since. As a result, a complex urban topography emerged, characterised by the simultaneity of different processes of peripheralisation and centralisation. Lefebvre described this process, from the example of the strongly industrialised and urbanised axis running across France, from Marseille in the south through Lyon and Paris to Le Havre in the north, while all the rest of the country was relegated to 'underdevelopment' by both economic development processes and state planning.[256]

Interestingly, Lefebvre linked this process of peripheralisation to the concept of colonisation: 'Where a dominated space is generated, organized and mastered by a dominant space – where there is periphery and centre – there is colonization.'[257] In a seminal article, Goonewardena and Kipfer reconstructed three distinct moments in Lefebvre's understanding of the concept of

---

254   Ibid., 65, 245ff.
255   Ibid., 247. Translation by author.
256   Lefebvre, *Production of Space*, 84.
257   Lefebvre, *De l'État*, vol. 4, 173–4. Translation by author.

colonisation.[258] In his texts of the 1950s and 1960s, he used the term 'colonisa-tion' as a metaphor for alienation. At the time, in collaboration with Guy Debord, he developed an understanding of colonisation of the everyday as a process of domination by the state and economic powers. This understanding changed in his texts on the urban in the late 1960s, in which he linked colonial and imperial questions to urban struggles and forms of spatial organisation in the imperial core.[259] For example, Lefebvre noted

> a kind of overall colonization of space by 'decision-making-centers'. Centers of wealth and information, of knowledge and power are begin-ning to create feudal dependencies. In this case, the boundary line does not divide city and country but cuts across the urban phenomenon, between a dominated periphery and a dominating center.[260]

Finally, in *De l'État*, where he wrote an entire chapter on 'Colonisations et colonisateurs'.[261] Lefebvre explicitly addressed theories of colonisation and imperialism, understanding 'colonisation' as a concept to describe the role of the state in organising hierarchical relations between dominant (central) and dominated (peripheral) social spaces.[262] Kipfer and Goonewardena have consistently developed these rather preliminary conceptual considerations to a postcolonial analytical framework and applied it exemplarily to public housing redevelopment projects in Paris and Toronto.[263]

In the larger global context, Lefebvre's dynamic and relational conception of centre and periphery allows us to connect a wide variety of struggles over centrality. Kipfer emphasises the 'discontinuous character of (the) urban revolution(s)' and reminds us that Lefebvre 'painted a world-wide tableau of struggle: a constellation of centralities produced by "near" and "far" peripheries'.[264]

This view is closely linked to the experiences of the worldwide revolts and struggles of the late 1960s. Lefebvre wrote:

> Should we forget that the last phase of war in dependent countries in Asia and Africa found its extension in the contestations and protests of youth,

---

258   Kipfer and Goonewardena, 'Urban Marxism and the Post-colonial Question'.
259   Ibid., 79.
260   Lefebvre, *Urban Revolution*, 113.
261   Lefebvre, *De l'État*, vol. 4, 172–210.
262   Kipfer and Goonewardena, 'Urban Marxism and the Post-colonial Question'.
263   Kipfer and Goonewardena, 'Lefebvre and "Colonization" '.
264   Kipfer, 'Pushing the Limits of Urban Research', 479.

women, intellectuals, the working class, the everyday, suburbs, in short, all peripheries, even those strangely close to the centers?[265]

However, this ' "world-wide front" against the planetary hegemony of imperial power was never consolidated, despite many attempts'.[266] The assembly of all the world's peripheries as the basis of a worldwide mobilisation was a widespread concrete utopia that has reappeared again and again in many forms to this day, especially in the anti- and alter-globalisation movements that formed in the late 1990s and the World Social Forums that arose from them.

The Urban Level as Mediation

How can these findings be applied to today's largely globalised and urbanised world? They condense into a picture of moving constellations of different processes of centralisation and peripheralisation, which can be depicted only on the middle, urban level, the level of mediation. How can such mediation function? On the one hand, urbanisation always increases connectivity and networking, and thus also enables or facilitates processes of socialisation, politicisation, and mobilisation. On the other hand, the struggle for centrality, as shown, also creates the conditions of mediation and a renewed centrality.

This mediating aspect of the urban becomes visible, for example, in alliances that bring together different organisations, action groups, and urban social movements in joint actions and activities, such as Social Justice alliances and Right to the City alliances, which have also organised as a national alliance, for example, in the United States. They explore new forms of cooperation across territorial boundaries that also introduce new, overarching, and inclusive practices and policies.

This political aspect of urban mediation also plays an important role for peripheral areas and territories of extended urbanisation. Roberto Luís Monte-Mór has shown for Brazil that extended urbanisation was accompanied by the development of an urban practice. The urban struggles for control of the collective means of reproduction and claims to citizenship that emerged in the 1970s in the larger centres began to extend to more remote places in the 1980s. Today, urban social movements also include, among others, indigenous peoples, rubber tappers, and landless workers.[267]

---

265   Lefebvre, *De l'État*, vol. 4, 238. Translated in Kipfer and Goonewardena, 'Urban Marxism and the Post-colonial Question', 98.
266   Lefebvre, *De l'État*, vol. 4, 247. Translation by author.
267   Monte-Mór, 'What Is the Urban in the Contemporary World?', 264–5.

Similarly, Martín Arboleda showed in his research on operational land-scapes of resource extraction in Colombia and Chile that these processes not only drove marginalisation and dispossession, but also enabled opportunities for encounters between previously isolated communities or individuals, thus generating new centralities.[268] This form of extended urbanisation requires not only energy and transportation infrastructure, but also sophisticated telecom-munication systems, internet connectivity, and radio and mobile phone signal coverage, which fostered not only physical mobility but also communication among local communities. The strong social mobilisations in many parts of Latin America against mining, agribusiness, logging, and energy and oil extrac-tion projects thus also created new forms of solidarity between local communi-ties and national and international advocacy networks, linking operational landscapes and large urban agglomerations in mutually transformative ways: 'Thus, it is precisely in the opening of avenues for increased communication and interaction where the emancipatory promise of planetary urbanization lies.'[269] In the same vein, Kipfer showed how resistance led by indigenous peoples to a pipeline project connecting a tar sand extraction site in the Canadian province of Alberta to global markets could connect various strug-gles along the pipeline, from the production site to metropolitan and intersti-tial spaces.[270] Similarly, Wilson showed how already the planning of the 'Plan Puebla Panamá', an overarching infrastructure project for southern Mexico and Central America, which was launched in 2001 and abandoned in 2008, sparked widespread local resistance, which in turn also forged new links between different groups and organisations, such as the movement fighting against airport development in the outskirts of Mexico City, and the resistance against the Isthmus of Tehuantepec megaproject in southern Mexico.[271] However, we must be aware that examples of successful mobilisations are juxtaposed with many other moments in which planetary peripheries are brutally repressed by politics, police, and military, and are ruthlessly exploited and economically marginalised.

Nevertheless, an urban potential is revealed here: that the urban level can mediate between the general level of global processes and the private level of everyday life. Goonewardena states that the concept of levels distinguishes Lefebvre's vision of the struggle for socialism: 'one that would be waged against the dominant logics of the "global" (level G), primarily but not exclusively on the intermediary "urban" terrain (level M), with the nourishment of the utopian

---

268   Arboleda, 'In the Nature of the Non-city'; Arboleda, 'Spaces of Extraction'.
269   Ibid., 118.
270   Kipfer, 'Pushing the Limits of Urban Research'.
271   Wilson, 'Plan Puebla Panama'.

energies released by the contradictions of "everyday life" (level P).[272] Thus, this mediation reveals for Lefebvre a 'possible-impossible', a concrete utopia: the reappropriation of space and time through the creation of a space-time unity within the framework of an urban *autogestion* that is itself part of a generalised *autogestion*.[273] We will return to this question in section 6.6.

The Urban as a Universal and Historical Category

On the basis of the reconstruction presented in chapters 3 and 4, we can formulate a general overview on the theorisation of the urban that Lefebvre unfolds. At the centre of this theory are the following three analytical operations or approaches to the social reality of the urban.

The space-time axis of urbanisation. This first operation shows how the historical city is destroyed by the process of urbanisation. The contradiction of city and country is dialectically sublated; the 'city' as a specific historical configuration, as a (delimitable) 'object', dissolves in the process of urbanisation. It survives only as an image, an ideology, a caricature of a city subject to the logic of industrial production.

Historical space-time configurations. From the overall perspective of the society, the second operation presents the same process as a succession of three historical sequences or fields: the rural, the industrial, and the urban. It becomes apparent that the dual process of industrialisation and urbanisation, with all the conflicts it generates, carries within the potential of a new society. Urbanisation becomes general and thus opens the possibility for the emergence of an 'urban society'. Lefebvre defines this urban society as a specific field or continent, as a comprehensive mode of production and life.

Space-time levels of social reality. This third operation presents the urban as a middle and mediating level between the level of abstract, general processes and the concrete-sensual level of everyday life. On this middle level, the specificity of the urban can be identified as a form, the form of *centrality*, which stands for assembly, meeting, and social innovation. This combination of level and form makes it possible to represent the complete urbanisation of society on the terrain: the urban is no longer bound to delimitable units, but forms a level of social reality on which the various centralities and peripheries can be mapped.

With this third operation, the question of the specificity of the urban in an urbanised world raised at the beginning finds a concise answer: the 'city' is a

---

272   Goonewardena, 'The Urban Sensorium', 67.
273   Lefebvre, *Urban Revolution*, 150, 179–80.

social form, centrality, which corresponds to a specific level of the social reality. The content of this form remains theoretically indeterminate and can only be determined empirically. It arises from the respective social relations and is the result of political conflicts and struggles. Under changed historical conditions, the content of the urban is socially redefined in each case.

Accordingly, the complete urbanisation of society does not mean that urban society becomes uniform and homogeneous, nor does it mean that the urban disappears. On the contrary, centrality is restored or re-created in many forms. It is in this historical process of dissolution and reconstitution that the specific quality of the urban first becomes apparent: it becomes productive by bringing together the most diverse elements of society and allowing them to interact with each other. Centrality thus constitutes an important social resource.

The dialectic of the urban is determined by the fundamental contradiction of centre and periphery. There is always a tendency for strong political and economic forces to monopolise, control, and limit access to centrality, thus excluding various social groups from centrality in many ways and pushing them into the periphery.

This finally raises the question of how inclusive forms of centrality can be produced, or, more generally, how the urban is produced under contemporary conditions. This question again leads to a radical change of the analytical perspective. It requires a more general concept and a more general theory that makes it possible to examine the production of the urban in its different dimensions. This is the concept of space and the theory of the production of space that Lefebvre elaborated in *The Production of Space*. This theory will be examined in more detail in the following chapter. Its consequences for the urban question will be explored in the discussion of differential space in section 6.4.

5

The Production of Space

The reconstruction of the theory of the production of space in chapters 3 and 4 has shown that Lefebvre developed a fundamentally new understanding of the urban. Beginning with his thesis of the complete urbanisation of society and the possibility of an urban revolution, he analysed the question of the urban from the general perspective of the entire society. From this vantage point, he observed the dissolution of the city and the transformation of the contradiction between city and country, and he saw on the horizon the emergence of the problematic of planetary urbanisation. This insight raised the question, what is 'the city' in an urban society, and how can the urban be understood in the context of complete urbanisation? Lefebvre found three answers to this question. First, he identified the urban as a specific level of social reality, which mediates between the near and the distant orders, between the private and the general levels. Second, he identified the form of the urban: centrality, which evolves through urbanisation into the contradiction between centre and periphery. Third, he recognised a 'dimensionality' of the urban: it is, at one and the same time, a practice, a strategy, and a text. It must then be asked *how* these different categories are linked to each other, and how the 'city' or the urban is produced.

Attempting to find an answer to this question again leads Lefebvre to a change of perspective, as it requires a more general approach that would be able to integrate the urban, the private, and the general in one overarching concept. This concept is 'space'.

In his analysis of space, Lefebvre proceeds in a way similar to his analysis of the city: he leaves the object behind him and focuses instead on the process of its production. As a result, Lefebvre presented what in many respects is indeed a 'revolutionary theory of social space', whose scope and implications are by no means yet exhausted.[1] Accordingly, *The Production of Space* forms the cornerstone of the present study.

The formulation 'production of space' is in this context anything but trivial. Space played only a subordinate role in humanities and social sciences well into the 1970s. Either it was taken as something self-evident and given, as a category that did not require further examination – as was the case in geography – or it was regarded as irrelevant, as it largely was in sociology and economics (see section 1.2). Given this situation, it is understandable that Lefebvre's book went unnoticed when it was first published in 1974. It was the 'spatial turn' in social sciences of the late 1980s that put the question of space on the agenda, and it took even longer until postmodern geography 'rediscovered' Lefebvre. The translation of *The Production of Space* into English in 1991 played a key role in this discovery, resulting in the paradoxical situation that Lefebvre became known in Anglo-American scholarship initially through his theory of the production of space, while his earlier texts on the city and the urban were not read more widely until a decade later.

This chapter introduces a new theoretical perspective: analysing how the urban is produced requires understanding of urban space. In his foreword to the third edition of *The Production of Space*, Lefebvre asks: 'How to think about the City (its widespread implosion-explosion, the "modern Urban") without conceiving clearly the space it occupies, appropriates (or "disappropriates")?'[2] Consequently, he argues for developing a general theory on the relationship between space and society.[3] The theory of the production of space is thus closely related to Lefebvre's earlier analyses of the process of urbanisation and the urban society, and it cannot be adequately understood without considering this relation: for Lefebvre, the 'production of space' always also means the 'production of urban space'. Originally, he wanted to give his book the title *Théorie de l'espace urbain* (Theory of urban space).[4]

The Production of Space is an extremely difficult book, and it raises some fundamental questions. In order to understand it, it is necessary to first enter into a debate about the nature of space that goes back to Greek philosophy. In his critical confrontation with various attempts to solve the enigma of space, Lefebvre developed a theory that understands space neither as a (material) object nor as a pure idea, but as a social process of production (section 5.1). This theoretical starting point that directly relies on his Marxist theoretical

---

1   Shields, *Lefebvre, Love and Struggle*, 7.
2   Lefebvre, 'Preface to the New Edition', 208.
3   Ibid.
4   Lefebvre, *Urban Revolution*, 195.

fundament and on his emphasis on action and praxis has manifold consequences. How does a society produce its space? How can this process be
grasped theoretically? Which aspects have to be taken into account? Lefebvre
embarked on a difficult search for a 'unified theory' (*théorie unitaire*) that
would unite different perspectives on this production process. As a result, he
designed a three-dimensional conception of the production of space that
brought together the previously separated concepts of physical, mental, and
social space (section 5.2). He finally found a double dialectical triad of terms
that he called dimensions, 'formants', or moments of the production of space:
first, perceived space (*espace perçu*) and spatial practice (*pratique spatial*);
second, conceived space (*espace conçu*) and representation of space (*représentation de l'espace*); third, lived space (*espace vécu*) and spaces of representation
(*espaces de représentation*). In sections 5.3 to 5.5, these three dimensions will be
explained in detail.

Understanding this double dialectical triad presents considerable difficulties.
First, Lefebvre's examples and illustrations of his theory are sometimes contradictory, which led to ambiguities and various misunderstandings. Second, he did
not reveal the sources of his three-dimensional conception. Third, his theory
interferes with other, similar three-dimensional conceptions. Therefore, I will
confront Lefebvre's theory with related or similar conceptualisations from critical rationalism and psychoanalysis. Finally, this reconstruction shows that the
foundations of Lefebvre's theory can be found in (French) phenomenology and
in Lefebvre's own theory of language (section 5.6). The final section, then, asks
how these three dimensions of the production of space are related to each other.
Here we can see the full effects of Lefebvre's three-dimensional dialectic, which
was elaborated in chapter 2. With its application to the production of space,
Lefebvre fully unfolds and develops this dialectic (section 5.7).

5.1 Space as a Product

(Social) space is a (social) product.[5]

Lefebvre announces the theory of the production of space in *The Urban
Revolution*. There, it is just a preliminary sketch on the political economy of
space (see section 7.1). But a broader claim quickly becomes visible: the elaboration of a general theory of the production of space.

---

5   Lefebvre, *Production of Space*, 26.

The production of space is not new in itself. Dominant groups have always produced a particular space, the space of the old cities, of the countryside (and what will become the 'natural' landscapes). What is new is the general and total production of social space.[6]

In *Espace et politique* (1974), the collection of lectures and articles subsequently added to *Le droit à la ville* (*Right to the City*), the first sketchy outlines of this new theory can be found, and in *The Survival of Capitalism* (1973) Lefebvre places the production of space in the larger context of the reproduction of society. These preliminary works culminate in his magnum opus *The Production of Space* (1974), in which he approaches the process of the production of space on a general level and analyses it not only as a historical phenomenon, but as a constitutive part of the production of society. In this sense, this work also claims to bring together his previous theorisations of everyday life, the urban, and the state in a general theory of the production of social space and social time.

Res Extensa *and* Res Cogitans

In the more recent theoretical debates on 'space', a central problem arises that is commonly understood in philosophy as the question of the 'ontology of space': What is space? Does space exist as such, is it an object to which inhere socially effective forces? Or is it merely an abstract, ideal concept? These questions refer to some of the fundamental philosophical traditions that have shaped Western thought to this day. Lefebvre develops his theory of the production of space in the critical examination of these traditions. In order to understand his theory, it is therefore necessary to briefly discuss this confrontation with Western philosophy (see also chapter 2).

The starting point of this discussion is René Descartes, who, in the history of philosophy, provided a decisive stage in the modern elaboration of the concept of space. Descartes had put an end to the old Aristotelian tradition, according to which space and time were seen as categories that allowed for the classification and naming of sensory facts. As Lefebvre points out, the status of these categories remained vague: they could either be regarded as a simple empirical procedure for grouping sensory facts, or they could be seen as generalities that stand above the realities of the bodily organs.[7]

---

6   Lefebvre, *Urban Revolution*, 155. Translation amended.
7   Lefebvre, *Production of Space*, 1.

Descartes broke with this view of space.[8] His concept of space was based on the radical separation of mind and body, of 'material things' and 'human cognition'. While the perceptible, according to Descartes, can in principle be doubted, even the fact that we ourselves have a body, that which thinks must exist at the time when it thinks: *cogito ergo sum*. This consideration led Descartes to define the two basic categories of his philosophy: the world splits into a creating-thinking substance or *res cogitans*, and into a material substance or *res extensa*. But how can these two substances be distinguished from each other? Descartes introduced a sort of 'spatial' criterion: while mental substances are bound to thinking, material substances have an extension, that is, they have length, width, and depth. This distinction consequently entails an objectivation of space: space, extension, and materiality become synonymous; they form three aspects of the same being, the *res extensa*, which underpins the reality of the perceptible world.

In this way, we encounter a philosophical problem that Lefebvre repeatedly addresses and vehemently criticises: the separation of body and mind and thus also of object and subject. He explains that in Descartes, space presents itself to the subject's mind as an object of thought, an object that dominates both the senses and bodies by containing them. As *res extensa*, space becomes an inert spatial milieu that contains people or things, actions, and situations. With Cartesian reason, space, for Lefebvre, entered the absolute: it did not appear as an intellectual construction or as an elaboration of the sensory, but as absolute, infinite, extrasensory, which could be grasped as an 'object' through a single act of intuition mediated through an absolute being – God.[9]

Absolute and Relational Space

From Lefebvre's point of view, the 'Logos' of the West after Descartes tried in vain to reassemble these separated parts. Is space a divine attribute? Is it the order inherent in the totality of existing things? This is how the question of space appeared to philosophers after Descartes, for Spinoza, Newton, and Leibniz.[10]

Baruch Spinoza regarded absolute space as an attribute or mode of being of the absolute being, hence of God. This space *as such*, defined as infinite, has no contours, because it has no content. It has neither a certain form, nor an

---

8   On the following, see also Werlen, *Sozialgeographie alltäglicher Regionalisierungen*, 161–3; Gosztonyi, *Der Raum*, 237–9.

9   Lefebvre, *Production of Space*, 1, 14, 293, 296–7.

10   Ibid., 1–2, 406.

orientation or direction. It is not the unrecognisable, but rather the indistinguishable.[11]

Isaac Newton came to similar conclusions from another perspective: he regarded space as God's 'sensorium'. However, this space did not only have metaphysical significance, as it did in Spinoza. It also served as the basis for Newton's epochal mechanics: space became the independent cause of the inertia of bodies – an idea which, according to Einstein, was one of Newton's greatest achievements.[12] Space plays an absolute role in this conception, insofar as it affects all material objects without their having an effect on it. Absolute space is, to a certain extent, the reference system on which the validity of Newton's mechanics depends. In contrast, relative space represents for Newton a measure or a movable part of absolute space, which is perceived by the senses through its position relative to other bodies. As an example of such a relative space, Newton takes a part of the earth's surface, or the atmosphere, whose position is fixed in relation to the earth. Only material substances and thus relative space are accessible to observation, but not 'pure', absolute space, which Newton understood accordingly as a spiritual unit that had to have a relationship with God.

Despite its oddities, this concept of space remained a central part of the foundation of physics until the beginning of the twentieth century, when the theory of relativity established a new, relational concept of space and time, which functions without absolute space. Whether the concept of absolute space represents a theoretical necessity for Newton's mechanics, or whether it is only a product of metaphysical thinking, remains controversial to this day. Einstein, in any case, took the view that Newton's concept of space was the only possible and, in particular, the only fruitful approach available to science at the time.[13]

The sharpest opposition to Newton's absolute space came from a contemporary, Gottfried Wilhelm Leibniz.[14] Leibniz approached the question of space through Aristotle, from whom he derived the concept of order, a concept which was to become central to his conception of space. He rejected Descartes's idea of a substantiality of space and the identification of all material things through their extension. He identified a second principle in bodies through which they resisted penetration, and he also recognised an internal, moving force within bodies. For Leibniz, therefore, extension was not the only specific

---

11   Ibid., 169.

12   Einstein, foreword to Jammer, *Concepts of Space*, xvi; Werlen, *Sozialgeographie alltäglicher Regionalisierungen*, 167–9; Gosztonyi, *Der Raum*, 329–31.

13   Einstein, foreword to Jammer, *Concepts of Space*.

14   See Werlen, *Sozialgeographie alltäglicher Regionalisierungen*, 179–81; Gosztonyi, *Der Raum*, 355–7.

characteristic of matter, and the materiality of space could not be inferred from the extension of bodies. He concluded that extension could not be a prerequisite of space, but was created intellectually. For Leibniz, extension relates to space as duration relates to time. Duration and extension are attributes of things, while time and space are to be regarded as outside of things and serve to measure them. For Leibniz, therefore, there is no substance that could be called space. Space, like time, is to be understood as a concept. From this line of argument Leibniz also criticised Spinoza's and Newton's conception of absolute space:

> These gentlemen maintain, therefore, that space is a real absolute being. But this involves them in great difficulties, for it appears that such a being must necessarily be eternal and infinite. Hence some have believed it to be God himself, or one of his attributes, his immensity. But since space consists of parts, it is not a thing that can belong to God.[15]

Leibniz confronted such ideas with a radically different conceptualisation: space, like time, is something relational. Time and space denote a mental order of things and phenomena, and thus the possibility of relating them to each other. Space is the order of simultaneous things, the order of togetherness or juxtaposition. Time, on the other hand, is the order of the succession of things. The basis of those orders cannot be determined empirically, nor are they accessible to perception. Space is therefore not built up from individual random sensory data and their associative connection, but is to be understood as a realisation of a conceived mental space based on perception.

In this conception, however, there remains an epistemological gap: how mental, conceived space is related to perception of reality remains unclear, as does the question of how the idea of space can arise at all. Thus, Leibniz's theory ultimately does not escape a need for God: the idea of space can only be conceived as something implanted by God.[16]

These profound debates about absolute and relational space were to continue to occupy scholars for a long time, from philosophy to physics to geography. In physics, the breakthrough came only with the theory of relativity, which finally made do without the hand of God. In the special theory of relativity Albert Einstein designed a relational unit of space, time, and matter, which also described the transformation of matter into energy. The mathematical basis for this was the 'four-dimensional spacetime' developed by Hermann Minkowski,

---

15 Leibniz, 'Leibniz's Third Letter', 14.
16 Gosztonyi, *Der Raum*, 370.

in which three-dimensional space is supplemented by the fourth dimension of time. He formulated the fundamental proposition: 'No one has noticed a place other than at a time and a time other than at a place.'[17] With his general theory of relativity, Einstein finally replaced the concept of the material object as the fundamental concept of physics with the concept of the 'field'. He discovered that the entire physical reality could be represented as a field whose components depend on four spatial-temporal parameters. Thus, in Einstein's words, 'the introduction of an independent (absolute) space is no longer necessary'.[18]

Space as Object and Space as Idea

If the old debate about space was set aside in mathematics and physics at the beginning of the twentieth century, it remained relevant in geography for much longer: thus Benno Werlen identifies a geo-deterministic spatial conception based on Newton's absolute space and counterposes it with an enlightened spatial conception in Leibniz's relational space, asserting that space 'as such' does not exist and that 'space' is accordingly to be understood as a concept.[19]

However, it cannot easily be deduced from Newton's conception of absolute space that perceptible space is a substance endowed with any active forces. For example, Einstein emphasises that both concepts of space, Newton's and Leibniz's, are free creations of human imagination, means devised for easier comprehension of sensory experiences.[20]

According to Einstein, Leibniz developed a 'psychologically simpler' concept of place. A material object or body occupies a certain 'place', that is, a part of the earth's surface identified by a name. 'Simple analysis' shows that this 'place' also could be a group of material objects. Does the word 'place' have a meaning independent of these material objects? 'If one has to give a negative answer to this question, then one is led to the view that space (or place) is a sort of order of material objects and nothing else.'[21]

But, Einstein continues, one could also think differently and imagine a box in which a definite number of objects are placed. This is a property of the material object 'box', which must be considered 'real' in the same sense as the box itself. This property could be called the 'space' of the box, and this term 'space' thus achieves a meaning which is freed from any connection with a

---

17   Hermann Minkowski, *Space and Time*, 40.
18   Einstein, foreword to Jammer, *Concepts of Space*, xvi.
19   Werlen, *Sozialgeographie alltäglicher Regionalisierungen*.
20   Einstein, foreword to Jammer, *Concepts of Space*, xv.
21   Ibid.

particular material object and appears as a superordinate reality to the world of the body.

> In this way by a natural extension of 'box space' one can arrive at the concept of an independent (absolute) space, unlimited in extent, in which all material objects are contained. Then a material object not situated in space is simply inconceivable.[22]

Following this line of argument, it could be concluded that geography and, to a certain extent, philosophy have misunderstood the theoretical construction of absolute and relational space. For Newton, absolute space was not, as in geography, a perceptible space, but only the final reference of his theory that was somehow connected with God. From this perspective, 'geographical space', the perceptible, given 'object' of geography, ultimately has nothing to do with Newton's concept of space, but with a naïve materialism that confuses the perceptible with the real. Whether space is regarded as a 'box' (Newton) or as a relational arrangement of relationships (Leibniz) does not change the status of this space in principle: it always remains a concept. The problem of the 'right' concept of space, then, appears to be fundamentally a question of the underlying theory: Newton's mechanics only functions in an absolute space, so for Einstein this space was 'right' in the sense that it was theoretically necessary.

Lefebvre sees this in a similar way, since he regards both concepts – Newton's and Leibniz's – as representations of space (see section 5.4). However, Newton's conception, which Einstein regarded as advantageous in terms of the theory of physics, presents itself as problematic with regard to social theory. Lefebvre interprets the concept of absolute space as a representation in which the (formal) container and the material content are indifferent to each other and therefore do not prescribe any detectable differences: each region of the container could contain anything. This results in a disaggregation; the container and what it contains become separated. This separation also extends to the contents, which likewise can be disaggregated into separate parts. The reflection is finally exhausted by counting the individual parts or things contained in the container. Lefebvre sees in this a 'logic of separation' which produces and at the same time justifies a strategy of separation.[23] For this reason, Lefebvre prefers Leibniz's thesis, which enables him to develop a dialectical concept of space-time (see section 5.2).

---

22   Ibid.
23   Lefebvre, *Production of Space*, 170.

Lefebvre also sees the problem of the geo-deterministic conception of space. But in contrast to Werlen, he does not associate this with Newton, but with Descartes: his separation between the thought and the material has led to a split of the contemplation of 'space', and space has been conceived of either as an abstract mental construction, or as a concrete 'object' endowed with natural forces. Abstraction and reification thus appear as two sides of the same coin. Having developed this analysis, Lefebvre then directs his critique at all conceptions of space in philosophy and the social sciences which have been based on this Cartesian separation.

The Space of Philosophy

Lefebvre's critique of the philosophical conceptions of space also applies to Immanuel Kant, who had taken up the Aristotelian concept of the category. Lefebvre criticises Kant for seeing space as an instrument of knowledge for classifying phenomena, and thus detached from the empirical as in the older conceptions. Space (as well as time) is thus linked to a priori knowledge of the 'subject', to its inner and ideal, that is, transcendental, structure.[24]

It was Hegel, he finds, who finally brought this idealistic philosophy of space to a head by making space into a fetish of the state. According to Hegel, historical time, animated by knowledge (the concept) and guided by consciousness (language and Logos), produces a space over which the state spreads and which it commands. This space appears as the product of a historicity that realises the archetype of the rational being in a coherent set of institutions, groups, and partial systems (law, morals, family, and so forth). These institutions occupy a national territory dominated by a state. Time thus solidifies and is fixed in the rationality inherent in space. The Hegelian end of history therefore consists of an immovable space, the place and milieu of fulfilled reason, in which time loses all meaning.[25]

In the phase succeeding Hegel, philosophy and practical activity could only attempt to restore time. Lefebvre here looks to, among other philosophical currents, Marx in particular, who conceived of historical time as a time of revolution, as a historicity driven by productive forces and guided by industrial, proletarian, and revolutionary rationality.[26]

But this led to a split of the contemplation of space and time: on the one hand, a philosophy of time and duration developed; on the other hand, an

---

24   Ibid., 2.
25   Ibid., 21.
26   Ibid., 21–3.

epistemology emerged that constructed an abstract space and thought about abstract spaces. The epistemology of the twentieth century accepted the status of space as a 'mental thing' or a 'mental place' and thus generalised the concept of 'mental space'. Lefebvre identifies this mental space in many theoretical approaches, from structuralism and phenomenology to linguistics, semiotics, and psychoanalysis. He vigorously criticises this mental space, because it gives priority to the *cogito*, the abstract subject of Cartesian philosophy, and creates a deep gap between the mind and social practice.[27]

The philosophical account on 'space' thus ultimately remained always bound to an (occidental) logos. Such a space can only be imagined as created either by God or by thinking, both of which Lefebvre must reject epistemologically: only God could create the space of the philosophers as his first work, and this applies both to the God of the Cartesians (from Descartes through Spinoza and Leibniz) as well as to the Absolute of the post-Kantians (Schelling, Fichte, Hegel).[28] Kant's version of understanding space as a priori is also idealistic, since this space can ultimately only emerge from thinking and not from practice. Lefebvre sees a fundamental philosophical problem with all these approaches: the idea that thought, starting from general concepts, can find the 'content' of space. For Lefebvre, this is an idealistic illusion that reduces matter and space to a representation (see section 2.3).[29]

From Lefebvre's materialist perspective, space is not merely a representation; it does not arise in the mind, as a philosophical abstraction, without a corresponding social practice – for him such an idea would be pure idealism. A space which is apparently 'neutral', 'objective', fixed, transparent, innocent, or indifferent is in his view the 'convenient establishment of an inoperative system of knowledge'. It is not simply an error that can be addressed by evoking the 'environment', ecology, nature, anti-nature, or culture. Rather, it is a whole complex of illusions, which can even cause us to forget that there is a subject that acts in order to maintain and reproduce its own living conditions.[30]

In his journey through the mental spaces of Western philosophy, Lefebvre thus confirms his fundamental critique of philosophy as a whole, and specifically his critique of speculative thinking and of the primacy of the spirit (see section 2.3). This philosophy comes to a dead end when it encounters the question of the 'subject' and the 'object' and their mutual relationship. The idea of a unity of the subject and object in humans or in 'consciousness' merely adds another philosophical fiction to the already long list of entities: when

---

27   Ibid., 3–6, 24.
28   Ibid., 73.
29   Ibid., 162.
30   Ibid., 94.

philosophy contemplated the subject without the object, as pure thinking 'I', and the object without the subject, as body-machine, it irrevocably separated what it sought to determine.[31] Philosophy was only able to overcome this separation through great effort: the subject and the object, the *res cogitans* and the *res extensa* of Descartes, the 'I' and the 'non-I' of the Kantians. For Lefebvre, however, this binarism exists only in the mental realm, and it empties life, thought, and society of everything that constitutes living activity.[32]

The Double Illusion: Transparency and Opacity

In previous attempts in Western thinking to grasp space theoretically, Lefebvre argues, the 'truth of space' remained ultimately hidden behind the double illusion of transparency and opacity, in which each term refers to the other, reinforces the other, and hides behind the other.[33]

In the illusion of transparency, which approaches the illusion of philosophical idealism,[34] space appears luminous, understandable, as a free field of action:

> The illusion of transparency goes hand in hand with a view of space as innocent, as free of traps or secret places. Anything hidden or dissimulated – and hence dangerous – is antagonistic to transparency, under whose reign everything can be taken in by a single glance from that mental eye which illuminates whatever it contemplates. Comprehension is thus supposed, without meeting any insurmountable obstacles, to conduct what is perceived, i.e. its object, from the shadows into the light; it is supposed to affect this displacement of the object either by piercing it with a ray or by converting it, after certain precautions have been taken, from a murky to a luminous state.[35]

In this illusion, the space elaborated by philosophy and epistemology is constituted solely in the mind. It is a transparent place, a logical milieu, ultimately a purely spiritual, mental space.[36] Its transparency is a result of thinking. It is produced by a system that possesses neither materiality nor residuals and offers itself like rational evidence to spiritual trial, as if it had the magical power to bring the 'object' out of

---

31   Ibid., 406.
32   Ibid., 39.
33   Ibid., 27, 92.
34   Ibid., 30.
35   Ibid., 28.
36   Ibid., 297.

the shadows and into the light without deforming it, simply by the fact of deciphering it. By suppressing any resistances, shadows, and their 'beings', knowledge places
itself in the service of power with an admirable lack of conscience, as Lefebvre
notes.[37] The illusion of transparency thus reveals itself to be a transcendental illusion. It is a kind of magic lure, but at the same time it refers to another lure that
serves as an alibi, as a mask: the illusion of opacity.[38]

The illusion of opacity, a realist illusion, comes very close to a naturalistic or
mechanistic materialism.[39] It is a naïve illusion that has long been denounced
by philosophy and linguistic theory under such terms as 'naturalness' or
'substantiality'. According to this critique, the gullibility inherent in 'common
sense' entails the deceptive conviction that 'things' are more effective than the
'subject', his thinking, his desire.[40]

> The illusion of substantiality, naturalness and spatial opacity nurtures its
> own mythology. One thinks of the space-oriented artist, at work in a hard
> or dense reality delivered direct from the domain of Mother Nature.
> More likely a sculptor than a painter, an architect sooner than a musician
> or poet, such an artist tends to work with materials that resist or evade his
> efforts. When space is not being overseen by the geometer, it is liable to
> take on the physical qualities and properties of the earth.[41]

The illusion of transparency thus finds its other side in the opposite illusion of
opacity. For Lefebvre, these two illusions are dialectically related to one another;
each contains and nourishes the other. In the transition from one illusion to
another, an oscillation arises that acquires its own significance, since the rational
is naturalised and nature is covered with a nostalgia that replaces reason:

> Symbolisms deriving from nature can obscure the rational lucidity which
> the West has inherited from its history and from its successful domina-
> tion of nature. The apparent translucency taken on by obscure historical
> and political forces in decline (the state, nationalism) can enlist images
> having their source in the earth or in nature, in paternity or in maternity.
> The rational is thus naturalized, while nature cloaks itself in nostalgias
> which supplant rationality.[42]

---

37   Ibid., 39–40.
38   Ibid., 29.
39   Ibid., 30.
40   Ibid., 29.
41   Ibid., 30.
42   Ibid.

For Lefebvre, (Western) philosophy, as a whole, has not been able to resolve the contradictions of conceptualising space. On the contrary, it has divided space: it became either the comprehensible, as the transparency of the spiritual absolute, or the incomprehensible, as the degradation of the spirit, as the absolute naturalness outside the spirit. The *espace lumineux*, the radiant, illuminated space, the cosmos, the pure spatial form, stands opposite the *espace ténébreux*, the shadow-filled, dark space, the world, space as substance.[43]

With this argument, Lefebvre follows the dialectical path of the young Marx in his confrontation with both (German) idealism and early substantialist materialism, a confrontation which can be found in concentrated form in the famous *Theses on Feuerbach* (see section 2.2): while idealism shifts the real into consciousness, into pure thought, and thus obstructs access to the material, practical-sensory world, 'naïve' materialism tries to grasp 'things' or 'substance' as such. But, for its part, such materialism fails to grasp the access to the subjective, creative, productive activity that lends form and meaning to 'things'.

It is significant here that Lefebvre does not direct this critique simply at Western philosophical thinking of the nineteenth century, but also at all contemporary philosophical and social-scientific reflections on space known to him. There are essentially two reasons for this: on the one hand, he sees all these reflections as based on positions which he rejects as 'reductionist' or 'idealist' (such as structuralism or phenomenology); on the other hand, historical-materialist approaches up to the end of the 1960s hardly ever seriously addressed the question of space. For them, time, historical development, and the revolutionary movement remained the decisive theoretical and practical questions (see section 6.4).

Lefebvre's (implicit) recourse to the *Theses on Feuerbach* is consistent in this respect, returning to the beginnings of Marx's critique and attempting on this basis to introduce space into a historical, dialectical, and materialist theory of society, and to develop a consistently spatial materialist-dialectical theory of society.

Producing Space

The remarks above make clear the thrust of Lefebvre's argument from the very beginning of his theoretical treatment of space. On the one hand, he consistently opposes any 'idealist' conception of space. Space could not emerge from conceptual thought, since this is not an immediately productive power. Space

---

43   Ibid., 405–6.

is not (only) a mental construct; it is also based in a concrete materiality.[44] On the other hand, he also rejects object materialism with its naïve belief in the substantiality of 'things': space is not a 'thing'; it cannot be grasped as an object.[45]

From a historical-materialist perspective, space is neither a 'subject' nor an 'object', but it is a social reality. This reality can only be understood as the result of a concrete (material) process of production, which must be analysed in the context of concrete, historical relations of production.[46]

These considerations lead directly to the concept of praxis as it was defined in section 2.2. 'Who talks, who acts, who moves in space?'[47] In Lefebvre's understanding, neither abstract ideas nor material things, but rather concrete subjects, individuals, or collectives produce space. What is sought, then, is a spatial theory of social practice that takes, as its starting point, subjects and their social relations and analyses these subjects' actions and situations.[48]

Lefebvre derives his central initial hypothesis from these considerations: social space is a social product.[49] 'Producing space' may be a confusing formulation, as Lefebvre himself admits. But he sets this term, consciously and provocatively, against the still-widespread idea that space exists before the 'things' that occupy and fill it. And at the same time, he refers to the concept of production in the broad sense, to the self-production of human beings (see section 2.2). Lefebvre thus no longer regards space (and time) as (more or less strongly modified) facts of 'nature' or of 'culture', but as historical products.[50]

The first consequence of this hypothesis is epistemological: if space is a product, then cognition should no longer be directed at space as such, and should not construct models or typologies of space, but should rather reproduce and explain its production. Correspondingly, the epistemological interest shifts from a 'science of space' to the exploration of the production of space.[51] Consequently, Lefebvre does not want to develop a critical theory of space, nor does he strive for a methodological deconstruction of the codes that relate to space. Instead, he seeks a reversal of the prevailing tendency, a change of

---

44   Lefebvre, *Urban Revolution*, 154.
45   Lefebvre, *Production of Space*, 90.
46   Lefebvre, *Urban Revolution*, 157; Lefebvre, *Production of Space*, 116.
47   Lefebvre, *Urban Revolution*, 191.
48   Ibid.
49   Lefebvre, *Production of Space*, 36.
50   Lefebvre, 'Preface to the New Edition', 207.
51   Lefebvre, *Production of Space*, 36–7, 404–5; Lefebvre, *Survival of Capitalism*, 18.

perspective from the consideration of space as a product to the analysis of its production.[52]

The partial products, the things that are localised in space, as well as the discourses on space, serve Lefebvre only as indications and testaments to this production process, which also includes processes of creating meaning. It is therefore not a question of revealing a specific space but of understanding space as a totality or generality that can no longer be examined only analytically, but has to be generated in and through theoretical recognition. Theory has rather to reproduce this generative process in a strong sense: theory can no longer be introduced into lived experience from the outside in a descriptive way, but must rather come from within experience, moving continuously from the past to the present and vice versa. Theoretical concepts encounter a present consciousness that knows no certainty and is as much ahead of an uncertain situation as it is behind it.[53]

With these considerations, Lefebvre makes a radical break with hitherto dominant ideas about space: there is no space before practice, and space itself, as a universal category, does not exist. 'Space' is produced, and to conceptualise 'space' it is necessary to grasp its process of production. This also entails a rejection of individualistic perspectives, since, for Lefebvre, 'production' is always a social, that is, collective, process.

Lefebvre sees himself as adopting a similar approach to space as Marx once took with regard to political economy. Marx's procedure, following the example of Hegel and the English economists (Adam Smith, David Ricardo), consisted in moving back from the results of production to the productive activity itself. This led him to carry out a critical analysis of social labour, the relations and the mode of production, instead of studying isolated objects or (produced) things. Accordingly, for Lefebvre, understanding space cannot be a question of looking at things in space but rather of analysing space as a social product and revealing the social relations associated with its production.[54]

This approach corresponds to the one that Lefebvre had already used so successfully in *The Urban Revolution*: to make a perspective shift from the 'object' (the city) to the process (urbanisation).

---

52 Lefebvre, *Production of Space*, 25–6.
53 Ibid., 37; Lefebvre, *Survival of Capitalism*, 20.
54 Lefebvre, *Production of Space*, 89, 115; Lefebvre, *De l'État*, vol. 4, 279–80.

5.2 Physical, Mental, and Social Space

There are always Three. There is always the Other.[55]

Social space is a social product. With this initial hypothesis, Lefebvre laid the groundwork for a new spatial theory of society. However, he thereby immediately creates a new problem: how exactly is space produced?

The philosophical starting point that Lefebvre wants to overcome has been explained in detail above: the duality of subject and object, of spirit and materiality, of mental and physical space, in which both poles ultimately remain in mere abstraction. For Lefebvre, this relation of two terms is reduced to an opposition, and it is defined by an effect of meaning: the effect of an echo, of a repercussion, of a mirror.[56] One refers to the other in an endless movement where the dialectic remains trapped, so to speak. To release the dialectic, Lefebvre requires a third concept in order to complete a triad.

This triad, however, crystallises only slowly, as the result of a long search process: in *The Right to the City* and *The Survival of Capitalism*, Lefebvre is still starting from a duality, distinguishing a mental space and a social space, or an *espace 'idéal'* ('ideal' space) based on mental, logical-mathematical categories, and an *espace 'réel'* ('real' space) – the space of social practice.[57]

It is only in *The Production of Space* that Lefebvre finds a triad, a triad of fields (*champs*) and their corresponding spaces: first, the physical field, nature, the cosmos, materiality and thus physical space, which is defined by the practical-sensory and the perception of nature. Second, there is the mental field, which includes logic and formal abstraction, and thereby also mental space, the logical-epistemological space defined by philosophy and mathematics. And, third, there is the social field, the field of projects and projections, of symbols and utopias, of the imaginary, and, as might be added, that of desire.[58] It is only in this triad that Lefebvre finds the 'real life' that Western philosophy has banned from its reflections.

Having found the triad of the physical, mental, and social fields, however, another problem arises: in conventional definitions, these three fields fall apart. What should one call the lines of separation which keep physical, mental, and social space at a distance from one another? Fault line, distance, cut, break? The names are not important: what matters for Lefebvre is the distance between

---

55   Lefebvre, *La présence et l'absence*, 143. Translation by author.
56   Ibid.
57   See also Lefebvre, *Production of Space*, 14.
58   Ibid., 6, 11, 27.

these three spaces.[59] The essential theoretical problem is thus to link these three fields with each other and to uncover their mutual relationships: what he is seeking is nothing less than a 'unified theory' (*théorie unitaire*) of physical, mental, and social space, which once again brings together these three spaces or fields that had until then been conceived of separately.[60]

In Search of a Unified Theory

Following Lefebvre's epistemological premises, a unified theory should not be established as an achieved 'totality', much less as a 'synthesis'. Nor can it be about constructing a system of spaces or a system of space, which would only refer to the discourse on space. For Lefebvre, the fundamental theoretical and methodological goal is to identify the essential elements or moments of the production of space, by distinguishing what has been mixed and reassembling what has been separated. He wants to demonstrate the production of space itself by bringing together the different 'spaces' and the modalities of their genesis in a single theory.[61]

A unified theory: this is an intentional terminological analogy to the old dream of a unified theory of physics that would succeed in bringing together molecular, electromagnetic, and gravitational forces. Lefebvre explains that the theory of material nature defines certain concepts on the most general and abstract level: 'energy', 'space', and 'time'. Through these three concepts, 'matter', 'nature', 'physical reality', or, to use an old term from philosophy, the 'substance' of this world, to which the earth and human beings with their consciousness belong, has found a certain unity. These three concepts and the theories they entail should not be mixed or separated. They only make sense in combination. Alone, they remain empty abstractions.[62]

It would therefore be an easy step to borrow this physical model in order to analyse social practice. Lefebvre, however, points out that physics can only provide limited help in the search for a unified theory of the production of space. Attempts in this vein have, so far, always led to failure. There is no reason to assume an isomorphism between social and physical energies, or between 'human' and physical force fields. Physics can serve as guidance, but not as a model.[63] Lefebvre thus seeks out approaches to a unified theory in other fields,

59   Ibid., 11, 14.
60   Ibid., 11–12, 21, 298.
61   Ibid., 16, 413.
62   Ibid., 11–12.
63   Ibid., 13–14.

with the Surrealists and Georges Bataille, but especially in Jacques Lafitte's reflections on the science of machines.[64] Although he finds interesting points of contact, he does not find a satisfactory solution.[65]

The Three Formants of the Production of Space

Finally, Lefebvre ventures to make his own proposal for a conceptualisation of the triad of the production of space: the 'perceived' (*le perçu*), the 'conceived' (*le conçu*), the 'lived' (*le vécu*). In spatial terms, he calls this triad 'spatial practice' (*pratique spatiale*), 'representation of space' (*représentation de l'espace*), and 'spaces of representation' (*espaces de représentation*). This double series of three terms designates, for Lefebvre, the foundational moments or formants of the production of space.[66]

The term 'formant' (*formant*) is a borrowing from musicology, where it denotes one of the characteristic partials of a sound. The term 'moment' (*moment*) has a more complex background: it refers, first, to a temporal aspect. Second, it refers to the dialectic in which thesis and antithesis can be understood as 'moments' of a dialectical process (see section 2.3). The dialectic moment marks the turning point of reality *and* concept, the starting point of negativity, which is fulfilled in sublation.[67] In volume 2 of his *Critique of Everyday Life*, Lefebvre also sketched out a 'theory of moments' (*théorie des moments*),[68] in which he contrasts the concept of the 'moment' with the concept of the 'situation', which has been developed and defined by Guy Debord and the Situationists.[69]

The production of space thus unites three such 'moments' or 'formants'. First, material production, the production of goods, of objects of exchange, a production determined by necessity. Second, it comprises the production of knowledge: the productive process here is considered at a higher level, as the result of accumulated scientific knowledge that permeates the working process and thus becomes materially effective, creative. And, finally, there is the freest creative process, the process of giving meaning, a poetic process that produces works, tied to pleasure and also sexuality, which announces the 'reign of freedom'.[70]

---

64   Lafitte, *Réflexions sur la science des machines*.
65   Lefebvre, *Production of Space*, 18–20.
66   Ibid., 40, 285, 369.
67   Lefebvre, *Critique of Everyday Life*, vol. 2, 343.
68   Ibid., 341–4.
69   See Hess, *Henri Lefebvre et l'aventure du siècle*, 215–17.
70   Lefebvre, *Production of Space*, 137.

The production of space can therefore be grasped analytically as the totality of three dialectically linked production processes that implicate one another:

1. Material production, which produces a spatial practice and thus also the perceivable aspect of space (*espace perçu*).
2. Knowledge production, which creates a representation of space and thus a conceived space (*espace conçu*).
3. Meaning production, which is tied to spaces of representation and which produces an experienced or lived space (*espace vécu*).

Central to this concept is the simultaneity of the three moments: space is simultaneously conceived, perceived, and lived. Although these three aspects should not be mixed together, they cannot be separated from one another. Each implies and hides the other, presupposes and assumes the other.[71] The three moments of the production of space must therefore not be considered in isolation. They only make sense together:

> That the lived, conceived and perceived realms should be interconnected, so that the 'subject', the individual member of a given social group, may move from one to another without confusion – so much is a logical necessity. Whether they constitute a coherent whole is another matter. They probably do so only in favourable circumstances.[72]

This triad must not be treated as an abstract model: either it captures the concrete (not the immediate), or it has only a limited meaning, that of ideological meditation among others.[73]

A double problem arises from these explanations. On the one hand, these terms fall from the sky, so to speak. Lefebvre does not introduce them and he does not deduce them from other concepts in *The Production of Space*. Nor does he offer any assistance to the reader that would allow for a reconstruction of their theoretical starting points. On the other hand, he does not even try to give a clear definition of these terms: instead, he feels his way in, sounds them out, tests their possible applications, in order to reformulate them again in the course of his reflections. Therefore, this and the following chapters will be concerned with examining the theoretical construction and testing the practical use of these terms, clarifying them and exploring their empirical fruitfulness.

---

71 Ibid., 14, 285, 356; Lefebvre, *De l'État*, vol. 4, 261.
72 Lefebvre, *Production of Space*, 40.
73 Ibid.

Social Space

We encounter the first difficulty in the concept of 'social space' itself, which remains in a nebulous indeterminacy at the very outset of *The Production of Space*. Without going into the origins of the term here, it is usually associated with social values in the social sciences. For Pierre Bourdieu, for example, social space is a purely abstract, 'mental' space in which social positions are reflected.[74] Benno Werlen defines it in a similar way, following Popper's theory of 'three worlds': social space for Werlen refers to the world of 'objective' social norms and values, establishing a connection between the physical-material world and the mental world, the 'subjective' world of pure thoughts (see section 5.6).[75] But Lefebvre does not use 'social space' in this sense. In attempting to clarify his usage, however, one runs into considerable difficulties of interpretation that cannot be resolved by citing and interpreting individual passages, and requires, instead, an argumentative approach which draws across the achievements of the book as a whole.

A first interpretation produces the following deduction: Lefebvre identifies a 'physical space' which is characterised by its materiality. As the discussion in section 5.1 has shown, however, this space is not a (material) object, not a space 'per se' – such an idea would correspond to a naïve materialism that Lefebvre explicitly rejects. On the other hand, there is a 'mental space', a space determined by theory, which exists only in the imagination. But, in Lefebvre's view, referring exclusively to this mental space runs the risk of a fall into pure idealism. He therefore contrasts the duality of these two 'spaces' with a concept that is both material and dialectical: a 'social space' that refers to social practice in the broadest sense. Social space, therefore, would be the dialectical third concept that overcomes and transforms the opposition of mental and physical space, of *res cogitans* and *res extensa*. According to this line of argument, then, both mental and physical space would be pure abstractions that Lefebvre criticises precisely because they do not refer to social practice. The term 'social space', on the other hand, would be the comprehensive term that designates the space produced by social practice. This first approach to the production of space thus results in the triad physical space–mental space–social space. However, these three moments do not express a simultaneity but a progression: the sublation of the contradiction of physical and mental space leads to social space.

At the same time, however, Lefebvre develops another dialectical triad that defines the contradictions inherent in social space: perceived space–conceived

---

74   See for example Bourdieu, 'Social Space and Symbolic Power'.
75   Werlen, *Society, Action and Space*.

space–lived space. This triad could be understood as the three aspects or moments that relate to the modalities of the production of space: perception, conception, and lived experience. This interpretation could be based, for example, on a passage in which Lefebvre explains his theory using the example of the human body, and which begins with the words: 'In seeking to understand the three moments of social space . . '.[76] These three aspects or moments of the production of space can, however, be assigned to certain 'spaces', in the sense that perception relates to a physical-material space, conception to a mental space, and experience to a social space – an assignment, incidentally, that Lefebvre himself makes. Thus, for example, in *De l'État*, he begins his exposition of the production of space with a brief characterisation of these three 'spaces', distinguishing a physical or material space, a mental space, and a social space 'in the proper sense', which – according to his usual formulation – should neither be separated nor mixed with one another.[77] Various similar examples can be found in *The Production of Space*.

Thus, Lefebvre defines the term 'social space' in two different ways. On the one hand, he defines it comprehensively in a 'broad sense' as a socially produced space, as a space of social practice. On the other hand, he uses the term 'social space' in a narrow or 'proper' sense, and contrasts it with physical-material and mental space. What adds to the confusion is the fact that Lefebvre usually uses the terms 'mental space' and 'physical-material space' critically, as became clear in section 5.1. In his understanding, these 'spaces' are in themselves pure abstractions. As a result, social space, in the narrow sense of the word, would also be an abstraction.

In this way Lefebvre creates an ambivalence that makes his texts significantly more difficult to understand, a problem that will be discussed again at a later point (see section 5.6). To avoid misunderstandings, I will stick to the first interpretation and will use the term 'social space' only in its comprehensive sense. In contrast to this, the terms 'physical-material space' and 'mental space' are to be understood critically throughout my text. This definition cannot be justified in a satisfactory way at this point. It is the result of a full examination of Lefebvre's theory of the production of space and is therefore only conclusively elaborated in section 8.1.

---

76   Lefebvre, *Production of Space*, 40.
77   Lefebvre, *De l'État*, vol. 4, 258–60.

5.3 Perceived Space: Spatial Practice

> Time is known and actualized in space, becoming a social reality by virtue
> of a spatial practice.[78]

> The spatial practice of a society secretes that space; it propounds and
> presupposes it, in dialectical interrelation; it produces it slowly and
> surely, as it masters and appropriates it. From the analytic standpoint,
> the spatial practice of a society is revealed through the deciphering of its
> space ... [Spatial practice] embodies a close association, within
> perceived space, between daily reality (daily routine) and urban reality
> (the routes and networks which link up the places set aside for work,
> 'private' life and leisure). [79]

Spatial practice produces an *espace perçu*, perceived space, the space of the
practical and sensory world. The term 'perception' might be misleading,
though. Perceived space does not refer to cognitive processes, and it does not
relate to the way human beings are mentally processing and interpreting stimuli received by our physical senses. Lefebvre uses this term in a purely material
sense, to describe how the human body receives sensory information. Perceived
space is thus the material aspect of space which is perceivable by human beings
with their five senses: sight, sound, smell, taste, and touch.

Perceived space is the space in which the actions of collective actors inscribe
themselves in the form of permanent objects and realities.[80] Spatial practice
projects all aspects, elements, and moments of social practice 'onto the terrain'
(see also section 4.2).[81] Spatial practice can thus be understood as the material
aspect of social practice.

Spatial practice includes production and reproduction, specific places and
spatial constellations that are inherent in every social formation. To ensure
continuity, it must have a certain cohesion, although not an intellectually elaborated logical coherence. This cohesion requires from each member of a society a certain spatial 'competence' and 'performance' – concepts borrowed by
Lefebvre from Noam Chomsky.[82] Lefebvre assumes that everyone knows
what is meant when we speak of a room, a street corner, a square, a market, a
cultural or shopping centre, a public space, and the like. These words of

---

78   Lefebvre, *Production of Space*, 218.
79   Ibid., 38.
80   Lefebvre, *De l'État*, vol. 4, 259.
81   Lefebvre, *Production of Space*, 8.
82   Chomsky, *Syntactic Structures*; Lefebvre, *Production of Space*, 33, 38.

everyday language distinguish specific spaces without isolating them and describe generally a social space. They correspond to a use of this space, and thus to a spatial practice that expresses it.[83]

In order to make possible a better understanding of the following discussion, we should refer here to Lefebvre's fundamentally new understanding of space: 'producing' space was a completely unusual idea at the time of the publication of *The Production of Space*. Furthermore, there is also a linguistic problem: '*espace*' and 'space' do not denote exactly the same thing in both everyday language and scientific contexts. In English the term 'space' is usually associated with a given physical-material or 'geographical' space. In the francophone humanities and social sciences, a more metaphorical use of the term '*espace*' has become established, which allows 'spatial' terms to be applied to the most diverse, even completely immaterial fields of meaning, as has already become apparent in our discussion of Bourdieu's definition of social space, which is not a material space, but a pure mental space in which social positions are reflected (see section 5.2). Lefebvre, in contrast, firmly adheres to a physical-material anchoring of the term '*espace*', which he explicitly set against abstract and 'idealist' conceptions of space (see section 5.1).

Material Space

What is then to be taken as the theoretical starting point of this spatial practice or this perceived (and thus material) space? As has already been made clear, a 'space' cannot be perceived without also being conceptualised mentally (see also section 5.4). Lefebvre does not assume that spatial practice can exist without a prior mental act, and therefore he needs to establish a theoretical starting point for understanding spatial practice.

This brings us back to the debate on absolute and relational space discussed in section 5.1. Lefebvre criticises Newton's concept of absolute space primarily because it creates an indifference between form and content. Leibniz, in contrast, postulated that space as such, 'in itself', is not 'nothing' nor 'something', nor the totality of things or the form of their sum: for Leibniz, space is what is indistinguishable. To be able to distinguish something, an orientation must first be introduced.[84] In Lefebvre's view, this is to be interpreted in the sense that space, in order to become distinguishable, must necessarily be occupied by a concrete body. Relative space can thus be understood as an abstract,

---

83   Lefebvre, *Production of Space*, 16.
84   Ibid., 169–70.

mathematical space, but also as a concrete, 'physical' space through which bodies exist and manifest their material existence.[85]

Although Lefebvre ascribes these considerations to Leibniz, they correspond more closely to those of the mathematician Hermann Weyl, to whom Lefebvre also makes explicit reference shortly following the passage discussed above. Weyl had made a major contribution to the mathematical formulation of the theory of relativity, and used mathematical operations to clarify the 'essence' of symmetries, which he investigated using a wide variety of examples, from shells and flowers to architecture and art. What appears as beauty or perfection in a social context, Weyl attributes to specific properties of matter.[86]

As Lefebvre notes with reference to Weyl, the 'properties' of space, symmetries, reflections, rotations, which can be defined in 'pure' mathematical terms, can also be understood as inherent properties of organic and inorganic nature, from the planets to crystals, electromagnetic fields and cell division to the form of shells and architectonic forms; they are thus not the result of pre-existent thinking that imposed these properties on the material bodies. In parallel with those insights, Lefebvre proposes that the characteristics of space are therefore determined by a body: qualities like right and left, high and low, central and peripheral are derived from a body in action.[87]

The relationship between space and nature is immediate and does not depend on the mediation of an external, spiritual, or divine power. The laws of space reside within space itself; they cannot be resolved into an inside–outside relationship. Lefebvre explains this using the example of shells, whose symmetries had been analysed stringently and affectionately by Weyl (1955): the shape of a shell is not the result of a finality, nor of 'unconscious' thinking or higher decision ('intelligent design' in today's terms). 'The poetry of shells . . . has nothing to do with some mysterious creative force, but corresponds merely to the way in which energy, under specific conditions . . . is deployed.'[88]

Lefebvre finds the considerations elaborated by Weyl so convincing that he applies them – with all due caution – to social space as well, taking as his starting point not matter in the physical sense but spatial practice: from spatial practice emerges a (material) social space that can only be understood genetically, that is, in the sequence of productive actions. Every reality given in space can therefore be represented and explained by a genesis in time. Conversely,

85   Ibid., 170.
86   Weyl, *Symmetry*.
87   Lefebvre, *Production of Space*, 171, 174.
88   Ibid., 172.

any activity that takes place in (historic) time produces a space, and only in space does it assume a practical reality and concrete existence.[89]

For Lefebvre, the question now arises as to how this 'occupation' of space occurs. Since relative space cannot be 'empty' – that is, having no previously existing, formal characteristics – it can only receive them through a living body, its energies, its actions. For Lefebvre, it is first and foremost the living body with its available energies that produces space. Conversely, the laws of space, of recognisability in space, are those of the living body and its expenditure of energy.

> This is a truly remarkable relationship: the body with the energies at its disposal, the living body, creates or produces its own space; conversely, the laws of space, which is to say the laws of discrimination in space, also govern the living body and the deployment of its energies.[90]

The Body as the Producer of Space

To summarise: space as such has no prior, 'transcendental' (in the sense of 'predetermined') existence. It is created only with and by a material 'content', 'matter' in the physical sense or, biologically speaking, a living body: every body is space, makes its space, and has its space.[91] The entire social space thus originates from the human body. The genesis of the 'far order' (see section 4.2) can be understood only on the basis of the order of the body.[92]

With this theory, Lefebvre wants to take consideration of the relations between subjects and objects beyond the old conceptions. He thus takes up the body again, together with space: for Lefebvre, Western philosophy denied and betrayed the body and actively contributed to the great metaphorisation that abandoned the body. But the living body, which is simultaneously 'subject' and 'object', does not allow for the separation of these concepts. Beyond philosophy and the discourse and the theory of discourse, the body asserts itself as the base and foundation, as the generator and producer of space.[93]

For Lefebvre, space – philosophically speaking – is neither a subject nor an object, nor is it a thing that can be treated like anything else. It is rather a 'frame of life' (*cadre de vie*). But this frame should not be confused with a picture

---

89   Ibid., 115, 171.
90   Ibid., 170.
91   Ibid.
92   Ibid., 405.
93   Ibid., 407, 384.

frame: space is social morphology. For lived experience, it is the form of the living organism itself, intimately connected with its functions and structures.[94] A 'human being' does not have social space – the space of society – in front of it or surrounding it like an image, a spectacle, or a mirror: it knows that it has a space and that it is in a space; it acts and situates itself in a space – or in a series of 'secreted' spatial shells that are mutually dependent and contain each other, and whose sequence explains social practice.[95] In this way, Lefebvre attempts to establish a consistently materialist conception of space: space as at once occupied and occupying, as a totality of places.[96]

The Space of Networks and Flows

On the basis of these conceptions, spatial practice can now be empirically observed and analysed: in architecture, urban planning, design, everyday life, and urban reality.[97] What does this spatial practice look like in contemporary society?

> It embodies a close association, within perceived space, between daily reality (daily routine) and urban reality (the routes and networks which link up the places set aside for work, 'private' life and leisure). This association is a paradoxical one, because it includes the most extreme separation between the places it links together. The specific spatial competence and performance of every society member can only be evaluated empirically. 'Modern' spatial practice might thus be defined – to take an extreme but significant case – by the daily life of a tenant in a government-subsidized high-rise housing project. Which should not be taken to mean that motorways or the politics of air transport can be left out of the picture.[98]

Perceived space is thus marked, modified, and transformed by networks, connections, and flows, roads, canals, railway lines, airlines, business connections, urban networks, and so on. The commodity, with its networks and markets, also forms a component of (practical) social existence and thus of spatial practice. On a worldwide scale, circuits and networks of exchange are formed and articulated. Additionally, there are markets on different scales

---

94 Ibid., 92–4.
95 Ibid., 294.
96 Ibid., 172.
97 Ibid., 413.
98 Ibid., 38.

(local, regional, national, global) and in different sectors: the commodity market, the labour market, the capital market, the land market, the art market, the market of signs and symbols – and finally the 'market of spaces'. Each of these markets has been consolidated over the centuries and concretised in a network. Accordingly, these markets are simultaneously connected and separated; they overlap and penetrate each other. Ultimately, they constitute a superordinate unit: the world market.[99]

In this sense, the world economy can be defined as a spatial practice, combining flows of energy, labour, goods, and capital, and so forth. The connections of these flows are ensured and programmed by institutions within the spatial framework of their operational range. Although each flow can be defined by its beginning, its end, and the distance between them, its effects occur only in relation to other flows. These flows are coordinated in an (urban) space.[100]

Accordingly, the production process can, for example, be defined as the 'space of work'. What does this space consist of? First of all, it consists of production units: companies, offices, farms. The various networks that connect these units are also part of this space. The agencies that govern these networks are not the same as those that regulate work, but they correspond to them. This creates a relative coherence that includes conflicts and contradictions. The space of work is thus the result of (repetitive) gestures and (serial) actions of productive labour, but also of the technical and social division of labour, and thus of local, national, and global markets and, finally, of ownership relations. This means, however, that the space of work only takes on contours and boundaries for and through abstract thinking. The space of work is a network among others, a space among others that penetrate each other.[101]

If one follows these considerations, then basically every social relationship produces a (its) social space: a social space can therefore be neither clearly defined nor clearly delimited. As Lefebvre notes, there is not one social space, but an indeterminate multiplicity of social spaces, for which the term 'social space' designates the uncountable totality. If these spaces were considered in isolation, each of them would remain a mere abstraction. As concrete spaces, however, as networks, as markets, they are articulated with each other. These spaces do not destroy each other but penetrate and overlap each other.[102]

Social spaces are thus not separate things whose edges collide. Although their visible boundaries (walls and enclosures) give rise to the appearance of

99 Ibid., 86, 341–2; Lefebvre, *De l'État*, vol. 4, 259.
100 Lefebvre, *Production of Space*, 347, 391.
101 Ibid., 191.
102 Ibid., 86.

separations, they actually only show the ambiguity and continuity of social spaces: the space of a room, a house, or a garden, although separated from social space by barriers and walls, by all the signs of private property, is therefore no less part of social space. These spaces are not empty 'milieus', containers that can be separated from their contents. Accordingly, the places in social space are not only next to each other, in contrast to those in natural space (see also section 6.1). They push into each other, they combine, they overlap, and sometimes they collide.[103] Thus social space appears in a diversity that Lefebvre compares with a millefeuille, a many-layered French puff pastry.[104] In his text 'A Thousand Leaves' Neil Brenner has taken up this metaphor to show the complexity of the geographies of uneven spatial development (see also section 4.5).[105]

In another example, Lefebvre tries to capture social space in a metaphorical reference to hydrodynamics to emphasise the temporal aspect more strongly:

> Great movements, vast rhythms, immense waves – these all collide and 'interfere' with one another; lesser movements, on the other hand, interpenetrate. If we were to follow this model, we would say that any social locus could only be properly understood by taking two kinds of determinations into account: on the one hand, that locus would be mobilized, carried forward and sometimes smashed apart by major tendencies, those tendencies which 'interfere' with one another; on the other hand, it would be penetrated by, and shot through with, the weaker tendencies characteristic of networks and pathways ... The hypercomplexity of social space should by now be apparent, embracing as it does individual entities and peculiarities, relatively fixed points, movements and flows and waves – some interpenetrating, others in conflict, and so on.[106]

These formulations make it clear that perceived space refers to the materiality of the world, is grasped by the five senses, and thus emanates from the body. At the same time, perceived space is generated by social practice and is thus based on the materiality of collective processes: through their spatial practice, through their movements, activities, and actions, people generate a complex social space which is constantly changing.

---

103   Ibid., 87, 88.
104   Ibid., 86.
105   Brenner, 'A Thousand Leaves'.
106   Lefebvre, *Production of Space*, 87–8.

5.4 Conceived Space: The Representation of Space

The theoretical error is to be content to see a space without conceiving it.[107]

Representations of space: conceptualized space, the space of scientists,
planners, urbanists, technocratic subdividers and social engineers, as
of a certain type of artist with a scientific bent – all of whom identify
what is lived and what is perceived with what is conceived. (Arcane
speculation about Numbers, with its talk of the golden number,
moduli and 'canons', tends to perpetuate this view of matters.) This is
the dominant space in any society (or mode of production).
Conceptions of space tend, with certain exceptions to which I shall
return, towards a system of verbal (and therefore intellectually worked
out) signs.[108]

As this quote indicates, *representations of space* arise on the level of discourse,
on the level of language as such, and they generate the *espace conçu*, the
conceived space. Language and discourse should not be interpreted too
narrowly in this context: Lefebvre also considers maps and plans or information conveyed through pictures or signs as representations of space.[109]

These representations are necessarily abstract, but they enter social and
political practice. As Lefebvre observes, it is to be expected that the relationships between objects and people, as defined in representations of space, take
on a practical meaning. This can be accomplished by means of building and
architecture – not in the sense of constructing an isolated building, but as a
project that fits into a spatial context or a texture and thus changes it. These
textures would be to some extent impressions or imprints of knowledge and
ideologies. Representations of space would therefore have a specific influence
of considerable importance on the production of space.[110]

To a certain degree, a representation of space is a necessary prerequisite for
any spatial practice, even if it can itself be inspired by this practice. As Lefebvre
states, it would be a great theoretical error to think that you can see a space
without conceiving it at the same time. Because, for Lefebvre, a 'representation
of space' means carrying out a mental act by assembling countless scattered
details and their relationships to one another into a whole, the totality of a

---

107   Ibid., 94.
108   Ibid., 38–9.
109   Ibid., 7, 233.
110   Ibid., 41–2.

'reality'.[111] The reality of spatial practice can therefore only be grasped from a mental space: 'who can grasp "reality" – i.e. social and spatial practice – without starting out from a mental space, without proceeding from the abstract to the concrete? No one.'[112]

Abstraction and Spatial Strategy

The representation of space is therefore initially a concept or a conception of space.[113] In Lefebvre's understanding, this concept is not located in space itself, nor does it contain any space: the concept of a dog does not bark. Representations of space denote and connote all possible spaces, both abstract and 'real'. As Lefebvre notes, however, the philosophical preoccupation with space has led to confusion, since philosophy has acted as if the concept of space itself could produce a space.[114] But in his understanding, reflections about space that take place outside of practice, on the level of pure knowledge, can produce nothing but empty talk. A social space does not exist without social practice, which not only consists of the application of concepts, but also includes ignorance, blindness, and lived experience.[115]

This is why Lefebvre clearly differentiates between a cognition of the production of space that tries to grasp space as a product and wants to shed light on this production process, and a 'spatial science' (*science de l'espace*), which has sought to establish itself in various disciplines, such as philosophy, geography, ecology, and even ethnology. This science oscillates between description and fragmentation, describing things in space and cutting out partial spaces from social space, such as the 'geographical' and the 'demographic' space, or the 'space of images' or 'musical space'. However, Lefebvre sees such theories of space as mere *representations of space*.[116] This distinction is significant because it reveals Lefebvre's understanding of his own theory, which he sees not as a *theory of space*, but as *a theory of the production of space*. It does not try to construct or design models but rather to understand the productive process itself. It analyses how concepts of space, or representations of space, are socially produced, and thus it includes a critique of this process and the concepts it produces.

So, in Lefebvre's understanding, spatial theories and scientific or

---

111　Ibid., 94.
112　Ibid., 415.
113　Ibid., 45.
114　Ibid., 299.
115　Ibid., 297, 415.
116　Ibid., 90–1, 104.

philosophical concepts belong to the representations of space.[117] However, this does not mean that he considers these representations to be irrelevant – on the contrary. Since representations of space are permeated with knowledge, they can become strategic instruments for the reduction of spatial practice and the imposition of an order on it. An example of this reduction, which Lefebvre repeatedly cites and criticises, is urban design and spatial planning, which assign a location to each activity on the terrain (see also section 6.3).[118] The conception of space on which these representations are usually based is that of the 'empty space': for technocrats, 'space is the site of their future exploits, the terrain of their victories, so to speak. Space is available. Why? Because it is almost empty or seems to be.'[119] Technocratic thought oscillates between the representation of an empty, geometric space, which they can occupy with their concepts, logics, and strategies, and the representation of a space finally filled by the results of these logics and strategies.[120] This thinking finds its incarnation in the plan and in the floor plan, which mediates between the mental activity that invents and the social activity that performs.[121]

Maps, too, contain and/or reveal a spatial strategy. An example of this is maps of scenic beauties, historical landscapes, and monuments, which are accompanied by a business rhetoric. Such maps indicate those places where insatiable consumption devours the remains of nature and the past, feeding on the signs of the historical and the original. The map legends, the codes that allow these documents to be read, are even more deceptive than things, because they are, so to speak, on a second level and are therefore less easy to see through.

Ideology and Cognition

As these examples have shown, representations of space are concepts, plans, images, and strategies that have an effect on social practice and thus influence, shape, and guide the production of space. These representations incorporate and implement knowledge. In this sense, knowledge is Janus-headed, since for Lefebvre cognition and ideology are combined in knowledge.[122] Representations of space (as well as of time) are thus part of the history of ideologies.[123]

---

117   Ibid., 41, 230.
118   Ibid., 45, 107.
119   Lefebvre, *Urban Revolution*, 154.
120   Ibid.
121   Lefebvre, *Production of Space*, 27–8.
122   Ibid., 41.
123   Ibid., 116.

However, the concept of ideology is in many ways an unclear concept, and Lefebvre struggled with it already in *La conscience mystifiée* published in 1936. He continued to use the term, but mostly in a rather vague way and with a certain unease. A detailed discussion of the question of ideology can be found in *Au-delà du structuralisme* (1971) and in *The Survival of Capitalism* (1973). Based on his reading of Marx, Lefebvre reconstructs a whole series of meanings that can be assigned to the term 'ideology': ideology is an incomplete, inverted reflection of 'reality'; a part of reality that is totalised by means of systematisation (extrapolation and reduction); a product of the social division of labour, especially between material and intellectual work; a set of images and representations that conceal the conflicts and contradictions of social practice; an ensemble of representations through which a (dominant) class realises its hegemony. Lefebvre concludes in *The Survival of Capitalism* that the concept of ideology is at an impasse: 'The effectiveness of ideology is undeniable, but it is limited: it masks the contradictions for and in consciousness (in representations). At worst, it postpones the effects of these contradictions. It cannot suppress them.'[124]

Lefebvre's fundamental critique of the concept of ideology is most obvious in his confrontation with Louis Althusser, whom he criticises not only for his structuralism and his turning away from dialectics but also for his dogmatism. In his famous text 'Ideology and Ideological State Apparatuses',[125] Althusser proceeds from the thesis that ideology represents the imagined relationship of individuals with the conditions of their real existence and thus all 'subjects' necessarily live within an ideology, because there is a practice only through and under an ideology: 'man is an ideological animal by nature.'[126] For Lefebvre, this theory is itself an ideology, and it exhausts itself in decoding and deciphering ideological messages. It no longer wants to change the world but reflects the world in a perfect mirror. In the process, the reference point of ideology, social practice, disappears, and with it also social contradictions.[127] Lefebvre sees this theory in clear contrast to Marx, who wanted to transform ideologies by means of revolutionary truth, which should first be introduced into theory and then into practice.[128]

Against the structuralist position of Althusser, who declared ideology to be an indispensable component of the 'subject', Lefebvre sets his strategy of cognition. As discussed in section 2.4, Lefebvre makes a clear distinction between

---

124   Lefebvre, *Survival of Capitalism*, 68.
125   Althusser, 'Ideology and Ideological State Apparatuses'.
126   Ibid., 171.
127   Lefebvre, *Everyday Life in the Modern World*, 391, 397.
128   Lefebvre, *La présence et l'absence*, 26.

knowledge (*le savoir*) and cognition (*la connaissance*), a distinction that plays an important role in the Latin languages and also in German, but can only be expressed with difficulty in English. For Lefebvre, cognition always starts from a critique and opens itself up to the possible, while knowledge is based on a strategy of reduction, and therefore of separation, and is connected to power and ideology. A strategy of cognition means, accordingly, to start from social practice, and to explore the production of society. This includes a critique of the production of space, and thus also a critique of knowledge. This critique must also destroy those ideologies of an abstract spatiality which do not reveal themselves as ideologies but present themselves explicitly as knowledge.[129]

On the Theory of Representation

To overcome the confusion of ideology and knowledge, Lefebvre uses another term: 'representation'. For him, it is a comprehensive term, one that he introduces in order to bring the concepts of knowledge and ideology together in a broader concept, as they are otherwise difficult to distinguish.[130] For Lefebvre, 'representation' designates a 'doubling of the real', a doubling of concrete activities through the deceptive horizons that representations unfold above practical reality.[131] But Lefebvre rejects the well-known thesis that representation is a pure reflex of reality and tries to develop a dialectical understanding of the relationship between 'appearance and reality' or 'truth and illusion': 'reality' is hidden, but it is made visible through its representation, and is being simultaneously changed in the process.[132]

In *The Production of Space*, Lefebvre outlined the concept of representation and applied it in a variety of ways but did not fully clarify it. A few years later, however, he did present a theory of representation in *La présence et l'absence*. It introduces a fundamental distinction that Lefebvre captures through the German terms of *Vorstellung* (imagination, conception) and *Darstellung* (depiction, delineation).[133] In the broadest (philosophical) sense, the concept of representation does not denote truth or falseness, neither does it signify presence (*la présence*) or absence (*l'absence*). Rather, it allows the dualism of signifier–signified and subject–object to be replaced by the triad of the represented, the representative, and the

---

129 Lefebvre, *Production of Space*, 10, 90, 367–8, 404.
130 Ibid., 45; Lefebvre, *La présence et l'absence*, 7, 26.
131 Lefebvre, *Metaphilosophy*, 18.
132 Lefebvre, *La présence et l'absence*, 27–8.
133 Ibid., 8, 26.

representation (*le représenté, le représentant, la représentation*).[134] What does a representation represent? Lefebvre explains the problem using the example of (social) labour that can be measured by the quantitative number of working hours. The abstract measure of labour time represents a productive activity, just as a curve represents a physical phenomenon. The mathematical function and the curve have no evident homology and no perceptible analogy with the phenomenon under consideration. Nevertheless, they allow you to recognise and grasp it. But what is the exact connection between the represented (the phenomenon) and the representation (the degree, the function, the curve)? It is an abstraction that reduces living social labour to a quantifiable and measurable amount, labour time. This measurement requires an instrument – the clock – and a unit of measurement – the hour. Working time, as a representation of social labour, also includes ideology: the idea that work can be measured by time serves to replace the cyclical time of the day with the linear and homogeneous time of the clock, and finally to measure abstract time with the equally abstract measurement of money.[135] The representation of labour in labour time and the idea of an equivalence of labour time and money ultimately form one of the foundational pillars of capitalism.

Against this background, representations of space can be more clearly analysed. Lefebvre uses the German terms *Darstellung* and *Vorstellung* to structure his analysis. As representations (*Darstellung*), they represent something, they make something visible. They privilege certain aspects and hide others. This raises the question of what is present and what is absent, what is shown and what remains hidden. What is not shown is often more important than what is shown. At the same time, representations of space have also an operative quality because they contain an idea (*Vorstellung*) and thus a guide to action: they not only describe and illuminate something, but also determine something. In this sense, the *conceived* contains not only theoretical and philosophical concepts but also representations that are used for strategic goals. Lefebvre continues to refer to these representations as ideologies.[136]

Representations of space can be particularly effective if they establish a new 'image of space'.[137] This is because we cannot act in a space without first having developed an idea of what that space is. In order to convey this idea, we need terms, pictures, and maps that depict this space and name it. They highlight something, they prescribe something, they guide action, they set a direction. As we know from Lefebvre, such representations are never innocent because they are always linked to power.

---

134   Ibid., 14, 26.
135   Ibid., 29, 32.
136   Ibid., 61.
137   See Schmid, 'The Trouble with Henri'.

5.5 Lived Space: Spaces of Representation

> An already produced space can be decoded, can be read. Such a space
> implies a process of signification.[138]

> Spaces of representation: space as directly lived through its associated
> images and symbols, and hence the space of 'inhabitants' and 'users', but
> also of some artists and perhaps of those, such as a few writers and
> philosophers, who describe and aspire to do no more than describe.
> This is the dominated – and hence passively experienced – space which
> the imagination seeks to change and appropriate. It overlays physical
> space, making symbolic use of its objects. Thus spaces of representation
> may be said, though again with certain exceptions, to tend towards
> more or less coherent systems of non-verbal symbols and signs.[139]

Spaces of representation are embodying complex symbolisms that are linked to the secret and subterranean side of social life, and also to art, which might provide a code of the spaces of representation.[140] But even if art and poetry, to a certain extent, determine these spaces of representation, we should not forget that for Lefebvre it is everyday life that takes shape in the spaces of representation, or, rather, gives them shape.[141]

> The space of representation is alive: it speaks. It has an affective kernel or
> centre: Ego, bed, bedroom, dwelling, house; or: square, church, grave-
> yard. It embraces the loci of passion, of action and of lived situations, and
> thus immediately implies time.[142]

Spaces of representation are thus lived, not conceived. They are qualitative, fluid, and dynamic and can be qualified in different ways: directional, situational, relational. They never strive for coherence or cohesion. They are imbued with the imaginary and symbolism, and they have a history: the history of a people and the history of every individual belonging to that people. Ethnology, anthropology, and psychoanalysis deal with these spaces of representation, whether they know it or not, along with childhood memories, dreams, images, and symbols. However, they often forget to confront these spaces of

---

138   Lefebvre, *Production of Space*, 17.
139   Ibid., 39. Translation amended.
140   Ibid., 33, 42.
141   Ibid., 116.
142   Ibid., 42. Translation amended.

representation with the representations of space that coexist, correspond, or interfere with them, and they neglect spatial practice even more.[143]

Representation of Space and Spaces of Representation

As the terms 'representation of space' and 'spaces of representation' show, space implies a double representation that refers either to the conceived or to the lived.[144] While the conceived generates representations of space that are founded on practical and scientific elements, the lived leads to spaces of representations that are imagined on the basis of the body and that are symbolised by the body.[145]

Spaces of representation are thus experienced or lived spaces that represent 'something'. In order to understand them it is crucial to think Lefebvre's concept through to the end: spaces of representation are not representations of space; they do not refer to a space itself, but to something else, a third thing: life or death, a divine or worldly power, a universal principle, and so forth. They represent social 'values', traditions, dreams – and, last but not least, individual and collective experiences. (See sections 6.2 and 6.3 for a detailed discussion of Lefebvre's own examples of spaces of representation.)

'Representational spaces', the English term that has prevailed for *espaces de représentation*' since Donald Nicholson-Smith's translation of *The Production of Space*, is therefore misleading. This is because 'representational' can take on various meanings, as evidenced by terms such as 'representational democracy' or 'representational art'. But spaces of representations do not belong to a specific 'type' of space in the sense that on the one hand, there are spaces that represent something, and, on the other, there is a whole series of other spaces that are determined by different characteristics, such as 'non-representational spaces' or 'formal spaces' or 'blue spaces' or any other kind of spaces. It has to be clear that *every* social space is also a space of representation because it always has a social meaning and refers to something, expresses or symbolises something. Lefebvre has therefore deliberately placed the two terms symmetrically: *représentation de l'espace* and *espaces de représentation*, to express the difficult-to-determine connection between these two aspects of representation.

How is it even possible that a space becomes a bearer of meaning? This is only possible because space itself is composed of diverse (material) elements,

---

143   Ibid., 41–2.
144   Ibid., 288.
145   Lefebvre, *De l'État*, vol. 4, 281.

which are related to each other both in thought and in practice. This results in a certain arrangement of these elements in space, and this arrangement can take on a certain meaning, which is then attributed to the corresponding space. However, this raises a central question for Lefebvre: do the non-verbal sets of signs and symbols, whether codified or not, systematised or not, belong to the same category as the verbal sets? Lefebvre also counts music, painting and sculpture, architecture, and theatre, or, for example, landscapes, among the non-verbal signifiers. For him, these non-verbal sets are all characterised by a 'spatiality' that is not reducible to the mental realm.[146]

The formation of a social space, in Lefebvre's sense, can ultimately be understood only if the common categories of the 'conscious' and the 'unconscious' are transcended, as well as the attributes assigned to those concepts. Thus, there is nothing more 'conscious' than the use of metaphors, for they are inherent in discourse and thus in consciousness. And nothing could be more 'unconscious' either, if we consider the content that subsequently manifests itself in the course of the use of words and concepts.[147] With this, the second term which Lefebvre uses to characterise the spaces of representation – lived space, *l'espace vécu* – comes into view.

Temps vécu *and* espace vécu

For Lefebvre, the lived (*le vécu*) cannot be understood in theoretical and historical terms without the conceived (*le conçu*). According to his understanding, it was only with the advent of Western philosophy that the conceived was separated from the lived, thus generating the fundamental contradiction between life and thought, between lived and conceived. However, they do not exist independently of one another: all social reality, all human experience and cognition, is characterised by a dialectical movement between the lived and the conceived.[148] But, as Lefebvre insists, the conflict between the lived without concept and the conceived without life has been methodologically and epistemologically persistent for a long time: some despise theoretical thought, and others entrench themselves in pure knowledge and 'theoretical praxis'; they do not descend to the lived, to the trivial occupation with social life. Some spare themselves thinking, and others disdain living.[149]

Rob Shields claims, without any proof, that Lefebvre took the 'central dualism'

---

146   Lefebvre, *Production of Space*, 62.
147   Ibid., 290.
148   Hajo Schmidt, *Sozialphilosophie des Krieges*, 169.
149   Lefebvre, *Survival of Capitalism*, 19–20.

of lived and conceived from Nietzsche and Spinoza.[150] Lefebvre, however, who discusses the lived as early as *Metaphilosophy*, refers to Jean-Paul Sartre and considers it a philosophical name for everyday life.[151] It has to be said that the concept of *vécu* has a long tradition in French philosophy, as well as in the humanities and social sciences. The lived is usually directly connected with (concrete) experience and everyday life, and in German is often referred to by the term *Lebenswelt* or 'life world' (for example in Husserl, Schütz, or Heidegger).

The connection of the 'lived' with 'space' and thus the concept of 'lived space' was introduced in the 1930s. Alexander Gosztonyi has shown in detail that this concept emerged in psychiatry partly due to the observations of anomalies in the experience of space, under hypnosis and under the influence of psychedelic substances.[152] The psychiatrist and phenomenologist Eugène Minkowski played a central role in this, as he conducted extensive research on 'lived time' and in this process also discovered 'lived space'. He established, for example, that there is not only a geometric (and thus measurable) distance, but also a lived distance that has completely different qualitative characteristics. He explains this, inter alia, using the example of night, in which the experienced space takes on a completely different nature than during the day.[153] These and other observations from clinical psychology were taken up and further developed by the French phenomenologist Maurice Merleau-Ponty in his famous work *Phenomenology of Perception*.[154] For him, space can only be experienced through its materiality. Space is not lived by placing one object next to another and determining their objective relationships, but rather as a flow of experiences that imply and explain each other, both simultaneously and successively. From the perspective of lived space, Paris is not a collection of perceptions or an object with 1,000 facets. Each perception on a journey through Paris – the cafés, the faces of the people, the trees along the quays, the bends of the Seine – is inscribed into the total being of Paris, and thus conveys a certain style or a certain meaning of Paris.

> And when I arrived [in Paris] for the first time, the first streets that I saw upon leaving the train station were – like the first words of a stranger – only manifestations of a still ambiguous, though already incomparable essence.[155]

150　Shields, *Lefebvre, Love and Struggle*, 9.
151　Lefebvre, *Metaphilosophy*, 70–1.
152　Gosztonyi, *Der Raum*, 943–5.
153　Eugène Minkowski, *Le temps vécu*, 366–8.
154　Merleau-Ponty, *Phenomenology of Perception*.
155　Ibid., 294.

The key here is that Merleau-Ponty is postulating, referring to Husserl, that experience and the lived world precede the known and the conceived:

> Everything that I know about the world, even through science, I know from a perspective that is my own or from an experience of the world without which scientific symbols would be meaningless. The entire universe of science is constructed upon the lived world, and if we wish to think science rigorously, to appreciate precisely its sense and its scope, we must first awaken that experience of the world of which science is the second-order expression.[156]

Lefebvre agrees with this position (but without mentioning Merleau-Ponty), as the following quote confirms: 'Like all social practice, spatial practice is lived directly before it is conceptualized.'[157] The lived and the conceived are thus both at the same time the expression and the foundation of practice. But the speculative primacy of the conceived in Western philosophy also makes practice disappear, together with life. For Lefebvre, the lived then forms the outer frontier of the Logos and the limit of philosophy as such.[158]

In the research tradition of clinical psychiatry or phenomenology, lived space is seen as the space apparent to an individual, depending on his or her own life history, experience, and state of mind. Lefebvre, however, does not argue from the perspective of psychology, nor does he share Merleau-Ponty's individualistic perspective. His starting point is historical materialism, and thus social practice, rather than the individual, forms the central reference point of his theory (see also section 5.6). Accordingly, Lefebvre's theory treats lived space, along with perceived and conceived space, as socially produced and thus as a historical product. The lived includes the body and subjectivity, but also what is lived socially and collectively.[159]

On the Reading and Writing of Space

There is no doubt for Lefebvre that there are spaces that represent 'something'. But between the signifier and the signified there is an inexhaustible field of shifts, distortions, fluctuations, and substitutions.[160] Does it therefore make

---

156   Ibid., lxxii.
157   Lefebvre, *Production of Space*, 34.
158   Ibid., 34, 288, 406.
159   Ibid., 61.
160   Ibid., 160.

any sense at all to speak of a writing and reading of space? Does space embody a discourse, or a language? Here, too, Lefebvre remains sceptical and answers with his famous '*oui et non*': yes, to the extent that a 'reader' deciphers and decodes a space, and a 'writer' expresses himself, inscribes his trajectory into space. On the other hand, however, social space is not a white sheet of paper on which someone could simply write a message. There is a great diversity of social spaces with very different origins, and thus also with different spatial codes. Space is overloaded with messages that get mixed up and create disorder.[161]

The very space that is created in order to be 'read' is then for Lefebvre the most deceptive of all spaces. The graphic effect of 'legibility' disguises strategic intentions and actions. This is most evident in monumentality, which always seeks to impose a readable certainty:

Monumentality, for instance, always embodies and imposes a clearly intelligible message. It says what it wishes to say – yet it hides a good deal more: being political, military, and ultimately fascist in character, monumental buildings mask the will to power and the arbitrariness of power beneath signs and surfaces which claim to express collective will and collective thought. In the process, such signs and surfaces also manage to conjure away both possibility and time.[162]

In addition to these monumental spaces there are also empty or neutral spaces and spaces overloaded with meanings:

Some 'over-signifying' spaces serve to scramble all messages and make any decoding impossible. Thus certain spaces produced by capitalist promoters are so laden with signs – signs of well-being, happiness, style, art, riches, power, prosperity, and so on – that not only is their primary meaning (that of profitability) effaced but meaning disappears altogether.[163]

If there is a text or a writing of space, it is in the context of conventions and orders: space indicates what is to be done and what is forbidden, and it contains multiple, often interfering instructions and regulations. However, these 'instructions' should not be confused with signs, because, for Lefebvre, they are

---

161   Ibid., 143.
162   Ibid.
163   Ibid., 160.

rather actions themselves, which take place in space and – to a limited extent – are prescribed by space, whereby 'obedience' is blind, spontaneous, 'lived':[164] 'space "decides" what activity may occur, but even this "decision" has limits placed upon it. Space lays down the law because it implies a certain order – and hence also a certain disorder.'[165]

Therefore, if there is such a thing as the 'reading of space', then it follows the production of space, and, for Lefebvre, this means the actions that produced the space in the first place. Nothing comes from 'space per se'. Only real or possible actions produce space, and not mental states, or better or less well told stories. And actions produce and reproduce 'meaning', even if the actors themselves are not aware of it.[166]

On the Semiotics of Space

Could there be a semiotics of space? This question was hotly debated at the time Lefebvre was working on his theory, and important contributions were made by a number of renowned theorists in architecture and semiotics.[167] Lefebvre, however, was highly critical of this proposed 'semiotics of space'. He did see some possibility, though, in the analysis of spatial textures. A texture implies meaning. But meaning for whom? For a 'reader'? No, says Lefebvre, rather for someone who lives and acts in a certain space, for a 'subject' equipped with a body, or for a 'collective subject'. The problem is to bring this experienced meaning to the level of the conceived, the (conceptually) grasped, without breaking it. A 'semiotics of space' therefore raises difficult questions. Any attempt to construct a procedure for deciphering social space always runs the risk of reducing this social space to a message and its use to a reading, thus avoiding both history and practice.[168]

Perhaps, Lefebvre suggests, specific codes have developed over time that allow the 'subjects' of a given society to access their space, to act in this space, and to understand it. This codification would then have been produced together with the corresponding space. From Lefebvre's point of view, the analysis of this code would be different than the work of specialists in the field: instead of insisting on a formal coherence of codes, they would have to be understood

---

164   Ibid., 143.
165   Ibid.
166   Ibid., 144.
167   See for example Greimas, *Sémantique structurale*; Barthes, 'Semiology and Urbanism'; Eco, *La struttura assente*; Choay, 'Sémiologie et urbanisme'.
168   Lefebvre, *Production of Space*, 7, 132.

dialectically. The spatial codes would have to be situated in a practical relation-ship, in the interaction of the 'subjects' with their space.[169]

Decoding space proves to be limited, however, as it immediately reveals a multiplicity of spaces, each of which in turn can be decoded in many ways. Moreover, Lefebvre asks himself whether non-verbal signs form an actual system at all, or whether they instead elude any coherent systematisation. The difficulty here is that symbols of space as such escape abstract knowledge. This knowledge without body and without temporality might be sophisti-cated and effective, but it proves to be 'irreal' in relation to lived realities.[170] Lefebvre also has reservations regarding a science of discourse that attempts to grasp the spoken, the unspoken, and the forbidden as the essence and meaning of the lived. Lived space would thus be reduced to a mere 'space of discourse' and thus to the text, the written, the readable, and the visible. However, in space the production of meaning and a practice of meaning cannot be reduced either to everyday discourse or to the text and the written language.[171]

Both discourse and semantic or semiotic categories such as message, code, or reading/writing can thus only be applied to already produced spaces, and leave two residuals: the body and power. On this side of the readable and visi-ble is the body, with its senses, and the actions of the body, suffering, desire, pleasure. Space is always perceived, lived, and thus also produced from the starting point of the body.[172] That which animates this body, its presence, is neither visible nor legible as such, nor is it the object of a discourse: 'This life reproduces itself within those who use the space, within their lived experience. Of that experience the tourist can grasp but a shadow, and the passive spectator remains just a phantom.'[173]

Beyond the readable is power: it cannot be decoded; it has no code. The state possesses all existing codes, manipulates them, makes them the tool of its strat-egies. The signifier and the signified of power coincide, implying violence and death.[174]

Space thus never says everything: its mode of existence, its practical 'reality', is radically different from that of a document or book.[175] Lefebvre is therefore sceptical of all (structuralist-inspired) approaches that attempt to generate a

---

169   Ibid., 17–18.
170   Ibid., 43, 130–1, 163.
171   Ibid., 135–6.
172   Ibid., 160, 135–6.
173   Ibid., 137. Translation amended.
174   Ibid., 162.
175   Ibid., 142–3.

theoretical (semiotic) knowledge of space:[176] 'The forbidden fruit of lived experience flees or disappears under the assaults of reductionism; and silence reigns around the fortress of knowledge.'[177]

The Reign of Logos

As has become clear, the distinction between the representation of space and spaces of representation must be made with great caution. It could lead to hasty divisions while, on the contrary, the aim must be to restore the productive unity of the process of meaning.[178] For between the conceived and the lived there is no division, no break, but nevertheless their relationship is subject to conflict. The dialectical movement between the conceived and the lived never stops.

It is uncertain, however, whether the distinction between the conceived and the lived can be generalised across different social formations.[179] For Lefebvre, this distinction is to be understood in a fundamentally historical sense. Thus, in Western practice, starting from Greece and Rome, this distinction is the result of a social process of abstraction in the course of which the reign of reason was established (see section 6.2). One of the great dramas of the European Logos was the devastating conquest of the lived by the conceived, and thus by abstraction.[180] With the rule of 'King Logos' (*Logos-Roi*) and the 'true' space, the conceived and the lived separated, as did the object and the subject. The theory of the arbitrariness of the sign further intensified this separation, as did theories addressing the signifier and the signified, the mental and the real.[181] Only art and poetry attempt to restore this unity. An example of this unity is the theatre, which includes a representation of space, the scenic space that corresponds to a certain conception of space, and a space of representation, a space that is mediated but experienced directly.[182]

For Lefebvre, lived space can ultimately only be grasped if the concept of space is linked to a social practice that includes both a spatial practice and a practice of meaning.[183]

---

176   Ibid., 132–3.
177   Ibid., 134.
178   Ibid., 42–3.
179   Ibid.
180   Lefebvre, *La présence et l'absence*, 7.
181   Lefebvre, *Production of Space*, 406–7.
182   Ibid., 175, 188.
183   Ibid., 137.

5.6 The Three Dimensions of the Production of Space

> A body that perceives, a direction that is conceived, a lived movement
> that paves the way to the horizon.[184]

With the material presented in this chapter so far, we have a first approximation of Lefebvre's three-dimensional theory of the production of space and the
dimensions, moments, or formants involved. But, as has also become clear,
these dimensions remain in a diffuse indeterminacy that opens up a large scope
for interpretation.

The starting point of the theory of the production of space is – to make it
clear once again – spatial practice, the perceived and perceivable space, and
thus the five senses, the body. This perception directly implies a conceived
space: we cannot perceive a space without having first (mentally) conceived it.
But this conception of space is always directed towards a goal and thus in turn
towards a spatial practice, and it is always connected with power. If, however,
the analysis of the production of space were limited to these two aspects only,
it would remain trapped in abstraction. For, in addition to the material aspect
of the practice and the concepts and rules that underlie it, this practice is always
also experienced and suffered, and that thus implies symbolism. This symbolism constitutes the third aspect of the production of space, the lived, which
refers dialectically to the other two dimensions of space. This third dimension
overlays the physical aspect of space, in that the material elements or their
arrangement become bearers of meaning. But it is also dialectically intertwined
with conceived space, which on the one hand itself contains symbolisms, but
on the other tends to determine and dominate lived space.

This first summary of the theory of the production of space leaves many
questions open, however, and for several reasons. First, Lefebvre did not fully
develop this theory and its categories. He unfolds his concepts and theoretical
constructions, and he explores the possibilities they offer. This experimenta-
tion, this 'thinking aloud', creates inconsistencies that cannot be resolved by
simply comparing individual passages. It makes it necessary to reconstruct the
underlying theoretical framework by considering the dynamics of Lefebvre's
own reflections and to descend into the epistemological foundations of his
overall project.

Second, there is the problem of basic terms and categories that Lefebvre
uses. Depending on the scientific discipline and theoretical approach, these
can mean very different things. Thomas Kuhn observed in the context of his

---

184   Ibid., 423. Translation amended.

analysis of paradigm shifts in the natural sciences that the transition from one paradigm to another can involve a 'gestalt-like' change, a reconfiguration of fundamental ideas and understandings.[185] Even though the old terms and methods are still used, they denote and measure something else. If one wants to understand Lefebvre's theory, one must, in a sense, slip into the new 'configuration' of his terminology and his epistemology and should not try to reach this theory starting from other approaches that use apparently similar terms, concepts, or theoretical constructions. Otherwise, confusion and misunderstanding are inevitable. Thus, there are several other 'three-dimensional' theoretical constructions of the 'world', such as Popper's 'three-world theory' or Lacan's three-dimensional 'Borromean knot', which have certain parallels with Lefebvre's approach, but are based on fundamentally different epistemological assumptions.

Third, there is the problem that Lefebvre did not fully disclose his own theoretical foundations and, in particular, only very sparsely revealed other approaches from which he drew inspiration. At the end of this chapter, the two central foundations of Lefebvre's three-dimensional theory of the production of space are clarified: first, the spatial concepts of French phenomenology; and second, Lefebvre's distinctive three-dimensional theory of language.

With these considerations in mind, a reasonably plausible and robust interpretation of the three-dimensional theory of the production of space can be presented.

The Architecture of Space

As we have seen, Lefebvre's theory is not concerned with space 'as such', but with a production process of space that he analytically examines from three perspectives. But how do they come together? In Lefebvre's work, there are many passages in which he explains the three-dimensional conception of his theory and gives examples. One such example is the production of the human body in modern society.[186] The relationship of a 'subject' to space also implies its relationship to its own body and vice versa. As Lefebvre points out, social practice in general presupposes the use of the body: the use of hands, limbs, sensory organs. Thus, social practice constitutes the perceptible or, in the psychological sense, the practical basis of the perception of the external world. The representation or the concept of the body, on the other hand, originates

---

185   Kuhn, *The Structure of Scientific Revolutions*.
186   See Lefebvre, *Production of Space*, 40.

from the predominant knowledge mixed with ideologies: the anatomical, the physiological, the illnesses and the cures, the relationship of the human body with nature, its environment, and its 'milieu'. The experienced, for its part, reaches a high degree of complexity and strangeness, because this is where 'culture' with its illusion of immediacy intervenes, through symbolisms based on traditions that often go back a long time. The lived 'heart' differs strangely from the imagined and perceived heart, Lefebvre notes ironically, and he suggests that this applies even more to sexuality.[187]

This example illustrates that 'space' is not a universal category for Lefebvre. In each historical epoch or social formation, the three moments or formants have a different influence on the production of space. The relations between the three moments are never simple and never stable.[188] It is also uncertain whether they form a coherent whole. Lefebvre suspects that under favourable circumstances a consensus, a common language, a unitary code could be established that would bring the three moments together in everyday life, as for example in sixteenth-century Venice:[189]

> The *representation of space* (the sea at once dominated and exalted) and *the space of representation* (exquisite lines, refined pleasures, the sumptuous and cruel dissipation of wealth accumulated by any and every means) are mutually reinforcing. Something similar may be said of the space of the canals and streets, where water and stone create a texture founded on reciprocal reflection. Here everyday life and its functions are coextensive with, and utterly transformed by, a theatricality as sophisticated as it is unsought, a sort of involuntary *mise-en-scène*. There is even a touch of madness added for good measure.[190]

The Space of Architecture

The example of Venice shows how, under certain historical circumstances, the production of space can produce extraordinary 'products' or 'works'. But what does such a work express? Who designed the architectural unity that encompasses every palazzo in the entire city? Obviously, no one: Venice was not planned in advance. And yet it was created by people, by definable social groups. The creation of Venice thus implies a political act. The creation of this

---

187   Ibid.
188   Ibid., 46.
189   Ibid., 40, 73.
190   Ibid., 74. Translation amended.

city cannot be separated from the system of trade and the dominance of a political caste, the merchant oligarchy, nor from the state of the productive forces and of social labour, the social relations that dominated them and the profits that the merchant oligarchy drew from labour. Venice is therefore also the result of the realisation of the social surplus product, the forerunner of capitalist surplus value. The tasteful and highly civilised use of this surplus product cannot hide its origin: the 'oeuvre' which is Venice is permeated by social labour.[191]

As this example shows, 'space' as a product often conceals more than it shows. In any case, to understand a particular space we require a comprehensive analysis of the production process that produces it. The following interpretative compilation on the production of 'modern' architectural space illustrates this.[192]

One could assume, writes Lefebvre, that the architect disposes of a piece of space that has been cut out of larger units. He would take it as 'given' and work on it in full freedom, according to his taste, techniques, ideas, and preferences. But things do not play out like this. For there is nothing innocent about the space that is granted to the architect and which he works on: it is a means to certain ends, it serves tactics and strategies, and it consists of plots of land that are themselves shaped by their relations to their surroundings. The role that is granted to the architect therefore always depends on the calculations of his clients, which he supposes but does not exactly know.[193]

It is on this basis that the architect pursues his professional activity. He designs his space, the conceived space. But, for Lefebvre, the architect's eye is no less neutral and innocent than the piece of land he has been given or the white sheet of paper on which he makes his first draft. The 'subjective' space of the architect is loaded with objective meanings. As a visual space it is reduced to the image: to the 'world of the image', the opposite of the imagination. The linear perspective developed since the Renaissance (see section 6.2) accentuates and justifies this reduction: it presupposes a fixed observer, an immobile field of perception, a permanent visual world. The architect thus has a certain representation of space that is linked to graphic elements. Those who make use of this conceived space consider it to be true although, or precisely because, it is geometric. In this way it becomes a place of objectification of projects. The most important criterion of the architectural project, which is 'unconsciously' determined by this conceived space, is its feasibility: the project must be quantifiable, profitable, communicable, in short: 'realistic'. The division and

191 Ibid., 77.
192 Ibid., 360-2.
193 Ibid., 360.

separation of labour, functions, needs, and things which are localised in physical space are thus framed precisely in this conceived space, which itself appears
as a place of knowledge: as something neutral and objective.[194]

Finally, those for whom there is not even a well-defined and clearly connoted
designation and who are called 'users' or 'inhabitants', either clumsily or mali-
ciously, must also be considered. Spatial practice marginalises them, even in
language. The word 'user' (*usager*) has something indefinite and suspect about
it. Use of what? One uses or utilises clothes, cars, houses. What is the use value
of space compared to exchange and its implications? And what does the word
'inhabitant' (*habitant*) mean? Everyone and no one. The elementary demands
of the (disadvantaged) 'users' and the (marginalised) 'inhabitants' are difficult
to express, although the symbols of their situation sometimes grab our attention. The space of the users is lived, not represented or conceived. In comparison to the abstract space of architects, the space of the users, the space of their
daily requirements, is a concrete space, and thus also a subjective space. It is a
space of 'subjects', not of calculus; it is a space of representation. Its origins lie
in the experiences of childhood, and it is marked by the conflict between the
inevitable, difficult process of growing up and an *immaturation* that leaves the
initial resources and reserves untouched. The 'private' is confirmed, stronger or
weaker, but always conflictual, against the public.[195] The representation of
space, as it is designed by scientists or urbanists, for example, can therefore
differ considerably from the space of representation that the inhabitants have
in their minds and which is an integral part of their social practice.[196]

Triads: Confusions and Contradictions

The description in the previous section has not yet provided the clarity we
hoped for. This is already evident as we identify the actors in the production of
space: Do the three dimensions of the perceived, conceived, and lived each
relate to one and the same person, as the first example of the human body
suggests? Or do they constitute different and distinguishable fields that are
occupied by different actors? The example of the space of architecture seems to
point to this second interpretation: here, the client or builder occupies spatial
practice, the architect designs representations of space, and the 'user' creates a
space of representation in and through everyday life.

---

194   Ibid., 361–2.
195   Ibid., 362.
196   Ibid., 93.

It would seem that the two examples present different perspectives on the production of space, and that the two 'conceptual triads' do not have the same theoretical status. As Lefebvre himself notes, the first triad – the perceived, the conceived, and the lived – refers to a subject that brings them together in a spatial practice.[197] In contrast, the terms of the second triad – spatial practice, the representation of space, and spaces of representation – refer to a social production process. The specific social context here is the division of labour, which implies a specialisation and thus also a separation of the different moments of the production of space. Accordingly, different actors are involved in these three moments – a phenomenon well known in architecture and urban planning: architects, planners, and scientists design and conceive concepts, plans, and models, maps and theories, and thus produce specific *representations of space*. There are then clients and addressees, that is, future potential users. If these representations of space are realised, they are materialised through and in a specific *spatial practice*. This process of implementation is not without problems, as it involves other actors who construct the designed buildings. Finally, the building or the urban ensemble is used and appropriated and it thus becomes a *space of representation*, which is appropriated by the users and incorporated into their everyday life.

It seems that these two examples presented above are expressing two different perspectives, depending on whether we are considering the concrete situation of an individual subject or that of social, collective actors. But the fact that Lefebvre equates the two conceptual triads and uses the terminology (almost) interchangeably suggests that he does not see things in this way. This example makes it clear how misleading selected passages of Lefebvre's text can be if they are not embedded in the overall context of the theory.

To bring the status of Lefebvre's three-dimensional thinking into closer focus, the following section compares apparently similar three-dimensional concepts from social theories in methodological individualism and from psychoanalysis. This shows how the individual and the collective can be thought through in combination and clarifies Lefebvre's approach.

The Problem of the Three Ontological Worlds

A first possible similarity to Lefebvre's three-dimensional conception lies in individualistic social theories that postulate three (separate) ontological worlds. Benno Werlen, the most important contemporary theorist of space in

---

197   Ibid., 230.

the German-speaking world, has developed a theory of space based on a similar three-world theory and accordingly constructed three different ontological concepts of space, which are separate but connected to each other.[198] His theory of space is embedded in the epistemology of methodological individualism and refers mainly to Karl Popper's objective epistemology and the subjective phenomenology of Alfred Schütz.

The basis of Werlen's theory is Popper's concept of three ontological worlds. According to this concept, the 'world' can be subdivided into three ontologically different 'partial worlds'. The first world is the physical world or the world of physical states. The second world is the world of the subjective states of consciousness of actors, or the mental world. Finally, the third world is the world of ideas in the objective sense, the world of possible objects of thought, the world of theories and their logical relationships, the world of arguments and problems as such.[199] This third world of objective ideas also includes language and knowledge (including potential knowledge that is not yet 'known'), as well as the social and institutions. With limitations, this third world can also be defined as a 'social world'. Behind this definition is the consideration that ideas or arguments, as long as they are only thought, belong to the second, that is, mental and subjective, world. But, as soon as they are communicated, they take on an external, objective character and are no longer dependent on the recognising subject. This external, objective character can therefore be interpreted as the social character of ideas and arguments in the true sense of the word.[200]

The first and third worlds are thus objectively given and independent of the subjective second world. However, this second world, the world of actors' subjective states of consciousness, assumes a mediating function: the physical world and the world of objective ideas are connected by the actors' personal experiences. This mediation is constructed in such a way that the subjective, mental second world is in mutual interaction or interrelation with the other two worlds through the acts of cognition and practical action.[201]

Werlen then interprets Alfred Schütz's phenomenological sociology in a similar way. Accordingly, he distinguishes three different worlds depending on the context of action. First, the physical world, nature, and material conditions, which also include the body of the acting person. Second, the subjective world, the available stock of knowledge of the actor, which is based on his or her experiences with the everyday world and therefore has a specific biographical

---

198   See Werlen, *Society, Action and Space.*
199   Ibid., 27; Popper, *Objective Knowledge.*
200   Werlen, *Society, Action and Space*, 28–9, 32.
201   Ibid., 27, 30.

character. And third, the social world, which includes all other actors, and, specifically, the way they give meaning to actions and artefacts; these are regarded as intersubjective and thus 'objective' meanings. They are detached from the actor's body and represented in the intersubjective context of meaning of the language system.[202] Through the consistent application of these considerations to 'space', Werlen comes to the conclusion that for each of the three ontological worlds a different concept of space must be developed.[203]

This Three Worlds Theory, which Werlen made explicit and which has latent resonances with many social theories, interferes in many ways with Lefebvre's theory of the production of space. At first glance, there appear to be many similarities; but on closer analysis there turn out to be fundamental differences. Thus, a puzzling image is created that makes it difficult to understand Lefebvre's theory and has proved to be a source of many misunderstandings.

The first confusion arises from the concepts of the mental and social worlds. For Popper, the mental world appears as something subjective, experienced, whereas the social world appears as objective, intersubjective, and thus socially generated. Lefebvre, however, understands the term 'mental' in reference to the Cartesian tradition and the materialist debate on idealism (see section 2.2), in the sense of ideal, intellectual, theoretically conceived, and thus 'objective'. According to Marx, concepts or ideas, if they have social validity – that is, if they are socially accepted – are objective 'forms of thought'.[204]

The 'objective' side is thus manifested in the production of representations of space as expressed in scientific concepts, maps, plans, and the like. They are oriented towards realisation and are connected with power. The 'subjective' side, on the other hand, refers to the spaces of representation or the lived spaces that Lefebvre connects with appropriation and experience. Thus, the concept of 'subjective' is reversed: for Lefebvre, mental space is objective – that is, socially valid – while social space in the narrow sense – that is, lived space – is experienced and endured, and is therefore subjective.[205]

The terms 'subjective' and 'social' seem here to be mutually exclusive. But this is only the case if 'subjective' is equated with 'individual', that is, if an individualistic perspective is adopted. This brings us to a second source of confusion, which arises from a disregard for a fundamental incompatibility: the incompatibility between an individualistic perspective, as adopted by Popper, Schütz, and Werlen, and Lefebvre's dialectical materialism.

At the centre of the individualist perspective is a recognising and acting

202   Ibid., 77, 82.
203   Ibid., 153–5.
204   Marx, *Capital*, vol. 1, 169.
205   Lefebvre, *Production of Space*, 298.

subject, which refers itself to the external, social, and physical world. Lefebvre, on the other hand, rejects the Cartesian separation of object and subject that underlies such a conception as idealistic. He starts from a dialectical and materialist conception of society, and thus from the contradiction between individual and society. In such a conception there is no 'subjective centre' of action: actions and actors are always both individual and social at the same time. Accordingly, both the 'mental' or 'conceived' as well as the 'social' or 'lived' are to be understood as present in this contradiction. 'Objective' concepts or 'thought forms' are always open to individual interpretation, and without this individual interpretation or appropriation they could not be socially effective at all. The lived, in contrast, is subjective, but socially produced. In this sense, the 'subjective' appears almost as the core of the social, that is, of social relationships and bonds, which always also contain 'feelings' – love, desire, anger, hate, grief, and so on – and thus are subjectively experienced and suffered. Humans are not only rationally calculating individuals, but always also emotional and therefore deeply social beings.

This results in a decentring of the 'worlds' or 'dimensions' of action: if Popper's conception is based on a 'linear' configuration with a centre (the recognising and acting ego) and two pairs of interactions with the 'outer world', then the 'world' in Lefebvre's work presents itself as a triangle spanned by three pairs of contradictions: between the lived and the conceived, between the conceived and the perceived, and between the perceived and the lived.

This conception of social reality is accompanied by Lefebvre's radical rejection of the idea of three separate ontological worlds. From his perspective, it would therefore be completely wrong to separate the three dimensions of the perceived, conceived, and lived, or even to construct three ontologically different 'spaces', spatial categories, or concepts of space. For Lefebvre, there is only one world that can be analytically represented as a dialectical unity of three moments or formants.

Space and Psychoanalysis

Another attempt to understand Lefebvre's three-dimensionality is to take up the apparent parallels with concepts of psychoanalysis and make them productive. As Gosztonyi notes, lived space is always something psychic.[206] Lived space is not identical with the space presented by the five senses, perceived through movement, even if it depends on it. Lefebvre also notes that the lived

---

206   Gosztonyi, *Der Raum*, 944.

contains the unconscious.[207] Therefore, it seems obvious to assume further starting points for Lefebvre's theory of the production of space in psychology and especially in psychoanalysis.

Virginia Blum and Heidi Nast have followed the traces of Lacan's psychoanalytic representations in *The Production of Space* from a feminist perspective, emphasising and criticising above all the heterosexuality and masculinity in both authors (see also section 6.3).[208] In the remarkable book *The Body and the City*, which attempts to combine geography and psychoanalysis, Steve Pile explores the possibilities and limits of a concordance between Freud, Lacan, Kristeva, and Lefebvre systematically and in detail. The starting point is Lefebvre's frequent use – and in Pile's eyes also his abuse – of psychoanalytic concepts, and his description of visual and phallic space (see section 6.3) and of mirror effects.[209] Pile's analysis, however, confuses the three spatial dimensions, and therefore cannot show the similarities and differences of the analysed approaches. He concludes his comparison of the different approaches by claiming there is a fundamental inconsistency or incompatibility between Lefebvre's categories and those of psychoanalysis. But on closer examination a stronger accordance could be found – especially between Lefebvre and Lacan – than Pile's reconstruction shows.

Over the course of his cryptic work, Jacques Lacan developed a kind of topology of psychic being. This topology contains three 'registers': the imaginary (*l'imaginaire*), the symbolic (*le symbolique*), and the real (*le réel*).[210] For Lacan, the imaginary is connected with desire and denotes the dimension of the perceived or imagined images. Lacan introduces it with the myth of Narcissus and explains it by means of the mirror stage of child development. If one only occupies the imaginary, one cannot say something about it, and someone who can say something about it is no longer entirely in the imaginary. In order for something to be said, the symbolic is added as a structuring instance that precedes every individual existence. The symbolic stands for the order of signifiers in a system of differential elements. It thus designates the linguistic dimension of psychic existence: without the symbolic nothing could be said. Finally, Lacan adds to these two registers the third concept, the real, an inaccessible place situated on this side of language. The real stands for the nonexistent, emptiness, absence, for a nothingness that is nevertheless not nothing, for the impossible, or for that which is always in the same place.

---

207   Lefebvre, *Production of Space*, 34.

208   Blum and Nast, 'Where's the Difference?'.

209   Pile, *The Body and the City*, 146–7.

210   The following account is based on Widmer, *Subversion des Begehrens*, 18–20, 153–5; and Pile, *The Body and the City*, 137–9.

In Lacan, these three registers join together to form a 'Borromean knot', a formal principle of the Christian doctrine of the Trinity, included in the coat of arms of the Borromeo family. The three registers can be represented as rings, arranged in such a way that one ring links the other two, which are not connected to each other. When one ring is detached, the other two rings are also left unconnected. The representation of this topology refers to three prerequisites of human existence. First, that there is something; that something is here and fixed – the real. Second, that something can be said – the symbolic, without which nothing could be said. And third, the imaginary is what holds things together, the consistency of the Borromean knot. According to Lacan, every statement happens within these three conditions. A position outside of this knot cannot exist.[211]

From this presentation of Lacan's three registers, we could easily establish a connection to the three formants of Lefebvre. The correspondences would then be as follows: the perceived and the real; the conceived and the symbolic; the lived and the imaginary. Prigge has hinted at this connection without, however, pursuing it further.[212] In Lefebvre's work, there is a passage where he explains the production of space with the three concepts of the practical, the symbolic, and the imaginary instead of the terms he otherwise uses.[213]

Pile, however, makes a different attribution of Lefebvre's formants and Lacan's registers. He distinguishes this triad as follows:[214]

1. *The real – spatial practices:* they embrace the organising principles of production, reproduction, and consumption which form the unconscious of society.
2. *The imaginary – representation of space:* this is tied to spatial practices, but exists as the way that those practices are represented; this is the realm of images, conscious and/or unconscious, perceived and/or imagined.
3. *The symbolic – spaces of representations:* they embody complex symbolisms, which have conscious and unconscious resonances, and are linked to 'underground social life'.

In Pile's interpretation, the categories of the spatial practices and the spaces of representations have become confused. As Pile himself states, the symbolic in Lacan is tied to language, and thus would have to correspond to Lefebvre's representation of space, while the imaginary would have to correspond to the

---

211   Widmer, *Subversion des Begehrens*, 153–4.
212   Prigge, 'Reading the Urban Revolution', 54.
213   Lefebvre, *Production of Space*, 74.
214   Pile, *The Body and the City*, 156–7.

spaces of representation. Here the concept of 'symbolism' obviously contributed to the confusion. As will be shown below, Lefebvre does not, as Pile does, link the 'symbolic' to the (linguistically) conceived, but to the lived experience. Lefebvre clearly distinguishes between the psychological function of the imaginary and the social function of the symbol. In Lefebvre's theory of language, the symbolic dimension is precisely what is 'unspoken', 'poetic', 'pictorial' in language, which is produced through connotations and metaphors. In his theory of space, he therefore links the symbolic to spaces of representation, whose symbolic meanings cannot be fully grasped analytically and linguistically, but are experienced and lived, and thus inexhaustible.

At the same time, however, it must be noted – and here Pile was undoubtedly on the right track – that Lefebvre explicitly did not understand his analysis as a psychological one. He criticised Lacan's theory for establishing a logical, epistemological, and anthropological priority of language in relation to space. At the same time, it places prohibitions, including the prohibition of incest, at the origin of society, rather than productive activity. It thus assumes an objective, neutral, and empty space in which only the space of speech and writing is generated.[215] Obviously, such assumptions cannot serve as a basis for a theory that proceeds from material social practice.[216]

Thus, Lefebvre's analysis is explicitly not to be interpreted as psychological – despite the extensive references and discussions that Lefebvre himself repeatedly leads on this theme. In the context of mirroring and reflection effects caused by the spaces of representation, for example, he writes that his theory treats certain relations that are usually regarded as 'psychic', that is, as connected with the psyche; here, however, he regards them as material, that is, as connected with the body-subject and the mirror-object.[217]

This cryptic formulation is made clearer by an example that Lefebvre repeatedly uses as a metaphor, the landscape. The power of a landscape does not come from what it offers visually, but from the fact that it presents us, as mirror and mirage, a simultaneously illusory and real image of a creative capacity that the ego, marvellously deceived for a moment, attributes to itself. This is also how the tourist illusion of understanding and participating in a work emerges, while passively absorbing an image by passing through a city, for instance Venice. This illusion at the same time obscures the concrete work and the productive activity that produced it.[218]

In another passage, Lefebvre distinguishes his own analysis of the

---

215   Lefebvre, *Production of Space*, 36.
216   See also Blum and Nast, 'Where's the Difference?', 562.
217   Lefebvre, *Production of Space*, 186.
218   Ibid., 189.

production of space from psychoanalysis in the following way: he himself treats a different question than psychoanalysis by exploring social practice as an extension of the body. He thus analyses the genesis of space in time as a historical production process.[219] Lefebvre's materialism is thus not psychologic at all, and he shares with French phenomenology a fundamental scepticism towards psychoanalysis. Bachelard, for example, writes: 'A psychoanalyst can of course study the human character of poets but, as a result of his own sojourn in the region of the passions, he is not prepared to study poetic images in their exalting reality.'[220]

The First Triad: On the Phenomenology of Space

The phenomenological criticism of psychoanalysis points to another promising hint for identifying the philosophical roots of Lefebvre's triad of the production of space. The phenomenological points of reference in Lefebvre are readily apparent in his key terms: the perceived, the conceived, the lived. 'Perception' is a central concept in phenomenology. How does a 'subject' perceive a picture, a landscape, a monument? Obviously, perception depends on this 'subject': a farmer does not see 'his' landscape in the same way as a city dweller who takes a walk there.[221] However, Lefebvre is quite sceptical about the phenomenological account of perception, and he therefore also puts the concept of spatial practice alongside it to show that perception does not only take place in the mind, but is embedded in a concrete, socially produced materiality.[222]

A clear phenomenological point of reference can also be seen in the concept of lived space. As already discussed in section 5.5, Maurice Merleau-Ponty developed in *Phenomenology of Perception* from 1945 a theory of perception that operates with the fundamental concepts of 'space', 'time', and 'lived world' (*monde vécu*).[223] Here, we already find the distinction between a lived world and a perceived world. As Merleau-Ponty asserts, science on the one hand refers to an experience of the world (and thus lived world) and, on the other, is a determination or explication of the perceived world. Accordingly, Merleau-Ponty distinguishes between first a physical space constituted by perception, second a geometric space that is intellectually grasped, and third a lived space, the mythical space, the space of dream, schizophrenia, and art, which is based

---

219   Ibid., 249.
220   Bachelard, *The Poetics of Space*, 42.
221   Lefebvre, *Production of Space*, 113.
222   See also ibid., 183.
223   Merleau-Ponty, *Phenomenology of Perception*, lxx.

on the relationship of the subject to one's world and which is anchored in the physicality of this subject.[224] We could say that this passage contains already a brief sketch of Lefebvre's triad, even if the theoretical fundaments are different. Lefebvre even uses the term 'geometric formant' in the same way as Merleau-Ponty (see section 6.3). In an inspiring essay, Eden Kinkaid reads *The Production of Space* alongside Merleau-Ponty's *Phenomenology of Perception*, explores their shared emphasis on bodily practices, and reveals the potential for a renewed critical phenomenology.[225] Lefebvre himself, however, did not directly disclose this relationship between his own concepts and the theory of Merleau-Ponty, although he had studied Merleau-Ponty intensively.[226]

However, Lefebvre refers explicitly to Heidegger and Bachelard for his triad of the production of space, and particularly emphasises their analyses on dwelling and the house.[227] In Heidegger's text, which Lefebvre used for his conception of dwelling (see section 4.3), there is a remarkable reflection on the 'essence' of space: 'When we speak of man and space, it sounds as though man stood on one side, space on the other. Yet space is not something that faces man.'[228] For Heidegger, space is neither an external object nor an inner experience. Rather, it can be derived from dwelling: 'Spaces open up by the fact that they are let into the dwelling of man.'[229] Heidegger then sees dwelling in close connection with building and thinking: building belongs to dwelling and receives its essence from it. In the same sense, but in a different way, thinking also belongs to dwelling:

> Building and thinking are, each in its own way, inescapable for dwelling. The two, however, are also insufficient for dwelling so long as each busies itself with its own affairs in separation, instead of listening to the other. They are able to listen if both – building and thinking – belong to dwelling, if they remain within their limits and realize that the one as much as the other comes from the workshop of long experience and incessant practice.[230]

With a little imagination, Lefebvre's concepts can be recognised here: perceived space can be seen in building, conceived space in thinking, and lived space in dwelling.

---

224   Ibid., 253–4, 304.
225   Kinkaid, 'Re-encountering Lefebvre'.
226   Lefebvre, 'Idéologie et vérité'.
227   Lefebvre, *Production of Space*, 120–1.
228   Heidegger, 'Building Dwelling Thinking', 358.
229   Ibid., 359.
230   Ibid., 362.

In this context, *The Poetics of Space*, Gaston Bachelard's classic phenomeno-logical analysis of lived space is of central importance. In this book Bachelard pursues the ambitious project of designing a phenomenology of the imagina-tion by means of poetic images of the 'felicitous space' in literature.[231] In this work, we can find arguments that also sketch out Lefebvre's three-dimensional concept. The images of the felicitous space seek to determine the human value of the spaces we love, the spaces we defend against adverse forces.

> Attached to its protected value, which can be a real one, are also imag-ined values, which soon become dominant. Space that has been seized upon by the imagination cannot remain indifferent space subject to the measures and estimates of the surveyor. It has been lived in, not in its positivity, but with all the partiality of the imagination.[232]

Here, then, we already find a first distinction between a 'real' (or also: material) aspect of space and an experienced or lived one, whereby it is clear that both aspects can refer to one and the same 'space': the 'felicitous space' not only is imagined or experienced, it also has a protective value, which thus corresponds to a spatial practice.

The third aspect of space, the conceived space, is also found in Bachelard, explicitly in contrast to the imagined space. In the context of an aesthetic of the hidden, which deals with chests, cupboards, and drawers, Bachelard writes:

> An empty drawer is *unimaginable*. It can only be *thought of*. And for us, who must describe what we imagine before what we know, what we dream before what we verify, all wardrobes are full.[233]

The following critical passage from Lefebvre reads like a continuation: 'Empty space in the sense of a mental and social void which facilitates the socialisation of a not-yet-social realm is actually merely a *representation of space*.'[234] Lefebvre himself suggests this reference when he notes that Bachelard crossed the spaces of representation in his dreams, distinguishing them from the representations of space elaborated by science.[235]

Thus, a first central reference point of the theory of the production of space is revealed: (French) phenomenology. Lefebvre is, however, critical of this

---

231   Bachelard, *Poetics of Space*, 30, 46.
232   Ibid., 46.
233   Ibid., 48.
234   Lefebvre, *Production of Space*, 190.
235   Ibid., 121.

approach, as in his eyes it is still too strongly influenced by Descartes's separation of subject and object. Accordingly, he criticises Husserl, the founder of phenomenology, as well as his disciple Merleau-Ponty, in particular because they too made the subjectivity of the ego the centre of their theory and thus could not overcome idealism.[236] Lefebvre's aim is, so to speak, to develop a materialist version of phenomenology – a project Merleau-Ponty pursued, but did not complete. To reach this goal, Lefebvre approaches the production of space from the point of view of social practice and thus understands the perceived, the conceived, and the lived as socially produced dimensions of human reality.

The Second Triad: Language and Space

After the first triad of perceived, conceived, and lived space has been clarified, the second triad of spatial practice, the representation of space, and the spaces of representation must also be illuminated.

As the term 'representation' suggests, this triad has something to do with language. In fact, as early as 1966, in the book *Le langage et la société*, Lefebvre presented his own theory of language orientated towards Nietzsche, and which, in many respects, broke with the semiotic approaches common at the time. In this book he analysed language in exactly the same dialectical way that he would later analyse space, and he developed a three-dimensional scheme that can be seen as a model or precursor to the theory of the production of space.

The starting point of his theory of language is Nietzsche's poetics and, in particular, his text 'On Truth and Lies in a Nonmoral Sense' from 1873.[237] Nietzsche, Lefebvre argues, was the only one to pose the problem of language correctly, by starting from what was really spoken and not from a 'model', and by linking meaning with values and knowledge with power from the very beginning (see also section 2.4).[238] Lefebvre makes special reference to the classical concepts of metonymy and metaphor, which took on radical meaning in Nietzsche. Words go beyond the immediate, the sensory, the chaos of impressions and sensations. They replace this chaos with an image or an audible representation, and thus create a metamorphosis. With the words of a language, we thus possess only metaphors of things, while concepts arise from an identification of the non-identical, and thus from an act of metony-

---

236   Ibid., 4, 22.
237   Ibid., 138.
238   Lefebvre, *Survival of Capitalism*, 77.

my.[239] Nietzsche wrote:

> We believe we know something about the things themselves when we
> speak of trees, colours, snow and flowers, and yet we possess nothing but
> metaphors for things – metaphors which correspond in no way to the
> original entities.[240]

For Nietzsche, each word thereby immediately becomes a concept

> precisely insofar as it is not supposed to serve as a reminder of the unique
> and entirely individual original experience to which it owes its origin; but
> rather, a word becomes a concept insofar as it simultaneously has to fit
> countless more or less similar cases – which means, purely and simply,
> cases which are never equal and thus altogether unequal. Every concept
> arises from the equation of unequal things.[241]

So, what is language? Lefebvre answers with Nietzsche's definition of truth:

> What then is truth? A movable host of metaphors, metonymies, and
> anthropomorphisms: in short, a sum of human relations which have
> been poetically and rhetorically intensified, transferred, and embellished,
> and which, after long usage, seem to a people to be fixed, canonical, and
> binding.[242]

Lefebvre sees metaphor and metonymy in the original sense as acts that become
rhetorical figures only through use. Accordingly, he conceives society as a
space and an architecture of concepts, forms, and laws whose abstract truth
asserts itself against the reality of the senses, the body, wishes, and desires.[243]
Out of these considerations, Lefebvre develops a theory of the three-
dimensionality of language.

The first dimension, which he calls the syntactic or syntagmatic dimension,
is the more or less classical dimension of linguistics and grammar. It defines the
formal rules of connection that determine the relationships between the signs
and their possible combinations – the syntax.[244]

---

239   Lefebvre, *Production of Space*, 138.
240   Nietzsche, 'On Truth and Lies in a Nonmoral Sense', 82–3.
241   Ibid., 83.
242   Ibid., 8; see also Lefebvre, *Production of Space*, 138.
243   Lefebvre, *Production of Space*, 137.
244   Lefebvre, *Le langage et la société*, 243.

Lefebvre distinguishes from this a 'paradigmatic' dimension. This term refers to Roman Jakobson, one of the most influential linguists of the twentieth century, who developed a two-dimensional theory of language.[245] Jakobson distinguished two ways of attributing a linguistic sign. The first is the combination or context: each sign consists of a combination of signs and/or appears in combination with other signs. Each linguistic unit thus serves as the context for simpler units and/ or appears in the context of more complex units. This first attribute of the sign, which corresponds to a metonymic process, can be related to the syntagmatic dimension. Jakobson distinguished a second linguistic operation from this: selection or substitution. This operation implies the possibility of replacing a terminus with another that is equivalent to the first one in one aspect and different from it in another. This second attribute of the sign, which corresponds to a metaphorical process, refers to a code, a system of meanings, the paradigms. Lefebvre accordingly calls this the paradigmatic dimension. Up to this point, Lefebvre's conception of language is rather conventional.

This changes when Lefebvre adds a third dimension to these two: the symbolic dimension. As Lefebvre admits, the concept of symbol is confusing, since it has different meanings. On the one hand, it refers to the formalised signs of mathematics, while on the other it is also loaded with images, emotions, affectivity, and connotations. Lefebvre turns to this second meaning of the term: the substantiality of the symbol, its ambiguities, and its complexity, which are part of the lived and living language.[246] Even philosophy, Lefebvre asserts, has not succeeded in renouncing images and symbols, or poiesis. Although it commits itself to discursive rigour, there is also ambiguity and misunderstanding in philosophy,

> a fortunate ambiguity, the chance of a misunderstanding. Discourse passes from master to disciple not *despite of*, but *on account of* these ambiguities and misunderstandings: on account of words that underlie discourse, and images or symbols that give impulse to concepts.[247]

Lefebvre here does not want to slide in any way into irrationality and mysticism, but, on the contrary, he sees the emotional and the 'irrational' as social facts. It is only with this intention that he wants to take up the symbol again and explore its meaning for the people of a society. Thus, the symbol enters into social structures and ideologies and serves as a support for emblems and

---

245   Jakobson, 'Two Aspects of Language'. See also Lefebvre, *Le langage et la société*, 210–17.

246   Lefebvre, *Le langage et la société*, 247–8.

247   Lefebvre, *Metaphilosophy*, 64.

fetishes. It forms the basis of the social imaginary, which often differs from the individual imaginary. For Lefebvre, a clear distinction must therefore be made between the psychological function of the imaginary and the social function of the symbol. For him, it is decisive that symbols are inexhaustible, and therefore cannot be formalised.[248]

Lefebvre applies this three-dimensional analysis in *Le langage et la société* to a variety of topics, such as need, consciousness, music, philosophy, the house, dwelling, or the world of objects. And he even presents a three-dimensional linguistic analysis of the 'traditional city': the *syntagmatic dimension* is determined by itineraries, connections, networks of relations; the *paradigmatic dimension* is made up of oppositions: city–countryside, inside–outside, centre–periphery, enclosure–gate; and the *symbolic dimension* includes monuments, style, historical memories, continuity. Lefebvre has already analysed the explosion of the traditional city (see chapter 3.3) according to these three dimensions: while the syntagmatic dimension becomes predominant, the paradigmatic dimension fades away, and the symbolic dimension almost disappears.[249]

It is obvious how to transfer this schema to 'space'. In fact, in other texts, Lefebvre postulates that activity in space establishes an order which, to a certain point, coincides with the order of words: thus, we can assign the *syntagmatic dimension* (articulations, concatenations, and connections) to *spatial practice*. The *paradigmatic dimension* and its binaries correspond to a *representation of space*. And the *symbolic dimension*, with its monuments and privileged places that symbolise the cosmos, the world, society, or the state, refers to *spaces of representation*.[250]

The Double Triad of the Production of Space

This chapter has sought to uncover the foundations of Lefebvre's theory of the production of space. Here, we can now draw a preliminary conclusion: Lefebvre conceives of 'space' as a production process that takes place in three dialectically intertwined dimensions. These dimensions are defined twice by Lefebvre and are therefore named twice. On the one hand, there is 'the perceived', 'the conceived', and 'the lived', concepts which can be related to (French) phenomenology. On the other hand, Lefebvre uses the terms of 'spatial practice',

---

248   Lefebvre, *Le langage et la société*, 253, 258, 269.
249   Ibid., 290.
250   Lefebvre, *Right to the City*, 116; Lefebvre, *Production of Space*, 117; Lefebvre, *De l'État*, vol. 4, 282.

'representation of space', and 'spaces of representation' derived from his own three-dimensional theory of language.

These three dimensions initially remain in a floating indeterminacy: true to his epistemological premises (see section 1.2), Lefebvre introduces them as approximations, whose scope he explores and which he then modifies in the course of his theoretical explorations. This approach requires from the reader a meticulous reconstruction of the entire theory.

First, Lefebvre explicitly does not assume three ontologically independent 'worlds', as in Popper's critical rationalism, but rather three dialectically connected dimensions of the production of space (and society; see section 7.4).

Second, despite certain similarities, Lefebvre's theory of the production of space is fundamentally different from psychoanalytical concepts: while these concepts treat psychological processes that take place within the individual, Lefebvre takes an external perspective and looks from the position of society as a totality. Psychic processes are also formed in social practice, of course, but Lefebvre does not attempt to trace these processes back to the 'interiority' of the individual. Instead, he is interested in the material aspects of these processes, and he tries to analyse them as part of their incorporation into social products, such as language or space.

Third, a central reference point of this theory lies in French phenomenology, especially Bachelard and Merleau-Ponty. Compared to these approaches, however, Lefebvre tries to maintain his dialectical-materialist point of view. This shifts the epistemological perspective from the recognising, acting, and experiencing subject to the social production of the processes of recognising, acting, and experiencing.

Fourth, there is a direct connection between the theory of the production of space and the theory of language developed by Lefebvre himself. The distinctiveness of this theory of language consists in its three-dimensional dialectical construction, but also in the 'symbolic dimension' oriented towards Nietzsche, which coincides with the concept of 'spaces of representation'. However, the theory of the production of space goes a step further than the three-dimensional theory of language: it attempts to encompass the entirety of social practice, and not only language as a partial aspect of this practice. Thus, it has to consider and to conceptualise the crucial elements of any 'theory of space': the materiality of social practice and the central role that physicality, and thus the human body, plays in it.

Finally, we must return to the question raised at the beginning of this section: does Lefebvre's theory of the production of space refer to the concrete situation of an individual subject or to social, collective actors? The considerations made here permit only one conclusion: it clearly refers to both,

which Lefebvre attempts to grasp as dialectically intertwined. Spatial practices, representations of space, and spaces of representation are the outcome
of individual *and* collective actions and experiences. Likewise, the perceived,
the conceived, and the lived are simultaneously individual *and* social, because
the individual is never alone, but, as a social being, always embedded in
society.

5.7 The Dialectic of the Production of Space

> The dialectic emerges from time and realises itself; it operates, in an
> unforeseen manner, in space.[251]

As elaborated in chapter 2, dialectics is the epistemological key to the entire
work of Henri Lefebvre. In his confrontation with the classics, he developed a
highly individual and original version of the dialectic, a 'triadic dialectic', which
is not only based on Marx and Hegel but also incorporates Nietzsche's poetics.
He repeatedly reviewed, revised, and further developed this particular version
of the dialectic in his work. It was only in *La production de l'espace*, however,
that he explored this three-dimensional dialectic in all its breadth and depth.
In this sense, the theory of the production of space constitutes a decisive stage
in the development of Lefebvre's epistemology.

It is precisely this core element of Lefebvre's theory, however, that poses the
greatest problems of interpretation. The Anglo-American discussion of his
work in particular is characterised by a poorly differentiated, sometimes functionalist ('Marxist'), and sometimes idealist ('Hegelian') understanding of his
dialectics.

A functionalist understanding can be seen, for example, in David Harvey,
who, after more than twenty years of Marxist analysis, finally dedicated a separate chapter to dialectics in *Justice, Nature and the Geography of Difference*.[252]
There he sets out eleven 'principles' of dialectic, even as he admits that setting
out principles is inherently contrary to dialectics. These principles refer extensively to processes, flows, and relations, as well as to 'things' and systems but
hardly at all to social contradictions. And at no point does Harvey mention the
key concept of dialectics that was so important to Lefebvre: the 'sublation of the
contradiction'. Harvey's understanding of dialectics is not unusual, however. It
is based essentially on Bertell Ollman's influential interpretation of Marx's

---

251   Lefebvre, *Production of Space*, 129. Translation amended.
252   Harvey, *Justice, Nature and the Geography of Difference*, 46–59.

dialectic. This is also characterised by a functionalist understanding, as is evident in his interpretation of the (dialectical) contradiction:

> Contradiction is understood here as the incompatible development of different elements within the same relation, which is to say between elements that are also dependent on one another. Consequently, their paths of development do not only intersect in mutually supportive ways but are constantly blocking, undermining, otherwise interfering with, and in due course transforming each other.[253]

It is obvious that Lefebvre's understanding of dialectics is far away from such a reductionist representation (see sections 2.3 and 2.4).

If in broad parts of the Anglo-American discussion the 'classical' form of dialectics remains misunderstood, the specific variant used by Lefebvre can only cause additional confusion. This is particularly evident in postmodern geography, where the theory of the production of space moved into the centre of interest, inevitably accompanied by interpretations of Lefebvre's three-dimensional dialectics. However, the eclectic character and multipolar perspective of the postmodern approach can only be reconciled with dialectical thinking with great difficulty. For example, Derek Gregory, in his book *Geographical Imaginations*, which provides one of the most influential postmodern interpretations of Lefebvre's theory to date, discusses the three dimensions of the production of space in detail.[254] They appear here as elements that are related to one another but ultimately exist independently. Finally, Gregory amalgamates fragments of theory from Lefebvre, Foucault, and Habermas to form a theoretical schema, the 'eye of power', in which not only social practice disappears but dialectics along with it.[255] In contrast, other representatives of postmodern geography, such as Edward W. Soja and Rob Shields, have made intensive efforts to decipher the nature of Lefebvre's dialectic, but have failed, not least because they could not free themselves from a Hegelian interpretation of the dialectic.

In contrast with these different interpretations, this chapter has revealed the dynamic and open-ended understanding of dialectics that Lefebvre developed over decades and brought to fruition in the production of space. This dialectic provides an analytical tool that can be used for a wide range of applications, and it has encouraged many efforts to analyse all sorts of questions in a dialectical way.

253 Ollman, *Dance of the Dialectic*.
254 Gregory, *Geographical Imaginations*, 403–5.
255 Ibid., 401.

The Space of Political Economy

It is obvious that Lefebvre's three-dimensional conception of the production of space is not fully compatible with a classical understanding of political economy, which is essentially reduced to two dimensions: the economic (material production processes) and the political (regulation, planning). Lefebvre was well aware of these difficulties, and for this reason did not develop a political theory of space, but a theory of the production of space (see the detailed discussion in section 7.1). It is therefore not surprising that David Harvey, who in his extensive work repeatedly took up Lefebvre's concepts and implemented them productively, experienced considerable problems with the three-dimensionality of Lefebvre's theory of the production of space.[256] He presents the three dimensions of the production of space as follows:

1. Material spatial practices refer to physical and material flows, transfers, and interactions that occur in and across space to ensure production and social reproduction.
2. Representations of space encompass all the signs and significations, codes, and knowledge that allow such material practices to be talked about and understood, whether they are expressed in everyday or academic terms.
3. Spaces of representation are mental inventions such as codes, signs, 'spatial discourses', utopian plans, imaginary landscapes, and also material constructs such as symbolic spaces, built environments, paintings, museums, and the like, which imagine new meanings or possibilities for spatial practices.

This representation does not initially pose any major problems, although the interpretation of the spaces of representation as 'mental inventions' raises some questions. However, the assignment of the two conceptual triads is revealing: Harvey assigns *experience* to spatial practice, *perception* to the representation of space, and *imagination* to the spaces of representation. This amounts to a confusion of perception and conception.[257] Harvey thus twice misses the content of Lefebvre's arguments: on the one hand, Lefebvre relates perception to spatial practice, which ultimately means that materiality is constituted in perception as such; on the other hand, he connects the representation of space with conception, and thus articulates it with abstraction. This confusion of concepts has no direct effect on Harvey's analysis, however, but only because the concepts of perceived, conceived, and lived space no longer appear in his

---

256   See Harvey, *Condition of Postmodernity*, 218–19.
257   Ibid., 220–1.

work. He breaks off his brief excursion into the dimensions of the production of space with the following argument: 'But to argue that the relations between the experienced, the perceived, and the imagined are dialectically rather than causally determined leaves things much too vague.'[258] He then turns to Bourdieu and attempts to achieve the reproduction of the objective conditions of productive practices through the concept of 'habitus'.

In Harvey's analysis of Lefebvre's theory of the production of space, two aspects are particularly noteworthy: first, his obvious incomprehension of the 'three-dimensionality' of the production of space; and second, his scepticism towards Lefebvre's dialectic. Clearly, Harvey shrinks back from pursuing the question of three-dimensionality, with which Lefebvre went beyond a narrow interpretation of Marxism and the limitations of the classical critique of political economy.

These limitations become clear in Harvey's explanation of postmodernism in his book *The Condition of Postmodernity*. Here he sees postmodernism as an aesthetic movement that resulted from the crisis of over-accumulation in the late 1960s and early 1970s.[259] Consequently, for Harvey, postmodernism is nothing other than the cultural logic of the regime of flexible accumulation raised following the economic crisis of Fordism. Although Harvey reconstructs the (cultural) history of space in the footsteps of Lefebvre to substantiate his thesis, his analysis is much more influenced by Fredric Jameson. Jameson had regarded postmodernism as the cultural logic of late capitalism, which he characterises by the incorporation of cultural production into the commodification process.[260]

However, Harvey's analysis does not address the fact that the 'cultural phenomena' conceptualised by postmodernism were not only produced by the logic of capital accumulation and the crisis of Fordism, but have their origins as well in various cultural, feminist, and urban social movements that were themselves constitutive for the crisis of Fordism. Harvey does indeed present the thesis that the countercultural movements of the 1960s created an environment of unfulfilled needs and repressed desires, which were then taken up by postmodernist popular cultural production and transformed into commodities. But he immediately relativises this statement with the counter-thesis that in order to maintain its markets, capitalism had to produce such desires and titillate individual sensibilities to create a new aesthetic.[261]

In the end, this statement appears to be only a slightly revised version of the classic theory of base and superstructure, which Lefebvre himself had fundamentally transformed with his theory of the production of space (see section

---

258   Ibid., 219.
259   Ibid., 327–8.
260   Ibid., 63; see also Jameson, 'Postmodernism'.
261   Harvey, *Condition of Postmodernity*, 63.

7.5). Thus, the three-dimensional concept of the production of space is a central criterion for distinguishing Harvey's and Lefebvre's seemingly related theoretical positions (see also section 7.1).

It should be noted, however, that Harvey's analyses do go beyond a narrow political-economic dualism. This is particularly evident in his historical analysis of the transformation of Paris under Baron Haussmann and the uprising which followed in the Paris Commune. Here, he uses his theoretical categories to examine not only class structures, capital circuits, real estate markets, land speculation, and state regulations but also everyday life, 'the urbanisation of consciousness', and 'the urban experience'.[262]

Dialectic or 'Trialectic'?

A completely different problem with Lefebvre's three-dimensional dialectic is apparent in the work of Edward W. Soja, who has provided the most important and influential consideration of Lefebvre's theory of the production of space to date.[263] Soja recognised early on that Lefebvre's dialectics no longer corresponded to 'classical' dialectics in essential points. He described the specificity of this new dialectics as follows: Lefebvre wanted to overcome the reductionism of binary terms, concepts, or elements, such as subject–object, natural–social, or bourgeoisie–proletariat. He persistently sought to crack them open by introducing a third term, a third possibility, or third moment, one that is not just a simple combination or an 'in between' position but something else that arises from the disordering, deconstruction, and tentative reconstitution of their presumed totalisation, and that produces an open alternative that is both similar and strikingly different.[264]

These formulations seem to be familiar. They can be seen as a possible interpretation of the classical idea of the 'sublation of the contradiction', as found in Marx and also in Lefebvre (see section 2.3). But Soja calls this other thing, this third moment that arises from the dialectical sublation, 'Thirding-as-Othering'. He emphasises that this is more than a mere dialectical synthesis à la Hegel or Marx, where the process is caught up in the 'totalising closure' of the temporal sequence of thesis, antithesis, and synthesis.[265] But while Soja considers it necessary to give this dialectic a new, postmodern name and to contrast it to 'classical' dialectics, the question inevitably arises as to what Soja understands by dialectics in general – and how he understands Lefebvre's dialectic in particular. Soja's view

262 Harvey, *Consciousness and the Urban Experience*.
263 Soja, *Postmodern Geographies*; Soja, *Thirdspace*.
264 Soja, *Thirdspace*, 60–1.
265 Ibid.

is illustrated by the fact that he defines 'Thirding-as-Othering' as a cumulative 'trialectic' that is open to a constant expansion of spatial knowledge. A confusion seems to be developing here. What at first appears to be a 'temporal' dialectic suddenly presents itself, by a mere redefinition, as a 'trialectic of spatial knowledge'. Soja thus apparently recognises a new, different dialectic in the theory of the production of space, which he is not, however, able to reconstruct.

The first difficulty lies obviously in understanding Lefebvre's shift of perspective from a 'classical' to a 'three-dimensional' dialectic. However, Lefebvre's conception is still a dialectic, and not a 'trialectic' – the Greek prefix *dia-* means not 'two' but 'through', and Hegel understood dialectics as a thinking based on the movement of contradictions. In addition, the indeterminacy or ambiguity in Lefebvre's use of the term 'social space' also plays a role here. Lefebvre uses the term 'social space' in a narrow sense, synonymously to 'lived space', but also in a wide sense to designate the totality of socially produced space (see section 5.2). From this ambiguity, Soja confusingly draws the conclusion that social space is the synthesis of mental and physical space, which contains and transcends these two spaces at the same time. According to Soja, this social space takes on two different qualities: 'It serves both as a separable field, distinguishable from physical and mental space, *and/also* as an approximation of an all-encompassing mode of spatial thinking.' In this sense, this space is a third space that is both distinguishable from other spaces and a transcending composite of all spaces. Soja calls this a 'Thirdspace'.[266]

In this Thirdspace, everything comes together: subjectivity and objectivity, the abstract and the concrete, the real and the imagined, the knowable and the unimaginable, the repetitive and the differential, structure and agency, mind and body, consciousness and the unconscious, and so on.[267] Soja compares this Thirdspace to the 'Aleph', an allegorical figure for the infinite complexity of space and time that appears in a short story by Argentine writer Jorge Luis Borges. The Aleph is one of the points in space that contain all other points.[268]

This all-inclusive simultaneity opens up endless worlds to explore and, at the same time, presents daunting challenges. Any attempt to capture this all-encompassing space in words and texts, for example, invokes an immediate sense of impossibility, a despair that the sequentiality of language and writing, of the narrative form and history-telling, can never do more than scratch the surface of Thirdspace's extraordinary simultaneities.[269]

266 Ibid., 62.
267 Ibid., 56–7.
268 Ibid., 54–6.
269 Ibid., 57.

Going further in his interpretation, Soja enters more dangerous waters: although social space in the wide sense contains all three 'spatialities' (the perceived, the conceived, and the lived) and therefore none of them is privileged a priori, Soja sees this third, lived space of representation as a strategic place from which all spaces can be encompassed, understood, and transformed simultaneously: 'Lived social space, more than any other, is Lefebvre's limitless Aleph, the space of radical openness, the space of social struggle.'[270] At the same time, however, Soja admits: 'Lefebvre never made explicit his strategic "preference" for the spaces of representation.'[271]

It seems as if Soja conceives of three independent 'spaces' or 'spatialities', which in a certain sense subversively sublate each other in this third space. He describes this 'Thirdspace' as a 'dominated space', the space of the periphery, which is filled with ideology and politics, the real and the imagined, with capitalism, racism, patriarchy, and other material spatial practices, and thus also as a strategic place for liberation and emancipation.[272]

This passage allows for no other conclusion than that Soja reifies the dimensions or moments of the production of space laid out by Lefebvre – Soja makes them, to a certain extent, into 'independent' spaces: there is a first, physical space; a second, mental space; and finally a third and comprehensive social space. This conclusion is supported by Soja's further elaborations, in which he distinguishes specific spatial 'epistemologies', each of which is intended to explore the first, second, or third space. In *Postmetropolis*, he then uses exactly this distinction to divide different approaches to urban research into three different epistemological categories.

Without going into further detail here, it should only be noted that according to Lefebvre it is impossible to see a space without conceiving it, and equally impossible to conceive it without having first experienced it (see sections 5.4 and 5.5). The result of our reconstruction of the theory of the production of space allows us to conclude that, according to Lefebvre's theory, there can be no 'third space', just as there can be no first or second. This is already indicated by the terminology, as preliminary and tentative its form may be: it is hardly conceivable that perception, thought, or experience alone, separate from one another, could constitute a social practice existing outside of abstraction. Logically, the perceived, the conceived, and the lived cannot form 'independent' spaces either, but only three dialectically connected moments or formants of the production of space. It is precisely in this conception that we find the quality and analytical strength of Lefebvre's theory.

---

270   Ibid., 68.
271   Ibid., 69.
272   Ibid.

A 'Spatial Dialectic'?

Soja is not alone in having difficulty coping with Lefebvre's three-dimensional dialectic. Rob Shields, who presented the first comprehensive account of Lefebvre's work in English, also had considerable problems with this dialectic. In his interpretation, partly inspired by Soja, he argues that Lefebvre did not fully exploit the significance of his *dialectique de triplicité*. The presentation of a 'triple dialectic' on the basis of a thesis with two antitheses, he writes, remains confusing.[273]

In Shields's view, the 'usual interpretation' of Lefebvre's dialectic runs as follows: affirmation (everyday practice and perception)–first negation (analytical theory and institutions)–second negation (lived moments). The three dimensions of the production of space figure here as three 'elements', which together are 'synthesized' together in a social 'spatialization'.[274] This view of Lefebvre's dialectics does indeed seem unworkable. It is worth asking, however, whether this line of interpretation has any defenders. Shields does not cite a single bibliographical reference to this 'usual interpretation'.

Shields now observes that the third term is treated by Lefebvre as a negation of the negation rather than an equal player with the first two terms. He proposes, therefore, that the three terms should be understood as follows: everyday perception–contradiction of practice and spatial theory–concepts relativised by a transcendent, entirely different, moment: creative, fully lived space. The totalising synthesis would then lie in a fourth transcendent term, what Lefebvre calls 'space' and what can best be understood as 'spatialisation'.[275]

This argument, however, only seemingly helps Shields avoid reification, and his dialectic makes strange turns. What Soja called the first, second, and third 'spaces' become here 'elements' that contradict each other – the first contradicts the second, and the third contradicts the other two – and which are finally spatialised in a totalising synthesis: from whatever perspective we might look at this process, only one 'total object' finally emerges, that consists of conflicting 'partial spaces' – and thus forms an absolute space. If space is understood as a 'synthesis', it can be nothing more than the absolute object that contains and immobilises all other objects as well as time – the end of history. Dialectic turns into its opposite; space remains trapped in Hegel's absolute knowledge (see section 2.3).

Thus, both Soja's and Shields's interpretations – despite their differences – ultimately return to Hegelian dialectics, a dialectic that inevitably ends in the

---

273   Shields, *Lefebvre, Love and Struggle*, 120.
274   Ibid.
275   Ibid.

absolute. Lefebvre was well aware of the consequences of Hegel's dialectic. Instead, starting out from Marx's materialism, he found his way through Hegel's Absolute and Nietzsche's poetics to another dialectic in which the three dialectical moments incessantly relate to one another. What remains obscured in Soja's and Shields's interpretations is Lefebvre's real innovation: the development of a three-dimensional dialectic.

A similar limitation can be found in Stuart Elden.[276] In his critique of Soja and Shields, he states that Lefebvre's conception neither replaces dialectical thinking nor means the introduction of space to dialectics. And he locates Lefebvre's problem with dialectical materialism in its tendency towards a linear, teleological vision of historical change. He argues that Lefebvre therefore does not make the third term into the result of dialectic, as a culmination. Rather, the synthesis can react to the first two terms. Nevertheless, one wonders whether such a construction could still be called dialectical, since dialectical thinking is fundamentally rooted on the dynamics of contradictions and cannot be reduced to the mutual 'interaction' of elements. Furthermore, Elden also claims that Lefebvre's concept of *dépassement* is more a translation of Nietzsche's 'overcoming' (*Überwinden*) rather than Hegel's or Marx's 'sublation'. Here, he refers to a passage from *De l'État*, which, however, is not concerned with questions of dialectics, instead addressing philosophy.[277] Lefebvre goes into this question in more detail in *La présence et l'absence*, where he states clearly that Nietzsche's 'overcoming' is not the same as Marx's and Hegel's 'sublation': overcoming destroys that from which it has arisen, while sublation at the same time negates and preserves it.[278]

As discussed earlier, the 'sublation of the contradiction' means (in Hegel, Marx, and Lefebvre) that the contradiction is overcome and preserved at the same time (see section 2.3). Taking a one-sided view to 'overcoming' ultimately leads to a flat, undialectical version of the contradiction. Elden's interpretation cannot be supported by Lefebvre's work: Lefebvre's dialectic consistently takes the figure of the contradiction as its starting point, and the term *Aufheben* is used – in German and with accompanying explanations – again and again at central points, right up through Lefebvre's final texts. Elden's account thus does not therefore significantly reduce the confusion surrounding Lefebvre's dialectic. To conclude, we need to return to Lefebvre's foundational conceptualisation of dialectics (see section 2.4).

---

276   Elden, 'Politics, Philosophy, Geography', 812; Elden, *Understanding Henri Lefebvre*, 37.
277   Lefebvre, *De l'État*, vol. 2, 171.
278   Lefebvre, *La présence et l'absence*, 95.

Lefebvre's Dialectical Triads

This chapter closes the great theoretical arc that can be traced from Lefebvre's early texts on dialectics through his account of metaphilosophy and arriving at his theory of the production of space.

In his early texts, Lefebvre had already encountered a fundamental problem in classical dialectics: the contradiction between being and consciousness. A central question was the starting point of dialectic: for Hegel this starting point was thinking, the speculative idea. Marx stood Hegel's dialectic 'on its feet' and gave priority not to the idea but to the material process of the production of society. But in this conception, Lefebvre, referring to Nietzsche, criticised the lack of the creative act, of art, of poetry, of *désir*. Thus, a three-dimensional dialectical figure emerged, in which three moments are dialectically connected to one another: the material social praxis (Marx), the word and thought (Hegel), and the creative, poetic act (Nietzsche). In this way, a triangle is formed by three pairs of contradictions, in which each moment is to be understood as a synthesis of the other two. With this, Lefebvre sketched out a new, three-dimensional, or triadic, version of the dialectic.

The 'classical' dialectic of affirmation and negation sets a starting point, the thesis. The antithesis marks the contradiction inherent to this starting point. The third term is the determination that was already laid out in the first term (the thesis) and that unfolds in time, striving for its completion and sublation. As it progresses, a dialectical movement of contradictions develops through the cascade of sublations. Lefebvre's triadic dialectic, on the other hand, posits three concepts at the start. Each of these concepts can be understood as a thesis, and each refers to the other two, and, without them, would have remained a mere abstraction. This triadic figure does not end in a synthesis, as it does in Hegelian dialectics. It combines three concepts which it differentiates without bringing them together in a synthesis: three concepts which interact with one another, in conflicts or in alliances.[279]

However, the idea that this could be a 'spatial dialectic', as Soja and Shields proposed, is misleading: such an interpretation misses the core of Lefebvre's dialectics, which is not limited to space. It is rather a general principle that Lefebvre applied to the most diverse fields (see sections 2.4 and 7.4). For example, the triad of form–structure–function appears regularly throughout his work. And we can also point out the fundamental triadic unity of Lefebvre's conception of space-time: space–time–energy.[280]

---

279   Lefebvre, *Rhythmanalysis*, 12.
280   See for example Lefebvre, *Le retour de la dialectique*, 42.

When applied to the production of space, this understanding of Lefebvre's dialectic leads to the following conclusion: a social space comprises not only a concrete materiality, but also a mental concept and a lived experience. The material practice in itself, without the thought that leads and represents it and without the lived, the emotions that are connected to it, as no existence from a social point of view. Pure thought is pure fiction: it comes from the world, from being, both material and lived, experienced being. And pure 'experience', finally, is pure mysticism: it has no real, that is, social, existence without the materiality of the body on which it is based and without the thought that structures and expresses it.

In consequence, the three moments of the production of space can only be understood as of equal value: space is simultaneously perceived, conceived, and lived. None of these dimensions can be set as an absolute starting point, as 'thesis': none is privileged. This space is by its very nature unfinished, because it is produced continuously, and therefore it is always bound to time.

6

On the History of Spaces

The previous chapter presented a detailed reconstruction of the theory of the production of space. The core of this theory consists in the three dialectically intertwined dimensions of the perceived, the conceived, and the lived, or, in spatial terms, spatial practice, the representation of space, and the spaces of representation. This double series of three terms revealed certain conceptual ambiguities. On the one hand, they arise from the dialectical character of these terms, which requires understanding them in the dynamics of their mutual interactions. On the other hand, it is also due to Lefebvre's metaphilosophical approach, which relates these three dimensions back to practice, thus making it necessary to always include the historical context in the analysis.

We therefore cannot understand the production of space universally but only in a given, concrete historical context. This context is, however, always ambiguous: for space is, first of all, a historical product; but this space is also always a space in the process of production. The production of space is thus to be understood as an ongoing process, embedded in a secular development, which also shifts the relationships between the three dimensions of the production process. The history of space has to be understood in this double perspective: as space in the process of production, and as a historical mode of producing space.

The first aspect, space in the process of production, is treated in Lefebvre's texts through numerous historical digressions in which he unfolds, complements, and develops his three-dimensional dialectic. As might be expected from Lefebvre, however, these digressions are not systematic case studies. True to his postulate of understanding concepts and categories in their historicity, he embeds them within the broad stream of his theoretical-historical explorations. Often, he illuminates only a particular aspect of an example in order to take it up again elsewhere. The fragmentary, essayistic, and poetic-polemical character of these digressions makes it sometimes difficult to determine the historical context more precisely – and thus offers starting points for diverse interpretations.

The following chapter shows how Lefebvre himself applies his three-dimensional dialectic to concrete historical situations, and how in doing so he also consolidates and specifies the theoretical construction of the three dimensions of the production of space. In this way, it provides essential insights into how Lefebvre's theory can be applied empirically and practically.

In addition, however, a second, overarching analytical point of view comes into play: the history of the production of space. Lefebvre's main work on the question of space, *The Production of Space*, has a historical structure of its own, and spans an enormous historical arc from antiquity to the present. It tells – or rather, reconstructs – not only histories of space, but also 'the history' of space, although it is written from an admittedly European perspective. The result is a history that also shows the genesis and historical development of capitalism in an unusual way.

Lefebvre's far-reaching historical approach requires a chapter exposition that runs parallel to the 'history of the city' presented in section 3.3. Its starting point is nature and the space of nature, which, to a certain extent, represent the raw material of the production of space (section 6.1). Against this background, the production of space means the creation of a 'second nature' produced by humans. Following the line of this guiding principle, Lefebvre unfolds the history of the production of space in Europe in three overarching historical sequences: it ranges from the 'absolute space' of European antiquity and the Middle Ages to the 'abstract space' of worldwide capitalism, and finally leads to the concrete utopia of a 'differential space' – the space of a possible urban society.

In Lefebvre's understanding, absolute space is a religious-political space charged with meanings that are not directed towards the intellect but towards the body (section 6.2). The 'original' unity of the lived and the conceived is increasingly split in the course of historical development from European antiquity through the Middle Ages to the Renaissance. The history of the production of space in Europe is thus above all a history of abstraction and thus also of the alienation that accompanies the unfolding of capitalism. This history flows into the modern, abstract space of the twentieth century.

This abstract space is shaped by industrial production and the (national) state (section 6.3). It is a 'homogeneous-fractured space' (*espace homogène-brisé*), which is determined by the homogenising control of the nation state, its comprehensive rationality, and the abstract logic of the commodity, and thus becomes interchangeable. At the same time, however, this space is fractured, since it is determined through the real estate market by diverse actors who buy and sell individual plots of land. To characterise this space, Lefebvre identifies three specific dimensions or formants: the geometric formant (conceived space), the visual formant (perceived space), and the phallic formant (lived space).

This abstract, homogeneous-fractured space contains fundamental contradictions, which push towards the emergence of a differential space (section 6.4). Lefebvre developed the concepts of difference and differential space in several steps. The starting point was his experience of the urban revolt in Paris in 1968, to which he dedicated his *Manifeste différentialiste*. He further developed his thoughts towards a 'theory of difference', which he condensed into the concept of differential space in *The Production of Space*. There he combined his theory of difference with a concrete material process: urbanisation. Differential space is thus nothing other than urban space. This opens up a new definition of the urban: it emerges from differences that themselves originate in urbanisation and which, dialectically speaking, represent the positive potential of urbanisation. The concept of 'differential space' thus allowed him to define urban space from a perspective that no longer focuses on the 'city' but on social space more generally. Therefore, the concepts of difference and differential space complement the concepts of centrality and mediation that were elaborated in chapter 4.

This leads us to what was laid out in chapter 3: the urban – as an abbreviation for urban society – is not a completed reality, nor is it a clearly definable moment, but, rather, a concrete utopia that points the way to a possible urban revolution (section 6.5). This requires bringing philosophy – and thus theory – 'into the world', a task that had challenged Lefebvre since he was a student (see also sections 2.4, 3.1, and 4.3): How can his theory be put into practice? What possibilities and what strategies can be developed from his theoretical findings? In the course of his long oeuvre, Lefebvre developed and refined a wide range of terms and concepts: urban strategy, counter-project, heterotopy and u-topia, (territorial) *autogestion* and urban democracy. He also participated on the development of concrete architectonic projects that have only been rediscovered in recent years. This concrete utopia is therefore not only theory, but also lived practice.

This reconstruction of the history of spaces provides an opportunity to read Lefebvre's history of the city and that of space in parallel (see chapter 4). The effect of the change of the analytical focus from the 'urban' to 'space' will be explored in more detail in section 6.6, where I attempt to bring together

Lefebvre's two great narratives: the urban revolution that heralds a possible urban society, and the production of space as the harbinger of the concrete utopia of differential space.

Finally, there remains the question of historiography, and, in particular, the specific presentation of the history of the production of space in Lefebvre. His presentation is not without problems. Since it refers only to Europe, it is correspondingly limited and one-sided, and, from today's point of view, it appears to be partially outdated. The postcolonial turn in readings of Lefebvre opens up the possibility of telling more diverse histories of space. This would then be no longer a history of the production of space, but a many-voiced history of the production of urban spaces: a (possible) collective project. This potential will be explored in the final chapter of the book (see section 8.3).

6.1 Space as a Historical Product

Destructurations and restructurations are followed in time and space,
always translated on the ground, inscribed in the practico-material,
written in the urban text, but coming from elsewhere: from history and
becoming.[1]

(Social) space is a (social) product: a fundamental consequence of this thesis is that space must be analysed in a historical context. The production of space is a historical process that changes in and with history. Space, as well as the processes that produce it, changes accordingly with a given society.[2] Programmatically, Lefebvre thus postulates that each society produces its own specific space, which can be treated as an 'object' for analysis and for general theoretical exposition.[3]

Space is thus fundamentally a historical product: the historical and its consequences, the 'diachronic', the etymology of places – that is, what happened there and changed a place – has inscribed itself into space. The past has left its traces – writings of time (*écritures du temps*). But this space with its connections and links is always also a space of the present, given as a totality that is in the process of production. Thus, production and product present themselves as two inseparable sides and not as two separable representations.[4] This consideration also explains Lefebvre's use of the terms 'space' and the 'production of

---

1   Lefebvre, *Right to the City*, 107.
2   Lefebvre, *Production of Space*, 27, 31, 46.
3   Ibid., 31.
4   Ibid., 37.

space' as synonyms throughout his work: Lefebvre always thinks of 'space' as a process, and thus as entangled with time.

It should be kept in mind that every social space is the result of a process with multiple aspects and movements. It is therefore not enough to simply examine the history of space, for the three-dimensionality of the production of space, as elaborated in the previous chapter, is constitutive for this history. As Lefebvre points out, the spatial practice of each social formation must be taken into account, as well as the representations of space and the spaces of representation. In particular, however, attention must be paid to the respective connections between these dimensions, to their fault lines, shifts, and interferences.[5]

According to Lefebvre, the relationship between space and the time that produces it is thus fundamentally different from the representations common in the historical sciences, where thinking makes a cut into temporality and halts the historical process. While historical analysis fragments and dissects the object of its analysis, Lefebvre's history of space sees the historical, the diachronic, the generative past as incessantly written into the present of the spatial. The history of space cannot, therefore, be separated from the history of time. Lefebvre is thus concerned with more than an analysis of the inscriptions of time, the uncertain traces of events in space. Space generated by time is always present, synchronous, and given as a whole, and Lefebvre's ambition is to grasp society's inscription of itself into space as the result and product of social activities in the process of action (*en acte*).[6]

Accordingly, Lefebvre does not begin his exploration of the history of space with a geographical description of natural space but rather with the study of natural rhythms, their changes, and their inscription into space by human actions. His starting point is the analysis of the spatio-temporal rhythms of nature transformed by social practices. This is where the investigation must start and try to understand social space as such, its genesis, and its form, with its specific times, the rhythms of everyday life. Lefebvre sees this double investigation of space and time as a combination of 'structure' and 'process', of invariances and change, of institutions and events.[7] A few years later, Lefebvre consequently supplemented *The Production of Space* with the book *Rhythmanalysis*, which explores precisely these times and rhythms of everyday life.

Lefebvre's history of space therefore does not address the production of

---

5   Ibid., 41, 110.
6   Ibid., 110, 117.
7   Ibid., 31, 117.

things and the history of their production. By extending it to space and time, the history of the production of space ultimately becomes the comprehensive history of society, indeed of humanity as such.[8] It becomes a summary, a 'compendium', an 'index' of history, encompassing the abstract and the concrete beyond philosophy. In this way, according to Lefebvre, it should be possible to relativise history instead of making it a substitute for metaphysics, an ontology of becoming.[9] Lefebvre links this analysis with a further ambition, which the title of the book *The Production of Space* does not openly announce: to recognise the genesis of contemporary society with and through the analysis of the production of space.[10] Starting from this history of space, Lefebvre ultimately wants nothing less than to expand and transform historical materialism.[11] These efforts can be seen in *The Survival of Capitalism* and especially in the four-volume work *De l'État*. We can postulate that from these various efforts a renewed general theory of society has indeed emerged, which will be examined in more detail in chapter 7.

Space and Mode of Production

The transformation of Marxism that Lefebvre hoped to achieve addresses in particular a concept central to any historical-materialist analysis: the mode of production. This concept poses considerable problems for Lefebvre in all his historical analyses, as has already become clear in the case of the history of the city (see section 4.4). This point is addressed again in section 6.6 and further developed in section 7.5. For now, suffice it to say that the mode of production plays a decisive role in the production of space for Lefebvre. He even advances the thesis that each mode of production, with its specific sub-variants, produces its own space and time. Within the framework of the respective mode of production, each society has formed its space, through the violence of wars and revolutions, through political and diplomatic cunning, and through labour. With the transition from one mode of production to another, a new space is thus also produced.[12] Lefebvre warns, however, against focusing too much on the internal characteristics of a mode of production as a totality. Through such an analysis the individual mode of production would be more comprehensible, but the transition from one mode of production to another becomes more

---

8   Ibid., 128.
9   Ibid., 129.
10   Lefebvre, 'Preface to the New Edition', 211.
11   Lefebvre, *Production of Space*, 128.
12   Ibid., 31, 46, 412.

difficult to understand.[13] It is, therefore, necessary to pay attention to both continuities as well as ruptures in the historical development and to analyse them accordingly.

However, the relation between the mode of production and the production of space is anything but clearly and unambiguously determinable. Lefebvre wants to show that the production of space is inherent in the modes of production, and that these are defined not only by class relations or by ideologies and forms of knowledge and culture, but also by the specific form of the production of space itself. Every mode of production 'has' its respective space. However, the characteristics of space cannot be traced back to the general characteristics of the mode of production, because space is based on political, social, and economic conditions, but cannot be reduced to these conditions.[14]

As Lefebvre notes, the history of space periodises the productive process in a way that 'does not exactly' correspond to the usual periodisations. While he continues to propose a classification of spaces that corresponds approximately to the sequence of modes of production according to Marx, he emphasises that this sequence as well as the characteristics of each mode of production can by no means be considered as evident and established.[15] Thus Lefebvre redefines the concept of the mode of production in a certain way: he treats it – without specifically naming it as such – as a mode of production of space.

> It is not the work of a day for a society to generate (produce) an appropriated social space in which it forms, presents and represents itself – a social space which is not identical with this society, and which indeed is its tomb and its cradle. This act of creation is, in fact, a *process*.[16]

Nature and the Production of Space

Lefebvre's history of the production of space begins with the 'space of nature' (*espace-nature*) – that is, space as it existed before humans entered history.

Lefebvre begins by immediately addressing a fundamental problem: what is nature? As he concedes, his understanding of 'nature' differs substantially from that of Marx. For Marx, the mastery of material nature was immediately

---

13   Lefebvre, *Urban Revolution*, 24.

14   Lefebvre, *Production of Space*, 46; Lefebvre, *De l'État*, vol. 4, 291, 296; Lefebvre, *State, Space, World*, 234, 236.

15   Lefebvre, *Production of Space*, 48; Lefebvre, *De l'État*, vol. 4, 291; Lefebvre, *State, Space, World*, 234.

16   Lefebvre, *Production of Space*, 34. Translation amended.

accomplished with its appropriation, which transforms material nature into human reality according to the desires and needs of human beings – including their own nature, their bodies, their needs, and desires. For Lefebvre, this idea is an optimistic hypothesis, an expression of the industrial rationalism of the nineteenth century. In the second half of the twentieth century, he insists, this hypothesis became untenable: the idea that the power of humans over nature combined technical domination with an aesthetic and ethical project broke down.[17]

Accordingly, Lefebvre sees a crucial implication of his initial thesis that (social) space is a (social) product in the fact that the space of nature irrecoverably disappears.[18]

> The fact is that natural space will soon be lost to view. Anyone so inclined may look over their shoulder and see it sinking below the horizon behind us. Nature is also becoming lost to *thought*. For what is nature? How can we form a picture of it as it was before the intervention of humans with their ravaging tools? Even the powerful myth of nature is being transformed into a mere fiction, a negative utopia: nature is now seen as merely the raw material out of which the productive forces of a variety of social systems have forged their particular spaces. True, nature is resistant, and infinite in its depth, but it has been defeated, and now waits only for its ultimate voidance and destruction.[19]

Nature is thus nothing other than the raw material for the production of space, a raw material that is transformed into a product, consumed, and destroyed by this production process itself: this is Lefebvre's central thesis on the history of space, a thesis that he advances again and again.[20]

Still, the space of nature remains the starting point common to all social spaces: the origin and the primordial of the social process. Every social space thus has a history that starts from nature, a primal and original condition that is always and everywhere endowed with particularities. But the space of nature does not disappear from the scene entirely. It remains the background of the painting and is therefore more than mere decoration. Every detail, every object of nature, is exploited by being turned into a symbol. In the process of social transformation, however, this space loses everything 'natural' about it. For when a society transforms, the materials for its transformation come from a

---

17   Lefebvre, *Survival of Capitalism*, 15.
18   Lefebvre, *Production of Space*, 30.
19   Ibid., 31.
20   Ibid., 84, 123, 128, 334.

social practice that pre-existed the transformation historically. The natural, the original in its pure state, is therefore never found again.[21] Does a 'nature park', for example, belong to the realm of the natural or to that of the artificial? Lefebvre thinks one could be uncertain. 'Nature', once predominant, becomes blurred and subordinate, while, conversely, the social character of space and the social relations it implies, contains, and veils, begin to assert themselves.[22] Ultimately, 'nature' can no longer be grasped – it escapes the commanding influence of rational action, of domination as well as appropriation. In *The Right to the City* Lefebvre asserts:

> Nature as such escapes the hold of rationally pursued action, as well as from domination and appropriation. More precisely, it remains outside of these influences: it 'is' what it flees: it is reached by the imaginary; one pursues it and it flees into the cosmos, or in the underground depths of the world.[23]

Later, in *The Production of Space*, he adds:

> It is becoming impossible to escape the notion that nature is being murdered by 'anti-nature' – by abstraction, by signs and images, by discourse, as also by labour and its products. Along with God, nature is dying. 'Humanity' is killing both of them – and perhaps committing suicide into the bargain.[24]

When God dies, so does nature. And thus we again find Nietzsche's phrase, which, for Lefebvre, has not lost any of its relevance (see section 2.4) and which will accompany us on the following journey through the history of spaces: a journey from nature to abstraction.[25]

From Nature to Second Nature

The history of space is a history of socially produced abstraction, from the space of nature to abstract space and beyond. Nature disappears in the course of this process, but not without being transformed into something

---

21 Ibid., 30, 110, 190.
22 Ibid., 83.
23 Lefebvre, *Right to the City*, 118.
24 Lefebvre, *Production of Space*, 71.
25 Ibid., 110.

new. For, dialectically speaking, the end of nature means nothing more than the creation of a new 'second nature'.[26] Thus the history of space includes not only the destruction of nature in the process of social abstraction, but also a movement from nature to 'second nature', an acquired and artificial nature.

Lefebvre conceives of this second nature as a social space, and as a social time. They are the results of social action upon 'first nature', the sensually perceptible conditions, matter, and energies. In this process, the produced space detaches itself from the space of nature and is transformed into a second nature based on productive social capabilities.[27] Nature, understood as the sum of particulars scattered in space and external to one another, disappears. But at the same time it is re-created, as second nature, as a produced space containing specific new qualities: gathering and encounter, the simultaneity of all that exists socially. This second nature, this produced space, is, for Lefebvre, therefore nothing less than the urban reality itself, the city as anti-nature or non-nature.[28]

With this line of reasoning, Lefebvre closes the circle: through the production of space and the creation of a second nature, he finds the urban society at a higher level, and with it a new definition of urbanisation as the production of a second, urban nature. The history of the production of space is thus nothing other than the history of urbanisation. This results in a doubling of the thesis of complete urbanisation (see section 3.2): as society urbanises, it creates a second nature, a social space and a social time. Finally, these formulations evoke striking parallels to Marx's classical figure of humans' self-creation from nature (discussed in section 2.2): humans, as social beings, create a second nature for themselves – second nature, produced space, urban reality.

These considerations outline the general argument of the following history of space: it leads from nature to abstraction, from space of nature to urban space. Like the history of urban society (see section 4.4), this history is conceived as a trilogy. It begins with 'absolute space', the space of the political city, and eventually leads, via 'abstract space', the space of industrial society, to urban 'differential space'.

---

26   Ibid., 409.
27   Ibid., 229, 330.
28   Lefebvre, *Survival of Capitalism*, 15; Lefebvre, *Production of Space*, 229, 368.

6.2 Absolute Space

> Absolute space was made up of fragments of nature located at sites
> which were chosen for their intrinsic qualities (cave, mountaintop,
> spring, river), but whose very consecration ended up by stripping them
> of their natural characteristics and uniqueness. Thus natural space was
> soon populated by political forces. Typically, architecture picked a site
> in nature and transferred it to the political realm by means of a
> symbolic mediation.[29]

Absolute space is first and foremost a religious-political space. It is charged with meanings that are directed not to the intellect but to the body, meanings that are experienced again and again through sanctions and emotions. This space is lived and not conceived; it is a space of representation rather than a representation of space. As soon as it is conceived, its magic weakens and finally disappears.[30]

Absolute space consists of sacred or damned places that are accentuated and marked, a monument, for example, or even a stone or a cave. The 'absolute' character of a space can be ritually connected to any place; it only needs a marking to identify it as such. Thus, this space generates forms and inserts into forms that summarise the universe: the square (mandala), the circle or sphere, the triangle, the cross – a rational volume occupied by a divine principle. In the ancient Greek version, absolute space can also be empty, like the opisthodomos of the Greek temple, the secret dwelling place of the divine – and of thought.[31]

The history of space that Lefebvre lays out follows the traces of this absolute space in Europe according to the classical sequence of modes of production: the analogue or anthropological space of the 'original' societies, the cosmological space of antiquity, the symbolic space of the European Middle Ages up to the perspectival space of the Renaissance. Lefebvre identifies a social process of abstraction in this sequence where the absolute character of space, the 'original' unity of the lived and the conceived, is increasingly pushed into the background or 'underground'. Lefebvre's history of Western space is thus above all a history of abstraction and thus also of alienation. It finally flows into the modern, abstract space of the twentieth century.

---

29 Lefebvre, *Production of Space*, 48.
30 Ibid., 48, 235–6.
31 Ibid., 237, 240.

Analogue Space

In the beginning was the Topos. Before – long before – the advent of the
Logos, in the chiaroscuro realm of primitive life, lived experience already
possessed its internal rationality; this experience was producing long
before thought space, and spatial thought, began reproducing the projection, explosion, image and orientation of the body. Long before space, as
perceived by and for the 'I', began to appear as split and divided, as a
realm of merely virtual or deferred tensions and contacts. Long before
space emerged as a medium of far-off possibilities, as the locus of potentiality. For, long before the analysing, separating intellect, long before
formal knowledge, there was an intelligence of the body.[32]

The starting point of absolute space is the 'analogue space',[33] or the 'anthropological space':[34] hunters, shepherds, and nomads are the first to mark and identify sites, which then enter into memory and are interpreted symbolically.
Social and mental activity casts its net over the space of nature, over the stream
and chaos of spontaneous phenomena. Practical activity and thus social space
inscribe themselves on nature like writing on a piece of scrap paper. This
implies a representation of space: the ability to recognise and name places.
Thus, a given space is subjected to definition, orientation, and hierarchy. The
original places (*topoi*) are directly present in nature. The peculiarities of the soil
(material nature, flora and fauna, the course of roads, and so forth) offer landmarks and field names and thus enter into the social and mental double grid of
word and practice. Between the places and networks of paths there are blank
patches, edges. Values are assigned to the paths: danger, safety, hope,
promise.[35]

For these societies, the social relationship of the body to space had an immediacy that was later lost. The way in which people measured and talked about
space conveyed to them a living image, a mirror of their bodies. This can be
seen, for example, in the units of measurement of space borrowed from the
body parts: foot, thumb (inch), arm (cubit), and so on. In this way, the body
was inserted into space.[36] The (only very slow and incomplete) introduction
of the abstract generality of the decimal system meant a revolution. It changed
the measure and thus the representation of space, and it was accompanied by a

---

32   Ibid., 174.
33   Lefebvre, *De l'État*, vol. 4, 283–4; Lefebvre, *State, Space, World*, 230.
34   Lefebvre, *Production of Space*, 192.
35   Ibid., 117–18; Lefebvre, *Urban Revolution*, 26, 117.
36   Lefebvre, *Production of Space*, 110.

tendency towards the quantitative, homogeneous, and thus also the disappearance of the body, which finally sought refuge in art.[37]

Cosmological Space

Cosmological space is connected with the ancient mode of production. In its Greek version it embodied a simple principle: unity. Referring to Viollet-le-Duc, Lefebvre sees in Greek architecture a unity of form, function, and structure.[38] The external appearance and the internal composition of the buildings cannot be distinguished from one another. The Greek space therefore has a strict form: the well-proportioned volumes testify to a coherent stability, the rational unity of Logos and cosmos.[39] 'Volume perceived and conceived, clarified by the light of the sun as by the light of understanding, is the Cosmos in epitome. This, whether that volume is vacant or occupied by thought.'[40] The polis, as a social as well as spatial hierarchy, integrates the different parts of urban society in its well-defined space, which is at once an end and a means, knowledge and action, natural and political. At the centre is the agora: it is empty so that citizens can gather here. At the top of the acropolis is the temple: it is an image – of nothing.[41]

The Roman space breaks with this Greek space. It is filled with objects and monuments, as the forum exemplifies. The form detaches itself from the structure, becomes a decorative element that corresponds to the function to be fulfilled. Rome, *urbs et orbis*, is represented as *imago mundi*, as an image of the world. The city gathers and concentrates that which is scattered around it and with which it is connected by the Roman streets. Embedded in nature in a well-defined location, it evokes a representation of space that does not refer to a specific space, but to the whole space, the world. Analogously, the pantheon, as a space of representation, symbolises not only the adoption of the gods of another people but also their space, thus conveying an understanding not only of the defeated gods but also of the spaces subordinated to the world empire. In contrast, Lefebvre also recognises spaces of representation determined by the female principle, which are not denied but integrated: spaces sunk into the earth, spaces of fertility and death.[42]

---

37   Ibid., 110–11.
38   Viollet-le-Duc, *Discourses on Architecture*.
39   Lefebvre, *Production of Space*, 238–9.
40   Ibid., 237.
41   Ibid., 237, 249–50.
42   Ibid., 111, 237–8, 243–4, 245.

Symbolic Space

With the medieval town a new symbolic space is created, which is filled with religious symbols. Lefebvre situates the transition from cosmological to symbolic space in the transition from Romanesque to Gothic.[43]

The *imago mundi* had survived, through the entire decline of the Roman Empire, to this point in time, a space representing an image of the world. Lefebvre sees this space realised in an exemplary manner in the underground religious spaces of the crypts. They contained wonderful paintings, which were not visible except when they were lit by candles on particular occasions. These paintings were not made to be seen, but to be *known* to exist:

> Cryptal art of this kind has nothing visual about it, and for those who think in the categories of a later time, projecting them into the past, it poses an insoluble problem. How can a painting remain out of sight? ... The answer is that these paintings were made not to be seen, but merely to 'be' – and so that they might be known to 'be' there. They are magical images, condensing subterranean qualities, signs of death and traces of the struggle against death, whose aim is to turn death's forces against death itself.[44]

In the twelfth century, this cosmological, political-religious space is shaken fundamentally. Lefebvre sees the Gothic cathedral as a shining example of this upheaval, which he interprets as an emancipation from the crypt and the cryptic space.[45] In reference to art historian Erwin Panofsky, Lefebvre sees these monuments as the realisation of a 'visual logic'.[46] In his analysis of Gothic cathedrals, Panofsky had shown that the introduction of new constructive elements, such as pointed arches or buttresses, could not be explained in terms of function alone, nor could it be explained solely by the desire to create a particular illusion. He saw them rather as a kind of manifestation or explanation, as a self-explanation and self-analysis of architecture, and in this sense as an expression of a 'visual logic': the classical cathedral sought to embody the totality of Christian, theological, scientific, and historical knowledge by putting everything in its place and leaving out what had not yet found its place. The scholastic spirit demands a maximum of explanation. It permits and demands a clarification of function through form as well as of thinking through

---

43   Lefebvre, *De l'État*, vol. 4, 284–5; Lefebvre, *State, Space, World*, 231.
44   Lefebvre, *Production of Space*, 254.
45   Ibid., 256.
46   See Panofsky, *Gothic Architecture and Scholasticism*, 58.

language.[47] As Lefebvre notes, Panofsky thus postulates a homology (not just an analogy) between philosophy and architecture.[48]

For Lefebvre, however, Panofsky did not follow this reasoning to its logical consequence. The visual logic contains the instruction that everything must be revealed. That which rises with it from the realm of shadows goes far beyond Gothic architecture and extends to the city, to political action, poetry, music, thinking. It is, in particular, a rebellion of the body. Thought and philosophy rise from the depths to the surface, but what emerges here is nothing more than a new space in Lefebvre's analysis: not a new place of the mind, an ideal or ideal space, but a new mental and social space.[49]

Lefebvre ascribes a central role in the production of this new space to the emergent cities. The new urban landscape reverses the former space: it rises up, emphasising the vertical. Against the ominous utopia of the underground world, it proclaims a confident and luminous utopia. Knowledge no longer serves an oppressive power but contributes to the strengthening of a reasonable power.[50] For Lefebvre, however, visual logic also has a threatening quality: visualisation comes to the fore, and abstraction, geometry, and logic enter a relationship with power.[51]

> The prestigious Phallus, symbol of power and fecundity, forces its way into view by becoming erect. In the space to come, where the eye would usurp so many privileges, it would fall to the Phallus to receive or produce them. The eye in question would be that of God, that of the Father or that of the Leader. A space in which this eye laid hold of whatever served its purposes would also be a space of force, of violence, of power restrained by nothing but the limitations of its means. This was to be the space of the triune God, the space of kings, no longer the space of cryptic signs but rather the space of the written word and the rule of history. The space, too, of military violence – and hence a *masculine* space.[52]

For Lefebvre, this secularised space, which appeared and spread in Western Europe in the twelfth century, represents the very cradle of accumulation and capitalism.[53] It is this space that becomes the arena of class struggle of the

---

47   Ibid., 103, 111–13.
48   Lefebvre, *Production of Space*, 258.
49   Ibid., 259–60.
50   Ibid., 256.
51   Ibid., 261.
52   Ibid., 262.
53   Ibid., 263.

urban bourgeoisie against the landed gentry.[54] Once again, Lefebvre argues in an original and daring way. As he notes, capital accumulation – that is, the productive reinvestment of capital as a cumulative process – is based on a number of preconditions, including scientific thought and technical knowledge, the growth of agricultural production, the commodity and money economy, and the existence of cities. These are preconditions that had already been realised in various societies but had taken particularly clear shape in Western antiquity. Why, Lefebvre asks himself, did the process of accumulation not begin until the European Middle Ages? Which preconditions had been missing before? Various answers have already been given to these questions, but they do not satisfy Lefebvre. As a consequence of these considerations, he now proposes a new answer: it was symbolic space that appeared and gradually spread in the twelfth century that made this accumulation process possible.[55]

Lefebvre understands this transition in the twelfth century primarily as a metamorphosis, as a shift, as the overthrow of the signifiers. What previously signified the forbidden in an immediate manner now refers only to itself as signifier and has lost its affective or magical signified. The medieval space has thus been not only deciphered but also emptied: social practice, without knowing where it was going, made space available for something else. This simultaneously spiritual and material, intellectual and sensory space, which had lost its sacral character and was filled with the signs of the body, thus became a place of accumulation of knowledge and then of riches. The cradle of accumulation was not so much the city as a community of citizens (as Max Weber emphasised; see section 1.1) but rather the marketplace or market hall.[56]

Lefebvre emphasises the novelty of the marketplace with its splendour of political and religious buildings. In ancient times, trade and merchants were something external to the city, alien to the political constitution, and were banished to the periphery. The basis of wealth remained land ownership and agriculture (see also the analysis of Marx and Engels in section 3.2). It was only the medieval revolution that brought trade into the city and installed it in the centre of the transformed urban space. In contrast to the agora or forum, access to the marketplace was free, and it opened up to the surrounding area, which was dominated and exploited by the city.[57]

This interpretation shows how the historical analysis itself generates new elements of theory. The marketplace becomes the new centre of the medieval

---

54   Lefebvre, De l'État, vol. 4, 285; Lefebvre, State, Space, World, 231.
55   Lefebvre, Production of Space, 262–3.
56   Ibid., 264.
57   Ibid., 265.

city, and this means that exchange becomes the dominant process in this society. In *De l'État*, Lefebvre develops this analysis further and shows that the act of exchange forms the foundation of capitalism, and that the place of exchange becomes the basis of the state, which intervenes to create and enforce appropriate regulations (see section 7.4).

Perspectival Space

The dissolution of feudalism and the rise of commercial capitalism engendered the city of the Renaissance and with it a new space: perspectival space, a homogeneous, clearly defined space with a horizon and a vanishing point.[58] In Lefebvre's analysis, perspective was not conceived and invented by the artists, as is suggested by many historians and art historians, but was produced by a spatial practice: the practice of the system of *métayage* (French) or *mezzadria* (Italian), which was introduced in Tuscany from the thirteenth century onwards. Under this system, an urban oligarchy of merchants and citizens bought land from feudal lords, replacing serfs with *métayers* or *mezzadri*, sharecroppers who had to cede part of the agricultural product they produced to the landowner.[59] This gave rise to a new social reality that was based on neither the city nor the country alone, but rather on their dialectical relationship in space. Thus, the bourgeoisie transformed the country and the landscape according to a preconceived plan, a model: the houses of the *métayers* were grouped around the palace where its owner occasionally stayed. Houses and palace were connected by avenues of cypresses:

> Symbol of property, immortality and perpetuity, the cypress thus inscribed itself upon the countryside, imbuing it with depth and meaning. These trees, the criss-crossing of these alleys, sectioned and organized the land. Their arrangement was evocative of the laws of perspective, whose fullest realization was simultaneously appearing in the shape of the urban piazza in its architectural setting. Town and country – and the relationship between them – had given birth to a space which it would fall to the painters, and first among them in Italy to the Siena school, to identify, formulate and develop.[60]

---

58 Ibid., 47, 79.
59 Ibid., 78–9; Lefebvre, *De l'État*, vol. 4, 286; Lefebvre, *State, Space, World*, 231.
60 Lefebvre, *Production of Space*, 78.

For Lefebvre, this example does not only show the material production of new social forms and relations, or the social production of material conditions. It also shows, specifically, that the new social forms do not only inscribe themselves into an already existing space, but that they produce a new space that is neither urban nor rural, but the result of the new relationship between city and country. This space corresponds to the middle on the space-time axis of urbanisation (see section 3.3).

Lefebvre sees the growth of the productive forces as the cause and base for this transformation, represented by certain social groups such as the urban oligarchy and parts of the peasantry. This led, in turn, to an increase in surplus products and thus wealth. Finally, the construction of new palaces and monuments allowed artists to express in their own way what they recognised: they discovered and theorised perspective because they were offered a perspectival space that had already been produced. At the end of this process, a new representation of space emerged: the visual perspective that appeared in the works of the artists and was designed by architects and later geometers. Thus, this specific knowledge came from a practice and was then elaborated, formalised, and connected with logical principles.[61]

Tuscan painters, architects, and theorists, starting from a social practice, used perspective to elaborate a representation of space which ultimately subordinated the extant spaces of representation and reduced them to symbolic representations of heaven and hell, of devils and angels. Perspective thus also marks the transition from a space of representation to a representation of space: the line of the horizon, the vanishing point, and the meeting of parallels in infinity defined a representation that was both intellectual and visual at the same time, further reinforcing the primacy of the gaze and the 'logic of visualisation' that were already emerging in the Gothic period.[62]

In this way, a common language, a consensus, a code, was created in the Western city in which the perceived, the conceived, and the lived formed a coherent whole. The establishment of this code, which lasted from the Italian Renaissance to the nineteenth century, meant that the inhabitants, as well as the architects and the politicians, stopped trying to get from the 'urban messages' to the code by deciphering reality. Instead, they took the opposite path from the code to the messages by producing a corresponding reality and discourse. This code defined the alphabet and language of the city, the elementary signs, their paradigms and syntagmatic connections. The facades were arranged to determine the perspectives. The entrances and windows were subordinated to the facades and perspectives; the streets and squares were arranged around the

---

61   Ibid., 79; Lefebvre, *De l'État*, vol. 4, 287; Lefebvre, *State, Space, World*, 232.
62   Lefebvre, *Production of Space*, 40–1, 119.

important buildings. According to their differing significance, the elements of this space, from the apartment to the monument, were arranged in a way that did not lose its charm until the end of the twentieth century. The code of this perspectival space made it possible to live in it, to understand it, and to produce it.[63]

How Is a New Space Produced?

I have presented these examples here in such detail because they exemplify Lefebvre's theoretical approach and style of argumentation. He looks at historical development from the perspective of the production of space, and thus often comes to explanations other than the 'usual' ones. He follows the production of space starting from the space of nature, and he analyses the relation between the conceived and the lived, their intimate entanglement and their slow separation throughout the history of the West, through the logic of visualisation in the Gothic period, the introduction of the marketplace and of capitalism in the cities, to the production of perspectival space and, it must be added, the radical separation of body and mind in philosophy, especially in Descartes's conception of space (see section 5.1).

These examples also impressively demonstrate Lefebvre's application of his regressive–progressive method, which he applies in his search for the 'origin' or the beginning of a given process, following a 'descending' line, in order to then reconstruct its historical development in an ascending movement (see section 3.1). They also illustrate the dual approach of genealogical and genetic analysis: with the genealogical analysis, Lefebvre identifies individual periods or modes of the production of space with their random events and contingencies. He then uses genetic analysis to reveal an overarching tendency, like the general process of abstraction and the unfolding of capitalism.

In this way, Lefebvre succeeds in analysing the history of the production of space, and thus in finding a different history and different determinants and explanations to those that were put forward in Marxist orthodoxy. This is particularly evident in the example of perspective, which he claims was developed from an already materially produced space and thus finds a 'true' historical-materialist explanation for developments in art. Lefebvre had himself examined the system of *métayage* or *mezzadria* in detail in the French Pyrenees in the 1950s, and then encountered it again during a visit to Tuscany.[64] It can serve as a prime example for his regressive–progressive method. In order to explore the

---

63 Ibid., 40–1, 47–8; Lefebvre, *De l'État*, vol. 4, 288; Lefebvre, *State, Space, World*, 232.
64 See Stanek, *Henri Lefebvre on Space*, 57–8.

origin (genealogy) of this system, he descended into the thirteenth century, detected a 'new' space, perspectival space, and then ascended again to reconstruct the history (genesis) of this space. As beautiful as this example of the 'discovery' of the perspective appears, it must be noted that the historical facts do not correspond to the course of this history. Brunelleschi painted his famous panels, which for the first time were based on a detailed and constructed central perspective, in 1410. Although the system of *mezzadria* in Tuscany originated in the thirteenth century, the specific architectural ensemble described by Lefebvre, consisting of a palazzo, the *casa da padrone* in the middle, and the houses of the sharecroppers, the *case da lavoratore*, arranged in a perspectival manner, was actually introduced in the sixteenth century.[65] Moreover, perspective did not originate in Tuscany alone. It was developed in a long process in various Italian cities in an active mutual exchange.

This example thus also shows the fundamental problem of a historical analysis of the production of space: what processes lead to the production of a 'new' space, and what role do the dialectically linked moments of the perceived, the conceived, and the lived play in this? In his 1981 foreword to the third edition of *La production de l'espace*, Lefebvre returns to this point, since he himself seems to have had doubts about his story. He states that the processes involved in the production of space are far away from the simplicity of a causal concatenation and asks what really happened in the invention of the perspective:

Was this new space conceived, engendered, produced by and for princes? For rich merchants? By a compromise? Or by the city as such? Several points are still unclear. The history of space (like that of social time) is far from exhausted![66]

6.3 Abstract Space

King Logos is guarded on the one hand by the Eye – the eye of God, of the Father, of the Master or Boss – which answers to the primacy of the visual realm with its images and its graphic dimension, and on the other hand by the phallic (military and heroic) principle, which belongs, as one of its chief properties, to abstract space.[67]

---

65   Lazzaro, 'Rustic Country House to Refined Farmhouse'; Stopani, '*Case da padrone*'; Lasansky, *Hidden Histories*.

66   Lefebvre, 'Preface to the New Edition', 210.

67   Lefebvre, *Production of Space*, 408.

As the previous chapter has shown, Lefebvre argues that since the Renaissance and the Renaissance city, from the sixteenth to the nineteenth centuries, there had existed an architectonic, urbanistic, and political code, a language based on classical perspective and Euclidean space, a language common to the inhabitants of the country as well as the cities, to authorities as well as artists. This code made it possible not only to 'read' a space, but also to produce it.[68] At the beginning of the twentieth century, however, a fundamental process of dissolution began.

The starting point for this new space was an event which, although unnoticed, was of central importance for Lefebvre:

> Around 1910 a certain space was shattered. It was the space of common sense, of knowledge (*savoir*), of social practice, of political power, a space thitherto enshrined in everyday discourse, just as in abstract thought, as the environment of and channel for communications; the space, too, of classical perspective and geometry, developed from the Renaissance onwards on the basis of the Greek tradition (Euclid, logic) and bodied forth in Western art and philosophy, as in the form of the city and town.[69]

Space in the usual sense of the word, as well as the codes that refer to space, was shaken and left as mere rubble: words, images, metaphors.[70]

Thus, a new space emerged: abstract space, simultaneously homogeneous and fractured. This is the space of the commodity and its overarching logic, and it is also the space whose cohesion is essentially determined by the state. At the same time, however, it is a fractured space divided into plots and influenced by a multitude of individual actors via the real estate market. This raises a number of additional questions related to the commodification of space and the role and functioning of the state, which will be treated in more detail in chapter 7.

This section, by contrast, examines the three-dimensionality of the production of space and shows how Lefebvre himself applies his categories. This analysis therefore follows the three constituent formants of abstract space. Lefebvre sees spatial practice as dominated by the visual, while the representation of this space is based on geometric homogeneity, and the spaces of representation are characterised by the phallic.[71] The geometric and

---

68 Ibid., 7, 17.
69 Ibid., 25.
70 Ibid.
71 Ibid., 288.

the visual complement each other in their contrariness, by aiming at the same effect in different ways – the reduction of the 'real'. On the one hand there is the map, which is situated in a void without other qualities, and on the other hand is the flattening of the mirror, the image, and the spectacle under a pure, icy gaze. The phallic joins in so that there is 'something' in this empty space, a signifier, whose signified is not emptiness but fullness, the fullness of a destructive force, and thus an illusion: the filling up by an object that is the bearer of myths.[72]

The Year 1910

The year 1910 is an almost mythical year for Lefebvre, which he evokes again and again in his texts.[73] This year marks for him a decisive turning point in the history of modern society and its space. What is so decisive about this year? In his afterword to *The Production of Space*, David Harvey links it to the eve of the First World War, the Russian Revolution, and a maelstrom of intellectual change.[74] But Lefebvre himself does not refer to these events. He refers to the collapse of reference systems (*référentiels*), and the challenge to the tonal system in music and to perspective in art and architecture. The breakthrough of the theory of relativity in physics led to the disappearance of the homogeneous Euclidean space and the absolute space of Newton. The historical city breaks apart, the family begins to dissolve, and the 'subject' of philosophy disappears: 'God is dead, and man, and even the devil; the "subject" defined by philosophy in the name of all individuals gets clouded.'[75]

Lefebvre detected the key to this new space in a painting. In Picasso's epochal painting *Les Demoiselles d'Avignon* from 1907, he sees the objectified end of the referential, of perspective, of the horizon line – and finds a new space, a space that is at once homogeneous and fractured.[76] It was in this painting that Picasso announced abstract space, the space of modernity. It is a space visualised to the last, subject to the dictatorship of the eye and the phallus. 'Picasso's cruelty toward the body, particularly the female body, which he tortures in a

---

72   Ibid., 287.

73   For example, ibid., 25, 30; Lefebvre, *Metaphilosophy*, 11, 129; Lefebvre, *Everyday Life in the Modern World*, 158–9; Lefebvre, *Right to the City*, 98–9; Lefebvre, *Le langage et la société*, 81; Lefebvre, *De l'État*, vol. 4, 285; Lefebvre, *State, Space, World*, 231.

74   Harvey, afterword to Lefebvre, *Production of Space*, 425.

75   Lefebvre, *La présence et l'absence*, 156. Translation by author; see also Lefebvre, *Critique of Everyday Life*, vol. 3, 146.

76   Lefebvre, *Production of Space*, 301.

thousand ways and caricatures without mercy, is dictated by the dominant form of space, by the eye and by the phallus – in short – by violence.[77]

Along with other modern painters such as Klee or Kandinsky, Picasso introduced not only a new way of painting but also a new, abstract 'spatiality': the object painted on the picture can be recognised in a legible and visible connection with what surrounds it, with the entire space of the image. The space detaches itself from the subject, from the emotional and expressive dimensions, and presents *itself* as significant.[78] Lefebvre emphasises, however, that these artists did not invent or even produce abstract space – but rather announced it. The appearance of this abstract space cannot be dated for Lefebvre. It is not specific events or institutions that put it into form. As Lefebvre remarks laconically: at the end of the twentieth century this space is 'here'.[79]

Homogeneous-Fractured Space

Why and how did a code that had been valid since the Renaissance shatter? And what are the characteristics of this new, abstract space? First of all, it should be noted that abstract space, for Lefebvre, is not the result of an ideology or a false consciousness, but of a practice: this space is a milieu of exchange, implying interchangeability, which tends to absorb use. It is in abstract space that the world of the commodity unfolds. It is a space of accumulation, calculation, planning, programming, and it is a space that is dominated – due to the worldwide reach of productive forces and scientific knowledge – by a tendency towards homogenisation (see also section 7.2).[80]

But this space is also fractured: by administrative divisions, by specialised techniques, by the sciences, which cut up and dissect space, with each discipline constituting its own space. In particular, however, space is 'pulverised' by the real estate market. Space, transformed into a commodity, is divided into plots, sold and bought.[81] Accordingly, Lefebvre calls this space 'homogeneous-fractured' (*homogène-brisé*) to emphasise its contradictory unity. Abstract space is at once homogeneous and fractured, all-encompassing and piecemeal. As a homogeneous space, it abolishes distinctions and differences, including those between inside and outside, and reduces them to the indifference of the visible and legible.

---

77   Ibid., 302.
78   Ibid., 304; Lefebvre, *De l'État*, vol. 4, 285–6; Lefebvre, *State, Space, World*, 231.
79   Lefebvre, *Production of Space*, 290, 302.
80   Ibid., 308, 393; Lefebvre, *Survival of Capitalism*, 17.
81   Lefebvre, *Production of Space*, 334–5, 355; Lefebvre, *Survival of Capitalism*, 21; Lefebvre, *De l'État*, vol. 4, 290–1; Lefebvre, *State, Space, World*, 233.

At the same time, the same space is crumbled, splintered, fractured. Parcelled out and sold in individual pieces, it becomes, on a practical level, a milieu of segregation; it disperses the elements of society, which is most evident in dwelling (see section 4.3). This homogenising space is to a certain extent polyscopic, forcing the most diverse fragments and elements into a unity. In this way, abstract space combines incoherence with coherence, separation with cohesion, flows and the transitory with the permanent, and conflictive social relations with an apparent logic.[82]

This fundamental contradiction is particularly evident at the strategic level. On the one hand, states and supranational corporations have the ability to pursue general strategic goals and to conceive and organise space on a planetary scale. On the other hand, their resources (production facilities, households) are always localised. This abstract space thus impinges on the lowest level, the local and localisable, the everyday, dwelling. But, at the same time, abstract space rests upon this lower level – it is the foundation of abstract space.[83]

For Lefebvre, however, it would be wrong to construct a hierarchy between two poles, with an *intended* unity of political power on the one hand and an *actual* dispersion of its elements on the other. The fragmentation of space is dominated by strategic intentions of the state and of private powers, who keep space in this paradoxical state of being connected and at the same time separated. The dispersed and fractional thus preserve a unity in the homogeneous: the space of power.[84]

These theoretical reflections relate directly to the concept of 'levels of social reality' that Lefebvre developed in *The Right to the City* and *The Urban Revolution* (see section 4.3). It is interesting and revealing to see how he develops the same idea in *The Production of Space* from a different angle. This doubling of the perspective allows us to better understand Lefebvre's theoretical construction: on the one hand, he looks from the general perspective of the production of space, identifies the historical space-time *configuration* of abstract space, and defines its specific properties; on the other hand, he looks at the *levels* of social reality and analyses the 'modes of operation' of abstract space on the general, the private, and the urban levels. These thoughts will be taken up in much more detail in section 8.2. In the following, the production of this abstract, homogeneous-fractured space will be analysed in more detail.

---

82   Lefebvre, *Production of Space*, 308–9, 334–5, 354–5.

83   Ibid., 355, 366; Lefebvre, *De l'État*, vol. 4, 290–1; Lefebvre, *State, Space, World*, 233–4.

84   Lefebvre, *Production of Space*, 365–6.

The Geometric Formant

I begin the analysis of abstract space, like Lefebvre himself, with the 'geometric formant' and thus with the representation of space.[85] The instrumental, homogeneous or rather homogenising characteristic of abstract space can best be represented in mathematics, logic, and strategy. It implies an ideology: the primacy of abstract unity.[86] The base of this representation is Euclidean space, which has long been regarded by philosophy as 'absolute'. Lefebvre sees this space as the privileged instrument for the reduction of space. It serves to reduce three-dimensional space to two dimensions and thus forms the base for blue-prints, maps, graphic illustrations, and projections.[87]

Abstract space is based on a theory of rationality and organisation, which Lefebvre – once again – dates to around 1910. This theory marked the beginning of a deep social crisis and also of attempts to solve this crisis, initially with organisational methods at the level of the company, and later on the general (national) level.[88] It is easy to identify two concepts in this description that were developed by the French Regulation school shortly after the publication of Lefebvre's work: Taylorism and Fordism. If Taylorism is characterised by the introduction of scientific methods of organisation into the production process at the company level, Fordism brought the extension of these methods of organisation to the nation-state level, with the Keynesian welfare state playing a key role in the process.[89]

Lefebvre attributes the introduction of these organisational methods into architecture and urban design and the development of a unitary conception (*conception unitaire*) of space to the famous Bauhaus school in Germany. Its members had understood that things in space, such as furniture and houses, form an entity and could not be produced without taking into account their relations to one another. They could not simply be put together like a collection of objects.[90] As he did with the introduction of perspective, Lefebvre also situates this 'discovery' in a concrete historical practice: around 1920, in the advanced industrial nations, a practical connection had already been established between industrialisation and urbanisation, between home and workplace. In Lefebvre's understanding, modern architecture developed this connection into a project and even a programme. Although this 'programme'

---

85   Ibid., 285–91.
86   Ibid., 355.
87   Ibid., 285.
88   Lefebvre, *Right to the City*, 98–9.
89   See for example Aglietta, *A Theory of Capitalist Regulation*.
90   Lefebvre, *Production of Space*, 124.

was considered both rational and revolutionary, the state, Lefebvre argues, had found no difficulty in making use of it.[91] For Lefebvre, then, the establishment of abstract space is closely linked to the state, which uses the production of space as a privileged means to impose its rationality. One of its central functions is to organise space, to regulate the flow of goods and people, and to control networks, for which it uses a significant amount of surplus value. Abstract space thus appears first and foremost as the space of a state bureaucratic order that is realised 'on the ground' and at the same time disappears in the transparent air of functional and structural 'legibility' – an order, therefore, that Lefebvre sees realised in both state capitalism and state socialism.[92] To his great disappointment, urban developments in the Soviet Union, in the so-called socialist countries, as well as in China and Cuba, did not differ in any significant way from those in capitalist countries. Their urbanistic projects, he argued, followed a clear anti-urban line.[93]

For Lefebvre, the most important instrument of the state for programming space besides national planning is '*urbanisme*'. This term is misleading, because 'urbanism' in English generally means an approach that deals with the city and urbanisation. In a narrower sense it can also mean a certain way of life, as in Louis Wirth's famous essay.[94] In French, in contrast, the term *urbanisme* denotes an academic discipline and a practice that roughly coincides with urban design and urban planning. Lefebvre takes this term more broadly – and also more polemically – and defines it as an activity that seeks to subject urbanisation and urban practice to the logic of the state. This claim, he argues, springs from a double illusion that he sees in close connection with the illusion of philosophy and the state.[95]

One side of this illusion is the idea of organising and administering a natural space that is apparently free and available and open to rational action. In reality, however, urbanism replaces an already inhabited space, an already existing urban practice, with a new order.[96] But urbanists, Lefebvre insists, do not know this practice, which they claim to organise – it is a blind field for them. They live it, they are in it, but they don't see it, and certainly cannot understand it as such, and thus they impose their own representations of space, and their own understanding of social life, of social groups and their relationships.[97]

---

91   Ibid.
92   Ibid., 317, 383; Lefebvre, *De l'État*, vol. 4, 263; Lefebvre, *State, Space, World*, 226.
93   Lefebvre, *Urban Revolution*, 111.
94   Wirth, 'Urbanism as a Way of Life'.
95   Lefebvre, *Urban Revolution*, 151, 153, 160.
96   Ibid., 163–4; Lefebvre, *De l'État*, vol. 4, 278–9; Lefebvre, *State, Space, World*, 228.
97   Lefebvre, *Urban Revolution*, 153.

The other side of the urbanist illusion lies in the belief that one system can produce a (new) totality.[98] For Lefebvre, urbanism is characterised by an analytical rationality whose aim is to create or restore coherence in an urban reality that it observes as chaotic. Urbanism thus creates a space that is presented as objective, scientific, neutral, and whose repressive logic appears as coherence:[99] 'Industrial practice, for example, has achieved a high degree of consistency and efficiency, mostly through planning and scheduling. Urban practice assumes it will follow this path.'[100] But this rationalism runs the risk of not recognising that coherence is a means and not an end, and is used to systematise the very logic that underlies the visible disorder and incoherence. For Lefebvre, the urban chaos that can be observed is only the result of the order imposed by urbanism.[101]

In a somewhat more nuanced distinction, Lefebvre sees quite different urbanistic tendencies.[102] But, in the end, he says, urbanism, whatever its colour, leads always to the reconstruction or reworking of the city:

> The city, or what remains of it, is built or is rearranged, in the likeness of a sum or combination of elements . . . while one may rationally look for diversity, a feeling of monotony covers these diversities and prevails, whether housing, buildings, alleged urban centres, organized areas are concerned. The urban, not conceived as such but attacked face on and from the side, corroded and gnawed, has lost the features and characteristics of the oeuvre, of appropriation. Only the constraints are projected on the ground, in a state of permanent dislocation.[103]

Urbanism leaves the city with nothing more than a collection of disjointed elements that are presented to the user as a compulsion – or as a spectacle: 'Before us, as a spectacle . . . are the dissociated and inert elements of social life and the urban.'[104]

---

98   Ibid.
99   Lefebvre, *Right to the City*, 98–9; Lefebvre, *Urban Revolution*, 164, 181.
100 Lefebvre, *Urban Revolution*, 58.
101 Lefebvre, *Right to the City*, 98–9; Lefebvre, *Urban Revolution*, 151, 158.
102 Lefebvre, *Right to the City*, 100–1; Lefebvre, *Urban Revolution*, 110–11.
103 Lefebvre, *Right to the City*, 127.
104 Ibid., 143.

The Visual Formant

The previous section highlighted some of the consequences of the geometric-abstract representation of space as presented in Lefebvre's critique of urbanism: the elements of social life are separated and presented to the gaze as a spectacle, like the merchandise in a shop window display. The geometric, planned space is thus doubled in a logic of visualisation that materialises in an exchangeable space that implies everydayness and spatial hierarchisation.[105] For Lefebvre, the perceptible side of abstract space is thus distinguished above all by its visibility. In the course of a long process, the senses of taste, smell, touch, and even hearing become blurred, and the visual gains dominance over the other senses.[106]

In Lefebvre's analysis, this visibility of abstract space, its 'visual logic', is closely linked to its commodity character. This aspect of spatial practice – the space of the commodity and space as commodity – is discussed in detail in section 7.2. Here we are concerned with the specific visual character of abstract space, which Lefebvre tries to summarise under the term 'visual formant'.

Abstract space is dominated by the visible: the visibility of people and things, of everything contained in space. Central to Lefebvre's line of argument is the mutual internal connection between abstraction and visualisation, and thus between the representation of space and spatial practice. The visual logic that materialises in perceived space contains a strategy. This strategy, which Lefebvre, following Panofsky's reflections, sees already realised in the Gothic cathedrals (see section 6.2), has reached the entirety of social practice in abstract space. Through assimilation and simulation, everything in social life becomes the deciphering of a message with the eyes, the reading of a text.[107] Lefebvre draws close connections here with the concepts of the dominance of the printed word formulated by Marshall McLuhan and the dominance of the spectacle analysed by Guy Debord.[108]

The visual character of abstract space works as a reducing force in spatial practice. The reduction starts with the already reduced dimensions of the geometric two-dimensional space, which is flattened to the surface, to a blueprint. This is, for example, the space that we perceive when driving a car, a space in which cars circulate like isolated atoms and which is reduced to a functional utility: speed, legibility, simplicity.[109]

---

105   Lefebvre, *De l'État*, vol. 4, 293; Lefebvre, *State, Space, World*, 235.

106   Lefebvre, *Production of Space*, 286.

107   Ibid., 75, 128, 286.

108   McLuhan, *The Gutenberg Galaxy*; Debord, *Society of the Spectacle*; Lefebvre, *Production of Space*, 286.

109   Lefebvre, *Production of Space*, 312–13.

Space is defined in this context in terms of the perception of an *abstract subject*, such as the driver of a motor vehicle, equipped with a collective common sense, namely the capacity to read the symbols of the highway code, and with a sole organ – the eye – placed in the service of his movement within the visual field. Thus space appears solely in its reduced forms. *Volume* leaves the field to *surface*, and any overall view surrenders to visual signals spaced out along fixed trajectories already laid down in the 'plan'. An extraordinary – indeed unthinkable, impossible – confusion gradually arises between space and surface, with the latter determining a spatial abstraction which it endows with a half-imaginary, half-real physical existence. This abstract space eventually becomes the simulacrum of a full space (of that space which was formerly full in nature and in history). Travelling – walking or strolling about – becomes an actually experienced, gestural simulation of the formerly urban activity of encounter, of movement amongst concrete existences.[110]

What Lefebvre shows here using the example of the highway tends to extend to the entire space. The normal or normalised abuse of the visual masks the fact that social space is also a field of practical action. View and image, the classical figures of the intelligible in the West, become a trap. They allow the simulation of diversity in social space, the simulacrum of the illuminating light – transparency.[111]

The eye, however, tends to relegate objects to the distance, to render them passive. That which is merely *seen* is reduced to an image – and to an icy coldness. The mirror effect thus tends to become general. Inasmuch as the act of seeing and what is seen are confused, both become impotent. By the time this process is complete, space has no social existence independently of an intense, aggressive and repressive visualization. It is thus – not symbolically but in fact – a purely visual space. The rise of the visual realm entails a series of substitutions and displacements by means of which it overwhelms the whole body and usurps its role. That which is merely seen (and merely visible) is hard to see – but it is spoken of more and more eloquently and written of more and more copiously.[112]

---

110   Ibid., 313.
111   Ibid., 75–6, 286, 288.
112   Ibid., 286.

Lefebvre sees the architects of classical modernism, above all Le Corbusier, as important representatives of this strategy of visualisation. In ever new polemics he scourges this architecture, in which he sees the culmination of the tendency towards abstraction, visualisation, and formal spatiality: walls lose their supporting function, interior space is liberated, buildings turn away from the street, exterior space is disarticulated. For Lefebvre, the great freedom of design proclaimed by Le Corbusier leads to the homogeneity of an architectural whole, the *machine à habiter*, conceived as the habitat of the human-machine, to the fractioning of space and to the disarticulation of its elements, thereby also dissolving the urbanistic unity, the street, indeed the entire city.[113]

> Le Corbusier ideologizes as he rationalizes – unless perhaps it is the other way around. An ideological discourse upon nature, sunshine and greenery successfully concealed from everyone at this time – and in particular from Le Corbusier – the true meaning and content of such architectural projects. Nature was in fact already receding; its image, consequently, had become exalting . . . In the realm of nature rediscovered, with its sun and light, beneath the banner of life, metal and glass still rise above the street, above the reality of the city. Along with the cult of rectitude, in the sense of right angles and straight lines. The order of power, the order of the male – in short, the moral order – is thus naturalized.[114]

The strategy of visualising social space implies a double logic of the processes of metonymy and metaphor (see section 5.7): the logic of metonymisation consists in the incessantly generated and imposed transition from the part to the whole. Thus, in a building composed of stacked volumes, both the observer and the inhabitant directly capture the relationship between the part and the whole and also themselves in this relationship. This space presupposes and enforces a homogeneity in the separation of places. In extreme cases it takes on a tautological form: the space contains the space, the visible contains the visible, and the box is packed in a box.[115]

The second logic inherent in this visualisation is based on an incessant metaphorisation: living bodies are represented by analogies, by images, signs, symbols; consumers are seduced by happy, smiling, embellished doublings of themselves, which empty them to the exact extent that the seduction corresponds to a 'need' which they themselves take part in shaping. In a spatial

---

113   Ibid., 303.
114   Ibid., 303–5.
115   Ibid., 98.

milieu reduced to optical components, the body no longer has any presence, it is only represented.[116] The abstraction of the sign separates the pure form from the impure content, the lived time, the time of the body, its warmth, its life and death: in its own way the image, like all signs, like the word, kills. 'Occasionally, however, an artist's tenderness or cruelty transgresses the limits of the image. Something else altogether may then emerge, a truth and a reality answering to criteria quite different from those of exactitude, clarity, readability, and plasticity.'[117]

The Phallic Formant

Facing this dual attack by the geometric and the visual, the *vécu* is emptied as well. The spaces of representation are dominated by a representation of space that is linked to knowledge and power, reducing these spaces to works, images, and memories whose content has been removed to such an extent that they can barely even bring symbolism to flower. At the same time, the objectified 'things-signs' (*choses-signes*) imply the non-recognition and misunderstanding of the perceptible, the sensual, the sexual. But even such a visualised space cannot become completely depopulated and filled only with images, with transitory objects. It demands a truly full object, an object-like 'absolute'. The phallic fulfils this service. This leads to a symbolism that operates with the arrogance of verticality:[118]

> Phallic erectility bestows a special status on the perpendicular, proclaiming phallocracy as the orientation of space, as the goal of the process . . . which instigates this facet of spatial practice.[119]

The verticality of skyscrapers adds a phallocratic arrogance to the visual, which exhibits itself, so that every observer recognises the authority. Verticality and height manifest in space the presence of a power capable of violence. And they also show that male domination has shaped this space, a martial and violent domination that has been valorised by the so-called virile virtues and spread by the norms inherent in this space: by the use and abuse of straight lines, right angles, and perspective.[120]

---

116   Ibid., Lefebvre, *De l'État*, vol. 4, 292; Lefebvre, *State, Space, World*, 234.
117   Lefebvre, *Production of Space*, 97.
118   Ibid., 49–50, 287.
119   Ibid., 287.
120   Ibid., 98, 409–10.

The masculine virtues which gave rise to domination by this space can only lead, as we are only too well aware, to a generalized state of deprivation: from 'private' property to the Great Castration. It is inevitable in these circumstances that feminine revolts should occur, that the female principle should seek revenge.[121]

This critique shows clear parallels to contemporary critiques by feminists. Lefebvre shared the feminist critique of the mythology and ideology of phallic power. He insisted, however, that the language of power should also be attacked, the symbol of which is not only the phallus but also the eye and the gaze, height, and size, the monumental and the centred space,[122] a critique that was also put forward in feminist geography of the 1990s (see section 1.4).

However, Lefebvre's analysis was also met with considerable criticism. For example, in an article that is still discussed today, Virginia Blum and Heidi Nast criticised the heteronormativity that runs through Lefebvre's work, which turns on an active-passive binary: 'His framework depends upon a heterosexuality that is fixed in a number of rigid gendered distinctions that wind up equating the paternal with activity, movement, agency, force, history, while the maternal is passive, immobile, subject to force and history.'[123] They also accuse Lefebvre of privileging 'masculine' agency and ignoring more mutable 'feminised' socio-spatial practices and struggles. This harsh judgement, however, would possibly be somewhat relativised if Lefebvre's texts on everyday life were also included. Blum and Nast at least admit that Lefebvre's work is groundbreaking because 'it charts the changing ways in which constructions of the maternal and the paternal have been paradigmatically extended across politics and space'.[124]

The Violence of Abstract Space

This analysis of abstract space with its three formants, the geometric, the visual, and the phallic, leads Lefebvre to the only possible conclusion: abstract space contains violence. As elucidated in section 2.4, for Lefebvre every abstraction is a powerful instrument and means of action, of domination, and thus also of destruction. Just as violence is inherent in the tool and the sign in general, it is

---

121   Ibid., 410.
122   Lefebvre, *Survival of Capitalism*, 73.
123   Blum and Nast, 'Where's the Difference?', 577.
124   Ibid.

also contained in abstract space, even while it appears rational, evident.[125] Abstract space thus has an effect, in the same way as abstraction unfolds effects in practice, in thought, and also in lived experience. As the sum of constraints, provisions, and regulations, social space has a normative-repressive effectiveness. Logic and logistics conceal this latent violence, which does not even have to show itself in order to become effective. Thus, abstract space appears as a repressive space above all else, but in a very cunning way. Repression soon manifests itself through reduction, then through functional localisation, hierarchisation, segregation, and finally even through art.[126]

However, it is not political power as such that produces this space; it merely controls its reproduction (see section 7.5). Political action knows how to use space in an instrumental way. The illusory transparency of space is ultimately nothing other than that of political power, which hides itself to a certain extent 'behind space' and at the same time shines through 'in space'. In the space of power, therefore, power does not appear as such. It is hidden behind the 'organisation of space'. It bypasses and shifts everything that opposes it by hidden or open violence.[127] The state, notes Lefebvre, has always expressed itself through void: 'empty space, broad avenues, plazas of gigantic proportions, open to spectacular processions'.[128]

Thus, the meanings of abstract space – alongside the stimuli for consumption – consist primarily of prohibitions. The forbidden triumphs. The symbol of this constitutive repression is the object that is presented to the gaze, but whose use is denied, as in a museum or in a shop window display. Most of these prohibitions are invisible. Grids and walls are only the borderline case of separation. More abstract signs and signifiers protect the spaces of the elites, the wealthy neighbourhoods, and the privileged places against unwanted intruders. The prohibition is the counterpart and wrapping of property, the negative appropriation of space under the regime of private property.[129]

This space has strange effects:

For one thing, it unleashes desire. It presents desire with a 'transparency' which encourages it to surge forth in an attempt to lay claim to an apparently clear field. Of course this foray comes to naught, for desire encounters no object, nothing desirable, and no work results from its action. Searching in vain for plenitude, desire must make do with words; with the rhetoric of desire. Disillusion leaves space empty – an emptiness that words convey.

---

125   Lefebvre, *Production of Space*, 299, 306.
126   Ibid., 318, 358.
127   See ibid., 320–1.
128   Lefebvre, *Urban Revolution*, 109.
129   Lefebvre, *Production of Space*, 319.

Spaces are devastated – and devastating; incomprehensibly so . . . 'Nothing is allowed. Nothing is forbidden', in the words of one inhabitant. Spaces are strange: homogeneous, rationalized, and as such constraining; yet at the same time utterly dislocated. Formal boundaries are gone between town and country, between centre and periphery, between suburbs and city centres, between the domain of automobiles and the domain of people. Between happiness and unhappiness, for that matter.[130]

If social space is shifted to the absolute, its practical character disappears. If abstract space is made into a fetish, it generates the abstraction of reflection, which is no longer capable of critique, and the abstraction of the 'users' from their presence, their lived experience, and their body, ultimately from themselves.[131]

The Critique of Modernism

The preceding explanations have shown how Lefebvre himself brings the three dimensions of the production of space into play and relates them to one another in a virtuosic way. He analyses how the three formants – the geometrical (conceived), the visual (perceived), and the phallic (lived) – produce a space in their dialectical interaction in which abstraction and violence are inherent. It becomes clear once again that none of the three dimensions can claim priority: they always work in mutual interaction.

However, Lefebvre's criticism of the architecture and urban planning of classical modernism, and especially of Le Corbusier, no longer has the originality and freshness that it had at the time of its publication. It is often lacking nuance and is partially uninformed – especially regarding the claimed continuity of the classical modernism of the 1920s and 1930s with the post-war period, but also in relation to the generalisation of the specifically French variant of Fordist urban development (see section 4.3). Moreover, modern architecture is much more diverse and complex than Lefebvre's highly stylised criticism would suggest. As Stanek notes, Lefebvre's critique eclipses 'other' modernisms, which were highly heterogeneous in their philosophical and artistic sources, images, and political goals. These include not only approaches that were heretical and dissident in relation to the modern mainstream, but also architectural production from socialist countries, from Latin America, Africa, and Asia.[132]

---

130   Ibid., 97.
131   Ibid., 93.
132   Stanek, 'Introduction: A Manuscript Found in Saragossa', xv, xxxiv.

Moreover, Lefebvre repeats at length a somewhat classic critique that has become a stereotype. As Stanek demonstrates, Lefebvre's analysis is strongly influenced by the discussion of the late 1960s and early 1970s in France, when criticism of modern architecture and functional urban planning, especially in the context of the 1968 movements, became widespread and almost mainstream, and new paths for a different architecture were being tested. Therefore, Lefebvre's critique shows parallels to postmodern critiques, as can be seen, for example, in the anthology 'Actualités de Henri Lefebvre', which appeared in 1994.[133] Furthermore, Lefebvre was frequently quoting famous architects who were identified with postmodernism, such as Robert Venturi, Charles Jencks, and Ricardo Bofill.[134] This is not surprising, however, since the criticism of the late 1960s is also an important starting point for postmodernism in architecture (see section 1.3).

However, it would be misleading to deduce from this an affinity of Lefebvre to postmodernism, because his critique reaches much deeper (see sections 1.3, 6.5, and 6.6). He is concerned not only with a different architecture but more generally with the development of capitalism: abstract space is a space dominated by the state, by capital, and by industrialisation. Lefebvre understands the abstraction of space as a concrete, socially effective process, which he encapsulates in the concept of the homogeneous-fractured space – an analytical figure that conceives of the state (and the system of states) together with the (world) market. The homogenisation and the commodification of this space go hand in hand. A more detailed political-economic analysis of the production of this abstract space follows in chapter 7.

6.4 Differential Space

Difference, a seemingly trivial term, proves its theoretical and practical
importance at every moment. It emerges on different paths . . . which
are the paths of difference.[135]

Lefebvre's history of the production of space progresses from the space of nature through absolute space to abstract space. In Lefebvre's dialectical triptych, the third tableau, which will actually reveal the meaning of this 'history of space', is still missing. For abstract space, despite – or perhaps because of – its

133   Coornaert and Garnier, 'Actualités de Henri Lefebvre'.
134   See for example Lefebvre, *Production of Space*, 144–5; Lefebvre, *Le temps des méprises*, 246–7. See also Stanek, *Henri Lefebvre on Space*, 205–7.
135   Lefebvre, *Le manifeste différentialiste*, 8. Translation by author.

abstractness, carries within itself a new space. In a dialectical movement, the crisis of the homogeneous-fractured space, whose dialectical contradiction is so perfectly expressed in Picasso's painting, engenders a new space.[136] Lefebvre calls this (still) utopian space 'differential space', or more precisely: 'differential space-time'.[137] While the abstract space strives for homogeneity and reduces existing differences, the new space can only emerge by accentuating differences. It will bring together what the abstract space separates: the elements and moments of social practice.[138]

This brings a new concept to the centre of the analysis: difference. Lefebvre's theory of difference is not linked to the poststructuralist and postmodern approaches that redefined the concept of difference in many ways in the 1970s and 1980s. Lefebvre has developed and applied an independent concept of difference over many years. It emerged in his work at the end of the 1960s, initially referring to the immediate context of the 1968 movement and taking up the demands of the women's movement, immigrant organisations, and regional movements for a difference in equality (*la différence dans l'égalité*).[139]

In 1970, Lefebvre wrote a manifesto on this subject, *Le manifeste différentialiste*, in which he postulates a 'right to difference'. He understands the concept as a critique of politics, philosophy, political economy, anthropology, ethnology, and also of art and literature, and he places this critique in the context of the 'great crisis' of the modern world.[140] For him, the right to difference implies first and foremost an invitation to the 'other' and to allow the 'other' to live differently: 'difference' stands as a counter-concept, as a concrete utopia of another – different – world. The right to difference thus implies a social project. It cannot be proclaimed and demanded in discourse but must be won in political struggle. And it also requires the renewal and expansion of Marxist thought.[141]

While Lefebvre treats the concept of difference in *Le manifeste différentialiste* in a more general social context, in *The Right to the City* and *The Urban Revolution* he relates it directly to the question of the urban. In *The Production of Space* it finally appears in a historically elaborated form as 'differential space'. Nevertheless, Lefebvre still regards his theory of difference as difficult and unfinished.[142] In the third volume of *The Critique of Everyday Life* he takes the

---

136   Lefebvre, *Production of Space*, 303.
137   Lefebvre, *Urban Revolution*, 170; Lefebvre, *Le manifeste différentialiste*, 129.
138   Lefebvre, *Production of Space*, 50, 52.
139   Lefebvre, *Critique of Everyday Life*, vol. 3, 109–10.
140   Lefebvre, *Le manifeste différentialiste*, 8, 11.
141   Lefebvre, *Critique of Everyday Life*, vol. 3, 110.
142   Lefebvre, *Production of Space*, 371.

next step in the further elaboration of the theory and places difference in the broader context of the transformations of everyday life.[143]

In this section, we will explore this differential space, trace its various characteristics, and investigate how such a space becomes possible. As stipulated in the introduction, this differential space is nothing other than urban space (see section 6.1). We are thus approaching urban society and urban space no longer from the perspective of urbanisation, but from the broader perspective of the production of space.

The conclusion of this section demonstrates the interplay of the three different approaches to the urban that Lefebvre developed in his various writings. First, the urban is constituted on a specific spatio-temporal level of social reality, the intermediate level, which mediates between the global, abstract level of general processes and the concrete-sensual level of everyday life. Second, the urban is a specific form that corresponds to this level: centrality that is constituted by encounter and public gathering. And third, on this urban level, depending on the historical situation, a specific space or a specific space-time is produced: differential space.

The Thesis of the Primacy of Space

In order to reach differential space, Lefebvre formulates a new 'strategic hypothesis' that complements the thesis of complete urbanisation (see section 3.2) and is intended to show its implications: it states that space has achieved relative autonomy as 'reality' as the result of a long process of the production of space. In modern societies, the practical and theoretical questions of space are therefore becoming increasingly important, and space itself is achieving a dominant position.[144] For Lefebvre, the problematic of space is as fundamental as the industrial revolution and the development of industrialisation:

> There is a certain similarity between the present situation, in both its practical and its theoretical aspects, and the one which came to prevail in the middle of the nineteenth century. A fresh set of questions – a fresh 'problematic' as the philosophers say – is in the process of usurping the position of the old problems, substituting itself for them and superimposing itself upon them without for all that abolishing them completely.[145]

---

143   Lefebvre, *Critique of Everyday Life*, vol. 3, 109–11.
144   Lefebvre, *Production of Space*, 39, 62, 412.
145   Ibid., 88.

For Lefebvre, the thesis of the primacy of space initially denotes a historical change of perspective from the 'historical' to the 'spatial'. Lefebvre can precisely date the moment of this change of perspective and thus the emergence of the long-neglected reality of the production of space: he sees the 'historical' role of the Bauhaus in having recognised this reality: 'It is then that socially the notion of space comes to the fore, relegating into shadow time and becoming.'[146] And he understands the programme of modern architecture, from Paul Klee to Le Corbusier, as a programme that consists in creating and producing space.[147] Finally, the expression of this shift from the historical to the spatial is the new role of urbanism, as discussed above, which formulates all problems of society as questions of space and transposes everything that comes from history and consciousness into spatial expressions.[148] The process underlying this new meaning of space is thus urbanisation. The political-economic consequences of this shift from the temporal to the spatial will be discussed in detail in section 7.1.

On the Dialectic of Space and Time

The strategic thesis of the primacy of space addresses a fundamental general question: the relationship between space and time. 'L'espace enveloppe le temps': space envelops time, writes Lefebvre.[149] Temporalities are necessarily local, which implies a relationship between places and their time. Social time is produced and reproduced through space, and it enters space with its characteristics and determinations: repetitions, rhythms, and cycles.[150] Phenomena such as growth, maturation, and ageing, which are often tied to a 'temporality' by analysis, cannot be separated from 'spatiality', which is itself an abstraction. Thus, space and time manifest themselves as different but inseparable. Time can be distinguished from space but cannot be separated from it. For Lefebvre, 'time in itself' and 'space in itself' are absurdities: they mirror each other, the one constantly referring to the other. They are one and the same reality, creating a double surface, a double appearance.[151] Accordingly, society can be conceived as a set of actions that take place in time, and highlight a space and are highlighted by it. Space and time thus alternately become signifier and

---

146   Lefebvre, *Right to the City*, 99.
147   Lefebvre, *Production of Space*, 124.
148   Lefebvre, *Right to the City*, 98–9.
149   Lefebvre, *Production of Space*, 339.
150   Ibid., 175, 339.
151   Ibid., 175, 181.

signified.[152] Actions denote a space and are designated by it: the space refers to time and time to space. In principle, these formulations mean nothing less than the attempt to restore the unity of action, space, and time. The parallels with the theory of relativity are obvious in this respect (see section 5.3).

This dialectic of space and time is also present in the dialectic of the exchange and use of space: the buyer of a space acquires not only an inhabitable volume, semiologically marked by the discourse of advertising and the signs of a certain 'distinction', but also a distance that connects a place with certain other places, the centres of commerce, work, pleasure, culture, and decision. This is where time comes to the fore, and although architects, builders, and even users try to compensate for the disadvantages of a certain place by signs of prestige, happiness, or 'lifestyle', the buyer ultimately acquires a certain use of time, which itself constitutes the use value of a space. The use of time entails comforts and inconveniences, gains and losses of time, in other words something other than signs: a practice.[153] Conversely, time materialises in space and is also discerned in space:

> In nature, time is apprehended within space – in the very heart of space: the hour of the day, the season, the elevation of the sun above the horizon, the position of the moon and stars in the heavens, the cold and the heat, the age of each natural being, and so on. Until nature became *localized* in underdevelopment, each place showed its age and, like a tree trunk, bore the mark of the years it had taken it to grow. Time was thus inscribed in space, and natural space was merely the lyrical and tragic script of natural time.[154]

But, with modernity, time disappears in social space. It becomes isolated, specialised, written on the measuring devices and on the clocks. Abstract space throws time back into a specific abstraction: lived time (*temps vécu*) is subordinated to economic space and reduced to labour time by defining it through the rationalised and localised gestures of work. In this way, time is reduced to the constraints of the use of space, and of transport networks.[155]

The primacy of the economic and even more so of the political entails the domination of space over time:

> Our time, then, this most essential part of lived experience, this greatest good of all goods, is no longer visible to us, no longer intelligible. It

---

152   Lefebvre, *Right to the City*, 131.
153   Lefebvre, *Production of Space*, 339.
154   Ibid., 95.
155   Ibid., 95, 393, 408.

cannot be constructed. It is consumed, exhausted, and that is all. It leaves no traces. It is concealed in space, hidden under a pile of debris to be disposed of as soon as possible; after all, rubbish is a pollutant.[156]

If it is true that time can be balanced against money, to be bought and sold like any object, then it disappears as such. For Lefebvre, it is precisely the modernist trinity of readability, visibility, and comprehensibility, and thus abstract space, which includes the disappearance of time, this irreducible good, in social norms: 'Time may have been promoted to the level of ontology by the philosophers, but it has been murdered by society.'[157] Once again, we find the great echo of Nietzsche: just as humans killed God and nature, they also kill time (see sections 2.4 and 6.1).

But time cannot be reduced, nor can desire and nature. It reappears as the greatest wealth, as a place and milieu of use, of pleasure. Abstract space does not succeed in drawing time into the sphere of exteriority, of signs and images. Time reappears as intimacy, interiority, subjectivity, and as cycles closely tied to nature and use: sleep, hunger, and so on. In time, the expenditure of affectivity, energy, and creativity is opposed to the passive consumption of signs. But this expenditure, this desire to 'do something', to 'create' something, can only be fulfilled in a space by producing a space. The 'real' appropriation of space is not compatible with the abstract signs of appropriation, which only mask domination.[158]

Once again, Lefebvre makes a remarkable reversal. According to a famous passage of Marx in the *Grundrisse*, the rule of labour time means an 'annihilation of space by time':

> While capital must on the one side strive to tear down every spatial barrier to intercourse, i.e. to exchange, and conquer the whole earth for its market, it strives on the other to annihilate this space with time, i.e. to reduce to a minimum the time spent in motion from one place to another.[159]

Both Harvey and Castells have followed this analysis (see section 1.2). In this context, Prigge also speaks of a 'temporalisation of space':[160] distances would no longer be measured in metres but in seconds and the entire space would be

---

156   Ibid., 95–6.
157   Ibid., 96.
158   Ibid., 393.
159   Marx, *Grundrisse*, 408.
160   Prigge, *Zeit, Raum und Architektur*, 32.

subject to the dictates of the machine cycle. But Lefebvre sees this exactly the other way around: time solidifies, materialises in space, and is thereby destroyed. If, for Marx, all commodities are 'merely definite quantities of *congealed labour time*',[161] then space, as the most comprehensive commodity for Lefebvre, becomes to a certain extent a congealed, and thus also destroyed, living time. This is the final consequence of his conception of alienation as the objectification of activity in the product: space as a product also contains its alienation from time, and thus from becoming, from life (see section 2.3).

The Spatial Turn and Postmodernism

Lefebvre's thesis of the primacy of space was taken up by postmodern geography, especially by Soja, and turned into a central topos of the 'spatial turn' in the social sciences (see section 1.3). However, it became clear in these considerations that although Lefebvre postulated a new social meaning of space, he was much more critical of this process than the postmodern geographers. He even saw the 'almost official priority of space over time' as an indication of a social pathology.[162] As the following warning shows, Lefebvre was well aware of possible misunderstandings in the application of his 'strategic hypothesis': he noted that knowledge had taken shape on the basis of general schemas, either timeless according to classical metaphysics, or, on the contrary, since Hegel, temporal ones that postulated the primacy of historical becoming over space, a theoretical situation that called for a reversal. Sometimes, this has been attempted on indefensible grounds, by asserting the primacy of geographical, demographic, or ecological space over time.[163] This passage can be read as a clear rejection of postmodern interpretations.

The postmodern misunderstanding of Lefebvre's thesis of the primacy of space is, however, more deeply rooted, namely in its conception of space and time. Anglo-American postmodern geography, in particular, has struggled to free itself from the old idea of a given and pre-existing space, an idea that Lefebvre had rejected so radically in his theory. This becomes particularly apparent in Soja's attempt to design an 'ontology of space', in which he speaks of a 'space in itself', which he then distinguishes from the 'actual social space': 'Space in itself may be primordially given, but the organisation, and meaning of space is a product of social translation, transformation, and experience.'[164] To distinguish the

---

161 Marx, *A Contribution to the Critique of Political Economy*, 272.
162 Lefebvre, *Right to the City*, 99.
163 Lefebvre, *Production of Space*, 414.
164 Soja, *Postmodern Geographies*, 79–80.

contextually given 'space in itself' from socially produced space, he even introduces a new concept: 'spatiality'. From this he then develops a 'trialectic of being',
in which 'spatiality', 'historicality', and 'sociality', as the three moments of his new
'spatial ontology', whirl around being like a spiral nebula.[165]

But this ontology is the opposite of Lefebvre's position: for him, there is no
space 'in itself', as should have become clear in this history of space. There is a
space of nature that existed prior to the entrance of humans into the world,
before there was a language, concepts, and 'history'. Since then, however,
human beings appropriated the space they found, changed it, made it into a
social space through and with their practice. This is the core of the theory of
the production of space.

Accordingly, Lefebvre's analysis is by no means limited to space. In his
theory of the production of space, time is included in the analysis from the very
beginning: first as historical time and thus as history, but also as practice, as
everyday life: 'What are the times and rhythms of daily life which are inscribed
and prescribed in these "successful" spaces favourable to happiness?'[166]
Lefebvre thus explicitly warned against a pure 'space analysis' and asserted that
only a 'rhythmanalysis' could complete the analysis of the production of space,
since knowledge of the use of space is directly linked to an analysis of rhythms
(see section 6.1).[167] It is Lefebvre's declared aim to wrest the relationship
between space and time from an abstract separation and to dissolve the confusion between these two different but linked concepts.[168]

The Contradictions of Space

The new problematic of space also shifts the social contradictions: '*The dialectic
is no longer attached to temporality*', explains Lefebvre.[169] Dialectical thinking
is based on time, though: contradictions express the forces which are opposed
to one another in history.[170] For Lefebvre, the 'Hegelian-Marxist revolution'
consists in the fact that time became the object of research and cognition on
humans, the aspect of becoming gained priority, and the consciousness of
humans acquired a historical dimension.[171]

---

165   Soja, *Thirdspace*, 71–2.
166   Lefebvre, *Right to the City*, 151.
167   Lefebvre, *Production of Space*, 356, 405.
168   Ibid., 351.
169   Lefebvre, *Survival of Capitalism*, 17.
170   Lefebvre, *Production of Space*, 298.
171   Lefebvre, *Sociology of Marx*, 27–8.

With the arrival of abstract space, however, the dialectic is no longer tied to history, to historical time, a temporal dynamic as expressed in the sequence of affirmation–negation–negation of negation. The contradictions of space thus cannot be grasped with the dialectics of Hegel or Marx, which are based on an analysis of historical time and temporality.[172] According to Lefebvre, what is now needed is a renewed dialectic – which he indeed developed with his own three-dimensional dialectic.

In order to understand this fundamentally changed situation, Lefebvre constructs a difference between the contradictions in space and the contradictions of space: contradictions in space would accordingly be the 'classical' contradictions of the social relations that are produced by history and historical time (see section 7.3). But these contradictions have their effects and their place in space, and thus become contradictions of space.[173]

These contradictions of space can be seen, as derived above, in the simultaneously homogeneous and fractured character of abstract space. Another important contradiction of space is the problem of centrality (see section 4.4): the dialectical movement between centrality and periphery, and between realised and virtual centrality.[174] From this, finally, follows the contradiction between domination and appropriation of space. This contradiction represents to a certain extent a 'spatial' version of the contradiction between use value and exchange value (see section 7.2).

The contradictions of space have arisen from history. Without eliminating the contradictions that come from historical time, they lift the old contradictions, in a worldwide simultaneity, to another level, take on a new meaning, denote 'something else'.[175] In his strategic hypothesis of the primacy of space, Lefebvre sees a long-term theoretical and practical project to indicate a path to the production of another space, the space of another social life and another mode of production.[176] From these contradictions of space a new space antagonistic to capitalism will thus develop: differential space.[177]

---

172   Lefebvre, *Survival of Capitalism*, 14; Lefebvre, *Production of Space*, 331.
173   Lefebvre, *Production of Space*, 333, 365.
174   Ibid., 331, 333. See also Lefebvre, *Survival of Capitalism*, 17–18.
175   Lefebvre, *Production of Space*, 129.
176   Ibid., 60.
177   Lefebvre, *De l'État*, vol. 4, 317–18; Lefebvre, *State, Space, World*, 248.

On the Theory of Difference

What are the properties of this differential space? And what does difference mean in the theoretical context of the production of space? First of all, a definition has to be made: Lefebvre distinguishes the concept of 'difference' from the concept of 'particularities'. Differences are active elements, while particularities remain isolated from one another.[178] Originally, in the space of nature, only particularities exist, as material elements linked to local conditions and circumstances, such as place and location, climatic and topographic conditions, the presence of natural resources, and so on. In this original state, differences do not present themselves to people as such: they exist isolated from each other; they are external, alien to each other. They manifest themselves in struggles between different ethnic and social groups that come into contact with each other throughout history. Such a process is always conflictual: the particularities encounter each other in deadly battles, in the course of which they threaten to disappear. Historically, the moment of confrontation has led to devastating attempts to destroy particularities economically, politically, and culturally – attempts that reached their climax in the modern world.[179] Transformed by these conflicts, the qualities that survive but are no longer separate from each other assert themselves: they can only present and re-present themselves in their mutual relations, whether these are conflictual or pacified. Their confrontation can thus lead to a mutual 'understanding', a certain knowledge and awareness of the 'other'. Thus, the concept of difference emerges as lived practice, and finally as an act of thinking.[180]

For Lefebvre, difference is an active and dialectical category. Therefore, it has to be distinguished from concepts such as 'originality', 'diversity', 'multiplicity', or 'distinction'.[181] All these and other similar terms denote, according to Lefebvre, the existence and, at best, the emergence or constitution of different social groups within a society. In this context, Lefebvre criticises particularly Bourdieu, whom he accuses of using the concept of 'distinction' to disguise elitist class and power relations instead of opening them up to critical practice.[182] In contrast to such attempts to identify the heterogeneity of a society, Lefebvre wants to explore the contradictory social process that is

---

178   Lefebvre, *Urban Revolution*, 37, 94; Lefebvre, *Production of Space*, 373; Lefebvre, *Critique of Everyday Life*, vol. 3, 111.

179   Lefebvre, *Le manifeste différentialiste*, 64–5; Lefebvre, *Critique of Everyday Life*, vol. 3, 111.

180   Lefebvre, *Le manifeste différentialiste*, 65.

181   Ibid., 66–7.

182   Lefebvre, *Critique of Everyday Life*, vol. 3, 114–15. See also Bourdieu, *Distinction*.

set in motion by differences, and the potentials that are unleashed or confined by this.

It is crucial to the understanding of Lefebvre's theory that he sees 'difference' not only as a concept, as an imaginary form, but first and foremost as a practice that is experienced. Differences are connected with actions, situations, discourses, and contexts; they are related to diverse networks of interaction, which overlap, interfere with each other, and also change in this process. Differences thus initiate a movement that ultimately also changes social relations.[183]

Differences can be determined more clearly in their historical development. The rural field is dominated by particularities. With industrialisation, the rural order is radically transformed and an overarching industrial system with a universal, rational, and efficient logic is installed, which also initiates the homogenisation of society. The particularities disappear, and with them the specificities of places. With urbanisation and the spread of the urban fabric, however, a new potential emerges: a new, differential space-time can be created in which particularities, places, situations, and local qualities are related to each other through diverse networks that face each other, overlap, connect, interfere, or compete with each other, finally turning them into urban differences. In this sense, difference denotes the potential of an urban society.[184] For Lefebvre, differential space – or differential space-time – is a possibility that can unfold in the here and now.

Differential space is thus the space of an urban society. What is central here is the differences that come to light and become established in space. As Lefebvre emphasises, however, they do not emerge from space as such, but from what gathers in space, what is confronted in and with urban reality: separations and space-time distances are replaced by oppositions, contrasts, superimpositions, and juxtapositions of different realities. The urban brings together; it creates the conditions for the freedom to create differences. It can thus be defined as a place where differences converge and explore each other, and in this process recognise and acknowledge each other.[185]

Urban life suggests meetings, the confrontation of differences, reciprocal knowledge and acknowledgement (including ideological and political confrontation), ways of living, 'patterns' which coexist in the city.[186]

---

183   Lefebvre, *Le manifeste différentialiste*, 65, 126, 129; Lefebvre, *Critique of Everyday Life*, vol. 3, 115.

184   Lefebvre, *Le manifeste différentialiste*, 127–8, 178–9.

185   Lefebvre, *Urban Revolution*, 96, 125, 173–4.

186   Lefebvre, *Right to the City*, 75.

The urban is thus a contradictory space-time, a place of collision and confrontation, a place where conflicts find expression.[187] The urban 'delivers the essence of social relationships: the reciprocal existence and manifestation of differences arising from or resulting in conflicts. Isn't this the justification and meaning of this rational delirium known as the city, the urban?'[188]

Minimal and Maximal Difference

To understand better the emancipatory and revolutionary potential of difference, Lefebvre introduced the distinction between minimal and maximal difference. Stefan Kipfer has pointed out how important this distinction is for the understanding of an urban society, since it reveals the fault line of abstract space.[189]

Lefebvre takes this distinction from the rules of logic. Minimal difference corresponds to variations within a defined area or field. It tends towards a formal identity, variations of the same – such as differences within a certain style, or different forms of detached houses in an otherwise homogeneous suburb. Here, Lefebvre refers to Gilles Deleuze's work *Repetition and Difference*, from which he takes the idea that the repetition of an element already generates a difference. From this idea he derives a logic of difference that in his understanding is at least partially consistent with the logic of dialectics.[190]

In contrast, maximal difference denotes differences between different fields, and thus qualitative differences, that is, different ways of life and forms of everyday life. In the same sense, Lefebvre also distinguishes between induced and produced differences: while induced differences remain within a given setting or existing system, produced differences cross the boundaries of a field, as in art, where in the transition from one field or genre to another something new is created. Maximal differences always contain surprises; they remain unpredictable, are potentially explosive, and can lead to questioning and challenging an existing social system.[191] By transgressing the existing boundaries of everyday life, maximal differences can also generate social inventions, and thus become a productive force – and likewise a driving force of the urban revolution (see below).

---

187   Lefebvre, *Urban Revolution*, 176.
188   Ibid., 118.
189   See Kipfer, 'Urbanization, Difference and Everyday Life'; Kipfer, 'How Lefebvre Urbanized Gramsci'.
190   Lefebvre, *Production of Space*, 372; Lefebvre, *Logique formelle*, xvii.
191   Lefebvre, *Production of Space*, 372–4, 395–6.

But the abstract, homogeneous-fractured space shows always the tendency to subordinate both chaos and difference, and to eliminate everything that is different, whether actual or potential. Often, it captures the differences at the very moment of their emergence, thus eliminating them.[192] The dominant social and political forces try to enclose and integrate differences, forcing them back into the system by restrictions and violence, or to push them to the fringes of society and the edges of the city, where they survive as externalities or as forms of resistance. In this way, maximal differences are tamed and domesticated, brought into order, and thus reduced to minimal differences. The result of this integration is ultimately indifference. Accordingly, there arises what Lefebvre calls a 'titanic struggle' between the homogenising and the differential forces.[193]

Hegemony and Incorporation

The conflicts between the homogenising and the differential forces of a society raise the question of the role of hegemony, for the production of abstract space presupposes the active role of the state (see section 7.4). In this point, Lefebvre refers to Antonio Gramsci and his understanding of hegemony, which includes not only the repressive violence of the state but also the use and instrumentalisation of culture and knowledge.[194] In this process, hegemony is directly linked to the production of space, which in Lefebvre's understanding has an operational and instrumental side that is realised through spatial strategies, planning and urbanism, concepts and representations of space. Stefan Kipfer has examined this connection between Gramsci and Lefebvre in detail.[195] He understands abstract space with its complex combination of integration and homogenisation on the one hand and fragmentation and segregation on the other as an urbanised form of hegemony.[196] In this context, the distinction between minimal and maximal differences marks a possible turning point from integration to resistance. Oppositional counter-strategies can only unfold their counter-hegemonic potential if they not only discursively point out the differences, but actively realise them in practice and thus transform them into

---

192   Ibid., 370–2; Lefebvre, *De l'État*, vol. 4, 321; Lefebvre, *State, Space, World*, 249–50.
193   Lefebvre, *Le manifeste différentialiste*, 49, 129–30; Lefebvre, *Production of Space*, 382.
194   Lefebvre, *Production of Space*, 10–11.
195   Kipfer, 'Urbanization, Difference and Everyday Life'; Kipfer, 'How Lefebvre Urbanized Gramsci'; Kipfer, Saberi, and Wieditz, 'Henri Lefebvre: Debates'.
196   Kipfer, 'How Lefebvre Urbanized Gramsci', 206.

maximal differences.[197] Andrew Shmuely, expanding on these reflections by Kipfer, has established connections to Raymond Williams's concept of incorporation, which he understands as a direct analogy to Lefebvre's concept of producing minimal differences.[198]

The problem of incorporating differences can be understood in many ways. For example, the rediscovery of the urban since the 1960s not only has had an emancipatory and sometimes explosive effect but has also been accompanied by a wide variety of forms of incorporation and domestication, the celebration of diversity and multicultural values, and even the staging and simulation of urbanity (see sections 3.5 and 4.5). Connected with this are manifold processes of integration and co-optation of parts of the former oppositional milieus. As Daniel Weiss and I have postulated, a 'new metropolitan mainstream' has emerged, which can be understood as a norm for the design of urban spaces that has been established worldwide, in both urban centres and urban peripheries, with spectacular architecture, skyscrapers, cultural flagship projects, condo towers, business parks, entertainment centres, and privatised public spaces, which are intended to create a maximally controlled, consumable urban atmosphere.[199]

This is also linked to a process that Kipfer and I have called the 'commodification of the urban'.[200] This term refers not only to the sale or use of smaller or larger plots of land, or the reservation of exclusive locations for certain population groups, but also to the process of the use of urban space as such. The entire space is sold – along with the people who populate it, as well as the social resources and the effects they produce. Urban life itself is drawn into the process of exploitation and is transformed in the process. This means that the qualities of urban space, the places of encounter and exchange, become part of economic dispositives and the systematic exploitation of gains in productivity. The process of this commodification of space is examined in more detail in section 7.1.

The concepts of minimal/induced differences and maximal/produced differences make it possible to distinguish these processes of homogenisation and commodification of space from attempts to create a differential space. This distinction therefore does not refer to 'big' or 'small' activities and actions, nor is it about the question of 'revolutionary action' versus 'everyday life'. For

---

197   Ibid., 205.
198   Shmuely, 'Totality, Hegemony, Difference'; Williams, *Marxism and Literature*.
199   See Schmid and Weiss, 'The New Metropolitan Mainstream'; Schmid, 'Henri Lefebvre, the Right to the City'.
200   Kipfer and Schmid, 'Right to the City/Bourgeois Urbanism'; Kipfer et al., 'Globalizing Lefebvre?'; Schmid, 'Henri Lefebvre, the Right to the City'.

Lefebvre himself had postulated that the revolution must come from everyday life – or else it would not really take place (see section 3.1). So, the question here is, rather, to what extent differences override integration and domestication and, however 'small', connect to a different, non-commodified transformation of everyday life. Buckley and Strauss, who approached Lefebvre's concept of difference from a feminist position, have pointed out that it is precisely these everyday forms of lived experience that could lay the foundation for a revolution in the urbanisation process.[201]

Difference and Poststructuralism

One of the great achievements of Lefebvre's theory of difference is that it establishes a direct link between the unfolding of differences and urbanisation, while also developing a practical-utopian perspective. In this respect, his theory differs from many other approaches that have dealt with difference and spaces of difference in the context of the poststructuralist turn.[202] Kipfer has shown in detail the differences between Lefebvre's dialectical and transformative theory and poststructuralist or postmodern concepts of difference.[203] While Lefebvre considers material interaction processes, poststructuralist concepts are primarily based on linguistic constructions. For example, Derrida's neologism *différance*, which serves as an important basis for the method of deconstruction, is based on language and the process of meaning.[204] The same applies to Lyotard's concept of *différend*, which refers to the communication process of language.[205] By contrast, for Lefebvre, 'difference' is not about a linguistic deconstruction of discourses. What distinguishes his analysis is rather that he ties his concept of difference to a concrete materiality and refers to a social practice.[206]

Consequently, most of the poststructuralist (and postmodern) contributions that have applied the concept of difference to the city do not refer to Lefebvre, and they also treat other questions, such as the explanation of segregation, place-making, and socio-spatial differentiation in urban areas, the analysis of how difference is constituted and negotiated in urban contexts, or

---

201   Buckley and Strauss, 'With, against and beyond Lefebvre'.
202   See also Jameson, *Postmodernism*, 340–2.
203   Kipfer, 'How Lefebvre Urbanized Gramsci'; Kipfer, Saberi, and Wieditz, 'Henri Lefebvre: Debates', 120; Kipfer et al., 'On the Production of Henri Lefebvre'.
204   Derrida, *Of Grammatology*.
205   Lyotard, *The Postmodern Condition*.
206   See also Gibson-Graham, *The End of Capitalism*, 74–6.

the various processes of the construction and constitution of identities.[207] 'Difference' is often used synonymously with terms such as 'diversity' or 'heterogeneity' – which Lefebvre expressly rejected (see above). In contrast to Lefebvre, these contributions are thus not primarily concerned with the production of the urban through differences, but, rather, understand urban space as an arena in which differences occur, whereby certain problems or potentials arise.

Difference as Productive Activity

The contradictions between abstract and differential space, and the incorporation of differences, have been taken up and made fruitful in many theoretical and empirical contributions. Japhy Wilson, for example, examined the violence of abstract space through the example of the controversies and struggles over the Plan Puebla Panamá, a massive infrastructure project for Mexico and Central America that ultimately failed. Greig Charnock and Ramon Ribera-Fumaz analysed the reduction of and the struggle for differences in the example of the strategic transformation of the Poblenou district in Barcelona into an 'innovation district'. Naomi Hanakata has studied in detail the production of differences in Tokyo, and together with Christian Schmid and Monika Streule has explored the incorporation of differences in Mexico City, Los Angeles, and Tokyo in a comparative perspective.[208] Following in Lefebvre's footsteps, Garnier has critically examined the 'Greater Paris' project, which has been gradually implemented beginning in the 2010s.[209] He showed how this overarching project took the homogenisation, fragmentation, and hierarchisation of urban space to extremes, depoliticising urban development to such an extent that the project ultimately met with little resistance.

The idea of a productive force of difference was also an important starting point for the analyses of ETH Studio Basel, which made 'difference' one of its central categories of analysis. In *Switzerland: An Urban Portrait*, it developed the conception of 'networks–borders–differences', in direct reference to Lefebvre, as an analytical instrument for the identification of different forms of urbanisation. It used this conception to design an urban typology of Switzerland,

---

207   Fincher and Jacobs, *Cities of Difference*; Fincher et al., 'Planning in the Multicultural City'.

208   Wilson, ' "The Devastating Conquest of the Lived by the Conceived" '; Charnock and Ribera-Fumaz, 'The Production of Urban Competitiveness'; Hanakata, *Tokyo*; Hanakata, Schmid, and Streule, 'Incorporation of Urban Differences'.

209   Garnier, ' "Greater Paris" '.

which also serves as a project of a (possible) urban Switzerland.[210] 'Networks' refers to the interactions that criss-cross a territory, and create a dynamic, multiscalar, hierarchical pattern of centres and peripheries. The term 'borders' refers to different constellations of territorial regulations: borders mark and designate a territory, demarcate power, and mark the control of that territory. Third, there are the 'differences' that unfold in everyday life. They are doubly determined: on the one hand, they indicate what comes together in a concrete space – different people with their social wealth, knowledge, and skills; on the other hand, differences are also generated through networking: the connection of different places, from near and far, can also create new differences. Urbanisation in this sense means the connection and articulation of different places and situations.[211]

In only slightly modified form, the term 'difference' then entered the analytical triad 'territory–power–difference' in the project *Specificity*.[212] The aim of this project was to develop an analytical framework to capture and explain the differences of urban areas and to show how and why each urban area develops specific characteristics. The interplay of differences in everyday life plays an important role in this context: every urban territory develops certain mechanisms to handle and treat differences, such as instruments of integration, incorporation, and domestication, as well as exclusion and oppression, leading to certain patterns of segregation and hierarchisation of social spaces. The concept of difference is used in this context as an analytical instrument that contributes to the comparison of urban territories.

Urban Space: Mediation, Centrality, Difference

The concept of differential space – or differential space-time – reveals the third important element of Lefebvre's understanding of the urban. It is the (provisionally) final answer to the big question of the specificity of the urban. As the previous reconstruction has shown, the urban appears in Lefebvre's theory in different ways. The analysis of urbanisation and urban society in chapter 4 had already explored two other concepts that designate important characteristics of the urban: 'mediation' and 'centrality'. How are these concepts related to difference?

The reconstruction of Lefebvre's theory of the production of space has

---

210 Diener et al., *Switzerland*.
211 Schmid, 'Networks, Borders, Differences'.
212 Diener et al., *The Inevitable Specificity of Cities*; Schmid, 'Specificity and Urbanization'.

revealed two main approaches on urban space, which are based on two hypotheses: first, the thesis of complete urbanisation, which leads to the idea of an urban society; and second, the thesis of the primacy of space, which discovers differential space. The two theses and the two concepts to which they lead are based on two complementary perspectives: on the one hand, the perspective of urbanisation, and on the other the perspective of the production of space. Accordingly, 'urban society' and 'differential space-time' denote basically the same thing: the potential and the possibilities for the development of industrial society, viewed from two different analytical perspectives. From the perspective of the production of space, 'difference' has proved to be constitutive, while the perspective of urbanisation has revealed two other concepts: 'centrality' and 'mediation'. This finally results in three aspects or moments of the urban, which will be presented here in their mutual interplay.[213]

The Urban Level: Mediation. The urban is a specific level or order of social reality. It is a middle and mediating level that is situated between the private level, the near order, everyday life, dwelling, and the global level, the distant order, the world market, the state, knowledge, institutions, and ideologies. This intermediate level mediates between the global and the private level. With the complete urbanisation of society, it is precisely this level of mediation that is threatened.

The Urban Form: Centrality. At the same time, centrality becomes apparent as a second fundamental characteristic of the urban. It creates a situation in which different things no longer exist separately, in which constraints and normalities dissolve. The centre is a place of encounter, communication, and information, a privileged place where everything converges. Centrality therefore does not describe a concrete geographical situation, but a pure form. Its logic stands for the simultaneity of people, things, and events that can be brought together around a point. The fundamental contradiction of centrality lies on the one hand in the relationship of the centre to the periphery, and on the other in the question of access to centrality.

The Urban Space-Time: Difference. With the historical analysis of the production of space, Lefebvre now establishes *difference* as a third moment of the urban. Differences are active elements: they can only present and re-present themselves in their mutual relations. The specific quality of urban space arises from the simultaneous presence of very different worlds and values, ethnic, cultural, and social groups, activities, and knowledge. Urban space creates the possibility of bringing all these different elements together and making them

---

213   See also Schmid, 'Networks, Borders, Differences'; Schmid, 'Henri Lefebvre, the Right to the City'; Kipfer et al., 'On the Production of Henri Lefebvre'.

fruitful. It is therefore crucial how these differences are experienced and lived in concrete everyday life. While the abstract, homogeneous, fractured space tends to commodify and homogenise, the differential space will accentuate the differences and bring together the previously separate elements and moments of social practice.

The three concepts of centrality, difference, and mediation are thus directly intertwined: urban space is a place of difference, and the urban means a differential reality. But differences cannot arise without people meeting each other, and thus without centrality. As an urban form, centrality brings differences together and consolidates them.[214] Conversely, centrality can also be understood as a totality of differences.[215] At the same time, however, differences cannot unfold without political and social mediation at the urban level, which makes it possible for differences to interact and develop their productive potential. These three concepts are thus directly linked to each other. Difference can only unfold its productive capacity when different people come together – that is, through centrality. But it also requires social cohesion and a mediating instance that differences can recognise and acknowledge each other and enter into a productive exchange.

One could also connect this triad 'centrality–mediation–difference' with another triad that Lefebvre has repeatedly employed: 'form–function–structure'. For Lefebvre, a form as such is empty and requires a content in order to exist; a function needs objects if it is to operate; and the structure arranges elementary units within a whole.[216] Lefebvre brought this triad together with the three dimensions of the production of space:

> The form corresponds approximately to the moment of communication – hence the realm of the *perceived*. The function is carried out, effectively or not, and corresponds to the directly experienced in a space of representation. The structure is *conceived*, and implies a representation of space.[217]

If we transfer these considerations on the urban, then centrality would be the urban form that allows for material interaction. Mediation would be the structure that regulates exchange and holds 'the whole' together. And difference could be understood as the 'urban function' that is socially constituted and experienced, that becomes productive through the dramas of everyday life and thus unfolds its emancipatory and revolutionary potential.

---

214   Lefebvre, *Urban Revolution*, 37, 173.
215   Lefebvre, *Right to the City*, 131.
216   Lefebvre, *Production of Space*, 401.
217   Ibid., 369. Translation amended.

These reflections conclude the discussion of the specificity of the urban. However, two important questions remain open. First, it must be clarified how these analytical concepts can be applied and introduced into practice. As became clear in the course of this reconstruction, the urban in all its facets is a utopia. How can such a utopia become concrete? The following section offers some answers to this question.

On the other hand, we must also return to the history of spaces: how can the great narrative of the history of the production of space from absolute to concrete to differential space be linked to the history of urbanisation? This question is treated in the concluding section 6.6.

6.5 The Urban as Concrete Utopia

The possible belongs to the real, considered in a dynamic way.[218]

What is the urban? This question, which formed our central starting point and was repeatedly explored from new perspectives in the course of this reconstruction, finds its final answer: the urban is, first, a level of social reality that mediates between the global and the private; second, it is a form, centrality, and thus a place of encounter, meeting, and interacting; and, third, it is a space-time in which differences interact in a productive way and through that interaction may generate social inventions. The theory of the urban, which at the beginning was still emerging from the 'blind field' (see section 3.2), thus becomes more and more elaborated. But how can this theory become practice?

> We have here . . . before us projected separately, on the ground, groups, ethnic groups, ages and sexes, activities, tasks, and functions, knowledge. Here is all that is necessary to create a world, an urban society, or the developed urban. But this world is absent, this society is before us only in a state of virtuality.[219]

What is needed is a practice that sets itself the goal of bringing together what is dispersed, dissociated, separated, in the form of simultaneity and encounter.[220] The great theoretical and practical project that Lefebvre envisioned, and which

---

218   Lefebvre, *De l'État*, vol. 2, 64. Translation by author.
219   Lefebvre, *Right to the City*, 143–4.
220   Ibid.

runs like a red thread through all his writings on the city and space, is to explore a possible path towards this urban world. But this project remains – as he himself notes – necessarily abstract in his writings. Although it opposes the abstraction of the dominant space, it will not overcome it. Only practice can reveal the path of the 'concrete'.[221]

What could this practice be? As a possible guideline, Lefebvre proposed a series of rights, which changed in accordance with his current engagements with the urban question. If he postulated first the 'right to the city', he then demanded the 'right to centrality', the 'right to difference', and finally the 'right to space' (see section 4.5).[222] What these calls have in common is their utopian character. They do not refer to a current situation but highlight a possibility that is inherent in contemporary society.

Urban space is thus a utopia. But it is not an abstract utopia inspired by philosophical and cosmological reflections, but a concrete utopia that has its starting point in spatial practice, takes shape through the real appropriation of a dominant space, and opens the possibility of creating a different space.[223] This concrete utopia has nothing in common with the abstract imaginary: 'It is real. It is at the very heart of the real, the urban reality that can't exist without this ferment.'[224] Lefebvre's transductive project thus crosses the gap between science and utopia, between reality and ideal, between the conceived and the lived. It attempts to overcome these oppositions by exploring the dialectical relationship of the 'possible-impossible'.[225]

David Harvey, who also undertook a brief excursion into the world of (architectural) utopias, accused Lefebvre of not making any concrete proposals for the realisation of urban utopia.[226] However, he was obviously unaware of an important part of Lefebvre's work that was not available in English for a long time. Lefebvre rejected big utopian projects, because they are too abstract and also too repressive, ultimately only supporting the violence of the state, but he outlined a whole range of possible approaches that could lead to another, different, urban world. They are based on appropriation and self-determination and also include concrete projects for urban development and architecture. This is where Lefebvre's proximity to architecture comes into its

221   Lefebvre, *Production of Space*, 419.

222   Lefebvre, *Urban Revolution*, 194, 150; Lefebvre, *Production of Space*, 64; *De l'État*, vol. 4, 317; Lefebvre, *State, Space, World*, 247–8.

223   Lefebvre, *Toward an Architecture of Enjoyment*, 141.

224   Lefebvre, *Urban Revolution*, 38.

225   Lefebvre, *Production of Space*, 60.

226   Harvey, *Spaces of Hope*, 182; see also Harvey, *Justice, Nature and the Geography of Difference*, 435.

own. Łukasz Stanek, in his book *Henri Lefebvre on Space*, has shown in detail that Lefebvre has discussed and collaborated with many architects and urban designers and was directly involved in many of the contemporary (French) debates about space and architecture. Accordingly, architectural and urban planning proposals are also to be found in his approaches.

This section discusses some of these concrete utopias. It begins with a semiotic and topological reflection on the dialectical concept of isotopy and heterotopy and explores the concept of concrete utopia, the impossible-possible, which illuminates the horizon of action and initially appears impossible, but which, potentially, might be realised in the here and now. It discusses various urban strategies and analyses two contributions that Lefebvre made to urban planning competitions, but which were long lost and have only recently been rediscovered and reappraised. Finally, it treats the concept of autogestion: the concrete utopia of the withering away of the state.

Isotopy, Heterotopy, U-topia

What might a differential urban space look like? Lefebvre initially approached this question on a semiotic level, taking up a conception developed by Algirdas J. Greimas: isotopy and heterotopy. Greimas had been looking for a topological semiotics, that is, a semiotics that deciphers space as a meaningful 'object'. He regarded space as a construction that refers to something other than itself. Starting from the simplest articulation, Greimas came to the conclusion that a place can only be grasped by what it is not, by fixing it in relation to another place. The appropriation of a 'topia' is thus only possible through the postulation of a heterotopy. In this way, space itself becomes a signifier that denotes something other than space itself.[227] This is precisely what Lefebvre meant with the term 'spaces of representation'.

Although Greimas came from a background in structural linguistics, and Lefebvre was very sceptical about both structuralism and the project of spatial semiotics (see section 5.5), he nevertheless took these considerations as the starting point for his conception of differential space.[228] Lefebvre used the terms isotopy and heterotopy for the deciphering of urban space and of time written in space, bringing together different logics and readings in a classification that refers to oppositions in space. Isotopy denotes analogous, comparable

227   Greimas, 'Pour une sémiotique topologique', 12. See also Greimas, *Sémantique structurale*, 96–8.

228   Lefebvre, *Right to the City*, 113; Lefebvre, *Urban Revolution*, 38, 172; Lefebvre, *Production of Space*, 163, 366.

spaces, places that are the same or equal. In the spaces created by state rationalism, Lefebvre sees a special form of isotopy: large straight lines, wide avenues,
empty spaces, wide-open perspectives, which signify an occupation of the
terrain while eliminating what was previously there. In contrast, heterotopy
stands for contrasting, differential places or spaces. It denotes the other place
and the place of the other, the place that is excluded and – dialectically speaking – simultaneously included through its exclusion. The difference between
isotopy and heterotopy must be understood dynamically because something is
always happening in urban space. Social conditions change; differences mount
and move towards conflict, or they weaken and destroy each other.

The distinction between isotopies and heterotopies presupposes the existence of a neutral or indifferent element: a place of passage between adjacent
places, a square, a street, a crossroads, or a garden or park. Lefebvre calls this
neutral element *coupure-suture* (cut-suture) because it separates and/or
connects two opposing heterotopies. In the alleyways, the suture is stronger
than the cut. The opposite is true for the highways that criss-cross urban
space.[229]

Finally, the duality of isotopy and heterotopy produces – according to
Lefebvre's three-dimensional dialectic – a third topos: the u-topia. This is the
non-place, the place of that which has no place and yet seeks a place, the place
of elsewhere. In urban space, the u-topia is everywhere and nowhere, it is the
absolute, the divine, the possible.[230] U-topia unites the near order with the far
order – it is a barely determined but well-conceived and (figuratively) imagined place:

> In general, this place, imagined and real, is found near the borders of
> verticality, the dimension of desire, power, and thought. Sometimes it is
> found deep within the subterranean city imagined by the novelist or
> poet, the underside of the city given over to conspiracy and crime.[231]

U-topias are thus spaces occupied by the symbolic and the imaginary. Places
like gardens and parks make this elsewhere visible, tangible, readable by referring to a double u-topia: absolute nature and pure artificiality.[232]

It is revealing that Michel Foucault, at virtually the same time as Lefebvre,
also developed a concept of *heterotopia*, and he also told a story of space. He
presented it in his 1967 lecture to the architects of the Cercles d'études

---

229   Lefebvre, *Urban Revolution*, 38, 128–9.
230   Ibid., 38, 131, 133; Lefebvre, *Production of Space*, 163.
231   Lefebvre, *Urban Revolution*, 130.
232   Ibid., 131; Lefebvre, *Production of Space*, 366.

architecturales entitled 'Des espaces autres', which was published much later but then became very influential, both in architecture and in geography.[233] However, Foucault's concept of heterotopia has a completely different starting point to that of Lefebvre: in his preface to *The Order of Things*, where he mentions the term briefly for the first time, Foucault uses it to denote a confusion that arises when very different things are brought together linguistically: 'Things are "laid", "placed", "arranged" in sites so very different from one another that it is impossible to find a place of residence for them, to define a *common locus* beneath them all.'[234] Sigurd Lax has pointed out that the term 'heterotopia' in medicine describes a phenomenon in which a specific human tissue appears in a completely different place than is usually expected.[235]

In his lecture, Foucault then applied this concept to a wide variety of places, such as cemeteries, brothels, prisons, barracks, psychiatric clinics, but also to cinemas and theatres, gardens, museums, libraries, and even ships. These are spaces that are connected to all other spaces, but in which behaviour deviating from the dominant norm is localised and ritualised. These specialised spaces allow practices and fulfil needs that are displaced from everyday life.

Foucault's heterotopia is very inspiring. However, it is a different concept than Lefebvre's space of heterotopy, which is characterised by the simultaneity of differences. Lefebvre's heterotopy is created by internal and external relationships; it does not delimit the 'other' and does not dislocate it into specialised spaces, but rather makes it visible and brings it right into the midst of society to make it productive. Difference in Lefebvre's sense cannot exist in separation; it needs interaction and encounter, sometimes including active confrontation.

The Concrete Utopia

How can such a heterotopic, differential space arise? Lefebvre insists that such a space does not simply emerge, but must be created and fought for:

A revolution that does not produce a new space has not realized its full potential; indeed it has failed in that it has not changed life itself, but has merely changed ideological superstructures, institutions or political apparatuses. A social transformation, to be truly revolutionary in

---

233   Foucault, 'Of Other Spaces'. For the discussion of Foucault's heterotopia, see for example Knaller-Vlay and Ritter, 'Editorial'; Soja, *Postmodern Geographies*.

234   Foucault, *The Order of Things*, xix.

235   Lax, ' "Heterotopia" '.

character, must manifest a creative capacity in its effects on daily life, on language and on space – though its impact need not occur at the same rate, or with equal force, in each of these areas.[236]

This quotation refers directly to a critique of actually existing socialism, in which Lefebvre notes that the astonishing creative fermentation in the 1920s in the Soviet Union failed even more dramatically in the field of architecture and urban planning than in other areas. And he wonders whether it is still legitimate to speak of socialism when there has been no architectural innovation and no specific space has been created.[237] As the journal *Not Bored!* has shown, this quote also contains a critique of the Situationists and their concept of *détournement*, in which an existing space is used for other purposes.[238] Lefebvre himself gives the example of the famous Les Halles, the buildings of the former wholesale market in the centre of Paris which were transformed into a gathering-place and a scene of permanent festival before being demolished between 1969 and 1971.[239] This kind of détournement might be of great significance, but it is not enough, Lefebvre remarks in his critique, for a community to install itself in morphologically older spaces that may not be suitable for a communal life. In order to end the domination of abstract space, he insists, the production of a new space is indispensable.[240]

This position may be contradicted vehemently. There are countless examples of groups and projects that have successfully installed themselves for a shorter or longer period of time in converted and reappropriated spaces. However, Lefebvre is not concerned with individual projects, as he argues from the broader theoretical perspective of society as a whole. The realisation of an urban society, in his view, requires a new way of producing space (section 7.3).

This urban space, which has yet to be created, is initially a utopia. But in Lefebvre's understanding, this utopia is not an abstract, merely imagined place, but a concrete and lived practice – in other words, a concrete utopia. While abstract utopias are the creations of technocrats who want to build a perfect city, the concrete utopia, or the u-topia, is negative. It negates the everyday, work, the economy of exchange as well as the state and the supremacy of the political. Such a u-topia attempts to develop a new space based on an architectural project.[241]

---

236   Lefebvre, *Production of Space*, 54.
237   Ibid., 54–5.
238   Not Bored!, 'Henri Lefebvre's "The Production of Space" '.
239   Lefebvre, *Production of Space*, 167.
240   Ibid., 168.
241   Lefebvre, *Toward an Architecture of Enjoyment*, 148.

Chris Butler and Łukasz Stanek have identified some parallels between Lefebvre's concrete utopia and Ernst Bloch, who had developed his own concept of concrete utopia in his three-volume work *The Principle of Hope*, which explores how a transformation of society might be achieved in reality.[242] In this work, he assembled a wealth of examples, from social utopias to technical, geographical, architectural, and artistic utopias. It was Bloch's response to Marx's and Engels's criticism of the abstract utopias of the early socialists, formulating a concrete utopia which could lead to a Marxist practice.

Lefebvre, however, does not make reference to Bloch. His u-topia is directly linked to urban practice and is intended to search for ways of shifting the impossible towards the possible. These ways include a transgression: 'In order to extend the possible, it is necessary to proclaim and desire the impossible. Action and strategy consist in making possible tomorrow what is impossible today.'[243] In this sense the urban – urban society – is a horizon, it is the possible, defined by a direction in which it can move. In order to achieve this potentiality, it is first necessary to remove or break through the obstacles that make it impossible in the present.[244]

Lefebvre's reflections on concrete utopia have been discussed relatively widely in various theoretical and disciplinary contexts.[245] An excellent overview of the debates in architecture and urban planning is provided by David Pinder, who follows in Lefebvre's footsteps on a journey through utopian spaces, in particular highlighting the connections between Lefebvre and the Situationists, and in doing so also sheds light on the contrasts within the 'Situationist International' (SI).[246]

The manifold actions and activities of the Situationists can be seen as another attempt to introduce a utopian practice into everyday life. Lefebvre worked closely together with them in the late 1950s, but was never a member of the SI himself (see section 2.1). He agreed with the Situationists on the original idea of producing new situations, an 'at once poetic, subversive and bold idea', which already 'contained a project of difference'.[247] The concept of the situation was also closely linked to his own theory of moments, which he had developed in the context of his studies on everyday life (see section 3.1). He interpreted the basic

---

242   Butler, *Henri Lefebvre*, 134–6; Stanek, *Henri Lefebvre on Space*, 193–4; Bloch, *The Principle of Hope*.

243   Lefebvre, *Survival of Capitalism*, 36.

244   Lefebvre, *Urban Revolution*, 17.

245   For example, by Gardiner, 'Utopia and Everyday Life in French Social Thought'; Sadler, *The Situationist City*; Kofman and Lebas, 'Recovery and Appropriation in Lefebvre and Constant'.

246   See Pinder, *Visions of the City*; Pinder, 'Reconstituting the Possible'.

247   Lefebvre, *Le temps des méprises*, 157. Translation by author.

Situationist concept of *dérive* as an experimental method for creating new situations, for instance through the actionist connection of neighbourhoods that were spatially separated. 'Unitary urbanism', a concept for the implementation of *dérive* on the architectural level, also sought to connect different neighbourhoods with each other, and to assemble a new unity of the city, but one constantly in motion and transformation.[248] The famous project 'New Babylon' by Constant Nieuwenhys, himself a member of the SI for a short time, which represented a concrete application of unitary urbanism, made a strong impression on Lefebvre, not only because it embodied a dialectical relationship between space and social practices, but also because it created an ambiance, an affectivity, and thus incorporated lived space into architecture.[249] But, as Lefebvre noted in an interview with Kristin Ross, the theory of unitary urbanism lost its meaning with the advent of urbanisation and the explosion of the city, and he began to look for a more comprehensive theory of the urban.[250] The Situationists, on the other hand, increasingly turned away from their productive experimental concepts and started a radical critique of urbanism, which has also left clear traces in Lefebvre's texts (see section 6.3).

Towards an Urban Strategy

As shown in chapter 4, urbanisation presented Lefebvre with new problems: how can the urban be realised in the face of complete urbanisation? In *The Urban Revolution*, he outlined possible approaches to an 'urban strategy' that could lead towards such a u-topian space.[251] This is a 'strategy of knowledge' which, following the method of transduction, is oriented towards the practical and based on a constant confrontation with experience. It aims to develop a general and coherent urban practice that would enable people to appropriate space and time.[252]

What does this urban strategy consist of? Lefebvre gave different answers according to the respective social and political constellations he encountered. In *The Right to the City* he starts with the inhabitants:

The inhabitants (which ones? – it's up to research and researchers to find them!) reconstitute centres, using places to restitute even derisory

---

248   Ibid.; Ross and Lefebvre, 'Lefebvre on the Situationists', 73, 75.
249   Lefebvre, *Le temps des méprises*, 243–4.
250   Ross and Lefebvre, 'Lefebvre on the Situationists', 77, 81.
251   Lefebvre, *Urban Revolution*, 135–50.
252   Ibid., 140.

encounters. The use (use value) of places, monuments, differences, escape the demands of exchange, of exchange value. A big game is played before us, with various episodes whose meaning is not always evident.[253]

In *The Urban Revolution*, he reflects about the spontaneous action groups that emerged in the wake of the 1968 movement:

> If at some time in the near future, the ephemeral becomes more prevalent, which is entirely conceivable, what would it consist of? In the activities of groups that are themselves ephemeral, that would invent and realize various works. Their own. In which their lives and their group existence would be realized and exhausted by momentarily freeing themselves of the everyday. But what works, what groups? The answer would render the fundamental question of creation irrelevant. Those groups, should they come into being, would invent their moments and their actions, their spaces and times, their works. And they would do so at the level of habiting or by starting out from that level (without remaining there; that is, by modelling an appropriate urban space).[254]

However, he adds, some attempts to make the impossible possible would still prove nothing, either by their success or by their failure. They would only gain importance in the course of a revolutionary upheaval. Under the current circumstances, the existing society would try to co-opt their concepts.[255]

In *De l'État*, Lefebvre sees the emergence of 'movements of users' (*mouvements d'usagers*) that revive the concept of use without reducing it to the simple consumption of space. These movements had become a worldwide phenomenon, he claimed, referring in particular to Japan, Italy, Spain, and the US. They would raise the hypothesis of a possible convergence between the demands for work and those that affect the entire space and thus everyday life.[256]

In *The Production of Space*, Lefebvre, starting from his critique of architecture, proposes an active, practical, and theoretical negation: the counter-project (*contre-projet*), the counter-plan (*contre-plan*), or the counter-space (*contre-espace*), a space of counter-culture – an initially utopian alternative, as Lefebvre concedes. These projects and plans are first of all a practice. When a population opposes a highway or an urban development project, when it demands public facilities, places for games or meeting places, a counter-space is introduced

---

253 Lefebvre, *Right to the City*, 129.
254 Lefebvre, *Urban Revolution*, 98–9.
255 Ibid., 99.
256 Lefebvre, *De l'État*, vol. 4, 271–3; Lefebvre, *State, Space, World*, 227.

into spatial reality: against the eye and the gaze, against the quantitative and the homogeneous, against power and arrogance, against a boundless expansion of the 'private', against specialised spaces and narrowly localised functions. For Lefebvre, this ability to elaborate counter-projects and to negotiate them with the 'authorities' is the measure of a 'real' democracy.[257]

A Space of Joy and Pleasure

How might such counter-projects look? What kind of architecture could implement the demand for a differential space? Lefebvre pursued this question in a manuscript that Łukasz Stanek found in Saragossa during his research and published in an English translation under the title *Toward an Architecture of Enjoyment*. This manuscript was commissioned in 1974 by Mario Gaviria, a Spanish urban sociologist, planner, and activist who had previously studied with Lefebvre in Strasbourg and was working on a study of touristic 'new towns'. Lefebvre, however, gave no practical guidance in this text, nor did he draft any concrete proposals; Gaviria ultimately found the manuscript too abstract and therefore did not even include it in his study.[258] Nevertheless, this manuscript raises the important problematic of the architectural project which had occupied Lefebvre since the 1950s. Lefebvre gave it the title *Vers une architecture de jouissance*, obviously inspired by Le Corbusier's book with the simple title *Vers une architecture* which has become one of the most famous manifestos of modern architecture.[259] The translation of the word '*jouissance*' with its erotic and sexual connotations caused some difficulties, and 'enjoyment' was ultimately chosen as the English equivalent. *Jouissance* also played a central role in the work of Jacques Lacan, but since no English term adequately captures its wealth of meanings, *jouissance* was always left untranslated in the English editions of Lacan's work. However, there is no direct reference to Lacan in the Saragossa manuscript, even though Lefebvre often refers to Lacan in his texts and even though the erotic and sexual moment, which was so important for Lacan, also resonates with Lefebvre.

Lefebvre positioned his manuscript in the theoretical context established in *The Urban Revolution*. First, it relates to the three fields or continents (the rural, the industrial, and the urban) and their three defining concepts: need–work–enjoyment (*jouissance*) (see section 3.4). Second, the text is situated in

---

257 Lefebvre, *Production of Space*, 349, 381–2, 419–20; Lefebvre, *De l'État*, vol. 4, 293; Lefebvre, *State, Space, World*, 235.

258 Stanek, 'Introduction: A Manuscript Found in Saragossa', xi–xii.

259 Le Corbusier, *Toward an Architecture*.

architecture, and thus on level P, the level of everyday life.[260] With this manuscript, Lefebvre closes an important gap in his work: while he had written extensively on level M (and thus on urbanism), and later also on level G (territorial planning), a more detailed discussion of architecture was missing so far.

Despite his intense preoccupation with concrete architectural projects, Lefebvre found few realised examples for the kind of architecture he was imagining. Since the end of the nineteenth century, he laments, functionalism, monotony, and boredom have dominated, and the combinations of repetitive elements point at best to minimal differences.[261] With a magic carpet, Lefebvre flies to temples, palaces, castles, monasteries, gardens from different centuries and continents, visits utopian places like Fourier's Phalanstère, and even makes a detour into the mists of London. At the end he lands on a beach:

> The elements are there: earth, air, the sun's fire, water . . . The earth culminates in the sea; the sky dissolves into the earth and the water. This surface of encounters is one of interference: the fine sand, its delicious fluidity. Here, bodies no longer experience water alone or earth alone, or air and sun in isolation – I almost said, abstractly. Each element plays a role, receives the others and protects itself from them by sheltering living bodies; water protects the sun and the sandy earth from the assaults of the sun, the waves (such a beautiful name, the waves, always repeated, always different, uncertain, unambiguous, individual, caressing, violent). Fire burns and consumes by its own force, water engulfs, and the air sweeps away and dries. Where they end, the beach begins. Transition, passages, encounters. A space of enjoyment . . . The total body begins to appear.[262]

Not architecture, then, but a beach. But Lefebvre himself exposes the idea that leisure spaces could form a 'counter-space' as a 'complete illusion': 'Leisure is as alienated and alienating as labour.'[263] And yet this space contains a promise and reveals a possible rupture.[264] Lefebvre concludes: 'An architecture of pleasure and joy, of community in the use of gifts of the earth, has still to be invented.'[265] In the early eighties, he wrote in the preface to the third edition of *La production de l'espace*: 'The project for creating a new space remains uncertain.'[266]

---

260   Lefebvre, *Toward an Architecture of Enjoyment*, 146.
261   Ibid., 16–18.
262   Ibid., 48–9.
263   Lefebvre, *Production of Space*, 383.
264   Ibid., 385.
265   Ibid., 379.
266   Lefebvre, 'Preface to the New Edition', 213.

So, even if Lefebvre could not give a concrete answer to the question of what a new architecture of pleasure might be, he took part in another competition in 1986, together with the architects Serge Renaudie and Pierre Guilbaud. The International Competition for the New Belgrade Urban Structure Improvement, organised by the City of Belgrade, was looking for proposals for the completion of the huge unfinished development area of Novi Beograd on the plateau west of the Sava River, the result of large-scale modernist urban planning. Their competition entry – 'The New Urban' – was retrieved by the architectural historian Ljilijana Blagojević and reprinted by Sabine Bitter and Helmut Weber in *Autogestion, or Henri Lefebvre in New Belgrade*.[267] In their contribution, which was already eliminated in the first round because it did not adhere to the competition's strict specifications, the three authors attempted to insert a different, more open, flexible, and communicative structure into the abstract urban structure of New Belgrade, which is dominated by the modernist grid of the 'mega-block'. The strategy of reconnection that the Situationists used in unitary urbanism is clearly visible: there are several new bridges over the Sava River that connect New Belgrade with historical Belgrade, as well as numerous new connections within New Belgrade.

The proposal aims to increase the complexity and dynamics of urban space, following three design principles:

1. In order to oppose the systematisation, homogenisation, and uniformity of abstract space and to increase the opportunities of communication and encounter, the proposal relies on the principle of a diversity of uses, structures, activities, and rhythms.

2. The principle of *imbrication* (meshing or overlap) attempts to create an 'active' situation in which interactions, interconnections, interferences, and interpenetrations of events become the new components of the city.

3. At the same time, however, the specificities of activities, functions, groups, and units should be preserved and not dissolve within a space of connectivity.[268]

This project comes closest to an architectural realisation of Lefebvre's ideas. It assembles almost all the u-topias that Lefebvre had developed over time, and also his u-topian calls to action: the right to the city, to centrality, to difference, to active participation, and to *autogestion*.

---

267   Renaudie, Guilbaud, and Lefebvre, 'International Competition'; Blagojević, 'The Problematic of a "New Urban" '; Blagojević, 'Novi Beograd'.
268   Renaudie, Guilbaud, and Lefebvre, 'International Competition'.

Autogestion and Urban Democracy

Finally, a concept that must be presented runs like a red thread through Lefebvre's texts: autogestion. This concept emerged in the context of the French discussions of the 1950s and 1960s and represented a general and fundamental demand for self-determination and self-determined spaces. Neil Brenner and Stuart Elden have written extensively about Lefebvre's concept of autogestion and have also shown that this term cannot be translated directly into English.[269] It refers to different forms of self-management in various areas of social and political life, in companies and also in state institutions themselves, right up to local and regional self-administration.

Klaus Ronneberger has traced the history of autogestion in detail. Its roots go back to the anarchist and anarcho-syndicalist circles of the early nineteenth century, especially to Proudhon, who had a strong influence on the French labour movement.[270] Jean Duvignaud has shown that Proudhon's ideas were disseminated in France by, among others, the sociologist Georges Gurvitch, who was one of the organisers of the Russian Soviets in 1917, and who later emigrated to France and initiated the journal *Autogestion* in 1966.[271] As Frank Georgi has analysed, the discussion on autogestion in France was strongly influenced by the Yugoslav model of socialism, which broke away from Stalinism in the early 1950s and decentralised the state decision-making process.[272] As Erić Zoran has shown, certain state functions were taken over by associations of free producers in this process.[273] The Serbo-Croatian term *radničko samoupravljanje* (workers' self-management) was ultimately translated into French as *autogestion*.

Michel Trebitsch judges that the relation of Lefebvre's theoretical project to the concept of autogestion should not be overestimated.[274] Nevertheless, the idea of autogestion runs through all of Lefebvre's work, in particular as a strategy that breaks not only with capitalism but also with the state mode of socialism. The roots of this idea can be traced back in Lefebvre's work to *Dialectical Materialism*, where he thematises the self-production of humans and raises the question of the practical implementation of the demand for the withering away of the state – the great utopia that had already been so prominently advocated

---

269   Brenner and Elden, introduction to Lefebvre, *State, Space, World*, 14, 37.
270   Ronneberger, 'Henri Lefebvre and the Question of Autogestion'.
271   Duvignaud, 'Georges Gurvitch'.
272   Georgi, *Autogestion, la dernière utopie*.
273   Zoran, 'The Third Way'.
274   Trebitsch, 'Henri Lefebvre et l'autogestion', 65–6.

by Marx and Engels, but which in no way became apparent in socialist countries.

Autogestion can thus be understood as a possible concrete utopia of the withering away of the state. A first detailed examination of the term can be found in Lefebvre's text 'Problèmes théorique de l'autogestion' from 1966 which forms the theoretical prelude to the first issue of the journal *Autogestion*. In this text, Lefebvre explains that autogestion continues the path of revolutionary spontaneity that underlies the Paris Commune, the Russian Soviets, and anarcho-syndicalism in the Spanish Civil War: 'Now, the form taken today by revolutionary spontaneity is no longer anarcho-syndicalism, it is *autogestion*.'[275] Autogestion constitutes itself as a force beyond the state, as an opening to the possible, which can restore use value and appropriation in relation to exchange value.[276]

The demand for autogestion reached a climax in French political discussions in 1968, and Lefebvre dedicated a chapter to it in his manifesto *The Explosion*, which refers directly to May 1968 in Paris.[277] He notes that the rallying cry of autogestion arose spontaneously to fill the void left by the state. It expresses a fundamental social need, and implicitly contains a general project that is directly linked to the question of everyday life. The protests, the strikes, the whole movement shook everyday life, but afterwards it was restored, and with it the social order based on it. Lefebvre therefore proposes autogestion to fundamentally transform everyday life and to lay the foundations for a different society.

In the 1970s, autogestion was widely discussed in France in leftist milieus outside the Communist Party. In *The Urban Revolution*, Lefebvre calls for an '*autogestion urbaine*' in a short section,[278] and at the end of *De l'État* he sketches the idea of an '*autogestion territoriale*', that is, the democratic control of the production of space and the affirmation of differences.[279] *Autogestion territoriale* could also be understood as a political complement to differential space. Its implementation requires an urban democracy, a concept that Lefebvre developed at the end of his life together with the Groupe de Navarrenx in the book *Du contrat de citoyenneté*.[280]

---

275   Lefebvre, *State, Space, World*, 142.
276   Ibid., 148–50.
277   Lefebvre, *The Explosion*, 84–90.
278   Lefebvre, *Urban Revolution*, 150.
279   Lefebvre, *De l'État*, vol. 4, 323–4; Lefebvre, *State, Space, World*, 250–1.
280   Lefebvre and Groupe de Navarrenx, *Du contrat de citoyenneté*.

Possible Urban Worlds

With the concepts of differential space-time, urban strategy, urban practice, the architecture of enjoyment, *autogestion territoriale*, and urban democracy, Lefebvre developed or refined a whole range of ideas in the 1970s that could be used for the production of a differential urban space. But Lefebvre was well aware that social relations would first have to change before such proposals could have a chance of being realised. In volume 3 of the *Critique of Everyday Life*, for example, he noted that the theory of difference had not been very well received.[281] And autogestion, too, lost some of its appeal when actually existing socialism collapsed in the 1990s and Yugoslavia broke apart in a terrible civil war. Nevertheless, autogestion continues to be discussed in France today.

Since Lefebvre always developed his concepts in direct confrontation with current social reality, they are necessarily a product of their time. Urbanisation, however, is constantly evolving. So it is necessary to go further, and to develop new counter-proposals and counter-projects, not only in architecture and urban planning, but also in and for public space, for the appropriation of urban spaces, for the creation of self-determined and self-organised cultural and social centres, in urban revolts and the often fleeting moments of actions and happenings, to search for maximum differences that can illuminate a horizon and expand the realm of the possible towards the impossible. Even if such movements and projects are ephemeral, their effects are often overlooked and underestimated. Many of these discussions and mobilisations, experiences in occupied squares, and provocative and often funny happenings and actions remain undocumented, and at best appear in newspaper articles, movement magazines, leaflets, and blogs, in photographs or narrations. One of the few publications that has collected such projects and thereby also established a connection to Lefebvre is *Possible Urban Worlds*, published by the International Network for Urban Research and Action (INURA).[282] What all these projects have in common is that they call for, propagate, and practise a self-determined appropriation of space and thus convey something very important: the hope for a different urban world.

---

281   Lefebvre, *Critique of Everyday Life*, vol. 3, 113.
282   INURA, *Possible Urban Worlds*.

6.6 Histories of Urban Spaces

> Time is known and actualized in space ... Similarly, space is known
> only in and through time.[283]

With the concrete utopia of urban, differential space, Lefebvre's history of the production of space comes to a close. It has uncovered a whole range of new insights into this complex process, some of which may seem confusing and have given rise to misunderstandings. This concluding section, therefore, summarises the various lines of argumentation.

In reviewing the production of historical spaces presented by Lefebvre, it has become clear that the contradictory formants of the production of space – the perceived, the conceived, and the lived – develop differently, while their mutual relations are also changing. Starting from a previously existing space, each formation of society produces its own space in the course of its historical development, which again becomes the starting point for the subsequent formation. Correspondingly, modern society has also produced its space, homogeneous-fractured abstract space with its three formants: the visual, the geometric, the phallic. In this abstract space, however, Lefebvre sees not only a threat, but also a potential, a 'possible-impossible', the concrete utopia of a new space: differential space, a space of heterotopy, in which differences develop, encounter each other, and in their interaction generate a new space. This differential space is nothing other than the space of urban society. This raises the question of how the 'history of the production of space' presented in this chapter is related to the 'history of the city' presented in chapter 3, a question that Lefebvre himself has left in the dark.

This brings us to the next problem of the historical schema of the production of space and, related to this, the periodisation of history. Lefebvre's diverse and sometimes disparate attempts to periodise history have repeatedly posed considerable difficulties for interpretation. First, this has to do with the general and thus also sweeping character of the 'periods' or 'modes of production' identified by Lefebvre. Second, the associative, essayistic procedure that Lefebvre employs, as well as the lack of heuristic and methodological criteria in his 'historiography', makes it difficult to assess their objectives. Third, Lefebvre seems to pursue different directions with these histories, which makes them more like illustrations of theses than accurate historical accounts of the city or of space. Fourth, the irritating idea arises that this sequence of 'modes of production' corresponds to a Hegelian philosophy of history that strives for a

---

283   Lefebvre, *Production of Space*, 218.

finality, an 'end of history'. This also raises the question of the epistemological status of these 'histories': what form of knowledge is conveyed by them and what should they show?

Finally, the most problematic side of these histories must also be addressed: their obvious Eurocentrism, which turns these histories of urban space into histories of the West rather than into a 'world history' or a 'history of capitalism', which could only be grasped if social developments outside Europe and especially colonialism were also included in the analysis. This requires a critical conclusion and at the same time consideration of a possible postcolonial reading of Lefebvre's theory. Such a critique also opens up the fundamental possibility of turning Lefebvre's theory and procedures into a collective project (see section 8.3).

On the Periodisation of History

As noted in the introduction, Lefebvre's texts on the city and on space contain several periodisations of history. The sequence of historical spaces presented in this chapter, or, more precisely, of modes of the production of space, distinguishes the following phases: analogous space, cosmological space, symbolic space, perspectival space, homogeneous-fractured space.

Their assignment to the classical modes of production is rather easy here: it starts with the 'original' societies (analogous space) and leads via the European antiquity of Greece and Rome (cosmological space) to the feudal mode of production in Western Europe (symbolic space). Between the latest of these and the twentieth century, however, there is a long gap that Lefebvre fills with perspectival space. Lefebvre himself noted that the space of perspective does not correspond to the classification of modes of production.[284] However, if we look at another periodisation that Lefebvre presented in *The Survival of Capitalism*, we learn that in the sixteenth century the rise of capitalism and the bourgeoisie was marked by fierce political struggles, and that this rise was reinforced and consolidated in the eighteenth century by the emergence of industry, which replaced manufacture.[285] In this sense, then, the space of perspective would correspond with merchant and industrial capitalism. Finally, the twentieth century brings with it the homogeneous and fractured space, and this would correspond to 'monopoly capitalism' in an orthodox periodisation. In *De l'État*, Lefebvre developed the concept of the 'state mode of production' for this phase, which will be discussed in section 7.5.

---

284   Lefebvre, *De l'État*, vol. 4, 285; Lefebvre, *State, Space, World*, 231.
285   Lefebvre, *Survival of Capitalism*, 60.

This periodisation interferes in a peculiar way with the 'history of the city' as it was elaborated in section 4.3. Here the sequence was as follows: political city, merchant city, industrial city, and this sequence could be extended to the 'world city' (see section 4.4). This periodisation of urban development is only partly consistent with the historical sequence of 'spaces': the phase of the 'political city' covers the entire period from the Neolithic Revolution to the Middle Ages. The merchant city corresponds to a part of the 'perspectival space', and the industrial city could partly be assigned to the homogeneous-fractured space – even if industrialisation began long before the 'rupture of 1910'. These individual periods can, however, also be assigned differently.[286]

However, one can ask whether Lefebvre intended a stringent periodisation at all. As was already made clear in the introductory discussion of the modes of production (see section 6.1), he is not interested in achieving a direct correspondence between an economically defined periodisation and the history of the production of space. He notes, for example, that medieval symbolism cannot be defined either by ground rent or by the relation between town and country. And he adds the criticism that reducing the aesthetic, the social, and the mental to the economic was a disastrous mistake that some 'Marxists' still perpetuate.[287]

What really stands out in this history of space is the way Lefebvre uses non-economic aspects for his periodisation. To give an example, he argues that the rise of capitalism is rooted not only, as in classical analyses, in the emergence of the world of commodities and capital accumulation, but also in the production of a new space that was essentially marked by an overthrow of the signifiers and the emergence of a 'visual logic', epitomised in Gothic cathedrals. And he understands the beginning of merchant capitalism in the Renaissance from the production of a specific, 'perspectival' landscape in Tuscany. In a similar way, he characterised modern, abstract space first and foremost with a painting by Picasso, which heralded its arrival and revealed its fundamental problematic.

Without going into further detail and attempting to sort these 'histories of space' (or rather: of 'occidental space') even more precisely, it still needs to be noted that these histories have their inconsistencies (see also section 3.3). They should not be taken at face value, but rather serve as outlines, to which Lefebvre attaches his historical digressions in an essayistic manner. Although the material he lays out is impressive, the presentation remains too cursory and too general for a profound historical analysis. But more than historical precision, what is of interest in this context is the procedure that Lefebvre exemplifies here: taking the production of space as a starting point for a historical analysis of social development.

---

286   See for example Gregory, *Geographical Imaginations*, 383.
287   Lefebvre, *De l'État*, vol. 4, 292; Lefebvre, *State, Space, World*, 234.

The Historical Scheme of the Production of Space

In my understanding, a similar approach is also recommended for the two comprehensive, three-part narratives that overlap with these periodisations, each telling a different 'history of space'. One narrative is the sequence of spatio-temporal fields or continents – the rural, the industrial, and the urban – discussed in section 3.4; the other is the sequence of historical spaces – the absolute, the abstract, and the differential – reconstructed above.

Here, too, there seems to be a direct connection between these two stories or sequences. Derek Gregory sees two overlapping narratives in these histories: a more positive strand (the history of the city) that exposes the horizon of urban society as a project of human self-realisation, and a much more negative one (the history of space) that traces the 'disembodiment' of space in the West.[288] This account, however, appears to be undialectical and does not correspond to the material presented here. Thus, both narratives contain emphatic critiques of the observed development, and both reveal a utopian hope: on the one hand, for urban society, and on the other, for differential space-time. Obviously, these narrative strands run in dazzling parallel.

It is therefore necessary to recall once again the main results of the earlier analysis in chapter 3: the rural field is determined by need, and it is the field in which the urban–rural contradiction takes shape. The industrial field is dominated by labour, and it produces urbanisation, which transforms the contradiction of city and country to that of centre and periphery. Finally, the urban continent emerges as a virtuality that might help pleasure and enjoyment to arise.

In contrast, the history of spaces describes a process of abstraction that is explicitly linked to the commodity and the development of capitalism: this process of abstraction begins with the Gothic that paves the way for a new space, the space of (capitalist) accumulation. With the Renaissance and the introduction of perspective in art, this space became increasingly abstract, along with the spread of capitalism and the commodity. This history also reveals a virtuality, the possibility of differential space. Here, the 'urban continent' and 'differential space' basically denote the same thing, namely the concrete utopia of an urban society, but viewed from different perspectives. What is both confusing and illuminating is that this shift in perspective is not due to the development of Lefebvre's thinking, but rather is laid out in parallel in most of his texts: thus the concept of differential space is already present in *The Right to the City*, and the spatio-temporal continents that Lefebvre

---

288   Gregory, *Geographical Imaginations*, 368.

apparently abandons in *The Production of Space* in favour of a new periodisation suddenly reappear in *De l'État*, where Lefebvre notes that the practical
transformation of the world has gone through three phases: the agrarian, the
industrial, and the urban.[289]

However, the status of these historical 'fields' does not seem to be the same.
The rural, the industrial, and the urban denote spatio-temporal configurations
whose transitions cannot be clearly delimited from one to the other and which
can also exist simultaneously. But no clear, sharply delineated transitions can
be identified between absolute, abstract, and differential space either, and here
too the question arises as to whether they characterise a clear historical
sequence at all. The main chapter titles in *The Production of Space*, which structure this history of space, provide a first hint at a different reading: 'From
Absolute Space to Abstract Space' – 'Contradictory Space' – 'From the
Contradictions of Space to Differential Space'. It can be concluded from this
that Lefebvre does not see this sequence rigidly, but rather as an overlapping set
of tendencies. He also postulates that no space is eliminated and disappears in
the course of the social process, not even the initial space of nature: 'something'
survives and continues to exist.[290] Accordingly, he does not assume, for example, that 'absolute space' is completely absorbed by abstract space. Rather, this
space is pushed underground and transformed into heterotopic places, places
of witchcraft and madness, places inhabited by demonic forces, fascinating,
cursed, and rediscovered much later by artists.[291]

These two histories of space can therefore be read in parallel. In a sense,
Lefebvre illuminates two sides of the same coin: if in the first narrative he analyses three different historical ways of life or modes of social practice, in the
second he is primarily concerned with representations – with the historically
determined relationship between representations of space and spaces of
representation.

Both narratives follow the same classical dialectical pattern of thesis, negation, negation of negation: one presents a history of the city that traces the
development and dissolution of the contradiction of city and countryside in
the wake of urbanisation. It reveals the potential of urban society. The second
starts from space as a general category and is essentially a history of the increasing domination of the commodity and the abstraction of the social, inseparably
linked to the production of a new space – abstract space. This history, like the
first, also opens up to a possibility, a concrete utopia of differential space.

---

289 Lefebvre, *De l'État*, vol. 4, 422.
290 Lefebvre, *Production of Space*, 403.
291 Ibid., 263.

Ultimately, therefore, these histories of space are deciphered not from the past, but from the future.

We can thus conclude that both histories of space constitute historical reconstructions which, true to the regressive–progressive method, descend from the present into the past, in order to then trace, in ascending order, the genesis of a historical process. In Lefebvre's view, such a reconstruction reveals the possible that is laid out in the present. This possible, this concrete utopia, is in both cases the urban.

The Urban Revolution and the Revolution of Space

In Lefebvre's urban utopia, the immanent dialectic of urban society lifts past and future to a new level:

> Perhaps, through this unitary and differential thought, we will enter a period that is no longer part of history, a time when particularities confronted one another, when uniformity struggled with heterogeneity. Gatherings, encounters, and meetings (although not without their specific conflicts) would supplant the struggle between separate and now antinomic elements.[292]

The urban as a higher unity in which time and space come together: Lefebvre sees the creation of such a spatio-temporal unity (*unité spatiotemporelle*) as one of many possible definitions of the urban and urban society.[293] The starting point for this would be lived space, and thus also 'private' space, which would again have to become a place of subjects. This would involve, first of all, the restoration of the body, and thus the restoration of a sensory-sensual space, a space of the voice, of smell, of hearing, of the non-visible.[294] Lefebvre discerns on the horizon, at the limit of possibilities, the space of the human being, as a collective work, as 'art': a planetary space as the social foundation of a transformed everyday life, open to the most diverse possibilities. In his own understanding, Lefebvre follows here the great utopia announced by Fourier, Marx, and Engels.[295]

In *The Urban Revolution* he outlines even a third historical triad leading to a new, radical humanism. This triad starts with an abstract humanism, based

---

292   Lefebvre, *Urban Revolution*, 40.
293   Ibid., 179–80, 186.
294   Lefebvre, *Production of Space*, 362–3.
295   Ibid., 422–3.

on an abstract image of the human being, presented and represented by classical philosophy; it transforms into a critical humanism that reveals the goal and the meaning of this development, and moves towards the third moment, unfolding into a developed humanism, the project of the plenitude of the human being as a totality.[296] In fact, Lefebvre understands this third moment as a 'posthistory': only with the urban revolution the true history of humanity begins – urban society and differential space-time are not reconcilable with capitalism.[297]

With this outlook we arrive at the end of the history of space (and the city) at the figure of the world revolution, which pervades large parts of Lefebvre's work as an undercurrent. This is not astonishing for a Marxist of his time, as the world revolution was the intensely debated goal of many activists and critical intellectuals for decades. These ideas can of course be critically examined, as Stathis Kouvelakis does with great sympathy for Lefebvre's project. We have to take into consideration, though, the fact that Lefebvre himself experienced historical moments in which the 'world history' could have taken another turn, particularly at the end of the 1960s, when revolts and upheavals erupted in so many places across the world that the possibility of a planetary change seemed not as utopian as in the decades before. This revolutionary moment vanished quickly, as we know, and in his 1973 book *The Survival of Capitalism*, Lefebvre engaged in the question of why and how capitalism is constantly reproducing itself (see section 7.4).

Nevertheless, these two histories of space and the city offer us a second, more tangible insight: urban space is a product that only emerges in the complex interplay of spatial practice, representation of space, and spaces of representation, or of the perceived, the conceived, and the lived. In Lefebvre's understanding, it is therefore crucial to re-create the city as an 'oeuvre' open to all parts of the population: to provoke a situation – the urban situation – in which the perceived, the conceived, and the lived come together again and form a unity, in which differences are recognised and acknowledged and thus become socially productive.

When have these privileged moments occurred, when people felt space and found the city? Lefebvre's answer to this question is revealing: historically, during the Italian Renaissance; closer to the present, in May 1968:

As if by a miracle, the everyday emerges by transforming itself. We are experiencing first how *their space has been occupied* by students, then by

---

296   Lefebvre, *Urban Revolution*, 72–3.
297   Ibid., 40.

the working class, with an attempt of *appropriating* it. In the course of this attempt, the complex relations of the social groups with their space are on display, the relation of individuals with their body, their speech, their voice.[298]

Two aspects seem particularly important in this moment of transformation. First, there is a direct connection between the urban, space, and everyday life. And second, this transformation happens when the three dimensions of the production of space coincide – and thus at very special moments: the festival, the revolt.

It is from this context that the meaning of Lefebvre's final formulation for his poetic, metaphilosophical project of a transcendence of reality is revealed: the 'revolution of space' (*révolution de l'espace*), which includes the urban revolution.[299] Ultimately, Lefebvre sticks to the poetic postulate: *Changer la vie!* Change life!

---

298   Lefebvre, *De l'État*, vol. 4, 273. Translation by author. See also Lefebvre, *Production of Space*, 56.

299   Lefebvre, *Production of Space*, 419.

7

The State and the Commodification of Space

The reconstruction developed in this book has uncovered essential elements of the theory of the production of space. In a first step, it recognised Lefebvre's three-dimensional dialectic as the epistemological foundation of the entire theory. Second, it explored the thesis of the complete urbanisation of society, which leads to a (possible) urban society on a planetary scale. Third, it has identified the urban as a specific level of social reality: a level of mediation, a middle level that mediates between the general level of the market and the state, on the one hand, and the private level of everyday life, on the other. This urban level is based on centrality, and thus on the dialectic of centre and periphery. In a fourth step, this reconstruction revealed Lefebvre's three-dimensional dialectic of the production of space: from a phenomenological perspective, social space can be understood as a contradictory unity of perceived space, of conceived space, and of lived space; from the perspective of language theory, it appears as the dialectical unity of spatial practice, the representation of space, and the spaces of representation. Fifth and finally, the history of the production of space was shown as it developed from the 'space of nature' to the abstract, homogeneous-fractured space of capitalism, a space subjected to the power of abstraction, the space of the commodity and the state. This abstract space contains within itself an urban potential, the space of difference, which shows a possible path towards an urban society.

This reconstruction has comprehensively addressed the questions of urbanisation, urban society, and the production of space. It has not yet shown, however, in what way the theory of the production of space is related to the basic categories of Marxist social theory, and thus whether it fulfils Lefebvre's claim to have developed a spatio-temporal and dialectical-materialist theory of society. The difficulties of such a theory have become apparent repeatedly in the course of this reconstruction: the fundamental problem lies in the fact that Marx and Engels only partially addressed the question of space in their works. On the one hand, this is a result of their strong focus on social change and the possibilities for a political revolution, and, connected to this, their emphasis on 'becoming' and historical development. On the other hand, Marxist analysis has increasingly narrowed itself down to a limited, economistic conception of production in the course of its later development (see section 2.2), which has made it difficult to approach new fields and questions.

In the course of his own theoretical work, Lefebvre continued to develop this Marxist analysis, and thus expanded its scope. At the time when Lefebvre was working on questions of the everyday, urbanisation, and the production of space, Marxism had hardly considered these questions at all. Lefebvre therefore not only was forced to introduce these questions into Marxist theory; he also had to change this theory accordingly in order to be able to address them. From this perspective it is an enormous achievement that Lefebvre held on to Marxism until the end of his career, not only calling for a renewal of Marxism, but also implementing this renewal in both empirical and theoretical work.

Lefebvre's consistent introduction of space or space-time into Marxist social theory had far-reaching theoretical consequences. It drove him repeatedly to expand, reformulate, and even create new definitions of central Marxist concepts and categories: for the critique of political economy, ground rent, productive forces, circuits of capital, exchange value and use value, concrete abstraction, the mode of production, the concept of base and superstructure, the question of social relations and their reproduction, and finally the theory of the state and its relationship to space.

Lefebvre's renewed spatio-temporal theory of society emerged only slowly and gradually in the course of his engagement with the questions of everyday life, urbanisation, space, and the state. A first and important step in this direction was the book *The Urban Revolution*, in which he sketched the basic outlines of a political economy of space. In *The Survival of Capitalism* he tackled a question that was then being raised for the first time: that of the reproduction of social relations. In *The Production of Space* he explored the commodity character of space and its development towards a concrete abstraction. Finally, in *De l'État*, Lefebvre not only presented a completely new theory of the state but also addressed the question of how social relations of production are constituted and revealed the fundamental act that establishes these relations in capitalism: the act of exchange.

The question of Lefebvre's Marxism, or, more precisely, the question of *what kind* of Marxism Lefebvre actually developed, has often been asked in the course of his theoretical trajectory. His broad and open conception of Marxist theory, which took him far beyond Marxist orthodoxy, has often been poorly understood. Although he had been one of the most important theorists of the French Communist Party before his expulsion in 1958, and published numerous introductions to Marx's work and Marx's thought into the 1970s, his theory of the production of space was often received without serious reference to basic Marxist categories.

All these theoretical innovations and their consequences are the subject of the present chapter. The starting point is the development of a new conception of the critique of political economy that constitutively integrates space into its theoretical construction and forms the materialist foundation of the theory of the production of space (section 7.1). Lefebvre analyses the central role of land and ground rent, and develops an extended understanding of the production of space as a productive force. Lefebvre recognised a second circuit of capital in the production of space, one which overlaps with and complements the first circuit of capital of the production of goods – a concept with which Lefebvre has fundamentally renewed political economy. David Harvey adopted this concept early on and made it the basis of his own spatial political economy. Lefebvre himself took another decisive step further towards a renewed spatio-temporal social theory, as he wanted to develop not (only) a political economy of space but also a comprehensive theory of the production of space. He thus showed how the entire social space is made into a commodity – that is, not only the land, but the entire space of the planet, including the elements formerly reserved for nature: water, air, the earth. Through this he also analysed how urban space itself, with its specific qualities, becomes a commodity.

Space becomes a commodity: all of space and everything it contains, along with the people that constitute it. Starting from this provocative statement by Lefebvre, the question arises as to what consequences the commodification of social space has for the social production process as a whole (section 7.2). Here it is necessary to take a closer look at the process of exchange, which is constitutive of capitalism, and thereby also analyse the dialectic of exchange value and use value. The commodity, after all, has a peculiar double character: on the one hand, it is a concrete, material use value; but on the other hand, it is an abstract, universal exchange value. Lefebvre develops from this a specific understanding of the relationship between exchange value and use value and applies it to the historical analysis of social development. Thus, he arrives at one of his fundamental concepts, which has already appeared several times in this text, but which can be analysed in more detail here: the 'concrete abstraction'. On a more general theoretical level, we once again encounter abstract space, the homogeneous and fractured space dominated by the state and the commodity (see section 6.3). With the concept of concrete abstraction, it now becomes possible to embed abstract space in the context of the (capitalist) production of value and the commodification of space. In the process it becomes apparent that, in abstract space, the dialectical contradiction of exchange value and use value is transformed and becomes the contradiction of domination and appropriation.

The contradiction of domination and appropriation raises the question of how domination of space becomes possible, and how power structures can inscribe themselves into social space. For an understanding of this process, the social relations that determine the production of space must also be examined (section 7.3). Building from the consideration that the commodity itself should be understood as a social relation, Lefebvre develops his own historical-materialist understanding of social relations through which he arrives at a highly provocative thesis that has been the subject of considerable debate: social relations of production only have a social existence if they also have a spatial existence and produce a corresponding space. Lefebvre concludes that every social relation is based on a material 'support' which is the foundation of the spatio-material order of society.

It is through the production of this material support that social relations are incorporated into space and are thereby also preserved. But who controls the production of the material support? This is where the state comes into play, as it has the important task of coordinating and controlling the production of space (section 7.4). This is also accompanied by a fundamentally new under-standing of the state: after Lefebvre had long advocated a rather orthodox Marxist conception of the state guided by the classic concept of base and super-structure, he came to a much more fundamental conclusion in De l'État: what is the foundation of a capitalist society? He finds an unusual and far-reaching answer to this question: at the heart of every capitalist society is the act of exchange, as both a concrete and an abstract act. The state has a very specific task in this regard: the equalisation of the unequal: the state is the great equal-iser that regulates and controls exchange. This idea ultimately becomes the core of a general spatio-temporal theory of society.

The final section of this chapter is concerned with a question that was widely debated in France in the early 1970s, after the failure of the great upheaval of May 1968: how are social relations reproduced? Lefebvre answers this question in a way that is not unexpected: in space, through the production of space (see section 7.5). The state now comes to the fore, taking up an increasingly domi-nant position in the course of social development. With the commodification of space, the state becomes the agent that directs and coordinates the produc-tion of space. Lefebvre recognises that a 'state space' is thereby created that even establishes a 'state mode of production'. The ever-increasing extension of urbanisation is only possible with an enormous expansion of state control and surveillance over the entire planet: the earth eventually becomes the new horizon of the production of space. Where is this development heading? Lefebvre leaves this question open; the production of space proves to be a permanent search process.

Over five sections, this chapter traces the fundamental reorientation undertaken by Lefebvre in building his spatio-temporal and materialist-dialectical theory of society. It also leads to new theoretical terrain because the introduction of space into Marxist theory changes this theory significantly, and Lefebvre had to develop new definitions for some of its foundational categories. The result of this enormous theoretical effort is a reformulation and expansion of Marxist theory that has not yet received its due recognition.

This chapter is old and new at the same time. I wrote it originally as an integral part of my dissertation, but then had to omit it both from the dissertation itself and from the resulting published book because, at the time, at the beginning of the twenty-first century, it was still not possible to discuss Marxist concepts so openly in German-language geography. This chapter, practically ready for publication, therefore lay in the drawer for almost two decades. Only now has it become possible to finally make this chapter, with only minor changes and revisions, available to an interested audience.

7.1 A Political Economy of the Production of Space

> It is possible to conceive of a 'political economy of space' which would go back to the old political economy and rescue it from bankruptcy, as it were, by offering it a new object: the production of space.[1]

In his texts on the city and on space, Lefebvre did not only develop a new theory of the production of (urban) space – he also sketched the outlines of a new political economy of space. This political economy goes much further than most accounts consider, and it contains an enormous potential that has yet to be utilised.

When Lefebvre began his work on urban space in the 1960s, a Marxist urban or spatial political economy did not yet exist. Moreover, Lefebvre's search for insight in classic Marxist texts, as he himself had noted in *Marxist Thought and the City*, had not been very productive (see section 3.2): Marx and Engels had

---

1 Lefebvre, *Production of Space*, 104.

only experienced the beginnings of urbanisation, and space was not (yet) a central problem for the economy at that time. Thus, Lefebvre began to sketch a possible political economy of space himself. He developed it quite consistently throughout all his work on urbanisation and the production of space, but only addressed it in relatively short and scattered inserts and digressions. This chapter therefore provides a detailed reconstruction of this political economy of space, showing how Lefebvre's most important insights into urban space are based on Marxist concepts, and how he himself was always developing these concepts further.

This account begins with the land question and the ground rent, which must be (re)introduced into political economy in order to theorise the production of space. Although Marx had started to develop a theory of ground rent, he went no further than the analysis of agricultural land. For Lefebvre, as for many theorists before and after him, this raised the question of how this theory could be applied to urban space. There are many ways of answering this question.[2] Lefebvre's path proceeded from the analysis of a single plot of land to the overall process of producing space. In doing so he tried to understand the (material) production of space itself as a productive process. He realised that the produced space is itself a productive force and can thus be incorporated into the schema of capital accumulation. Lefebvre thereby developed, in short sketches in *The Urban Revolution* and *The Production of Space*, the idea that the production of space constitutes a second circuit of capital that overlaps and complements the first circuit of the production of goods. This second circuit not only absorbs the shocks and crises of the first circuit, but also represents a long-term capital investment that further advances the urbanisation process and fundamentally changes space-time configurations across the world.

Lefebvre always took these considerations into account in his analyses, but he did not fully develop them. It was David Harvey who, building on precisely these insights from Lefebvre, presented a more detailed political economy of space in *The Limits to Capital*. As will be shown, however, Lefebvre's ambition went much further: he did not (only) want to develop a political economy of space – his aim was to produce a (comprehensive) theory of the production of space.

From this broader perspective, Lefebvre considered not only the production of the built environment like Harvey but the entire (planetary) urban space. He thus postulated, for example, that in the course of capitalist development all of space (and not only the land) would become an object of exchange, would

---

2 See for example Brede, Dietrich, and Kohaupt, *Politische Ökonomie des Bodens und Wohnungsfrage*; Harvey, *Limits to Capital*; Haila, *Urban Land Rent*.

become exchange value and thus a commodity. This includes, on the one hand, elements such as air, water, and the landscape, which were long available for free, but with the expansion of capitalism have had to be produced to an ever-greater extent and thus have taken on the character of commodities whose use must be paid for. On the other hand, however, the qualities of urban space collectively produced by people are also commodified and therefore also acquire an exchange value that can be appropriated privately by means of ground rent. Through these considerations, which are only today reaching their full meaning, Lefebvre went beyond classical political economy and began to develop a comprehensive spatio-temporal analysis of the production of capitalist society.

The Trinity Formula: Labour, Capital, and Land

To introduce space into Marxist analysis requires, first of all, addressing the question of land. Lefebvre, however, does not find a systematic elaboration of this question in Marx's political economy. He sees in the core of *Capital* a binary dialectical model based on the contradiction of labour and capital, of proletariat and bourgeoisie, and thus of wage and profit. With this contradiction, however, a third historical concept disappears: the earth, and thus the landowning class, ground rent, agriculture, the city. In this binary scheme, as Lefebvre notes, the space of social practice goes unnoticed, and time plays only a modest role: it is reduced to the measure of social labour. The binary schema of labour–capital itself is ultimately situated in a purely abstract, mental space.[3] Lefebvre thus regards the contradiction between capital and labour, the foundation of Marx's theory, as a mere mental abstraction: it is only in the context of his examination of the philosophy of space (see section 5.1) that this provocative statement discloses its full critical potential. Basically, Lefebvre denies that this binary abstract schema has any relation to reality.

According to Lefebvre, resistance to this schema emerges primarily from social reality itself. On a global level, none of land ownership, the political importance of landowners, or ground rent have disappeared.[4] The abstract opposition of labour and capital thus only becomes concrete when its material-ity is taken into account, and this materiality can only be grasped when space (and time) and thus also land and land ownership are included in the analysis. The essential lines of argumentation of this chapter can be derived from this short formula.

---

3   Lefebvre, *Production of Space*, 324.
4   Ibid.

Nevertheless, the starting point of Lefebvre's renewed spatio-temporal theory of society is still from Marx. As is well known, Marx had written extensively on the question of ground rent. The third volume of *Capital* contains an unfinished but important section on the theory of ground rent.[5] In its forty-eighth chapter, Lefebvre finally finds the extension he was looking for, the 'trinity formula': labour, capital, land.

Lefebvre sees this formula as nothing less than the constitutive triad of capitalist society.[6] He interprets it as follows: there are three elements, aspects, or 'factors' in the capitalist mode of production and bourgeois society – the earth ('Madame la Terre'), capital ('Monsieur le Capital'), and labour (the proletariat). Accordingly, there are also three forms of revenue: ground rent, profit, and wages.[7]

But, for Marx, this 'trinity formula' was meant ironically:

> Capital-profit (or better still capital-interest), land-ground-rent, labour-wages, this economic trinity as the connection between the components of value and wealth in general and its sources, completes the mystification of the capitalist mode of production, the reification of social relations, and the immediate coalescence of the material relations of production with their historical and social specificity: the bewitched, distorted and upside-down world haunted by Monsieur le Capital and Madame la Terre, who are at the same time social characters and mere things.[8]

With his 'trinity formula', Marx criticised the mystification of the bourgeois economy, which understood capital, land, and labour as equal sources of social wealth, which were compensated for their share in wealth creation with interest, ground rent, and wages, respectively.[9] But, for Marx, this idea was the highest expression of 'commodity fetishism': he regarded interest and ground rent as means of appropriating social surplus value, the real source of which can only be human labour (see section 7.2). With regard to ground rent, he brought this view to the most concise formulation: 'And now to take land, inorganic nature as such . . . in its primeval wilderness. Value is labour. So surplus-value cannot be earth.' Surplus value cannot be earth; soil itself does not produce value. According to the Marxist law of value, value (and thus also surplus value) can arise from human labour alone. Just like interest (as revenue

---

5   Marx, *Capital*, vol. 3, 882–907.

6   Lefebvre, *Survival of Capitalism*, 8.

7   Lefebvre, *Production of Space*, 324–5.

8   Marx, *Capital*, vol. 3, 968–9.

9   Ibid., 954.

on capital), ground rent is a skimming off of surplus value originally produced by human labour.

Lefebvre sees this connection very clearly. Marx argues, according to Lefebvre, that the political power in capitalist society understands that the elements of that society – land ownership, wage labour, and capital – are at once connected and separated under its control. These three closely related elements are presented as different sources of 'revenues'. This would seem to legitimise the 'revenues' from capital and land ownership instead of showing that they are only components of surplus value (generated by labour). This means, Lefebvre argues, that there is a direct connection between social practice and its representations: 'The representations conceal the concrete situation, while "expressing" it in their own particular way. One cannot dissociate ideology from practice by "presenting" it separately.'[10] Thus, Lefebvre considers the question of land ownership and ground rent to be highly relevant to the social production process and the production of surplus value. Although he agrees with Marx that the source of social wealth lies in the generation of a surplus product, he does not assign land a merely passive, derivative, or subordinate role. In order to clarify this role, we must first delve deeper into Marx's theory of ground rent.

Differential Rent

How does ground rent come into existence according to Marx's theory of value? In his comments on ground rent,[11] Marx developed a concept that was to occupy generations of theorists in the future. However, his reflections are incomplete, particularly because he confined himself essentially to land in its agricultural use; industry and cities were largely ignored, which is a major problem for applying this concept in an industrialised and urbanised society.

As Marx notes, land ownership under capitalist conditions means that certain persons exercise a monopoly over certain portions of the earth, just as any owner of goods has a monopoly over his goods. Accordingly, the landowner can collect ground rent from the person who uses and works his land, whether it is arable land, forest, a mining area, a building plot, or even a body of water. Ground rent is thus the form in which landed property is economically valorised.[12] But how much can a landowner demand for the use of his land?

---

10 Lefebvre, *Survival of Capitalism*, 69.
11 Marx, *Capital*, vol. 3, 917–50.
12 Ibid., 1046–7, 654–5.

David Ricardo had already postulated that ground rent results from the difference between the yields of two different pieces of land, and how those yields can result from identical amounts of capital or labour.[13] Marx developed from this idea his concept of differential rent: differences in fertility and the location of different pieces of land lead to corresponding differences in the yield of the labour or capital employed on them. These two factors can also work in opposite directions, since soil can be well situated and not very fertile, or vice versa.[14]

This statement is based on the assumption that a product is sold at the price at which it can still be produced on the least productive soil. Products that are produced on better soil are produced more cheaply, but can be sold at the same price, and thus a 'surplus profit' is created – that is, an additional profit that is achieved without any additional use of capital. The essential point of Marx's argument is that this surplus profit can be absorbed by the landowner as ground rent. This rent is based solely on the monopolisation of natural power, and it arises from the difference between the individual production price of individual capital and the general production price of the capital invested in the corresponding sector of production[15] – hence the term differential rent.

In the space of nature, the decisive moments of this differential, 'fertility' and 'location', are given; they are found and can be exploited accordingly. Marx calls this form of rent 'differential rent I'. But he also shows that these natural conditions are already modified in agricultural production, and that this is done through productive labour: by investing additional capital in the soil, the yield of the soil can be increased temporarily or permanently, such as by means of fertilisation, levelling of the soil, drainage, setting up irrigation systems, and so forth. This transforms the earth from mere matter into 'earth-capital',[16] which allows the generation of additional surplus profit, which can also be appropriated by the landowner as differential rent. Marx calls this form of rent 'differential rent II'.

One could therefore say that differential rent I is dependent on the unequal earning power of land for reasons that are independent of capital, whereas differential rent II is generated only by the additional capital incorporated into the land.[17] However, this is primarily an analytical distinction, since the two forms of differential rent are closely linked.[18] What is most important in this

---

13   Ibid., 788.
14   Ibid., 789.
15   Ibid., 785.
16   Ibid., 757.
17   Ibid.
18   Harvey, *Limits to Capital*, 353–5.

context is that the return on land can be increased by investment. This applies not only to the fertility of the soil, but also to the location, which is also 'produced', since it depends, among other things, on the quality of transport access to a piece of land. If better transport links are created, such as through new roads, railways, or shipping connections, then products can be transported more cheaply and, above all, more quickly. In this way, the time to reach the markets can be reduced, and completely new markets can be opened up.

> It is finally clear that the progress of social production in general has on the one hand a levelling effect on location as a basis for differential rent, since it creates local markets and improves location by producing means of communication and transport; while on the other hand it increases the differences of geographical location, by separating agriculture from manufacture and forming great centres of production, while also relatively isolating the countryside.[19]

In the example of the produced location, Marx thus clearly recognised that differential rent depends not only on the capital invested on a single plot of land, but also to a large extent on production as a social process and thus also on the social production of space, whereby he explicitly refers to the urbanisation process: on the one hand, to the formation of large centres; and, on the other hand, to the 'relative isolation' of the countryside – in other words, a form of peripheralisation.

As already suggested by Marx, this general schema of differential rent can now be applied to non-agricultural land:

> Wherever rent exists, differential rent always appears and always follows the same laws as it does in agriculture. Wherever natural forces can be monopolized and give the industrialist who makes use of them a surplus profit, whether a waterfall, a rich mine, fishing grounds or a well-situated building site, the person indicated as the owner of these natural objects, by virtue of his title to a portion of the earth, seizes this surplus profit from their functioning capital in the form of rent.[20]

---

19   Marx, *Capital*, vol. 3, 789–90.
20   Ibid., 908.

Social Space as a Productive Force

Based on these considerations, a bridge can be built from agricultural land to industrial or urban land. For here it is no longer a matter of the 'fertility' of a plot of land, but rather – in Lefebvre's understanding – of the 'productivity' of space, or more precisely: the productivity of the arrangement of the elements of material production in space.

The question of differential rent and productivity dependent on the qualities of a piece of land thus also touches on the concept of the productive forces. Marx understood productive forces as the entirety of human and material factors which, in a metabolic process with nature, cause the appropriation of nature by humans in the production process. The productive forces include, on the one hand, human labour and, on the other, the means of production available to labour. The latter include nature (soil, water, air, raw materials, and so on) and the primary products obtained from it, as well as the means of labour, that is, tools and machinery, means of transport, the organisation of labour, techniques, and finally also knowledge.[21]

For Marx, nature was thus one of the productive forces.[22] As shown in section 6.1, however, the production of space leads to the creation of a second nature; the space of nature is transformed into a produced, social space. It is now clear that this produced space, this second nature, is as much a productive force in Lefebvre's understanding as the initial nature that it displaces and replaces.[23]

But in what sense can produced space represent a productive force? To answer this question, Lefebvre refers back to the essential characteristic of the urban phenomenon: centrality (see section 4.4). The city becomes productive by bringing together the elements necessary for production: 'It centralizes creation.'[24] The urban does not produce in the same way as agriculture and industry. But it is nevertheless productive in gathering and redistributing people and goods. Lefebvre compares urban space with manufacturing, which has become a productive force by bringing together in one place labour and (technical) tools that had previously been scattered.[25] For Lefebvre, then, urban space becomes a productive force by combining previously dispersed and disjointed elements into a new, more productive entity. Transferred to the level of the entire (urban) society, social space itself can thus be understood as a productive force.

---

21   See also Lefebvre, *Production of Space*, 69.
22   Ibid., 343.
23   Ibid., 349.
24   Lefebvre, *Urban Revolution*, 117.
25   Ibid., 173. See also Lefebvre, *De l'État*, vol. 4, 269.

Marx addressed precisely this consideration from the point of view of the spatial concentration of labour and means of production:

> A large number of workers working together, at the same time, in one place (or, if you like, in the same field of labour), in order to produce the same sort of commodity under the command of the same capitalist, constitutes the starting-point of capitalist production. This is true both historically and conceptually.[26]

For Marx, cooperation in industry, the simultaneous use of a larger number of workers who systematically work alongside and with one another, meant a revolution in the material conditions of the labour process: buildings, warehouses, tools, machinery can be used together in the labour process.[27] Furthermore, cooperation allows for a division of labour: instead of having the various operations carried out by a single craftsman in a chronological sequence, they are detached from one another, isolated, and placed next to one another in space. Each of these operations is assigned to a different craftsman, and all craftsmen together perform all the operations at the same time: 'The different stages of the process, previously successive in time, have become simultaneous and contiguous in space.'[28]

The spatial contraction of the space of production, the conglomeration of workers, the assembly of different work processes, and the concentration of the means of production thus result simultaneously in a 'constriction of the sphere of space [*Raumsphäre*] of labour and an extension of its sphere of effects [*Wirkungssphäre*]', which saves a lot of 'incidental expenses [*faux frais*]' and increases productive power.[29] From this follows the basic principle that has become known under the term 'agglomeration economies' that arise precisely because the diverse elements of the production process are brought together. This process is also addressed by Lefebvre.[30]

Engels had already described this process in his famous passage in *The Condition of the Working Class in England*:

> The greater the town, the greater its advantages. It offers roads, railroads, canals; the choice of skilled labour increases constantly, new establishments can be built more cheaply, because of the competition among

---

26 Marx, *Capital*, vol. 1, 339.
27 Ibid., 455–6.
28 Ibid., 465.
29 Ibid., 446. Translation by author.
30 Lefebvre, *State, Space, World*, 242.

machinists who are at hand, than in remote country districts, whither timber, machinery, builders, and operatives must be brought; it offers a market to which buyers crowd; communication with the markets supplying raw material or demanding finished goods. Hence the marvellously rapid growth of the great manufacturing towns.[31]

This passage vividly summarises an understanding of agglomeration economies that is still valid today (see section 3.5).

With the introduction of the machine, an additional element enters the production process: while the labour force was the starting point of production in the workshop, in the factory it is the working tool, the machine, which becomes its new starting point.[32] In his analysis of the production of space, Lefebvre refers to precisely this concentrating characteristic of the machine, basing his analysis not only on Marx but also on Charles Babbage, who had himself inspired Marx.[33] According to Lefebvre, the importance of the machine lies in the fact that it forms a device that functions differently from a tool or the grouping of tools in a workshop: energy is supplied to the machine (water, steam, electricity) and it consumes this energy in a sequence of productive operations. The worker now operates the machine instead of handling a tool. This results in a radical but contradictory change in the productive process: while labour is more and more divided and parcelled out, the machine forms an ever-expanding, more coherent, unified, and productive unit. Since its beginnings in the windmill and the loom, the machine has presented a fundamentally new characteristic, a new rationality: the automation of the productive process.[34]

Lefebvre then compares these characteristics of the machine with the city: in a certain sense, the city itself forms a comprehensive machine. In a process of productive consumption, it consumes natural energies. Over the centuries, the city's spatial dispositions have been transformed, as have its external relations: water supply and sewage disposal, lighting, transportation, energy supply, information, and so on. Thus, urban productivity has increased incessantly, thanks to the proximity and the integration of the elements necessary for the production process. The city is, therefore, a machine, but, at the same time, it is also more: it is a produced space, a second nature that has a use value for society.[35]

---

31   Engels, *The Condition of the Working Class in England*, 326.
32   Marx, *Capital*, vol. 1, 464–5.
33   Lefebvre, *Production of Space*, 344.
34   Ibid.
35   Ibid., 345.

These considerations only develop their full potential, however, by bringing in the urbanisation process and the expansion of the 'urban fabric': the thesis of complete urbanisation means that the industrial system is extended over the entire territory (see section 3.2). This increases not only the productive effects of spatial concentration but also the effects of the expansion of production networks and infrastructure: the advantages of spatial concentration can thereby be extended to a larger area. Marx had already recognised this process:

> Just as a certain number of simultaneously employed workers is the material pre-condition for the division of labour within manufacture, so the number and density of the population, which here corresponds to the collection of workers together in one workshop, is a pre-condition for the division of labour within society. Nevertheless, this density is more or less relative. A relatively thinly populated country, with well-developed means of communication, has a denser population than a more numerously populated country with badly developed means of communication. In this sense, the northern states of the U.S.A. for instance, are more thickly populated than India.[36]

In Lefebvre's line of argument, space itself becomes a decisive aspect of the production process: the material arrangement and spatial organisation of the elements of the production process, the flow of materials and energy, the networks of transport and information are essential components of the productivity of this production process. From this perspective, urbanisation always means the production of a new industrial arrangement. At the same time, (urban) space under capitalism is not a passive container indifferent to its content but itself becomes productive. Space is simultaneously a product of the capitalist mode of production and a political-economic instrument for increasing productivity.[37]

This idea of the instrumental function of the production of space under capitalism is one of Lefebvre's central theses. It appears repeatedly in his texts and has a number of theoretical consequences. The instrumental role of space applies not only to the concentration of labour and the means of production – and thus to the phenomenon of agglomeration economies and 'big cities' – but to the entire social space. If the 'urban fabric' expands ever further, then the entirety of urban space must accordingly be understood as a productive force.

---

36 Marx, *Capital*, vol. 1, 472–3.
37 Lefebvre, *Production of Space*, 129; Lefebvre, *De l'État*, vol. 4, 270.

These considerations now have two consequences that will be discussed in the following two sections. First, the (material) production of space itself is to be understood as a productive process, which in turn generates surplus value and thus must be introduced into the schema of capital accumulation. Second, social space itself (and not only land) becomes an object of exchange, and thus a commodity.

The Second Circuit of Capital

To better understand the productive effect of the production of space, Lefebvre reassesses another basic concept of Marx's law of value: fixed capital.[38] In Marx's schema, fixed capital is that part of capital which does not flow directly into the production process but is used to maintain production, such as machinery and equipment, buildings (factories, plants, offices), and infrastructure (roads, energy supply, and so on). In contrast to raw materials, which are consumed in the production process and flow directly into the product, a part of the value of fixed capital remains fixed and thus immobilised for a shorter or longer period of time.[39]

Lefebvre now adopts this concept of fixed capital in order to anchor the production of space in value theory. In the light of the above considerations, it becomes clear that, for Lefebvre, fixed capital cannot be limited to the firm's tools, machines, and buildings alone. It also extends to investments in space – in the past, for example, in canals and railways, later, in motorways and airports, but also in radar surveillance of the airways (satellite communication networks did not exist when Lefebvre wrote this text) – and to all types of infrastructure, facilities, and equipment. These represent not only material infrastructures but also – analogous to the organisation of labour – the incorporation of knowledge into social reality on a planetary scale.[40]

Productive investment in space thus becomes a central aspect of the entire production process. For Lefebvre it forms a second circuit that runs parallel to the capital circuit in industrial production.[41] For a long time, he notes, this second circuit was only a backward sector of industrial and financial capital. Land belonged to the remnants of a historical class – the aristocracy – and production in the real estate sector was dominated by artisanal enterprises. But

---

38   Lefebvre, *Production of Space*, 345.
39   See also Harvey, *Limits to Capital*, 204–7.
40   Lefebvre, *Production of Space*, 345.
41   Lefebvre, *Urban Revolution*, 159.

with industrialisation, capitalism also took possession of the land and mobilised the real estate sector.[42]

This second circuit absorbs the shocks in the first: as soon as economic crises occur, capital flows into the second circuit.

> As the principal circuit – current industrial production and the movable property that results – begins to slow down, capital shifts to the second sector, real estate. It can even happen that real-estate speculation becomes the principal source for the formation of capital, that is, the realization of surplus value. As the percentage of overall surplus value formed and realized by industry begins to decline, the percentage created and realized by real-estate speculation and construction increases. The second circuit supplants the first, becomes essential.[43]

The production of space thus becomes a new sector of capitalist production that attracts capital from the 'classical' sectors – the production of the means of production and consumer goods.[44] This process accelerates whenever these sectors show the slightest signs of weakness.[45] As Lefebvre clearly recognised, however, this second sector not only offers a solution to the problem of stagnant or blocked capital accumulation in times of economic crisis but also creates considerable problems of its own. This second sector hardly has any multiplying effects: capital is immobile and tied up for the long term, which means that the turnover time of capital is extended. These problems drive capital to destroy both old and new spaces so that investment cycles do not slow down.[46]

With the concept of the second sector or circuit of capital, Lefebvre has sketched the intersection of his theory of the production of space with Marx's theory of value. Although he left it in this preliminary form, the concept has had a significant influence on debates in urban and spatial theory. It became the starting point for David Harvey's theory of the production of the built environment, with Harvey developing his own theory precisely along Lefebvre's line of argumentation (see section 1.2).[47] Harvey, however, defined this second circuit of capital more precisely and more narrowly than Lefebvre. In Harvey's version, it takes shape in the form of the 'built environment', specifically for

---

42   Lefebvre, *Production of Space*, 335.
43   Lefebvre, *Urban Revolution*, 160.
44   Lefebvre, *Production of Space*, 335.
45   Lefebvre, *Urban Revolution*, 159.
46   Lefebvre, *Production of Space*, 336; Lefebvre, *Urban Revolution*, 160.
47   Harvey, *Limits to Capital*.

companies (factories, offices), for private individuals (housing), and for infra-structure (roads, electricity, and so on).[48] This second circuit differs from the first circuit not only in its immobility, but also in its different temporality: the time horizon is oriented towards long-term investments, and thus to the future rather than the present.[49]

The production of the built environment thus implies a productive invest-ment of capital that drives the urbanisation process and fundamentally changes the space-time configurations of the world. As a consequence, the spatio-temporal barriers of the production process lose their significance, and thus the globe shrinks: a process that Harvey calls 'space-time compression'.[50] But at the same time the fundamental problem of this second circuit arises from the fact that capital is immobilised in a material infrastructure that conflicts in the long term with the dynamics of technological change and capital accumu-lation. The value of investment in the built environment becomes uncertain, and the continuous circulation of capital is threatened by serious collapse. The second circuit thus offers only a temporary way out of the crisis tendencies inherent in capitalism.[51]

On a concrete level, however, this long turnover time of capital in the second circuit also means that the material structures of the built environment deter-mine the direction of urbanisation for a long time to come. They can only be changed in the short term with significant losses and often also with corre-sponding material destruction.[52]

Neil Brenner has expressed this dialectical contradiction with the formula 'fixity and motion'.[53] He treated this contradiction in a much broader context, focusing not only on the material production process and investments in the built environment, but also on the central role of the state in the production of space. He thus also sheds light on institutional arrangements and territorial scales. These interrelationships are discussed in more detail in section 7.5.

The Commodification of Social Space

Lefebvre does not stop, however, with an outline of the second circuit of capi-tal. The instrumental use of the production of space for increasing productivity

---

48   Ibid., 408.
49   Ibid., xvi.
50   Harvey, *Condition of Postmodernity*.
51   Harvey, *Limits to Capital*, xvi.
52   See also Schmid, 'Specificity and Urbanization'.
53   Brenner, 'Between Fixity and Motion'; Brenner, *New Urban Spaces*.

has additional consequences, which need further exploration: social space itself is drawn into the process of capitalist exploitation.

> Not too long ago, a localized, identifiable space, the soil, still belonged to a sacred entity: the earth. It belonged to that cursed, and therefore sacred, character, the owner (not of the means of production, but of the Home), a carryover from feudal times. Today, this ideology and the corresponding practice are collapsing. Something new is happening.[54]

What is this new development? Space itself is being mobilised for commodification. This strategy goes much further than simply selling space 'bit by bit'.[55] Space itself, and no longer just the land, becomes exchange value.

This process begins with the land, which must first be removed from that classic, stable type of ownership based on inheritance – something that is not possible without concessions to the landowners and which generates the form of ground rent. Mobilisation then extends to space, the subsoil and the volumes above the ground: the entire space becomes exchange value. But exchange implies interchangeability: space becomes a commodity, assumes an apparently autonomous reality, becomes comparable to other things, such as a quantity of sugar or coal. Its exchange value is expressed in money, and this means that the space can be bought and sold. While in the past it was a piece of land that was bought or sold, today volumes are bought and sold: apartments, rooms, floors, terraces, and all sorts of facilities.[56]

The typical resident is thus reduced to the function of a buyer of space who realises its surplus value.[57] Space becomes a global object, the supreme product, the final object of exchange:

> The deployment of the world of commodities now affects not only objects but their containers, it is no longer limited to content, to objects in space. More recently, space itself has begun to be bought and sold. Not the earth, the soil, but *social space*, produced as such.[58]

In this passage, it seems that Lefebvre himself is frightened by his discovery: the production of space is no longer just a question of land and ground rent, as

---

54 Lefebvre, *Urban Revolution*, 155.
55 Ibid.
56 Lefebvre, *Production of Space*, 336–7.
57 Lefebvre, *Urban Revolution*, 156.
58 Ibid., 154.

the entire social space becomes exchange value – 'living' space together with its inhabitants.

Lefebvre uses tourism, among other things, as an example to illustrate this process: Tourism is nothing more than a 'consumption of space' – an unproductive form of consumption. Entire regions – in the mountains, by the sea, historical cities – are dominated by the tourism and leisure industry and subjected to a kind of 'neo-colonialism'. These regions only serve to be consumed, in the economic and literal sense, with all their elements – from the landscape to the historical buildings and even entire cities.[59] The inhabitants of these areas become, on the one hand, service providers who are supposed to make life pleasant for tourists, and, on the other hand, real-life extras who 'populate' touristic towns and landscapes. In the same way, urban centres also become commodities: 'The urban center is not only transformed into a site of consumption; it also becomes an object of consumption, and is valued as such.'[60] This includes the commodification of urban qualities produced by the inhabitants of and visitors to an area. It can be seen, for example, in all kinds of meeting places, lively public spaces, creative cultural and/or economic milieus which attract many people and also generate a greater demand for housing, office space, shops, restaurants, and spaces for a wide range of other uses. This demand is absorbed through the real estate market and differential rent. The concept of gentrification, however, which is the one most often applied to these phenomena, focuses primarily on the absorption of the 'rent gap', that is, the absorption of the surplus value by differential rent.[61] How this surplus value is generated, however, is not discussed. Lefebvre's reflections now make it possible to analyse the commodification of social space and thus also the generation of value – of urban value – as a social process on a general level (see also section 4.4).[62]

The New Scarcities

Another consequence of this process of the commodification of social space is the production of 'new scarcities' (*nouvelles raretés*), as Lefebvre calls them: certain once-scarce goods are comparatively abundant due to industrial production, while conversely once-abundant 'natural' goods, such as vegetation, air, light, water – which previously had no 'value' because they were not products – become scarce. Since it is no longer possible to take them directly

---

59 Lefebvre, *Production of Space*, 58, 122, 353.
60 Lefebvre, 'Dissolving City, Planetary Metamorphosis', 567.
61 See Smith, *The New Urban Frontier*.
62 See Schmid, 'Lefebvre, the Right to the City'.

from the inexhaustible reservoir of nature, they now have to be produced themselves. They thus become commodities whose use must be paid for.[63]

These goods or 'elements', among which Lefebvre includes (geographical) location, thus become social elements of space. In this process, urban space is detached from the space of nature, which itself becomes a scarce commodity, and, conversely, scarcity becomes localised and spatialised: 'Everything thus affected by scarcity has a close relationship to the Earth: the resources of the land, those beneath the earth (petroleum) and those above it (air, light, volumes of space, etc.), along with things which depend on these resources, such as vegetable and animal products and energies of various kinds.'[64] When these 'elements' begin to circulate within the production system, they fall into the domain of political economy. But, Lefebvre asks: does this political economy still have anything to do with classical political economy?[65]

'Space in its entirety enters the modernized capitalist mode of production, there to be used for the generation of surplus value.' The earth, underground resources, and the air above the ground – all become products and (productively consumed) productive forces. The urban fabric and the various networks of communication and exchange become means of production. The city and all its facilities are fixed capital. All space is consumed productively, as are industrial plants, machines, raw materials, and the labour force.[66] This also applies to centralities, which gather the constitutive elements of society within a limited territory to productive effect.[67]

These points can already be found roughly sketched in Marx, who wrote:

> One section of society here demands a tribute from the other for the right to live on the earth, just as landed property in general involves the right of the proprietors to exploit the earth's surface, the bowels of the earth, the air and thereby the maintenance and development of life. The rise in population, and the consequent growing need for housing, is not the only factor that necessarily increases the rent on buildings. So too does the development of fixed capital, which is either incorporated into the earth or strikes root in it, like all industrial buildings, railways, factories, docks, etc., which rest on it.[68]

---

63   Lefebvre, *Production of Space*, 329. See also Lefebvre, *Urban Revolution*, 151, 161.
64   Lefebvre, *Production of Space*, 329.
65   Ibid., 330.
66   Ibid., 347.
67   Ibid., 333.
68   Marx, *Capital*, vol. 3, 909.

And he adds:

> Two elements come into consideration here: on the one hand the exploi-
> tation of the earth for the purpose of reproduction or extraction, on the
> other hand the space that is required as an element for any production
> and any human activity.[69]

Lefebvre concludes that the production process must therefore be viewed from
the perspective of society as a whole and not just from the perspective of the
individual enterprise:

> In the recent past, there was no other way to conceive of 'production' other
> than as an object, located somewhere in space: an ordinary object, a machine,
> a book, a painting. Today, space as a whole enters into production as a prod-
> uct, through the buying, selling, and exchange of parts of space.[70]

Political economy must therefore no longer be concerned with things in space
but must become a political economy of space and its production.[71]

This reversal of perspective from the production of things in space to the
production of space itself (see section 5.1) has incalculable consequences, not
only for the analysis of 'space' but also for the analysis of social development.
The production of 'things in space' was still connected to 'classical' questions
such as the ownership of the means of production, the control and management of the production process, and the conflict between capital and labour.
But a focus on the production of space poses new analytical problems:[72] the
opposition between the productive and the non-productive consumption of
space, between capitalist 'consumers' (*utilisateurs*) and collective 'users'
(*usagers*),[73] or even between capitalist domination and the self-determined
appropriation of space (see section 7.2).

Lefebvre developed these thoughts well beyond Harvey's theoretical focus.
As became clear above, he is not only interested in the second circuit of capital,
the real estate sector, or the production of the built environment. The process
of the commodification of space goes much further, taking on aspects that were
– hitherto (and subsequently) – ignored. Elements originally considered 'natural', such as light, air, water, or landscape, are increasingly drawn into the

---

69   Ibid.
70   Lefebvre, *Urban Revolution*, 155.
71   Lefebvre, *Production of Space*, 299.
72   Ibid., 334.
73   Ibid., 359.

capitalist process of commodity production as a result of ongoing urbanisation. It becomes clear that commodification ultimately and potentially encompasses the entire (planetary) space. Neil Brenner and I developed our concepts
of planetary urbanisation and extended urbanisation precisely by following
this line of argument.[74]

Additionally, however, the commodification of space also extends to exploit-
ing the advantages in productivity that result from the production of social
space. These include, for example, the advantages of agglomeration, which are
the consequences of many individual decisions, activities, and actions, but
which have a collective benefit. In a broader sense, it also includes all the
advantages arising from centralities that are generated by the efforts and activities of the people themselves. Thus, the increased productive force of urban
space is commodified and the urban, as a collective product, is appropriated
privately. Urban space itself becomes a commodity. The consequences of this
commodification of space will be discussed in the next section.[75]

The Production of Space in the Narrow and Wide Sense

With these reflections on the second circuit of capital, the mobilisation of
space, centrality, and the 'new scarcities' Lefebvre sketched the outlines of a
political economy of space. It would thus be possible – according to Lefebvre
– to return to political economy and, in order to save it from bankruptcy, to
propose a new object of study: the production of space.[76]

But Lefebvre intentionally does not pursue this project any further: he sees
the political economy of space merely as a result of an even stronger theory –
the theory of the production of space. He assumes 'without hesitation' that this
theory will replace 'classical' political economy with its abstract growth
models.[77]

Two different conceptions of space appear in these deliberations: first, the
theory of the production of space broadly speaking, as presented in chapter 5;
and second, the political economy of space, or the production of space in a
narrow sense. This narrow conception was still the background of the analyses
in *The Urban Revolution*, in which Lefebvre developed the outlines of a political economy of space. There he defined the concept of the 'production of space'
as follows:

---

74 Brenner and Schmid, 'Towards a New Epistemology of the Urban?'.
75 See also Schmid, 'Lefebvre, the Right to the City'.
76 Lefebvre, *Production of Space*, 104.
77 Ibid., 350.

Capitalism appears to be out of steam. It found new inspiration in the conquest of space – in trivial terms, in real estate speculation, capital projects (inside and outside the city), the buying and selling of space. And it did so on a worldwide scale.[78]

However, it soon turned out that this narrow conception limited the scope of his theory. In *The Production of Space*, he made a new attempt to develop a general theory of the production of space, consistently following his earlier reflections on the narrow and the broad concept of production (see section 2.2). This led to a broadening of the problematic and a change in perspective from the political economy of space – that is, the question of its material production – to the production of social space and thus the question of the production and reproduction of society. His extended analysis of the production of space considers not only the produced objects in space – and the labour process that creates these objects – but also the production of the entire social space, the production of the living conditions, the material foundations of life as such.

In this sense, *The Production of Space* marks a decisive crossroads in the historical-materialist discussion of space: while David Harvey, starting from Lefebvre, designed a political economy of space through his theory of the production of the built environment, Lefebvre, in contrast, attempted to comprehensively renew Marxist theory from the perspective of the broad concept of space.[79] In his new approach, Lefebvre sees the only chance to preserve the Marxist thesis of the fundamental importance of the productive forces while at the same time freeing it from productivism and from the dogmatism of quantitative growth.[80]

7.2 Space as Concrete Abstraction

> Capitalism . . . has produced abstract space, which includes the 'world of commodities', its 'logic' and its worldwide strategies, as well as the power of money and that of the political state.[81]

Space becomes a commodity, the entirety of space, with everything that it contains, including the people who constitute it: with this conclusion, elaborated in the last section, Lefebvre goes beyond a critique of political economy

---

78 Lefebvre, *Urban Revolution*, 155.
79 See also Lefebvre, 'Preface to the New Edition', 209.
80 Lefebvre, *Production of Space*, 410.
81 Ibid., 53.

in the narrow sense and begins a comprehensive analysis of the production of capitalist society. The commodification of space revealed in this analysis refers to the foundations of Marx's theory, to its central categories of value, labour, and the commodity character of labour, and to the commodity as a constitutive element of capitalist societies.

For Lefebvre, however, these categories conceal a fundamental problem, because they can be viewed from two different angles: On the one hand, capitalism can be seen as a system based on the exchange of goods, on the universality of the commodity and on circuits of capital. On the other hand, the 'actors of the drama' can be analysed: the companies, the banks, the promoters, the authorities – all those who are able to intervene and exert their influence. Capitalism thus becomes either a nearly closed, coherent system, or a simple sum of separate activities. In this way, the unity of capitalism is bracketed, along with its diversity and contradictions.[82] However, as Lefebvre emphasises repeatedly, there can never be a completely closed system, only attempts at systematisation. These attempts always start from concrete actors who strive to give the chaos of contradictions a cohesive character and who rely on control mechanisms such as ideologies, institutions, language, contractual systems, and so on.[83]

In order to forge an analytical connection between these two aspects of capitalism – the system and the actors – it is not enough just to construct concepts; they must also be freed from their ontological fixation and be understood from the perspective of social reality itself. In expanding his theory, Lefebvre therefore follows a procedure that he has successfully applied many times: to trace the genesis of concepts in the historical process, in the dialectics of mental abstraction and concrete reality (see section 2.4 and chapter 6). A concept that brings this dialectic into a contradictory unity serves Lefebvre as a 'key to the real': the 'concrete abstraction'.[84]

Although the concept of 'concrete abstraction' is only introduced here, it appears in Lefebvre's work in various contexts: thus, for example, 'everyday life', the 'urban', and also the 'worldwide' (*le mondial*) are understood by Lefebvre as concrete abstractions.[85] It is only in *The Production of Space* and *De l'État*, however, that Lefebvre fully developed this concept and its application.

Łukasz Stanek has traced the concept of concrete abstraction throughout Lefebvre's work, and he also shows how Lefebvre applied this concept in his

---

82   Ibid., 10.
83   Lefebvre, *Survival of Capitalism*, 66–7.
84   Lefebvre, *De l'État*, vol. 3, 63.
85   Lefebvre, *Urban Revolution*, 87; Lefebvre, *Production of Space*, 341.

own empirical work.[86] On a theoretical level, Stanek demonstrates the connection to Hegel's 'concrete universal', and he follows the analysis that Marx had laid out in the *Grundrisse* when he contrasted concrete, living labour with generalised, abstract labour, and thus with labour as a commodity. These connections make it possible to place the concept of concrete abstraction in a broader theoretical context.

Lefebvre himself reveals the source of his understanding of concrete abstraction explicitly in *De l'État*: he had developed it from the first chapter of *Capital*.[87] However, in this chapter, where Marx sets out the foundations of his theory of the capitalist laws of motion, traces the enigmatic character of the commodity, and explains the law of value in its elementary form, the concept of concrete abstraction cannot itself be found. What can be found in this first chapter, however, are foundational reflections on exchange value and use value, and on the commodity character of labour under capitalism. The thorough analysis of the commodity, the dialectical relationship between exchange value and use value, and the form of exchange finally lead Lefebvre to his own understanding of concrete abstraction as a relativised, dialectical concept that opens up to 'becoming' and social practice (see section 2.3).[88]

Lefebvre's concept of concrete abstraction, however, reveals an 'epistemological gap' in *Capital*, the gap between the lived and the conceived.[89] Lefebvre argues that Marx reduced the multiplicity of human reality to a mathematical form and thus obscured important moments and aspects.[90] Consequently, he attempts to break open the formal rigour that Marx had given to his theory in order to make it fruitful for changing social practice. This yields rich rewards, as it allows us to see the commodification of space in its wider social context.

Since Marx's time, the dialectical contradiction between exchange value and use value has become even more acute: for Lefebvre, today it is in space that this opposition especially manifests itself and increasingly puts use value itself in question. As the following section considers, the dialectical contradiction of exchange value and use value is thus transformed into the contradiction of domination and appropriation.

---

86   Stanek, 'Space as Concrete Abstraction'; Stanek, *Henri Lefebvre on Space*, 133–5.
87   Lefebvre, *De l'État*, vol. 3, 63.
88   Ibid., 61.
89   Hajo Schmidt, *Sozialphilosophie des Krieges*, 335; Lefebvre, *Une pensée devenue monde*, 121–2.
90   Lefebvre, *De l'État*, vol. 3, 22.

Commodity, Exchange Value, and Use Value

When Marx wanted to reveal the mode of operation of capitalist society, Lefebvre noted, he started with the commodity, an abstraction of 'theological subtlety'.[91] Marx wrote:

A commodity appears at first sight an extremely obvious, trivial thing. But its analysis brings out that it is a very strange thing, abounding in metaphysical subtleties and theological niceties.[92]

For Marx, the commodity was something 'ambiguous', for it contains both use value and exchange value. First of all, the commodity is a thing that satisfies human needs through its properties – whatever they may be, and whether they originate from 'the stomach, or the imagination, makes no difference'.[93] The use value is realised only in use, in consumption:

The usefulness of a thing makes it a use-value. But this usefulness does not dangle in mid-air. It is conditioned by the physical properties of the commodity, and has no existence apart from the latter.[94]

Use values are the material content of wealth, and this content can have many properties. To discover the different sides and the different ways of using things is therefore the 'work of history'.[95]

In a capitalist social formation, the use value is also the material carrier of exchange value. The exchange value is therefore the mode of expression, the manifestation of a content that can be distinguished from it, a quantity that contains 'not an atom of use-value'.[96] The goods thus have a concrete, material side – the use value – and a general, abstract side – the exchange value. Exchange values abstract from the material properties of the objects to which they refer. They express a sameness: the quantitative relationship in which different use values are exchanged for one another.[97] Thus, a good never has its exchange value in isolation, but always only in the exchange ratio to another,

---

91 Ibid., 19.
92 Marx, *Capital*, vol. 1, 163.
93 Ibid., 125.
94 Ibid., 126.
95 Ibid., 125.
96 Ibid., 128.
97 Ibid., 125–7.

different commodity.[98] In general terms, this relationship can be summarised in the term 'equivalence': this term indicates that different quantities of different things can be exchanged for each other, that is, have the same value. In the course of social development, a specific commodity has emerged, which functions as the general equivalent for all other commodities: money.[99]

But what is the relationship through which commodities are exchanged against each other? How does exchange value actually appear? In Marx's analysis, the exchange value of a commodity is the expression, manifestation, or 'form of appearance' of a 'value' objectified in this commodity.[100] What constitutes this value? For his answer, Marx draws on the labour theory of value of classical political economy, as advocated by Adam Smith and David Ricardo, among others. It states that commodities have a 'value' because human labour is objectified in them. It is from these and other considerations – which I cannot go into here – that Marx finally derives his famous 'law of value', the foundation of all classical Marxist analysis: the value of a use value is determined by the quantity of socially necessary working time needed to produce it: 'As values, commodities are simply congealed quantities of human labour.'[101]

Marx now treats labour in an analogous way. On the one hand, labour is a concrete productive activity – the 'expenditure of human brain, nerve, muscle and sense organs',[102] whose usefulness is reflected in the use value of a product.[103] On the other hand, labour is pure abstraction, abstract labour that is reduced to a measure: the socially necessary working time to produce a certain product.

The complete sameness of different forms of labour is the result of an abstraction from their real differences, a reduction to the common character they possess as an expenditure of abstract human labour.[104] Thus nothing remains of the products of labour but the same 'ghostly incarnation of abstract human labour'.[105] Things only represent the human labour spent in their production. The value of a commodity is to a certain extent the 'crystal' of this abstract human labour, and the exchange value is the necessary form of appearance of this value.[106]

---

98   Ibid., 154.
99   Ibid., 162–3.
100 Ibid., 140–1.
101 Ibid., 141.
102 Ibid., 164.
103 Ibid., 153.
104 Ibid., 169.
105 Ibid.
106 Ibid., 127.

The Concrete Abstraction

Marx took the contradiction between exchange value and use value as the central theoretical starting point for his concepts: the commodity is a product of social labour that is intended to be exchanged and is therefore endowed with a double value: use value and exchange value.[107] Lefebvre sees this distinction between exchange value and use value in Marx as a logical opposition, as two complementary poles constituting a single concept with a double aspect.[108] Contrary to a common interpretation, however, for Lefebvre, it is not the use value that constitutes the exchange value, but rather the opposite: it is the exchange value that generates the use value.[109] For, as a logical opposition, the two terms belong together inseparably: without the term 'exchange value' the term 'use value' would have no meaning whatsoever. Thus, the use value does not exist before the exchange, but arises only with it and through it. Admittedly, only use allows exchange: a thing that someone uses can be sold. It takes on an exchange value precisely because it has a use value. For Lefebvre, however, use does not coincide with use value. For thousands of years, water, air, and soil had no practical value, although the whole world made use of them. They became use values in the very moment they were produced to be sold, that is, the moment they assumed an exchange value.[110]

Although this is undoubtedly an inspiring interpretation, it does not correspond to Marx's understanding:

A thing can be a use-value without being a value. This is the case whenever its utility to man is not mediated through labour. Air, virgin soil, natural meadows, unplanted forests, etc., fall into this category.[111]

This seemingly insignificant difference characterises Lefebvre's understanding of the dialectic as a historical process. Concepts cannot claim an ontological status – rather, they are fundamentally bound to a social practice.[112] They are to be understood from their historicity; their real content develops only in and with a social practice. Here Lefebvre draws a direct comparison to Marx's abstract labour as expressed in the law of value: this abstract labour has

---

107   Lefebvre, *Production of Space*, 402.

108   Lefebvre, *De l'État*, vol. 3, 27.

109   Ibid., 28; Lefebvre, *Production of Space*, 329. See also Hajo Schmidt, *Sozialphilosophie des Krieges*, 190.

110   Lefebvre, *De l'État*, vol. 4, 275.

111   Marx, *Capital*, vol. 1, 131.

112   Hajo Schmidt, *Sozialphilosophie des Krieges*, 195.

nothing to do with a mental, scientific, or epistemological abstraction, because it has a social existence.[113] But abstraction does not become concrete through the intentional transition from concept to action, like a plan or a project. The abstract always concretises and realises itself in and through a social practice.[114]

In Lefebvre's understanding, the pair of terms exchange value/use value thus forms an initially abstract, logical opposition that only develops into a concrete dialectical contradiction and thus into a concrete abstraction in and through social practice. The distinction between exchange value and use value thus has a practical meaning: if you consume your product yourself, you cannot offer it on the market. Conversely, exchange implies the suspension of use, the sometimes permanent loss of the product, the curbing of desire in the expectation of exchange. In the course of history, however, the abstract, logical relationship between use value and exchange value has tended to become reality, to become conflictual and thus dialectical.[115] In a bitter struggle, exchange value prevails over use value: 'Exchange wrests use from its limits, but also from immediate enjoyment.'[116]

Thus not only does exchange value generate use value as its logical correlate, but the use of the commodity also changes with the emergence of exchange value: it loses its immediate totality, defines and realises itself no longer in itself, but only in its confrontation and relationship with exchange value. And, following Lefebvre's dialectic, with the concept of exchange value emerges its correlate as well: the lived, *le vécu*, which separates itself from the conceived, *le conçu* (see section 5.5).[117]

Lefebvre explains this relationship between use and exchange through the example of sexual relations, which are subject to material exchange in two ways: marriage and prostitution. Whereas in prostitution, use is paid for directly, in marriage, it is regulated by formally stipulated rules, which may also include material exchange (gifts, inheritance). Under these conditions, use separates and distances itself from exchange and becomes the domain of passion, revolt, poetry. Expressed in general and abstract terms, this movement can be summarised in the contradiction between use and exchange.[118]

Here, again, we see Lefebvre's specific approach and interpretation. For Marx, use was not a problem: so far as a commodity is a use value, there is

---

113   Lefebvre, *Production of Space*, 307.
114   Lefebvre, *De l'État*, vol. 3, 59.
115   Ibid., 27.
116   Ibid., 28. Translation by author.
117   Ibid., 33.
118   Ibid., 29.

'nothing mysterious about it'.[119] For Lefebvre, on the other hand, use is dialectically linked to social abstraction through exchange value. If one follows Lefebvre's logic, exchange and exchange value alienate a product from the person who uses it. Use then loses its immediate totality and is reduced to the lived, the *vécu*. It therefore makes a big difference whether something is bought or has to be bought, or whether it is freely available and can be appropriated collectively.

The Form of Exchange

As this reconstruction makes clear, the concrete abstraction of the commodity is not just an abstract fantasy, nor a mental category. It is the result of an activity: exchange. This means, at the same time, that this abstraction does not have a predetermined existence but develops historically. It can thus also be understood as a concrete, historical process.

Exchange has developed in thought as well as in social practice, in space and time.[120] Here, Lefebvre explicitly follows Marx's approach in developing the concept of social labour in *Capital* and in his preceding work *A Contribution to the Critique of Political Economy* of 1859. Lefebvre argues that Marx showed that the idea and the concept of social labour only appeared in the eighteenth century, when the division of labour had reached such an advanced stage that the various partial work tasks formed a unity in real practice – that is, social labour had emerged. Before that, people had also worked, but this fact did not enter into philosophical 'consciousness' – it was not considered worthy of mention in philosophy and in discourses on human beings.[121]

For Lefebvre, it was the merit of Marx to have traced the reasons for the emergence of social labour and to have identified its essence: social labour is not a substance or a 'reality' but a pure form: the form of exchange. This form has a polar structure – exchange value and use value – and certain functions. But a dialectical paradox remains at its core, an almost empty spot, an absence: the form of exchange that guides social practice.[122]

In Lefebvre's view, this almost pure and, to a certain extent, logical form is similar and related to other forms: identity and difference, equivalence, coherence, reciprocity, repetition.[123] Here, Lefebvre explicitly emphasises the parallel

119   Marx, *Capital*, vol. 1, 163.
120   Lefebvre, *Production of Space*, 100.
121   Ibid.; Lefebvre, *Metaphilosophy*, 50–1.
122   Lefebvre, *Production of Space*, 100.
123   Ibid.

nature of the exchange of material goods and the exchange of signs, that is, language and discourse: the form of material exchange does not say what is exchanged. It only determines that 'something' that has a use is also an object of exchange. And the form of non-material communication does not say which sign is exchanged, but rather it demands a repertoire of different signs, a message, a channel, a code. Similarly, the form of logic does not say what is coherent or what is thought but demands formal coherence so that thinking can even occur.[124]

In the same way, for Lefebvre concrete abstractions such as commodities, labour, or money are forms that have a social existence but require content in order to exist socially.[125] Viewed in isolation, 'in itself', the commodity, even on a worldwide scale, does not have the capacity for practical existence. It therefore remains an abstraction, even if – as a thing – it is endowed with a terrible, to a certain extent lethal, power. The 'world of commodities' cannot exist by itself. It requires labour, productive activity. Every commodity is the product of the division of labour, of technology, of the expenditure of energy. In this sense, in order to become concrete, the concept of the commodity must materialise, and for Lefebvre this means that it requires a spatialisation: the commodity also includes a space.[126]

The Concrete-Abstract Space

Just as Marx had done with the commodity and labour, Lefebvre conceptualises social space as a concrete abstraction. Like exchange and labour, the capitalist form of social space has only developed gradually, and it also is something close to a logical form. It requires a content, and it cannot be understood without its content. But it should be understood through abstraction, beyond any defined content.[127]

So, what is the form of social space for Lefebvre? Gathering, assembly, simultaneity[128] – in other words, centrality, as he introduced and defined it in *The Urban Revolution* (see section 4.4). This is where he had also defined the urban as a pure form, with a polar structure (centre–periphery). And, like social space, the urban was also conceived in this text as a concrete

---

124   Ibid., 100–1.
125   Ibid., 306.
126   Ibid., 342.
127   Ibid., 100.
128   Ibid., 101.

abstraction.[129] This parallel with the analysis of the commodity reveals the full scope of the concept of social space: it is the general category that encompasses the specific, historical category of urban society (see sections 3.4 and 8.2).

The qualities of social space come from the processes that constitute it: production, and thus activity, labour. But the social labour that produces this space is itself a concrete abstraction: on the one hand, it is general and abstract; on the other, it is concrete, and thus, as a consequence of the division of labour, divided and fragmented.[130] Space produced in this way also has an abstract-concrete character: abstract because its existence is only achieved through the interchangeability of all its constituent elements, concrete because it is socially real and localised as such. This is precisely the space which is simultaneously homogeneous and fractured (see section 6.3).[131]

This is how social space finally acquires its double determination: on the one hand, 'reality', 'natural substance', the milieu of accumulation, commodity, and capital; on the other hand, 'irreality', transparency.[132] Thus, we find the theoretical origin of the 'double illusion of space' that Lefebvre took as the starting point for his analysis of the production of space (see section 5.1).

The concept of concrete abstraction thus provides a dialectical resolution to this apparent paradox: in the process of social abstraction through exchange, the 'reality' of social space loses its material, autonomous form of appearance.[133] Social space tends to become absolute, like every 'thing' that has become a commodity through exchange. But the thing does not reach the absolute, because it cannot free itself from activity, use, need, from its 'social existence'.[134] Even if exchange, circuits, and networks occupy the worldwide space, use and consumption keep their local character: a certain person, with a certain schedule, seeks a certain satisfaction. The paradigmatic contrast between exchange and use, between the abstract, worldwide circuits and the concrete places of production and consumption, thus becomes a dialectical contradiction through *spatialisation*.[135] Use reappears, and does this in an intensified conflict with exchange, because it too implies appropriation, and therefore time as well. The contradiction between use value and exchange value

---

129 Lefebvre, *Urban Revolution*,118.
130 Lefebvre, *Production of Space*, 129.
131 Ibid., 341–2.
132 Ibid., 129.
133 Ibid.
134 Ibid., 83.
135 Ibid., 341–2.

thus becomes a contradiction between appropriation and domination in space.[136]

Domination and Appropriation

With his conception of the contradiction between appropriation and domination, Lefebvre again reaches the limits of Marx's understanding of the relationship between humans and nature. Marx did not, in Lefebvre's view, clearly distinguish between these two concepts: humans would appropriate nature simply by dominating material nature through labour and technology and subordinating it to their needs. In this sense, appropriation would thus mean transforming nature through and for human use: 'Thus nature was converted directly from an enemy, an indifferent mother, into "goods".'[137]

For Lefebvre, however, appropriation is closely linked to lived experience. It includes the affective realm, the imaginary, dreams, the body, pleasure, and enjoyment – and thus also space. For Lefebvre, an appropriated space resembles a work of art. It is often a monument or a building – and a landscape, a square, or a street can be 'appropriated' as well. Yet it is not easy to determine how, through what processes, and for whom a space is appropriated.[138]

Lefebvre sees the 'farmhouse' or the 'village' as typical examples of an appropriated space, and in this context, he refers to the studies of Amos Rapoport (1972) and Gaston Bachelard (1987):[139] 'Peasant houses and villages speak: they recount, though in a mumbled and somewhat confused way, the lives of those who built and inhabited them.'[140]

Appropriation and domination still coincide in these examples of the rural field. The development of capitalism, however, brought about their separation, and thus the dialectical contradiction between domination and appropriation. Domination is not only created by political forces, by wars and conquests – it is particularly intensified by the fact that space becomes a commodity.[141]

A prime example for this contradiction is the beach, a privileged place of pleasure and enjoyment, introduced or discovered with modernity: a space located at the intersection of the elements, sun, air, sea, earth (see section

---

136   Ibid., 356.
137   Ibid., 165.
138   Ibid.; Lefebvre, *De l'État*, vol. 3, 30.
139   Rapoport, *House Form and Culture*; Bachelard, *The Poetics of Space*.
140   Lefebvre, *Production of Space*, 165.
141   Ibid.

6.5).[142] The use of the beach lies in accepting it as a gift, through and with the presence of the body:

> Children use it in a different way than lovers or athletes or the elderly. There is a multiplicity of uses, according to the bodies and the use of the body. The body appropriates this space with ease, which is part of the pleasure.[143]

But this actual or potential use comes into collision with exchange and the exchange value of the beach, which can be owned, occupied, sold, and thus also fenced off, reserved, forbidden. Property and exchange value fight against those forms of appropriation and particularly against the living body and lived experience in a visible, readable, and evident way.[144]

The example of the beach makes it clear that with the domination of space the body is also fragmented, dispossessed, and expropriated. The reappropriation of the body is thus closely connected with the appropriation of space.[145] In this way, the beach becomes a symbolic value for Lefebvre: it symbolises the struggle for differential space, for use, for the body, and for pleasure. 'Sous les pavés, la plage!' (Under the paving stones, there is the beach!) – this slogan of the French movement of May '68 could be read also in Lefebvre's sense.

The production of space accompanies the renewed importance of 'nature' as a source of use values. 'For Marx nature was *the only true wealth*.'[146] For Lefebvre, this statement remains true as long as first and second nature are not arbitrarily separated: 'The supreme good is time-space.'

This brings us back to the contradiction between abstract space and differential space, which was discussed in detail in sections 6.3 and 6.4. In the general formulation presented here, this appears as a contradiction between the domination and the appropriation of social space. But how can the appropriation of space become realised? To answer this question, the concrete power structures that are incorporated into space through the process of the production of space must be addressed – those power structures that resist, and even actively hinder, the appropriation of space.[147]

---

142 Lefebvre, *De l'État*, vol. 4, 277–8; see also Lefebvre, *Toward an Architecture of Enjoyment*, 48–9.

143 Lefebvre, *De l'État*, vol. 4, 278. Translation by author.

144 Ibid.

145 Lefebvre, *Production of Space*, 167–8.

146 Ibid., 350.

147 Lefebvre, *State, Space, World*, 245.

7.3 Space and Social Relations

> Marx identified the most general form of social relations, namely the
> form of exchange.[148]

In the previous section, (capitalist) space was considered as a concrete abstraction: on the one hand it is concrete, material, use value; and on the other it is abstract, exchangeable, exchange value. From this fundamental contradiction arises the contradiction between the domination and appropriation of space. It would therefore be obvious to develop suitable strategies, tactics, and designs for the appropriation of space – as in fact many architects, urbanists, and sociologists have striven to do. But this is not what Lefebvre proposed (see section 6.5), for in his view in most cases the answers would come up short and fall into the trap of fighting symptoms without questioning the underlying power relations. We must therefore continue to ask: How might the domination of space actually work? How can power structures inscribe themselves into space? How does the dialectic of exchange value and use value become a spatial reality?

These questions foreground another central Marxist concept: the social relations of production. For Lefebvre, concrete abstraction has a real existence in social relations of production, that is, in concrete relations of exploitation and domination, authority, and power.[149] However, this concept has often been somewhat obscured in the academic debate. Marx used the term *Produktionsverhältnisse* (relations of production) to denote those social relations that are constitutive for a mode of production, that is, the social relations that determine the production, exchange, and consumption of products.[150] In English translations this therefore often appears as 'social relations of production' or in French as *rapports sociaux de production*, in order to prevent misunderstandings. In shorthand use, these terms are often reduced to 'social relations' (or *rapports sociaux*), which can lead to new misunderstandings, because 'social relations' is a very broad category that of course goes far beyond the narrow focus of the production process.

Like Marx, Lefebvre understands social relations as concrete, material relations, and he consistently incorporates them into his spatio-temporal theory of society. In doing so, he arrives at a highly provocative and controversial thesis: social relations of production only have a social existence if they also have a spatial existence.

---

148   Lefebvre, *Production of Space*, 82.
149   Lefebvre, *Survival of Capitalism*, 51.
150   Lefebvre, *Production of Space*, 32; Lefebvre, *De l'État*, vol. 4, 307.

What exactly is the mode of existence of social relationships? Are they substantial? natural? or formally abstract? The study of space offers an answer according to which the social relations of production have a social existence to the extent that they have a spatial existence; they project themselves into a space, becoming inscribed there, and in the process producing that space itself. Failing this, these relations would remain in the realm of 'pure' abstraction – that is to say, in the realm of representations and hence of ideology: the realm of verbalism, verbiage and empty words.[151]

This famous thesis has been met with enthusiastic approval, but also with vehement opposition. If it is regarded by some as evidence of the primordial significance of space, for others it is proof of the reifying character of Lefebvre's theory of space (see also sections 1.2 and 6.4). Edward W. Soja took this quotation as the starting point for his widely discussed and controversial thesis on the central importance of space for social processes.[152] Benno Werlen countered this thesis by arguing that the social content of social relations cannot be spatial because its social component is immaterial.[153] He derived from this argument the criticism that space had been reified – in Soja but also in Lefebvre. However, a closer analysis of the concept of social relations will show that both interpretations, that of Werlen as well as that of Soja, are not tenable, as neither of them fully appreciates how Lefebvre defines social relations.

What do social relations mean for Lefebvre? Before *The Survival of Capitalism*, he had hardly ever treated the question of the constitution of social relations in any detail, and, in this text, he approaches this question primarily from the point of view of their reproduction (see section 7.5). In *The Production of Space*, he formulates and substantiates his thesis of the spatiality of social relations quoted above, but, ultimately, it remains unclear what social relations actually are – this is one of the reasons for the cryptic character of this book.

It is only with *De l'État* that Lefebvre redefines social relations from the point of view of the commodification of space. Here, he returns to the question of what a commodity actually is and how it is constituted. For Marx, as for Lefebvre, the commodity is a social relationship, but this is veiled in everyday reality. Marx addresses this phenomenon using the concept of the 'commodity fetish'. As shown in the previous section, the commodity has a contradictory character: as a use value, it is a thing that has useful properties and is therefore

---

151   Lefebvre, *Production of Space*, 129.
152   Soja, *Postmodern Geographies*, 127–8; Soja, *Thirdspace*, 45–6.
153   Werlen, *Society, Action and Space*, 4.

needed and used by people. At the same time, however, the commodity is exchange value, and thus an abstract value, which is measured by the labour time spent in its production. Things thus become mere quantities that are detached from their materiality and use. Their essential qualities are thus overlaid (or fetishised) by exchange, and thus the social relations that were involved in their production are obscured or veiled. The consequence of this argument is that the commodity, as a concrete abstraction, is itself a social relationship.

Starting from this understanding of the commodity as a social relationship, the issue to consider is the role of the materiality that underlies this relationship: how do social relations inscribe themselves into space? Lefebvre concludes that every social relation is based on a 'material support' that constitutes the foundation of the spatial-material order of society, and thus identifies a new dialectic of determination and openness.

The Commodity Fetish: Commodity as a Social Relation

According to Lefebvre, a social relation can be understood neither simply as such, nor through the individuals involved, but only in its contradictory unity: the practical 'I' is inextricably individual *and* social.[154] The actors are therefore simultaneously individual and collective, since they are always members of a social group or class.[155]

In order to explore the mystery of social relations under capitalism, Lefebvre goes back once again to the foundation of social reality that is at once simple and yet so difficult to understand: exchange. He argues that Marx himself had recognised the form of exchange as the most universal form of a social relation, that he understood it as action that implies a relationship. But this relationship does not reveal itself as such, for it is to a certain extent hidden in the exchanged things that conceal, shift, and mirror this social relationship.[156] Marx addressed this peculiar characteristic of the commodity, as well as the dialectic of exchange value and use value, in the first chapter of *Capital*, through the concept of the commodity fetish.

Lefebvre sums up the concept of the commodity fetish as follows: products that are reduced to the common measure of money do not tell the truth about themselves. On the contrary, they lie by disguising the productive labour and the social labour time they contain, as well as the social relations of

---

154   Lefebvre, *Production of Space*, 61.
155   Ibid., 57.
156   Ibid., 82; Lefebvre, *De l'État*, vol. 3, 19, 22.

exploitation and domination on which they are based. The product becomes a fetish, it becomes 'more real' than reality and productive activity. The product thereby conceals something very important – pleasure – and it lies by means of appearances and illusions, the signs and meanings it carries and supports. Lefebvre sees Marx's strength precisely in the fact that he tore off the mask of things and revealed the social relations inherent in them.[157] In order to reach that point, Marx had to shatter the certainties of an epoch, the confidence in things and 'reality':

> The 'positive' and the 'real' have never lacked for justifications or for strong supporting arguments from the standpoint of common sense and of everyday life, so Marx had his work cut out when it fell to him to demolish such claims.[158]

For Marx, the enigmatic character of the commodity lay in the social form of the commodity itself. Its mystery lies in the fact that it reflects back to people the social character of their own labour as natural properties of the produced things, and thus the social relationship between producers and workers appears as a relationship between things that is situated beyond themselves. In this way, the products of labour become 'sensual-extrasensory' things, social things – commodities:[159]

> I call this the fetishism which attaches itself to the products of labour as soon as they are produced as commodities, and is therefore inseparable from the production of commodities.[160]

As Marx sees it, this phenomenon is based on the fact that the product contains a double relation, a double opposition: the inner opposition inherent in the commodity is that between use value and value (as a measure of labour time contained in it; see section 7.2). But in the relationship of exchange this opposition is represented by an external relation, by the equivalence of the different exchanged things, and thus by an abstraction.[161] But this abstraction then appears to be the actual essence of things. Marx illustrates this strange twist with the following example:

---

157   Ibid., 80–1.
158   Ibid., 82.
159   Marx, *Capital*, vol. 1, 165.
160   Ibid.
161   Ibid., 159.

If commodities could speak, they would say this: our use-value may interest men, but it does not belong to us as objects. What does belong to us as objects, however, is our value. Our own intercourse as commodities proves it. We relate to each other merely as exchange-values.[162]

In the abstract reality of the world of commodities, things are detached from their concrete, material quality and become mere quantities, pure values. In the exchange economy, however, it is precisely this abstract side of exchange values that takes on the appearance of the 'essence' of things: in the value of a product, the labour spent in its production appears as a material property.[163] Marx formulates this fetish character even more pointedly in the following quotation:

So far no chemist has ever discovered exchange-value either in a pearl or a diamond. The economists who have discovered this chemical substance ... nevertheless find that the use-value of material objects belongs to them independently of their material properties, while their value, on the other hand, forms a part of them as objects. What confirms them in this view is the peculiar circumstance that the use-value of a thing is realized without exchange, i.e. in the direct relation between thing and man, while, inversely, its value is realized only in exchange, i.e. in a social process.[164]

To crown it all, Marx quotes Shakespeare: 'To be a well-favoured man is the gift of fortune; but reading and writing comes by nature.'[165]

It is precisely these passages which Lefebvre takes up when he postulates that the commodity is not an abstraction *despite* its character as a 'thing' but, on the contrary, *because* it is a social 'thing' – that is detached from its materiality, from its use, from productive activity, from the need it is supposed to satisfy. The commodity is hidden in the department stores and warehouses. But it does not conceal a mystery analogous to that of nature. Its mystery is entirely social: money, property, the cycle of 'demand–money–satisfaction'. The commodity asks to appear, to exhibit itself visibly and legibly in the shop windows and displays:

Once it is apparent, there is no call to decode it; it has no need of deci-pherment after the fashion of the 'beings' of nature and of the

---

162   Ibid., 176–7.
163   Ibid., 165.
164   Ibid., 176–7.
165   Ibid., from *Much Ado about Nothing*, Act 3, Scene 3.

imagination. And yet, once it has appeared, its mystery only deepens. Who has produced it? Who will buy it? Who will profit from its sale? Who, or what purpose, will it serve? Where will the money go? The commodity does not answer these questions; it is simply there, exposed to the gaze of passers-by, in a setting more or less alluring, more or less exhibitionistic, be it in a nondescript small shop or in a glittering department store.[166]

The commodity, therefore, contains two intertwined relationships: use implies a relationship between a person and a thing, while exchange is a social process and implies a relationship between persons. Or, as Lefebvre observes: production doubles into the production of things and the production of relations, where one goes hand in hand with the other.[167] In social practice, however, these relations are topsy-turvy, as Marx writes: to the producers, 'the relations connecting the labour of one individual with that of the rest appear, not as direct social relations between individuals at work, but as what they really are, material relations between persons and social relations between things.'[168] What is hidden behind the commodity fetish, though, is the social relations between people that result from the social process of labour and exchange. In this sense, they are always material relations, because they are necessarily bound to a concrete materiality, that of the labour process and its products.

As Lefebvre points out, the formal relationship established through exchange has nothing in common with a merely mental relationship as conceived in positivist thinking. It does not remain 'in the air'. For it always has a content, a material object. Nevertheless, the formal side of exchange unfolds above the content, the objects that change while the form remains.[169] As a result, this means that the commodity, as a concrete abstraction, does not simply imply or constitute a social relation: the commodity itself is a social relation. And it is precisely this social character of the commodity that the thing simultaneously contains and conceals.

But this does not yet answer the initial questions: What is the materiality of this social relation? How do social relations maintain their existence? Where does a social relation exist if it is not realised in a concrete situation? What is its status as it waits for its realisation?[170]

---

166   Lefebvre, *Production of Space*, 340.
167   Lefebvre, *De l'État*, vol. 3, 54.
168   Marx, *Capital*, vol. 1, 165.
169   Lefebvre, *De l'État*, vol. 3, 23.
170   Lefebvre, *Production of Space*, 401.

The Material Support of Social Relations

For Lefebvre, it is clear that social relations must have a material base, located in a sensible world:

> Social relations are achieved from the sensible. They cannot be reduced to this sensible world, and yet they do not float in air, they do not disappear into transcendence. If social reality suggests forms and relations, if it cannot be conceived in a way homologous to the isolated, sensible or technical object, it does not survive without ties, without attachment to objects and things. We must insist on this methodologically and theoretically important point.[171]

This means, in consequence, that no social relation can exist without a material support (*support matériel*), without a material foothold or backing.[172] The French term *support* denotes, approximately, an 'underpinning', 'layer', or 'foundation'. Here, I have chosen to use the term 'support' to express its general technical use as a thing that bears the weight of another thing and thus supports it and keeps it upright.

How does this material support work? The answer that Marx gave in his exploration of the mysterious nature of the commodity remains incomplete for Lefebvre: the commodity as both concrete and abstract 'thing/not-thing' (*chose-non-chose*). The thing, the product of social labour, being both exchange value and use value at the same time, contains and disguises social relations. It is the support of these conditions. But, as a commodity, it ceases to be a thing. Insofar as it remains a thing, it becomes an 'ideological object', overloaded with meanings. As a commodity, then, it dissolves in social relations and has only an abstract existence. This goes up to the point where one is tempted to see in the commodity only signs and signs of signs (that is, money).[173]

Where, in all this, has concrete, sensuous materiality gone? Marx writes that the use values or the physical bodies of commodities represent the joining of two elements: materials from nature and labour. If one subtracts the entirety of all useful work contained in these physical bodies, a material substrate always remains that is naturally present without human intervention. Human beings can only proceed in production as does nature itself; they can only change the forms of the materials.[174]

---

171   Lefebvre, *Right to the City*, 103.
172   Lefebvre, *Production of Space*, 401.
173   Ibid., 402.
174   Marx, *Capital*, vol. 1, 133.

For Lefebvre, however, this 'material substrate' does not offer a satisfactory answer: the question of the material support cannot be completely solved by reference to the durability of the material.[175] The central problem lies precisely in the relationship between the social relation and the 'material support' that carries and promotes it.[176]

Lefebvre sees a better answer in his concept of social space. This space is also a thing/not-thing: Neither material nor mental reality, social space does not dissolve into abstractions and does not consist in a collection of things in space or in a sum of occupied places. It is neither a space-sign (*espace-signe*) nor an ensemble of signs concerning space. It has a different actuality than the abstract signs and the real things it envelops. It has a starting point: the space of nature, physical space. On this foundation, a society produces successive and jumbled layers of networks which transform the space of nature, replace it, and threaten to destroy it. These networks are always materialised, but their materiality takes various forms: paths, roads, railway lines, telephone lines, and the like. Each of these material supports establishes a specific network, and thus a space, which is also a product that in turn is exchanged, used, and consumed. The material supports find their meaning and finality only in and through this space.[177]

Lefebvre explains these considerations by analogy to language: just as there is no thinking and no reflection without language, there is likewise no language without material support – the senses, mouths, ears, masses of air set in motion, voices, and signs as articulated utterances. There is therefore a space of language that presupposes the lips, the ears, the articulatory functions. But its material conditions are not sufficient to define this space: It is a space of actions and interactions, of expressiveness and power, of latent violence and revolts. It is a space of discourse, but it does not coincide with the discourse on space or the discourse in space. This space of speech envelops the space of the body and develops with the space of traces, of what is written, prescribed, and inscribed.[178]

Similarly, neither kilograms of sugar nor metres of fabric can be considered material support for the general existence of the commodity. What must instead be taken into account are all the shops and warehouses where these things are stored, the ships, trains, and trucks that move them, and the transport routes they take. These objects constitute relational networks and commodity chains in space. The world of commodities would have no 'reality' without the entirety of these points of connection and insertion.[179] In Lefebvre's

---

175 Lefebvre, *Production of Space*, 402.
176 Ibid., 401.
177 Ibid., 402–3.
178 Ibid.
179 Ibid., 403.

understanding, social relations of exchange exist socially only in the sense that they are projected onto the terrain and are materialised in concretely localised transport networks, markets, and centres.[180]

This is how social space realises social relations and thus incorporates relations of power. This applies both to the relations of production (the division of labour and the organisation of labour) and, for example, to gender relations. Social space contains these relations and assigns the activities that constitute them to their corresponding place; it 'localises' them. Not without failures – as Lefebvre remarks ironically.[181]

The 'texture of space' gives a place to abstract, 'placeless' social actions. Spatial practice is determined by this texture: the subject perceives space as an obstacle, as a resistant materiality, sometimes as relentlessly hard as a concrete wall, which is not only extremely difficult to change, but also subject to draconian rules that forbid any change.[182]

The Spatial-Material Order of Society

Social relations, understood as concrete abstractions, are incorporated into social space. The mode of production projects them onto the terrain. They have a real existence only in and through social space. Their material support is spatial.[183] Using formulations like these, which run like a red thread through *The Production of Space*, Lefebvre attempts to trace the connection between social space and social relations.

In other words, this means that social relations inscribe themselves into space, solidify themselves in space, produce a spatial texture, which in turn determines action by 'assigning a place' to it, defining its possibilities and limits – whereby, and this is decisive, it is not only the materiality itself that determines action, but also the rules that are imposed on this materiality – and the violence that these rules are bound up with (see section 7.4).

How does this determination of social space work? For Lefebvre – by recourse to Marx – this question can only be clarified by bringing the process of production and its inherent rationality into focus. This rationality demands a series of successive actions in order to reach a concrete 'goal' (such as to produce an object). The process of production creates a temporally and spatially sequenced order of operations whose results coexist in space. Spatial elements

---

180   Ibid., 120.
181   Ibid., 32.
182   Ibid., 57.
183   Ibid., 333, 404.

are set in motion: the body, the hands, the eyes, but also materials (stones, wood, and so on) and equipment (tools, weapons, language, commands, and so on). The active mind creates relational orders between these elements of material action, relations of simultaneity. This incessant transition from temporality (sequences, the chain of events) to spatiality (simultaneity, synchronisation) defines – even more than the constants and invariants – every productive activity. The formal relationships that allow separate actions to form a coherent whole cannot be separated from the material conditions of individual and collective action, whether the act in question is displacing a rock, hunting big game, or producing an object of any kind.[184]

Social space is the result of a sequence of operations; it encloses the produced things and contains their relationships in their coexistence and simultaneity, in their relative order and/or disorder.[185] A space thus contains highly diverse natural and social objects, networks, and paths that enable the exchange of material things and information. Social labour transforms them and changes their situation to that of a spatio-temporal totality, even if it does not affect their materiality or their natural state, such as that of an island, a river, or a hill.[186]

Social space thus connects the various aspects of practice by coordinating them or, more precisely, by uniting them in a practice.[187] The production of space thus follows a logic of the general form of simultaneity. Every spatial order is based on the mental juxtaposition and material assemblage of elements whose simultaneity is produced.[188]

This simultaneously material and mental spatial order is set by predetermined conditions. Every social space was fixed before the arrival of the individual or collective actor who seeks to appropriate this space. This presupposed, previously established existence of space determines the presence, action, and discourse, and the competence and performance of the actors. And yet, by presupposing the existence of space, the actors' presence, action, and discourse also negate it.[189]

Following this analysis, the rationality of space does not result from a quality or characteristic of human activity in general, of human labour as such, of 'human beings' or social organisation. On the contrary, the rationality of space is the origin and the immediate, inherent source of the rationality of action, an origin which is hidden but nevertheless included in the inevitable empirical

---

184   Ibid., 71.
185   Ibid., 73.
186   Ibid., 77.
187   Lefebvre, 'Preface to the New Edition', 209.
188   Ibid.
189   Lefebvre, *Production of Space*, 57.

reality of those who use their hands and tools, coordinate their movements, and expend their energies.[190]

The determination of the material support is only relative, however. It cannot be claimed, says Lefebvre, that from the beginning the capitalist mode of production 'ordered' its spatial extension, which today encompasses the entire planet. A society appropriates the pre-existing, previously formed space and arranges it according to its intentions. Lefebvre conceives the production of space as an evolutionary process, as a process of genesis: space is created by successive waves that (discontinuously) create one layer of space after another.[191]

Accordingly, for Lefebvre there can be no exact, predetermined correspondence between social relations and spatio-temporal relations.[192] There is a distance between the material support and the social relations that materialise through and in it, a distance that is filled by illusions and ideologies. This is precisely why space is not transparent and cannot be grasped directly (see section 5.1).[193] Lefebvre also emphasises that the connection between the material support and social relations always requires a separate analysis, an implication-explication of its genesis: a critique of the institutions, substitutions, transfers, and metamorphoses that transform space.[194]

Between Determination and Openness

The influences on this theorisation of the historical transformation of space cannot be overlooked: if space is the synchronous order of things, time is their diachronous order. Here Lefebvre adopts aspects of Leibniz's relational definition of space and time (see section 5.3). However, he does not understand space as the result of mental acts through which things are brought into a spatial order; space would thus only be conceived. He sees this order as the result of a (diachronic) sequence of material operations, and thus this order is actively produced and materialises in space and as space. At the same time, this material order produced as the result of action once again becomes the precondition for action, which is the immanent source of its rationality.

Against this background, the thesis presented at the beginning of this section is illuminated and relativised:

---

190   Ibid., 71–2.
191   Lefebvre, 'Preface to the New Edition', 209, 211; Lefebvre, *Urban Revolution*, 127.
192   Lefebvre, 'Preface to the New Edition', 211.
193   Ibid., 209.
194   Lefebvre, *Production of Space*, 404.

Any 'social existence' aspiring or claiming to be 'real', but failing to produce its own space, would be a strange entity, a very peculiar kind of abstraction unable to escape from the ideological or even the 'cultural' realm. It would fall to the level of folklore and sooner or later disappear altogether, thereby immediately losing its identity, its denomination and its feeble degree of reality.[195]

This thesis is ultimately nothing more than Marx's famous dictum, applied to the production of space: 'Men make their own history, but they do not make it just as they please; they do not make it under circumstances chosen by themselves, but under circumstances directly encountered, given and transmitted from the past.'[196]

Placing this in the context of the preceding reconstruction of Lefebvre's theoretical structure, we can summarise as follows: to carry out a materialist analysis of social processes always also means including the material conditions of these processes. Although they are not sufficient to explain action, they are nevertheless its prerequisites. These material conditions are always tied to the concrete physical aspect of space, which forms the material support of action and thus also of social relations.

But this material support is not natural: it is to an increasing degree produced by society. Social actors produce the conditions of their actions in space and as space. In this way, however, social conditions are also incorporated into space. So, what applies to produced 'things' also applies to produced space – it implies, contains, and conceals social relations.[197]

We can therefore now resolve the debate on the reification of space, discussed in the introduction to this section. For Lefebvre, social relations are not pure ideas or abstract values, nor are they immaterial structures; they do not float in the air, but are rather constituted by concrete activities, such as labour or exchange. Thus, the social does not exist without the material, the human body and the material objects and tools of activity. The material and the social are always dialectically intertwined. This also makes it clear that Lefebvre does not reify space, because he does not assume space as pre-existing and substantialised. On the contrary, he conceives of space not as an 'object' or as a 'system of objects' but as a process. As he emphasises again and again, space is not a 'thing'. Just as the isolated observation of produced things 'as such' obscures the social conditions of their production and thus turns the commodity into a

---

195   Ibid., 53.
196   Marx, *The Eighteenth Brumaire of Louis Bonaparte*, 103.
197   Lefebvre, *Production of Space*, 82.

fetish, the trap of space 'as such' is also set: the trap of spatiality and spatial fetishism.[198] This is also a clear answer to Soja, who, in his ontology of space, tried to separate a 'space as such' from the social space – 'spatiality' (see sections 1.3 and 5.7).

This reading is found even more explicitly in the following quotation: 'Space has no power "in itself".[199] Spatial practice does not create life, it merely regulates it, and the contradictions of space are not determined by space 'as such'. It is the social contradictions that generate the contradictions of space; they come to light through space.[200] Lefebvre insists that his theory and its key articulations must be understood in their entirety, and he strongly objects to the concept of 'space' being used in a trivial manner, without analysis.[201]

For Lefebvre space is, first, the space of social practice and, second, it is to be analysed in its entirety. He therefore understands and treats space not as a material object or thing, but as an ensemble of social actions: for him, social space 'incorporates' social actions, the actions of subjects who are both collective and individual, who are born and die, who suffer and act.[202] This produced space is deprived of everything natural. It is conceived as a 'living' space or as a 'process space', which is simultaneously produced in the perceived, in the conceived, and in the lived dimensions of social life.

7.4 The State and the Act of Exchange

Space . . . becomes the seat of power.[203]

Lefebvre's materialist understanding of social space incorporating the entirety of social relations takes a further step towards a spatio-historical theory of society: through the production of the material support – transport routes, buildings, infrastructure, and so on – social relations are incorporated into material space and thus preserved. But this once again raises more questions: How is this incorporation of social relations achieved? Who controls the production of the material support? Lefebvre concludes that this requires an actor able to hold together the entirety of elements that enter the process of the production of space. And this actor is the state.

---

198   Ibid., 90.
199   Ibid., 358.
200   Ibid.
201   Ibid., 420.
202   Ibid., 33–4.
203   Lefebvre, *Survival of Capitalism*, 83.

Lefebvre had already approached the question of the state in *The Production of Space*, but it was only in *De l'État* that he explored this question in depth and developed an original theory of the state. In doing so, he fundamentally challenged his previous understanding of the state, abandoned the classical Marxist base–superstructure concept, and moved in the direction of a radical new conception of state theory. He again started with exchange, but this time, he analysed it not only as a social relation (see section 7.3) but also as a concrete act, the act of exchange. What happens in exchange? And what is the state's role? Lefebvre arrives at a momentous answer: the state is the central regulator and at the same time the great equaliser that makes exchange possible, that controls and secures it. This is an extraordinary conception, which also enabled Lefebvre to think of social relations as the foundation of a renewed understanding of the state.

At almost the same time as Lefebvre, the Paris Regulation school proposed a quite similar conception of statehood and social relations: its conception of regulation is based on an identification and analysis of social relations of production; its core thesis is that the contradictions of social relations are temporarily resolved through specific arrangements of regulation. However, the Paris Regulation school does not go beyond an instrumentalist understanding of the state that is still strongly influenced by Althusser.[204] There are also different conceptions and understandings of social relations and regulation in other strands of the broad theoretical current of the regulation approach.

But Lefebvre captures the nature of social relations in a different way from the regulation approach: he once again applies his three-dimensional dialectics, which he had already used to such success in the analysis of the production of space. From this three-dimensional perspective, a social relation can be understood simultaneously in its perceived, conceived, and lived dimensions, thus creating entirely new possibilities for theorisation. To this day, however, Lefebvre's conception has still not been adopted in urban studies and in the social sciences more broadly, and the connections and parallels to the regulation approach have not yet been elucidated in any detail.[205]

Lefebvre's texts on the state, which will be discussed below, have to date had only a limited reception. In France, their importance has not been recognised, and they have not been available in other languages as, for legal reasons, *De l'État* has not yet been translated, or even reprinted. An excellent and detailed reconstruction and analysis of Lefebvre's theory of the state can be found in the

---

204   See for example Aglietta, *A Theory of Capitalist Regulation*; Alain Lipietz, 'From Althusserianism to "Regulation Theory"'.

205   See Schmid, 'Urbane Region und Territorialverhältnis'; Schmid, 'Raum und Regulation'.

book by Hajo Schmidt, that I partly use for the following analysis.[206] Corell Wex has also analysed the spatiality of Lefebvre's conception of the state in his dissertation.[207] Neil Brenner and Stuart Elden have extensively addressed the question of the state in Lefebvre. In the collected volume *State, Space, World* they have compiled a careful selection of Lefebvre's texts and commented on them in detail.[208] Finally, in many of his texts, Neil Brenner has taken up Lefebvre's concepts of state and space, developed them further, and incorporated them into his own approach to the scale question and 'state space', while also highlighting the central role of the state in the production of space.[209]

The Critique of the Base–Superstructure Concept

In his famous foreword to *A Contribution to the Critique of Political Economy*, Marx writes:

> In the social production of their existence, men inevitably enter into definite relations, which are independent of their will, namely relations of production appropriate to a given stage in the development of their material forces of production. The totality of these relations of production constitutes the economic structure of society, the real foundation, on which arises a legal and political superstructure, and to which correspond definite forms of social consciousness. The mode of production of material life conditions the general process of social, political and intellectual life.[210]

According to Hajo Schmidt, these lines, which have been cited over and over again, contain the essence of a new paradigm of a philosophico-scientific historicism and, simultaneously, the germ of its theoretical decay.[211] Even if they were commented on and modified in Marx's later work, they still form the historical-materialist foundation, the starting point and canon of Marxist orthodoxy, according to which the relations of production, that is, material social relations, form the necessary economic structure of a society, which is independent of the will of human beings. Together with the productive forces, the entirety of the relations of production form a firmly established unit – the

---

206   Hajo Schmidt, *Sozialphilosophie des Krieges.*
207   Wex, 'Logistik der Macht'.
208   See Lefebvre, *Space, State, World.*
209   In particular, see Brenner, *New State Spaces*; Brenner, *New Urban Spaces.*
210   Marx, *A Contribution to the Critique of Political Economy*, 263.
211   Hajo Schmidt, *Sozialphilosophie des Krieges*, 173–4.

'economic base'. Above this base rises a political and legal superstructure that encompasses the state, culture, and social consciousness, which in a dogmatic reading appears as a mere reflection, as a superficial appearance of the economic base. Of course, this dogmatic understanding of base and superstructure has been heavily criticised, contested, debated, and modified ever since its appearance, and cannot be discussed further here.

Lefebvre also strongly criticised the economism, productivism, and the dogmatism of orthodox interpretations of Marx from early on and challenged the idea of the dominance of the productive forces over the relations of production as well as a static conception of the mode of production (see sections 3.4, 6.1, and 6.6). But despite this criticism, Lefebvre remained attached to the classical base–superstructure concept for a long time. Precisely because he repeatedly and vehemently attacked the state in both its 'state-capitalist' and 'state-socialist' variants (see the following section), he saw in the state merely an ultimately superfluous superstructure that would be swept away by the proletarian revolution. Engels's famous phrase of the 'withering away of the state' was also a recurring metaphor in Lefebvre's work, expressing the actual goal of the world revolution.

This view is particularly evident in his *Sociology of Marx* of 1966, where Lefebvre presents his first elaborated theory of the state. Here, he regards the state as a fragment of society that adds further superfluous functions to the socially necessary functions.[212] In this way, the state rises above society and, using its bureaucracy and its authority, pursues its own interests. But, Lefebvre asserts, the state could not abstract from the real society which serves as its base, from classes and class struggles, because, although it possesses its own reality, which tends to become independent, it is nevertheless determined by the dominant social relations. Accordingly, the state serves the ruling classes, mediating between their different fractions when their rivalries threaten the existence of society.[213] Schmidt describes this first theory of the state by Lefebvre as rather conventional, not just because of its only weakly moderated instrumentalist view of the state, but also because it limits itself to the critique of the modern (bourgeois) state and the normative specification of the concept of proletarian revolution.[214]

Although Lefebvre paved his own way towards a more open and at the same time more dialectical understanding of history and society with his *Metaphilosophy* and his investigations into everyday life and urban society, his

---

212   Lefebvre, *Sociology of Marx*, 123–86.
213   Ibid., 124.
214   Hajo Schmidt, *Sozialphilosophie des Krieges*, 167.

dualistic view of state and society remained present in his work for a long time and also shows through in *The Production of Space*. Nevertheless, his understanding of the state gradually became more dynamic and concrete as a result of the social upheavals and revolts of the late 1960s and the political debates that followed. In the mid-1970s, Lefebvre presented *De l'État*, his great work on the state, which not only put the question of the political on a new foundation but actually completed his analyses of everyday life, urban society, and the production of space. Here, he finally confirmed that the reduction of aesthetic, social, and mental phenomena to the economic had been a disastrous mistake, one that certain 'Marxists' were still perpetuating.[215]

The starting point of his new theory of the state is an explicit critique of the base–superstructure concept which, he argues, implies a separation of the political and the economic. Lefebvre now sees a fundamental dilemma in this separation: either the political is reduced to the economic, or the political is posited as a specific category. The latter would mean that the political would detach itself from the economic base and create its own base, such as sovereignty or legitimacy, which would thus be elevated to the absolute.[216] The first position would be a relapse into a philosophical materialism, the second a reversion to Hegelian idealism. Lefebvre then also argues that in separating 'base' and 'superstructure', Marx in fact repudiated his own analysis.[217]

Consequently, in his new conception, Lefebvre no longer sets the political against the base, but seeks to explore it through a better understanding of the base itself. He thereby seeks to uncover the proper social foundations of the modern state: social relations.[218] This way out of the double impasse of the base–superstructure conception follows a hint that Marx himself had offered in a passage from *A Contribution to the Critique of Political Economy* that immediately precedes the one quoted above:

> Neither legal relations nor political forms could be comprehended either by themselves or on the basis of a so-called general development of the human mind, but on the contrary they originate in the material conditions of life.[219]

In his new conception of the state, Lefebvre regards statehood as part of social relations, and again he starts with exchange, as he did in the last section. This

---

215   Lefebvre, *State, Space, World*, 235.
216   Lefebvre, *De l'État*, vol. 3, 14.
217   Ibid., 29.
218   Ibid., 16.
219   Marx, *A Contribution to the Critique of Political Economy*, 262.

time, however, it is not a question of the materiality of social relations but the fundamental question of how a social relation is constituted at all.

Exchange as the Cell and Social Bond of Society

As already established in this chapter, social relations are not materialised in things 'in themselves', in their brute materiality, but in exchange, thus in their interchangeability. As we noted, though, exchange for Lefebvre is not something purely mental: in order to be able to exchange, those who exchange come into contact with each other. For Lefebvre, the act of exchange forms in a way the 'cell' of (capitalist) society. For the term 'cell of society' Lefebvre refers to Marx, without further discussion.[220]

In the act of exchange, actors bring a material reality, their bodies, their hands, their tools, and their products. They come into contact with each other. And this contact, this interaction, which also includes information, changes them at the same time. In this way, the act of exchange constitutes an immediate relationship, it binds the actors together to a certain extent. For Lefebvre, exchange therefore forms the social tie (*lien social*) of a society. Here, Lefebvre makes explicit reference to Nietzsche, who, in accordance with Marx, also emphasised the importance of material exchange as the fundamental social bond of developed societies.[221] The concept of 'social bond' was also common in French philosophy and early sociology, and can be traced back to Rousseau's *On the Social Contract*.

Lefebvre's new conception of statehood thus begins with a fundamental act: exchange as an elementary reality, as a cell of society. This incorporates the starting point for his analysis: a social bond that establishes a fundamental social relation. But exchange, in which unequal things are compared and exchanged, implies an abstraction – the exchangeability, that is, the equivalence of unequal things – which is simultaneously conceived and realised in the act of material exchange. The social bond constituted by the act of material exchange thus develops through abstraction: it involves the abstract and links it with the practical act of exchange. In this way abstraction is realised in the social act. The daily concatenation of exchange, buying and selling, ultimately produces and reproduces social relations.[222]

What is particularly important in this theoretical construction is that

---

220 Lefebvre, *De l'État*, vol. 3, 19.
221 Ibid., 19, 35, 55.
222 Ibid., 20, 38, 55–7.

Lefebvre does not only consider the purely material side of exchange, the exchange of objects produced by labour. For a material exchange to even occur, it requires verbal communication, confrontation, comparison, language and discourse, signs and exchange of signs – that is, a mental exchange. And this relationship of exchange also includes an exchange of feelings and passions, which the encounter simultaneously unleashes and chains.[223]

In this simultaneous presence of material, mental, and affective exchange, it is easy to recognise the fundamental dimensions of Lefebvre's theory – the perceived, the conceived, and the lived. Here, then, this triad is applied to the act of exchange, and in doing so Lefebvre demonstrates an application of his three-dimensional dialectics that goes beyond the production of space. Thus, in principle, every social relation can be captured in this three-dimensionality.

The State, the Equalisation of the Unequal, and the Violence of Exchange

Exchange thus forms a dialectical unity of these three fundamental moments or dimensions of social reality, unfolding as follows. The first dimension is the material form of exchange that the produced thing initiates, supports, and transports. This material exchange implies a social relation between the actors of exchange, but in everyday practice this relationship escapes consciousness.[224]

The second – the intellectual or mental – dimension is based on a logic: the logic of equivalence which socially realises the abstract logic of the commodity. It is this logic that enables the practical solution to the fundamental problem of exchange: the equalisation of the unequal (*l'égalisation de l'inégal*).[225] The equalisation of different products and of the various forms of labour objectified in them does not take place without conflict, however: the exchange ultimately remains unequal. Lefebvre ascribes great importance to this conflictual aspect: the two actors face each other as enemies. Each party hopes to obtain the other's product under the best conditions, at the 'best price'. The parties exert pressure on each other, argue – 'haggle' – which borders on quarrelling. The establishment of a relationship of exchange therefore also requires a certain coherence: an agreement between the exchangers which takes the form of

---

223 Ibid., 20, 22.
224 Ibid., 20.
225 Ibid., 23.

money and at the same time also the form of a contract or quasi-contract, which can be written or verbal. This contract declares that the exchangers accept the conditions of the exchange, and that means, first of all, the assumed or real equivalence of the exchanged products. It is only by accepting this equivalence that the products become exchangeable and thus become commodities.[226] Exchange thus also implies a legal quality, which is doubled into a moral aspect, an ethics of exchange: rational conviction, the incessant call for honesty, or even honour, in the course of transactions. Thus, the market is organised by introducing new elements: the order of the market, the settlement of conflicts, the legal status that guarantees contracts.[227] As a conclusion, the 'architecture of society', for Lefebvre, is built on the following three pillars: First, logic or knowledge. Equivalence is a formal relationship that maintains cohesion and coherence in material relations of exchange. Second is morals, which constitutes an ethics of exchange relations. And third, the law: the act of exchange brings with it a tacit or formal contract that determines its conditions and consequences.[228]

Finally, these two moments, the material form of exchange and the intellectual or conceived form (based on logic, morals, and law), are joined by a third moment of coercion and violence inherent in the act of exchange. These are inherent in the acceptance of the conditions, which are necessarily unequal. Equality in inequality is revealed in the employment contract as much as in the marriage contract, both of which imply power and violence.[229] It is thus also a social coercion that is usually explicit and even institutionalised: moral, social, and political control is exercised at the place of exchange. Thus, the place of exchange demands the presence of authority: police and court, political and/or religious authorities that guarantee the conditions of this exchange while also pursuing their own objectives. A hierarchy of guarantors and guardians of this order soon constitutes and perpetuates itself around the marketplace. 'What order? The equivalence of non-equivalents.'[230] The concatenations of exchange and the operation of markets are thus superimposed by hierarchical powers crowned by a political power: the state.[231]

What, then, are social relations? This question has now been clarified to such an extent that it can be answered with some precision: social relations are always the product of the mutual interactions of humans. Marx had written:

---

226   Ibid., 21–3, 54.
227   Ibid., 23.
228   Ibid., 55.
229   Ibid., 21–2, 24, 28–9.
230   Ibid., 21.
231   Ibid., 24.

'What is society, irrespective of its form? The product of the mutual interaction of humans.'[232] In Lefebvre, just as in Marx, social relations are always also material relations, because these are relations which people enter into in their concrete, material life. In capitalist societies, this material life is based on social production and social exchange. The corresponding social relations are therefore necessarily conflictive. They are based on material contradictions, which are stabilised by knowledge, morals, and law and which always include direct or indirect violence. In their totality, social relations constitute the state, the 'great equaliser', as a guarantor of the equivalence of the non-equivalent.

Towards a Spatio-Temporal Theory of the State

Drawing on these analyses, Lefebvre distils his central conception of the state:

> The law of the form and the fundamental power [of the state] is the crushing of the unequal, the different, the content, i.e. the equalisation of the unequal and the equivalence of the non-equivalent.[233]

Following this line of argument, Lefebvre finally arrives at a new definition of the state: the state decides on the various chains of equivalence. It defines them, and defines itself through them. In this way, the state brings these abstractions into a concrete existence, the state that is itself an abstraction endowed with terrible and very concrete powers. Finally, it also produces the broadest chain of equivalence, the worldwide system of the states (see section 4.3).[234]

With his new theory of the state, Lefebvre transcends Marx's conception as well as his own earlier one. He himself concedes that in his own works on Marxism and everyday life, the accounts of the commodity and use value were incomplete, precisely because they did not place an emphasis on the coercion and violence inherent in relations of reciprocity and equivalence.[235] This coercion emanates from the state and takes place in a space. There is thus a close connection between state and space. Indeed, Lefebvre states that the state is connected to space by a complex relationship that changes over time.[236] In this relationship of state and space, two moments can be distinguished: first, a market – that is, a complex ensemble of commercial relations and

---

232   Marx, 'Letter to Pavel Vasilyevich Annenkov', 96. Translation amended.
233   Lefebvre, *De l'État*, vol. 3, 24. Translated by author.
234   Ibid., 58.
235   Ibid., 35.
236   Ibid., 259.

communication networks – and second, the violence of political power.[237] Both moments are, as we have seen, spatially bound: space serves as the material support for these networks, and the force of the state as the 'guarantor of the equivalence of the non-equivalent' extends over a specific space.[238] In Lefebvre's analysis, these moments have been historically linked in the production of the specific space of the nation state. Thus, according to Lefebvre, the nation state cannot be defined either as a personalised substance or as a pure ideological fiction, because its mode of existence is defined by its relationship with a (material) space.[239] The importance of this relationship between state and space for Lefebvre can be seen in the fact that, towards the end of his four-volume opus *De l'État*, he dedicates an entire chapter to it that once again summarises the production of space. This close linkage between state and space is examined in more detail in the following section.

7.5 Space, the State, and the Reproduction of Society

> 'Change life!' 'Change society!' These precepts mean nothing without
> the production of an appropriate space.[240]
> To change life, however, we must first change space.[241]

The question of how social relations are incorporated into social space, raised in the previous two sections, directly implies another question: how are social relations reproduced? 'Generations come and go, men change, but the "structural" relations persist. How and why is this possible? Where is re-production produced?'[242]

It is both theoretically and politically revealing that the question of the reproduction of social relations was not discussed more widely until the early 1970s. This obviously had to do with the political debates of the time: at the end of the 1960s, the 'world revolution' seemed to be on the agenda. In many countries all over the world, in the East and the West, in the North and the South, protests and revolts erupted that fundamentally challenged existing social relations. But the revolution soon vanished and the old relations were restored. Why did capitalism prove to be so robust and durable? Why did it not collapse? How were the existing social relations restored?

---

237 Lefebvre, *Production of Space*, 112.
238 Ibid., 347.
239 Ibid., 112.
240 Ibid., 59.
241 Ibid., 190.
242 Lefebvre, *Survival of Capitalism*, 50.

A long-lost manuscript by Marx, 'Results of the Direct Production Process',[243] played a major role in the debates on the reproduction of social relations, particularly in France, where it was published only in 1970.[244] In this text, which is a kind of summary and conclusion to the first volume of *Capital*, Marx for the first time addressed the question of the reproduction of capital, which he placed in the context of the accumulation of capital.

The debates of the 1970s, however, quickly moved away from this text and sought other answers. Louis Althusser formulated the concept of the 'ideological state apparatuses', which exist alongside the repressive state apparatus (government, administration, military, police, courts, prisons) and ensure the reproduction of social relations (see section 5.4). Among the ideological state apparatuses Althusser counted churches, schools, the family, the judiciary, the parties, interest groups, and the media (press, radio, television, and so on) as well as the cultural ideological state apparatus (literature, art, sport, and so on). His famous essay 'Ideology and Ideological State Apparatuses', originally published in 1971, was part of a larger manuscript that was published posthumously under the title *On the Reproduction of Capitalism*.

Another answer to the question of the reproduction of social relations came from the Regulation school, which was concerned with the regulation of social relations and recognised in these practices the basic mechanisms of the reproduction of the relations of production. In the course of the 1970s and 1980s, the Regulation school developed into a broad stream of analysis that was taken up and further developed not only in France but also in German- and English-speaking countries (see also 1.3 and 8.3).

Other theorists have also addressed the question of reproduction, including Pierre Bourdieu, with his concepts of habitus and social and cultural capital, and Yves Barel, who published a large-scale study examining 'social reproduction'.[245] Feminism raised the question of the reproduction of social relations in a more radical way, and explored why systematic oppression and discrimination against women was so difficult to change.

Lefebvre, too, began to address the question of the reproduction of social relations in the late 1960s, although he rightly emphasised that he had already

---

243   There was some confusion about where this manuscript was originally intended to be placed in *Capital*, vol. 1. In an early outline it appeared as the final chapter 6 of the book. The English translation of this manuscript in *Karl Marx, Frederick Engels: Collected Works* therefore has the title 'Chapter Six: Results of the Direct Production Process'. See also Hecker, foreword to *Capital*, vol. 1.

244   It had, however, already been published in German and Russian in 1933; see Hecker, foreword to *Capital*, vol. 1, 14.

245   Barel, *La reproduction sociale*.

implicitly raised the problem in his critical analysis of everyday life, citing *The Right to the City*, *Le manifeste différentialiste*, and *Au-delà du structuralisme*.[246] Reflections on the concept of the reproduction of social relations can also be found in *Everyday Life in the Modern World* and ultimately became the central theme of the essay collection *The Survival of Capitalism*.[247] This concept subsequently played a prominent role in *The Production of Space* and *De l'État*.

In *The Survival of Capitalism*, Lefebvre raises the question of reproduction in all its vastness. Where are social relations reproduced? The company, the workplace, and labour relations could not, he argues, be the sites for the reproduction of social relations, since the world proletariat (understood in the broadest sense) nevertheless unshakably and relentlessly continues to resist capitalism.[248] Lefebvre also goes through the whole range of proposals put forward by social sciences so far: culture, language, science itself, and so on, only to find that although these areas are all involved in one form or another in the reproduction of social relations, they cannot explain them in isolation: for Lefebvre, in these analyses 'totality was and is badly conceived'.[249] His subsequent reflections on everyday life, the city and the state, in which he recognises essential elements of the reproduction of society, led him finally to the following conclusion:

> It is not only the entire society that becomes the place of reproduction of social relations . . . but also the entire space.[250]

The initial programmatic question – how did capitalism survive? – thus finds an equally programmatic answer: by seizing space, by producing space. The space that is drawn into the exploitation of capital is produced, bought, and sold (see section 7.1) – this space actively reproduces the relations of production.[251]

The thesis that the production of space implies the reproduction of social relations brings the role of the state into focus, a role that for Lefebvre became increasingly important in the course of the development of capitalism. The state does not simply have an active role to play. The state, the great equaliser, as pointed out in the preceding section, in effecting the 'equalisation of the unequal', also becomes involved in guiding and controlling the production of

---

246   Lefebvre, *La survie du capitalisme*, 7, 58.
247   Lefebvre, *Everyday Life in the Modern World*, 35.
248   Lefebvre, *Survival of Capitalism*, 81.
249   Ibid., 78. Translation amended.
250   Ibid., 90–1.
251   Ibid., 20.

space. Lefebvre recognises that in this way a 'state space' is created, which even establishes a 'state mode of production'. Neil Brenner has taken up and developed this idea of state space, and he has also shown how this concept can be fruitfully applied to the analysis of current developments.[252]

The Reproduction of Social Relations

In his reflections on the reproduction of society, Lefebvre draws on Yves Barel's definition:[253] the concept of reproduction denotes a structure which is capable of self-reproduction, thereby reproducing its own preconditions and elements.[254] Therefore, we have to understand the conditions under which the activities that produce objects reproduce themselves, restart, resume their constitutive relationships, or, on the contrary, change through gradual modifications or leaps.[255]

In Marx's analysis, three aspects of reproduction were central: the reproduction of the means of production, the reproduction of the labour force, and, broadly, the reproduction of capital itself as the restoration of the material conditions of the productive process and as the foundation of capital accumulation. Marx discussed this third aspect of reproduction in another long-lost text entitled 'Results of the Direct Production Process'. Here he first sums up once again the main lines of argument of the first volume of *Capital*: the product of capital is the commodity, and capitalist production is the production of surplus value.[256] Only at the very end of the text does Marx come to the crux of the matter: capitalist production not only is the production of surplus value, but also includes the production and reproduction of capital. In this sense, capital is self-valorising value, or value that gives birth to capital.[257] According to this view, capital provides the material for its own reproduction.

Thus, capitalist production implies not only the reproduction of the relations of capital but also their expansion on an ever-growing scale:

In the same proportion as the social productive power of labour develops, along with the capitalist mode of production, the pile of wealth confronting the worker grows, as *wealth ruling over* him, as *capital*, the world of wealth expands vis-à-vis the worker as an alien and dominating

---

252   See Brenner, *New State Spaces*; Brenner, *New Urban Spaces*.
253   Barel, *La reproduction sociale*, 19.
254   Lefebvre, *Survival of Capitalism*, 46.
255   Lefebvre, *Everyday Life in the Modern World*, 18.
256   Marx, 'Chapter Six: Results of the Direct Production Process'.
257   Ibid., 461.

world. At the opposite pole, and in the same proportion, the worker's subjective poverty, neediness and dependency develop.[258]

The capital relation thus expands more and more, includes new production sectors and world regions, and thus incorporates more and more people. Under these conditions, how can a revolution occur at all? In this text, for Marx it is the further development of the capital relation itself, together with the productive forces, the conditions of production and the relations of circulation, which creates the real conditions of a new, antagonistic mode of production, and thus also the material base of a transformed life process and a new social formation.[259]

For Lefebvre, however, these passages reveal a contradiction in Marx's thinking, which could not have been apparent at the time. Marx believed that the limits of capitalism lay within capitalism itself and that a mode of production only disappeared when it had developed all the productive forces inherent in it. The productive forces would thus constantly collide with the narrow limits of the existing capitalist relations of production, and the revolution would finally explode these limits:[260] 'Marx seems to have thought that growth arrives at a sort of threshold which either condemns it to stagnation or which it crosses in a revolutionary manner.'[261] The question of the reproduction of social relations thus did not appear as an additional problem in its own right but rather was understood within this process.[262]

But it turned out that capitalism did not reach these limits in the hundred years after the appearance of *Capital*. The working class did not remain in the 'negative', and no immovable bourgeoisie has confronted it. The bourgeoisie, the proletariat, and the state have all changed. And, as though they have been set in motion, and changed over time, the essential core of the relations of production has nevertheless been reproduced.[263]

For Lefebvre, the reproduction of social relations denotes precisely this ability of capitalism to survive its critical moments and to restore its constitutive elements. The 'actors' of exchange, the circumstances of exchange, the exchanged goods, and also the way in which they are reproduced can all change, together with society, without the initial and fundamental social bond of exchange disappearing.[264]

---

258   Ibid., 463.
259   Ibid., 466.
260   Lefebvre, *Survival of Capitalism*, 20.
261   Ibid., 45.
262   Ibid.
263   Ibid., 20.
264   Lefebvre, *De l'État*, vol. 3, 38; Lefebvre, *Survival of Capitalism*, 72.

Why was capitalism able to survive? Lefebvre examines the debates in the young Soviet Union and traces the significance of the nation and the nation state for the reproduction of social relations, as shown by Trotsky. In Wilhelm Reich he finds the radical counter-thesis that the family is the central place of reproduction of the overall system of relations. Finally, the question of reproduction was suffocated by the Second World War and by Stalinism.[265]

> The central question began to appear on the horizon following the second world war, but with such amazing slowness that it did not actually emerge from the mists until after May 1968. No less than *three* reconstructions of capitalist social relations within half a century were needed before these reconstructions could become the 'object' of reflection, of critical consciousness.[266]

The questions then arise as to why there is any problem to consider in relation to the reproduction of capitalist relations of production that is independent of the problem of the emergence and development of these relations, why Marx himself recognised this problem so late, and why it subsequently remained obscured – or actively repressed – for so long.[267] This, first of all, requires a closer look at the question of the capitalist mode of production.

The Mode of Production

The concept of the reproduction of social relations is closely linked to the concept of the mode of production, which Marx defines as the totality of the productive forces and the relations of production of a historical social formation. Just as the productive forces – that is, technical progress and quantitative growth – cannot in Lefebvre's understanding determine or explain a society, the mode of production cannot be conceived as a fixed ensemble of social relations. The theoretical reconceptualisation of social relations (see section 7.4) and the question of the reproduction of these relations thus forces Lefebvre to reformulate and open up the concept of the mode of production.

For some Marxists, mode of production is the answer to everything. This concept, in so far as it concerns capitalism, has been omnipresent ever

---

265   Lefebvre, *Survival of Capitalism*, 49–50.
266   Ibid., 50.
267   Ibid., 51, 71.

since it was first formulated in epistemology and theory, and it has eliminated or subjugated all others. It is carefully toughened up, in the name
of the perfect science. It is presented as *totality*, pre-existing that which it
encompasses, including the social relations.[268]

Social relations are thus only defined and theoretically understood through
and in the mode of production. From this point of view, one cannot pose the
problem of their reproduction, because it is inherent in the mode of production: 'The discussion would appear to be academic. Which came first, the relations of production or the mode of production?'[269]

If the concept of the mode production is dogmatically fixed, Lefebvre
explains, then history and any kind of process is removed from the equa-
tion. Capitalist society then presents itself as a closed system that, according to the principle of 'all or nothing', can only either maintain its own
conditions or collapse:[270] the successors of Marx, Lenin, and Trotsky
'have resolutely kept proclaiming the end of the process, the final catas-
trophe. But they have not understood it for what it really is.'[271] The history
of the emergence of capitalism, as well as its internal development and
possible transformation, was thus omitted. Lefebvre illustrates this with
the example of the relationship between primitive (or original) accumulation and industrialisation, which can only be depicted as a concrete
history in its development. This history implies a very specific entanglement of continuity and discontinuity, and presents itself in retrospect as
a highly dramatic sequence of shifts, transformations, and transfers of
wealth and power: ' "Subjects", "agents" confront and attack each other,
while knowledge, techniques and wealth (in short, capital and the conditions of bourgeois society) accumulate around them and by means of
them.'[272] Here, Lefebvre asks: Can capitalism even be definitively understood? And, if so, from what historical moment must theoretical thinking
consider the mode of production as constituted in its totality?[273] From his
historical vantage point Marx could only describe the genesis and constitution of competitive capitalism. But was the capitalist mode of production already fully realised at the time Marx analysed it? As Lefebvre
comments, 'To answer no implies that competitive capitalism, with its

---

268   Ibid., 59.
269   Ibid., 59–60.
270   Ibid., 60.
271   Ibid., 11.
272   Ibid., 60.
273   Ibid.

laws and its blind self-regulation, was at that time still not capitalism. To answer yes creates utter confusion.'[274]

The shift of analytical emphasis to the mode of production not only corresponds to the petrification of Marxist thought, but also means that coherence is given priority over contradictions. In contrast, placing the emphasis on the relations of production and their reproduction means bringing contradictions and thus social conflicts into focus, analysing what happens to them and what results from them.[275] Lefebvre returns here to the insight already elaborated in *Metaphilosophy* (see section 2.4): if the reproduction of social relations is the result of a strategy and not of a pre-existing system, and if this strategy aims to constitute this system in the first place, rather than merely securing or confirming it, then it follows that 'the "real" cannot be enclosed'.[276]

Lefebvre thus argues for a radical opening of the concept of the mode of production, as has already become clear in sections 3.3, 6.1, and 6.6. His various attempts to identify other 'modes of production' or 'modes of life' led him, among other things, to the rural, industrial, and urban field, and to absolute, abstract, and differential space-time. To a certain extent, these concepts can be read as experiments with which he wanted to comprehensively illuminate and understand the processes of urbanisation and the commodification of space as discussed above. The concept of the reproduction of social conditions now allows him to go a decisive step further.

The Production of Space as Reproduction of Social Relations

As Lefebvre emphasised, the production of space is in many ways bound up with the production and reproduction of society:[277] it is an important part of the productive forces (section 7.1), and it also affects the relations of production, since space itself, with its flows, networks, and circuits, becomes a commodity (section 7.2); it becomes an ideology and an instrument of political power; and, finally, it also enters into the production of surplus value, the realisation of surplus value (the organisation of everyday life and consumption), and the allocation of surplus value (ground rent). In this way, the production of space becomes, at a certain moment, the dominant process and the essential instrument of a generalised reproduction of social relations.

Section 7.3 showed how, in Lefebvre's understanding, social relations

---

274   Ibid., 61.
275   Ibid., 63.
276   Ibid., 90.
277   See also Lefebvre, *State, Space, World*, 242.

'inscribe themselves on the terrain' and create the conditions for action 'in space'. It has also become clear how the produced texture of space determines action. Social relations materialise and solidify in space and in this way reproduce themselves – or so one could conclude. But Lefebvre does not see things as simply as that. For space is not, in his view, a 'substance', not an object based on an independent logic that can be distinguished by the 'subjects'. Nor can it be considered as simply a consequence or a result of processes or activities. It is not the passive place in which social relations take place, the milieu in which they solidify, or even the sum of the procedures for their continuation. No. Space has an active, operational, instrumental side: knowledge and action. It is, in an active sense, a medium, a mediator: hegemony uses space as a means to assert itself.[278]

Lefebvre's thesis should therefore be seen in the light of this 'active space': in this view, the production of space becomes a means of reproducing social relations. Societies reproduce themselves by producing 'their' spaces.[279]

This concept of 'active' space explains the homogeneous-fractured character of abstract space (see section 6.3): how can these two formally incompatible characteristics – homogeneous and fractured – come together at all and constitute a 'whole'? For Lefebvre, the answer cannot be found in space as such, in space as a thing or as a collection of things, facts, or concatenation of facts, in space as 'milieu' or 'environment'. For such a space would again be a 'neutral' space, situated before or outside a social practice: a mental space and, as such, a space turned into a fetish. 'Only an *act* can hold – and hold together – isolated fragments in a homogeneous totality. Only an action can prevent dispersion, like a fist clenched around sand.'[280] But who controls this action? Who can develop and implement this strategy? This actor is the state. For the state is the agent that for the most part controls the production of space (see section 7.4). This active role of the state in the production of space was already revealed in the discussion of urbanism (see section 6.3).

Here, the role of the state in the production of space becomes central: only the state is able to hold these different spaces together and to impose a rationality – its own rationality – on the chaos of different relations between individuals, groups, and class fractions. And its privileged instrument is the production of space. The economy is thus spatially transformed, as the state controls flows and stocks and ensures their coordination: flows of energy, raw materials, labour power, goods, trade patterns, and so forth, and stocks of capital,

---

278 Lefebvre, *Production of Space*, 11, 411.
279 Ibid., 12.
280 Ibid., 320.

investments, machines, technologies, stable clusters of jobs and enterprises, and so on.[281]

State Space

Thus, a space slowly emerges that is controlled and dominated by the state – Lefebvre calls this a 'state space' (*espace étatique*). The nation states, each bound to certain territories, are the actual administrators of these spaces; they intervene and act as dominant powers through the production of these spaces. The state does not limit itself, therefore, to regulating the social existence of the people by institutional and administrative means. It proceeds in a more indirect, but no less efficient, way, using the privileged instrument of the production of space.[282]

State space is the result of a long historical development in which the nation state becomes increasingly dominant and finally becomes the principal actor in the production of space. In the course of development, the state binds itself to space through a complex and shifting relationship. The production of state space, which is directly bound to the nation state, can be described according to the triadic formula in the three moments or formants of perceived, conceived, and lived space.[283]

First, the state produces a national territory, and thus the material support of its own space, a physical space determined by networks, circuits, and flows, by roads, canals, railways, and commercial and financial circuits. In this material space, the actions of generations of people and of political forces produced durable realities and thus have left their marks . . .[284]

Second, the conception of the state is based on a representation of space – a space of hierarchically ordered institutions, of laws and conventions. The social architecture of this space is the state itself, a concrete abstraction, 'full of symbols, the source of an intense circulation of information and messages, "spiritual" exchanges, representations, ideology, knowledge, bound up with power'.[285]

Third, state space is also a lived space that contains representations of the state and is maintained by 'values' conveyed by the national language. In this social space there is a minimum of consensus: 'Every French person knows

---

281   Lefebvre, *State, Space, World*, 226.
282   Lefebvre, *De l'État*, vol. 3, 303, 415.
283   Lefebvre, *State, Space, World*, 250.
284   Ibid., 224–5.
285   Ibid., 224.

what he is talking about when he is referring to the town hall, the post office, the police station, the prefecture, the *département*, a member of the National Assembly, the grocery store, the bus and the train, train stations and bistros.'[286]

So, as Lefebvre notes, the socialisation of the productive forces, of production and society has taken place in capitalism as foreseen by Marx. In the process, a space has been created that is social in the sense that it is determined by connections, networks, and circuits. But this 'socialisation' and 'nationalisation' of space had an unexpected outcome. For the state has not only used already existing spaces, integrating older spaces and destroying them in the process, but has also increasingly taken over the management of these spaces; it comprehensively controls the land, and the underground with all its resources, as well as airspace, and has thus produced its own space. Every state has a space, and every state is itself a space.[287]

The State Mode of Production

According to Lefebvre, these developments ultimately lead to the emergence of a new mode of production: the state mode of production (*mode de production étatique*).

Lefebvre sees three essential aspects realised in this mode of production:[288]

1. Through its control, the state reinforces the homogeneous (geometric) character of space and thus establishes a decisive counterpart to the 'fractured' space determined by commodification and the dominance of private interests. It is only through the massive intervention of the state that the homogeneous-fractured, abstract space can come into being at all.
2. This space can also be defined as optical and visual. The human body disappears in a space that is reduced to its optical components and corresponds only to a series of images, in which the body no longer has a presence but is merely represented.
3. This is also a phallic space dominated by high-rise buildings and their arrogance.

In this account, two important aspects of Lefebvre's earlier analyses reappear: on the one hand, this is abstract space and its three central characteristics or

---

286 Ibid., 225.
287 Ibid., 225, 241.
288 Ibid., 234.

formants – the geometric, the visual, and the phallic (see section 6.3); on the other hand, the direct relationship between state space and urbanisation – state space is generated by the production of the urban fabric and all sorts of infrastructures, and thus by urbanisation.

According to Lefebvre, the conditions for this new mode of production were laid down after the First World War, with the Bauhaus, the beginnings of urbanism, and spatial planning. However, the state mode of production was subsequently realised in very different ways around the world:

> Announced by the New Deal and fascism, fully realised by Stalin . . . the state mode of production was generalised around the 1960s, in an unequal way, but worldwide.[289]

This concept, which combines Fordism and actually existing socialism, but which at the same time goes far beyond them, brings together East and West, North and South, state socialism and state capitalism, social democratic and bourgeois policies in one mode of production. Lefebvre's detailed analyses include the US, Mexico, France, Chile, Portugal, Yugoslavia, Italy, Spain, England, Algeria, the socialist people's republics, Japan, the Federal Republic of Germany, Senegal, and China.[290] Across these very different examples, he sees clear similarities: the state controls and administers, it protects and secures, it kills.[291] Here, Lefebvre also articulates a clear critique of the social democratic class compromise, which, in his view, contributed to the consolidation of the state mode of production, a critique that also applies to the Western European left, and that of France especially, because they did not challenge this compromise.[292] Lefebvre addresses all these and many other questions in great detail in volumes three and four of De l'État.[293]

Lefebvre's analyses end in the 1970s and therefore do not address neoliberal developments. Lefebvre would undoubtedly find his insights confirmed, however, if he could see all the urban megaprojects across the globe, controlled and subsidised by the state, and the massive extension of infrastructure systems still pushing state space to its limits today, for example in China's Belt and Road Initiative.

---

289   Lefebvre, De l'État, vol. 3, 22. Translation by author.
290   Ibid., 301–3.
291   Ibid., 373.
292   See also Brenner and Elden, introduction to Lefebvre, State, Space, World, 18–20.
293   A very precise presentation and discussion can be found in ibid. See also Brenner, 'Global, Fragmented, Hierarchical'; Brenner, New State Spaces; Brenner, New Urban Spaces.

Planetary Urbanisation: The Production of Space as a Search Process

This state mode of production is not stable, though. It is constantly confronted with new contradictions, because the state cannot control the entire process of the production of space – therein lies the paradox of the state:

> The political power which holds sway over 'men', though it dominates the space occupied by its 'subjects', does not control the causes and reasons that intersect within that space, each of which acts by and for itself.[294]

In this way, a space is created which is determined by more or less independent causes whose effects coexist in space, such as pollution, the near exhaustion of resources, and the destruction of nature.[295] The earth as a planet thus becomes the new horizon of the production of space: urbanisation has created a planetary space, and the colonisation of space is driven to the most extreme strategic consequences, including the occupation of the sea and threats that encompass the totality of planetary space.[296] This development is directly related to the state and to state space, because the planetary spread of urbanisation is only possible through the massive intervention of (nation) states, through their manifold infrastructure projects and their regulatory control, also coordinated internationally.

In his last text, published in May 1989 in the French monthly journal *Le monde diplomatique*, Lefebvre addresses these phenomena. The text bears the poetic title 'Quand la ville se perd dans une metamorphose planétaire' (When the city is lost in a planetary metamorphosis) and sums up once again the essential points of his analyses of urbanisation. Here, he extends his thesis of complete urbanisation to the entire planet by making the case for the 'planetarisation of the urban': 'Soon, only islands of agricultural production and concrete deserts will remain on the Earth's surface.'[297]

The ongoing commodification of space, the urbanisation of the planet, the worldwide extension and intensification of production networks, the depletion of resources, and their planetary effects, from the climate crisis to the biodiversity and the food crises, which Lefebvre had not yet experienced, give these analyses a new urgency today. It is precisely these considerations that became the starting point for the concept of 'planetary urbanisation' which, in

---

294 Lefebvre, *Production of Space*, 413.
295 Ibid.
296 Lefebvre, *De l'État*, vol. 4, 320.
297 Lefebvre, 'Dissolving City, Planetary Metamorphosis', 567.

considering these planet-wide processes, calls for a decentring perspective on urbanisation.[298]

Nevertheless, it is crucial that this transformation of space is understood neither as an accident nor as a conscious and desired goal of political and economic transformations.[299] For Lefebvre, it is much more the case that it is the transformation of space itself which can provide insights into these processes. He writes that space itself puts society to the test – an insight he calls *l'épreuve de l'espace*. This term, which could be translated as 'testing through space' or 'trial by space', describes a kind of determined indeterminacy or a materialist account of fate. For Lefebvre, it replaces the 'classical conception of fate' and the 'judgement of God':[300]

> With its confrontations and clashes, trial by space does not unfold in the same way for all historical formations, for things are affected by each formation's degree of rootedness in nature and by each's natural peculiarities, as well as by the relative strength of its attachments to the historical realm . . . There is no escaping a fate that weighs equally on religion and churches, on philosophy with its great 'systems' – and, of course, on dialectical (and historical) materialism . . . The hypothesis of an ultimate and preordained meaning of historical becoming collapses in the face of an analysis of the strategies deployed across the surface of the planet. At the terminal point as at the origin of this process of becoming is the Earth, along with its resources and the objectives that it holds out. Formerly represented as Mother, the Earth appears today as the centre around which various (differentiated) spaces are arranged. Once stripped of its religious and naïvely sexual attributes, the world as planet – as planetary space – can retrieve its primordial place in practical thought and activity.[301]

The earth as a planet therefore marks the ultimate horizon of the production of space. In Lefebvre's simultaneously subtle and adamant dialectic, however, the result of this development remains undetermined. The production of space is a collective and conflict-laden search process: the horizon remains open.

---

298   See Merrifield, *The Politics of the Encounter*; Brenner and Schmid, 'Towards a New Epistemology of the Urban?'; Schmid, 'Journeys through Planetary Urbanization'.
299   Lefebvre, *De l'État*, vol. 4, 319.
300   Lefebvre, *Production of Space*, 416.
301   Ibid., 417–18.

8

A Spatio-Temporal Theory of Society

The aim of this book was to reconstruct Henri Lefebvre's theory of the production of space. This reconstruction has shown that this theory contains the outline of a general theory of society that consistently conceives society in its spatio-temporal dimensions. The key to understanding Lefebvre's theory is a specific, triadic conception of dialectics, which runs through the entire theory as a basic epistemological orientation. On this basis, Lefebvre builds his theory of social practice in space and time.

The aim of this concluding chapter is to outline the three central categories of Lefebvre's theoretical construction which we have explored separately throughout the book and to present them in their overall context. I call these categories, following Lefebvre, spatio-temporal dimensions, spatio-temporal levels, and spatio-temporal configurations of social reality.

The category of spatio-temporal *dimensions* of social reality relates to the fundamental aspects of every social practice: the perceived, the conceived, the lived. Lefebvre overlays these three phenomenological terms with three corresponding terms derived from linguistic theory: spatial practice, the representation of space, and the spaces of representation. The production of space can thus be understood analytically as the totality of three dialectically linked production processes that imply each other: the production of material conditions, the production of knowledge, and the production of meanings (section 8.1).

The second category, the spatio-temporal *levels* of social reality, relates to the social context of the production of space. It, too, follows a threefold subdivision into a general level or distant order, a private level or near order, and an intermediate and mediating level, the level of the urban. These three levels are not fixed, but change according to processes of social development. Thus, the general level shows a tendency towards *mondialisation* and gradually expands to a planetary scale. The private level is also transformed, and thus everyday-ness emerges as a specific form of social life. Between these two levels lies the urban level, which is transformed by the process of urbanisation that sublates the contradiction between city and country (section 8.2).

The third category, the spatio-temporal *configurations* of social reality, relates to the historicity and temporality of the production of space. These configurations denote relatively stable modes of producing space in time. Lefebvre elaborated this category only in a very general way. It is based on the concept of the mode of production, which he repeatedly subjected to critique and further developed (section 8.3).

It could be said that these three categories taken together constitute the core of Lefebvre's theory of the production of space. In an encompassing sense, then, this theory includes Lefebvre's theorisations of the everyday life, of the state, and of the urban.

Assembling this matrix of three categories, however, does not necessarily follow Lefebvre's intentions, since he explicitly refused to provide any sche-matic and thus necessarily reductionist and 'prosaic' presentation of his concepts. He never brought the 'elements' of this matrix together in this form. Nonetheless, I present this matrix as the result of my theoretical reconstruction in order to critically appropriate and further develop his theory.

8.1 Spatio-Temporal Dimensions

The space-time dimensions form the core of the theory of the production of space, from which the other elements and categories of the theory can be deci-phered. These dimensions – Lefebvre also calls them formants or moments – are doubly determined and therefore also doubly named: on the one hand, there is the triad of spatial practice, representation of space, and spaces of representation; on the other hand, there is perceived, conceived, and lived space. This double series of terms points to a double perspective, a double approach: on the one hand phenomenological, on the other linguistic.

Given these categories, it remains for us to clarify a central question that has repeatedly arisen in the course of this book and which has also caused consid-erable confusion in the reception of Lefebvre's theory: the question of the status and constitution of these three spatio-temporal dimensions and their internal relationships.

A Dialectical Conception of Space and Time

Like most contemporary theories of space, Lefebvre starts from a relational conception of space and time: 'space' stands for simultaneity, the synchronous order of social reality; 'time', on the other hand, for the diachronic order and thus the historical process of the production of society.[1]

This formulation clarifies both the relationship to some other relational space-time conceptions and how Lefebvre's theory differs from them (see section 5.1). Whereas Leibniz's philosophy conceptualised the spatio-temporal order of (physical-material) 'things' and Einstein's physics theorised the relations among space, time, and energy, Lefebvre conceives of space and time as relational categories of society.

In this context, 'society' means neither a spatio-temporal totality of 'bodies' or of 'matter', nor a sum of actions or practices. At the centre of Lefebvre's materialist theory are people in their corporeality and sensuality, with their sensations and imaginations, their thinking and their feelings, human beings who relate to each other through their actions and practices.

A 'human being' is not only an individual, but a fundamentally social being that can only be understood from its embeddedness in society. None of the characteristics of human beings belong to them as individuals alone. Their practice is a social one, their senses and perceptions have developed historically and thus socially, thought and language are social products, and sensations are also socially formed. The knowledge of human beings, of their thinking, acting, and feeling, is thus inseparably bound to the knowledge of society: individual and society are dialectically related to each other and, in Lefebvre's understanding, can only be understood through this dialectic.

Lefebvre builds his theory of the production of social space and social time on these basic assumptions. In this understanding, space and time are not purely material realities, they are not a philosophical apriorism and they cannot be reduced to pure concepts, but are integral aspects of social practice. Lefebvre sees them as social products: they are the result and precondition of the production of society.

To understand this theory, it is first necessary to detach oneself from a common understanding of space, which imagines 'space' as an independent, material given, existing 'in itself' or 'as such'. Lefebvre counters such an understanding with the concept of the 'production of space', which understands 'space' as bound to a historically produced social reality. It follows from this

---

1 For other conceptions of space, see Harvey, *Justice, Nature and the Geography of Difference*; Werlen, *Society, Action and Space*.

that, epistemologically, space can never be assumed to exist 'in itself'. The starting point of the production of space is a space-time configuration that Lefebvre
calls *espace nature*, space of nature. By this, however, he understands a 'state' or
a 'world' that eludes human access: in this world there is not yet any social
practice, and there is no knowledge of this world, which is therefore not yet a
'social world'. From today's perspective, this space of nature can be studied and
reconstructed scientifically, but its 'meaning', its 'sense', remains unknown.

Consequently, space and time are not universally given, but can only be
understood as socially produced within a given society. In this sense, space and
time are not only relational, but also fundamentally historical. This requires an
analysis that attends to social formations, power relations, and contradictions.
True to Lefebvre's regressive–progressive method, the starting point of this
historical analysis is the present.

It is crucial to see that this radical conception of social space and social time
or social space-time breaks with various other conceptions of space and time.
Thus, space and time are not given, they are not a cognitive apriorism as
conceived by Kant. Nor do they have an existence 'in themselves', as is so often
assumed in geography, including critical and postmodern geography. From
this point of view, it also makes no sense to develop an 'ontology' of space,
because there is no 'universal' space-time that can somehow be fixed or
constructed, but only a constantly changing process of the production of society, and thus also of space and time.

The Dialectical Trinity of the Human Being

Lefebvre marks the phenomenological approach to the three dimensions of the
production of space with the concepts of the perceived (*perçu*), the conceived
(*conçu*), and the lived (*vécu*). This trinity is both individual and social: it is
constitutive not only for the self-production of the human being, but also for
the self-production of society. All three terms denote active processes that are
both individual and social.

1. Perceived Space (*espace perçu*): 'space' has a perceptible aspect that can be
   grasped with the senses. This perception cannot be reduced to contem-
   plative, distant observation, but forms an integral part of every social
   practice. It encompasses everything that presents itself to the senses, that
   is, not only seeing, but also hearing, smelling, touching, tasting. This
   sensually perceptible aspect of space relates directly to the materiality of
   the 'elements' that constitute a 'space'.

2. Conceived Space (*espace conçu*): a space cannot be perceived without first having been conceived mentally. The bringing together of the elements to form a 'whole', which is then considered or described as 'space', presupposes a mental act that is connected with the production of knowledge.

3. Lived Space (*espace vécu*): the third dimension of the production of space is living or experiencing space. This dimension describes the world as it is experienced by people in their everyday practice. Lefebvre is categorical on this point: lived, practical experience cannot be exhausted by theoretical analysis. Something more is always left over, a remainder, a residuum. In his view, this 'rest' is also the most valuable part of human existence that can only be expressed by artistic means.

From the phenomenological perspective, the production of space is thus based on a three-dimensionality that can be identified in every social process. Lefebvre demonstrated this with the example of exchange: exchange, as the historical origin of commodity society, is not exhausted in the (physical) exchange of objects. In order for a material exchange to occur at all, it requires verbal communication, confrontation, comparison – that is, language and discourse, signs and the exchange of signs, a mental exchange. The relationship of exchange also contains an affective aspect, an exchange of feelings and passions (see section 7.3).[2]

Thus, the triad of the perceived, the conceived, and the lived underpins a specific version of materialist phenomenology, which can be understood as a further development of theories of the French phenomenologists Maurice Merleau-Ponty and Gaston Bachelard (see section 5.7).[3]

The Dialectical Trinity of Language

Lefebvre superimposes on this first, phenomenological triad of the production of space a second triad, for which he uses the terms 'spatial practice', 'representation of space', and 'spaces of representation'. These terms can be derived from Lefebvre's three-dimensional theory of language, which he developed in *Le langage et la société* (see section 5.6). In this book, Lefebvre distinguishes between a syntagmatic, a paradigmatic, and a symbolic dimension of language. The syntagmatic dimension refers to the formal rules of connection that define

---

2   Lefebvre, *De l'État*, vol. 3, 20, 22.
3   Merleau-Ponty, *Phenomenology of Perception*; Bachelard, *The Poetics of Space*.

the relationships between the signs and their possible combinations. The paradigmatic dimension implies the possibility of substituting one term with another that is equivalent to the first in one aspect, yet different from it in another. The assignment of signs in this way refers to a code, a system of meanings or paradigms. Finally, the symbolic dimension refers to the emotional aspect of a society. Lefebvre understands symbols as social products that cannot be fully captured by scientific analysis.

Lefebvre later applied these linguistic criteria to the three-dimensional analysis of the production of space:

1. Spatial Practice (*pratique spatiale*): this term refers to the concept of praxis that Lefebvre had elaborated in his engagement with the classics of German dialectics, and which denotes the entirety of social activity and social interaction (see section 2.2). The term 'spatial' in this context means a focus on the aspect of the simultaneity of activities. In analogy to the syntagmatic dimension of language, spatial practice denotes the order that results from the linking or concatenation of elements or activities but, unlike language, not in a temporal sequence, but in simultaneity, and thus in space. In concrete terms, this could be networks of interaction and communication as they arise in everyday life (such as the daily linkage of home and workplace) or in the production process (networks of production and exchange). These networks are in turn based on a material support: the networks of streets and roads, the dwellings and production sites, and so on, which together constitute an urban fabric (see section 7.3).

2. The Representation of Space (*représentation de l'espace*): this term refers to the theory of representation that Lefebvre introduces in order to bring together the concepts of knowledge and ideology, which are difficult to distinguish, in a broader concept. The representation of space is thus a representation that depicts and defines a space. Representations of space arise at the level of discourse, of language as such, and thus include verbalised forms such as descriptions, definitions, and, in particular, (scientific) theories of space. Furthermore, Lefebvre also includes maps and plans, information conveyed through images and signs. The specialised disciplines of the production of these representations are architecture, urbanism, and spatial planning, but also the social sciences (and, here especially, geography). These representations have an operational side: they are meant to guide action, and to regulate the production of space.

3. The Spaces of Representation (*espaces de représentation*): Lefebvre formulates the third dimension of the production of space as a terminological

inversion of the 'representations of space'. These are spaces that designate 'something'. Spaces of representation thus refer not to space itself, but to something else: a divine power, the Logos, the state, the masculine or feminine principle, and so on. This dimension of the production of space refers to the process of meaning that is attached to a (material) symbol. The symbols of space can be taken from nature, such as plants or topographical formations, they can be artefacts, buildings, and monuments, they can also arise from a combination of both, such as 'cultural landscapes'. Spaces of representation are constituted by experiences. An important, joyful, or traumatic event can therefore become inscribed in a space. What is important here is that Lefebvre is not referring to individual experiences, but to socially produced spaces of representation. Any investigation must therefore not seek to reveal individual preferences but to identify social constellations, experiences, and imaginaries.

According to this schema, (social) space can be analytically investigated on three dimensions. First, it presents itself on the dimension of (spatial) practice as a concatenation or interconnection of activities or interactions, which in turn are based on a certain material support (morphology, built environment). Second, this spatial practice can be defined and delimited linguistically as 'space' and then forms a representation of space. This representation is at the same time a foundation, an order, or a frame of reference for understanding and interaction, which allows for (spatial) orientation and thus at the same time co-determines action. And third, the physical terrain, thus constituted, can itself become the bearer of meanings. Thus a (spatial) symbolism emerges that contains and evokes social norms, values, and experiences.

The Three Production Processes of Space

The double determination of the three dimensions of the production of space through a superimposition of two sets of three terms indicates parallel approaches to a (triple) production process: the production of material conditions, the production of knowledge, and the production of meaning.

1. Material production leads to the creation of material realities that are accessible to the senses and thus to perception. However, these conditions only develop a 'meaning' in the context of a spatial practice that makes use of them. This spatial practice constitutes a perceptible space, and, conversely, it presupposes the perception of a space. In this sense,

Lefebvre conceives of 'space' comprehensively: it is a space of interaction that includes the activities of the people who produce this space, use it, animate it, and populate it. From this point of view, a street, for example, forms a different 'space' at different times of the day or night.

2. The production of knowledge gives rise to representations of space and thus to a conceived space. Lefebvre assumes an active knowledge that permeates the production process and thus becomes materially effective, generative. Social conceptions determine and define what a 'space' is. These conceptions or constructions of space are formed by social conventions that determine which elements are related to each other and which are excluded or marginalised, conventions that are 'learned', but are not immutable, and are often contested and fought over and negotiated in discursive (political) engagement. This is therefore a social production process that is linked to power relations. In a broad sense, representations of space thus include not only linguistic forms, representations, and images but also social rules and ethics.

3. Finally, there is the third process, that of the production of meaning. This is a poetic process that heralds the 'realm of freedom' and transcends the other two dimensions. The production of meaning imbues spaces with a symbolic order and thus turns them into spaces of representation. These spaces are experienced or lived and not conceived.

This should make it clear that the theory of the production of space does not analyse 'the space' or 'spaces', but active production processes that take place in time. 'Space' is continuously produced and reproduced; it is thus to be understood in an active sense: the object of analysis is not the arrangement of (material) objects and artefacts, but the generation of practical, mental, and symbolic relations between 'objects' and activities.

One can therefore never assume the existence of clearly fixed, 'frozen' spaces. A space changes as soon as one of its dimensions changes. This change does not necessarily have to be a material one. Spaces can be socially redefined or given new meanings or used in a different way, and are then also to be regarded as different spaces.

Ultimately, however, the language remains treacherous: the term 'space' suggests a fixed object, just as in common understanding the three aspects of space (the perceived, the conceived, and the lived space) tend to be seen as having a certain 'autonomous' existence. Consequently, the term 'space' should be replaced by the term 'production of space', and we should speak of dimensions, moments, or formants of the production of space.

The Threefold Dialectic of the Production of Space

One of the central questions of this three-dimensional conception concerns the relationship between the three dimensions of the production of space. As shown by selected readings of leading representatives of Anglo-American geography, this relationship has been interpreted in highly diverse ways (see section 5.7). The reconstruction carried out here has yielded a clear answer in this respect: Lefebvre assumes a contradictory unity of the three moments of the production of space. The alternative terms 'formants' or 'moments' of the production of space indicate that this unity is dialectically conceived. These dimensions are equivalent or simultaneous. From a theoretical point of view, there can be no privileging of any one of the dimensions.

However, this does not mean that the relationship among these dimensions is the same in all societies. The identification of their relationship can only result from a historical analysis and accordingly can only claim validity for specific societies or spatio-temporal configurations.

This means that Lefebvre introduces a three-dimensional dialectical schema in which each dimension contradicts the other two. This results in a triple contradiction and a three-sided determination. Together, these dimensions form a self-contained triangle in which each dimension is both the starting point and the end point of the dialectical movement. Lefebvre thus developed a completely new triadic dialectic. Where the 'classical' forms of dialectics in Hegel or Marx start from two concepts that contradict each other and sublate each other in a third concept, this 'three-dimensional' dialectic sets in motion three elements that become effective at the same time. Lefebvre's three-dimensional dialectic thus forms a triangle spanned by three pairs of contradictions.

The Contradictions of the Production of Space

This dialectic can perhaps be better understood through its contradictions than through its elements. From this perspective, the production of space is put into motion through the triad of three contradictions.

The first contradiction marks the dialectic of sensory perception and mental conception, or, in philosophical terms, of being and consciousness. In other words, it describes the mutual interaction between the material order and the representations of this order: on the one hand, spatial practice forms the (perceptible) starting point of representations of space; on the other hand, these representations serve to influence and change spatial practice (and thus material reality), as in planning processes or architectural design.

A second contradiction is found in the dialectic of representations of space and spaces of representation, or between language and meaning. Language tries to express meanings and sensations, but at the same time it also structures them. The distinction between conceived space and lived space thus proves to be extremely difficult. For, on the one hand, conceived space always contains connotations that lead beyond the narrow horizon of the actually designated and refer to something that is 'lived' and 'experienced'. On the other hand, the space of representation is often permeated by representations of space, by a 'code' that 'prescribes' the attributions and interpretations that are 'valid' in a certain social context. This dynamic relationship opens up an epistemological gap in the precise distinction between these two types of representation.

The third contradiction arises from the relationship between sensory perception and lived experience. It is true that experience may appear completely detached from materiality, as a kind of inner world projected onto an outer world. But Lefebvre is explicitly not concerned with such purely psychological processes. Rather, he emphasises the fact that (everyday) experience is always bound to a physicality and thus also to the material world. The meaning, the symbolism of spaces of representation, cannot be separated from their materiality and thus spatial practice, as it is directly linked to the experiencing of this materiality. Social practice therefore always includes a material aspect and also the social meaning contained (experienced and produced) in this practice.

Analysing the Production of Space

How can this three-dimensional conception of space be used analytically and applied empirically? Because this conception allows us to examine all kinds of spaces, at all scales, from a street corner to a neighbourhood or an extended landscape, up to the planet, it can be used in a wide variety of ways. It offers a general theoretical framework that creates an awareness of the dynamics and relevant aspects of the production of space, which could be helpful in many different kinds of analyses.

The quality of this conception lies precisely in the fact that it goes beyond political-economic analyses and also includes processes of meaning and experience that are usually treated in anthropology, cultural studies, architecture, literature, and art. The concept of lived space is an important key to understanding the collective nature of experience and the (symbolic) meaning of spaces, which with this conception can be directly linked to political-economic aspects of the production of space. In addition, the concept of conceived space, or the representation of space, allows us to examine the incorporation of power into the production of space. It is crucial, however, that these representations are not viewed in isolation from material reality, but are related back to social practice, activities, and actions. For the starting point of these representations is always social practice in everyday life.

There are many ways to apply this three-dimensional conception in empirical research.[4] Many have done this using various qualitative methods from cultural anthropology, sociology, and social geography, or with sophisticated triangulations of different methods, which is very productive but also very time-consuming.[5] ETH Studio Basel developed a combination of methods that operates with the triad 'networks–borders–differences' and also integrates cartographic procedures constitutively in the analysis (see section 6.4).[6] In another research project, we applied this three-dimensional conception to the analysis of urbanisation processes and accordingly examined material production processes, processes of territorial regulation, and processes of socialisation and the production of meaning in their interplay (see below).[7]

Finally, the utopian and revolutionary moment inherent in this three-dimensional conception of the production of space should be mentioned: in a socially appropriated space, the three moments of the production of space come together to form a unity, thus producing a differential space-time that can be experienced in an immediate way. This can happen at certain festivals and events, for example, but also during social revolts and actions, and perhaps explains why these moments are experienced as so intense and liberating.

8.2 Spatio-Temporal Levels

The dialectical three-dimensionality of the production of space can be considered as the fundamental aspect of Lefebvre's theory. However, it is not sufficient to analytically differentiate spaces or space-times. From a general theoretical point of view, the development of society leads to all kinds of spaces: every constellation of actors, every group or institution (from the family to the nation state) generates a social practice and thus produces its 'own' specific space. It is

4   Stanek, *Henri Lefebvre on Space*; Schmid, 'The Trouble with Henri'.

5   Streule, *Ethnographie urbaner Territorien*; Stanek, 'Architectural Project and the Agency of Representation'.

6   Diener et al., *Switzerland*.

7   Schmid et al., 'Towards a New Vocabulary of Urbanisation Processes'; Schmid and Streule, *Patterns and Pathways of Urbanization*; Schmid and Topalović, *Extended Urbanisation*.

obvious that these spaces cannot be clearly demarcated from each other, because they overlap and interpenetrate, a fact that confronts any empirical analysis with an infinite multiplicity of interwoven spaces, a situation that Lefebvre aptly compared to a millefeuille, a French puff pastry (see section 5.3). This raises the question of how analysis of space-time configurations can be further theoretically structured, in order to facilitate their interpretation.

Lefebvre clearly saw this problem, and he therefore introduced the category of 'spatio-temporal levels of social reality', which range from the concrete-sensual to the abstract-general level. He thus analytically subdivided the production of space into three levels according to the degree of abstraction entailed in the underlying social realities: first, a distant order or general level (G); second, a near order or private level (P); and third, a mixed, middle, or mediating level, the level of the urban (M). This category of levels provides an analytical perspective on otherwise highly diverse processes. Lefebvre did not finish developing this category of levels, leaving it as theoretical sketches, digressions, and fragments in various parts of his work. They have to be further developed in order to enable empirical application.

Everyday Life, the Urban, the State

To better understand these levels, it is necessary to recall the relational definition of space that forms the foundation of Lefebvre's conception (see section 5.1): a relational space refers to the synchronous order of things, and thus the order of social reality as simultaneity. The terms chosen by Lefebvre for the levels of social reality, the 'near order' and the 'distant order', suggest that the synchronous order of social reality can be analytically divided into a near, practico-sensual order and a distant, abstract order. These two orders correspond to two of Lefebvre's central fields of research: everyday life and the state. In addition to these two levels, he constructed a third, middle level that lies between the two orders and articulates them with each other: the urban is the connecting, mediating level of social reality. With the category of levels, all four central topics of Lefebvre's later work can be embedded in a general framework: everyday life, the urban, the state, and space.[8]

These levels are not self-contained but interpenetrate each other. They can be identified in any space-time configuration, whether we consider a neighbourhood, a region, or an even larger configuration. The levels thus form an analytical grid that allows us to further differentiate the three dimensions of

---

8   On this, see also Goonewardena, 'The Urban Sensorium'.

social reality. In turn, the three dimensions of social reality can be identified and analysed on each of these three levels.

First, these three levels are produced by specific *spatial practices*: on the private level P, this includes inhabiting, which is related to the processes of social reproduction and consumption. Then there is labour as a concrete activity, which constitutes a very important part of everyday life, although Lefebvre did not address and theorise it further. For level P, then, *everyday activities and practices* are central, and with them time, the modulations and rhythms of everyday life, the times of the day, the seasons. Additionally, we have to analyse the sites and material spaces in which these everyday practices take place, office buildings, factories, workshops, studios, apartment blocks, single-family houses, villas, shanties, and also the objects and instruments used in these activities, such as tools, machinery, furniture, appliances, up to the private automobile.[9]

In contrast, the urban level M is determined by the *connections* of everyday activities. Lefebvre specifically mentioned commuting between home and work. In a more general sense, however, all movements can be considered that link the different places of everyday life with one another, and thus generate urban spaces, from shopping to leisure activities to all other kinds of family, social, cultural, political, and economic activities. Of particular importance are the nodes of these networks, which constitute a wide variety of *centralities*. These centralities connect not only the various activities of urban space, but also activities associated with near and distant orders, and thus level P and level G.

On the general level G, the *global production process* and related practices take place. They generate planetary networks of production, trade, exchange, finance, and communication that constitute the world market and the capitalist world system. These networks require a corresponding material support: buildings, infrastructure (airports, motorways, railway networks, pipelines, and so on) and global means of communication (fibre optic cables, satellite systems, mobile phone connections, and so on).

Second, the three levels are determined by different *representations of space*. These are concepts, images, and ideologies anchored in concrete social relations, which are realised through corresponding territorial regulations and spatial strategies on the terrain, incorporating power relations into space.[10]

Level G is determined by abstract institutions and authorities, the world market and global capitalism, the nation state with its symbols, laws, and

---

9   See Ross, *Fast Cars, Clean Bodies.*
10   See Schmid, 'Specificity and Urbanization'.

regulations, but also language with its rules and forms of expression, ethics, morals, religions, worldviews, political orientations, and so on, as well as universal 'rationalities' and 'logics', class logics, logics of power and control.[11] The regulation of this general level presupposes overarching concepts and planning systems, especially spatial planning and various forms of international and national instruments of coordination, which are able to design and implement large-scale strategies.

At the level M, laws, rules, and strategies regulating 'urban space' come into play. These are based on representations, such as the city plan and the map, which directly or indirectly determine what belongs to the 'city', simply by what they do or do not show, what is present and what is absent. The first representations of cities were not yet abstract maps, but perspectival images, a combination of vision and concept, artwork and science. They constructed and constituted 'the city' as a totality.[12] This representation, this 'image of the city', still shapes the idea of the urban as a bounded unit, even if the urban form has long since dissolved. Due to the fragmentation of urban space, the classical discipline of urban design has been replaced by bureaucratic forms of urban and regional planning – 'urbanism' in Lefebvre's understanding – which are strongly dominated by the nation state and thus level G (see section 6.3).

Finally, in relation to representations of space, level P is primarily determined by private initiatives and projects that may lead to the fragmentation and commodification of space. It is the level of architecture in the narrow sense, or, in the absence of strong state rules and norms, of diverse forms of urban informality and popular urbanisation (see section 7.1).

Third, the three levels constitute *spaces of representation* that are linked to experiences and thus to lived space. The 'superior powers' are represented by diverse monuments, religious sites, government buildings, large-scale urban planning projects, but especially also through wide, empty, open spaces, huge squares and avenues that are suitable for marches and parades. Level P comprises all private buildings, which, with their respective styles and insignia, represent the preferences and affiliations of their inhabitants and users. They are often dominated by standardised and globalised commercial styles. Finally, the urban level M comprises all those places that remain if we leave out all elements of the levels P and G, that is, streets, squares, avenues, public buildings, cultural venues, meeting places, schools, hospitals, and so on. These buildings and the spaces they form are the 'sites' of the urban, which allow

---

11   Lefebvre, *Urban Revolution*, 78.
12   Ibid., 12–13.

people to connect and meet, and which have a great influence on whether and how urbanity can emerge and be lived.

The three levels of social reality are not fixed and static, because they are constantly produced and reproduced. Each can be associated with distinctive historical processes. Historically, on the level P, 'everydayness' emerged through industrialisation and modernisation, enforced by state regulations and an industrial rationality. Level G also changed: in the course of the nineteenth century, an imperialist system of nation states was gradually imposed through revolutions and wars, and a comprehensive capitalist world market came into being. As a result, this distant order expanded to worldwide scale and overlaid and encompassed the national states in a process Lefebvre called *mondialisation*.[13] The intermediate level M was simultaneously transformed by the process of urbanisation: cities began to radiate further into their surroundings, developed into centres of economic, social, and cultural life, and formed catchment areas and spheres of influence, while the urban fabric and urban practices extended across all borders until urban reality began to dominate ever larger parts of the planet.

This dynamic perspective clarifies that the concept of levels of social reality should not be confused with the concept of *scale*: the levels of social reality are always multiscalar and they cannot be related to a single scale. Level G is not confined to the nation state, because it always includes global practices, networks, and regulations. Level M is characterised by the urbanisation process, which is a cross-border process that transcends neighbourhoods, municipalities, and regional and national borders. In the same sense, level P is not simply limited to an individual plot of land or apartment; everyday life today has become a multiscalar reality determined by regional, national, and global networks of migration and exchange.

In order to better understand this interplay of levels, the processes of *mondialisation*, urbanisation, and the production of the everyday will be examined in more detail below.

Mondialisation *and Globalisation*

Level G or the distant order is constituted by institutions and authorities that have emerged historically. While nation states form central frameworks for this distant order, they are, however, not independent entities, because the general level G has been expanding to worldwide scale since the nineteenth

---

13   Lefebvre, *De l'État*, vol. 4, 95.

century and thus shows the tendency towards *mondialisation*. A capitalist world system emerged, with its manifold networks, linkages, and mutual dependencies. States were drawn into this system and at the same time produced it themselves through the joint creation of international agreements, institutions, and bodies.

In the period following the Second World War this worldwide system of national states became formalised and crystallised into a tripartite world order: a market-oriented capitalist first world, a state capitalist second world, and a 'third world' dominated by colonial and postcolonial dependences, unequal exchange relations and terms of trades, and an imposed international division of labour. This rigid capitalist world order fundamentally changed in the 1970s, and, through various upheavals, a contradictory and heterogeneous neoliberal model of development was established. Lefebvre already mentioned two basic principles that determined this new model: *neoliberalism*, which allows private enterprises a maximum of private initiative, and *néo-dirigisme*, characterised by the increased reliance on specialists and technocrats.[14] In the course of the 'long 1980s', additional processes occurred: the gradual unleashing of the international financial system; the ongoing microelectronic revolution with all its effects on the production and labour process, on everyday life and global communication; the formation of a new international division of labour; and, finally, the collapse of the Eastern bloc and the demise of actually existing socialism.

These processes set in motion a dramatic transformation of level G, which was captured in the English-language literature by the term 'globalisation'. As explained in detail in section 4.3, globalisation is not the same as *mondialisation*. While the term *mondialisation* was coined at the beginning of the twentieth century to describe the worldwide expansion of capitalism, 'globalisation', in the narrower sense, means the formation of 'horizontal' global communication and production networks, and with it the establishing of a new world order with a more flexible global spatial division of labour that differs fundamentally from the rigid world order of the post-war period.

Globalisation thus means, first, a (global) *spatial practice* in its manifold gradations and shades, from the intensification of global flows of commodities and the formation of global production networks to the massive increase in global connectivity through the expansion of the means of transportation and communication, leading to the latest round of space-time compression.

At the same time, globalisation has to be analysed as a concept or as a *representation of space*. As Harvey has shown, the term itself emerged only in the

---

14   Lefebvre, *Urban Revolution*, 78.

1980s.[15] The term 'globalisation' is by no means neutral, nor are its effects limited to the discursive level, but it is in fact used to enforce certain interests and activities. Globalisation is structured and advanced by a wide variety of regulations that are negotiated and defined by supranational organisations and institutions. This also includes – and this is often forgotten – a global language, 'world English', which has been established across the world only in the past few decades. Together, all these sets of rules and regulations constitute a constantly shifting, contradictory, conflict-ridden 'world order'.

The process of globalisation also involves the transformation of social meanings and 'values' that are attached to certain symbols, thus producing *spaces of representation* that convey and express a kind of 'global' experience. The most obvious example is the skyline, which visibly symbolises the power and influence of global corporations, and at the same time expresses the emergence of global cities and world cities as command centres of the world economy. The skyscraper as a symbol of economic dominance is not new; as is well known, it already figured on the Chicago skyline by the end of the nineteenth century and subsequently left its mark on several North American metropolises. On a global scale, however, skyscrapers only emerged in the 1980s, and their construction was fiercely contested in some places, notably Paris and London.[16] This trend was accelerated by the emerging global cities in Asia, such as Hong Kong, Singapore, Shanghai, or Dubai, which became the new models of the global age. These spaces not only represent the dominance of global capitalism, but also convey a 'global experience' that can be seen, for example, in the globalised style of airports, hotel chains, and holiday resorts, or in the omnipresence of international brands. These spaces of representation are also linked to an experience that Lefebvre had already mentioned and that has increasingly come to the fore in recent years: widespread precarisation and dispossession and the experience of powerlessness in the face of this distanced and highly abstract world order.

These examples show that globalisation is, first of all, not a fundamentally new process, and secondly does not constitute a new 'level' but rather a shift in scale or a multiplication of scales: the general level G is organised no longer predominantly within the framework of the nation state, as in the post-war order, but through a complex, interdependent interplay of scales, from the planetary to the national and regional down to the local scale. In this sense, globalisation could be seen as the latest phase of *mondialisation*. It would be a very interesting task to examine different processes of *mondialisation* and

---

15 Harvey, *Condition of Postmodernity*.
16 Glauser, *Vertical Europe*.

thereby also identify different historical phases of 'world making', as Stanek and Madden have suggested.[17]

The Production of Everyday Life

On the opposite side of the analytical grid of levels of social reality are the specific, concrete everyday practices that constitute level P. In Lefebvre's understanding, the everydayness which characterises this level in the contemporary period only emerged with industrialisation, modernisation, and the establishment of the world of commodities, in which state intervention and regulation played a decisive role. The state not only regulates the process of consumption through norms and rules, but also intervenes directly in the economic process of production and reproduction, through the creation of infrastructure, through housing construction and the operation of diverse social, cultural, and educational institutions.

Lefebvre situates this everyday life between the poles of 'habitat', a term that refers to the alienation caused by rationalist urban planning and housing construction, and a utopian 'dwelling', which stands for appropriation and self-determination. Habitat thus appears as a functionalised, parcelled, and fragmented spatial practice that is reduced to the mere functions of reproduction and consumption.

Level P has changed massively since Lefebvre wrote. The various forms of dwelling and urban living can no longer be reduced to the alternatives of (state or collective) apartment blocks and (private) detached houses, which Lefebvre – as well as Castells – described and analysed in detail in France in the 1960s and 1970s. Globalisation and urbanisation have changed everyday life in many ways, with the massively increased spatial mobility of people through various global migration processes, through the computerisation and digitalisation of the world of work and the private sphere, with the internet, smart phones, and social media, which make it possible to establish and maintain relationships across large distances. Urbanisation has also led to a multiplication of concrete urban situations and to a great variety of ways of living and dwelling. With the increasing spatial mobility of people, new forms of multi-local living, and of circular and temporary migration, of both affluent and precarious social groups, are also emerging. Thus, a simultaneously globalised and urbanised everyday life is emerging, with manifold social, gender, ethnic, cultural, and economic divisions and disparities. This has led to unprecedented degrees of

---

17   Stanek, *Architecture in Global Socialism*, 30–2; Madden, 'City Becoming World'.

exclusion and dispossession in very different contexts, and it has also instituted new forms of alienation. At the same time, this changed everyday life is – under favourable conditions – also enabling new possibilities of social exchange and new ways of experiencing differences.

Urbanisation and the Production of the Urban

Finally, the urban enters the picture as a middle, mediating, and mixed level of social reality. The urban forms the starting point and the hinge of the entire theory of the production of space. The discussion of the question of how the urban is produced in an urbanised world led Lefebvre to the conclusion that the 'city' is not (any longer) a bounded unit but constitutes a level of social reality that mediates between the level of abstract, general processes and the concrete-sensual level of everyday life. The concept of levels was thus a key point in the transition from Lefebvre's theory of the urban to his theory of the production of space.

Historically, cities in very different societies formed spatio-temporal entities that were clearly defined politically, socially, and economically and were often demarcated from the 'outside', both practically and symbolically, by material structures such as city gates, city walls, and ramparts. Cities could have different roles and meanings, serving as material and symbolic centres, or as seats of political, religious, and cultural power, and their relationship to the countryside varied widely (see sections 3.2 and 3.5). With the industrialisation of society, however, the process of urbanisation began that ultimately led to the disintegration of the historical space of the city, the transformation of the countryside, and the sublation of the contradiction of city and countryside. Just as in the case of *mondialisation*, a shift and multiplication of scales can be observed at the urban level: urbanisation transcends local, regional, and national borders and tends towards a planetary horizon. According to Lefebvre, this process leads, ultimately, to the complete urbanisation of society.

The concept of the urban level makes it possible to identify the urban without having to demarcate it as a territory. This is a decisive advantage when the morphological, social, economic, cultural, political, and institutional borders of the 'city' or the 'urban region' are blurring. The analysis can thus advance by examining traces of urbanisation and forms of the urban throughout a given territory, and by identifying new territorial differentiations resulting from urbanisation processes beyond urban agglomerations.

Lefebvre interpreted the process of urbanisation in the context of the entire society as a collision or fusion of levels G and P, whereby the (former) cities lose their previous (relative) autonomy and independence. On the one hand, industrialisation and the world market follow a universal economic rationality determined by technology, which is implemented and driven by various state actors and international agencies. This results in a tendency of homogenisation: the particularities of place and location are diminishing, and the distinction between urban and rural areas is disappearing.[18] On the other hand, space is commodified, parcelled out, and subjected to the logic of individual economic actors. The result is an abstract, homogeneous-fractured space in which the specific qualities of the urban are destroyed (see sections 6.3 and 7.2).

In Lefebvre's analysis, however, this process of dissolution simultaneously recreates the urban in a dialectical movement: urbanisation generalises the potentiality of the urban and leads to its reassertion. Lefebvre understands urbanisation as a dialectical process that on the one hand has destructive effects, but on the other also generates new potentials and possibilities. In this sense, the urban revolution appears as a concrete utopia that moves via many different paths towards an urban society.

On the dimension of *spatial practice*, urbanisation transforms the dense and socially mixed historical urban centres in a process of implosion and explosion. On the one hand, this leads to an enormous concentration of people, activities, and capital in urban centres, whereby certain economically and politically privileged centres develop into centres of decision-making and control. On the other hand, the expansion of urban areas scatters centrality, and various new centralities emerge in the former peripheries. This extends the *dialectic of centre and periphery* to the entire planet (see sections 4.5 and 7.1).

At the level of the *representation of space*, the image of the city disintegrates, and the regulation of the urbanisation process becomes fragmented, which reduces the capacity of the urban level to mediate between the near and the distant orders. The double domination by the world market and the state threatens the possibilities of a self-determined appropriation of urban space. The general contradiction between exchange value and use value is finally transformed in space into the *dialectic of domination and appropriation* (see sections 4.5 and 7.2).

As a *space of representation*, the experienced urban space is overwhelmed by the homogenising forces of the state and of commodification. The role of the urban as a place where differences are created and become productive is threatened. This leads to the *dialectic of homogenisation and differentiation* (see section 6.4).

---

18   Lefebvre, *Urban Revolution*, 79.

With these three concepts of centrality, mediation, and difference, Lefebvre offers three approaches to a renewed understanding of the urban. However, he does not bring these three aspects together as formants of the production of space, but treats them as three different analytical elements: as urban form (centrality), as urban level (mediation), and as urban space-time (difference). He thus develops three different perspectives on the urban, which are closely related: difference as the generating force of the urban can only unfold when different people and activities come together – in other words, through central-ity. But centrality requires social interaction and thus mediation so that it is accessible to all parts of the society; centrality as place of meeting and encoun-ter can also contribute to mediation. And, finally, differences also presuppose mediation, so that they can flourish and enter into productive exchange.

Centrality

Urbanisation can be understood as a specific *spatial practice* that is located above the practical-sensual and below the abstract realms. This is the practice of *movement* in space, which connects the diverse activities of everyday life with each other. Through these movements, permanent or fleeting networks of action and interaction emerge, which generate more or less complex urban spaces. These networks are not evenly distributed across space. Meshes form and nodes emerge where different lines of interaction converge. These nodes also connect different kinds of networks, as well as near and distant places. Thus, centralities emerge, as places of meeting, encounter, and exchange, of communication and information, places which can generate surprises and support innovation.

Therefore, centrality in Lefebvre's understanding does not describe a concrete geographical situation, but a pure form. Its logic stands for the synchronicity of people, things, and events that can be brought together at a single point. From a theoretical point of view, the (social) content of centrality remains undetermined. Accordingly, different centralities can emerge, as can sectoral and specialised centralities; they might be multiscalar, with different ranges that link diverse activities. This makes it clear that centralities also artic-ulate the three levels G, M, and P with each other. Global networks could be directly linked with local networks, thus interacting with one another.

With globalisation and planetary urbanisation, a seemingly paradoxical situation arose that can be explained by the double process of implosion–explosion. On the one hand, privileged global centres of decision-making and power developed, while, on the other, centrality was dispersed: the expansion of the urban fabric and the development of infrastructure and means of transportation and communication led to an intensification and dense layering of networks. Opportunities were created for new centralities to develop in hitherto peripheral locations. Edge cities and business parks, megaprojects and new towns, entertainment centres and leisure parks were constructed in the urban peripheries. Additionally, outside the dense agglomerations, new centralities also emerged at important transport hubs and intersections, at places of raw material production or at tourist sites, and new global production locations were installed, such as 'special economic zones' and 'enterprise zones'. The resulting hierarchical and polycentric system of centralities can take very complex spatial forms.

Centres, however, never stand alone. Every centre inevitably generates peripheries (both near and distant). Processes of *centralisation* are therefore always associated with processes of *peripheralisation*. The development and strengthening of centrality involves processes of displacement and thus the exclusion of various social groups from centrality, who are driven to urban peripheries in the process. At the same time, peripheralisation also occurs in other areas whose economic, social, and cultural energies and activities are diminishing, leading to a loss or relocation of activities and selective emigration. Peripheralisation can affect established industrial regions, sparsely populated and/or agricultural areas, remote and poorly connected areas, and many more. Centre and periphery no longer form coherent territories, but archipelagos that are interdependent in various ways. On a planetary scale, uneven urbanisation generates very different kinds of centralities and peripheries.

Because centrality generates privileged and potentially productive places, it is always contested. Lefebvre vividly described the struggles for centrality of the Paris Commune of 1871 and of May 1968. Many more urban struggles across the world have erupted about access to centrality and exclusion from centrality in recent decades. They fight for the creation, maintenance, and defence of popular centralities that represent an urban value created by the people themselves. The transformation, commodification, and sometimes even complete destruction of such centralities not only affect the residents and (small) businesses of these places but directly or indirectly concern the entire population of an urban region. Lefebvre's call for a right to centrality expresses these different moments: it is about the right of access to the material and immaterial resources of centrality, to the possibilities and opportunities of the centre – the right to a renewed urbanity.

Mediation

Urbanisation has a second important consequence. Urban areas disintegrate into countless disjointed fragments, creating sprawling and dispersed urban landscapes that can extend across different political-territorial entities: communes, regions, provinces, even nations. Urbanisation thus transcends scale, and urban areas are criss-crossed by multiple borders and boundaries, leading to fragmentation and a loss of political coherence and social cohesion.

This has a direct impact on the *representation* of urban space. Since the city is no longer a distinct morphological, social, economic, or political unit, there are many ways to define and delimit a specific urban space. This is also the main reason why so many different definitions of the city or the urban coexist today. Depending on the chosen perspective and approach, different urban units have been defined, whether in scientific research, planning, media, or politics: agglomeration, urban region, metropolitan region, conurbation, megaregion, and so on. Each of these terms defines a certain space and constitutes a certain representation of space. These terms are always associated with a certain intention, a (political) interest in a specific definition of the urban (as a political unit, as an economic catchment area or labour market, as a planning unit, as a socio-cultural entity, and so on), and imply corresponding strategies of inclusion and exclusion. Accordingly, these representations of space must also be read politically: they are meant to promote and guide action, and they are used to design spatial strategies that can advance the reorganisation and re-scaling of territorial regulations. For Lefebvre, representations of space are always linked to power and involve the incorporation of power structures into the production of space.

The urban level is thus determined by different interests and power constellations, but it interferes also with the other two levels G and P, and thus with state definitions and regulations (such as definitions of 'urban' and 'rural' areas, which are subjected by different territorial regulations) and private interests and initiatives. The urban level is thus the level where different strategies interact and collide, and it becomes a privileged arena and nexus for struggle but also constitutes the very stakes of that struggle.[19] The appropriation of space, the development of the urban, and the metamorphosis of everyday life come into direct conflict with the state and diverse private interests.[20] Thus the contradiction of exchange and use value in space becomes the contradiction of *domination and appropriation* (see section 7.2).

---

19   Ibid., 91; Lefebvre, *Production of Space*, 386.
20   Lefebvre, *Production of Space*, 387.

The specific role of the urban level is to facilitate a mediation of the different interests and bring together and moderate the countless disjointed urban fragments. To reach this goal, Lefebvre proposed an 'urban strategy', a strategy of territorial self-organisation and urban autogestion. Such a strategy presupposes political mobilisations and also new forms of political and social organisation. Various urban movements, such as Right to the City alliances, have created links between different social groups in urban regions and thus formed a new, mediating unity of the urban. In the same vein, activisms and resistances against large-scale infrastructure projects and resource extraction sites have opened pathways to increased communication and interaction between groups and organisations in different places, and thereby also created a mediation between the three levels: the private, the urban, and the general.

Difference

With urbanisation, the implosion–explosion of urban areas, and the parallel processes of centralisation and peripheralisation, the experience of urban space is shattered. Urban space, with its floating centralities and overlapping regulations, this simultaneously fractured and homogeneous space, in which many people are constantly on the move, no longer constitutes a unity but is splintered into fragments and broken shards. What can 'the urban' mean under these conditions, what 'urban experience' can it convey?

The (experienced) meaning of the 'city' – as well as of the 'country' – is never homogeneous, but always characterised by ambiguities, ruptures, and superimpositions, and the 'city' (and the 'country') thus becomes the object of manifold utopias and dystopias. The urban experience can provoke resolute rejection, in which case the city appears or is portrayed as a place of chaos, vice, and crime. In contrast, Lefebvre empathically evoked desire, heterotopy, meetings, encounters, interactions, the longing for the Other, the unexpected, the new. He condensed these aspects into the concept of difference.

Lefebvre understands differences as active elements that can only present and re-present themselves in their mutual relations. The specific quality of urban space thus arises from the simultaneous presence of very different worlds and values, of ethnic, cultural, and social groups, activities, and knowledge. Urban space creates the possibility of bringing all these different elements together and making them socially productive. It is therefore crucial how these differences are experienced and lived in concrete everyday life: Lefebvre's concrete utopia is a space-time in which differences recognise each other, acknowledge each other, and thus become socially productive.

However, these differences are constantly threatened by state control and commodification and thus by a tendency towards homogenisation. In his analysis, Lefebvre conceptualised this opposition in the contradiction between abstract space and differential space. Abstract space is tied to the industrial field, and it is the space that results from the collision and fusion of the general level G and the private Level P. It is therefore a homogeneous-fractured space (see above). This space rests on a rationality that represents space as isotropic, as an empty container that can be filled with people, objects, industries, buildings, flows, and networks. Such ideas and representations motivate spatial strategies of homogenisation that destroy differences.[21] Whereas abstract space tends to homogenise, differential space accentuates differences and brings together hitherto separate elements and moments of social practice. Thus emerges what Lefebvre calls a heroic struggle between *homogenisation* and *differentiation*.

This struggle is constantly fomented by urbanisation. On the one hand, the commodification of the urban reduces differences; but on the other, urbanisation processes and urban transformations can in turn also generate new connections and new urban potentials. This differentiating process is two-sided: on the one hand, urbanisation creates the possibility of bringing together diverse people in one place and thus has the potential to support the development of differences; on the other hand, it also connects different places and enables the exchange of different people and experiences. What is crucial, therefore, is what people make of these situations and moments – whether they develop the urban potential inherent in urbanisation and realise the concrete utopia of differential space by creating places where differences can be realised and lived.

The struggle for difference includes resistance against the commodification and privatisation of urban space and at the same time the creation of possible urban worlds. These can be initiatives that create meeting places, cultural spaces, places of exchange and encounter, that are open to diverse people. They also involve initiatives to reclaim public spaces, streets, and squares, to fight for open spaces, for places to experiment, for the preservation and strengthening of neighbourhoods with their social networks and their diverse economic and social resources. Mobilisations, demonstrations, and occupations play an important role here, generating new experiences of solidarity, inclusion, and lived difference. It is precisely these moments, in which difference is actively experienced, that can fundamentally change the lives of those involved.

---

21   Lefebvre, *Urban Revolution*, 48.

Articulating the Levels

With this summary, it has become clear that Lefebvre's theory of the production of space can be used to analyse very different phenomena and processes, on the level of everyday life, on the level of the urban, and on the level of general processes and regulations. On each level, certain 'realities' come into view that cannot be depicted on the other levels. Everyday life opens the view to social reproduction, family life, gender division, sexual life, daily routines and rhythms, and also to everyday dramas, experiences of poverty, exclusion, discrimination, and racism. The general level directs attention to 'the whole', to the planet, the capitalist world system, unequal development on a large scale, global power relations, states, and the global system of states. In between is the urban level with its contradictions: centralisation and peripheralisation, domination and appropriation, differentiation and homogenisation.

It is important to understand that these three levels do not represent 'spaces'. It would be misleading to imagine level P as a house, level G as a nation state, and level M as a 'city' or 'urban region'. These levels of social reality are not territorially bounded, they are constitutive of any space, and they do not exist independently of each other. Rather, they are articulated and intertwined in many ways. They are units within a larger whole, and they express a complexity which is differentiated yet structured within a totality.[22]

The great quality of Lefebvre's concept of levels lies precisely in the fact that it allows us to analyse the urban without being forced to delimit it spatially. We thus can proceed with an urban analysis without boundaries. The urban level is potentially boundless, but nevertheless structured. There are breaks and transitions, centralities, differences, mediations. This conception makes it possible not only to bring together the most diverse aspects but also to connect various struggles and actions with each other, opening up to a planetary horizon.

Many mobilisations and struggles facilitate and push this interconnection of levels. Even if they are engaged with questions and problematics directed at the general level, such as Black Lives Matter or Extinction Rebellion, they also work practically at the urban level, through the creation of formal or informal regional and local organisational structures, through forging connections or establishing centres, and through generating shared experiences of difference. They also inevitably have an impact on everyday life, which they transform and transcend in often unexpected ways. In this sense, urban struggles cannot be reduced to one aspect, level, or dimension. With

---

22   Lefebvre, *Critique of Everyday Life*, vol. 2, 119.

his multiple demands and calls – the right to the city, the right to centrality, the right to difference, the right to space – Lefebvre attempted to grasp analytically the various facets of the urban and to formulate concrete (urban) utopias to inform collective action.

8.3 Spatio-Temporal Configurations

The third category of Lefebvre's analysis, space-time configurations of social reality, brings together the two categories discussed so far – the dimensions and the levels of social reality – in a concrete space-time. Space-time configurations can be understood as specific units that we want to investigate empirically, and which we therefore necessarily have to delimit analytically. These space-time configurations can be understood as open totalities that have emerged historically and are constantly evolving.

Lefebvre made his own historical analyses of space-time configurations from a large-scale perspective. One could say he studied the space-time of Europe, from Greek antiquity to the end of Fordism. As elaborated in chapters 3 and 6, Lefebvre tells two different 'histories' of this overarching space-time configuration: one is about the development of the 'city and the urban', the other concerns the 'history of space'. Both stories are based on a double periodisation: on the one hand, Lefebvre uses a category he calls 'fields' or 'continents'; on the other hand, he explicitly refers to a periodisation according to the 'classical' Marxist scheme of modes of production.

Two basic problems run through Lefebvre's histories. First, like most proponents of Western Marxism of his time, his lens is focused on the world of the West, and he includes colonialism only to a limited extent. Second, typical of all twentieth-century Marxism, the question of the philosophy of history and thus of the finality of history arises, a question that Lefebvre repeatedly discusses, and which always leads him implicitly or explicitly to the figure of world revolution.[23]

Considering Lefebvre's main concepts, the category of space-time configurations of social reality is the one that needs to be revised and extended most radically. Further development should, first, develop a procedure that makes it possible to identify and empirically analyse concrete spatio-temporal configurations; and, second, find (collective) ways to expand Lefebvre's theory in order to address today's postcolonial questions.

---

23   See particularly Lefebvre, *La fin de l'histoire*.

Modes of the Production of Space

The most general 'unit' of space-time configurations is what Lefebvre calls 'fields', 'continents', or simply 'spaces'. He vaguely connects them with the concept of the mode of production, although this concept obscures rather than illuminates the particularity of Lefebvre's units, since he understands them in a more comprehensive sense as ways of thinking, acting, and living.

In his history of 'the city' told in *The Urban Revolution*, Lefebvre approaches these general space-time configurations as spatio-temporal fields or continents. On the one hand, the term 'continent' has an epistemological connotation, and might be related in one way or another to Althusser's conception of 'continent of knowledge', even if Lefebvre does not mention him in this context (see section 3.4). On the other hand, these terms also suggest that this configuration has not only a temporal-historical but also a spatial-geographical extension. The term 'field' evokes references to practices, as expressed in the term 'field of practice'. Lefebvre distinguishes three such fields: the rural, the industrial, and the urban fields. The rural field is determined by need, and it is the field in which the urban–rural contradiction takes shape. The industrial field is dominated by labour, and it produces urbanisation, which transforms the contradiction of city and countryside into that of centre and periphery. Finally, as a virtuality, as a possibility, the urban continent emerges, and with it the time and space of pleasure and enjoyment.

In *The Production of Space* Lefebvre constructs a similar history of three spaces that can be related to these fields or continents: absolute, abstract, and differential space. This triad describes an overarching historical process of social abstraction: absolute space is first and foremost a religious-political space that is experienced rather than conceived and is charged with meanings that are not addressed to the intellect but to the body, meanings that are experienced through sanctions and emotions. In the progression of Western history, Lefebvre identifies a social process of abstraction in which the absolute character of space, the 'original' unity of the experienced and the conceived, is increasingly pushed into the background or 'underground'. This process of abstraction culminates in the abstract space of the twentieth century, a homogeneous-fractured space that is on the one hand homogenised by a universal rationality, and on the other parcelled out and traded as a commodity (see section 6.3). Finally, the concrete utopia of differential space announces the space of urban society, a space determined by differences that recognise and acknowledge each other and, in this way, become socially productive.

These two histories of the city and of space can be read in parallel, and, in a sense, they illuminate two sides of the same coin: one is a history of the Western city that traces the dialectical movement of the urban–rural contradiction and thereby brings to light three different ways of life or forms of social practice. The second analyses the history of the space-time of the West and is primarily concerned with the historically determined relationship between representations of space and spaces of representation. It is essentially a history of the rise of the commodity and the abstraction of the social, which is inseparably linked to the production of a specific space, namely abstract space. Both histories eventually open up onto a possibility, a concrete utopia: urban society, differential space-time (see section 6.6). These histories are thus reconstructions that, true to Lefebvre's regressive–progressive method, start from the present and descend genealogically into the past in order to then ascend again to grasp the genesis of a historical process. In Lefebvre's understanding, such a reconstruction reveals what is possible in the future, a future that is inherent in the present.

Lefebvre does not propose a clear historical succession of these fields or spaces: they can overlap in both time and space. Thus, absolute space does not disappear completely through the rise of abstract space. It is displaced into the underground and the unconscious, into a space of the dissident, the hidden, and the forbidden. Analogously, the rural, the industrial, and the urban can exist simultaneously.

In a precise sense, then, these fields, continents, and spaces are to be understood as modes of the production of space. Seen from the point of view of the philosophy of history, they can also be understood as pre-capitalism, capitalism, and post-capitalism. In the general form in which Lefebvre presents them, they can be highly inspiring, but are not necessarily suitable for framing further concrete empirical research. They reveal the possibilities of social development but – at the same time – the limits of a project that seeks to understand world history in all its vastness and dreams of the world revolution. Such large-scale projects necessarily have their gaps and blind spots. In Lefebvre's case, despite his broadly conceived and internationally oriented investigation, which in *De l'État* includes a lot of additional historical material, he only touches on a topic that has become increasingly important in recent years: the history of colonialism. How can a history of urbanisation be understood without shedding light on colonisation? And how can a 'history of space' proceed without a polyphonic 'history of spaces' that are, in fact, so divergent and different across the world? Thus, any theoretical construction of historical space-time configurations must necessarily consider the investigation and representation of the diverse and unequal urban worlds that exist today, their asynchronicities and inequalities.

The Production of Space-Time Configurations

Lefebvre himself clearly saw the analytical problems that his conceptualisation of space-time configurations created. In his texts on the city and on space, he already juxtaposed his two large, superordinate narratives (the history of the Western city and the history of the space-time of the West) with a more conventional periodisation following the historical sequence of the classical modes of production. In doing so, he tried more or less successfully to assign space-time configurations associated with the level M (political city, commercial city, industrial city) and the level G (analogue space, cosmological space, symbolic space, perspectival space, homogeneous-fractured space) to certain historical modes of production. Not unsurprisingly, however, these classifications led to considerable inconsistencies, since the histories of cities and territories do not simply coincide with these overarching political, social, and economic constellations, but have their own dynamics. These periodisations are therefore more illustrations of a possible analytical procedure than stringent historical analyses (see section 6.6).

In fact, the mode of production, one of the central concepts of classical Marxism, proved to be one of the biggest obstacles to the development of the theory of the production of space. Over the years, Lefebvre repeatedly circled around this obstacle until he dissolved the rigid conceptualisation of base and superstructure and conceived the concept of modes of production as an ensemble of social relations. Consequently, he moved the question of the development and reproduction of social relations into the foreground and particularly highlighted their contradictions and lines of conflict (see sections 7.4 and 7.5).

Closely related to these efforts was his development of the concept of 'state space', which makes it possible to think of the category of space-time configuration in a more concrete, but also more open, way. He conceived of the 'state' not only as a nation-state but as a multiscale entity, reaching from the planetary scale down to the neighbourhood scale and including all 'floors' of the state structure. He thus conceptualised scale as a vertical, hierarchically stratified 'envelope' of the state. With this conception he achieved a decisive opening of state theory: even if for him the national scale still represented the most important institutional unit of the state, it was far from being the only scale of state interventions and strategies. This led him to his central insight that statehood effectively permeates space, an insight he expressed with the term 'state space' (see section 7.5). It was precisely this conception that Neil Brenner masterfully further developed in his own theory and applied empirically in his further work.[24]

---

24   Brenner, *New State Spaces*; Brenner, *New Urban Spaces*.

Lefebvre's conception also establishes a link to the regulation approach. Greig Charnock has rightly pointed out that the neo-Marxist structuralist background of the regulation approach, partly based on Althusser, does not appear compatible with Lefebvre's undogmatic and open thinking.[25] However, the regulation approach is not a monolithic edifice. Some of Althusser's 'rebellious' sons and daughters have taken a different path, especially Alain Lipietz and Danièle Leborgne with their more open understanding of regulation oriented towards a dialectical relationship between structure and agency, which lends itself well to analyses of space-time configurations.[26] As explained in section 7.4, the concept of 'social relations of production' forms the hinge that makes it possible to combine Lefebvre's theory with certain variants of the regulation approach.[27] While the regulation approach delivers a detailed conception of the social relations of production and gives insights into the variations of regulation, Lefebvre's theory allows him to think of scale and levels together and to link them with the production of material space, the production of knowledge (and thus of representations and regulations), and the production of meaning.

Based on such considerations, Jean-Noël DuPasquier, Daniel Marco, and I developed the regulation approach further to make it applicable to an analysis of urban and regional developments. We extended the concept of social relations to include the concept of 'territorial relation' (*rapport territorial*).[28] A territorial relation describes the ensemble of social actors, power geometries, and contradictions that determine the ownership and use of land. It governs and generates the rules and procedures that regulate land use and the production of the built environment and thus also determine what will be localised in which part of the territory. However, the rules, according to which the territory is organised and the process of urbanisation is steered, are never unequivocal: they are constantly challenged and contested, and are in a contradictory balance between explicit and implicit, customary and modern, legal and illegal, formal and informal procedures. Based on these considerations, we subsequently developed at ETH Studio Basel the broader concept of 'territorial regulation'.[29]

---

25   Charnock, 'Challenging New State Spatialities'.

26   Alain Lipietz and Jenson, 'Rebel Sons: The Regulation School'; Alain Lipietz, 'Accumulation, Crises, and Ways Out'; Alain Lipietz, 'From Althusserianism to "Regulation Theory" '; Leborgne and Alain Lipietz, 'New Technologies, New Modes of Regulation'.

27   See also Schmid, 'Raum und Regulation'.

28   DuPasquier and Marco, *Régulations fordiste et post-fordiste en Suisse*; Schmid, 'Urbane Region und Territorialverhältnis'; Schmid, 'Raum und Regulation'; Schmid, 'Specificity and Urbanization'.

29   See Diener et al., *The Inevitable Specificity of Cities*; Schmid, 'Specificity and Urbanization'; Karaman et al., 'Plot by Plot'.

The analysis of the territorial relation can be used for a periodisation of urban development by distinguishing a succession of different 'paradigms of urbanisation'. With this term we designate a period in which territorial relations are relatively stable in time, and thus leads to more or less consistent forms of territorial regulations and patterns of urbanisation.[30]

Analysing Space-Time Configurations

By further developing this approach, it becomes possible to analyse territorial development in time and space. In the project 'Patterns and Pathways of Urbanisation', we developed a procedure for identifying and analysing specific space-time configurations by applying a horizontal and a vertical analysis, as already described by Lefebvre in his studies on rural sociology (see section 3.1).[31] The 'horizontal' or synchronic analysis seeks to grasp the present situation of a concrete urban territory. This synchronic analysis aims at developing a comprehensive understanding of the expansion and interweaving of urban processes, and identifying the resulting pattern of urban configurations. This intellectual operation freezes the urban process to discern its manifold characteristics and thus examines the structure of an urban territory as it is at a given moment. A second, 'vertical' or diachronic analysis follows the pathways of urbanisation and reconstructs the decisive lines of development of this urban territory. This analysis reveals the path dependency of the territory as well as the important ruptures and changes and leads to a periodisation of the urbanisation process by identifying a succession of paradigms of urbanisation. By combining these two analytical operations, any given urban territory can be understood as the materialisation of an ensemble of specific urbanisation processes that are articulated with each other.

This conception allows researchers to analyse more openly defined space-time configurations, adaptable to concrete research questions and case study areas. In such an understanding, space-time configurations are by principle open in time and space. The goal is not trying to define the 'limits' of an urban space, but analysing the succession and overlapping of various urbanisation processes thus enabling the researcher to develop a better understanding of these processes, and to uncover the underlying problematics and potentials.

---

30   Schmid, 'Global City Zurich'; Schmid and Streule, *Patterns and Pathways of Urbanization*.

31   Schmid, 'Patterns and Pathways of Global Urbanization'; Schmid et al., 'Towards a New Vocabulary of Urbanisation Processes'; Schmid and Streule, *Patterns and Pathways of Urbanization*.

Taken together, these efforts add up to an open theoretical and empirical approach that offers a dynamic, multidimensional, and multi-level analysis of emerging territories of urbanisation.

Globalising Lefebvre

Finally, we have to cope with the second basic problem of Lefebvre's category of space-time configurations, the limiting and sometimes misleading effects of his Eurocentric historiography, and thus have to globalise Lefebvre.[32] He writes his histories of space from the perspective of the spatio-temporal development of France, with its specific developmental features and political and social idiosyncrasies, even though in his later work, especially in De l'État, he also addresses global developments, analysing a wide variety of states. In particular, he also takes up questions of colonisation and neocolonialism.

From today's perspective, it is obvious that the history of the city and of space cannot be encapsulated in the history of Paris and the Pyrenees. Lefebvre's Eurocentric focus is part of a long tradition of research and concept building in urban studies that strongly privileged Western urbanisms, and often treated all other examples of urbanisation and urban design as 'deviations'.[33] There were of course always urban scholars working all over the world and also approaches that took seriously variations in urbanisation, but they mostly did not attract much attention from the Western academic industry.[34] This situation was fundamentally changed by late-twentieth-century interest in dependency and world systems theories, and, since the beginning of the twenty-first century, the rise of postcolonial urban studies. Scholars from different regional contexts have proposed concepts and strategies for global urban studies, and argued for the need to analyse the very different trajectories of urban spaces that do not conform to the hitherto dominant Western models of development.[35] Postcolonialism is undoubtedly the most important approach to urban studies (and more broadly to the analysis of spatio-temporal developments) of the past two decades: it has already produced an enormous amount of new knowledge, addressed new problematics, and fundamentally changed the understanding of urban development. It has also led to the development of new tools and methods of analysis. These include, in particular, new comparative approaches that

---

32   See Kipfer et al., 'Globalizing Lefebvre?'.

33   See Roy, 'Who's Afraid of Postcolonial Theory?'

34   See Robinson, Ordinary Cities; Robinson, 'Global and World Cities'.

35   See, among many others, Robinson, Ordinary Cities; Roy and Ong, Worlding Cities; Simone, For the City Yet to Come.

enable further possibilities for analysing and better understanding the diverse and complex contemporary urban world.[36] Postcolonial approaches, moreover, play an important role not only in the analysis of urbanisation in former colonies, but also in Western metropolises by showing how Europe itself was shaped by colonialism and imperialism.[37]

This has significant implications for any further development of Lefebvre's categories. Wing-Shing Tang notes that Lefebvre's account has clear limitations, especially with regard to the history of colonisation, and calls for a geographical and historical widening of his analysis.[38] Goonewardena and Kipfer come to a similar conclusion:

> Our concern with Lefebvre's histories of city and space is not that they are rooted in European experiences or that the concepts they yielded are impossible to disentangle from these experiences (they can be). The problem is that they make it all but impossible to understand how worldwide relations (including the links between colonial and imperial cities) have overdetermined or mediated urbanization and the formation of abstract space in the modern world (including Europe).[39]

As Kipfer notes, Lefebvre's work is fundamentally open to a conception of historical transformation as multi-temporal, where continuity and discontinuity may relate to each other in tension. He argues that Lefebvre is committed to a multipolar world of knowledge creation, and that he provides us with important resources for spatio-temporal analyses outside Europe.[40]

Lefebvre's concepts are already being applied to many developments and questions outside the West, and increasingly also contribute to postcolonial analyses. To activate these resources, however, we have to go beyond Lefebvre, as his work gives us few clues about variations in urbanisation and the different histories of space in different parts of the world. This creates the need for a double decentring that combines postcolonial and planetary perspectives. Ultimately, this no longer results in a history of space, but in polyphonic histories of spaces – a possible collective project that brings together theory and practice.

---

36   Robinson, *Comparative Urbanism*.
37   For Lefebvrian analyses, see Kipfer, 'The Fractures of Worldwide Urbanization'; Kipfer, 'Pushing the Limits of Urban Research', Kipfer and Goonewardena, 'Henri Lefebvre and "Colonization"'.
38   Tang, 'Where Lefebvre Meets the East', 87.
39   Kipfer and Goonewardena, 'Urban Marxism and the Post-colonial Question', 105.
40   Kipfer, 'The Fractures of Worldwide Urbanization', 289.

8.4 Staying in Motion

One final question remains to be answered: What is to be done with this theory of the production of space? What are its possible futures? As explained in the introduction to this book, there are fundamentally different ways of approaching the work of Henri Lefebvre. First, it can be used as a rich theoretical source for a wide variety of concepts, ideas, and inspirations, often treated as only loosely related. This has been done extensively, with more or less commitment to Lefebvre's theory, and with uncertain results. The problem with this approach, as has become clear again and again in the course of this reconstruction, is that it results in an incomplete, often misleading understanding of the key terms and concepts. This may well lead to creative misunderstandings and interesting new conceptions, but the theoretical consequences and value of such interpretations remain unclear. This is less about insisting on precise theoretical exegeses and the 'clarity' of the theory and much more about the limited results of such uses of this theory. As Lefebvre himself stated, his theory is not to be understood simply as a picture frame that can be fitted onto a study. As we could experience in our own research projects, this theory can have important effects by generating theoretical connections and hypotheses that guide research; by directing attention to 'blind fields' or unrecognised and unexplored developments and processes; by helping to recognise and cross invisible analytical borders; and by providing inspiration for further thinking.

A second possible approach to Lefebvre's theory would be to attempt to grasp and apply it in its entirety. However, Lefebvre himself was constantly developing it further; his work was always in motion, in a dialectic, transductive interplay between theory and practice. So, this work must never come to a stop, otherwise it would contradict Lefebvre's own premise that totality cannot be exhausted. And, above all, it would negate the great potential for transformation that Lefebvre's theory had identified.

A third possibility, then, is to take this work as setting a direction for enquiry. This would be a form of appropriation that would creatively use the openness of the theoretical constructions, in the sense of the maieutic approach of stimulating critical thinking through the cooperative argumentative dialogue that Lefebvre himself held in such high esteem. It is this approach that I have chosen to adopt in appropriating his work and that consequently determines not only the analysis and perspective I have taken throughout this book, but also my assessment here of the outlook for further development of Lefebvre's theory.

At the end of this reconstruction of the theory of the production of space, with an expanded and deepened understanding of this theory to hand, we arrive once more at a beginning – of a further analysis. From my point of view, and in the spirit of Lefebvre's own practice, there are two ways in which this might be taken forward. First, the theoretical resources uncovered here are best made fruitful through empirical applications. As has become clear, all areas of society can be examined from the perspective of this theory, since it is – in both its design and its ambition – a general theory of society.

Second, this theory offers enormous freedom, because it does not present preconceived concepts. Lefebvre's radical critique of representations has an incredibly liberating and generative effect. To think of society in space and time, and to seek to analyse the production of space and time, means first of all to critically question the existing representations of space and time – and thus our concepts and terms, our images and maps, our definitions. It is to make ourselves aware that these are not 'truths' but tools, and also interventions in political confrontations. We have to push aside entrenched preconceptions, prescriptions, and ideologies that condition our thinking in order to remain alert to the developments unfolding before our eyes. Following Lefebvre, we cannot recognise spaces and times without having first conceived them, and we cannot conceive them without having experienced them.

In conclusion, further development of Lefebvre's theory is a necessary element of the theory itself. This should be undertaken in an undogmatic way and in dialectical interaction with both practice and empirical research. Lefebvre develops his categories and concepts on a formal level, explains them with examples, makes them shimmer as if in a kaleidoscope, and thereby gives them metaphilosophical depth. This poetic indeterminacy gives rise to problems in any concrete application, but it involves also a productive theoretical openness.

In my own work on and with this theory, mostly in collective projects, we have always looked for new ways of creatively responding to the stimuli and challenges of Lefebvre's theory. We have realised that it is important to take seriously Lefebvre's transductive procedure and his dialectical method: it advises us to include our everyday experiences in developing theory, and thus to keep our thinking constantly in motion.

At the very end of the magisterial and perplexing oeuvre which is *The Production of Space*, Lefebvre insisted that he was not constructing a new theoretical system but rather proposing a direction, nothing more and nothing less: the senses perceive something, a direction is theoretically conceived, a lived movement paves a way to the horizon.

Acknowledgements

I would like to express my deepest thanks to Jennifer Robinson for her friendship, her encouragement, her inspiration, and also for her great support in the revision, translation, and editing of this book. I am very grateful to my colleagues and friends Neil Brenner, Kanishka Goonewardena, Lindsay Howe, Stefan Kipfer, and Łukasz Stanek for their valuable comments and suggestions. Special thanks to Benno Werlen, who, in 1991, encouraged me to start a PhD on Lefebvre's theory under his supervision. I would also like to thank Zachary Murphy King for his long-standing and productive collaboration in the translation of this book. I am likewise grateful to Sebastian Budgen, Jeanne Tao, and Verso Books for their support and patience with this project.

This book is the result of an intellectual project that spans four decades. I would like to thank all those colleagues, friends, and collaborators who accompanied me on my journey through urban theory, research, and practice for their inspiration, support, and friendship.

Bibliography

Works by Henri Lefebvre

Lefebvre, Henri. 'Au-delà du savoir'. In *Le Jeu de Kostas Axelos*, edited by Henri Lefebvre and Pierre Fougeyrollas, 12–13. Montpellier: fata morgana, 1973.

Lefebvre, Henri. *Au-delà du structuralisme*. Paris: Anthropos, 1971.

Lefebvre, Henri. *Critique of Everyday Life*. Vol. 1, translated by John Moore. London: Verso, 1991. First published: *Critique de la vie quotidienne*. Vol. 1, *Introduction*. Paris: Grasset, 1947.

Lefebvre, Henri. *Critique of Everyday Life*. Vol. 2, translated by John Moore. London: Verso, 2002. First published: *Critique de la vie quotidienne*. Vol. 2, *Fondements d'une sociologie de la quotidienneté*. Paris: L'Arche, 1962.

Lefebvre, Henri. *Critique of Everyday Life*. Vol. 3, translated by Gregory Elliott. London: Verso, 2006. First published: *Critique de la vie quotidienne*. Vol. 3, *De la modernité au modernisme (pour une métaphilosophie du quotidien)*. Paris: L'Arche, 1981.

Lefebvre, Henri. *De l'État*. Vol. 1, *L'État dans le monde modern*. Paris: Union Générale d'Éditions, 1976.

Lefebvre, Henri. *De l'État*. Vol. 2, *Théorie marxiste de l'état de Hegel à Mao*. Paris: Union Générale d'Éditions, 1976.

Lefebvre, Henri. *De l'État*. Vol. 3, *Le mode de production étatique*. Paris: Union Générale d'Éditions, 1977.

Lefebvre, Henri. *De l'État*. Vol. 4, *Les contradictions de l'état modern*. Paris: Union Générale d'Éditions, 1978.

Lefebvre, Henri. *Dialectical Materialism*. Minneapolis: University of Minnesota Press, 2009. First published: *Le matérialisme dialectique*. Paris: Alcan, 1939.

Lefebvre, Henri. 'Dissolving City, Planetary Metamorphosis'. In *Implosions/ Explosions: Towards a Study of Planetary Urbanization*, edited by Neil Brenner, 566–70. Berlin: Jovis, 2014.

Lefebvre, Henri. *Du rural à l'urbain*. Paris: Anthropos, 1970.

Lefebvre, Henri. *Everyday Life in the Modern World*. Translated by Sacha Rabinovitch. New York: Harper & Row Publishers, 1971. First published: *La vie quotidienne dans le monde modern*. Paris: Gallimard, 1968.

Lefebvre, Henri. *L'existentialisme*. Paris: Éditions du Sagittaire, 1946.

Lefebvre, Henri. *The Explosion: Marxism and the French Upheaval*. Translated by A. Ehrenfeld. New York: Monthly Review Press, 1969. First published: *L'irruption – de Nanterre au sommet*. Paris: Anthropos, 1968.

Lefebvre, Henri. *La fin de l'histoire: Épilégomènes*. Paris: Les Éditions de Minuit, 1970.

Lefebvre, Henri. *Hegel, Marx, Nietzsche: or, The Realm of Shadows*. Translated by David Fernbach. London: Verso, 2020. First published: *Hegel, Marx, Nietzsche ou le royaume des ombres*. Paris: Casterman, 1975.

Lefebvre, Henri. 'Henri Lefebvre par lui-même'. In *Les philosophes français d'aujourd'hui par eux-mêmes: Autobiographie de la philosophie française contemporaine*, edited by Gérard Deledalles and Denis Huisman, 282–301. Paris: Centre de Documentation Universitaire, 1963.

Lefebvre, Henri. 'Idéologie et vérité'. *Les Cahiers du Centre d'Études Socialistes* 20 (1962): 7–16.

Lefebvre, Henri. *Introduction to Modernity*. Translated by John Moore. London: Verso, 1995. First published: *Introduction à la modernité: Préludes*. Paris: Éditions de Minuit, 1962.

Lefebvre, Henri. *Key Writings*, edited by Stuart Elden, Elizabeth Lebas, and Eleonore Kofman. London: Bloomsbury Revelations, 2003.

Lefebvre, Henri. *Le langage et la société*. Paris: Gallimard, 1966.

Lefebvre, Henri. *Logique formelle, logique dialectique*. 2nd ed. Paris: Anthropos, 1969. First published: Paris: Éditions sociales, 1947.

Lefebvre, Henri. *Le manifeste différentialiste*. Paris: Gallimard, 1970.

Lefebvre, Henri. *Le marxisme*. Paris: Presses Universitaires de France, 1948.

Lefebvre, Henri. *Marxist Thought and the City*. Translated by Robert Bononno. Minneapolis: University of Minnesota Press, 2016. First published: *La pensée marxiste et la ville*. Paris: Casterman, 1972.

Lefebvre, Henri. *Metaphilosophy*. Translated by David Fernbach. London: Verso, 2016. First published: *Métaphilosophie: Prolégomènes*. Paris: Éditions de Minuit, 1965.

Lefebvre, Henri. 'Les nouveaux ensembles urbains. Un cas concret: Laq-Mourenx et les problèmes urbains de la nouvelle classe ouvrière'. In *Du rural à l'urbain*,

109–28. Paris: Anthropos, 1970. First published: In *La Revue française de sociologie*, no. 1–2 (1960): 186–201.

Lefebvre, Henri. *Une pensée devenue monde . . . Faut-il abandonner Marx?*. Paris: Arthème Fayard, 1980.

Lefebvre, Henri. 'La pensée et l'esprit'. *L'Esprit* 1 (1926).

Lefebvre, Henri. 'Perspectives on Rural Sociology'. In *Henri Lefebvre: Key Writings*, edited by Stuart Elden, Elizabeth Lebas, and Eleonore Kofman, 111–20. London: Continuum, 2003. First published: 'Perspectives de la sociologie rurale'. *Cahiers Internationaux de Sociologie* 14 (1953): 22–40.

Lefebvre, Henri. 'Preface to the New Edition'. In *Henri Lefebvre: Key Writings*, edited by Stuart Elden, Elizabeth Lebas, and Eleonore Kofman, 206–13. London: Continuum, 2003. First published in *La production de l'espace*, 3rd ed. Paris: Anthropos, 1986.

Lefebvre, Henri. *La présence et l'absence: Contribution à la théorie des representations*. Paris: Casterman, 1980.

Lefebvre, Henri. *Problèmes actuels du marxisme*. 3rd ed. Paris: Presses Universitaires de France, 1963. First published: 1958.

Lefebvre, Henri. *La proclamation de la Commune, 26 Mars 1871*. Paris: Gallimard, 1965.

Lefebvre, Henri. *The Production of Space*. Translated by Donald Nicholson-Smith. Oxford: Blackwell, 1991. First published: *La production de l'espace*. Paris: Anthropos, 1974.

Lefebvre, Henri. *Qu'est-ce que penser?*. Paris: Publisud, 1985.

Lefebvre, Henri. *Le retour de la dialectique: 12 mots clefs pour le monde moderne*. Paris: Messidor/Éditions sociales, 1986.

Lefebvre, Henri. *Rhythmanalysis: Space, Time and Everyday Life*. Translated by Stuart Elden and Gerald Moore. New York: Continuum, 2004. First published: *Éléments de Rythmanalyse*. Paris: Syllepse, 1992.

Lefebvre, Henri. *The Right to the City*. In *Writings on Cities*, edited by Eleonore Kofman and Elizabeth Lebas, 63–182. Oxford: Blackwell, 1996. First published: *Le droit à la ville*. Paris: Anthropos, 1968.

Lefebvre, Henri. *The Sociology of Marx*. Translated by Norbert Guterman. New York: Columbia University Press, 1982. First published: *Sociologie de Marx*. Paris: Presses Universitaires de France, 1966.

Lefebvre, Henri. *La somme et le reste*. Paris: La Nef de Paris, 1959.

Lefebvre, Henri. *State, Space, World: Selected Essays*. Edited by Neil Brenner and Stuart Elden. Minneapolis: University of Minnesota Press, 2009.

Lefebvre, Henri. *The Survival of Capitalism: Reproduction of the Relations of Production*. Translated by Frank Bryant. New York: St. Martin's Press, 1976. First published: *La survie du capitalisme: La reproduction des rapports de production*. Paris: Anthropos, 1973.

Lefebvre, Henri. *Le temps des méprises*. Paris: Stock, 1975.

Lefebvre, Henri. 'Theoretical Problems of *Autogestion*'. In Henri Lefebvre, *State, Space, World: Selected Essays*, edited by Neil Brenner and Stuart Elden, 138–52. Minneapolis: Minnesota University Press, 2009. First published: 'Problèmes théorique de l'autogestion'. *Autogestion* 1 (1966): 59–70.

Lefebvre, Henri. *Toward an Architecture of Enjoyment*. Edited by Łukasz Stanek. Translated by Robert Bononno. Minneapolis: University of Minnesota Press, 2014.

Lefebvre, Henri. *The Urban Revolution*. Translated by Robert Bononno. Minneapolis: University of Minnesota Press, 2003. First published: *La révolution urbaine*. Paris: Gallimard, 1970.

Lefebvre, Henri. *La Vallée de Campan: Étude de sociologie rurale*. Paris: Presses Universitaires de France, 1963.

Lefebvre, Henri. 'Vers un romantisme révolutionnaire'. *La Nouvelle Revue Française* 58 (1957): 644–72.

Lefebvre, Henri. *Writings on Cities*. Edited by Eleonore Kofman and Elizabeth Lebas. Oxford: Blackwell, 1996.

Lefebvre, Henri, and Groupe de Navarrenx. *Du contrat de citoyenneté*. Paris: Syllepse, 1990.

Lefebvre, Henri, and Norbert Guterman. *La conscience mystifiée*. Paris: Gallimard, 1936.

Other Works Cited

Aglietta, Michel. *A Theory of Capitalist Regulation: The US Experience*. Translated by David Fernbach. London: Verso, 2000 [1976].

Ajzenberg, Armand, Hugues Lethierry, and Léonore Bazinek. *Maintenant Henri Lefebvre*. Paris: L'Harmattan, 2011.

Allen, John. *Lost Geographies of Power*. Oxford: Blackwell, 2003.

Allen, John, and Michael Pryke. 'The Production of Service Space'. *Environment and Planning D: Society and Space* 12, no. 4 (1994): 453–75.

Alonso, William. *Location and Land Use: Toward a General Theory of Land Rent*. Cambridge, MA: Harvard University Press, 1964.

Altenhoff, Wolfgang. Foreword to *Sprache und Gesellschaft*, by Henri Lefebvre, 9–15. Düsseldorf: Schwann, 1973.

Althusser, Louis. *For Marx*. Translated by Ben Brewster. London: Allen Lane, 1969 [1965].

Althusser, Louis. 'Ideology and Ideological State Apparatuses (Notes towards an Investigation'. In *Lenin and Philosophy and Other Essays*, translated by Ben Brewster, 85–126. New York: Monthly Review Press, 1971 [1970].

Althusser, Louis. 'Lenin and Philosophy'. In *Lenin and Philosophy and Other Essays*, translated by Ben Brewster, 11–41. New York: Monthly Review Press, 1971 [1968].

Althusser, Louis. *On the Reproduction of Capitalism: Ideology and Ideological State Apparatuses*. Translated by G. M. Goshgarian. Verso: London, 2014 [1995].

Amin, Ash, and Nigel Thrift. 'Neo-Marshallian Nodes in Global Networks'. *International Journal of Urban and Regional Research* 16, no. 4 (1992): 571–87.

Anderson, Perry. *Considerations of Western Marxism*. London: Verso, 1976.

Andresen, Knut, and Bart van der Steen, eds. *A European Youth Revolt: European Perspectives on Youth Protest and Social Movements in the 1980s*. Basingstoke: Palgrave Macmillan, 2016.

Arboleda, Martín. 'In the Nature of the Non-city: Expanded Infrastructural Networks and the Political Ecology of Planetary Urbanisation'. *Antipode* 48, no. 2 (2016): 233–51.

Arboleda, Martín. *Planetary Mine: Territories of Extraction under Late Capitalism*. London: Verso, 2020.

Arboleda, Martín. 'Spaces of Extraction, Metropolitan Explosions: Planetary Urbanization and the Commodity Boom in Latin America'. *International Journal of Urban and Regional Research* 40, no. 1 (2016): 96–112.

Attoh, Kafui A. 'What *Kind* of Right Is the Right to the City?'. *Progress in Human Geography* 35, no. 5 (2011): 669–85.

Axelos, Kostas. *Vers la pensée planétaire: Le devenir-pensée du monde et le devenir-monde de la pensée*. Paris: Éditions de Minuit, 1964.

Bachelard, Gaston. *The Poetics of Space*. Translated by Maria Jolas. London: Penguin, 1964 [1958].

Bairoch, Paul. *Cities and Economic Development: From the Dawn of History to the Present*. Translated by Christopher Braider. Chicago: University of Chicago Press, 1988 [1985].

Barel, Yves. *La reproduction sociale: Systèmes vivantes, invariance et changement*. Paris: Anthropos, 1973.

Barthes, Roland. 'Semiology and Urbanism'. In *The Semiotic Challenge*, translated by Richard Howard, 413–18. New York: Hill & Wang, 1988 [1967].

Bartolovich, Crystal. 'Introduction: Marxism, Modernity and Postcolonial Studies'. In *Marxism, Modernity and Postcolonial Studies*, edited by Crystal Bartolovich and Neil Lazarus, 1–19. Cambridge: Cambridge University Press, 2002.

Bathla, Nitin. 'Delhi without Borders'. In *Extended Urbanization: Territories, Processes, Struggles*, edited by Christian Schmid and Milica Topalović. Basel: Birkhäuser, 2023 (forthcoming).

Bauer, Jenny. *Differentielles Denken, heterogene Räume und Konzepte von Alltäglichkeit*. Bielefeld: transcript Verlag, 2015.

Bauer, Jenny. *Geschlechterdiskurse um 1900: Literarische Identitätsentwürfe im Kontext deutsch-skandinavischer Raumproduktion.* Bielefeld: transcript Verlag, 2016.

Benjamin, Walter. 'Paris, the Capital of the Nineteenth Century'. In *Selected Writings 1935–1938*, edited by Howard Eiland and Michael W. Jennings, translated by Edmund Jephcott and Howard Eiland, 32–49. Cambridge, MA: Harvard University Press, 2002 [1935].

Benko, George, and Ulf Strohmayer, eds. *Space and Social Theory: Interpreting Modernity and Postmodernity.* Oxford: Blackwell, 1997.

Berke, Deborah, and Steven Harris, eds. *Architecture of the Everyday.* New York: Princeton Architectural Press, 1997.

Bernhard, Maxie, Benedikt Korf, Tim Fässler, Meret Oehen, Nicola Siegrist, Livia Zeller, and Gary Seitz. *Geografe nüme schlafe! Kritische Lehre in der Geographie, früher und heute.* Zurich: Geographisches Institut der Universität Zürich, 2020.

Berry, Brian, and John D. Kasarda. *Contemporary Urban Ecology.* London: Macmillan, 1977.

Bertuzzo, Elisa. *Archipelagos: From Urbanisation to Translocalisation.* Berlin: Kadmos, 2019.

Bertuzzo, Elisa. *Fragmented Dhaka: Analysing Everyday Life with Henri Lefebvre's Theory of Production of Space.* Stuttgart: Franz Steiner Verlag, 2009.

Best, Ulrich. 'The Debate about Berlin Tempelhof Airport, or: A Lefebvrean Critique of Recent Debates about Affect in Geography'. In *Urban Revolution Now: Henri Lefebvre in Social Research and Architecture,* edited by Łukasz Stanek, Christian Schmid, and Ákos Moravánszky, 283–99. Farnham: Ashgate, 2014.

Bitter, Sabine, and Helmut Weber. *Autogestion, or Henri Lefebvre in New Belgrade.* Berlin: Fillip Editions and Sternberg Press, 2009.

Blagojević, Ljiljana. 'Novi Beograd: Reinventing Utopia'. In *Urban Revolution Now: Henri Lefebvre in Social Research and Architecture,* edited by Łukasz Stanek, Christian Schmid, and Ákos Moravánszky, 301–18. Farnham: Ashgate, 2014.

Blagojević, Ljiljana. 'The Problematic of a "New Urban": The Right to New Belgrade'. In *Autogestion, or Henri Lefebvre in New Belgrade,* edited by Sabine Bitter and Helmut Weber, 119–34. Berlin: Fillip Editions and Sternberg Press, 2009.

Bloch, Ernst. *The Principle of Hope.* 3 vols. Translated by Neville Plaice, Stephen Plaice, and Paul Knight. Cambridge, MA: MIT Press, 1986 [1938–1947].

Blokland, Talja, Christine Hentschel, Andrej Holm, Henrik Lebuhn, and Talia Margalit. 'Urban Citizenship and Right to the City: The Fragmentation of Claims'. *International Journal of Urban and Regional Research* 39, no. 4 (2015): 655–65.

Blondel, Maurice. *L'action. Essai d'une critique de la vie et d'une science de la pratique*. Paris: Presses Universitaires de France, 1950.

Blum, Virginia, and Heidi Nast. 'Where's the Difference? The Heterosexualization of Alterity in Henri Lefebvre and Jacques Lacan'. *Environment and Planning D: Society and Space* 14, no. 5 (1996): 559–80.

Borden, Iain. *Skateboarding, Space and the City*. Oxford: Berg Publishers, 2001.

Borden, Iain, Joe Kerr, Alicia Pivaro, and Jane Rendell. *The Unknown City: Contesting Architecture and Social Space*. Cambridge, MA: MIT Press, 2002.

Bourdieu, Pierre. *Distinction: A Social Critique of the Judgement of Taste*. Translated by Richard Nice. Cambridge, MA: Harvard University Press, 1984.

Bourdieu, Pierre. 'Social Space and Symbolic Power'. *Sociological Theory* 7, no. 1 (1989): 14–25.

Brede, Helmut, Barbara Dietrich, and Bernhard Kohaupt. *Politische Ökonomie des Bodens und Wohnungsfrage*. Frankfurt: Suhrkamp, 1976.

Brenner, Neil. 'Between Fixity and Motion: Accumulation, Territorial Organization and the Historical Geography of Spatial Scales'. *Society and Space* 16, no. 4 (1998): 459–81.

Brenner, Neil. *Critique of Urbanization: Selected Essays*. Basel: Birkhäuser, 2016.

Brenner, Neil. 'Global, Fragmented, Hierarchical: Henri Lefebvre's Geographies of Globalization'. *Public Culture* 10, no. 1 (1997): 135–67.

Brenner, Neil. *Implosions/Explosions: Towards a Study of Planetary Urbanization*. Berlin: Jovis, 2014.

Brenner, Neil. 'The Limits to Scale? Methodological Reflections on Scalar Structuration'. *Progress in Human Geography* 25, no. 4 (2001): 591–614.

Brenner, Neil. *New State Spaces: Urban Governance and the Rescaling of Statehood*. Oxford: Oxford University Press, 2004.

Brenner, Neil. *New Urban Spaces: Urban Theory and the Scale Question*. New York: Oxford University Press, 2019.

Brenner, Neil. 'A Thousand Leaves': Notes on the Geographies of Uneven Spatial Development'. In *Leviathan Undone? The New Political Economy of Scale*, edited by Roger Keil and Rianne Mahon, 27–49. Vancouver: University of British Columbia Press, 2010.

Brenner, Neil. 'The Urban Question as a Scale Question: Reflections on Henri Lefebvre, Urban Theory and the Politics of Scale'. *International Journal of Urban and Regional Research* 24, no. 2 (2000): 361–78.

Brenner, Neil, and Stuart Elden. 'Henri Lefebvre in Contexts: An Introduction'. *Antipode* 33, no. 5 (2001): 764–8.

Brenner, Neil, and Stuart Elden. 'Henri Lefebvre on State, Space, Territory'. *International Political Sociology* 3, no. 4 (2009): 353–77.

Brenner, Neil, and Stuart Elden. Introduction to *State, Space, World: Selected*

Essays, by Henri Lefebvre, 1–48. Minneapolis: University of Minnesota Press, 2009.

Brenner, Neil, and Nikos Katsikis. 'Is the Mediterranean Urban?'. In *Implosions/ Explosions: Towards a Study of Planetary Urbanization*, edited by Neil Brenner, 428–59. Berlin: Jovis, 2014.

Brenner, Neil, and Nikos Katsikis. 'Operational Landscapes: Hinterlands of the Capitalocene'. *Architectural Design* 90, no. 1 (2020): 22–31.

Brenner, Neil, Peter Marcuse, and Margit Mayer, eds. *Cities for People, Not for Profit: Critical Urban Theory and the Right to the City*. New York: Routledge, 2012.

Brenner, Neil, Jamie Peck, and Nik Theodore. 'Variegated Neoliberalization: Geographies, Modalities, Pathways'. *Global Networks* 10, no. 2 (2010): 182–222.

Brenner, Neil, and Christian Schmid. 'Planetary Urbanization'. In *Urban Constellations*, edited by Matthew Gandy, 10–13. Berlin: Jovis, 2011.

Brenner, Neil, and Christian Schmid. 'Towards a New Epistemology of the Urban?' *City* 19, no. 2–3 (2015): 151–82.

Brenner, Neil, and Christian Schmid. 'The "Urban Age" in Question'. *International Journal of Urban and Regional Research* 38, no. 3 (2014): 731–55.

Brenner, Neil, and Nik Theodore, eds. *Spaces of Neoliberalism: Urban Restructuring in North America and Western Europe*. Malden, MA: Blackwell, 2002.

Brugmann, Jeb. *Welcome to the Urban Revolution: How Cities Are Changing the World*. New York: Bloomsbury USA, 2009.

Buckley, Michelle, and Kendra Strauss. 'With, against and beyond Lefebvre: Planetary Urbanization and Epistemic Plurality'. *Environment and Planning D: Society and Space* 34, no. 4 (2016): 617–36.

Burkhard, Bud. *French Marxism between the Wars: Henri Lefebvre and the 'Philosophies'*. New York: Humanity Books, 2000.

Butler, Chris. 'Abstraction beyond a "Law of Thought" ': On Space, Appropriation and Concrete Abstraction'. *Law and Critique* 27, no. 3 (2016): 247–68.

Butler, Chris. *Henri Lefebvre: Spatial Politics, Everyday Life and the Right to the City*. New York: Routledge, 2012.

Carter, Harold. *The Study of Urban Geography*. London: Edward Arnold, 1977.

Castells, Manuel. *The City and the Grassroots: A Cross-Cultural Theory of Urban Social Movements*. Berkeley: University of California Press, 1983.

Castells, Manuel. *City, Class and Power*. London: Macmillan, 1978.

Castells, Manuel. *The Informational City: Information Technology, Economic Restructuring, and the Urban-Regional Process*. Oxford: Basil Blackwell, 1989.

Castells, Manuel. *Luttes urbaines et pouvoir politique*. Paris: Maspero, 1973.

Castells, Manuel. *La question urbaine*. Paris: Maspero, 1972.

Castells, Manuel. *The Urban Question: A Marxist Approach*. Translated by Alan Sheridan. London: Edward Arnold, 1977 [1972].

Castells, Manuel, Eddy Cherki, Francis Godard, and Dominique Mehl. *Crise du logement et mouvements sociaux urbains: Enquete sur la region parisienne*. Paris: Mouton, 1978.

Castells, Manuel, and Francis Godard. *Monopolville*. Paris: Mouton, 1974.

Castriota, Rodrigo. 'Extractivism and Urban Struggle: Carajás, Amazonia, Brazil'. In *Extended Urbanization: Territories, Processes, Struggles*, edited by Christian Schmid and Milica Topalović. Basel: Birkhäuser (forthcoming).

Castriota, Rodrigo, and João Tonucci. 'Extended Urbanization in and from Brazil'. *Environment and Planning D: Society and Space* 36, no. 3 (2018): 512–28.

Castro, Roland. *Civilisation urbaine ou barbarie*. Paris: Plon, 1994.

Catterall, Bob. 'Citizen Movements, Information and Analysis: An Interview with Manuel Castells'. *City* 2, no. 7 (1997): 140–55.

Chan, Felicity. *Tensions in Diversity: Spaces for Collective Life in Los Angeles*. Toronto: University of Toronto Press, 2022.

Charnock, Greig. 'Challenging New State Spatialities: The Open Marxism of Henri Lefebvre'. *Antipode* 42, no. 5 (2010): 1279–1303.

Charnock, Greig, and Ramon Ribera-Fumaz. 'The Production of Urban Competitiveness: Modelling 22@Barcelona'. In *Urban Revolution Now: Henri Lefebvre in Social Research and Architecture*, edited by Łukasz Stanek, Christian Schmid, and Ákos Moravánszky, 157–71. Farnham: Ashgate, 2014.

Chase, John, Margaret Crawford, and John Kaliski, eds. *Everyday Urbanism*. New York: Monacelli Press, 1999.

Choay, Françoise. 'Sémiologie et urbanisme'. In *Le sens de la ville*, edited by Françoise Choay et al., 9–30. Paris: Éditions du Seuil, 1972.

Chomsky, Noam. *Syntactic Structures*. The Hague: Mouton, 1957.

Christaller, Walter. *Central Places in Southern Germany*. Inglewood Cliffs, NJ: Prentice-Hall, 1966 [1933].

Cohen, Robert B. 'The New International Division of Labor, Multinational Corporations and Urban Hierarchy'. In *Urbanization and Urban Planning in Capitalist Society*, edited by Michael J. Dear and Allen J. Scott, 287–317. New York: Methuen, 1981.

Coornaert, Monique, and Jean-Pierre Garnier, eds. 'Actualités de Henri Lefebvre'. Special issue, *Espaces et Sociétés* 76 (1994).

Coronil, Fernando. 'Beyond Occidentalism: Toward Nonimperial Geohistorical Categories'. *Cultural Anthropology* 11, no. 1 (1996): 51–87.

Coronil, Fernando. 'Towards a Critique of Globalcentrism: Speculations on Capitalism's Nature'. *Public Culture* 12, no. 2 (2000): 351–74.

Costes, Laurence. *Henri Lefebvre: Le droit à la ville*. Paris: Ellipses, 2009.

Couling, Nancy. 'Ocean Space and Urbanisation: The Case of Two Seas'. In *Urbanisation of the Sea*, edited by Nancy Couling and Carola Hein, 19–32. Rotterdam: NAI010 Publishers, 2021.

Couling, Nancy, and Carola Hein, eds. *Urbanisation of the Sea: From Concepts and Analysis to Design*. Rotterdam: NAI010 Publishers, 2021.

Cox, Kevin R., ed. *Urbanization and Conflict in Market Societies*. London: Methuen, 1978.

Cunningham, Frank. 'Triangulating Utopia: Benjamin, Lefebvre, Tafuri'. *City* 14, no. 3 (2010): 268–77.

Datta, Ayona, and Abdul Shaban. *Mega-urbanization in the Global South: Fast Cities and New Urban Utopias of the Postcolonial State*. London: Routledge, 2017.

Davidson, Mark. 'Displacement, Space and Dwelling: Placing Gentrification Debate'. *Ethics, Place and Environment* 12, no. 2 (2009): 219–34.

Davidson, Mark. 'Gentrification as Global Habitat: A Process of Class Formation or Corporate Creation?'. *Transactions of the Institute of British Geographers* 32, no. 4 (2007): 490–506.

Davis, Mike. *Ecology of Fear: Los Angeles and the Imagination of Disaster*. New York: Metropolitan Books, 1998.

Dear, Michael J. 'Les aspects postmodernes de Henri Lefebvre'. *Espaces et Sociétés* 76 (1994): 31–40.

Dear, Michael J. *The Postmodern Urban Condition*. Oxford: Blackwell, 2000.

Dear, Michael J. and Allen J. Scott, eds. *Urbanization and Urban Planning in Capitalist Society*. New York: Methuen, 1981.

Debord, Guy. 'Perspectives for Conscious Alterations in Everyday Life'. In *Situationist International Anthology*, edited and translated by Ken Knabb, 68–75. Berkeley: Bureau of Public Secrets, 1981 [1961].

Debord, Guy. *The Society of the Spectacle*. Translated by Donald Nicholson-Smith. New York: Zone Books, 1994 [1967].

Derrida, Jacques. *Of Grammatology*. Translated by Gayatri Chakravorty Spivak. Baltimore: Johns Hopkins University Press, 1976 [1967].

Deutsche, Rosalyn. *Eviction: Art and Spatial Politics*. Cambridge, MA: MIT Press, 1996.

Deutsche, Rosalyn. 'Uneven Development: Public Art in New York City'. *October* 47 (1988): 3.

Diani, Mario, Henrik Ernstson, and Lorien Jasny. ' "Right to the City" and the Structure of Civic Organizational Fields: Evidence from Cape Town'. *Voluntas, International Journal of Voluntary and Nonprofit Organizations* 29, no. 4 (2018): 637–52.

Diener, Roger, Liisa Gunnarsson, Mathias Gunz, Vesna Jovanović, Marcel Meili, Christian Müller Inderbitzin, and Christian Schmid, eds. *Territory: On the Development of Landscape and City*. Zurich: Park Books, 2016.

Diener, Roger, Manuel Herz, Jacques Herzog, Marcel Meili, Pierre de Meuron, Christian Schmid, and Milica Topalović, eds. *The Inevitable Specificity of Cities*. Zurich: Lars Müller Publishers, 2015.

Diener, Roger, Jacques Herzog, Marcel Meili, Pierre de Meuron, and Christian Schmid, eds. *Switzerland: An Urban Portrait*. Basel: Birkhäuser, 2006.

Dierwechter, Yonn. 'Lefebvre's Modernities: Informality, Planning and Space in Cape Town'. In *Planning in a Global Era*, edited by Andy Thornley and Yvonne Rydin, 189–210. Abingdon: Ashgate, 2002.

Dikeç, Mustafa. *Badlands of the Republic: Space, Politics, and Urban Policy*. Malden, MA: Blackwell, 2007.

Dolenec, Danijela, Karin Doolan, and Tomislav Tomašević. 'Contesting Neoliberal Urbanism on the European Semi-Periphery: The Right to the City Movement in Croatia'. *Europe-Asia Studies* 69, no. 9 (2017): 1401–29.

Domaradzka, Anna. 'Urban Social Movements and the Right to the City: An Introduction to the Special Issue on Urban Mobilization'. *Voluntas, International Journal of Voluntary and Nonprofit Organizations* 29, no. 4 (2018): 607–20.

Dörfler, Thomas. 'Antinomien des (neuen) Urbanismus: Henri Lefebvre, die HafenCity Hamburg und die Produktion des posturbanen Raumes'. *Raumforschung und Raumordnung* 69, no. 2 (2011): 91–104.

Dörfler, Thomas. *Gentrification in Prenzlauer Berg? Milieuwandel eines Berliner Sozialraums seit 1989*. Bielefeld: transcript Verlag, 2010.

DuPasquier, Jean-Noël, and Daniel Marco. *Régulation fordiste et post-fordiste en Suisse depuis 1937*. Geneva: Unité pour l'étude de la régulation en Suisse, 1991.

Duvignaud, Jean. 'Georges Gurvitch: Une théorie sociologique de l'autogestion'. *Autogestion* 1 (1966): 5–12.

Eco, Umberto. *La struttura assente*. Milan: Bompiani, 1968.

Edensor, Tim. *Geographies of Rhythm: Nature Place Mobilities and Bodies*. London: Ashgate, 2010.

Einstein, Albert. Foreword to *Concepts of Space: The History of Theories of Space in Physics*, by Max Jammer, xiii–xvii. Cambridge, MA: Harvard University Press, 1954.

Elden, Stuart. 'Mondialisation before Globalization: Lefebvre and Axelos'. In *Space, Difference, Everyday Life: Reading Henri Lefebvre*, edited by Kanishka Goonewardena et al., 80–93. New York: Routledge, 2008.

Elden, Stuart. 'Politics, Philosophy, Geography: Henri Lefebvre in Recent Anglo-American Scholarship'. *Antipode* 33, no. 5 (2001): 820.

Elden, Stuart. *Understanding Henri Lefebvre*. London: Continuum, 2004.

Elias, Amy J., and Christian Moraru, eds. *The Planetary Turn: Relationality and Geoaesthetics in the Twenty-First Century*. Evanston: Northwestern University Press, 2015.

Engels, Frederick. *Anti-Dühring*. In *Karl Marx, Frederick Engels: Collected Works*, vol. 25. New York: International Publishers, 1987 [1878].

Engels, Frederick. *The Condition of the Working Class in England*. In *Karl Marx, Frederick Engels: Collected Works*, vol. 4, 295–583. New York: International Publishers, 1975 [1845].

Engels, Frederick. *The Housing Question*. In *Karl Marx, Frederick Engels: Collected Works*, vol. 23, 317–91. New York: International Publishers, 1988 [1873].

Erensü, Sinan, and Ozan Karaman. 'The Work of a Few Trees: Gezi, Politics and Space'. *International Journal of Urban and Regional Research* 41, no. 1 (2017): 19–36.

Es, Evelien van, Gregor Harbusch, Bruno Maurer, Muriel Pérez, Kees Somer, and Daniel Weiss, eds. *Atlas of the Functional City: CIAM 4 and Comparative Urban Analysis*. Zurich: gta Verlag, 2014.

España, Kike. *Die sanfte Stadt*. Translated by Gerald Raunig. Wien: transversal texts, 2021.

Fenster, Tovi. 'The Right to the Gendered City: Different Formations of Belonging in Everyday Life'. *Journal of Gender Studies* 14, no. 3 (2005): 217–31.

Fernandes, Edesio. 'Constructing the Right to the City in Brazil'. *Social and Legal Studies* 16, no. 2 (2007): 201–20.

Fichte, Johann Gottlieb. *The Science of Knowledge*. Edited and translated by Peter Heath and John Lachs, 97. Cambridge: Cambridge University Press, 1982 [1795].

Fincher, Ruth, Kurt Iveson, Helga Leitner, and Valerie Preston. 'Planning in the Multicultural City: Celebrating Diversity or Reinforcing Difference?' *Progress in Planning* 92 (2014): 1–55.

Fincher, Ruth, and Jane Jacobs. *Cities of Difference*. New York: Guilford Press, 1998.

Fisher, Robert, Yuseph Katiya, Christopher Reid, and Eric Shragge. 'We Are Radical: The Right to the City Alliance and the Future of Community Organizing'. *Journal of Sociology and Social Welfare* 40, no. 1 (2013): 157–82.

Fishman, Robert. *Bourgeois Utopias: The Rise and Fall of Suburbia*. New York: Basic Books, 1987.

Florida, Richard. *Cities and the Creative Class*. New York: Routledge, 2005.

Foucault, Michel. 'Of Other Spaces'. Translated by Jay Miskowiec. *Diacritics* 16, no. 1 (1986): 22–7.

Foucault, Michel. *The Order of Things: An Archaeology of the Human Sciences*. London: Routledge, 2002.

Frehse, Fraya. 'For Difference "in and through" São Paulo: The Regressive-Progressive Method'. In *Urban Revolution Now: Henri Lefebvre in Social Research and Architecture*, edited by Łukasz Stanek, Christian Schmid, and Akos Moravánszky, 243–62. Farnham: Ashgate, 2014.

Frehse, Fraya. *O tempo das ruas na São Paulo de fins do Império*. São Paulo: EdUSP, 2005.

Friedmann, John. 'The Right to the City'. In *Rethinking the Latin American City*, edited by M. Morse and J. Hardoy, 139. Baltimore: Johns Hopkins University Press, 1993.

Friedmann, John. 'The World City Hypothesis'. *Development and Change* 17, no. 1 (1986): 69–83.

Friedmann, John, and Goetz Wolff. 'World City Formation: An Agenda for Research and Action'. *International Journal of Urban and Regional Research* 6, no. 1 (1982): 309–44.

Fujita, Masahisa, Paul Krugman, and Anthony Venables. *The Spatial Economy: Cities, Regions, and International Trade*. Cambridge, MA: MIT Press, 1999.

Gardiner, Michael. *Critiques of Everyday Life: An Introduction*. London: Routledge, 2000.

Gardiner, Michael. 'Everyday Utopianism: Lefebvre and His Critics'. *Cultural Studies* 18, no. 2–3 (2004): 228–54.

Gardiner, Michael. 'Utopia and Everyday Life in French Social Thought'. *Utopian Studies* 6, no. 2 (1995): 90–123.

Garnier, Jean-Pierre. ' "Greater Paris": Urbanization but No Urbanity – How Lefebvre Predicted Our Metropolitan Future'. In *Urban Revolution Now: Henri Lefebvre in Social Research and Architecture*, edited by Łukasz Stanek, Christian Schmid, and Ákos Moravánszky, 133–55. Farnham: Ashgate, 2014.

Garnier, Jean-Pierre. *Une violence eminemment contemporaine*. Paris: Agone, 2010.

Garreau, Joël. *Edge City: Life on the New Frontier*. New York: Doubleday, 1991.

Georgi, Frank. *Autogestion, la dernière utopie*. Paris: Publications de la Sorbonne, 2003.

Gibson-Graham, Julie Katherine. *The End of Capitalism (as We Knew It): A Feminist Critique of Political Economy*. Malden, MA: Blackwell, 1996.

Giddens, Anthony. *The Constitution of Society: Outline of the Theory of Structuration*. Berkeley: University of California Press, 1986.

Gilbert, Liette, and Mustafa Dikeç. 'Right to the City: Politics of Citizenship'. In *Space, Difference, Everyday Life: Reading Henri Lefebvre*, edited by Kanishka Goonewardena et al., 250–63. New York: Routledge, 2008.

Ginsburg, Theo, Hansruedi Hitz, Christian Schmid, and Richard Wolff, eds. *Zürich ohne Grenzen*. Zurich: Pendo, 1986.

Glaeser, Edward. *Triumph of the City: How Our Greatest Invention Makes Us Richer, Smarter, Greener, Healthier, and Happier*. New York: Tantor, 2011.

Glauser, Andrea. *Vertical Europe: The Sociology of High-Rise Construction*. Frankfurt am Main: Campus Verlag, 2020.

Goonewardena, Kanishka. 'The Country and the City in the Urban Revolution'. In *Implosions/Explosions: Towards a Study of Planetary Urbanization*, edited by Neil Brenner, 219. Berlin: Jovis, 2014.

Goonewardena, Kanishka. 'Henri Lefebvre'. In *The Wiley-Blackwell Companion to Major Social Theorists.* Vol. 2, *Contemporary Social Theorists,* edited by George Ritzer and Jeff Stepnisky, 44–64. Chichester: Wiley-Blackwell, 2011.

Goonewardena, Kanishka. 'Marxism and Everyday Life: On Henri Lefebvre, Guy Debord, and Some Others'. In *Space, Difference, Everyday Life: Reading Henri Lefebvre,* edited by Kanishka Goonewardena et al., 117–33. New York: Routledge, 2008.

Goonewardena, Kanishka. 'Planetary Urbanization and Totality'. *Environment and Planning D: Society and Space* 36, no. 3 (2018): 456–73.

Goonewardena, Kanishka. 'The Urban Sensorium: Space, Ideology and the Aestheticization of Politics'. *Antipode* 37, no. 1 (2005): 46–71.

Goonewardena, Kanishka, and Stefan Kipfer. 'Spaces of Difference: Reflections from Toronto on Multiculturalism, Bourgeois Urbanism and the Possibility of Radical Urban Politics'. *International Journal of Urban and Regional Research* 29, no. 3 (2005): 670–8.

Goonewardena, Kanishka, Stefan Kipfer, Richard Milgrom, and Christian Schmid, eds. *Space, Difference, Everyday Life: Reading Henri Lefebvre.* London: Routledge, 2008.

Goswami, Manu. *Producing India: From Colonial Economy to National Space.* Chicago: University of Chicago Press, 2010.

Gosztonyi, Alexander. *Der Raum: Geschichte seiner Probleme in Philosophie und Wissenschaft.* Freiburg: Karl Alber, 1976.

Gottdiener, Mark. *The Social Production of Urban Space.* Austin: University of Texas Press, 1985.

Gregory, Derek. *Geographical Imaginations.* Cambridge, MA: Blackwell, 1994.

Gregory, Derek, and John Urry, eds. *Social Relations and Spatial Structures.* London: Macmillan, 1985.

Greimas, Algirdas Julien. 'Pour une sémiotique topologique'. In *Sémiotique de l'espace,* edited by Centre de Mathématique, Méthodologie et Informatique. Paris: Denoël/Gonthier, 1979.

Greimas, Algirdas Julien. *Sémantique structurale: Recherche de méthode.* Paris: Larousse, 1966.

Groupe Genève 500 mètres de villes en plus. *Genève, projet pour une métropole transfrontalière.* Geneva: L'Âge d'Homme, 2013.

Haila, Anne. *Urban Land Rent: Singapore as a Property State.* Oxford: Wiley-Blackwell, 2016.

Hanakata, Naomi. *Tokyo: An Urban Portrait.* Berlin: Jovis, 2020.

Hanakata, Naomi, Christian Schmid, and Monika Streule. 'Incorporation of Urban Differences in Tokyo, Mexico City, and Los Angeles'. *City* (forthcoming).

Harloe, Michael, ed. *Captive Cities: Studies in the Political Economy of Cities and Regions*. Chichester, NY: Wiley, 1977.

Harootunian, Harry. *History's Disquiet: Modernity, Cultural Practice and the Question of Everyday Life*. New York: Columbia University Press, 2000.

Harrison, John, and Michael Hoyler, eds. *Megaregions: Globalization's New Urban Form?* Cheltenham: Edward Elgar, 2015.

Hart, Gillian. 'Relational Comparison Revisited: Marxist Postcolonial Geographies in Practice'. *Progress in Human Geography* 42, no. 3 (2018): 371–94.

Hartmann, Roger, Hansruedi Hitz, Christian Schmid, and Richard Wolff. *Theorien zur Stadtentwicklung*. Oldenburg: Geographische Hochschulmanuskripte, 1986.

Harvey, David. Afterword to *The Production of Space*, by Henri Lefebvre, 425–34. Translated by Donald Nicholson-Smith. Oxford: Blackwell, 1991.

Harvey, David. *A Brief History of Neoliberalism*. Oxford: Oxford University Press, 2005.

Harvey, David. *The Condition of Postmodernity: An Enquiry into the Origins of Cultural Change*. Oxford: Blackwell, 1989.

Harvey, David. *Consciousness and the Urban Experience: Studies in the History and Theory of Capitalist Urbanization*. Baltimore: Johns Hopkins University Press, 1985.

Harvey, David. *Explanation in Geography*. London: Edward Arnold, 1969.

Harvey, David. *Globalization and the Body*. Basel: Birkhäuser, 1998.

Harvey, David. *Justice, Nature and the Geography of Difference*. Oxford: Blackwell, 1996.

Harvey, David. *The Limits to Capital*. Oxford: Blackwell, 1982.

Harvey, David. *Rebel Cities: From the Right to the City to the Urban Revolution*. London: Verso, 2012.

Harvey, David. 'The Right to the City'. *New Left Review* 53 (2008): 23–40.

Harvey, David. *Social Justice and the City*. London: Edward Arnold, 1973.

Harvey, David. *Spaces of Hope*. Edinburgh: Edinburgh University Press, 2000.

Harvey, David. *The Urbanization of Capital: Studies in the History and Theory of Capitalist Urbanization*. Baltimore: Johns Hopkins University Press, 1985.

Haug, Frigga. 'Alltagsforschung'. In *Historisch-kritisches Wörterbuch des Feminismus*, vol. 1, 6–14. Hamburg: Argument Verlag, 2003.

Haug, Frigga. 'Questions Concerning Methods in Feminist Research'. In *Deconstructing Feminist Psychology*, edited by Erica Burman, 115–39. London: Sage, 1998.

Hecker, Rolf. Foreword to *Das Kapital 1.1: Resultate des unmittelbaren Produktionsprozesses*, 7–17. Berlin: Dietz Verlag, 2009.

Hegel, Georg Wilhelm Friedrich. *G. W. F. Hegel, Morceaux choisis*. Edited and translated by Norbert Guterman and Henri Lefebvre. Paris: Gallimard, 1938.

Hegel, Georg Wilhelm Friedrich. *Lectures on the History of Philosophy*. Vol. 2, translated by E. S. Haldane and Frances H. Simson. Lincoln, NE: University of Nebraska Press, 1995 [1840].

Hegel, Georg Wilhelm Friedrich. *The Phenomenology of the Spirit*. Translated by A. V. Miller. Oxford: Oxford University Press, 2004 [1807].

Hegel, Georg Wilhelm Friedrich. *The Science of Logic*. Translated and edited by George di Giovanni. Cambridge: Cambridge University Press, 2010 [1813–16].

Heidegger, Martin. 'Building Dwelling Thinking'. In *Basic Writings: From Being and Time (1927) to the Task of Thinking (1964)*, edited by David Farrell Krell New York: HarperCollins, 1993 [1951].

Heidegger, Martin. 'The Origin of the Work of Art'. In *Basic Writings: From Being and Time (1927) to the Task of Thinking (1964)*, edited by David Farrell Krell. New York: HarperCollins, 1993 [1935].

Hertzog, Alice. 'Movement and Urban Fabric along the West African Corridor: Cotonou, Benin'. In *Extended Urbanization: Territories, Processes, Struggles*, edited by Christian Schmid and Milica Topalović. Basel: Birkhäuser (forthcoming).

Hess, Rémi. *Henri Lefebvre et la pensée du possible: Théorie des moments et construction de la personne*. Paris: Economica-Anthropos, 2009.

Hess, Rémi. *Henri Lefebvre et l'aventure du siècle*. Paris: Éditions A. M. Métailié, 1988.

Hetherington, Kevin. *Expressions of Identity: Space, Performance, Politics*. London: Sage, 1998.

Highmore, Ben. *Everyday Life and Cultural Theory: An Introduction*. London: Routledge, 2002.

Highmore, Ben. *The Everyday Life Reader*. London: Routledge, 2002.

Highmore, Ben. *Ordinary Lives: Studies in the Everyday*. London: Routledge, 2010.

Hirsch, Joachim, and Roland Roth. *Das neue Gesicht des Kapitalismus: Vom Fordismus zum Post-Fordismus*. Hamburg: VSA, 1986.

Hitz, Hansruedi, Roger Keil, Ute Lehrer, Klaus Ronneberger, Christian Schmid, and Richard Wolff, eds. *Capitales Fatales: Urbanisierung und Politik in den Finanzmetropolen Frankfurt und Zürich*. Zurich: Rotpunkt, 1995.

Hitz, Hansruedi, Christian Schmid, and Richard Wolff. 'Boom, Konflikt und Krise'. In *Capitales Fatales: Urbanisierung und Politik in den Finanzmetropolen Frankfurt und Zürich*, edited by Hansruedi Hitz et al., 208–82. Zurich: Rotpunkt, 1995.

Hitz, Hansruedi, Christian Schmid, and Richard Wolff. 'Urbanization in Zurich: Headquarter Economy and City-Belt'. *Environment and Planning D: Society and Space* 12, no. 2 (1994): 167–85.

Hitz, Hansruedi, Christian Schmid, and Richard Wolff. 'Zurich Goes Global:

Economic Restructuring, Social Conflicts and Polarization'. In *Social Polarization in Post-industrial Metropolises*, edited by John O'Loughlin and Jürgen Friedrichs, 95–131. Berlin: Walter de Gruyter, 1996.

Hobsbawm, Eric. *The Age of Extremes: A History of the World, 1914–1991*. New York: Pantheon, 1994.

Holm, Andrej, and Dirk Gebhardt, eds. *Initiativen für ein Recht auf Stadt*. Hamburg: VSA, 2011.

Horn, Philipp. 'Indigenous Peoples, the City and Inclusive Urban Development Policies in Latin America: Lessons from Bolivia and Ecuador'. *Development Policy Review* 36, no. 4 (2018): 483–501.

Horn, Philipp, Paola Alfaro d'Alençon, and Ana Claudia Duarte Cardoso. *Emerging Urban Spaces: A Planetary Perspective*. Cham: Springer, 2018.

Huchzermeyer, Marie. 'The Legal Meaning of Lefebvre's the Right to the City: Addressing the Gap between Global Campaign and Scholarly Debate'. *GeoJournal* 83, no. 3 (2018): 631–44.

Hughes, Jonathan, and Simon Sadler. *Non-plan: Essays on Freedom Participation and Change in Modern Architecture and Urbanism*. New York: Routledge, 2000.

IG Rote Fabrik, ed. *Bewegung tut gut: Rote Fabrik*. Zurich: Limmat Verlag, 2021.

INURA, ed. *Possible Urban Worlds*. Basel: Birkhäuser, 1998.

INURA and Raffaele Paloscia, eds. *The Contested Metropolis: Six Cities at the Beginning of the 21st Century*. Basel: Birkhäuser, 2004.

Islar, Mine, and Ezgi Irgil. 'Grassroots Practices of Citizenship and Politicization in the Urban: The Case of Right to the City Initiatives in Barcelona'. *Citizenship Studies* 22, no. 5 (2018): 491–506.

Jacobs, Jane. *The Death and Life of Great American Cities*. New York: Random House, 1961.

Jakobson, Roman. 'Two Aspects of Language and Two Types of Aphasic Disturbances'. In *Fundamentals of Language*, edited by Roman Jakobson and Moris Halle, 69–96. New York: Mouton de Gruyter, 1956.

Jameson, Fredric. 'Postmodernism, or the Cultural Logic of Late Capitalism'. In *New Left Review* 146 (1984): 53–92.

Jameson, Fredric. *Postmodernism, or, the Cultural Logic of Late Capitalism*. London: Verso, 1991.

Jameson, Fredric. *Valencies of the Dialectic*. London: Verso, 2009.

Jay, Martin. *Marxism and Totality: The Adventures of a Concept from Lukács to Habermas*. Berkeley: University of California Press, 1986.

Jencks, Charles A. *The Language of Post-modern Architecture*. New York: Rizzoli, 1977.

Kanai, Juan Miguel. 'On the Peripheries of Planetary Urbanization: Globalizing

Manaus and Its Expanding Impact'. *Environment and Planning D: Society and Space* 32, no. 6 (2014): 1071–87.

Kanna, Ahmed. 'Urban Praxis and the Arab Spring'. *City* 16, no. 3 (2012): 360–8.

Karaman, Ozan, Lindsay Sawyer, Christian Schmid, and Kit Ping Wong. 'Plot by Plot: Plotting Urbanism as an Ordinary Process of Urbanisation'. *Antipode* 52, no. 4 (2020): 1122–51.

Katsikis, Nikos. 'From Hinterland to Hinterglobe: Urbanization as Geographical Organization'. PhD diss., Harvard University, 2016.

Katsikis, Nikos. 'Operational Landscapes of Primary Production: The US Corn and Soy Belt'. In *Extended Urbanization: Territories, Processes, Struggles*, edited by Christian Schmid and Milica Topalović. Basel: Birkhäuser (forthcoming).

Katznelson, Ira. *Marxism and the City*. Oxford: Clarendon Press, 1993.

Kegler, Karl R. 'Zentrale Orte: Transfer als "Normalisierung" '. *ACME* 15, no. 1 (2016): 36–80.

Keil, Roger, and Rianne Mahon, eds. *Leviathan Undone? Towards a Political Economy of Scale*. Vancouver: UBC Press, 2010.

Keil, Roger, and Klaus Ronneberger. 'Going up the Country: Internationalization and Urbanization on Frankfurt's Northern Fringe'. *Environment and Planning D: Society and Space* 12, no. 2 (1994): 137–66.

Keith, Michael, and Steve Pile. *Place and the Politics of Identity*. London: Routledge, 1993.

Kelly, Michael. 'Demystification: A Dialogue between Barthes and Lefebvre'. *Yale French Studies* 98 (2000): 79–97.

Kelly, Michael. 'The Historical Emergence of Everyday Life'. *Sites: The Journal of Twentieth-Century/Contemporary French Studies revue d'études français* 1, no. 1 (1997): 77–91.

Kelly, Michael. *Modern French Marxism*. Baltimore: Johns Hopkins University Press, 1982.

Kemal, Bahriye. *Writing Cyprus: Postcolonial and Partitioned Literatures of Place and Space*. New York: Routledge, 2020.

King, Anthony, ed. *Culture, Globalization and the World System: Contemporary Conditions for the Representation of Identity*. Basingstoke: Macmillan, 1993.

Kinkaid, Eden. 'Re-encountering Lefebvre: Toward a Critical Phenomenology of Social Space'. *Environment and Planning D: Society and Space* 38, no. 1 (2020): 167–86.

Kipfer, Stefan. 'Fanon and Space: Colonization, Urbanization, and Liberation from the Colonial to the Global City'. *Environment and Planning D: Society and Space* 25, no. 4 (2007): 701–26.

Kipfer, Stefan. 'The Fractures of Worldwide Urbanization: Insights from the Literary World'. In *Implosions/Explosions: Towards a Study of Planetary Urbanization*, edited by Neil Brenner, 288–305. Berlin: Jovis, 2014.

Kipfer, Stefan. 'How Lefebvre Urbanized Gramsci: Hegemony, Everyday Life, and Difference'. In *Space, Difference, Everyday Life: Reading Henri Lefebvre*, edited by Kanishka Goonewardena et al., 193–211. New York: Routledge, 2008.

Kipfer, Stefan. 'Neocolonial Urbanism? La Rénovation Urbaine in Paris'. *Antipode* 48, no. 3 (2016): 603–25.

Kipfer, Stefan. 'Preface to the New Edition'. In Henri Lefebvre, *Dialectical Materialism*, translated by John Sturrock, xiii–xxxii. Minneapolis: University of Minnesota Press, 2009.

Kipfer, Stefan. 'Pushing the Limits of Urban Research: Urbanization, Pipelines and Counter-colonial Politics'. *Environment and Planning D: Society and Space* 36, no. 3 (2018): 474–93.

Kipfer, Stefan. 'The Relevance of Henri Lefebvre in the 1990s'. Paper presented at the panel 'Henri Lefebvre: Theoretical, Analytical, and Political Perspectives' at the meeting of Research Committee 21 of the International Sociological Association, World Congress of Sociology, Montreal, 1998.

Kipfer, Stefan. *Le temps et l'espace de la (dé)colonisation: Dialogue entre Frantz Fanon et Henri Lefebvre*. Paris: Eterotopia France, 2019.

Kipfer, Stefan. 'Urbanization, Difference and Everyday Life: Lefebvre, Gramsci, Fanon and the Problematic of Hegemony'. PhD diss., York University, 2004.

Kipfer, Stefan. 'Why the Urban Question Still Matters: Reflections on Rescaling and the Promise of the Urban'. In *Leviathan Undone? Towards a Political Economy of Scale*, edited by Roger Keil and Rianne Mahon, 67–83. Vancouver: UBC Press, 2010.

Kipfer, Stefan, and Kanishka Goonewardena. 'Henri Lefebvre and "Colonization": From Reinterpretation to Research'. In *Urban Revolution Now: Henri Lefebvre in Social Research and Architecture*, edited by Łukasz Stanek, Christian Schmid, and Ákos Moravánszky, 93–109. Farnham: Ashgate, 2014.

Kipfer, Stefan, and Kanishka Goonewardena. 'Urban Marxism and the Postcolonial Question: Henri Lefebvre and "Colonisation" '. *Historical Materialism* 21, no. 2 (2013): 76–116.

Kipfer, Stefan, Kanishka Goonewardena, Christian Schmid, and Richard Milgrom. 'On the Production of Henri Lefebvre'. In *Space, Difference, Everyday Life: Reading Henri Lefebvre*, edited by Kanishka Goonewardena et al., 1–23. New York: Routledge, 2008.

Kipfer, Stefan, and Richard Milgrom. 'Henri Lefebvre – Urbanization, Space and Nature: Editors' Preface'. *Capitalism Nature Socialism* 13, no. 2 (2002): 37–41.

Kipfer, Stefan, Parastou Saberi, and Thorben Wieditz. 'Henri Lefebvre: Debates and Controversies'. *Progress in Human Geography* 37, no. 1 (2013): 115–34.

Kipfer, Stefan, and Christian Schmid. 'Right to the City/Bourgeois Urbanism'. Paper prepared for the International Network of Urban Research and Action, Toronto, 2004.

Kipfer, Stefan, Christian Schmid, Kanishka Goonewardena, and Richard Milgrom. 'Globalizing Lefebvre?'. In *Space, Difference, Everyday Life: Reading Henri Lefebvre*, edited by Kanishka Goonewardena et al., 285–305. New York: Routledge, 2008.

Klaus, Philipp. 'Die Bedrohung durch die Stadt'. In *Bewegung tut gut: Rote Fabrik*, edited by IG Rote Fabrik, 357–66. Zurich: Limmat Verlag, 2021.

Kleinspehn, Thomas. *Der verdrängte Alltag: Henri Lefebvres marxistische Kritik des Alltagslebens*. Giessen: Focus-Verlag, 1975.

Knaller-Vlay, Bernd, and Roland Ritter. 'Editorial'. In *Other Spaces: The Affair of Heterotopia, Dokumente zur Architektur 10*, 14–21. Graz: Galgiani, 1998.

Knierbein, Sabine. *Die Produktion zentraler öffentlicher Räume in der Aufmerksamkeitsökonomie*. Wiesbaden: VS Verlag für Sozialwissenschaften, 2010.

Knierbein, Sabine. 'Public Space as Relational Counter Space: Scholarly Minefield or Epistemological Opportunity?'. In *Public Space and Relational Perspectives: New Challenges for Architecture and Planning*, edited by Chiara Tornaghi and Sabine Knierbein, 42–63. London: Routledge, 2015.

Knierbein, Sabine, and Tihomir Viderman. *Public Space Unbound: Urban Emancipation and the Post-political Condition*. London: Routledge, 2018.

Kofman, Eleonore, and Elizabeth Lebas. 'Lost in Transposition – Time, Space and the City'. In Henri Lefebvre, *Writings on Cities*, 3–60. Oxford: Blackwell, 1996.

Kofman, Eleonore, and Elizabeth Lebas. 'Recovery and Appropriation in Lefebvre and Constant'. In *Non-plan: Essays on Freedom, Participation and Change in Modern Architecture and Urbanism*, edited by J. Hughes and Simon Sadler. Oxford: Architectural Press, 2000.

Kollektiv Quotidien. *Lefebvre for Activists*. Hamburg: Adocs Verlag, 2020.

Konau, Elisabeth. *Raum und soziales Handeln: Studien zu einer vernachlässigten Dimension soziologischer Theoriebildung*. Stuttgart: Enke, 1977.

Krätke, Stefan. 'The New Urban Growth Ideology of "Creative Cities"'. In *Cities for People, Not for Profit: Critical Urban Theory and the Right to the City*, edited by Neil Brenner, Peter Marcuse, and Margit Mayer, 138–49. New York: Routledge, 2012.

Ku, Agnes Shuk-mei. 'Remaking Places and Fashioning an Opposition Discourse: Struggle over the Star Ferry Pier and the Queen's Pier in Hong Kong'. *Environment and Planning D: Society and Space* 30, no. 1 (2012): 5–22.

Kuhn, Thomas S. *The Structure of Scientific Revolutions*. Chicago: University of Chicago Press, 1962.

Kuymulu, Mehmet Bariş. 'Reclaiming the Right to the City: Reflections on the Urban Uprisings in Turkey'. *City* 17, no. 3 (2013): 274–8.

Lafitte, Jacques. *Réflexions sur la science des machines*. Paris: Librairie Bloud & Gay, 1932.

La Llata, Silvano De. 'Operation 1DMX and the Mexico City Commune'. In *City Unsilenced: Urban Resistance and Public Space in the Age of Shrinking Democracy*, edited by Jeffrey Hou and Sabine Knierbein, 173–85. New York: Routledge, 2017.

Lantz, Pierre. 'La fin de l'histoire: Nietzsche et Lefebvre'. *Futur antérieur* 18 (1993): 19–28.

Lasansky, Medina D. *Hidden Histories: The Alternative Guide to Florence and Tuscany*. Florence: Didapress, 2018.

Lax, Sigurd F. ' "Heterotopia" from a Biological and Medical Point of View'. In *Other Spaces: The Affair of Heterotopia, Dokumente zur Architektur 10*, edited by Bernd Knaller-Vlay and Roland Ritter, 119–23. Graz: Galgiani, 1998.

Lazzaro, Claudia. 'Rustic Country House to Refined Farmhouse: The Evolution and Migration of an Architectural Form'. *Journal of the Society of Architectural Historians* 44, no. 4 (1985): 347–67.

Leborgne, Danièle, and Alain Lipietz. 'New Technologies, New Modes of Regulation: Some Spatial Implications'. *Environment and Planning D: Society and Space* 6, no. 3 (1988): 263–80.

Le Corbusier. *The Athens Charter*. New York: Grossman Publishers, 1973 [1943].

Le Corbusier. *Toward an Architecture*. Translated by John Goodman. Los Angeles: Getty Research Institute, 2007 [1923].

Lehrer, Ute, and Roger Keil. 'From Possible Urban Worlds to the Contested Metropolis: Research and Action in the Age of Urban Neoliberalism'. In *Contesting Neoliberalism: Urban Frontiers*, edited by Helga Leitner, Jamie Peck, and Eric. S. Sheppard, 291–310. London: Guilford Press, 2007.

Lehtovuori, Panu. *Experience and Conflict: The Production of Urban Space*. Farnham: Ashgate, 2010.

Leibniz, G. W. 'Leibniz's Third Letter'. In *Correspondence/G. W. Leibniz and Samuel Clarke*, edited by Roger Ariew, 14–17. Indianapolis: Hackett, 2000.

Lethierry, Hugues. *Agir avec Henri Lefebvre*. Lyon: Chronique sociale, 2015.

Lethierry, Hugues. *Penser avec Henri Lefebvre*. Lyon: Chronique sociale, 2009.

Lévi-Strauss, Claude. *The Savage Mind*. Translated by George Weidenfeld and Nicholson Ltd. Chicago: University of Chicago Press, 1966 [1962].

Lipietz, Alain. 'Accumulation, Crises, and Ways Out: Some Methodological

Reflections on the Concept of Regulation'. *International Journal of Political Economy* 18, no. 2 (1988): 10–43.

Lipietz, Alain. 'From Althusserianism to "Regulation Theory" '. In *The Althusserian Legacy*, edited by E. Ann Kaplan and Michael Sprinker, 99–138. London: Verso, 1993.

Lipietz, Alain. *La société en sablier: Le partage du travail contre la déchirure sociale*. Paris: La Découverte, 1996.

Lipietz, Alain, and Jane Jenson. 'Rebel Sons: The Regulation School'. *French Politics and Society* 5, no. 4 (1987): 17–26.

Liss, Jon. 'The Right to the City: From Theory to Grassroots Alliance'. In *Cities for People, Not for Profit: Critical Urban Theory and the Right to the City*, edited by Neil Brenner, Peter Marcuse, and Margit Mayer, 250–63. New York: Routledge, 2012.

Lopes de Souza, Marcelo. 'From the "Right to the City" to the Right to the Planet'. *City* 19, no. 4 (2015): 408–43.

Lopes de Souza, Marcelo. 'Which Right to Which City? In Defense of Political-Strategic Clarity'. *Interface: A Journal for and about Social Movements* 2, no. 1 (2010): 315–33.

Lopes de Souza, Marcelo, and Barbara Lipietz. 'The "Arab Spring" and the City: Hopes, Contradictions and Spatiality'. *City* 15, no. 6 (2011): 618–24.

Lüscher, Rudolf M., and Michael Makropoulos. 'Vermutungen zu den Jugendrevolten 1980/81, vor allem zu denen in der Schweiz'. In Rudolf M. Lüscher, *Einbruch in den gewöhnlichen Ablauf der Ereignisse*, 123–39. Zurich: Limmat Verlag, 1984.

Lyotard, Jean-François. *The Postmodern Condition: A Report on Knowledge*. Translated by Geoff Bennington and Brian Massumi. Minneapolis: University of Minnesota Press, 1984 [1979].

Madden, David J. 'City Becoming World: Nancy, Lefebvre, and the Global–Urban Imagination'. *Environment and Planning D: Society and Space* 30, no. 5 (2012): 772–87.

Marcus, Greil. *Lipstick Traces: A Secret History of the Twentieth Century*. Cambridge, MA: Harvard University Press, 1989.

Marcuse, Peter. '"Dual City": A Muddy Metaphor for a Quartered City'. *International Journal of Urban and Regional Research* 13, no. 4 (1989): 697–708.

Marcuse, Peter. 'Whose Right(s) to What City?' In *Cities for People, Not for Profit: Critical Urban Theory and the Right to the City*, edited by Neil Brenner, Peter Marcuse, and Margit Mayer, 24–41. New York: Routledge, 2012.

Martínez López, Miguel A. 'Between Autonomy and Hybridity: Urban Struggles within the 15M Movement in Spain'. In *Urban Uprisings: Challenging Neoliberal Urbanism in Europe*, edited by Margit Mayer, Catharina Thörn, and Håkan Thörn, 253–82. London: Palgrave Macmillan, 2016.

Marx, Karl. *Capital: A Critique of Political Economy*. Vol. 1, translated by Ben Fowkes. London: Penguin Books, 1976 [1867].

Marx, Karl. *Capital: A Critique of Political Economy*. Vol. 3, introduced by Ernest Mandel, translated by David Fernbach. London: Penguin Books, 1981 [1894].

Marx, Karl. 'Chapter Six: Results of the Direct Production Process'. In *Karl Marx, Frederick Engels: Collected Works*, vol. 34, 355–467. New York: International Publishers, 1994 [1933].

Marx, Karl. *A Contribution to the Critique of Political Economy, Part One*. In *Karl Marx, Frederick Engels: Collected Works*, vol. 29, 257–417. New York: International Publishers, 1987 [1859].

Marx, Karl. *The Difference between the Democritean and Epicurean Philosophy of Nature*. In *Karl Marx, Frederick Engels: Collected Works*, vol. 1, 25–105. New York: International Publishers, 1975 [1841].

Marx, Karl. *Economic and Philosophical Manuscripts*. In *Early Writings*, translated by Rodney Livingstone and Gregor Benton, 279–400. London: Penguin, 1974 [1844].

Marx, Karl. 'The Eighteenth Brumaire of Louis Bonaparte'. In *Karl Marx, Frederick Engels: Collected Works*, vol. 11, 99–197. New York: International Publishers, 1979 [1852].

Marx, Karl. *Grundrisse: Foundations of the Critique of Political Economy*. Translated by Martin Nicolaus. London: Penguin Books, 1973 [1858].

Marx, Karl. 'Letter to Pavel Vasilyevich Annenkov'. In *Karl Marx, Frederick Engels: Collected Works*, vol. 38, 96–106. New York: International Publishers, 1982 [1846].

Marx, Karl. *Morceaux choisis de Karl Marx*. Edited and translated by Norbert Guterman and Henri Lefebvre. Paris: Gallimard, 1934.

Marx, Karl. *The Production Process of Capital*. In *Karl Marx, Frederick Engels: Collected Works*, vol. 30. New York: International Publishers, 1988 [1863].

Marx, Karl. *Theses on Feuerbach*. In *Karl Marx, Frederick Engels: Collected Works*, vol. 5, 3–5. New York: International Publishers, 1975 [1845].

Marx, Karl, and Frederick Engels. *The German Ideology*. In *Karl Marx, Frederick Engels: Collected Works*, vol. 5. New York: International Publishers, 1975 [1845].

Massey, Doreen. *Space, Place and Gender*. Minneapolis: University of Minnesota Press, 1994.

Massey, Doreen. *Spatial Divisions of Labour: Social Structures and the Geography of Production*. Basingstoke: Macmillan, 1984.

Massey, Doreen, and John Allen, eds. *Geography Matters! A Reader*. Cambridge: Cambridge University Press, 1987.

Mattos, Carlos A. de, and Felipe Link, eds. *Lefebvre revisitado: Capitalismo, vida cotidiana y el derecho a la ciudad*. Santiago de Chile: RIL editores – Instituto de Estudios Urbanos y Territoriales, 2015.

Mayer, Margit. 'Neoliberal Urbanism and Uprisings across Europe'. In *Urban Uprisings: Challenging Neoliberal Urbanism in Europe*, edited by Margit Mayer, Catharina Thörn, and Håkan Thörn, 57–92. London: Palgrave Macmillan, 2016.

Mayer, Margit. 'The "Right to the City" in Urban Social Movements'. In *Cities for People, Not for Profit: Critical Urban Theory and the Right to the City*, edited by Neil Brenner, Peter Marcuse, and Margit Mayer, 63–85. New York: Routledge, 2012.

Mayer, Margit, Volker Brandes, and Roland Roth, eds. *Stadtkrise und soziale Bewegungen: Texte zur internationalen Entwicklung*. Cologne: Europäische Verlagsanstalt, 1978.

Mayer, Margit, Catharina Thörn, and Håkan Thörn. *Urban Uprisings: Challenging Neoliberal Urbanism in Europe*. London: Palgrave Macmillan, 2016.

McCann, Eugene J. 'Race, Protest and Public Space: Contextualizing Lefebvre in the U.S. City'. *Antipode* 31, no. 2 (1999): 163–84.

McLeod, Mary. 'Everyday and "Other" Spaces'. In *Feminism and Architecture*, edited by Debra L.Coleman, Elizabeth Ann Danze, and Carol Jane Henderson, 3–37. New York: Princeton Architectural Press, 1996.

McLeod, Mary. 'Henri Lefebvre's Critique of Everyday Life'. In *Architecture of the Everyday*, edited by Deborah Berke and Steven Harris, 9–29. New York: Princeton Architectural Press, 1997.

McLeod, Mary. 'Mary McLeod Interviewed by Gevork Hartoonian'. In *Global Perspectives on Critical Architecture*, edited by Gevork Hartoonian, 109–20. Farnham: Ashgate, 2015.

McLuhan, Marshall. *The Gutenberg Galaxy: The Making of Typographic Man*. Toronto: University of Toronto Press, 1962.

Meili, Marcel. 'Is the Matterhorn City?'. In *Implosions/Explosions: Towards a Study of Planetary Urbanization*, edited by Neil Brenner, 103–8. Berlin: Jovis, 2014.

Mels, Tom. *Reanimating Places: A Geography of Rhythms*. London: Routledge, 2016.

Mendras, Henri. *The Vanishing Peasant: Innovation and Change in French Agriculture*. Translated by Jean Lerner. Cambridge, MA: MIT Press, 1970 [1967].

Merleau-Ponty, Maurice. *Phenomenology of Perception*. Translated by Donald A. Landes. London: Routledge, 2012 [1945].

Merrifield, Andy. 'Lefebvre and Debord: A Faustian Fusion'. In *Space, Difference, Everyday Life: Reading Henri Lefebvre*, edited by Kanishka Goonewardena et al., 176–89. New York: Routledge, 2008.

Merrifield, Andy. *Henri Lefebvre: A Critical Introduction*. London: Routledge, 2006.

Merrifield, Andy. 'Lefebvre, Anti-Logos, and Nietzsche: An Alternative Reading of the Production of Space'. *Antipode* 27, no. 3 (1995): 294–303.

Merrifield, Andy. *Metromarxism: A Marxist Tale of the City*. London: Routledge, 2002.

Merrifield, Andy. *The New Urban Question*. London: Pluto Press, 2014.

Merrifield, Andy. *The Politics of the Encounter: Urban Theory and Protest under Planetary Urbanization*. Athens, GA: University of Georgia Press, 2013.

Merrifield, Andy. 'The Right to the City and Beyond'. *City* 15, no. 3–4 (2011): 473–81.

Meyer, Kurt. *Henri Lefebvre: Ein romantischer Revolutionär*. Vienna: Europaverlag, 1973.

Meyer, Kurt. 'Rhythms, Streets, Cities'. In *Space, Difference, Everyday Life: Reading Henri Lefebvre*, edited by Kanishka Goonewardena et al., 147–60. New York: Routledge, 2008.

Meyer, Kurt. *Von der Stadt zur urbanen Gesellschaft: Jacob Burckhardt und Henri Lefebvre*. Munich: Wilhelm Fink, 2007.

Middleton, Sue. *Henri Lefebvre and Education*. Abingdon: Routledge, 2014.

Milgrom, Richard. 'Lucien Kroll: Design, Difference, Everyday Life'. In *Space, Difference, Everyday Life: Reading Henri Lefebvre*, edited by Kanishka Goonewardena et al., 264–81. London: Routledge, 2008.

Minkowski, Eugène. *Le temps vécu, études phénoménologiques et psycho-pathologiques*. Paris: Payot, 1933.

Minkowski, Hermann. *Space and Time*. Montreal: Minkowski Institute Press, 2012.

Mitchell, Don. 'Revolution and the Critique of Human Geography: Prospects for the Right to the City after 50 Years'. *Geografiska Annaler: Series B, Human Geography* 100, no. 1 (2018): 2–11.

Mitchell, Don. *The Right to the City: Social Justice and the Fight for Public Space*. New York: Guilford Press, 2003.

Mitscherlich, Alexander. *Die Unwirtlichkeit unserer Städte: Anstiftung zum Unfrieden*. Frankfurt am Main: Suhrkamp, 1965.

Monte-Mór, Roberto Luís. 'Extended Urbanization and Settlement Patterns'. In *Implosions/Explosions: Towards a Study of Planetary Urbanization*, edited by Neil Brenner, 109–20. Berlin: Jovis, 2014.

Monte-Mór, Roberto Luís. 'Modernities in the Jungle: Extended Urbanization in the Brazilian Amazonia'. PhD diss., University of California, Los Angeles, 2004.

Monte-Mór, Roberto Luís. 'What Is the Urban in the Contemporary World?'. In *Implosions/Explosions: Towards a Study of Planetary Urbanization*, edited by Neil Brenner, 260–7. Berlin: Jovis, 2014.

Monte-Mór, Roberto Luís, and Rodrigo Castriota. 'Extended Urbanization: Implications for Urban and Regional Theory'. In *Handbook on the Geographies of Regions and Territories*, edited by Anssi Paasi, John Harrison, and Martin Jones. Cheltenham: Edward Elgar, 2018.

Müller-Schöll, Ulrich. *Das System und der Rest: Kritische Theorie in der Perspektive Henri Lefebvres*. Mössingen-Talheim: Talheimer, 1999.

Ng, Mee Kam, Wing-Shing Tang, Joanna Lee, and Darwin Leung. 'Spatial Practice, Conceived Space and Lived Space: Hong Kong's "Piers Saga" through the Lefebvrian Lens'. *Planning Perspectives* 25, no. 4 (2010): 411–31.

Nietzsche, Friedrich. 'On Truth and Lies in a Nonmoral Sense'. In *Philosophy and Truth: Selections from Nietzsche's Notebooks of the Early 1870's*, translated by Daniel Breazeale, 79–91. Atlantic Highlands, NJ: Humanities Press, 1990 [1873].

Nietzsche, Friedrich. *The Will to Power*. Translated by Walter Kaufmann and R. J. Hollingdale. Edited and with commentary by Walter Kaufmann. New York: Vintage Books, 1968.

Nigg, Heinz, ed. *Wir wollen alles, und zwar subito! Die Jugendunruhen in der Schweiz und ihre Folgen*. Zurich: Limmat Verlag, 2001.

Not Bored!. 'Henri Lefebvre's "The Production of Space" '. *Not Bored!* 30 (1999): 65–76.

Nüssli, Rahel, and Christian Schmid. 'Beyond the Urban–Suburban Divide: Urbanization and the Production of the Urban in Zurich North'. *International Journal of Urban and Regional Research* 40, no. 3 (2016): 679–701.

Ollman, Bertell. *Dance of the Dialectic: Steps in Marx's Method*. Chicago: University of Illinois Press, 2003.

Osborne, Peter. *Politics of Time: Modernity and Avant-Garde*. New York: Verso, 1995.

Panofsky, Erwin. *Gothic Architecture and Scholasticism: An Inquiry into the Analogy of the Arts, Philosophy and Religion in the Middle Ages*. New York: Meridian Books, 1957.

Park, Robert E., Ernest W. Burgess, and Roderick D. McKenzie. *The City*. Chicago: University of Chicago Press, 1925.

Peck, Jamie. 'Economic Rationality Meets Celebrity Urbanology: Exploring Edward Glaeser's City'. *International Journal of Urban and Regional Research* 40, no. 1 (2016): 1–30.

Peck, Jamie. 'Struggling with the Creative Class'. *International Journal of Urban and Regional Research* 29, no. 4 (2005): 740–70.

Peck, Jamie, and Adam Tickell. 'Neoliberalizing Space'. *Antipode* 34, no. 3 (2002): 380–404.

Peet, Richard, ed. *Radical Geography: Alternative Viewpoints on Contemporary Social Issues*. London: Methuen, 1977.

Petropoulou, Chryssanthi. 'From the December Youth Uprising to the Rebirth of Urban Social Movements: A Space–Time Approach'. *International Journal of Urban and Regional Research* 34, no. 1 (2010): 217–24.

Phillips, Martin. 'The Production, Symbolization and Socialization of Gentrification: Impressions from Two Berkshire Villages'. *Transactions of the Institute of British Geographers* 27, no. 3 (2002): 282–308.

Pickvance, Christopher G., ed. *Urban Sociology: Critical Essays*. London: Tavistock, 1976.

Pile, Steve. *The Body and the City: Psychoanalysis, Space, and Subjectivity*. London: Routledge, 1996.

Pinder, David. 'Reconstituting the Possible: Lefebvre, Utopia and the Urban Question'. *International Journal of Urban and Regional Research* 39, no. 1 (2015): 28–45.

Pinder, David. *Visions of the City: Utopianism, Power and Politics in Twentieth-Century Urbanism*. Edinburgh: Edinburgh University Press, 2005.

Pluciński, Przemysław. 'Henri Lefebvre's Second Life: The Real Utopia of the Right to the City in Contemporary Poland'. *History of European Ideas* 46, no. 8 (2020): 1107–21.

Popper, Karl R. *Objective Knowledge: An Evolutionary Approach*. London: Clarendon Press, 1972.

Porter, Libby, and Kate Shaw. *Whose Urban Renaissance? An International Comparison of Urban Regeneration Strategies*. London: Routledge, 2013.

Porter, Michael E. *Competitive Advantage*. New York: Free Press, 1985.

Poster, Mark. *Existential Marxism in Postwar France: From Sartre to Althusser*. Princeton: Princeton University Press, 1975.

Préteceille, Edmond. 'Is Gentrification a Useful Paradigm to Analyse Social Changes in the Paris Metropolis?' *Environment and Planning A: Economy and Space* 39, no. 1 (2007): 10–31.

Prigge, Walter, ed. *Peripherie ist überall*. Frankfurt am Main: Edition Bauhaus, Campus, 1998.

Prigge, Walter. 'Reading the Urban Revolution'. In *Space, Difference, Everyday Life: Reading Henri Lefebvre*, edited by Kanishka Goonewardena et al., 46–61. New York: Routledge, 2008.

Prigge, Walter. *Urbanität und Intellektualität im 20. Jahrhundert: Wien 1900, Frankfurt 1930, Paris 1960*. Frankfurt am Main: Campus, 1996.

Prigge, Walter. 'Urbi et orbi – zur Epistemologie des Städtischen'. In *Capitales Fatales: Urbanisierung und Politik in den Finanzmetropolen Frankfurt und Zürich*, edited by Hansruedi Hitz et al., 176–87. Zurich: Rotpunktverlag, 1995.

Prigge, Walter. *Zeit, Raum und Architektur: Zur Geschichte der Räume*. Cologne: Deutscher Gemeindeverlag/W. Kohlhammer, 1986.

Purcell, Mark. 'Excavating Lefebvre: The Right to the City and Its Urban Politics of the Inhabitant'. *GeoJournal* 58, no. 2 (2002): 99–108.

Purcell, Mark. *Recapturing Democracy: Neoliberalization and the Struggle for Alternative Urban Futures*. New York: Routledge, 2008.

Rapoport, Amos. *House Form and Culture*. Inglewood Cliffs, NJ: Prentice-Hall, 1969.

Raulin, Anne. 'La vie quotidienne, entre colonisation et émancipation'. *L'Homme et la Société* 185–6, no. 3 (2012): 19–32.

Redfield, Robert. 'The Folk Society'. *American Journal of Sociology* 52 (1947).

Renaudie, Serge, Pierre Guilbaud, and Henri Lefebvre. 'International Competition for the New Belgrade Urban Structure Improvement'. In *Autogestion, or Henri Lefebvre in New Belgrade*, 1–71. Berlin: Fillip Editions and Sternberg Press, 2009.

Roberts, John. *Philosophizing the Everyday: Revolutionary Praxis and the Fate of Cultural Theory*. London: Pluto Press, 2006.

Robinson, Jennifer. *Comparative Urbanism: Tactics for Global Urban Studies*. Oxford: Wiley-Blackwell, 2022.

Robinson, Jennifer. 'Feminism and the Spaces of Transformation'. *Transactions of the Institute of British Geographers* 25, no. 3 (2000): 285–301.

Robinson, Jennifer. 'Global and World Cities: A View from Off the Map'. *International Journal of Urban and Regional Research* 26, no. 3 (2002): 531–54.

Robinson, Jennifer. *Ordinary Cities: Between Modernity and Development*. New York: Routledge, 2006.

Robinson, Jennifer. 'Thinking Cities through Elsewhere: Comparative Tactics for a More Global Urban Studies'. *Progress in Human Geography* 40, no. 1 (2006): 3–29.

Rolnik, Raquel. 'Ten Years of the City Statute in Brazil: From the Struggle for Urban Reform to the World Cup Cities'. *International Journal of Urban Sustainable Development* 5, no. 1 (2013): 54–64.

Ronneberger, Klaus. 'Henri Lefebvre and the Question of Autogestion'. In *Autogestion, or Henri Lefebvre in New Belgrade*, edited by Sabine Bitter and Helmut Weber, 89–118. Berlin: Fillip Editions and Sternberg Press, 2009.

Ronneberger, Klaus. 'Henri Lefebvre and Urban Everyday Life: In Search of the Possible'. In *Space, Difference, Everyday Life: Reading Henri Lefebvre*, edited by Kanishka Goonewardena et al., 134–46. New York: Routledge, 2008.

Ronneberger, Klaus. *Peripherie und Ungleichzeitigkeit: Pier Paolo Pasolini, Henri Lefebvre und Jacques Tati als Kritiker des fordistischen Alltags*. Berlin: Adocs Verlag, 2015.

Ronneberger, Klaus, and Christian Schmid. 'Globalisierung und Metropolenpolitik: Überlegungen zum Urbanisierungsprozess der neunziger Jahre'. In *Capitales Fatales: Urbanisierung und Politik in den Finanzmetropolen Frankfurt und Zürich*, edited by Hansruedi Hitz, Roger Keil, and Ute Lehrer. Zurich: Rotpunktverlag, 1995.

Ross, Kristin. *Communal Luxury: The Political Imaginary of the Paris Commune*. London: Verso, 2015.

Ross, Kristin. *The Emergence of Social Space: Rimbaud and the Paris Commune*. Minneapolis: University of Minnesota Press, 1988.

Ross, Kristin. *Fast Cars, Clean Bodies: Decolonization and the Reordering of French Culture*. Cambridge, MA: MIT Press, 1995.

Ross, Kristin. *May '68 and Its Afterlives*. Chicago: University of Chicago Press, 2002.

Ross, Kristin, and Henri Lefebvre. 'Lefebvre on the Situationists: An Interview'. *October* 79 (1997): 69–83.

Rossi, Aldo. *The Architecture of the City*. Cambridge, MA: MIT Press, 1982 [1966].

Rössler, Mechthild. *'Wissenschaft und Lebensraum': Geographische Ostforschung im Nationalsozialismus*. Berlin: Dietrich Reimer Verlag, 1990.

Roy, Ananya. 'Urbanisms, Worlding Practices and the Theory of Planning'. *Planning Theory* 10, no. 1 (2011): 6–15.

Roy, Ananya. 'What Is Urban about Critical Urban Theory?'. *Urban Geography* 37, no. 6 (2016): 810–23.

Roy, Ananya. 'Who's Afraid of Postcolonial Theory?' *International Journal of Urban and Regional Research* 40, no. 1 (2016): 200–9.

Roy, Ananya, and Aihwa Ong, eds. *Worlding Cities: Asian Experiments and the Art of Being Global*. Malden, MA: Blackwell, 2011.

Ruddick, Sue, Linda Peake, Gökbörü Tanyildiz, and Darren Patrick. 'Planetary Urbanization: An Urban Theory for Our Time?' *Environment and Planning D: Society and Space* 36, no. 3 (2018): 387–404.

Sadler, Simon. *The Situationist City*. Cambridge, MA: MIT Press, 1998.

Sartre, Jean-Paul. *La critique de la raison dialectique*. Paris: Gallimard, 1988.

Sassen, Saskia. *Cities in a World Economy*. Thousand Oaks, CA: Pine Forge Press, 1994.

Sassen, Saskia. *The Global City: New York, London, Tokyo*. Princeton, NJ: Princeton University Press, 1991.

Saunders, Peter. *Social Theory and the Urban Question*. London: Hyman, 1981.

Sawyer, Lindsay, Christian Schmid, Monika Streule, and Pascal Kallenberger. 'Bypass Urbanism: Re-ordering Center-Periphery Relations in Kolkata, Lagos and Mexico City'. *Environment and Planning A: Economy and Space* 53, no. 4 (2021): 675–703.

Schäfer, Christoph. *Die Stadt ist unsere Fabrik: The City Is Our Factory*. Leipzig: Spector Books, 2010.

Schmid, Christian. 'Analysing Extended Urbanisation: A Territorial Approach'. In *Urbanisation of the Sea*, edited by Nancy Couling and Carola Hein, 93–106. Rotterdam: NAI010 Publishers, 2021.

Schmid, Christian. 'The Dialectics of Urbanisation in Zurich'. In *Possible Urban Worlds*, edited by INURA, 216–25. Basel: Birkhäuser, 1998.

Schmid, Christian. 'Extended Urbanization: A Framework for Analysis'. In *Extended Urbanization: Territories, Processes, Struggles*, edited by Christian Schmid and Milica Topalović. Basel: Birkhäuser (forthcoming).

Schmid, Christian. 'Global City Zurich: Paradigms of Urban Development'. In *The Global Cities Reader*, edited by Neil Brenner and Roger Keil, 161–9. New York: Routledge, 2006.

Schmid, Christian. 'Henri Lefebvre's Theory of the Production of Space: Towards a Three-Dimensional Dialectic'. In *Space, Difference, Everyday Life: Reading Henri Lefebvre*, edited by Kanishka Goonewardena et al., 27–45. New York: Routledge, 2008.

Schmid, Christian. 'Henri Lefebvre, the Right to the City, and the New Metropolitan Mainstream'. In *Cities for People, Not for Profit: Critical Urban Theory and the Right to the City*, edited by Neil Brenner, Peter Marcuse, and Margit Mayer, 42–62. New York: Routledge, 2012.

Schmid, Christian. 'Journeys through Planetary Urbanization: Decentering Perspectives on the Urban'. *Environment and Planning D: Society and Space* 36, no. 3 (2018): 591–610.

Schmid, Christian. 'Networks, Borders, Differences: Towards a Theory of the Urban'. In *Implosions/Explosions: Towards a Study of Planetary Urbanization*, edited by Neil Brenner, 67–81. Berlin: Jovis, 2014.

Schmid, Christian. 'Patterns and Pathways of Global Urbanization: Towards Comparative Analysis'. In *Implosions/Explosions: Towards a Study of Planetary Urbanization*, edited by Neil Brenner, 51–77. Berlin: Jovis, 2014.

Schmid, Christian. 'Raum und Regulation: Henri Lefebvre und der Regulationsansatz'. In *Fit für den Postfordismus? Theoretisch-politische Perspektiven des Regulationsansatzes*, edited by Ulrich Brand and Werner Raza, 217–42. Münster: Westfälisches Dampfboot, 2003.

Schmid, Christian. 'Researching the City with Video'. In *Rebel Video: The Video Movement of the 1970s and 1980s, London–Basel–Bern–Lausanne–Zurich*, edited by Heinz Nigg, 229–52. Zurich: Scheidegger & Spiess, 2015.

Schmid, Christian. 'Specificity and Urbanization: A Theoretical Outlook'. In *The Inevitable Specificity of Cities*, edited by Roger Diener, Manuel Herz, Jacques Herzog, Marcel Meili, Pierre de Meuron, Christian Schmid, and Milica Topalović, 287–307. Zurich: Lars Müller Publishers, 2015.

Schmid, Christian. *Stadt, Raum und Gesellschaft: Henri Lefebvre und die Theorie der Produktion des Raumes*. Stuttgart: Franz Steiner Verlag, 2005.

Schmid, Christian. 'Travelling Warrior and Complete Urbanization in Switzerland: Landscape as Lived Space'. In *Implosions/Explosions: Towards a Study of Planetary Urbanization*, edited by Neil Brenner, 138–55. Berlin: Jovis, 2014.

Schmid, Christian. 'The Trouble with Henri: Urban Research and the Theory of the Production of Space'. In *Urban Revolution Now: Henri Lefebvre in Social Research and Architecture*, edited by Łukasz Stanek, Christian Schmid, and Ákos Moravánszky, 27–48. Farnham: Ashgate, 2014.

Schmid, Christian. 'Urbane Region und Territorialverhältnis: Zur Regulation des Urbanisierungsprozesses'. In *Unternehmen Globus: Facetten nachfordistischer Regulation*, edited by Michael Bruch and Hans-Peter Krebs, 224–53. Münster: Westfälisches Dampfboot, 1996.

Schmid, Christian, Ozan Karaman, Naomi C. Hanakata, Pascal Kallenberger, Anne Kockelkorn, Lindsay Sawyer, Monika Streule, and Kit Ping Wong. 'Towards a New Vocabulary of Urbanisation Processes: A Comparative Approach'. *Urban Studies* 55, no. 1 (2018): 19–52.

Schmid, Christian, Łukasz Stanek and Ákos Moravánszky. 'Theory, Not Method: Thinking with Lefebvre'. In *Urban Revolution Now: Henri Lefebvre in Social Research and Architecture*, edited by Łukasz Stanek, Christian Schmid, and Ákos Moravánszky, 1–24. Farnham: Ashgate, 2014.

Schmid, Christian, and Monika Streule, eds. *Patterns and Pathways of Urbanization: A Comparative Approach*. Basel: Birkhäuser (forthcoming).

Schmid, Christian, and Milica Topalović, eds. *Extended Urbanisation: Territories, Processes, Struggles*. Basel: Birkhäuser (forthcoming).

Schmid, Christian, and Daniel Weiss. 'The New Metropolitan Mainstream'. In *The Contested Metropolis: Six Cities at the Beginning of the 21st Century*, edited by Raffaele Paloscia and INURA, 252–60. Basel: Birkhäuser, 2004.

Schmidt, Alfred. *Beiträge zur Marxistischen Erkenntnistheorie*. Frankfurt am Main: Suhrkamp, 1969.

Schmidt, Alfred. 'Henri Lefebvre and Contemporary Interpretations of Marx'. In *The Unknown Dimension: European Marxism since Lenin*, edited by D. Howard and K. E. Klare, 322–41. New York: Basic Books, 1972.

Schmidt, Hajo. *Sozialphilosophie des Krieges: Staats- und subjekttheoretische Untersuchungen zu Henri Lefebvre und Georges Bataille*. Essen: Klartext, 1990.

Schnaidt, Claude. 'Les marxistes ont-ils un projet urbain?' *Société française* 29 (1988): 59–63.

Schoenberger, Erica. 'From Fordism to Flexible Accumulation: Technology, Competitive Strategies, and International Location'. *Environment and Planning D: Society and Space* 6, no. 3 (1988): 245–62.

Schwab, Jens Peter. *'L'homme total': Die Entfremdungsproblematik im Werk von Henri Lefebvre*. Frankfurt: Lang, 1983.

Scott, Allen J. *Regions and the World Economy: The Coming Shape of Global Production, Competition, and Political Order*. Oxford: Oxford University Press, 1998.

Scott, Allen J., and Edward W. Soja, eds. *The City: Los Angeles and Urban Theory at the End of the Twentieth Century*. Los Angeles: University of California Press, 1996.

Scott, Allen J., and Michael Storper. 'The Nature of Cities: The Scope and Limits of Urban Theory'. *International Journal of Urban and Regional Research* 39, no. 1 (2015): 1–15.

Seigworth, Gregory, and Michael Gardiner. 'Rethinking Everyday Life: And Then Nothing Turns Itself Inside Out'. *Cultural Studies* 18, no. 2–3 (2004): 139–59.

Sheringham, Michael. *Everyday Life: Theories and Practices from Surrealism to the Present*. Oxford: Oxford University Press, 2006.

Shields, Rob. *Lefebvre, Love and Struggle: Spatial Dialectics*. London: Routledge, 1999.

Shields, Rob. *Places on the Margin: Alternative Geographies of Modernity*. London: Routledge, 1992.

Shmuely, Andrew. 'Totality, Hegemony, Difference, Henri Lefebvre and Raymond Williams'. In *Space, Difference, Everyday Life: Reading Henri Lefebvre*, edited by Kanishka Goonewardena et al., 212–30. New York: Routledge, 2008.

Simmel, Georg. 'Metropolis and Mental Life'. In *The Sociology of Georg Simmel*, 409–24. New York: Free Press, 1950 [1903].

Simone, AbdouMaliq. *For the City Yet to Come: Changing African Life in Four Cities*. Durham, NC: Duke University Press, 2004.

Simonsen, Kirsten. 'Bodies, Sensations, Space and Time: The Contribution from Henri Lefebvre'. *Geografiska Annaler: Series B, Human Geography* 87, no. 1 (2005): 1–14.

Situationist International. 'Editorial Notes: Critique of Urbanism'. In *Guy Debord and the Situationist International: Texts and Documents*, edited by Tom McDonough, translated by John Shepley, 103–14. Cambridge, MA: MIT Press, 2002 [1961].

Smith, Neil. *The New Urban Frontier: Gentrification and the Revanchist City*. New York: Routledge, 1996.

Soja, Edward W. *Postmetropolis: Critical Studies of Cities and Regions*. Cambridge, MA: Blackwell, 2000.

Soja, Edward W. *Postmodern Geographies: The Reassertion of Space in Critical Social Theory*. New York: Verso, 1989.

Soja, Edward W. *Thirdspace: Journeys to Los Angeles and Other Real-and-Imagined Places*. Cambridge, MA: Blackwell, 1996.

Soja, Edward W., and Miguel Kanai. 'The Urbanization of the World'. In *The Endless City*, edited by Ricky Burdett and Deyan Sudjic, 54–69. London: Phaidon, 2006.

Spivak, Gayatri Chakravorty. *A Critique of Postcolonial Reason: Toward a History of the Vanishing Present*. Boston: Harvard University Press, 1999.

Spivak, Gayatri Chakravorty. *Death of a Discipline*. New York: Columbia University Press, 2003.

Staeheli, Lynn A., Lorraine Dowler, and Doris Wastl-Walter, eds. 'Social Transformation, Citizenship, and the Right to the City'. *GeoJournal* 58, no. 2–3 (2002): 73–223.

Stanek, Łukasz. 'Architectural Project and the Agency of Representation: The Case of Nowa Huta, Poland'. In *Urban Revolution Now: Henri Lefebvre in Social Research and Architecture*, edited by Łukasz Stanek, Christian Schmid, Ákos Moravánszky, 265–81. Farnham: Ashgate, 2014.

Stanek, Łukasz. *Architecture in Global Socialism: Eastern Europe, West Africa, and the Middle East in the Cold War*. Princeton, NJ: Princeton University Press, 2020.

Stanek, Łukasz. *Henri Lefebvre on Space: Architecture, Urban Research, and the Production of Theory*. Minneapolis: University of Minnesota Press, 2011.

Stanek, Łukasz. 'Introduction: A Manuscript Found in Saragossa'. In *Toward an Architecture of Enjoyment*, by Henri Lefebvre, xv–xxxiv. Minneapolis: University of Minnesota Press, 2014.

Stanek, Łukasz. 'Space as Concrete Abstraction: Hegel, Marx, and Modern Urbanism in Henri Lefebvre'. In *Space, Difference, Everyday Life*, edited by Kanishka Goonewardena et al., 62–79. New York: Routledge, 2008.

Stanek, Łukasz, Christian Schmid, and Ákos Moravánszky, eds. *Urban Revolution Now: Henri Lefebvre in Social Research and Architecture*. Farnham: Ashgate, 2014.

Stewart, Lynn. 'Bodies, Visions, and Spatial Politics: A Review Essay on Henri Lefebvre's *The Production of Space*'. *Environment and Planning D: Society and Space* 13, no. 5 (1995): 609–18.

Stopani, Renato. *'Case da padrone': L'edilizia signorile nella campagna toscana ai primordi della mezzadria*. Florence: Editoriale gli archipressi, 2001.

Storper, Michael. *The Regional World: Territorial Development in a Global Economy*. New York: Guilford, 1997.

Streule, Monika. *Ethnographie urbaner Territorien*. Münster: Westfälisches Dampfboot, 2018.

Streule, Monika, Ozan Karaman, Lindsay Sawyer, and Christian Schmid. 'Popular Urbanization: Conceptualizing Urbanization Processes beyond Informality'. *International Journal of Urban and Regional Research* 44, no. 4 (2020): 652–72.

Sugranyes, A., and C. Mathivet, eds. *Cities for All: Proposals and Experiences towards the Right to the City*. Santiago de Chile: Habitat International Coalition, 2010.

Sünker, Heinz. *Bildung, Alltag und Subjektivität*. Weinheim: Deutscher Studien Verlag, 1989.

Swyngedouw, Erik A. 'The Mammon Quest: "Glocalisation", Interspatial Competition and the Monetary Order: The Construction of New Scales'. In *Cities and Regions in the New Europe: The Global-Local Interplay and Spatial Development Strategies*, edited by Mick Dunford and Grigoris Kafkalas, 39–67. London: Belhaven Press, 1992.

Swyngedouw, Erik A. 'Neither Global nor Local: "Glocalization" '. In *Spaces of Globalization*, edited by Kevin R. Cox. New York: Guilford, 1997.

Tabb, William K., and Larry Sawers, eds. *Marxism and the Metropolis*. New York: Oxford University Press, 1978.

Tang, Wing-Shing. 'Town-Country Relations in China: Back to Basics'. *Eurasian Geography and Economics* 60, no. 4 (2019): 455–85.

Tang, Wing-Shing. 'Where Lefebvre Meets the East: Urbanization in Hong Kong'. In *Urban Revolution Now: Henri Lefebvre in Social Research and Architecture*, edited by Łukasz Stanek, Christian Schmid, and Ákos Moravánszky, 71–91. Farnham: Ashgate, 2014.

Thörn, Håkan, Margit Mayer, and Catharina Thörn. 'Re-thinking Urban Social Movements, "Riots" and Uprisings'. In *Urban Uprisings: Challenging Neoliberal Urbanism in Europe*, edited by Margit Mayer, Catharina Thörn, and Håkan Thörn, 3–56. London: Palgrave Macmillan, 2016.

Topalov, Christian. 'A History of Urban Research: The French Experience since 1965'. *International Journal of Urban and Regional Research* 13, no. 4 (1989): 625–51.

Topalović, Milica, ed. *Hinterland: Singapore and Urbanisms beyond the Border*. Basel: Birkhäuser (forthcoming).

Topalović, Milica. 'Palm Oil: A New Ethics of Visibility for the Production Landscape'. *Architectural Design* 86, no. 4 (2016): 42–47.

Tornaghi, Chiara, and Sabine Knierbein, eds. *Public Space and Relational Perspectives: New Challenges for Architecture and Planning*. London: Routledge, 2014.

Trebitsch, Michel. 'Henri Lefebvre et l'autogestion'. In *Autogestion, la dernière utopie*, edited by Frank Georgi, 65–78. Paris: Publications de la Sorbonne, 2003.

Trebitsch, Michel. Preface to *Critique of Everyday Life*, Vol. 1, by Henri Lefebvre. Translated by John Moore, ix–xxviii. London: Verso, 1991.

Trebitsch, Michel. Preface to *Critique of Everyday Life*, Vol. 2, by Henri Lefebvre. Translated by John Moore, ix–xxix. London: Verso, 2002.

Trebitsch, Michel. Preface to *Critique of Everyday Life*, Vol. 3, by Henri Lefebvre. Translated by Gregory Elliott, vii–xxxiv. London: Verso, 2006.

Trezib, Joachim Nicolas. *Die Theorie der zentralen Orte in Israel und Deutschland*. Berlin: De Gruyter, 2014.

Uitermark, Justus. 'Looking Forward by Looking Back: May Day Protests in

London and the Strategic Significance of the Urban'. *Antipode* 36, no. 4 (2004): 706–27.

Uitermark, Justus, Walter Nicholls, and Maarten Loopmans. 'Cities and Social Movements: Theorizing beyond the Right to the City'. *Environment and Planning A: Economy and Space* 44, no. 11 (2012): 2546–54.

UNESCO. *Urban Policies and the Right to the City*. Paris: UNESCO, 2006.

UN-Habitat. *The Right to the City: Bridging the Urban Divide*. Rio de Janeiro: World Urban Forum/United Nations, 2010.

Vacchelli, Elena, and Eleonore Kofman. 'Towards an Inclusive and Gendered Right to the City'. *Cities* 76 (2018): 1–3.

Vaiou, Dina, and Ares Kalandides. 'Practices of Solidarity in Athens: Reconfigurations of Public Space and Urban Citizenship'. *Citizenship Studies* 21, no. 4 (2017): 440–54.

Veltz, Pierre. *Mondialisation, villes et territoires: L'économie d'archipel*. Paris: Presses Universitaires de France, 1996.

Venturi, Robert. *Complexity and Contradiction in Architecture*. New York: Museum of Modern Art, 1966.

Venturi, Robert, Denise Scott Brown, and Steven Izenour. *Learning from Las Vegas*. Cambridge, MA: MIT Press, 1972.

Viollet-le-Duc, Eugène Emmanuel. *Discourses on Architecture*. Vol. 1, translated by Henry van Brunt. Boston: James R. Osgood, 1875 [1863].

Vogelpohl, Anne. 'Henri Lefebvres "Recht auf Stadt" feministisch denken: Eine stadttheoretische Querverbindung von 1968 bis heute'. *sub\urban, Zeitschrift für kritische Stadtforschung* 6, no. 2–3 (2018): 149–58.

Vogelpohl, Anne. *Urbanes Alltagsleben: Zum Paradox von Differenzierung und Homogenisierung in Stadtquartieren*. Wiesbaden: Springer-Verlag, 2012.

Waite, Geoffrey. 'Lefebvre without Heidegger: "Left-Heideggerianism" qua contradictio in adiecto'. In *Space, Difference, Everyday Life: Reading Henri Lefebvre*, edited by Kanishka Goonewardena et al., 94–114. New York: Routledge, 2008.

Walton, John. 'Urban Sociology: The Contribution and Limits of Political Economy'. *Annual Review of Sociology* 19 (1993): 301–20.

Weber, Alfred. *Theory of the Location of Industries*. Translated by Carl J. Friedrich. Chicago: University of Chicago Press, 1929 [1909].

Weber, Max. *The City*. Translated by Gertrud Neuwirth and Don Martindale. London: The Free Press, 1966 [1921].

Wentz, Martin, ed. *Stadt-Räume: Die Zukunft des Städtischen*. Frankfurt am Main: Campus, 1991.

Werlen, Benno. *Society, Action and Space: An Alternative Human Geography*. Translated by Gayna Walls. London: Routledge, 1993 [1987].

Werlen, Benno. *Sozialgeographie alltäglicher Regionalisierungen, Band 1: Zur Ontologie von Gesellschaft und Raum*. Stuttgart: Franz Steiner, 1995.

Wex, Corell. 'Logistik der Macht: Henri Lefebvres Sozialtheorie und die Räumlichkeit des Staates'. PhD diss., University of Marburg, 2000.

Weyl, Hermann. *Symmetry*. Princeton, NJ: Princeton University Press, 1952.

Whyte, William H. Jr, ed. *The Exploding Metropolis*. Berkeley: University of California Press, 1993.

Widmer, Peter. *Subversion des Begehrens: Eine Einführung in Jacques Lacans Werk*. Vienna: Turia + Kant, 1997.

Williams, Raymond. *Marxism and Literature*. Oxford: Oxford University Press, 1977.

Wilson, Japhy. ' "The Devastating Conquest of the Lived by the Conceived": The Concept of Abstract Space in the Work of Henri Lefebvre'. *Space and Culture* 16, no. 3 (2013): 364–80.

Wilson, Japhy. 'Notes on the Rural City: Henri Lefebvre and the Transformation of Everyday Life in Chiapas, Mexico'. *Environment and Planning D: Society and Space* 29, no. 6 (2011): 993–1009.

Wilson, Japhy. 'Plan Puebla Panama: The Violence of Abstract Space'. In *Urban Revolution Now: Henri Lefebvre in Social Research and Architecture*, edited by Łukasz Stanek, Christian Schmid, and Ákos Moravánszky, 113–31. Farnham: Ashgate, 2014.

Wilson, Japhy. *Reality of Dreams: Post-neoliberal Utopias in the Ecuadorian Amazon*. New Haven, CT: Yale University Press, 2021.

Wilson, Japhy, and Manuel Bayón. 'Black Hole Capitalism'. *City* 20, no. 3 (2016): 350–67.

Wilson, Japhy, and Manuel Bayón. 'Concrete Jungle: The Planetary Urbanization of the Ecuadorian Amazon'. *Human Geography* 8, no. 3 (2015): 1–23.

Wirth, Louis. 'Urbanism as a Way of Life'. *American Journal of Sociology* 44, no. 1 (1938).

Wolff, Richard. 'A Star Is Born: Rote Fabrik Cultural Centre'. In *Possible Urban Worlds*, edited by INURA, 226–31. Basel: Birkhäuser, 1998.

Wong, Kit Ping. 'Territorially-Nested Urbanization in China: The Case of Dongguan'. *Eurasian Geography and Economics* 60, no. 4 (2019): 486–509.

Zoran, Erić. 'The Third Way: The Experiment of Workers' Self-Management in Socialist Yugoslavia'. In *Autogestion, or Henri Lefebvre in New Belgrade*, 135–50. Berlin: Fillip Editions and Sternberg Press, 2009.

Index